Taiwan's Development Experience:
Lessons on Roles of Government and Market

TAIWAN'S DEVELOPMENT EXPERIENCE: LESSONS ON ROLES OF GOVERNMENT AND MARKET

Edited by

Erik Thorbecke
Cornell University

Henry Wan, Jr.
Cornell University

KLUWER ACADEMIC PUBLISHERS
BOSTON / DORDRECHT / LONDON

Distributors for North, Central and South America:
Kluwer Academic Publishers
101 Philip Drive
Assinippi Park
Norwell, Massachusetts 02061 USA
Telephone (781) 871-6600
Fax (781) 871-6528
E-Mail <kluwer@wkap.com>

Distributors for all other countries:
Kluwer Academic Publishers Group
Distribution Centre
Post Office Box 322
3300 AH Dordrecht, THE NETHERLANDS
Telephone 31 78 6392 392
Fax 31 78 6546 474
E-Mail <services@wkap.nl>

 Electronic Services <http://www.wkap.nl>

Library of Congress Cataloging-in-Publication Data

Taiwan's development experience : lessons on roles of government and
  market / edited by Erik Thorbecke, Henry Wan.
       p.   cm.
   Papers presented at a conference held at Cornell University,
  Ithaca, New York on May 3 and 4, 1996
    Includes index.
    ISBN 0-7923-8513-6
    1. Taiwan--Economic conditions--1975- Congresses. 2. Taiwan-
  -Economic policy--1975-   Congresses. 3. Industrial policy--Taiwan
  Congresses.   I. Thorbecke, Erik, 1929-   . II. Wan, Henry Y.
  HC430.5.T3825 1999
  330.95124'9--dc21

TABLE OF CONTENTS

LIST OF CONTRIBUTORS TO THIS VOLUME
(with their affiliations at the time of the conference)

Adelman, Irma — University of California, Berkeley

Amsden, Alice H. — Massachusetts Institute of Technology

Bhagwati, Jagdish — Columbia University

Chen, Po-Chih — National Taiwan University

Fei, John C.H. — Chung-Hua Institution for Economic Research

Fu, Tsu-tan — Institute of Economics, Academia Sinica

Galenson, Walter — Cornell University

Harberger, Arnold C. — University of California at Los Angeles

Kuo, Shirley W.Y. — Minister of State, Republic of China

Lin, Justin Yifu — Peking University and Hong Kong University of Science and
  Technology

Oyejide, T. Ademola — University of Ibadan

Ranis, Gustav — Yale University

Sadli, Mohammad — University of Indonesia

Shea, Jia-Dong — Institute of Economics, Academia Sinica

Shei, Shun-Yi — Institute of Economics, Academia Sinica

Thee, Kian Wie — The Indonesia Institute of Sciences

Thorbecke, Erik — Cornell University

Tsiang, Grace — University of Chicago

Wan, Henry — Cornell University

Yu, Tzong-shian — Chung-Hua Institution for Economic Research

PREFACE

The year 1995 marked fifty years of development of the Taiwanese economy after the end of the Japanese rule in Taiwan. Given the fact that two of the key architects of Taiwan's development strategy, T. C. Liu and S. C. Tsiang were longtime faculty members at Cornell University and the continuing interest in and involvement by past and present Cornell faculty in studying Taiwan's performance led us to think that the time was ripe to organize a conference. We felt that an appropriate theme for this conference would be "The Role of Government and Markets in Development with a Special Emphasis on the Relevance of the Taiwanese Performance to Development Theory and Policy". This topic has attracted different interpretations and spirited exchanges, especially recently, as professional interest in East Asia and the high performing economies in Asia increased following the publication of the World Bank's volume on the East Asian Miracle. Observers differed in the lessons to be learned from the East Asian Miracle: some emphasize the Korean state intervention and guidance as crucial success elements whereas others stressed Hong Kong's record under laissez faire.

We hoped that a conference organized at Cornell University would provide an appropriate forum for an impartial and in-depth appraisal of the economic development performance of Taiwan over the course of the last half century. Since the Liu and Tsiang Proposal for reform (1954) had a major impact on the course of Taiwan's economic history during this period and is likely to be relevant for current reform efforts in other developing countries as well, we also felt that it would be appropriate to have the conference honor the memory of our late colleagues.

We made a very special effort to invite authorities representing a variety of different viewpoints and expertise, including scholars from PRC and from opposition circles within Taiwan, to attempt to provide as objective and critical an appraisal of the Taiwanese experience as possible. Still another reason for holding a conference is the fact that since Taiwan is not a member of the U.N. family, its development history has not been scrutinized to the same extent as its neighbors and other developing countries.

The conference took place at Cornell University, Ithaca, New York, on May 3 and 4, 1996. In addition to a keynote address by Jagdish Bhagwati on "The Miracle that Did Happen: Understanding East Asia in Comparative Perspective", the papers were presented in four different areas: 1) Key macro economic policies and reforms in Taiwan's development; 2) the Liu-Tsiang policy proposals and follow-up; 3) the role of agriculture, industrial policy, human capital and labor institutions in Taiwan's development; and, 4) relevance and potential applicability of the Taiwanese development experience to other Third World regions. The conference ended with a panel discussion on "Alternative interpretations of the economic development of Taiwan". Since the conference was held just before the onset of the

Asian Financial Crisis, we added an Epilogue chapter addressing Taiwan' response to the cirsis. The conference was cosponsored by the department of Economics, the East Asian program and the Program on Comparative Economic Development at Cornell University, together with the Institute of Economics, Academia Sinica and the Chiang-Ching-kuo Foundation, in Taiwan. The scale and the scope of the conference would have had to be drastically reduced had it not been for the generous support from the last two institutions.

As usual, in an undertaking such as this one, many individuals played a key role in insuring the success of the conference. In this preface we can only mention a few of them, i.e. Yih-hsing Pao and K. T. Li whose extraordinary efforts in obtaining resources were vital to the success of the conference; Shirley Kuo who provided crucial institutional and historical background information, as well as Samuel Hsieh, J. D. Shea and T. S. Yu who were there when we needed them. Chung-Cheng Lin was an active participant of the panel discussion on Alternative Interpretations of the Economic Development of Taiwan. In addition, on the Cornell front, Professors Randy Barker and Tapan Mitra were strongly supportive of this effort from the outset. Finally three personal friends of T. C. Liu and S. C. Tsiang, namely, Gregory Chow, Anthony Koo and Lawrence Lau, actively participated in the conference.

Last but certainly not least we owe a great debt of gratitude to Gail Canterbury who before, during and after the conference handled all logistical arrangements with great skill and dedication and to Jessica Vivian who did an outstanding job of editing this volume.

Erik Thorbecke and Henry Wan, Ithaca, NY

PART I
INTRODUCTION

1 OVERVIEW: THE LESSONS FROM TAIWAN: RELEVANCE, LIMITATIONS AND TRANSFERABILITY

Erik Thorbecke and Henry Wan

The objective of this chapter is to provide a general overview of the major themes and issues presented in the various chapters of this volume. In the process we attempt to draw some general lessons from the Taiwanese performance over the last half century for development theory and policy based, largely, on the chapters that follow. In a related way, we also attempt to highlight, distill and synthesize some of the major features and characteristics of the Taiwanese experience so aptly brought out by the participants in their respective chapters. In this chapter we distill the main lessons that can be learned from the Taiwanese experience up to the onset of the Asian Financial Crisis. In turn, the Epilogue reviews and analyzes the specific Taiwanese institutions and policies that largely protected the economy from the massive socioeconomic devastation the Asian Financial Crisis brought on its neighbors.

The main features of the Taiwanese development experience are scrutinized under five interrelated themes and domains: 1) Outward-orientation vs. inward-orientation; 2) Sources of growth; 3) Dynamic balanced growth process: the interaction between agricultural and non-agricultural sectors; 4) The role of government in the transition to a more market-oriented economy; and, 5) The potential transferability of the Taiwanese development experience to developing countries.

In addition to highlighting the essential contributions of the papers, we also bring out the views and contributions, whenever relevant, of our two distinguished former colleagues whom we honor at this conference — T. C. Liu and S.C. Tsiang — under each of the above headings.

1.1   Outward-orientation vs. Inward-orientation

At the beginning of the 1950s, the government was faced with the difficult choice between inward-looking and outward-looking policies. Both of these options were problematic. Factors weighing in favor of adopting an inward-looking strategy were i) the prevailing ideology of the time as reflected by Prebisch, Singer and Mahalanobis, among others, who strongly advocated the development of infant industries through import substitution policies; ii) the loss of the historical markets of Japan and mainland China; and iii) the sizable trade deficits that Taiwan was confronted with at that time. In contrast, the factors that seemed to argue in favor of an outward-looking strategy were the limited size of the domestic market, which was clearly too small to be depended upon as a source of sustained growth (Kuo, Chapter 3), and the enlightened views of a few liberal economists, particularly S.C. Tsiang, as we will see shortly.

The conventional, but not universal, view is that the import substitution phase was short-lived and that the transition from import substitution to export promotion occurred in the second half of the 1950s and very early 1960s. Some authors (including Fei and Chu, Chapter 9) consider that the export orientation phase covered the period 1962-80 before giving way to the present phase, which they called the "Science and Technology Orientation." There appears to be a strong consensus that "exports were the true essential factor contributing to the rapid growth and successful labor absorption, and that export expansion was a dominant source of manufacturing growth after the 1960s" (Kuo, Chapter 3: 63). However it might be inappropriate to think of trade as the engine of growth; rather, exports should be seen as a lubricant for growth and vice versa. There is much evidence that a two-way linkage between growth and trade prevailed. In this sense, it may be more accurate to talk about the trade-growth nexus in Taiwan's development (Ranis, Chapter 5).

During an early phase of Taiwan's development, and probably up to 1966, an agricultural growth-export nexus prevailed. A number of factors, such as investment in physical infrastructure, combined with institutional infrastructure such as primary education, the JCRR and Farmers' Associations, led to a steady rise of total agricultural productivity. During this period the argument for causation runs mainly from domestically generated productivity change to agricultural export opportunities. The rapidly increasing ability to capture foreign markets was largely a function of increased international competitiveness occasioned by domestic productivity growth (Ranis, Chapter 5).

During the subsequent phase, until the mid 1970s, a pronounced shift occurred in the composition of exports from agriculture, or land-based, to industrial, or labor-based exports, concentrated initially in textiles, synthetic fiber, apparel, wood, and leather products. The emergence of a two-way nexus between the two mutual hand-maidens of domestic growth and export performance can be witnessed during this period.

In the present high-tech period, Taiwan's output and export mixes became increasingly skilled labor-, capital- and, ultimately, technology-intensive. In this most recent period, Taiwan's exports underwent a very rapid structural adjustment.

In particular, the share of intermediate products readily useable as final products, (i.e. machinery and equipment, electric and electronic machinery, chemical materials and, most pronouncedly, precision instruments) replaced consumer non-durable goods as the main export category, rising from about 26 percent of total export value in 1986 to over 44 percent in 1995, while the share of consumer non-durable goods dropped from about 35 percent to 13 percent in the same period (see Fu and Shei, Chapter 10; Chen, Chapter 11: 236). Changes in the relative labor costs between Taiwan and its major competitors appear the primary reason for this rapid and drastic shift in export composition.

The above described changing composition of exports suggests strongly that it followed closely a pattern of dynamic comparative advantage that theory would have predicted. Exporters climbed, in a rapid but gradual way, the product cycle ladder. Following the dictates of dynamic comparative advantage and moving up the products' cycle ladder are two major features of the development story of Taiwan. This contrasts markedly with the pattern we observe in many other developing countries, where attempts to leapfrog many rungs of that ladder have, more often than not, been unsuccessful (Lin, Chapter 7).

It is relevant to note that much credit was given to T.C. Liu and S.C. Tsiang for first advocating in the early 1950s and continuing to advocate those export promotion policies that were, at last, largely put in effect in 1959 (Little, 1979). S.C. Tsiang, in particular, realized early on the dangers — if not the fallacy — of the fashionable development strategies at that time, such as the Mahalanobis emphasis on heavy industries in economic planning, and the Prebisch-Singer proposal for import substitution. In his 1949 *Economica* paper ("Rehabilitation of Time Dimension in Investment in Macrodynamic Analysis"), Tsiang regarded such strategies as wasteful and unnecessary. They were wasteful because heavy industries have payback periods much too long to be afforded by developing economies, and they are unnecessary because exports of light industries can exchange for the products of the "basic" industries.

About 1954, when Tsiang argued for a realistic exchange rate, Defense Minister Yu objected that the main Taiwanese exports then were sugar and rice, both of their demand determined by quotas, and thus not very elastic. What such export-pessimists overlooked was the potential to export goods like textiles, processed foods and simple manufactured goods in the future. Ultimately the principal backer of the reform proposals of Liu and Tsiang in Taiwan was K.Y. Yin, an engineer by training, who initially dismissed private entrepreneurs as unsophisticated and usually not well informed. Tsiang met Yin in 1952 and gave him Meade's *Planning and the Price Mechanism*. Yin was so impressed that he assigned all his subordinates to read that book and invited Liu and Tsiang to study the exchange rate system, in 1954. Their proposals for liberalizing the exchange rate was adopted in 1958 and finally implemented in 1960.

An alternative — still revisionist — view claimed by Amsden (Chapter 4) is that a more or less continuous process of selective import substitution and export promotion has prevailed in Taiwan over the last half century. A variety of measures were used to protect certain domestic industries against imports, while other measures were used to encourage exports in other sectors. The combined impact of these measures was to "get the prices wrong," i.e. to create an artificial gap between price and marginal cost at the level of the firm. In this context, it is relevant to note that Tsiang relied extensively in his theoretical work on marginal equivalence conditions. But clearly, in his appreciation of Meade, he did recognize the importance of externalities, and hence the theoretical justification to use shadow prices rather than market prices for resource allocation (which is another way of "getting prices wrong"). What he was always guarding against were "government failures," in which, in the name of correcting for externalities, or pursuing dynamic comparative advantage, rent-seekers would exploit the system for their own benefit. Judging from the poor track record of Taiwan in protecting its automobile industry through import substitution, we can readily understand the reasons for his concern.[1]

1.2 Sources of Growth

Recent studies have tended to demystify the "East Asian Miracle" by suggesting that the rapid growth of East Asian newly industrialized economies in the past decades depended on resource accumulation with little improvement in efficiency, and that such growth was not likely to be sustainable, as the history of Soviet economic growth suggests (Krugman, 1994; Kim and Lau, 1994; Young, 1995). More specifically, Kim and Lau obtain a growth rate of Total Factor Productivity (TFP) for Taiwan (1953-90) of only 1.2 percent annually, more or less comparable to the estimate of Young (1995) of 1.5 percent (1970-85). The results of these studies imply that economic growth in Taiwan (and of course, more generally, in the East Asian NIEs) is predominantly due to factor accumulation — mainly capital. Given that the real GNP in Taiwan grew at 8.6 percent between 1952 and 1994, the above estimates of TFP growth suggest that only between one sixth and one seventh of GNP growth could be accounted for by the residual efficiency gains.

Of course, any estimates of TFP growth are crucially dependent on the form of the production function used to derive these estimates, as well as on an accurate measurement of the capital and labor inputs. Capital over time has to be adjusted for vintage and quality improvements and labor inputs have to be appropriately modified to reflect human capital (skill and knowledge) enhancement. It is therefore not surprising that different methodologies (i.e. functional specifications) and estimates of inputs yield a wide range of outcomes. Thus, for example, Pack (1992) obtains a rate of growth of TFP for the manufacturing sector of 5.3 percent a year in Taiwan (1961-1987) compared to only 1.7 percent (1966-90) obtained by Young (1995).

If we accept that TFP growth was relatively limited, then the predominance of the economic growth that occurred is attributable to capital accumulation and human capital enhancement. As Bhagwati delicately puts it, if "the remarkable growth performance can be explained overwhelmingly by high rates of investment, the miracle ceases to exist: a miracle dissolves the way a paradox is lost as soon as it is explained." (Bhagwati, Chapter 2: 22). This immediately suggests, but leaves unanswered, the question of how the Taiwanese economic system was able to absorb such enormous increases to its initial factor endowments. As Pack (1992) indicated, the capital stock until 1987 doubled roughly every five years and the labor force every 14 years and "to deploy productively this many additional resources in so short a period is quite remarkable and a major characteristic of the economy to be explained" (Pack, 1992, p. 79).

What allowed the avoidance of diminishing returns to such enormous additions to an initially small stock of capital? Is the growth of physical and human capital accumulation itself a miracle that requires an explanation?

Perhaps the beginning of an answer to this question lies in examining the role of institutions in the development process. Followers of the New Institutional Economics school would postulate that the development process can best be analyzed and described within a broader meta-production function that includes, besides the conventional capital and labor inputs, a variable reflecting the institutional framework. The role of institutions can be scrutinized at different levels of aggregation. At the most general level, Fei and Chu (Chapter 9) suggest that the "development" of Taiwan can be interpreted broadly as a process of modernization through the democratization of the political institutions and through the marketization of economic institutions. They define the latter term as "an evolutionary replacement of the 'centralism of political command' by the competitive market mechanism which automatically coordinates privatized decisions of families and firms in the society" (Fei and Chu, Chapter 9: 117). Central to both processes above is liberalization. Their optimistic conclusion that liberalization has promoted modernization is explained by the fact that the traditional Eastern (Chinese) cultural values are consistent with the requirements of modernization, which has a Western origin. Routinized innovations in products and processes that characterize a modern economy necessitate "a healthy metabolism — i.e. the timely birth of new firms and products and the timely death of those which have become obsolete... Creation is a meaningful end in itself in the modern society, much more important than the static resource allocation efficiency of the Pareto variety" (Fei and Chu, Chapter 9: 185).

At a lower and more mundane level of aggregation, one key feature of Taiwan's institutional development has been the importance of small scale enterprises (SSE) in the agricultural and subsequently industrial development of Taiwan. Between 1966-70 and 1986, the absolute growth in the number of firms appears extraordinary, especially in fast-growing sectors such as plastics and electronics. Pack, who studied the evolution of small firms, concluded that they were an important component in the explanation of the growth of TFP (recall that his estimate of the growth rate of TFP ranged between 5 and 7 percent per annum between 1957 and 1982). He argued that small firms are likely to have 1) exhibited great flexibility and movement among product lines; 2) managed employees more intensively to obtain high and growing productivity from a given set of factors; 3) allowed the benefits of considerable subcontracting and the realization of economies of scope; and, 4) tapped the ability of many innovative and skillful entrepreneurs (Pack, 1992, pp. 105-106). It is generally agreed upon that a strong entrepreneurial penchant is a national personality trait in Taiwan (Tsiang, Chapter 12).

In turn, Fu and Shei (Chapter 10) emphasize the interlinkages between agricultural exports and the rest of the economy in triggering and generating the vast pool of entrepreneurs that led to the rapid industrialization process. They conclude that "it was the increasing share of market oriented exports of private business and agriculture that fostered the incentives and opportunities for improvisers who sped up the process of Taiwan's industrialization especially between the mid 1960's and the mid 1970's." The adoption of unskilled labor intensive production processes combined with a relative absence of scale economies gave rise to a predominance of low cost small scale firms capable of competing internationally (Ranis, Chapter 5).

As part of the modernization process, a more competitive environment and more market-friendly institutions evolved. Some of these institutions, such as the stock market and banking system reforms (to facilitate entry), were initiated by the government, while others evolved as a natural by-product of the modernization process and the transition from a traditional government-traditional society nexus to a modern government-modern society nexus (Fei and Chu, Chapter 9).[2] The main impact of the more competitive environment and modern market institutions is likely to have reduced transaction costs significantly and improved the internal organizational efficiency of firms (i.e. Leibenstein's X-efficiency). It can be hypothesized that a strong and reciprocal interaction prevailed between the process of capital accumulation and the changing institutional framework, somewhat analogous to the two-way relationship between exports and growth — one being the handmaiden of the other.

Another related source of growth that is only very imperfectly reflected or captured by factor accumulation per se are the positive externalities linked to the technology transfer and imports of machinery and equipment that lead to "learning by doing" benefits. Engineers and skilled workers learn from interacting with the new technology and, to the extent that they are mobile across firms and industries, spillover effects result that are external to the individual firms or even individual industries adopting the new vintage technologies. Tsiang (Chapter 12) describes in some detail the tremendous public and private investment in education and skill-enhancement that occurred in Taiwan over the last half century.

One area of possible controversy is the role played by (and the relative importance of) Confucian norms and values in lubricating the modernization process in inducing market-friendly policy and institutional changes. Kuo (Chapter 3) argues that some deeply rooted Chinese philosophical principles form the basis of persistent pragmatic policies in Taiwan (such as "growth with equity," "growth with stability" and, in the early days, "balanced growth of agriculture and industry"). Fei and Chu (Chapter 9) go even further in concluding that a cultural approach (i.e. the consistency of Chinese values with the Western modernization process) can explain the political-economic miracle of Taiwan, i.e. the fact that democratization and marketization took place more smoothly in the transformation process than in the vast majority of other contemporary LDCs. Bhagwati (Chapter 2), in contrast, rejects the notion that "Confucian values" have provided the necessary fuel to ignite the East Asian miracle. In his words, the problem is that the very same Confucian values that were supposed to be a hindrance to development are now advanced as having been the engine of growth in East Asia! Besides, as with culture generally, values matter but in ways that are not obvious or decisive. Clearly this is not an issue that we can resolve at this time.

1.3 Smooth Intersectoral Structural Transformation: Dynamic Balanced Growth

The process of dynamic intersectoral structural transformation in Taiwan is characterized by its smoothness, gradualism and rapidity. One is tempted to refer to it as dynamic balanced growth — in contrast with static balanced growth characteristic of pre-liberalization India — except for the fact that the concept of "balanced growth" has been used in so many different and often contradictory ways that it might be misleading.

The interaction between the agricultural and the non-agricultural sectors throughout the Taiwanese development process is extremely enlightening. In the early phase of Taiwan's development, the agricultural sector played a very crucial and fundamental role in the takeoff stage. One of the key contributions of the agricultural sector consisted of providing an agricultural surplus to finance the incipient industrialization process. Taiwan represents a textbook example of a country that solved admirably well the set of issues related to the size, timing and form of the mechanism through which a potential agricultural surplus is converted into a net flow of resources benefiting the rest of the economy.[3] Given the initial conditions that prevailed in the 1950's (say after the land reform), the question Taiwan confronted was how to make the aggregate contribution of agriculture to the socioeconomic development process as effective as possible over the long run. To be successful, the process of capturing the surplus needed to be delicately planned. The goal should be to generate a reliable and continuous flow of *net* resources from agriculture into the rest of the economy throughout much of the structural transformation.

The critical lesson learned from the Taiwanese example, and a few other countries that were successful in achieving both growth and equity throughout their development history, is that a continuing *gross* flow of resources should be provided to agriculture in the form of such elements as investment in physical infrastructure (irrigation and road network), inputs, research and credit, combined with appropriate institutions (such as JCRR and Farmers Associations) and price policies to increase this sector's productivity and potential capacity of contributing an even larger flow to the rest of the economy. It is much easier to extract a net surplus from increasing production than from stagnant or falling output (Thorbecke and Morrisson, 1989). The policy and institutional package implemented in Taiwan, largely in the late 1940's and 1950's, yielded a gross flow of resources and an institutional setting that made possible a sustained growth of agricultural output and productivity. This allowed the government, in turn, to siphon off a larger *gross* flow of taxes and revenues (mainly through the hidden rice tax) from increasing agricultural production so as to generate a *net* transfer to the rest of the economy.

In a very natural and gradual way, the early industries relied on backward linkages (i.e. agricultural inputs) to process food for export, followed in close order by textile and leather products and other simple manufactured consumer goods in the 1960's. These early industries were all highly labor-intensive and played a crucial role in absorbing productively the labor that was gradually released from agriculture. Again, a key lesson from the Taiwanese development experience is that the rate at which labor was released from agricultural production (as a result of the spectacular growth of labor and land productivity) coincided with the rate at which this labor could be productively absorbed in the new industries.

Taiwan never experienced the phenomenon, typical in much of the Third World, of massive rural-to-urban migration resulting in large-scale un- and underemployment and squatters' settlements around the large metropolitan centers resulting from a much greater labor outflow of agricultural labor than could possibly be absorbed in the formal industrial sector (the fact that more often than not these countries followed import-substitution policies leading to a choice of capital-intensive technologies further aggravated the employment problem). This is another feature of dynamic balanced intersectoral growth.

A well functioning labor market can make a major contribution to growth, while one that is subject to rigidities and imbalances may constitute a source of blockage. The behavior of the labor market in Taiwan has been a major factor in promoting the country's rapid economic development. The massive unemployment that characterizes much of the developing world has never been a problem in Taiwan. Intersectoral shifts of manpower have taken place smoothly in response to economic requirements —particularly from agriculture to manufacturing to services. The changes in the occupational structure imply an improvement in quality, which would not have been possible without a large investment in education (Galenson, Chapter 13).

Another related key characteristic of Taiwan's development process was rural industrial decentralization through, e.g., the provision of rural transportation and power and rural industrial estates. This process of rural industrialization undoubtedly helped keep labor costs down, reduce the social costs of urbanization, encourage the development of medium and small scale firms and, ultimately, bring about an improvement in the distribution of income during this period of accelerated growth. The location of firms close to sources of rural labor made it possible for industrial labor (often young females) to bicycle in or be bused in for the day, returning to their rural households at night, thereby minimizing transport and transaction costs (Ranis, Chapter 5).

After the labor surplus was exhausted and wage rates started rising, the center of gravity of the economy moved increasingly towards more sophisticated industries higher up on the product cycle's ladder. Instead of leap-frogging this ladder — as Indonesia appears to be attempting today — the present stage of science-based and high-tech industries evolved quite naturally, in line with the dictates of dynamic comparative advantage.

1.4 The Role of Government

During the last half century, in the transition to a more market-oriented economy, the government intervened through a variety of measures that can be grouped into three broad categories, i.e. institutional changes and reforms; public investment; and policies. In what follows, we highlight the various forms of government intervention, first, at the macroeconomic level and then at the sectoral level in agriculture and industry, respectively.

1.4.1 Macroeconomic Foundations

In the immediate post-World War II period, Taiwan was confronted with hyper-inflation (prices rose at an annual rate of 500% per annum in 1946-48 and then accelerated to 3000% in the first half of 1949). Hence, the most urgently needed objective was price stabilization, which was achieved through a combination of monetary reform, a foreign exchange reform, preferential interest rate deposits and a balanced budget. In particular, the preferential interest rate deposit scheme at the outset yielded a compound annual interest rate of 125 percent (which was still below the inflation rate in 1950) and was very successful in mobilizing rural savings and breaking the back of inflation.

This scheme was the brain child of S.C. Tsiang, who opposed the erroneous but popular belief, at that time, that a low interest rate policy would stimulate investment, facilitate growth and lower the price level. He proposed this scheme initially in an article written in 1947. T.C. Liu and S.C. Tsiang also advocated interest rate deregulation forcefully. As a consequence, they were labeled as "high interest rate scholars" by those groups (e.g. businessmen) who stood to benefit from subsidized loans (Shea, Chapter 8). This label was clearly unfair to both of them. Tsiang mentioned in his Reminiscences (in Chinese) that what he disagreed with were subsidized loans at *negative* real interest rates, as was practiced in Korea. His reasons were simple and direct. In an economy at an early phase of development, few would save when faced with negative interest rates over a long period of time. Under those circumstances loans would have to be financed through the continuous use of an inflationary tax, which could have led to unpredictable and undesirable political outcomes in Taiwan. Secondly, the demand for loanable funds at negative real interest rates would create such an excess demand that the consequent rationing process could become controversial and corruptive. The following approximate translation from a paper by S.C. Tsiang (Tsiang, 1985) reflects his philosophy in a transparent way:

> When exporters find business unprofitable, their hired "pens" ask the Central Bank to create money and lend them funds at subsidized rates. This would cause wages and prices to shoot up at home, reducing the real worth of subsidized loans. This would accelerate the domestic inflation rate compared to the inflation rate abroad which, in turn, would force the government to devalue the currency... Who would recommend such a convenient shortcut to get rich quickly?.... But if someone wins, others must lose. The losers are the bank depositors. They lose because their current income is debased. They also lose because the purchasing power of their savings falls... For self-preservation, they withdraw their deposits and banks can no longer intermediate.

Throughout the 1950s Taiwan experimented with a variety of exchange control systems, including a multiple exchange rate system. For much of that period the exchange rate was overvalued. T.C. Liu and S.C. Tsiang strongly recommended that the exchange rate be unified at an equilibrium level. However, at the outset, this recommendation was not accepted by the authorities who were concerned that a unified, equilibrium exchange rate would lead to a depreciated NT dollar that would fuel domestic inflation and increase government import expenditures. Ultimately, in 1958, their suggestions were adopted. This marked the beginning of the export-promotion era in Taiwan (Shea, Chapter 8).

Balancing the budget was a necessary condition to achieve and sustain an internal monetary equilibrium (marked by stable prices) and an external equilibrium in terms of balance of payments equilibrium. Although budget deficits occurred during only seven of the thirty-six years from 1952 to 1988, they occurred mostly in the period before 1963 (Yu, Chapter 6). It is not until the major fiscal reform of 1972-74 that the fiscal structure was on a sound and stable footing. T.C. Liu was the main architect of the tax reform. The government had invited him to chair the Tax Reform Commission, at a cabinet rank. As this task entailed the closing of loopholes and the ending of corruptive practices, it was a thankless task that only his vision, energy, prestige and dedication could make as successful as it became. Largely as a result of Liu's efforts, with the assistance of S.C. Tsiang, Taiwan became one of the few economies that enjoyed a balanced — if not surplus — government budget, at least until the late 1980s.

In the subsequent period, Taiwan let its currency depreciate in line with the popular ideology of "export first," or "all out for exports" in the society (Shea, Chapter 8). There was a strong reluctance on the part of the authorities to let the NT dollar appreciate when the balance of payments was in surplus. This brought about a massive increase in foreign currency reserves, which, incidentally, were criticized by S.C. Tsiang who publicly advised against this particularly policy.

It is interesting to note that the growth of GNP was negatively correlated with inflation and exports over the period 1960-1995 — at statistically significant levels of confidence (Yu, Chapter 6).

Two interesting features of the Taiwanese macroeconomic strategy worth noting are: 1) the design and implementation of government policies were done gradually in a very pragmatic way, instead of "cold turkey" — especially when the adoption of certain economic policies would not only entail economic changes but also social and institutional changes (Kuo, Chapter 3: 44); and 2) the macro-economic reform sequence took place in the following order: a) price and monetary stabilization in the early 1950s, b) limited trade liberalization and achievement of a unified and equilibrium exchange rate in the late 1950s, c) fiscal reforms resulting in a sustainable balanced budget in the early 1970s and d) liberalization of the capital market only very recently. What is perhaps surprising is the very long period of time over which these reforms occurred when compared with the demands placed on typical developing countries today in terms of adopting a full-fledged package of stabilization and structural adjustment measures over the very short run.

In retrospect, monetary and interest rate liberalization, the exchange rate policy and a balanced budget based on major fiscal reforms were the main pillars supporting the macroeconomic foundations that were so crucial to the sustained development process of the Taiwanese economy.

1.4.2   The Role of Government in Agriculture

In section 3, the role of agriculture in the takeoff phase was analyzed. In turn, the role of the government can be quickly and briefly described. First, the key institutional and institutional changes involved were the major land reforms completed in the early 1950s; the JCRR, acting as a Super Ministry of Agriculture and Rural Development in providing hands on, as well as indicative comprehensive planning for that sector; the process of farmers' education; and, finally, the Farmers Associations. The latter inspired Dr. Chan (a former chairman of JCRR) to assert that

> the scene of Taiwanese FA's should be the most lively description of Taiwanese development experience... When all things were done, the farmer would join other farmers in the FA's to have snacks, to smoke, to talk and laugh and then go home with their oxcart. When I visited South and Southeastern Asian countries, the site of loneliness for the local farmers was in sharp contrast with Taiwanese farmers. (as quoted in Fu and Shei, Chapter 10: 209);

In terms of public investment, the bulk of the foreign aid resources provided by US aid, which in the early days amounted to between approximately one third and one half of total domestic investment (Kuo, Chapter 3: 53), went to expand infrastructure largely in the rural areas benefiting agriculture. Finally, the "hidden rice tax" was used in combination with a few other policies to turn the terms of trade against agriculture and siphon off the surplus necessary for the industrial takeoff.

A crucial turning point occurred around 1973-75, when the government switched from a strategy of taxing agriculture to one of increasingly supporting it. This transition is typical of countries graduating from the status of developing to that of developed nations. What is perhaps more surprising is the degree and extent of protection as compared to many more developed countries. The weighted average nominal rate of agricultural protection in Taiwan in 1980 was higher than in every member country of the EEC (except Italy), while it was below that of South Korea and Japan. A very approximate order of magnitude of the social costs of agricultural protectionism were estimated at about 1% of GNP (Thorbecke, 1992). Since this is not a one shot cost but a reduction in the growth rates of GNP over an extended transitional period, these costs are not marginal. Clearly in this second stage of Taiwan's agricultural development the role of agriculture changed from a resource supporting sector to a dependent and protected sector enjoying resources from the general economy. An argument can be made that the social benefits of the agricultural sector in terms of water resources preservation, soil erosion prevention, soil purification, health and recreation, protection of wildlife, supply of oxygen, and purification of the air more than exceed the social costs (Fu and Shei, Chapter 10).

1.4.3   The Role of Government in Industry

There is no question that the government intervened in the industrial sector. Where analysts differ is on the extent of that intervention; its form; what motivated the design of the industrial policy; whether that industrial policy was in fact effective in altering the composition of industrial output; how corruptive the intervention was; and whether it ultimately contributed to or hindered Taiwan's overall development.

On one side Amsden (Chapter 4) argues forcefully that "getting the prices wrong" in Taiwan's early postwar history had a significant impact on the growth of specific industrial sectors, in particular, cotton textiles, and that Taiwan's greater export orientation after 1961 "cannot be equated with a lesser governmental role, although the nature of that role changed in the direction of more targeting of strategic industries and 'selective seclusion' of the economy" (Amsden, Chapter 4: 95).

On the other side many observers would argue that, in general, industrial intervention was not particularly effective (a blessing in disguise?) — although some mistakes were made such as the promotion of an automobile industry. Furthermore, the industrial strategy that was followed consisted of a mixed bag of measures — some quite desirable and others objectionable on efficiency grounds.

In what follows, we undertake a quick overview of the major policy measures affecting industrial growth. First, at the institutional level, the Trade Associations that the government helped to establish played a key role. These associations often evolved into successful subcontracting networks. A good example of such a network is the one that evolved in the Taiwanese machine tools industries in the 1970s. This network consisted of a large number of relatively small firms that became increasingly export-dependent (given the small size of the domestic market). In order to be competitive, particularly in the US market, these machine tool producers had to excel on cost control, punctuality of delivery and readiness to adapt to the vagaries of the market. Through subcontracting, the standardization of submodules of production activities could occur. In fact, the small size of the firms was a real advantage in accommodating and adapting to the needs of particular clients, such as the car manufacturers (Lin and Wan, 1996).

In terms of public investment projects-cum-institutions promoted by the government one should mention the Export Processing Zones and subsequently the Industrial — essentially Science and High Technology — Parks. These two initiatives proved to be very successful and can be rationalized on the ground that some of the positive externalities and spillover effects of the adoption of state-of-the-art technologies by firms are not directly captured by these firms. In other words, the marginal social productivity of increased new vintage technology adoption by firms as the result of the existence of these processing zones and industrial parks is likely to exceed significantly the private benefits accruing to these same firms.

Finally, in the domain of policies, the government used a whole plethora of measures, such as subsidized interest rates, fiscal incentives attached to export performance and many others to encourage selective industrial development. In addition, Taiwan has maintained over its whole history a system of Four-Year Indicative Plans. In the process, distortions were introduced and mistakes made. A few of the protected and subsidized industries — particularly some state enterprises — turned into white elephants. However, a most interesting finding is that only a relatively weak correlation could be found between the *planned* annual growth rates of specific industries during any given Four-Year Plan and the *realized* annual growth rates of these same industries during that same Four-Year Plan period or even subsequent period. This led Chen (Chapter 11) to conclude that "the Economic

Plans of Taiwan did not predict the relative growth rates of the major products accurately... Either the industrial policies of Taiwan were not consistent with the targets of the government or the industrial policies were not successful" (Chen, Chapter 11: 244).

In the same study Chen argues that it is easy to find some products actively encouraged by government policies leading to successful development and it is also easy to find some industries that succeeded with little support from the government or failed with a lot of government support. Therefore, case studies of only one or a small number of industrial products can be quite misleading (Chen, Chapter 11). Although many policies were aimed at some specific industries at the outset, many of them were soon extended to other industries that requested the same privileges (such as those for strategic industries in 1982). Hence, if the policy package was not discriminatory in favor of or against some industries, they did not lead to major distortions.

In summary, a conclusion that would appear to be relatively robust is that the more general comprehensive policies and institutional changes — particularly at the macroeconomic level — were much more instrumental in influencing the pattern of industrial development than were specific industrial policies.

1.5 Comparison of the Taiwanese Development Experience with that in Other Parts of the Developing World and Its Potential Transferability

Four chapters compare the Taiwanese performance with that of other developing regions and address the issue of the potential transferability of the Taiwanese model to these other developing regions.

In his chapter on "What Can Sub-Saharan Africa Learn from the Taiwanese Development Experience?," Oyejide (Chapter 16) reminds us that it is important to recall that sub-Saharan Africa in the mid 1990s represents a mosaic, and that it is no longer possible, if it ever was, to talk of the continent as undifferentiated whole. He also reminds us that to draw lessons from the successful development experience of Taiwan, it is essential to relate it to both the initial conditions which set the stage for it and the development strategy and policies that contributed to the performance. In the late 1940s, Taiwan was a small, labor abundant, natural resource poor but human-resource rich economy; it was shaped by a clear ethnic homogeneity further welded together by the realistic fear of a powerful external adversary. Its endowment of human resources was significantly enriched by an educational system that stressed equality of access and opportunity and, in the process, obtained a relatively high level of literacy and a well-educated population, most of whom had emigrated from the mainland. Another legacy of colonialism was the development of infrastructure in rural Taiwan complemented by a set of rural institutions. Finally, a series of land reform measures starting in the 1940s led to a very equal distribution of land. The broadly shared vision of the importance of economic growth and development for the survival of both government and the state were underpinned and facilitated by an enduring and stable political system.

Turning to sub-Saharan African (SSA) development, Oyejide (Chapter 16) argues that, whereas SSA performance was not significantly different from that of other developing countries during the 60s and early 70s, it subsequently worsened progressively both relative to its earlier performance and that of other developing countries. By the 1970s, Africa had fallen off the "growth trajectory" of all developing nations. Initial conditions were and still are clearly unfavorable: the typical African economy is small, in terms of both population and GNP, and has very limited human resources and a very rapidly growth population. Dynamism in the agricultural sector is severely limited by the extremely low level of technology, the lack of rural infrastructure and the discriminatory policies against that sector. Most SSA countries contain heterogenous populations in which ethnic and racial conflict continue to impede efforts at nation building and maintaining political and social stability. Political power is often used to benefit the government and its close allies. The region is also plagued by a very large debt overhang.

Although the initial conditions that characterize the SSA economies and the unfavorable external environment contributed to their poor economic performance since the 1970s, the region's choice of development strategy and policies probably played a much more important role in explaining its economic stagnation. The region pursued an inward oriented development strategy and relied on large budget deficits, overvalued exchange rates, high inflation and negative real interest rates that discouraged private savings. Agriculture was significantly discriminated against, manufacturing was a favored sector relying on industrial parastatals nurtured behind high protectionist walls.

This was the background against which the wide range of policy reforms was adopted and implemented, in varying degrees, in many SSA countries starting in the early 1980s. While there has been some progress on the macroeconomic front, most countries are still far from the "policy frontier." The SSA development strategy must address the important issue of the relative roles of the state and private agents in the development process. While an outward-oriented development strategy typically regards the private sector as the main spring of economic growth, it is not necessarily optimal to limit the role of the state to that of only providing support for and accommodation to the private sector. The Taiwanese experience suggests that the state should also provide adequate public services and incentives to promote knowledge and the acquisition and diffusion of more advanced technology. Seeking refuge in a "minimalist" state would amount to abandoning the quest for sustainable and equitable growth.

At the sectoral level, the anti-agriculture bias has to be reduced and agricultural productivity improved. The strategy for promoting agricultural development must go well beyond repairing the distorted incentive structure. It should increase investment and rural infrastructure, and promote input and credit supply, technological innovation, and agricultural extension services. Promoting export-oriented industrialization requires restructuring, altering the industrial incentive regime to help exporters, and using appropriate proactive measures to assist exporters to overcome the difficulties of gaining access to information and technology. Regarding an outward oriented development strategy, discussion of import liberalization in the context of SSA continues to confront the twin question of "how much? how soon? The problem is that SSA countries rely on trade taxes as important sources of government revenue and are concerned about deindustrialization.

Oyejide (Chapter 16) concludes that although it may be wiser to rely on more market- and free trade-oriented policies and minimize interventionist policies, the experience of Taiwan shows that certain proactive and interventionist measures can play a significant role in the development process, e.g. investment in agricultural infrastructure and technology, and strong and focused measures to establish footholds and bridge-heads in appropriate foreign markets for manufactured exports.

Adelman (Chapter 14), in her chapter comparing Korea and Taiwan, also emphasizes the importance of initial conditions, including the institutional and polity environment, as key determinants of economic development performance. The development process is path dependent, in a pattern of causality that runs from initial conditions to institutional structures and policies. In her very detailed historical comparison of performance, she reaches a number of conclusions. First, in both countries, she argues that the import-substitution strategy was very successful both from an economic growth and social development perspective. The second phase of labor-intensive export-oriented industrialization from 1967 to 1972 in Korea and from 1958-1972 in Taiwan was likewise phenomenally successful, leading to high growth, rapid industrialization, rapid labor absorption, substantial increases in economic welfare and reductions in inequality in both countries. The third phase emphasized heavy and chemical industry (HCI), a drive that was initiated during a particularly inauspicious period, marked by significant adverse exogenous shocks from world markets. These industries are energy and import-intensive and the oil shocks raised the cost of operating these industries very substantially and induced stagflation in the OECD countries, negatively affecting the world demand for imports.

Adelman argues that, notwithstanding those unfavorable exogenous shocks, both countries continued their spectacular growth and export performance. Much of the debate on industrial policies hinges around the question of whether the HCI effort helped or hindered Korea's progress. In a recent book, Stern et al. (1995) evaluate the Korean HCI drive and conclude that at worst, detrimental effects were small and at best, HCI may well have accelerated Korea's industrialization. Following the liberalization of the 1980s and the progress made by then, the private sector could well have undertaken these initiatives without government assistance. However, they point out that the post-1985 acceleration of heavy industrial exports such as steel and automobiles would not have been possible without the earlier HCI program of the 1970s. What could perhaps be inferred is that for a country with a rapidly developing private sector, temporary protection followed by general liberalization could well accelerate the hazardous transition to more complete technologies which then lead to faster accumulation of specific industrial skills. Whether the same inference can be made with respect to Taiwan is more debatable.

During the next phase of economic liberalization and globalization (from 1984 to the present) performance continued to be spectacular in both countries. Although significant improvements in social welfare occurred during this period, Adelman claims that the relationship between income distribution and development in Taiwan and Korea has given rise to an *inverted* Kuznets curve, with the initial stages of industrialization marked by egalitarian growth and the later stages characterized by unequalizing growth.

In conclusion, Adelman argues that the governments of both countries adopted a dirigiste stance with respect to the private sector. Their development strategies were implemented through a mixture of carrots and sticks that were both discretionary and nondiscretionary. Both used market incentives as well as direct controls to attain their goals. A key issue is why government intervention appears to have led to superior economic results in Taiwan and Korea in contrast with most other developing countries. The following hypotheses in support of this contention are offered: 1) leadership commitment to economic development started at the very top, with technocrats wielding substantial influence and a great deal of autonomy; 2) both countries espoused sound economic policies in accordance with their dynamic comparative advantage; 3) they excelled in their administrative capacities and bureaucracies; 4) they developed dynamic entrepreneurial capabilities and industrial organizational structures, though the latter differed as among the two countries; 5) the governments of both countries took a long range view; 6) policies and strategies were pragmatic and flexible; 7) the design of policy involved continued vigilance with key indicators closely monitored.

While initial conditions, development strategies and institutions were largely similar in both countries, there were also important contrasts between them. First, there were two important differences in development strategy: 1) in Taiwan the import substitution phase was characterized by agricultural-development-led-industrialization in contrast to Korea, where agricultural development never played the same dynamic role; 2) the dynamics of Taiwan's changes in trade and industrialization policies especially during the HGI drive corresponded more closely to her changing comparative advantage than did Korea's.

With regard to macroeconomic management, although both countries relied on a high-investment high-growth strategy the monetary and fiscal policies of Taiwan were considerably more conservative than those of Korea. Evidently the historical memory of hyperinflation on the mainland was a key reason for the tremendous emphasis on maintaining stable prices. Another difference, particularly in the earlier development phase, was that the rate of national savings in Taiwan exceeded its investment rate — in contrast with Korea, where the domestic investment rate can continue to exceed its savings rate by significant percentage implying, of course, a greater reliance on foreign savings.

With regard to institutional development, the primary difference between the two countries is in their industrial organization and structure. While the distribution of firms in manufacturing is rather similar, Korean firms are aggregated into business groups (conglomerates or *chaebols*) for which there is no counterpart in Taiwan. One likely explanation is that Taiwan initially was endowed with more entrepreneurial and managerial talent than was Korea. The conglomerate and group structure was a way to economize on these scarce skills.

Harberger (Chapter 15) undertakes a careful examination of the contrasting economic growth performance and development strategies followed by East Asia and Latin America on the basis of a number of different statistical indicators. Economic growth has been much faster in East Asia than in Latin America; it has been strongly export-led and has given rise to economies with a significantly higher concentration in manufactures than has emerged in Latin America. While it can be argued that most of Latin American growth has also been export led, this growth often stemmed from exogenous forces like international commodity price booms. Only occasionally in Latin America does one find policies conducive to a pattern of exports more fully exploiting its comparative advantage. Besides the obvious better performance of the East Asian economies with respect to investment and controlling inflation, one finds that these countries have also exercised considerably more discipline in their macroeconomic policies, relying much less on the banking system to finance their government and maintaining significantly greater control over the expansion of total banking system credit.

Another difference stressed by Harberger is that the East Asian countries exhibited remarkably low real exchange rate variability while for the Latin American countries it was remarkably high. This difference in variability is largely related to the predominance of primary products in the production and trade patterns of the Latin American region. Finally, an analysis of the sources of economic growth indicated that the East Asian economies enjoyed a much higher rate of investment as well as rate of return to capital. The combination of these two factors yields a median contribution of capital to growth, since the 1960s, amounting to an outstanding 4 percent per annum, compared with less than 2 percent for Latin America. The other surprisingly big difference is in the contribution of total factor productivity to overall GNP growth, whose median level was almost three times higher in Asia than in Latin America (2.7% per year compared to 1%).

Sadli and Thee (Chapter 17) emphasized three successful aspects of Taiwan's development experience that could be fruitfully transferred to Indonesia, mainly, the rapid reduction of corruption, the successful promotion of economically viable and highly competitive small and medium scale enterprises and the acquisition and adaptation of foreign industrial technologies.

Although in contrast with many other parts of the world, and in particular with sub-Saharan Africa, the proceeds of corruption in Indonesia tended to be reinvested domestically, a lesson that Indonesia could profitably learn from Taiwan is to build more distance between government officials and the private sector to reduce the susceptibility of those officials to private bribery and undue influence. Increased deregulation and privatization would encourage a greater competition and hopefully thereby reduce corruption.

Taiwan's very successful experimentation with small and medium scale enterprises demonstrated to the developing world that a successful performance in manufactured exports is not necessarily dependent on large-scale enterprises. Here the main lesson for Indonesia is that the policy stance favoring large conglomerates is not a necessary prerequisite for sustaining the present momentum of Indonesia's manufactured exports. In fact, the Indonesian government should do more to reduce the institutional biases against small firms.

Taiwan has demonstrated that a useful instrument for the acquisition and adaptation of foreign technologies consists of relying on multinational corporations as sources of industrial technologies and knowledge about international marketing. Finally, Taiwan's highly effective science and technology (S&T) infrastructure could be copied in Indonesia if the government played a more important role in promoting S&T infrastructure and by establishing S&T institutes and think tanks.

1.6 Notes

1 Today, Tsiang's critics might say that "government failures" are fairly minor and rare and that hence greater government intervention might have internalized more externalities. Thus, Tsiang was overprudent. While history cannot be replayed, we believe that it is reasonable to speculate that government failure could have been worse in Taiwan, had it not been for Tsiang's call for prudence.

2 Specific examples of institutions initiated or encouraged by the government are discussed in Section 1.4.

3 Taiwan, of course, had a longstanding historical experience with the process of agricultural surplus extraction as President T.H. Lee so clearly analyzed in his classic study. (Lee, 1971)

1.7 References

Kim, J.-I. and L.J. Lau, 1994. "The Sources of Economic Growth of East Asian Newly Industrialized Countries." *Journal of the Japanese and International Economies* 8: 235-271.
Krugman, P., 1994. "The Myth of Asia's Miracle," *Foreign Affairs* 73(6): 62-78.
Lee, T.H., 1971. *Intersectoral Capital Flows in the Economic Development of Taiwan, 1895-1960.* Ithaca, NY: Cornell University Press.
Lin, Yongchih, 1995. "Technology Acquisition in a Developing Economy: Case Studies of the Taiwanese Machine Tool Industry", mimeo, Cornell University.
Little, Ian M.D., 1979. "An Economic Reconnaissance," in W. Galenson (ed.), 1979. *Economic Growth and Structural Change in Taiwan: The Post-War Experience of the Republic of China.* Ithaca, NY: Cornell University Press.
Pack, H. 1992. "New Perspectives on Industrial Growth in Taiwan", in: G. Ranis (ed.), *Taiwan: From Developing to Mature Economy*, Boulder, CO: Westview Press, pp. 73-120.
Stern, J.J., Kim, J.-H., Perkins, D.H. and Yoo, J.-H., 1995. *Industrialization and the State: The Korean Heavy and Chemical Industry Drive.* Cambridge, MA: Harvard University Press.
Thorbecke, Erik, 1992. "The process of agricultural development in Taiwan: transition from developing to mature economy," in G. Ranis (ed.), *Taiwan: From Developing to Mature Economy*, Boulder, CO: Westview Press: pp. 15-72.
Thorbecke, Erik and Christian Morrisson, 1989. "Institutions, Policies and Agricultural Performance: a Comparative Analysis", *World Development*, Special Issue: 1485-1498.
Tsiang, S.-C., 1985. *Lessons from the Economic Development of Taiwan: Growth Amidst Stability.* Taipei: Commonwealth. (In Chinese).
Young, A., 1995. "The Tyranny of Numbers: Confronting the Statistical Realities of the East Asian Growth Experience," *Quarterly Journal of Economics* 110(3): 641-680.

2 THE "MIRACLE" THAT DID HAPPEN: UNDERSTANDING EAST ASIA IN COMPARATIVE PERSPECTIVE

Jagdish Bhagwati[1]

I am honored by the invitation to give the Keynote speech at this celebratory Conference in honor of Professors Liu and Tsiang. But I am also intimidated: the many distinguished economists assembled here are scholars who know so much more than I do about the subject that I have been asked to address that my participation in the Conference will earn me an unrequited transfer rather than mere gains from trade.

Perhaps the most productive task I might undertake would be to address the lively debate in recent years over the issue of the East Asian "miracle," in which Taiwan has been a major player. What factors explain this phenomenon? What lessons can the laggard, reforming countries draw from this analysis? Drawing on a historical contrast between India, whose experience I know fairly well from my own research, and East Asia, whose experience I know almost as well from others' research, I plan to argue the following (among many other things):

- that the recent contention (by Paul Krugman, drawing on the Allwyn Young calculations of TFP and growth accounting,[2] but in fact going back, as I say below, to T.N. Srinivasan in his comments, based on Jong-Il Kim and Larry Lau's earlier TFP calculations instead, on the World Bank study of East Asia) that there was no "miracle" misconstrues what is miraculous about the East Asian growth experience;

- that the miracle consisted in the enormous growth in rates of private investment in these countries, to levels that are almost certainly unparalleled in the experience elsewhere, now or historically;

- that this "fundamental" cannot be explained without assigning a major explanatory role to the region's outward orientation, i.e. to its "export promoting" (EP) as distinct from an "import substituting" (IS) trade strategy;
- that, in turn, the growth of export earnings also led to this investment being "implemented" with increasing imports of newer-vintage capital equipment, which embodied significant technical change, whose social contribution exceeded its cost, providing therefore a double whammy (i.e. both high rates of private investment induced by exports and returns from technical change embodied in imports) that raised growth to "miracle" levels over a sustained period;
- that the excess of the social contribution by newer-vintage-capital-goods over their international cost was the larger because of the phenomenally high levels of literacy and education that characterized the East Asian countries, thus reinforcing the second source of contribution to growth noted above;
- that direct foreign investment (DFI), like trade, was equally productive in East Asia, reflecting the high returns to the EP strategy, whereas the IS countries both attracted less sustained inflows of DFI and got less therefrom;
- that "industrial policy," or what Alice Amsden has called "getting prices wrong," has little to do with East Asia's growth and may have even harmed it;
- that this mighty engine of growth, based on outward orientation, must be contrasted with the sluggish locomotive that India's IS-strategy-burdened economy registered, to appreciate the thesis I advance; and
- that the East Asian "model" has already been adopted with dramatic results by the NECs, having traveled west from the NICs, and India in South Asia stands poised to profit from a shift to it as the reforms initiated in 1991 are intensified.

2.1 A Miracle or Not?

At the outset, permit me to examine the issue whether there was a miracle or not.[3] To my knowledge, many of us christened the East Asian experience of near and actual double-digit growth rates over nearly a quarter century a miracle; and I have often thought that ours must be a dismal science indeed if anytime a country does remarkably well, we call it a miracle!

Some of the recent critics who contend that the East Asian miracle is a myth seem to take the theological view that a miracle is a phenomenon that cannot be explained. Since growth accounting suggests (what cannot but have been apparent to the scholars of East Asia) that the remarkable growth performance can be explained overwhelmingly by high rates of investment, the miracle ceases to exist: a miracle dissolves the way a paradox is lost as soon as it is explained.

But then there are also those who argue more substantively that the central role played by investment and the absence of significant TFP gains in East Asia means that there was no "miracle" in the different sense that we do not need to invoke or infer some silver bullet or an alchemy such as a wondrous "industrial policy" that we must all imitate or Max Weberite "Asian values" to account for East Asia's special performance.

Thus, let me cite T.N. Srinivasan who fully anticipated the later Krugman contention that there was "no miracle." In a forceful commentary on the draft of the World Bank study on the East Asian miracle, he argued as early as July 1993:[4]

...the analysis of Jong-Il Kim and Larry Lau suggests that *there was no TFP* growth in the NIC's. They conclude that "*the hypothesis that there has been no technical progress (or increase in efficiency) in the Newly Industrialized countries during the post-war period cannot be rejected.* By far the most important source of economic growth...is capital accumulation accounting for more than 80 per cent of their economic growth." (Jong-Il Kim and Lawrence J.Lau, "The Sources of Economic Growth of the Newly Industrialized Countries on the Pacific Rim," Stanford University (processed), December 1992.) ...Thus, one does not have to look beyond the neoclassical explanations based on *fundamentals*...to understand East Asian growth. **There is no mystery or miracle.**

And, in a subsequent letter to Michael Bruno, a few months later, he went on to argue that, therefore, "...the 'culture' and 'authoritarianism' hypotheses...ought to be firmly rejected," and that, in any event, other direct arguments could lead one to reject such "exceptionalism" hypotheses.

Equally, Ian Little, in an illuminating recent pamphlet on the subject, has argued that "exceptionalism" in the shape of "industrial policy" need not be cited either to explain the East Asian miracle, given the enormous and conventional role of investment, while also claiming that, in any event as I say below on the basis of his persuasive arguments, direct analysis of the role of industrial policy suggests that it was neither necessary for East Asia's performance nor harmless to it.[5]

My own view is that, even if the TFP calculations are taken seriously, the East Asian miracle, in the sense of "exceptionalism of outcomes" simply gets to be the miracle of East Asia's phenomenal increase in investment rates, i.e. it becomes an "exceptionalism of the fundamental of investment."[6] More to the point, since the East Asian investment rate increased in the private sector (whereas similar rises in investment rates occurred in the postwar period in the public sector in the former socialist countries, the latter resulting in blood, sweat and tears but not in growth), the real miracle that requires explanation is that of the phenomenal rise in private investment rates on a sustained basis to high levels, unparalleled as far as I know in any other region or historical period.

2.2 Explaining the Miracle: A Synopsis of My Thesis

In providing this "exceptional-private-investment"-centered explanation, which must be the critical starting point in any explanation of East Asia's miracle or exceptional performance, I will turn today to the region's outward orientation, especially to the adoption of the export-promoting (EP) strategy, and the substantial inducement to invest that the increasingly accessible world markets provided, while contrasting it with the adoption of the import-substituting (IS) strategy in India which, I shall argue, impaired instead the private inducement to accumulate by limiting it to that provided by the demand generated by the domestic (agricultural) growth rate.[7]

In turn, I will also argue that the flip side of the EP strategy was the exceptional export earnings which enabled the increased private investments to absorb increased imports of newer-vintage capital equipment whose social marginal product exceeded their international prices, yielding a "surplus" and hence an added boost to the East Asian growth.

Then again, this surplus must have been increased, and the miracle enhanced, by the increment in the social marginal product resulting from the high levels of primary education and literacy, as also the increases in higher education, that could interact meaningfully with the accumulation and imports-of-embodied-technology process that the outward orientation had unleashed and fed.

2.3   Dismissing Conventional Exceptionalism Arguments

But before I develop this argument, let me mention, only to reject, some of the conventional "exceptionalism" arguments that surface from time to time, especially those concerning the region's authoritarian politics, Confucian culture or industrial policy.

The exceptionalism cited to explain away the East Asian performance has taken some strange forms. For instance, it used to be asserted that Hong Kong and Singapore were small "city states" and therefore somehow were not subject to the economic laws applying to other "normal" nations. Of course, many nations around the world are even smaller on dimensions such as population. Again, coming from India, I recall exceptionalism being applied similarly to explain India's lack of performance: we were an exceptionally "large" country, so what could we expect? Of course, we then had to contend with Brazil and, now, we see China which is even larger (in population) pushing ahead rapidly. But the less outrageous claims of exceptionalism are no more persuasive.

2.3.1   Authoritarianism

The commonest and superficially plausible assertion, of course, is that East Asia prospered because it had authoritarian rule and that democracy is inimical to growth. It is hard to see authoritarian rule however as either a necessary or a sufficient condition for efficiency or for growth. Indeed, the historical record, as also recent postwar experience across nations, underlines the tenuous, even false, nature of such claims.

I suspect that these claims were a result of the Harrod-Domar style of thinking when the postwar period of planning began.[8] If one treated the marginal capital-output ratio as more or less a technological parameter, as the major development economists of the time such as Paul Rosenstein-Rodan and Jan Tinbergen did, then all policy action was concentrated on raising the average savings rate to increase investment and hence the growth rate.[9] If public sector saving was considered to be the principal agent for raising the savings ratio, then it was evident that the authoritarian states would be at an advantage over democracies: the former could create the necessary surplus through heroic fiscal efforts that the latter, dependent on popular support, could not. Interestingly, both the Marxist and the Harrod-Domar models produced the same presumption.

But, of course, the reality turned out to be otherwise. For one thing, the East Asian miracle reflects private, not public, savings and investment: its sustained and extraordinary increase itself must be explained by reference to the East Asian policy framework. At the same time, more generally, the variations in growth performance across countries have tended to reflect, not just differences in rates of investment, but also dramatic differences in the marginal capital-output ratio. The latter, in turn, reflects the policy framework and its effects on efficient use of resources. Again, I would argue that the policy framework relevant here includes incentives and democratic processes that both enable and motivate effective participation by the citizenry in the growing economy.

Returning to East Asia, it might still be argued that authoritarian structures permitted these countries to make the right policy choices, uncluttered by democratic pressures. So, if I believe that the EP strategy was at the heart of the East Asian miracle, then the choice of this strategy and its execution with a steady hand must be attributed to the authoritarian structures. But the choice of policy by these non-democratic governments could well have been for the IS strategy, as was the case in many other countries in Africa, Latin America, Eastern Europe, and within Asia itself (as in Indonesia).

I have seen no truly compelling explanation of why the East Asian nations, uniquely among the developing nations at the time, chose the EP strategy, on which I have made plain that I plan to lay heavy duty to explain the miracle. Do not count out luck, however. Pertinent examples include the fact that the economists we honor today happened to render the right advice to Taiwan; that Saburo Okita, as Head of the Economic Planning Agency, propelled Japan itself towards exports-orientation in the late 1950s in teeth of widespread elasticity pessimism; that, by contrast, the influential Indian planner P.C. Mahalanobis in the late 1950s,[10] aided by some of India's distinguished economists, propelled the economy towards the harmful IS strategy precisely by taking elasticity pessimism too seriously.[11]

Did East Asia's proximity to Japan, which has followed a similar EP strategy historically, help by diffusing the ideas more readily to the region? But, if so, why did that influence stop right at the four "little tigers"? Besides, the region is proximate also to China which, at least at the time, was considered alongside India to be a potential superstar in development, so that the IS strategy might have been considered to be equally diffusible to East Asia!

Similar objections can be raised against the hypothesis that these were "island" economies which "naturally" looked outwards, like Japan, and thus embraced the EP strategy. Have we not heard of Jamaica under Manley or of Indonesia under Sukarno and the early Suharto? If all these hypotheses collapse under the weight of scrutiny, it is easy to understand the implausibility of the more farfetched contention that authoritarianism explains the choice by East Asia of the EP strategy; nothing more needs to be said on the subject.

2.3.2   Confucian Values

The notion that "values" have provided the necessary fuel to ignite the East Asian miracle has appeal to the Weberites and to Prime Minister Lee Kuan Yew of Singapore. It is not that values cannot matter in affecting economic performance: that would be a vulgar and untenable position to take. The problem is rather that the very same Confucian values that were supposed to be a hindrance to development in the Far East are now advanced as having been the engine of growth there: an ex post explanation that seems contrived rather than compelling. Indeed, culture and values seem rarely to provide a strong causal explanation of economic performance and are generally overwhelmed by conventional economic factors in producing or inhibiting economic performance.

Thus, contrast South with North Korea: surely both had identical values at the outset. Or compare East and West Pakistan, both Islamic: the contrasts in their performance before the creation of Bangladesh were striking. Or array the European and Latin American Catholic countries on their growth rates in the postwar period: the differences among them are again quite striking, just as they are among the aggregated Christian countries.

Moreover, an acquaintance with the literature on what the culturalists have said about the critical importance of culture and values to development will make economists generally skeptical of the assertions in regard to the claims in behalf of cultural determinism and its iron grip on development. In particular, many of these claims turn out to be specious, the alleged differences being themselves a product of differences in economic opportunity and circumstance. Thus, for example, in the context of Japan, James Fallows had argued, in a series of influential articles on Japan where he sought "containment" of Japan and (citing Rudi Dornbusch's earlier proposal in the New York Times to give Japan import targets and to whip it with across-the-board tariffs in case of noncompliance) asked for punitive tariffs on Japan of 20-25 percent,[12] that one cannot expect Japan to open markets through rules and must impose import targets (i.e. VIEs) on them because the Japanese are not into abstract thinking and prefer to deal with concrete quantities (such as VERs in trade) rather than rules (as at the GATT). Of course, as anyone familiar with Japanese trade history knows, the VERs were imposed on Japan, starting in the 1930s, because we did not wish them to trade by rules: their exports were growing too fast for our industries' comfort. The Japanese learned to trade by quantities, rather than by rules, because we would not let them export by rules: it was our demands, not their culture, that was the culprit.[13]

Let me also cite my favorite quote on misguided cultural inferences. In 1915, an Australian productivity expert invited to Japan had the following to say to the government about the Japanese workforce:

> My impression as to your cheap labour was soon disillusioned when I saw your people at work. No doubt they are lowly paid, but the return is equally so; to see your men at work made me feel that you are a very satisfied easy-going race who reckon time is no object. When I spoke to some managers they informed me that it was impossible to change the habits of national heritage.

Such examples could be multiplied readily from our own time, of course.

2.3.3 Industrial Policy

It is harder to dismiss, however, the exceptionalism attributed by some, especially Robert Wade and Alice Amsden,[14] to the industrial-policy interventions of East Asia. I do think that there is a beneficial role to be assigned to governmental interventions in the East Asian miracle, in the early take-off period of the 1950s when these economies (as also India) were being kicked up into a bastardized, Rosenstein-Rodan-Vishny-Schleifer, superior equilibrium, as I will argue below. However, the notion that interventions, especially in the nature of industrial policy, played a systematically beneficial role for decades thereafter (and furthermore that outward orientation played a passive, not an active, role in explaining export and economic performance) is not persuasive to me, though it has gained my colleague Dani Rodrik as a convert or, perhaps I should say, as a victim.

With Alice Amsden at this conference, I realize that I am bearding the lion in her own den, if I may mix my metaphors genderwise. But let me make two critical observations. First, even if industrial policy was important, the metaphor that it amounts to "getting prices wrong" is inappropriate. Two propositions are essential to making good policy: one must always get one's prices right; and, in the presence of market failures, the right prices which economists call shadow prices will generally differ from market prices. To combine those propositions into the proposition that one must generally get prices wrong (because presumably there are market failures) is to add two positives to get a negative: a generally invalid procedure despite the philosopher Sidney Morgenbesser's classic response in rich Yiddish to Noam Chomsky (when Chomsky argued that two positives did not make a negative in any language): Ya, Ya?

But linguistics aside, I have a more serious reservation. Of course, contrary to the claims made by the revisionists who embrace industrial policy, the fact that the East Asian superperformers, with the exception of Hong Kong, had interventions, including in the credit and trade markets, was well known to many of us who wound up assigning little role to this bit of information in the well known OECD studies directed by Ian Little, Maurice Scott and Tibor Scitovsky in the late 1960s and in the NBER studies in the early 1970s directed by me and Anne Krueger. We may have been wrong, but we were certainly not ignorant.

The real issue is therefore whether these interventions can be regarded as having had a substantial, and a positive, effect. Here, the Bhagwati-Krueger NBER project finding for South Korea was that, when quantified into ad valorem equivalents — a procedure I admitted was not very satisfactory from an analytical viewpoint — the diverse quantity interventions and subventions did not significantly alter the pattern of incentives that world market prices would have provided.[15]

The World Bank analysis of the East Asian miracle[16] has subsequently argued that, contrasted with expectations of sectoral patterns predicted from endowments (as estimated in ways that can be disputed), there is no conclusive evidence that the sectoral developments were different from the predictions and, for South Korea, the evidence is conclusively so since the sectors growing most during 1968-1988 were the labor-intensive ones whereas the governmental interventions were, if anything, in favor of other sectors. The World Bank study thus concluded: "the quantitative importance of government intervention to alter the structure of production is not confirmed at the sectoral level."[17]

This conclusion, of course, is correct as a "central tendency" and does not mean that specific sectors were not influenced by the activist industrial policy. Thus, Little (page 19) has argued that "common sense tells one that the timing, scale and pattern of investment in heavy industry — especially cars, shipbuilding, and petrochemicals — was markedly different from what would have occurred under laissez faire (or under some non-selective industrial promotion)." It is pertinent therefore that the sectors favored by the industrial-policy proponents in South Korea are precisely the ones with lagging productivity performance. Little quotes the recent Dollar and Sokoloff finding that "TFP growth in the most capital-intensive sectors (many the object of industrial policy promotion) was less than half that in the most labor-intensive sectors. Electrical goods; rubber, leather and plastic products; furniture; and clothing and footwear all show above average TFP growth."[18]

In addition, I find particularly compelling Little's qualitative arguments, based on his intimate knowledge of Taiwan and South Korea, which militate against the thesis that industrial policy was both comprehensive and, where applied, also beneficial. Thus, let me quote just a few of the many telling examples he gives for South Korea, right after he has measured the social returns from Korean heavy industry and found them to be "bad news for heavy industry fundamentalists, and those who stress the importance and value of the government's industrial policies":[19]

In 1975 I led a small team which investigated on behalf of the Asian Development Bank the performance of 28 randomly selected medium-size firms which had received loans from the Medium Industry Bank. Since the bank was government-owned it might be thought that our sample firms were selectively promoted. This was not so. The government's guidelines to the bank gave priorities which covered every kind of industry except non-traded luxury consumer goods. (The bank agreed that confectionery was probably the only exclusion.) This, incidentally, suggests that the extent to which the government directed finance (because it owned the banking system) is sometimes exaggerated by the revisionists.

The main steel company, POSCO (the only important state enterprise in the industries mentioned), has had low financial returns throughout its 20 year life despite heavy subsidization of its non-traded inputs, including the real interest rate which has been negative throughout most of its life. It has also received protection (the import tariff on steel was 25% until recently).Despite this, pre-tax income as a percentage of assets averaged only 4.6% from 1973-87....POSCO may even have had negative social returns.

I find myself therefore in sympathy with Little's conclusion that industrial policy in South Korea cannot be regarded as successful. His retort to Wade seems quite persuasive to me:[20]

"[The revisionists] do not question the proposition that industrial policy was successful [because government leadership fixed some market failure or another]. To quote Wade (1990, pp.305-6): '... the balance of presumption must be that government industrial policies, including sectoral ones, helped more than hindered. To argue otherwise is to suppose that economic performance would have been still more exceptional with less intervention which is simply less plausible than the converse.' Since the less interventionist Hong Kong, Singapore, and Taiwan grew faster than Korea, it is unclear why Wade thinks it simply less plausible that less intervention would have been better, given also the widespread failure of government industrial policies elsewhere. I find it simply more plausible that Korea grew fast despite its industrial policies, than because of them."

2.4 Why the Miracle Happened

So, having assessed and found unpersuasive the three most popular views about the miracle's source, let me turn to my own thesis, which I sketched earlier in the barest outline.

I must confess that it was suggested to me while contemplating the contrasts between the Indian and the East Asian experience. I hope to persuade you that this sort of "comparative economics" is revealing in a way which many-country regressions (regressing, say, growth rates in 100-plus countries on proxies for natural resources, openness of the economy *et al.* on the RHS of the estimated equation) are not. I find it difficult to see what I can reliably learn by putting Poland, Outer Mongolia, Venezuela, India and Singapore, among many others, on one regression line. While running such regressions can be suggestive of hypotheses one has not thought of, I am afraid that their ability to persuade is crippled by the twin facts that the cross-country data are generally not conceptually commensurate and comparable whereas the context within which these data must be understood and assessed is vastly different across countries. The inevitable destiny of such regressions across 100-plus countries is thus to be dismissed by serious scholars as irrelevant when they do not conform to one's intuitions and theories, and to be cited as corroboration when they do.

I believe that the stylized "story" of the East Asian miracle, and its absence in India, can be told in two Phases. I emphasize the fact that my account is a sketch of what I think to be the essential elements of the analysis; it therefore builds on stylized facts as I understand them, whereas a complete account would have to bring in many details that I cannot possibly encompass or even claim to know.

2.4.1 Phase I

The first Phase of enhanced Indian, and East Asian,[21] growth during the 1950s must principally be explained, I believe, by reference to the Rosenstein-Rodan argument that Vishny and Shleifer have now formalized in their fine article in the *Journal of Political Economy* as a case of multiple equilibria. In his classic 1943 *Economic Journal* article, which is arguably the most beautiful piece of creative writing on development, Rosenstein-Rodan was basically arguing that, for developing countries stuck in a Nash equilibrium with low levels of investment, there existed a superior cooperative equilibrium with higher levels of investment and growth.

The Indian planners, in formulating the First Five Year Plan (1951-56), basically were exploiting this insight. This was an indicative Plan, without the straitjacket of controls and targeted allocations that would presumably reflect the contours of the superior equilibrium. In fact, it is absurd to imagine that anyone, either in India or East Asia, could have worked out such a Rosenstein-Rodan-Vishny-Schleifer equilibrium even if there had been complete information to do so! What did happen instead was that the large component of public spending on infrastructure which was built into these indicative programs made the government's commitment to kicking the system up into some bastardized version of the Rosenstein-Rodan-Vishny-Shleifer equilibrium quite credible to the private sector, triggering the self-fulfilling private sector investment response that lifted the economy into higher investment and growth rates.[22]

2.4.2   Phase 2
But, at the end of the 1950s, the policies of the two regions diverged in ways that would set them dramatically apart in their economic performance. The critical difference was that India turned to the IS strategy, East Asia to the EP strategy.

A. Inducement to Invest: India thus handicapped the private inducement to invest, while East Asia wound up enhancing it. India turned inwards, starting with the balance of payments crisis in 1956-57 which precipitated the imposition of exchange controls which then became endemic to the regime, reflecting the currency overvaluation that implies the effective pursuit of an IS strategy. Again, the explicit pursuit of an IS strategy was also desired, reflecting the economic logic of elasticity pessimism that characterized the thinking of India's planners.

The result was that the inducement to invest in the economy was constrained by the growth of demand from the agricultural sector, reflecting in turn the growth of that sector. But agriculture has grown almost nowhere by more than 4 percent per annum over a sustained period of over a decade, so that increment at the margin in India's private investment rate was badly constrained by the fact that it was cut off from the elastic world markets and forced to depend on inevitably sluggish domestic agricultural expansion. Thus, it became customary for Indian economists to talk about "balanced growth" and about the problem of raising the investment rate which, by the mid-1980s, was still in the range of 19-20 percent.

By contrast, the East Asian private investment rate began its takeoff to phenomenal levels because East Asia turned to the EP strategy. The elimination of the "bias against exports," and indeed a net (if mild) excess of the effective rate for exports over the effective exchange rate for imports (signifying the relative profitability of the foreign over the home market), ensured that the world markets were profitable to aim for, assuring in turn that the inducement to invest was no longer constrained by the growth of domestic market as in the IS strategy. Private domestic savings were either raised to match the increased private investment by policy deliberately encouraging them or by the sheer prospect of higher returns.

This argumentation is not easy to defend once you face up to what my student Don Davis, now at Harvard, has called the "tyranny of Stolper-Samuelson": for, when this theorem holds, wages and rentals on capital are inversely related.[23] When exports are labor-intensive, the EP strategy may be expected to raise the wage of labor but depress the return to capital, thus depressing, not raising, the inducement to invest. Clearly, therefore, the force of Stolper-Samuelson argument must be broken: as indeed it can be by relaxing one or more of the assumptions underlying that theorem.

Thus, Davis suggests that the forces of comparative advantage may be argued to have been sufficiently strong as to make East Asia specialize in the production of the labor-intensive goods. This "decouples factor returns from the factor price frontier for the capital intensive good, leaving wages and rentals dependent only on productivity in the labor intensive good and the price of that good. In moving from autarky to free trade, both factor prices can rise, inducing an accumulation 'miracle'." Another way out would be to assume productivity differences across countries, as in Ricardian theory. In this case, "if we assume that the relative productivity gap of East Asia relative to the rest of the world is largest in the capital intensive sectors, and that trade serves to close this gap, then it is again possible for both wages and rentals to rise."[24]

While therefore it is possible to formalize the argument I have made that the EP strategy increased the inducement to invest, I must also address Dani Rodrik's recent objection that exports were a relatively small part of the economy at the outset so that EP strategy could not have resulted in any significant impact, and therefore the source of the investment must be found in governmental subventions and interventions whereas the growth of trade is simply a passive result of the growth induced by these other factors. But this argument is totally unpersuasive because East Asia would have run into precisely the problem of demand constraint that India was afflicted with if an IS strategy had been followed, with the efficacy of these other policies in generating investment seriously impaired. Moreover, the ultra-EP strategy, with its mild bias in favor of the export market and the policy-backed ethos of getting into world markets, meant that the export incentives must have played a major role in influencing investment decisions, not just in the exporting industries, but also in the much larger range of nontraded but tradeable industries.[25] In any event, the growth of exports from East Asia was so phenomenal that the share of initial exports in GNP quickly rose to levels that would lay Rodrik's objection to rest, even if it were conceptually correct.

B. The Imports of Newer-Vintage Equipment: The flip side of the process was, of course, the generation of substantial export earnings that enabled the growing investment to be implemented by imports of equipment embodying new technical change.

Now, if the Social Marginal Product (SMP) of this equipment exceeded the cost of its importation, there would be a "surplus" that would accrue as an income gain to East Asia and would also, as I argue below, boost the growth rate. For this argument to hold, however, the international cost of the newer-vintage equipment must not reflect fully its SMP for East Asia. In a competitive international market for equipment, therefore, I must assume that East Asia was a small player whose higher SMP did not pull up the world price to reflect the higher SMP. I.e. that East Asia could, even without "piracy" and "theft" of intellectual property (which was widespread in the region until the new WTO regime), get embodied technology at bargain prices. This seems a reasonable assumption to make, especially when one sees that the world prices of the last-but-one vintage equipment fall drastically due to rapid obsolescence in the presence of quick product innovation: just think of your PCs. (To understand fully the foregoing point, note that an economy in 1970 such as Soviet Russia's which was confined to using its own 1930s-vintage technology in equipment would not lose to East Asia which could use a heuristically 20 times more productive 1960s technology if East Asia had to pay a 20 times greater price for it. The surplus arises because East Asia pays, say, only a 5 times greater price in world markets for equipment that is 20 times more productive in East Asia.)

This argument is illustrated in Figure 2.1 in a simple diagram, with the SMP curve for increasing imports of the vintage capital equipment for East Asia put against the international cost of importing it, the striped area then representing the surplus that accrues to East Asia.

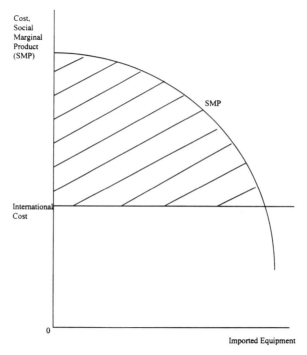

Figure 2.1   Social marginal product of imported equipment and surplus accruing East Asia

But there may also be another reservation about this argument's effect on the growth rate, as distinct from its effect on income. It is fair to say that, thanks to the focus on the steady state in Solow-type models, it has now become fashionable to assert that the gains from trade, like any allocative efficiency gains, amount to one-time gains, not affecting the growth rate. This is however wrongheaded as a general assertion. Thus, consider the simple Harrod-Domar corn-producing-corn growth model with labor a slack variable. If allocative efficiency regarding land use (say, from one inefficient farm to another efficient farm) leads to a greater return to the total amount of ("invested") corn being put into the ground, the marginal capital-output ratio will fall, ceteris paribus, and lead to a permanently higher growth rate. Similarly, it takes no sweat for a firstrate theorist to construct models where trade in capital goods leads to higher growth rates, without building in externalities etc. and relying exclusively on the fact that they can be imported more cheaply than constructed under autarky.

T.N. Srinivasan has extended the Mahalanobis-type putty-clay model to include trade and demonstrated precisely this.[26] Thus, he assumes (in place of just one capital and one consumer good in the autarkic version) that there are two of each class of goods, with the marginal product of capital constant in each sector as in the Harrod-Domar model. The social utility function and the function that transforms the output of the two investment goods into aggregate investment are Cobb-Douglas. There is no intersectoral (i.e. between the consumer goods and the capital goods sectors), as against intrasectoral (i.e. between the two goods in each sector), mobility of capital: this is the clay assumption.

Assuming that all four goods are produced under autarky, that free trade is undertaken at fixed terms of trade, and that the share of investment going to augmenting capacity in each of the two sectors is fixed exogenously, Srinivasan then demonstrates plausibly that free trade in consumer goods (but with autarky continuing in investment goods) will raise welfare relative to autarky but not affect the growth rate of income or utility. On the other hand, freeing trade in investment goods will have a positive effect on transitional as well as on long-run (steady state) growth effect, and also a beneficial welfare effect relative to autarky. The vulgar belief that trade gains cannot affect the growth rate is thus easily disposed of.

However, how does one reconcile the "surplus" argument with the findings that TFP growth has been a negligible factor in East Asia? So, is my story plausible but not borne out by the facts, as is often the case with our most interesting theories? I think not.

Thus, consider precisely the case where the imported equipment is 20 times more productive in Period 2 than in Period 1, but its price is only 5 times as high. If the valuation of this equipment is at domestic (producer) opportunity cost, as it should be, then it will indeed be priced 20 times higher than the older-vintage equipment of Period 1, so the measure of capital contribution at the level of the industry will rise commensurately and I presume that the estimated TFP growth in the industry will be zero: in that case, my thesis about the surplus is totally compatible with measured TFP emerging as negligible. But, of course, if the equipment is priced at its international cost, then I presume that TFP growth will pick up three-fourths of the gain that accrues from the "surplus" of SMP over the international cost. My guess then is that, in East Asia, the former was the case. This might have been, not because the accountants were smart and valued Period 2 equipment at domestic opportunity cost, but because I guess that much of the imported equipment may have gone through importing trading firms which collected the three-fourths premium rather than the producing firms.

2.4.3 Literacy and Education
The role of literacy and education comes in precisely at the stage of the second step in my story above. For, the productivity or SMP of the imported equipment would

be greater with a workforce that was literate and would be further enhanced if many had even secondary education. Thus, as shown in Figure 2.2, the SMP curve could shift to the right with literacy and education, leading to greater surplus for any given international cost of newer-vintage equipment.

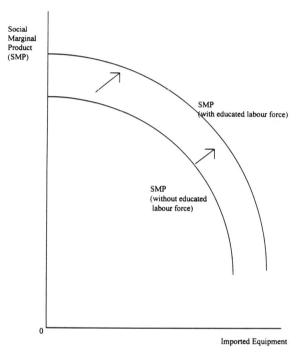

Figure 2.2   Impact of education on social marginal product of imported equipment

Here again, there will be much that is scholarly on this subject at the Conference, but I may cite Little (page 23) using the pretext that a Lecture justifies the informality of argumentation that a Conference paper does not:

It was largely from the experience of conducting this [1975, South Korean] survey, involving visits to the [28 randomly selected] firms ranging from 1.5 to 3.5 hours, that my own impressions of such matters as the acquisition of technology and skills on the part of the labour force. . .were formed. I also visited a number of high exporting medium-size labour-intensive firms in Taiwan in 1976. . . . Two points are mainly relevant in the present context. First the technology was simple, non-proprietary and easily acquired. . . . Secondly, both Korean and Taiwan workers were very quick to learn. Employees would usually reach the expected high level of productivity within a few weeks. This would probably not have been the case if the standards of primary education had not been high.

Of course, as these economies grew rapidly, the demand for secondary and higher education in turn would rise and a virtuous circle would follow: primary education would enhance the growth that the EP strategy brought whereas the enhanced growth would demand and lead to a more educated workforce. I see therefore primary education and literacy as playing an enhancing, rather than an initiating, role in the EP-strategy-led East Asian drama, again contrary to what I think Dani Rodrik has suggested in yet another analysis of the role of education in development.

Thus, my story combines in its own way three major elements, in that order: (i) the enhanced inducement to invest due to the EP strategy; (ii) the benefit from the surplus of domestic SMP over international cost of imported newer-vintage capital equipment; and (iii) the raising of this SMP by the presence of a literate workforce. But if the main plot is this, the story has doubtless many sub-plots. I will end on just one of them, especially as the analysis dates back to the early 1970s and to the NBER project, underlining the richness of the argumentation at the time that is hard to find in the somewhat caricatured accounts provided in the revisionist critiques.

2.4.4 Direct Foreign Investment (DFI)

In my synthesis volume[27] for the NBER Project findings, I had noted that among the advantages of the EP strategy, which the Project had found beneficial, one had to count the fact that trade barriers-jumping DFI in the IS countries was likely to be limited for these countries by the size of the domestic market by which it was motivated — there are shades here of the inducement-to-invest argument I have made today, but only in the faintest strokes. Secondly, such DFI as was attracted in the IS countries was also likely to be less productive because it would be going into economic regimes characterized by significant trade distortions that could even generate negative value added at socially-relevant world prices — a possibility that was discussed by me (based on an extension to the DFI issue of the contribution by Harry Johnson to the theory of immiserizing growth in tariff-distorted economies)[28] and then nailed down in well known articles into a certainty under certain conditions by Hirofumi Uzawa and by Richard Brecher and Carlos Diaz Alejandro independently.

I did say earlier that we all cite the many-country regressions when they go our way. So, let me mention that both these (thoroughly plausible in terms of their economic rationale) hypotheses have been examined, with some success, in cross-country regressions by another former student of mine, V.N.Balasubramanyam and his co-authors.[29] So, this element of explanation may also be added to the explanation of East Asia's superior performance relative to that of the IS-strategy-plagued countries.[30]

2.4.5 The Westward Diffusion

So, I conclude by noting that the East Asian alchemy seems to have been traveling westwards, lifting the economic performance of the NECs such as Indonesia and Thailand, and India now seems finally poised, with its economic reforms in the direction of global integration, to profit from it almost a quarter of a century late.

The miracle of East Asia can thus be explained; and having explained it, we can reproduce it. In that sense, it is more magic than miracle. But I will settle for magic, which is no less a spectacle than a miracle, and more consonant with our rational age.

2.5 Notes

1   This is the text of the Keynote speech delivered on May 3, 1996 at Cornell University on the occasion of the Conference on "Government and Market: The Relevance of the Taiwanese Performance to Development Theory and Policy" in honor of Professors Liu and Tsiang. I am thankful for many discussions I have had over the years with Ian Little, Martin Wolf, Don Davis, Vivek Dehejia, Magnus Blomstrom and T.N. Srinivasan on the issues raised by the East Asian experience. In making the final revisions, I have also profited from the contributions of many of the participants at the Cornell Conference, among them Irma Adelman, Erik Thorbeke, Arnold Harberger, John Cheh, Larry Lau, Gus Ranis and Henry Wan.

2   Krugman has advanced this argument in a number of newspapers and magazines, but the chief source is an article in Foreign Affairs , entitled "The Myth of Asia's Miracle," in the November/December 1994 issue.

3   T.N.Srinivasan, "Trade Orientation, Trade Liberalization and Economic Growth", Yale Economic Growth Center, mimeo, 1996, has recently suggested that the characterization of the Far Eastern performance as a miracle owes to Robert Lucas's lecture on "Creating a Miracle," followed by the World Bank's well known study entitled The East Asian Miracle, both in the early 1990s. However, Srinivasan is not correct. The characterization of the East Asian experience as a miracle, in the sense of an extraordinary performance, predates Lucas for sure. Thus, writing in the late 1980s in my book, *Protectionism* (MIT Press: Cambridge, Mass., 1988, p.98)), I myself had remarked on the Far Eastern experience as a miracle, in the context of arguing that everyone tended to see the miracle as produced by their preferred prescriptions: "...how could an economic miracle have occurred if policymakers had not followed our preferred policies? Recalling that public goods have the property that I can enjoy them without depriving you of your pleasure, I have formulated the following law: Economic miracles are a public good: each economist sees in them a vindication of his pet theories." I have no doubt that others have also used the word "miracle" in this sense, both generally and in relation to the East Asian experience, much before Lucas and the World Bank.

4   This quote is from a widely-circulated internal memo to the team in charge of the World Bank study, and is dated July 21, 1993. Italics are in the original; boldface has been added.

5   See the recent pamphlet by Ian Little, "Picking Winners: The East Asian Experience," Social Market Foundation Occasional Paper, London, 1996. I consider the subject of industrial policy in depth later in the Lecture.

6   In my analysis below, I explain why the inducement to invest was so high as to yield this exceptional investment performance. However, the accommodating increase in domestic savings also had to be remarkable and hence may be treated also as part of the miracle. As far as I can tell, the governments played a role in facilitating this process.

7   This element of my thesis was outlined in a Letter to the Editor, "Private Investment and the East Asian 'miracle,'" *The Financial Times*, January 15, 1996, apropos of Michael Prowse's column which had mentioned the Krugman views in *Foreign Affairs*. Krugman is wrong in arguing that there is no miracle in East Asia because the high growth can be explained by reference to "fundamentals" such as investment, while forgetting that the miracle lies precisely in these fundamentals being so exceptional: the fundamentals are themselves to be explained. In drawing an analogy between the USSR and East Asia to argue that the latter will grind to a halt the way the former did, Krugman also misses critically important differences between the two areas. The Soviet growth reflected exceptionally high levels of public saving and investment, set within a policy framework where incentives to use resources efficiently and to innovate (both endogenously and through imported technology via trade and investment) were both crippled, so that we would have quite rapidly the observed phenomenon of sagging and then sinking growth rates as illustrated dramatically by Padma Desai's Figure 1.1 (especially for 1955-1979) in her well known analysis,

Growth Retardation in The Soviet Economy: Problems and Prospects, Basil Blackwell: Oxford, 1987. By contrast, the East Asian experience is strongly built on exceptionally high private investment and saving, and high levels of absorption of foreign technology , explaining (in the manner outlined in the Lecture below) why the growth process has been sustained over a much longer period and the prospects are equally quite different from those that overtook the Soviet Union.

8   I have developed this theme at greater length in my 1994 Rajiv Gandhi Memorial Lecture, "Democracy and Development: New Thinking on an Old Question," published in a slightly abbreviated version in the *Journal of Democracy* , October 1995. The full text is published in the *Indian Economic Review*, Vol.30(1), 1995, pp.1-18.

9   That the marginal capital-output ratio would be constant in the Harrod-Domar model with slack labour force, which would be the case if we also assumed a Lewis surplus-labour economy, is consonant with the point I am making in the text about the capital-output ratio being taken by planners as virtually a technological parameter independent of the policy framework and its effects on efficiency.

10 See, in particular, P.C. Mahalanobis, "The Approach of Operational Research to Planning in India," *Sankhya*, Vol.16, 1-2, pp. 3-130.

11 I can testify to Saburo Okita's role personally, having gotten to know him in Tokyo in 1962 , and I discussed these questions in depth with him, when he and I were Secretaries to the Japanese and the Indian Groups of Wise Men, respectively, to promote Indo-Japanese research collaboration, trade and investment. Okita was Head of the Economic Planning Agency at the time. The Indian economists who worked with models that formally assumed elasticity pessimism to discuss developmental strategy, drawing policy lessons therefrom, and who therefore may properly be credited with the failures of India's developmental efforts, included K.N.Raj and Amartya Sen. For further discussion of the harmful role of economists in misguiding India's economic policy, see my Radhakrishnan Lectures at Oxford, *India in Transition*, Clarendon (Oxford University) Press, Oxford, 1993.

12 In a New York Times op.ed. article on February 22, 1996, provocatively titled by them "What Buchanan owes Clinton," I noted that Pat Buchanan had picked up his specific trade policy proposals from mainstream policy wonks and others, many uncomfortably close to the current administration. Thus, for instance, Buchanan has asked for a 10% across-the-board tariff against Japan, a moderate proposal compared to the 20-25 % tariff argued for by Fallows, and in a tone that is less alarmist and accusatory than that adopted by the leading Japan-baiting economists.

13 I have discussed this issue in my Harry Johnson Lecture, published as The World Trading System at Risk, Princeton University Press, 1991.

14 Cf. Alice Amsden, *Asia's Next Giant: South Korea and Late Industrialization*, New York, Oxford University Press, 1989; and Robert Wade, *Governing the Market: Economic Theory and the Role of the Government in East Asian Industrialization*, Princeton University Press, Princeton, 1990.

15 This finding was based on the South Korea study in the NBER project by Charles Frank, Kwang Suk Kim and Larry Westphal (South Korea, Columbia University Press: New York, 1975) and discussed in my overall synthesis volume, *The Anatomy and Consequences of Exchange Control Regimes*, NBER, Ballinger & Co.: Cambridge, Massachusetts, 1978.

16 *The East Asian Miracle, Economic Growth and Public Policy*, Oxford University Press, 1993.

17 Ibid., page 333, quoted in Little, op.cit., page 19.

18 Little, op.cit., page 19, citing David Dollar and Kenneth Sokoloff "Patterns of Productivity Growth in South Korean Manufacturing Industries, 1963-1979", *Journal of Development Economics*, Vol.33, pp. 309-327.

19 Little, *op. cit.*, page 22; the following quotes are from pp. 22-24.

20 Little, *op. cit.*, page 12.

21 Phase I may be set in part of East Asia as dating into the early 1960s; but this is a matter of judgment and detail of little consequence to my argument. Besides, Phase I may even be considered absent in Hong Kong, which had the unique advantages of an abundant entrepreneurial class and an entrepot economy that was already outward oriented from the outset. I might add that the notion that East Asia's investment growth in Phase 1 did not depend on outward orientation or EP strategy in trade will come as no surprise to any scholar in the field, though it is sometimes presented as if it was a modern discovery that somehow discredits those who talk of the critical role of EP strategy (which applies, of course, to Phase 2).

22 Dani Rodrik seems to share broadly this view of how private investment rose but seems to err in two ways. He seems to suggest, presumably in sympathy with the Amsden-Wade thinking, that the bureaucrats could figure out the sectoral contours of the superior equilibrium, a presumption that I find ludicrous, especially having seen the best bureaucrats in India confess to their inability to choose industrial favorites on any rational grounds. Moreover, he extends the argument well beyond the 1950s whereas, as I argue later in the text, this makes little sense.

23 I am drawing here on the preliminary draft of Don Davis's paper," 'Miracles of Accumulation': Models of Trade and Growth in East Asia," Department of Economics, Harvard University, January 1996.

24 Don Davis, ibid., page 2. Davis proceeds to formalize these ideas in a dynamic framework, more appropriate to the accumulation problem at hand.

25 Rodrik also seems to think it pertinent that the export incentive, in the shape of the real exchange rate, did not continue improving. However, it is not necessary for it to be improving continuously for the export incentives to operate. Thus, an excess of the effective exchange rate for exportables over that for importables (as distinct from continuous increase in this difference) will suffice to provide a continuing incentive for the export over the home markets. Cf. Dani Rodrik, "Getting Interventions Right: How South Korea and Taiwan grew Rich" *Economic Policy*, April 1995. Martin Wolf has also critiqued Rodrik's anti-EP-strategy argumentation, as also the Krugman argumentation, in two excellent recent Columns in the *Financial Times*, "The Tyranny of Numbers" and "A Lesson for the Chinese."

26 See his "Comment on 'Two Strategies for Economic Development: Using Ideas and Producing Ideas", by Romer,' Proceedings of the World Bank Annual Conference on Development Economics 1992, World Bank, Washington D.C., 1993. Srinivasan also makes the valid point that the Mahalanobis-Feldman putty-clay models are among the earlier examples of "endogenous" growth theory since the growth rate is determined by the discretionary policy choice of the share of investment goods being allocated to the capital goods sector. The neglect of the considerable literature on such models by the originators of the current endogenous growth theorists is to be attributed to the fact that these theorists have come to their models from the Solow model and have no acquaintance with the growth models that came up in the context of developmental problems in the 1960s. Of course, most of us are rediscovering great ideas all the time!

27 Bhagwati, 1978, op. cit.

28 See Jagdish Bhagwati, "The Theory of Immiserizing Growth: Further Applications," in Michael Connolly and Alexander Swoboda (eds), *International Trade and Money*, Toronto University Press: Toronto, 1973.

29 See, in particular, V.N. Balasubramanyam and M.A.Salisu, "EP, IS and Direct Foreign Investment in LDCs", in A. Koekkoek and L.B.M.Mennes (eds), *International Trade and Global Development: Essays in Honour of Jagdish Bhagwati*, Routledge: London, 1991, for the former hypothesis; and V.N.Balasubramanyam, M.A.Salisu and David Sapsford, "Foreign Direct Investment and Growth in EP and IS countries," *Economic Journal*, January 1996, for an indirect test of the latter hypothesis (explaining growth as the dependent variable).

30 Of course, as Magnus Blomstrom has reminded me, I should also note that there is considerable evidence at the micro level of beneficial spillover effects from DFI, including from several studies he has undertaken in developing countries. Reconciling this evidence with the contention that there is little evidence of TFP in the Lau-Young type studies remains an unresolved issue, however.

2.6 References

See Notes.

PART II
KEY MACRO POLICIES AND REFORMS IN TAIWAN'S DEVELOPMENT

3 GOVERNMENT POLICY IN THE TAIWANESE DEVELOPMENT PROCESS: THE PAST 50 YEARS

Shirley W. Y. Kuo

The Republic of China on Taiwan has achieved one of the world's highest rates of growth over the past 50 years. Its development has been characterized by rapid growth, stable prices, low unemployment, and equitable income distribution.

Over the past four decades, from 1952 through 1994, the real GNP grew at an average rate of 8.6 percent per annum, and the real per capita GNP grew at 6.3 percent. As a result, per capita GNP in Taiwan increased from about US$100 to US$12,500 during this period. The annual inflation rate was 4.3 percent on average, and since 1965 the unemployment rate has been below 3 percent.

It is a well-known story that the Taiwan economy went through the stages of import substitution, export promotion, and technology and knowledge intensification. Over the past five decades, the economic center of gravity shifted from agriculture to industry and, within industry, from labor-intensive light manufacturing to capital- and skill-intensive manufacturing. Exports and imports have played a crucial role in the development of Taiwan. With exports of US$111.7 billion and imports of US$103.6 billion in 1995, the Republic of China was the fourteenth largest trading country in the world.

Economic development has brought improvements in living standards in many areas, including education, sanitation, transportation and communications, and housing. From 1945 to 1995 the percentage of senior high-age youths actually in school increased from 28.3 percent to 92.4 percent, and the percentage of junior college- and university-age youths in school increased from 11.3 percent to 45.3 percent. Life expectancy lengthened from 58.6 years to 74.5 years. The widespread diffusion of public utilities brought benefits to even the poorest and most isolated families. For example, the percentage of houses equipped with electric lighting island-wide grew from 33 percent in 1949 to 99.7 percent in 1994. The gap between urban and rural sectors in the most basic needs, such as primary education, life expectancy, and possession of refrigerators and televisions, has become very small (see Appendix 1). In short, economic development over the past five decades has brought in its wake significant welfare benefits: higher per capita income, higher employment rate, higher productivity, and higher standard of living (Kuo, 1983a).

It is well known that government policies have played a vital role in the success of Taiwan's economic development. Before going into detail, some characteristics of these government policies will be identified.

First, government policies adopted in Taiwan over the last 50 years were, in general, a result of case-by-case innovations instituted in response to impending economic problems.[1] Yet, when we look back, we see them as if they were systematically designed, since they seem to form a consistent long-term package. They constitute a kind of linear movement in the direction of liberalization and internationalization, contributing greatly to the economic development of Taiwan. Needless to say, not all government policies made positive contributions. Some negative effects generated by previous policies were, however, dealt with by remedial policies later on. For example, during the period 1985 to 1987, the systematic gradual appreciation policy adopted by the Central Bank created a massive inflow of foreign exchange and a skyrocketing surge in stock prices. This led to a significant relaxation of foreign exchange controls, especially in the direction of capital outflow, in July 1987 (see section IX.3). Also, quite often, the policies adopted in response to impending problems were quietly abandoned or retained in name only after the problems disappeared. For example, a special export loan program for financing exports at preferential interest rates was initiated in the early period. The proportion of loans granted under this program was gradually reduced; and finally, in the early 1980s, banks stopped offering export loans at preferential rates. However, the name "export loans" has been maintained up to the present, although the amount of loans extended under this program has been negligible (0.3 percent of total loans in 1996).

Second, some deeply rooted Chinese philosophical principles formed the basis of persistent pragmatic policies in Taiwan. A generally accepted ideology can be seen in popular phrases such as "growth with equity" (均富), "growth with stability" (穩定中求成長), and, in the early days, "balanced growth of agriculture and industry." Thus, the policies were, in general, pragmatic in terms of economic development.

Third, the design and implementation of government policies in Taiwan were in general done gradually, instead of "cold turkey." There were many obstacles to be overcome; in particular, the adoption of certain economic policies not only entailed economic changes, but also social and institutional changes. Thus, resistance from vested interests and conservatives was sometimes strong. Also, in the course of design, it was not easy to identify the complicated cause and effect relationships, especially since various effects would appear only after different time lags. Furthermore, policies by nature had a "no free lunch" character. That is, even a good policy was inevitably associated with some adverse side effects, which was the price that a good policy had to pay. The adverse side effects were sometimes over-emphasized to such an extent that a good policy was rejected. These obstacles had to be overcome again and again in the past.

This paper attempts to discuss how and what government policies contributed to the nation's economic success. I would like to focus on certain policies that played an essential role in crises, that stimulated a faster transition, and that helped to shape fruitful tendencies. The following are the essential government policies of the past 50 years that I will try to cover:

1. Emphasis on Market Economy and Balanced Growth
2. Stabilization Policies of the early 1950s
3. Utilization of U.S. Aid
4. Factors for High Savings
5. Land Reform
6. Import Substitution Policies
7. Export Promotion Policies
8. Anti-inflation Policies during the Oil Crises
9. Financial Liberalization
10. Policies for High-Tech Industries
11. Policies on Infrastructure
12. Current Issues

3.1 Emphasis on Market Economy and Balanced Growth

The promotion of political and social stability was a prerequisite for Taiwan's successful development, and the emphasis on the market economy, based on a free economic system, was crucial. In particular, the institutional environment after the late fifties was such that entrepreneurs were free to seek profits and workers were free to pursue their best interests. This free economic system developed an essential dynamic force which stimulated the economy to grow rapidly.

The government advocated balanced growth, and the interdependence of agriculture and industry was strongly emphasized. Policies aimed at improving equity between rural and urban regions were manifested in an emphasis on rural irrigation, electrification, education, transportation, and other types of rural construction. As a result, the irrigation system was diffused over most of the island's cultivated area. Electrification was extended to practically every home. Education was spread widely and promoted to males and females alike. Excellent road and rail networks spread throughout the island. The mileage of rural roads increased rapidly. Technical assistance through the Joint Commission on Rural Reconstruction, and through farmers' associations, was enhanced. Thus were laid sound foundations for a marked spatial dispersion of economic development. Past industrial development was extremely rural-oriented so as to provide the advantages of easier acquisition of raw materials, rural laborers, and cheaper land. This brought about the relatively dispersed character of Taiwan's industrialization.

3.2   Stabilization Policies of the Early 1950s

3.2.1   *Hyper-Inflation*

Toward the end of World War II, Taiwan was subject to intense bombing by the allies and was isolated from the outside world. Production decreased, external trade was at a standstill, there was a serious shortage of commodities, and inflation reached serious rates.

Prices in Taiwan rose at an annual rate of 500 percent in 1946-48 and then accelerated to about 3,000 percent in the first half of 1949. The inflation in Taiwan during this period was mainly due to the following reasons: (1) extension of big loans for rehabilitation and reconstruction, (2) colossal government expenditures, and (3) the vicious inflation on mainland China. Although the purpose of automatic adjustment of the exchange rate of the old Taiwan dollar against the Chinese National Currency was to ward off the impact of the rapid depreciation of the Chinese currency, for many reasons the adjustment was not enough to be really effective. Furthermore, there was no way to stop the influx of capital from the mainland; consequently, this measure failed to achieve the expected result of suppressing the inflationary trend in Taiwan.

At this stage, the most urgently needed action, more vital than any other, was thus price stabilization. Stabilization policies were implemented by various measures, among which monetary reform, preferential interest rate deposits, and a balanced government budget were essential (Kuo, 1983a). Those three measures will be discussed below.

3.2.2   *Monetary Reform and Other Measures*

(A) Reform. The New Taiwan Dollar Reform was put into effect on June 15, 1949, when the economy was suffering from hyper-inflation. The old Taiwan currency was devalued at a rate of 40,000 to one, and the value of the New Taiwan dollar was linked up with that of the U.S. dollar at the rate of NT$5 to US$1. The new currency was backed by 100 percent reserves in gold, silver, and foreign exchange, and the ceiling on the issuance of currency was set at NT$200 million.

These stipulations, if strictly enforced, would unquestionably have inspired the confidence of the people in the currency and prevented the resurgence of inflation. However, due to a big government deficit, advances from the Bank of Taiwan, which was functioning as the central bank at that time, continued to accumulate. By the end of December 1949, currency issuance was close to the ceiling of NT$200 million, causing a rapid depreciation of the new currency and a steady rise in the price of the U.S. dollar in the black market. In July 1950, the maximum issuance limit was abolished. By December 1950, issuance of the N.T. dollar had reached NT$267 million, and the black market price of the U.S. dollar had risen to NT$16.

(B) Gold Savings Deposits. During this early period, from May 1949 to December 1950, a noteworthy financial measure taken by the government to check inflation was the redemption of gold. The redemption of gold was done in the form of "gold savings deposits," with deposits redeemable in gold in one month at the official price, which was set lower than the market price of gold. Due to the continuous rise of prices, however, a large discrepancy soon developed between the official

and market prices of gold. From June 1, 1950, Patriotic Savings Coupons were allotted against gold savings deposits, and the number of coupons thus allotted varied daily in accordance with the discrepancy between the official and market prices of gold. These Patriotic Savings Coupons were replaced by Patriotic Bonds after July 16, 1950. The liquidity of the Coupons and Bonds was very low. Since their maturity was two years for the Coupons and seventeen years for the Bonds, the allotment of these securities was actually a disguised increase in the price of gold. The gold savings deposits, which were designed to absorb currency and to dump gold for price stabilization, were finally suspended on December 27, 1950 (Pan et al., 1968).

(C) Other Measures. After that, new financial measures were incorporated in two decrees: (1) "Measures Governing Control of Gold and Foreign Currencies" and (2) "Prohibition of Importation of Luxury Goods." The former, while permitting the possession of gold and foreign currencies, prohibited the free buying and selling of these items. The purpose was to outlaw black market dealings and strengthen foreign exchange and foreign trade controls. The latter decree was designed to check the outflow of gold and foreign currencies through rigid suppression of smuggling and prohibition of illicit remittances and the trading of imported luxury goods. The authorities believed that prevention of smuggling and prohibition of imported luxury goods would help eradicate the black market dealings in gold and foreign currencies.

In addition to these, the following measures are noteworthy. As of December 19, 1950, an importer, when applying for import exchange allocation, was required to put up a marginal deposit equivalent to 50 percent of the amount of foreign exchange he was applying for. On March 23, 1955, the requirement was raised to 100 percent. This requirement, which was not abolished until June 29, 1964, was originally designed as a foreign exchange control measure, but because of its usefulness in calling in a sizable amount of money supply in circulation, it became one of the important monetary tools of the government. Frequently, the amount of foreign exchange that an importer applied for would be several times the amount that was eventually approved, and it would usually take several weeks for an application to be processed and approved. Thus, the requirement for a marginal deposit could freeze a large amount of currency for a considerable period of time.

3.2.3   Interest Rate Policy

(A) Preferential Interest Rate Savings Deposits. Another very important measure promoting stabilization was the introduction of "preferential interest rate savings deposits" in March 1950. Due to the hyper-inflation prevailing at the time, the duration of the deposits was set very short, starting with one month at the outset. Deposits received by the banks had to be transferred to the Bank of Taiwan. Loans could be given to the depositors based on their deposit certificates, but the amount of a loan could not exceed 70 percent of the amount of the deposit.

The principal characteristic of the preferential interest rate savings deposits was their high interest rate. At that time, the yearly interest rate on one-year time deposits was 20 percent. The interest rate on these new deposits was 7 percent per month, which, if compounded, would amount to 125 percent per year. Although the interest rate was actually still below the inflation rate in 1950, the setting of such a high interest rate required intelligence and determination on the part of the government.

The preferential interest rate savings deposits were very effective. After the inauguration of these deposits, the amount of time deposits in all banks increased to NT$35 million from just NT$2 million, in eight months. The interest rate was later lowered from 7 percent per month to 3.5 percent per month, and then to 3 percent per month in late 1950. However, this reduction resulted in a decrease in deposits, and the interest rate was again raised to 4.2 percent per month. The interest rate was then gradually reduced, dropping to 2 percent per month by November 1952. At that time, preferential interest rate savings deposits accounted for 44 percent of the money supply.

(B) Longer-Term Preferential Interest Rate Savings Deposits. After 1953 the government gradually implemented longer-term preferential interest rate savings deposits, and the amount of these longer-term deposits increased gradually. On March 5, 1956, the authorities established a new kind of time deposit that matured in six months or one year, bearing monthly interest rates of 1.5 percent and 1.8 percent, respectively, and that could not be accepted as security for loans. These rates were higher than those on deposits that matured in one month and three months, bearing monthly interest rates of 0.85 percent and 1 percent, respectively, and that could be accepted as security for loans. Due to the higher interest rates on these longer-term deposits, their volume increased significantly. At the end of 1956, deposits in one-year accounts comprised 27 percent of total deposits (Table 3.2.1).

On July 16, 1957, the Bank of Taiwan began to accept time deposits maturing in two years, and also abolished the one-month deposits. The interest rate on deposits of three-month duration was further lowered to 0.85 percent per month, and the monthly rate on deposits of two-year duration was fixed at 1.8 percent. During 1958, the total amount of one-year deposits more than doubled (Pan et al., 1968)

At the end of 1958, the authorities suspended preferential interest rate savings deposits. Total outstanding deposits at that time amounted to NT$1,500 million, or 29 percent of the money supply. In a period of about nine years, from March 1950 to the end of 1958, the financial authorities had relied on these savings deposits to call in a tremendous amount of idle funds from the market, thus contributing greatly to the stability of the island's economy during these years.

(C) From Inflation to Stability. The inflation rate slowed immediately after monetary reform was instituted, with prices increasing only 300 percent in 1950. Compared with the 3,000 percent increase experienced in the first half of 1949, this was a great success. Inflation was controlled further after 1951, and hyper-inflation was overcome by 1952. The inflation rate was brought down to 8.8 percent in 1953, 2.4 percent in 1954, and 2 percent in 1961. Although it took 12 years to accomplish this, the contribution of monetary reform and other measures to price stabilization and to general economic development was great.

(D) Differing Opinions of Intellectuals. During the period of high interest rates and then the period of lowering interest rates, there were heated arguments from many quarters. Those who favored a low-interest-rate policy were of the opinion that it would stimulate economic growth; that it would lower the cost of production, and hence, the prices of finished products; that regulation of interest rates would

Table 3.2.1   Rates of Preferential Interest Deposits

(percent per month)

Effective Date	Usable as Collateral						Not Usable as Collateral		
	Half Month	One Month	Two Months	Three Months	Six Months	One Year	Six Months	One Year	Two Years
Mar. 25, 1950	—	7.00	—	—	—	—	—	—	—
Apr. 17, 1950	6.0	7.00	8.0	9.00	—	—	—	—	—
Jul. 1, 1950	3.0	3.50	4.0	4.50	—	—	—	—	—
Oct. 1, 1950	—	3.00	3.3	3.30	—	—	—	—	—
Mar. 26, 1951	—	4.20	4.5	4.50	—	—	—	—	—
Apr. 28, 1952	—	3.80	4.0	4.00	4.2	—	—	—	—
Jun. 2, 1952	—	3.30	—	3.60	3.9	—	—	—	—
Jul. 7, 1952	—	3.00	—	3.20	3.4	—	—	—	—
Sep. 8, 1952	—	2.40	—	2.60	2.8	—	—	—	—
Nov. 30, 1952	—	2.00	—	2.15	2.3	—	—	—	—
Apr. 10, 1953	—	2.00	—	2.15	2.3	3.0	—	—	—
Jul. 16, 1953	—	1.50	—	1.70	2.0	2.5	—	—	—
Oct. 10, 1953	—	1.20	—	1.30	1.5	2.0	—	—	—
Jul. 1, 1954	—	1.00	—	1.10	1.3	1.6	—	—	—
Mar. 5, 1956	—	0.85	—	1.00	1.3	1.6	1.50	1.80	—
Jun. 18, 1956	—	0.85	—	1.00	—	—	1.50	1.80	—
Jul. 16, 1957	—	—	—	0.85	—	—	1.35	1.65	1.80

Source: Pan et al., 1968.

serve to secure a supply of financial capital for equity investment; and that the prerogative of government enterprises to obtain low-interest loans from government banks was only a way of subsidizing their products and services, which were frequently sold at lower prices.

Discounting entirely the points mentioned above, those who favored high interest rates claimed that the functions of interest rates should be to provide inducement for savings and to channel them to banking institutions for capital investment, and to allocate the capital to different, competitive uses. With the short supply of capital in Taiwan, a high interest rate, determined by the market demand for capital, would tend to direct capital investment to more efficient enterprises, so that less efficient enterprises might not have the same chance to expand. Conversely, if the interest rates were arbitrarily fixed, the result would be indiscriminate allocation of the limited supply of capital, permitting the diversion of a part of the funds into less productive uses.

(E) The Government's Decision. Amidst these differing opinions, the government gradually reduced interest rates. Market interest rates also gradually declined. This was mainly attributable to the increase in national income and in the savings of the people, and to the relative stability of prices. At the same time, after the period of runaway inflation was over, many enterprises went bankrupt due to poor management and the excessive burden of interest payments. Private money lenders learned a lesson from these changes and began to favor depositing their money with banks instead of earning interest from private borrowers. The size of the curb market was reduced accordingly. Bank deposits increased greatly under these circumstances, making it possible for the authorities to lower interest rates further.

3.2.4   The Balanced Government Budget

During this period, the authorities concerned concentrated on eliminating factors that could cause economic instability. On the fiscal side, a great effort was made to achieve a balanced budget. A part of U.S. aid was efficiently utilized to supplement the government's deficits up until 1961. The government budget, inclusive of transfer receipts, actually was in surplus every year even before 1961, which provided an important source of funds for investment in infrastructure (Table 3.2.2).

Table 3.2.2   Foreign Transfers and Government Current Surplus*

Period	Foreign Transfers to the Government Sector as Percent of Government Expenditure	Government Current Surplus Net of Foreign Transfers as Percent of Government Expenditure	Government Current Surplus Inclusive of Foreign Transfers as Percent of Government Expenditure	Government Expenditure as Percent of GNP
1951–56	29.4	–5.8	23.6	18.6
1956–61	21.1	–7.0	14.1	20.8
1961–66	7.9	1.3	9.2	19.2
1966–71	0.2	16.2	16.4	18.7

Source: Directorate-General of Budget, Accounting and Statistics, Executive Yuan, *National Income of the Republic of China* (1981, 1995).

*: Government current surplus = Current revenue minus current expenditure

In conclusion, the experience of Taiwan featured an anti-inflation policy that was implemented through three dimensions: first, an elimination of inflationary psychology by the implementation of monetary reform; second, an absorption of money supply by the manipulation of interest rates and other measures; and third, the maintenance of a sound government budget. The policies for these three dimensions were effectively implemented over the period 1949-58, and the hyper-inflation of the early 1950s was thus effectively cured. Although it took a decade to accomplish, the success of this anti-inflation policy laid down a sound foundation for continuing rapid growth in the following decades.

3.3 Utilization of U.S. Aid

Scholars who have studied U.S. aid consider the assistance extended to the Republic of China as a successful example of aid utilization (Jacoby, 1966). U.S. aid started in 1951 and ended in 1965. The annual amount received during this period was, in total, US$1,372 million.

3.3.1   U.S. Aid as Domestic Savings

Foreign aid is different from foreign investment and loans in that it is an inflow of transfers that the economy does not have to pay back. Therefore, in the national accounts of the Republic of China, foreign transfer payments (mostly U.S. aid) are treated as a part of domestic savings. Government savings were positive all throughout the period simply because it received a considerable amount of transfer payments from abroad in the form of U.S. aid. (When these transfers are subtracted, government savings before 1964 become negative, showing that the government was in deficit prior to that year).

For the whole economy, U.S. aid was an important source of disposable domestic savings, as it comprised 40 percent to 68 percent of all disposable domestic savings realized prior to 1961 (Table 3.3.1).

3.3.2   Allocation of U.S. Aid

U.S. aid was used mainly to expand infrastructure, including electricity, transportation, and communications, rather than to support education and sanitation. Foreign investment other than U.S. aid was very rare before 1960. U.S. aid comprised more than 30 percent of domestic investment each year, sometimes reaching more than 50 percent, and was the main financial source of domestic investment before 1961 (See column (2)/(3) of Table 3.3.2).

From the standpoint of the overall economy, we see from Table 3.3.3 that the distribution of U.S. aid investment from 1951 to 1965 was 67 percent in public enterprises, 6 percent in private enterprises, and 27 percent in mixed enterprises. The public enterprises which used the largest shares of U.S. aid were electricity, transportation, and communications. As for investment provided by local currency project aid to the manufacturing industry, we find that the distribution was 22 percent in public enterprises, 32 percent in private enterprises, and 46 percent in mixed enterprises (Table 3.3.3).

Table 3.3.1   Source of Disposable Domestic Savings (U.S. Aid and Domestic Savings)

(NT$ million)

		Private Disposable Savings (1) = (2) + (3)			Gov't Disposable Savings (4) = (5) + (6)			
		(1)	(2)	(3)	(4)	(5)	(6)	
		Private	Domes-	U.S. Aid	Govern	Domes–	U.S. Aid	
	Dispos-	Dispos-	tic	to	Dispos–	tic Gov't	to Gov-	Corpo-
	able Do-	able	Private	Private	able	Savings	ernment	rate
Year	mestic Savings	Savings	Savings	Sector	Savings		Sector	Savings
1951	1,290	519	483	36	458	−244	702	313
1952	1,812	330	303	27	939	−87	1,026	543
1953	2,253	520	484	36	1,134	−112	1,246	599
1954	2,112	523	524	−1	1,185	−257	1,442	404
1955	2,860	802	778	24	1,515	−125	1,640	543
1956	2,748	986	994	−8	1,076	−357	1,433	686
1957	3,178	1,173	1,170	3	1,059	−218	1,277	946
1958	4,208	1,655	1,299	356	1,781	−282	2,063	772
1959	4,830	1,712	1,355	357	1,932	−485	2,417	1,186
1960	7,063	2,871	2,670	201	2,492	−518	3,010	1,700
1961	8,492	4,010	3,422	588	2,392	−957	3,349	2,090
1962	6,854	4,534	3,949	585	1,177	−432	1,609	1,143
1963	11,205	7,230	6,667	563	1,202	−24	1,226	2,773
1964	14,266	10,151	9,668	483	1,475	1,153	322	2,640
1965	16,243	9,400	8,792	608	2,690	1,983	707	4,153

Source: Directorate-General of Budget, Accounting and Statistics, Executive Yuan, *National Income of the Republic of China*, 1981.

Note: Domestic government savings = government current account revenue minus government current expenditure exclusive of U.S. aid.

Regarding the distribution of U.S. dollar project aid in manufacturing investment, the figures show a higher percentage for public enterprises and a lower percentage for private ones: 49 percent and 32 percent, respectively.

Although a greater portion of U.S. aid was spent on the public sector, the growth rate of private investment was much higher than that of public investment. The contribution of U.S. aid to the private sector was made through both infrastructural construction and direct local currency project aid to the manufacturing industry (Table 3.3.4).

U.S. aid was really an indispensable factor in the economic development of Taiwan. However, such financial injection was only to be a "necessary but not sufficient" factor. That U.S. aid could have helped bring about such tremendous achievements in Taiwan was due largely to the diligent and economic character of the Chinese people, political stability, and the efficient policies implemented by the government.

Table 3.3.2   U.S. Aid Inflow as a Percentage of Domestic Savings and Domestic Investment

Year	Domestic Savings (exclusive of U.S. Aid) (NT$ million) (1)	U.S. Aid Inflow (NT$ million) (2)	Domestic Investment (inclusive of U.S. Aid) (NT$ million) (3)	atio of Domestic Savings to Domestic Investment (%) (1)/(3)	Ratio of U.S. Aid Inflow to Domestic Investment (%) (2)/(3)
1951	1,193	586	1,779	67.1	32.9
1952	1,586	1,057	2,643	60.0	40.0
1953	2,034	1,190	3,224	63.1	36.9
1954	1,930	2,111	4,041	47.8	52.2
1955	2,700	1,298	3,998	67.5	32.5
1956	3,158	2,366	5,524	57.2	42.8
1957	4,244	2,111	6,355	66.8	33.2
1958	4,411	3,047	7,458	59.1	40.9
1959	5,295	4,437	9,732	54.4	45.6
1960	7,889	4,729	12,618	62.5	37.5
1961	8,935	5,048	13,983	63.9	36.1
1962	9,506	7,227	13,733	69.2	30.8
1963	14,838	1,112	15,950	93.0	7.0
1964	19,880	−791	19,089	104.1	−4.1
1965	21,979	3,567	25,546	86.0	14.0

Source: Directorate-General of Budget, Accounting and Statistics, Executive Yuan, *National Income of the Republic of China*, 1981.

Notes : 1. Domestic savings refers to the savings generated domestically, exclusive of foreign transfer receipts. 2. As U.S. aid was terminated in 1965. Column (2) includes a small amount of foreign capital inflows after 1961; before that year, it refers mostly to U.S. aid.

Table 3.3.3   Distribution of Project Aid (1951–1965)

		Percentage of Distribution		
		Public Sector	Private Sector	Mixed
Whole economy	U.S. dollar project aid	79.5	6.9	13.6
	Local currency project aid	59.3	5.6	35.0
	Total	66.7	6.1	27.2
Manufacturing industry	U.S. dollar aid	48.9	32.4	18.7
	Local currency project aid	22.1	32.2	45.7
	Total	41.0	33.0	26.0

Source: Calculation from CIECD data.

Table 3.3.4   Gross Investment in Private and Public Sectors

(%)

Period	Percentage Distribution				Growth Rate	
	Private Sector	Public Sector	Public Enterprises	Govern-ment	Private Sector	Public Sector
1951–56	53.4	46.6	34.7	11.9	12.0	7.8
1956–61	50.6	49.4	37.0	12.4	16.7	10.8
1961–65	63.1	36.9	25.9	11.0	19.7	6.4

Source: Directorate-General of Budget, Accounting and Statistics, Executive Yuan, *National Income of the Republic of China*, 1981.

3.4   Factors for High Savings

The achievement of a high savings rate in the early period was a decisive factor in the successful development of Taiwan. In this section, we try to examine the causes of the rapid increase in the saving ratio based on a typical economic theory. That is, savings is a function of income and interest rate. It is a fundamental natural phenomenon that the propensity to save increases as income grows. We also note that at lower income levels, savings will possibly increase as interest rates rise. Reflecting this theory, Taiwan's postwar experience shows that factors contributing to the island's higher savings rate were a speedy growth of the economy and high real interest rates. In addition, sound government fiscal policies also contributed greatly to domestic savings. These points will be successively elaborated below.

3.4.1   Speedy GNP Growth

The Taiwan economy was restored to its prewar level by 1951, and after that the economy grew at a high speed. The average annual growth rate of GNP between 1951 and 1955 was 9.7 percent, between 1956 and 1960, 7.0 percent, and between 1961 and 1965, 10.1 percent. This high GNP growth rate generated higher incomes, which naturally increased the propensity to save.

3.4.2   High Real Interest Rates

One of the characteristics of the 1950s was a high interest rate policy that was adopted as an anti-inflation measure. Although the interest rate was brought down gradually, the rate in real terms was generally high during the 1952-65 period. The high real interest rate was realized because of two factors: a high nominal interest rate, and a reduced inflation rate. Actually, hyper-inflation was overcome by 1952; inflation was brought down to 8.8 percent in 1953 and 2.4 percent in 1954, although it took several more years to really overcome high price increases. Thus, the success in price stabilization contributed greatly to the increase in savings (Table 3.4.1).

Table 3.4.1   Real Interest Rate (1951–1965)

		(percent per annum)
	Nominal*	Inflation Rate	Real Interest
Year and Month	Interest Rate −	(by WPI) =	Rate

Year and Month		Nominal* Interest Rate	Inflation Rate (by WPI)	Real Interest Rate
1951	March	69.6	66.0	3.6
1952	April	63.8	23.1	40.7
1953	April	42.6	8.8	33.8
	July	34.5	8.8	25.7
	Oct.	26.8	8.8	18.0
1954	July	21.0	2.4	18.6
1955		21.0	14.1	6.9
1956		21.0	12.7	8.3
1957		21.0	7.2	13.8
1958		21.0	1.4	19.6
1959	Jan.	20.7	10.3	10.4
1961	March	19.0	3.2	15.8
	June	15.8	3.2	12.6
1962	Aug.	14.4	3.0	11.4
1963	July	12.7	6.5	6.2
1964	March	11.4	2.5	8.9
1965		11.4	−4.6	16.0

Source: Economic Research Department, The Central Bank of China, *Taiwan Financial Statistics Monthly* (Dec. 1956, 1961 and 1966); DGBAS, Executive Yuan, *Commodity-Price Statistics Monthly, Taiwan Area, the Republic of China* (June 1982).
Notes: * 1951 March: Three month rate for preferential deposits.
    1952 April: Six month rate for preferential deposits.
    1953 April-1958: One year rate for preferential deposits.
    After 1959 Jan.: Two year rate for fixed savings deposits.

3.4.3   High Government Savings

The sources of disposable domestic savings are shown in Table 3.3.1 above. It is very impressive that government savings (government current account revenue minus current account expenditure) registered such a large amount, even exceeding private savings for the period 1952-56. The high rate of government savings was probably not caused by heavy taxation, but by very restrictive government consumption. For tax revenues were a very low percentage of GNP: 10.0 percent in 1951-55, 11.7 percent in 1956-60, and 10.1 percent in 1961-65. The income tax was particularly low; the business income tax and individual income tax combined comprised only 1.53 percent, 1.56 percent and 1.17 percent of the GNP, respectively, in those periods. A large part of the agricultural surplus accrued to the government in the form of a "hidden rice tax" through government purchases at the government purchasing price, which was far lower than the market price. The hidden rice tax exceeded the total income tax of the whole economy almost every year before 1963 (Lee, 1971a). Thus light taxation enabled the industrial sector to retain a large part of its profit for further investment. Basically, however, it was restrictive government consumption that made it possible to have light taxation.

The high rate of government savings was possible because of sound fiscal policies which were implemented with firm determination.[2] The determination to cure inflation and to maintain a balanced budget can be seen, for example, in the statements of Mr. Chen Chen, then Governor of Taiwan Province and later "Premier" (Ho, 1965).

As the bitter lesson of inflation was well taken by the government, the issuance of paper currency was strictly controlled. The annual budget was carefully prepared and executed. In addition to the reform of the monetary system, several important measures were carried out by the government to counter the problems of increasing public expenditures. These included the launching of a tax reform program; an increase in monopoly profits; a speeding up of the disposal of properties received from the Japanese; an increase in spending for positive purposes and a reduction in spending for passive purposes; the maintenance of a balanced budget; and the establishment of a sound budgeting system (Chang et al., 1968).

The above observations show us the following: the Taiwan economy started to grow at a high rate right after World War II, with net investment comprising more than 10 percent of NNP every year. During the 1950s, however, the net savings rate was low, only around 5 percent of the NNP. U.S. aid was the main source of funds to fill the gap. High investment made the economy grow rapidly, which in turn boosted the savings rate to a high level. The economy reached the "take-off" stage in 1961-63, when the net savings rate began to exceed 10 percent of the NNP.

Factors contributing to the generation of a higher savings rate were essentially a speedy growth of the economy, a high real interest rate, and a firm determination to implement sound government fiscal policies.

3.5 Land Reform

Land reform in Taiwan has produced significant effects on the economy. Land reform was carried out in three phases: rent reduction, sale of public land, and the "Land-to-the-Tiller" program.

The rent reduction program was implemented in 1949. It legally limited the amount of farm rent on private tenanted land to 37.5 percent of the harvest. Before the implementation of this program, tenant farmers in Taiwan had to pay a land rent amounting to more than 50 percent of the total harvest. Therefore, the new rental rate reduced the land rent paid by tenants by more than 15 percent. The program also provided farmers with more security on lease contracts.

The sale of public land to tenant farmers was successfully implemented in 1953, and was followed by the redistribution of excess private tenanted land to the tenant-cultivators (Lee, 1969). The area transferred from landlords to tenants through the public land sale program, and the area bought by the tenants through the "Land-to-the-Tiller" program, amounted to 71 percent of the total area of public and private tenanted land (Chang, 1965).

The most significant factors which resulted from land reform and contributed to multiple cropping are as follows: (1) changes in tenancy conditions, (2) changes in the size of landholdings, and (3) changes in production patterns. These will be analyzed one by one.

3.5.1 Changes in Tenancy Conditions

After land reform, tenancy conditions were altered significantly. The ratio of owner-farmers to total farm families increased from 36 percent in 1949 to 60 percent in 1957. Owner-farmers and part owner-farmers owned more than 83 percent of all farmland in 1957.

Land reform had a significant impact on agricultural production. Rent reduction tended to encourage multiple cropping, and tenants benefited not only from lower rents but also from increased production beyond standard levels. The superiority of an owner-farmer system over a tenancy system was obvious as seen from per family, per person, and even per hectare income: the farm income of the tenant was only three-fourths that of the other two categories. Therefore, significant changes in tenancy conditions provided a strong incentive for production increases, and facilitated the more efficient utilization of the agricultural labor force.

3.5.2 Changes in the Size of Landholdings

Land reform led to an equalization of property and a smaller-scale farming system. Before the implementation of land reform, landholdings of more than 3 hectares comprised 42 percent of the total area; after implementation, they dropped to only 23 percent of the total area. Conversely, landholdings of 1 hectare or less, which originally comprised 25 percent of the total, increased to 35 percent. This indicates that land reform resulted in a reorganization of the economic structure of the farm in the direction of smaller-scale farming. The smaller size of farm units naturally brought about more intensive use of labor, and, consequently, more labor-intensive production of vegetables and fruits.

3.5.3 Changes in Production Patterns

After land reform, the farmers had greater choice regarding the cultivation of crops because, as owner-cultivators, they were under no obligation to produce rice for rental payments. Thus, the land reform tended to reduce the relative share of rice production and to increase the share of other crops, including vegetables, fruits, livestock, and poultry. Moreover, technological changes in agriculture after land reform were largely centered on the intensive use of land with more labor input (Tables 3.5.1 and 3.5.2).

Table 3.5.1   Farm Yields by Category of Farmers in 1963

(NT$)

Category	Per Family	Per Person	Per Hectare
Owner-farmer	34,853	4,019	26,998
Part owner	39,095	4,274	25,252
Tenant	29,877	3,038	17,754

Source: Chi-lien Hwang, *Wages and Incomes of Agriculture Workers in Taiwan* (Taipei: National Taiwan University, The Research Institute of Rural Socio-Economics, 1968).

Table 3.5.2 Indices of Land and Labor Productivity in Agricultural Production

(%)

Year	Land Area	Land Productivity	Labor Input	Labor Productivity
1950	100.0	100.0	100.0	100.0
1955	100.7	121.5	107.6	113.2

Source: Chi-lien Hwang, *Wages and Incomes of Agriculture Workers in Taiwan* (Taipei: National Taiwan University, The Research Institute of Rural Socio-Economics, 1968).

In short, after land reform, changes in tenancy conditions, in the size of landholdings, and in production patterns all greatly contributed to the development of multiple-crop farming and agricultural diversification.

3.6 Import Substitution Policies

At the beginning of the 1950s, the government was faced with a difficult choice between inward-looking and outward-looking policies. Both policy choices were problematic. From the inward-looking point of view, the size of the domestic market was clearly too small to be depended upon as a source of sustained growth, and from the outward-looking viewpoint, the ready markets of Japan and mainland China were no longer available. At the same time, surpluses of rice and other agricultural products were substantially reduced by increased domestic demand caused by the abrupt population increase resulting from the influx of people from the mainland.

Despite the obstacles to inward-looking measures, import controls had to be implemented for two reasons. By 1951 Taiwan was confronted with a sizable trade deficit, which was to continue throughout the 1950s. Numerous small enterprises had started up business immediately after the war, partly by acquiring old Japanese facilities and producing simple manufactures of poor quality but at high cost. Many of these enterprises not only encountered difficulties in marketing abroad, but also had to compete with the superior Japanese products that re-entered Taiwan. Under these conditions, import substitution policies were adopted.

Import substitution policies were reflected in the adoption of a foreign exchange policy and in the implementation of a pricing policy to encourage domestic production of substitutes for imported goods. The adoption of a multiple exchange rate system, the over-valuation of the New Taiwan dollar, and the maintenance of higher prices of import goods vs. export goods during this period all favored import substitution. These dimensions will be discussed below.

3.6.1   The 1950s Foreign Exchange Policy

(A) Exchange Settlement Certificates. In 1949, when monetary reform was put into effect, a functionally simple exchange rate was adopted. The operation was such that amounts of domestic currency in exchange for foreign money were given partly in cash, at a rate of NT$5 to US$1, and partly in exchange settlement certificates

(ESCs). These ESCs were freely negotiable on the market and could be sold to the Bank of Taiwan at the official rate. For importers, foreign exchange was approved rather liberally, and ESCs were sold for the importation of permissible items at the official rate. However, because of the large trade deficit and continued inflation, applications for foreign exchange soon outgrew the available supply. The official supply price of ESCs was repeatedly devalued.

(B) A Multiple Exchange Rate System. In 1951, along with substantial currency devaluation, a multiple exchange rate was introduced. Goods imported by the public sector, along with plant and important raw materials and intermediate inputs imported by the private sector, were afforded a lower official rate; imports of other goods were afforded a higher ESC rate. Earnings from major exports, such as sugar, rice, and salt, were given a lower ESC rate than private export earnings. After 1951 the New Taiwan dollar became overvalued due to continuous inflation, which hampered exports and encouraged imports and import substitution.

(C) A Simple Exchange System. The revision of the foreign exchange system in November, 1958, was decisive and paved the way for a move to a simple exchange system. The essence of this revision was to allow exchange settlement certificates to be applied to all kinds of exports and imports. In addition, the price of exchange settlement certificates was fixed at a level close to the market price. The Taiwan Sugar Corporation, which earned more than a half of the island's total foreign exchange, was permitted to sell its ESCs at a price very close to the market price. Furthermore, from August, 1960, the price of an ESC incorporated the official basic foreign exchange rate. After this, the market exchange rate was gradually stabilized at the rate of NT$40 to US$1. The Taiwan Sugar Corporation earned a large amount of foreign exchange in 1963 due to the high international sugar price that year. Making use of this abundance of foreign exchange, the government abolished the ESC system. The direct exchange settlement system thus came into being, and the over-valuation of the New Taiwan dollar was ended.

3.6.2 High Prices of Import Goods vs. Export Goods

Due to various reasons, mostly import restrictions and high tariffs, the price ratio of import-substituting goods to export goods went up appreciably in the beginning of the 1950s. This was manifested in a dramatic rise in the relative price of cotton textiles to rice, which increased from 2:1 during 1949-50 to 4-5:1 in 1951-52 (Lee, 1971b). This change was of particular significance, because rice was Taiwan's main agricultural product and an export commodity, while textiles were important imports. Import substitution of textile goods received significant support from the rise in the domestic price of such goods (Lin, 1973).

Import substitution was not only encouraged through foreign exchange measures and pricing, but also through allocation of raw materials and financial support. Mr. K.Y. Yin, then vice chairman of the Taiwan Production Board, an organization in charge of U.S. aid, emphasized the long-run comparative advantage for development. He organized a joint textile group to give full support to the expansion of cotton fabric production by providing necessary raw materials to manufacturing firms through U.S. aid and the allocation of funds. Thus, the textile industry grew rapidly.

3.6.3   A Change to Export Promotion

Some export promotion measures were in fact started in the early 1950s. For example, a system of tax rebates for reimbursing import duties on raw materials was introduced in 1954. A system offering a certain proportion of foreign exchange earnings for the import of raw materials was initiated in 1956. Basically, however, the overvaluation of the currency and the multiple exchange rate structure tilted policy in favor of import substitution.

Easy import substitution soon came to an end due to the limited domestic market and urgently needed foreign exchange earnings. By 1958 the investment climate was gloomy and more fundamental policy changes were called for. Development strategy was then turned toward export promotion.

3.7   Export Promotion Policies

A change in policy from import substitution to export promotion was made in 1956-60, due to the limited domestic market and the urgent need for foreign exchange earnings. Important measures taken in this respect are seen in the enactment of a 19-point Economic and Financial Reform, the Statute for Encouragement of Investment, tax reductions and rebates, and a special export loan program.

3.7.1   Nineteen-Point Economic and Financial Reform

The essential elements of the 19-point Economic and Financial Reform were as follows:
1) A thorough review of various control measures adopted in the past, for the purpose of liberalizing those measures.
2) The provision of preferential treatment for private business in the areas of taxation, foreign exchange, and financing.
3) Reform of the tax system and tax administration to enhance capital formation.
4) Reform of the foreign exchange and trade systems in order to establish a unitary exchange rate, and to liberalize trade controls.
5) A broadening of measures to encourage exports, to improve procedures governing the settlement of foreign exchange earned by exporters, and to increase contacts with foreign business organizations.

3.7.2   Investment Incentives

The Statute for Encouragement of Investment was enacted pursuant to the above 19-point supporting measures. The main purposes of this Statute were to facilitate the acquisition of plant sites and to provide tax exemptions and deductions. The salient points of the Statute for Encouragement of Investment may be described as follows:
1) *Income tax holiday*: The strongest incentive was the "five-year tax holiday" set forth in Article 5, whereby a productive enterprise conforming to the Statute's criteria was exempted from income tax for a period of five consecutive years.
2) *Business income tax*: The maximum rate of income tax, including all forms of surtax payable by a productive enterprise, would not exceed 18 percent of its

total annual income, which was much less than the 32.5 percent maximum for ordinary profit-seeking enterprises.

3) *Tax exemption for undistributed profit*: The amount reinvested for productive purposes was deductible from taxable income.

4) *Tax deduction for exports*: Within certain limits, a deduction from taxable income of 2 percent of annual export proceeds was offered.

5) *Exemption or reduction of stamp tax*: This tax was either waived or reduced in a large number of cases.

The development of industry toward export expansion in the early 1960s was still slow. In 1965, the Statute was revised and its scope was expanded. The Kaohsiung Export Processing Zone was set up; within this zone, no duties were imposed on imports. Development strategy at this time became entirely export-oriented.

3.7.3 Tax Reductions and Rebates

The reduction of taxes under the Statute for Encouragement of Investment, and the tax and duty rebates for exports, amounted to a large proportion of levied taxes, as shown in Table 3.7.1.

Table 3.7.1   Tax Rebates as % of Corresponding Tax and Total Tax Revenue

(%)

	Tax Rebates as % of Corresponding Tax			Tax Rebates as % of Total Tax Revenue	
Period	Income Tax	Customs Duties	Commodity Tax	Tax Rebates of Income Tax Customs Duties Commodity Tax for Exports and Investment	Tax Rebates of Customs Duties and Commodity Tax for Exports
1955-60	—	5.9	3.0	1.5	1.5
1961-65	16.7	25.2	17.8	10.4	8.6
1966-70	18.7	39.6	21.8	15.2	13.4
1971-75	15.7	67.3	35.7	26.7	24.2
1976-80	13.6	44.3	33.9	19.6	17.2
1981-85	18.5	33.7	8.8	11.8	7.9
1986-90	20.2	17.2	4.3	8.2	3.4
1991-94	15.1	4.4	0.1	4.2	0.4

Source: Department of Statistics, Ministry of Finance, *Yearbook of Financial Statistics of the Republic of China*, 1993, 1994.

Tax rebates for exports were applied mainly to customs duties and commodity taxes, while the credit for investment included the income tax. The largest rebates of customs duties and commodity taxes on exports, in percentage terms, were enacted in the period of 1971-75, amounting to 67.3 percent and 35.7 percent, respectively, of the corresponding taxes (Table 3.7.1). We note that those percentages were gradually reduced. They dropped to 17.2 percent and 4.3 percent, respectively, in the period of 1986-90, and to 4.4 percent and 0.1 percent in the period of 1991-94.

The ratio of rebates of customs duties and commodity taxes for exports in total tax revenue also underwent a gradual decline, falling from 24.2 percent in the period of 1971-75 to only 0.4 percent in the period of 1991-94 (Table 3.7.1). The management of tax rebates was a typical case of environment-led government policy. We can see the gradual change in the direction of liberalization and internationalization.

3.7.4   Favorable Interest Rates

A special export loan program was initiated in the early period, and preferential interest rates for export financing have been available since that time. However, the proportion of loans granted under this preferential interest rate program has been relatively small. In the 1980s, outstanding loans extended for exports declined to only about 1 percent of the total outstanding amount. Since the early 1980s, banks have stopped offering export loans at preferential rates. However, the name "export loans" has been maintained, and a very small amount of loans have continued under this name (see Table 3.7.2).

Table 3.7.2   Preferential Interest Rate Export Loans

Period	Preferential Rate Export Loans (in millions of NT dollars)	Total Loans (in millions of NT dollars)	Percentage of Preferential Rate Export Loans to Total Loans
1972-75	7,689	188,845	4.1
1976-80	11,521	480,406	2.4
1981-85	19,143	1,012,934	1.9
1986-90	16,368	2,232,512	0.7
1991-95	19,112	5,712,165	0.3

Source: Economic Research Department, The Central Bank of China, *Financial Statistics Monthly, Taiwan District,The Republic of China*, various years.

3.7.5   Real Effective Exchange Rate

The foreign exchange rate system was converted from a fixed system to a floating system in February 1979. The value of the New Taiwan dollar has fluctuated since that time, but the fluctuation has been very mild.

The real effective exchange rate (with 1980 as the base year) was under 100 for the entire period of 1976-81, indicating that in terms of the weighted foreign exchange rate, with the relative price change (domestic prices against foreign prices) taken into account, the value of the New Taiwan dollar was favorable to foreign trade during these six years (Table 3.7.3).

We also note that Taiwan's economic environment immediately before the two oil shocks was such that prices had been particularly stable for some time, and that speedy export growth was creating a large physical demand on the one hand and inducing money supply growth on the other. Both oil crises occurred in the midst of this environment. Strong demand plus available money supply easily absorbed the higher intermediate costs. The government measures adopted in the wake of these oil crises will be discussed in detail later.

Table 3.7.3 Real Effective Exchange Rate of the New Taiwan Dollar (1980=100)

Year	Export Weighted	Trade Weighted
1960	103.7	100.3
1961	102.2	100.1
1962	104.9	103.7
1963	112.8	109.5
1964	114.8	113.3
1965	107.9	106.5
1966	105.0	105.3
1967	103.5	105.0
1968	101.6	105.4
1969	97.6	102.8
1970	95.8	100.8
1971	89.5	95.9
1972	86.3	89.6
1973	94.1	95.4
1974	112.7	113.8
1975	99.6	101.3
1976	97.8	99.7
1977	93.4	94.2
1978	88.3	87.3
1979	93.3	93.3
1980	100.0	100.0
1981	99.7	99.9

Source: International Monetary Fund, *International Financial Statistics*, 1981; DGBAD, Executive Yuan, *Commodity-Price Statistics Monthly*, December 1981; Department of Statistics, Ministry of Finance, *Monthly Statistics of Exports and Imports*, December 1981.

Notes : 1.The index of the real effective exchange rate is the index of the effective exchange rate adjusted for inflation differentials which are measured by wholesale prices of nonfood manufactures.
2. Weighted by data of nine major trading countries.

In concluding this section, we may note that exports were the true essential factor contributing to the rapid growth and successful labor absorption of the past, and that export expansion was the dominant source of manufacturing growth after the 1960s. From the late 1950s, export expansion was emphasized and various export promotion schemes were implemented. Through the 19-point Economic and Financial Reform and the Statute for Encouragement of Investment, outward-looking trade policies were emphasized and carefully designed. Nominal rates of protection, exchange rates, investment policy, tax rebates, and trade loans all provided favorable incentives for export promotion. Thus, outward-looking government economic policies and measures contributed greatly to the successful transition growth in Taiwan. However, slow adjustment of foreign exchange rates during the 1970s laid the foundation for generating inflation in the wake of the two oil crises.

3.8   Policies on Growth and Inflation in the Wake of the Oil Crises

The quadrupling of oil prices in November 1973 had significant effects on the world economy, as oil was not only used as a prime energy source but also as a primary material input for countless products. The shock manifested itself in worldwide stagflation, in balance of payments deficits for most non-OPEC countries, and in deterioration in the terms of trade of oil importing countries. The second oil crisis in 1979 hampered the recovering world economy, causing the growth rate to decline and the inflation rate to rise again.

This section is aimed at analyzing the government measures taken in response to the oil shocks.

3.8.1   Growth and Inflation in the 1970s
(A) The First Oil Crisis. The performance of the Taiwan economy in the 1960s was characterized by rapid growth and stable prices. During 1961-71, the real GNP grew at an annual average rate of 10.2 percent. Prices were stable, increasing at an annual average of 1.6 percent measured by the wholesale price index, 2.9 percent by the consumer price index, and 3.6 percent by the GNP deflator. This outstanding performance was interrupted by the 1973 oil crisis.

The abrupt 22.9 percent rise in prices in 1973 was a severe shock, although the growth rate remained high that year. In 1974 the inflation rate jumped to 40.6 percent, and the growth rate dropped to 1.1 percent. This was quite a new experience for the Taiwan economy. Various drastic government measures were taken in response. In 1975 inflation came under control and dropped to a negative 5.1 percent, and the economy recovered to register a 4.2 percent growth. Thereafter, the Taiwan economy enjoyed renewed rapid growth with stable prices. For the three post-oil-crisis years, 1976-78, the average growth rate was a high 12.4 percent, and inflation was a low 3.0 percent. Taiwan enjoyed a prosperous and stable period before the second oil crisis (Table 3.8.1).

(B) The Second Oil Crisis. The rise of oil prices in 1979 and 1980 again shocked the Taiwan economy. Prices rose at annual rates of 13.8 percent in 1979 and 21.5 percent in 1980. On the other hand, the growth rate declined to 8.1 percent in 1979 and 6.6 percent in 1980. Thus, the inflation rate during the second oil shock was about half that of the first shock, and the reduction in the growth rate was also smaller. No widespread and drastic government measures were adopted this time; only mild monetary steps were taken. The economy adjusted itself gradually in the environment of tighter money. In 1981 the inflation rate was brought down to 7.6 percent; but the growth rate was not very high, just 5.5 percent. Although the recorded growth rate for the first half of 1982 was only 3.5 percent, the inflation rate became negative in June 1982.

Table 3.8.1   Fluctuations of Growth and Inflation Rates

(%)

| Year | GNP Growth | Rate of Inflation | | |
		Wholesale Prices	Consumer Prices	GNP Deflator
1961-71 (annual average)	10.2	1.6	2.9	3.6
1971	12.9	0.02	2.8	3.1
1972	13.3	4.5	3.0	5.8
1973	12.8	22.9	8.2	14.9
1974	1.1	40.6	47.5	32.3
1975	4.2	−5.1	5.2	2.3
1976	13.5	2.8	2.5	5.6
1977	9.9	2.8	7.0	6.2
1978	13.9	3.5	5.8	4.7
1979	8.1	13.8	9.8	11.3
1980	6.6	21.5	19.0	16.1
1981	5.5	7.6	16.3	12.1
1982/II*	3.5	−0.3	3.7	4.5

Source: DGBAS, Executive Yuan, National Income of the Republic of China (1981), Commodity-Price Statistics Monthly, Taiwan Area, the Republic of China (July 1982), Quarterly National Economic Trends, Taiwan Area, the Republic of China (May 1982).
Note: * The second quarter of 1982.

3.8.2   Causes of Inflation

(A) Cost-Push and Demand-Pull. The two inflationary periods of 1973-74 and 1979-80 can be explained as having been induced by both cost-push and demand-pull. The cost-push side will be explained first. Among four components of cost — wages, profits, cost of intermediate inputs, and indirect taxes — wages were not a factor of cost-push in Taiwan at that time, because the island's labor market was quite competitive and able to generate a market-determined wage rate. Cost-push due to profit maximization was not significant either, because monopoly power in Taiwan was not generally strong. The cost of intermediate goods depended heavily on import prices, as intermediate inputs comprised about 70 percent of manufactures and about 40 percent of these intermediates were imported. According to the cost-price model constructed by the present writer (Kuo, 1983b), the quadrupling of oil prices alone will incur about a 40 percent cost-price increase if all the increments are transferred to the downstream industry. Various econometric models based on observations for the past two decades or so show that import price changes accounted for about 50 percent of all past price changes. However, since a large part of the rise in oil prices in 1973 and 1974 was absorbed by the government-owned Chinese Petroleum Corporation and Taiwan Power Company,

only a small portion of the 40.6 percent inflation rate that occurred in 1974 could be explained by the increase in the oil price.

Second, the presence of demand-pull can be seen from the high growth rates in the money supply, which were mostly generated one year prior to the rise in prices. That is, a 37.9 percent growth rate in the money supply in 1972 preceded a 22.9 percent price rise in 1973, and a 49.3 percent growth in the money supply preceded a 40.6 percent price rise in 1974. Likewise, the 34.1 percent growth in the money supply in 1978 apparently led to price increases in 1979. The only exception was the inflation of 1980 which was not preceded by a large monetary growth in the previous year. Generally speaking, the close relationship between the money supply (M_1) and the rate of inflation can be observed in Fig. 3.8.1, where the two variables are depicted in terms of money supply per unit of output and rate of inflation. This relationship seems to show that "money matters" in the Taiwan case for the period 1971-81 (Table 3.8.2).[3]

Table 3.8.2   Inflation Rates and Changes in Import Prices and Money Supply

(percent per annum)

Year	Change in Wholesale Price Index (Year Average Comparison)	Change in Import Price Index (Year Average Comparison)	Growth Rate of Money Supply, M_1 (End of Year Comparison)
1961-71 (annual average)	1.6	1.7	17.9
1970	2.7	3.6	11.3
1971	0.02	5.1	24.8
1972	4.5	8.0	37.9
1973	22.9	22.1	49.3
1974	40.6	47.0	7.0
1975	−5.1	−5.0	26.9
1976	2.8	2.1	23.1
1977	2.8	7.7	29.1
1978	3.5	9.2	34.1
1979	13.8	16.6	7.0
1980	21.5	20.2	19.9
1981	7.6	8.6	11.1
1982/June	−0.4	−1.5*	7.8

Source: DGBAS, Executive Yuan, National Income of the Republic of China (1981), Commodity-Price Statistics Monthly, Taiwan Area, the Republic of China (July 1982), Quarterly National Economic Trends, Taiwan Area, the Republic of China (May 1982); Economic Research Department, The Central Bank of China, Financial Statistics Monthly, Taiwan District, the Republic of China (May 1982 and July 1982).

Note: * The second quarter of 1982.

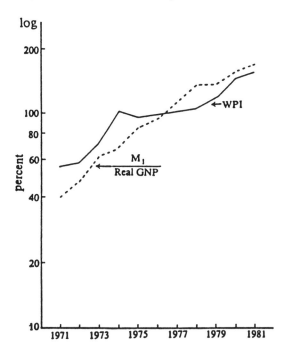

Figure 3.8.1 **Relationship Between Money Supply Per Unit of Output and Rate of Inflation (1971–1981=100)**

(B) Sources of Change in the Money Supply. Given the above observation, we would like to consider how this large money supply was created. Sources of change in the money supply can be decomposed into three categories: changes in net foreign assets, changes in net claims upon the government, and changes in banks' excess loans. These three sources are determined respectively by changes in the balance of payments, changes in government deposits and withdrawals, and changes in banks' loans and investment minus changes in deposits and banks' net worth.

For the four critical years of 1972, 1973, 1977, and 1978, when the money supply increased by close to or more than 30 percent, we note three things from the decomposition: first, that the increase in net foreign assets was the dominant source; second, that the performance of the government sector was a stabilizing force rather than an expansionary factor, especially since the portion of the money supply absorbed by government deposits was high in 1973 and 1978; and third, that in 1973 a high rate of excess bank loans, together with a large increase in net foreign assets, forced an almost 50 percent increase in the money supply. The contribution made by banks' excess loans to the increase in money supply in 1978, however, was only about one third of that due to the net increase in foreign assets.

(C) Trade Surplus and Balance of Payments. In the previous section, we observed that the net increase in foreign assets was the decisive factor in generating a high growth rate of the money supply. In this section, we would like to further examine this change. One characteristic was that in the four critical years of rapid monetary growth, the trade surpluses were particularly large in terms of percentage

of GNP: 8.2 percent in 1972, 6.8 percent in 1973, 5.5 percent in 1977, and 8.3 percent in 1978. Such large trade surpluses not only created a vast pool of additional money, but also caused a large portion of domestic savings to flow out to foreign countries.

Trade surpluses can be attributed to a superiority in export competitiveness. The competitiveness of exports is affected by two factors: relative prices and foreign exchange rates. The change in the competitiveness of exports can be measured by the real effective exchange rate. When the real effective exchange rate is greater than 100, competitiveness in that year is lower than in the base year; when the real effective exchange rate is less than 100, competitiveness in that year is superior to that of the base year. From Table 3.8.3 we see that whether we use exports or two-way trade as weights, the real effective exchange rate in the 1970s stayed below 100 except in 1974, when prices skyrocketed. This shows that during the 1970s, except for 1974, export competitiveness, in terms of relative prices and foreign exchange rates combined, was favorable to exports. We should also note that the real effective exchange rates in 1972 and 1978 were especially low, generating large trade surpluses which in turn resulted in a vast expansion of the money supply.

Table 3.8.3   Real Effective Exchange Rate

(%)

Year	Real Effective Exchange Rate (EER/PPP)	
	Export Weighted	Trade Weighted
1970	95.8	100.8
1971	89.5	95.9
1972	86.3	89.6
1973	94.1	95.4
1974	112.7	113.8
1975	99.6	101.3
1976	97.8	99.7
1977	93.4	94.2
1978	88.3	87.3
1979	93.3	93.3
1980	100.0	100.0
1981	99.7	99.9

Source: International Monetary Fund, International Statistics (1981); DGBAS, Executive Yuan, Commodity-Price Statistics Monthly, Taiwan Area, the Republic of China (Dec. 1981); Department of Statistics, Ministry of Finance, Monthly Statistics of Exports and Imports, the Republic of China (Dec. 1981).

Note: 1. Export weights are based on the export value of the nine largest exporting countries in that year.
2. Trade weights are based on trade value of the nine largest trading countries in that year.

From the above observations, we know that Taiwan's economic environment immediately before the two oil shocks was such that prices had been particularly stable for some time, and that speedy export growth was creating a large physical demand on the one hand and inducing money supply growth on the other. Both oil crises occurred in the midst of this environment. Strong demand plus the available money supply easily absorbed the higher intermediate costs. The two periods of high inflation in the 1970s were thus largely caused by demand-pull and, to a lesser extent, by cost-push.

3.8.3 Government Policies

The government measures taken in response to the first oil crisis were mostly implemented in 1974. In order to cope with the skyrocketing inflation rate, they were rather active and drastic. This was a rare case of a "cold turkey" treatment. The measures for the second oil crisis, which were taken after 1979, were comparatively mild and gradual. Measures taken in response to these oil crises will be successively discussed below.

(A) Government Measures in the Wake of the First Oil Crisis. Government measures taken in the wake of the first oil crisis can be categorized as a high interest rate policy, a one-shot adjustment of oil prices, significant tax reductions, and heavy public spending.

a) **High Interest Rate Policy.** As prices started to rise in 1973, interest rates were raised in April and July of that year. As a result of these two increases, the secured loan rate rose by two percentage points to 13.25 percent, and the discount rate by one and three quarters points to 11.75 percent. However, the price index continued to rise at a monthly rate of about 4 percent in the second half of 1973. Inflationary expectations became widespread over the entire island. Time and savings deposits started to decrease in October 1973. Finally, in January 1974, inflation soared at a monthly rate of 12.9 percent. At this juncture "Stabilization Measures" were promulgated on January 27, 1974. The high interest rate policy was implemented as one of the two essential components of the "Stabilization Measures."

The characteristics of this interest rate policy can be described as follows: first, a significant one-shot rise in interest rates: on January 27, 1974 deposit rates were raised by 33.4 percent on average, and loan rates by 25.8 percent (Table 3.8.4); second, a greater rise in shorter-term interest rates than in longer-term interest rates; third, a greater rise in deposit rates than in loan rates; and fourth, an allowance for the new deposit rates and bond rates to be applicable to all previous deposits and previously issued public bonds. The effectiveness of this interest rate policy resulted in a prompt and continuous increase in time and savings deposits after February 1974.

b) **A One-Shot Adjustment of Oil Prices.** As a government monopoly enterprise, the Chinese Petroleum Corporation had enjoyed a considerable rate of profit up until the outbreak of the oil crisis, which allowed it to absorb a part of the cost increase. However, the increase in the oil price was much more than the Chinese Petroleum Corporation alone could absorb.

Table 3.8.4   Changes in Interest Rates on January 27, 1974

(% per annum)

	Date of Change		Rate of Change
	Oct. 24, 1973	Jan. 27, 1974	(%)
Deposit rate			
1 month	7.00	10.00	42.9
3 months	8.00	11.50	43.8
6 months	9.00	12.50	38.9
9 months	9.50	13.00	36.8
1 year	11.00	15.00	36.4
2 years	11.50	15.00	30.4
3 years	12.00	15.00	25.0
Weighted average rise in deposit rate			33.4
Loan rate			
Unsecured	13.75	17.50	27.3
Secured	13.25	16.50	24.5
Weighted average rise in loan rate			25.8

Source: Economic Research Department, The Central Bank of China, *Financial Statistics Monthly, Taiwan District, The Republic of China*, December 1981.

Table 3.8.5   Changes in Domestic Prices of Fuel Oil and Electricity (%)

Year	Changes in the Price of Fuel Oil	Changes in the Price of Electricity
1971	2.6	0.5
1972	2.0	−0.6
1973	0	2.1
1974	88.4	78.7
1975	2.8	3.9
1976	0	−1.2
1977	2	20.9
1978	0.5	−0.3
1979	44.7	11.5
1980	71.3	45.3
1981	23.1	35.4

Source: Council for Economic Planning and Development, Executive Yuan, *Economic Situation*, 1979 and 1981.

On January 27, 1974, the domestic prices of oil and related products were raised to meet the higher costs of oil products. This was the other essential part of the "Stabilization Measures." In order to eliminate the psychology of inflation, which had prevailed for several months, a one-shot adjustment rather than a gradual change was adopted. Prices were raised by an average of 88.4 percent for various kinds of oil products, and the price of electricity was increased 78.7 percent. Inflation skyrocketed in January and February of 1974 to reach a monthly rate of 12.9 percent in those two months. These policies — the one-shot oil price adjustment together with the rise in interest rates on January 27, 1974 — were very effective. They started to bring the inflation rate down in March 1974, and kept it dropping continuously in each month thereafter, as can be seen in Table 3.8.6. Thus, the inflation that occurred after the first oil crisis was under control by 1975, with the inflation rate that year falling to a negative 5.1 percent.

Table 3.8.6   Inflation Rates in 1974

Year and Month	Changes in WPI	
	(Comparison with the Previous Month) (% Per Month)	(Comparison with the Same Month of Previous Year) (% Per Annum)
1973 May	0.9	
June	2.0	
July	3.1	
Aug.	4.5	
Sep.	4.6	
Oct.	4.3	
Nov.	2.8	
Dec.	4.6	
1974 Jan.	12.9	52.0
Feb.	12.9	67.4
Mar.	−1.8	62.8
April	−3.0	58.2
May	−1.8	54.1
June	−1.1	49.3
July	−0.9	43.5
Aug.	−0.1	37.1
Sep.	−0.9	29.9
Oct.	−1.4	22.8
Nov.	−1.5	17.6
Dec.	−0.1	12.3

Sources: Economic Research Department, The Central Bank of China, *Financial Statistics Monthly, Taiwan District, the Republic of China*, January 1974, January 1975.
Directorate-General of Budget, Accounting and Statistics, Executive Yuan, *Commodity-Price Statistics Monthly, Taiwan Area, the Republic of China*, No. 139, July 1982.

c) **Tax Reductions.** Tax reductions in 1974 were mainly designed to reduce the cost of products and to promote a faster recovery of the economy. Major reductions were directed at income taxes, customs duties, commodity taxes, and harbor dues.

The income tax law was amended in October 1974 to raise the exemption levels for individual and business income taxes. The income brackets for the business income tax were also amended. It has been estimated that this change reduced individual income tax receipts by NT$460 million but increased the business income tax by NT$100 million. Thus, the net reduction in income taxes in 1974 was estimated to be NT$360 million.

The tariff rate adjustment in 1974 lowered duties on 200 import items and raised them on only 7 items. At the same time, the Executive Yuan utilized its authority to greatly reduce the tariff rates on many imports. These reductions were estimated to amount to NT$6,740 million, or 25 percent of the total tariff revenue in 1974.

According to tax regulations, the commodity tax should be based on the "taxing price," which is determined by the wholesale price of the taxed commodity. In order to reduce the commodity tax, the "taxing prices" of sugar, cement, and oil products, which accounted for about one half of total commodity taxes paid, were frozen in July 1973. The reduction in 1974 tax receipts caused by this freeze was estimated to equal 28 percent of the total commodity tax revenue collected that year.

Table 3.8.7 gives a general picture of the 1974 tax reduction. The total tax reduction that year was estimated to be NT$11.11 billion, which was equivalent to 12.9 percent of total tax revenue and 2.1 percent of the GNP. Thus, the tax reduction in 1974 was quite significant.

Table 3.8.7   Estimated Tax Reductions in 1974

Taxes	Tax Revenues (NT$ billion)	Estimated Tax Reductions (NT$ billion)	Percentage of Tax Reductions (%)
Income taxes	15.77	0.36	2.3
Customs duties	26.66	6.74	25.3
Commodity taxes	13.90	3.94	28.3
Harbor dues	5.88	0.07	1.2
Total	86.45	11.11	12.9

Source: Economic Planning Council, Executive Yuan, "An Estimation of Tax Reductions in 1974" (mimeo.).

d) Public Spending — The Ten Major Projects. The Ten Major Construction Projects started in 1973 and ended in 1978. They included six transportation projects, three heavy industry projects, and one nuclear power generation project. Investment in the Ten Major Projects comprised 4.5 percent of total investment in the years 1973 and 1974, and about 20 percent in 1975 and 1976. Actually, the Ten Major Projects were not designed to counter the business cycle or any other such phenomenon, but rather to develop infrastructure and heavy industry. The opportune timing of this public spending was a nice coincidence. Thus, the implementation of the Ten Major Projects contributed greatly to Taiwan's rapid recovery in 1975 and to prosperous growth thereafter (Table 3.8.8).

Table 3.8.8   Investment in the Ten Major Projects and GNP Growth Rate

(%)

Year	Percentage of Investment in the Ten Major Projects in Total Investment	Growth Rate of GNP
1973	4.5	12.8
1974	4.5	1.1
1975	19.3	4.2
1976	19.6	13.5
1977	13.1	9.9
1978	8.1	13.9

Source: Council for Economic Planning and Development, Executive Yuan, *An Evaluation of Ten Major Projects*, 1979; Directorate-General of Budget, Accounting & Statistics, Executive Yuan, *National Income of the Republic of China*, 1981.

(B) Policies in the Wake of the Second Oil Crisis. The impact of the second oil crisis was comparatively mild in terms of increased inflation and reduced growth rate. However, the process of adjustment this time took longer than in the previous crisis. No radical government measures were undertaken this time; the mild and gradual measures that were adopted were directed to the more rational pricing of oil and its products, and a foreign exchange rate determined more by market forces. These points will be elaborated on below.

   a) **Pricing of Oil and Its Products.** After the one-shot increase in oil and electricity prices in 1974, their domestic prices were kept relatively low in order to prevent serious price fluctuations, lessen the economic burden of low-income people, and maintain the competitiveness of manufactured exports. As a result of the low-price policy for energy, manufacturing firms were slow to adjust and improve their equipment and production processes. Consequently, the entire manufacturing structure adjusted rather slowly to the oil-induced changes of the 1970s.

   After the second oil crisis, greater reliance was placed on the price mechanism. Domestic oil prices have been allowed to change in a manner more reflective of import costs. During 1979-81, prices of both oil and electricity were raised every year. However, much room was still left for improvement in the use of the price mechanism to promote more efficient energy use and to encourage further energy conservation.

   b) **Foreign Exchange.** In order for the foreign exchange rate to reflect the market rate more closely, the foreign exchange system was converted from the original fixed-rate system to a floating rate system in February 1979. After that, the value of the New Taiwan dollar changed more frequently: six times in 1979, 17 times in 1980, 39 times in 1981, and 32 times in the first eight months of 1982. However, the fluctuations were very mild.

   The exchange rate was set by the Foreign Exchange Center, which based its decisions on the cumulative excess demand or excess supply of foreign exchange, counting from the day when the foreign exchange banks cleared their balance with the Central Bank of China. Since August 12, 1981, when the New Taiwan dollar was devalued by 4.6 percent against the U.S. dollar in one day, the change in the real effective exchange rate has also been taken into consideration in the determination of the exchange rate. This is done in order to prevent over-valuation or under-valuation of the New Taiwan dollar.

c) Fiscal Policies. No particularly active fiscal policies were implemented during this period. This was partly due to the desire to prevent a crowding out of money by heavy public investment, and partly due to the fact that the government budget, the current account of which had been in surplus every year for more than a decade, started to show a deficit after 1980.

Although the impact of the second oil shock was large, prolonged, and widespread, it approached its end in 1982. By August 1982, inflation had been brought down significantly and the Taiwan economy had started to bottom out.

3.9   Financial Liberalization

Liberalization took place as a process of gradual change during the transition of the Taiwan economy, leaving some markets under substantial control until the end of the 1970s. The financial market was one of these. At the beginning of the 1980s, however, liberalization and internationalization were adopted as a national policy because of the need to adjust to new circumstances. Liberalization and internationalization covered three areas: (1) price deregulation, including a move to abolish interest rate controls and a switch from a pegged to a floating foreign exchange rate system, (2) relaxation of restrictions on capital movements, and (3) allowing the entry of new competitors and a broader scope of financial activities.

3.9.1   Background of Interest Rate and Foreign Exchange Liberalization
Interest rate and foreign exchange liberalization in Taiwan can be divided into two stages, one starting in the early 1980s and the other beginning in 1985. The first stage of liberalization occurred in response to the new circumstances that followed the oil crises and the resulting period of international financial disorder. The second stage of liberalization was prompted by the buildup of massive foreign exchange reserves and high money supply growth, both generated by a huge trade surplus. Although the backgrounds of the two stages of liberalization were somewhat different, the basic aim was the same: to place greater reliance on the price mechanism for the adjustment of imbalances.

The current account surplus (and excess savings) amounted to 4.9 percent of the GNP in 1982. This percentage increased to 8.7 percent in 1983 and then continued upward, reaching 22.4 percent in 1986. The continuous current account surpluses in these years created a massive amount of foreign exchange reserves. Although the Central Bank carried out intensive sterilization, the accumulation of foreign exchange reserves produced heavy pressure on the money supply.

Another factor leading to the second stage of liberalization was instability of the U.S. dollar and other foreign currencies; that is, instability of the dollar, the Deutsche mark, and the Japanese yen following the "G5" meeting of September 1985. The New Taiwan dollar started to appreciate against the U.S. dollar due both to Taiwan's large trade surplus and to the depreciation of the dollar in the international market. Under these new circumstances, a relaxation of import restrictions and a further reduction of tariffs were actively implemented. By this time, also, society had reached a consensus on the need for financial liberalization and internationalization. Various measures directed toward the liberalization of interest rates, foreign exchange, and capital were adopted beginning in late 1985.

3.9.2 Interest Rate Liberalization

(A) The First Stage Interest Rate Liberalization. Deregulation of the money market was the first step in interest rate liberalization. The money market, which was officially established in 1976, had not functioned very actively until 1980. The interest rate ceiling on money market rates was lifted by the promulgation of the "Essentials of Interest Rate Adjustment" in 1980, which permitted the free setting of interest rates on CDs and money market instruments. The resulting expansion of the money market in the 1980s paved the way for further interest rate liberalization. Also, the permissible range of the interbank call rate was gradually expanded, making it possible for the rate to reflect the excess reserves in the banking system.

According to the Banking Law at that time, the maximum rates for all kinds of deposits were prescribed by the Central Bank of China. At the same time, in order to move closer to market-determined interest rates, official interest rates were adjusted much more frequently than before, 10 times from November 1980 to September 1982. As can be seen in Fig. 3.9.1, the movement of interest rates during this period

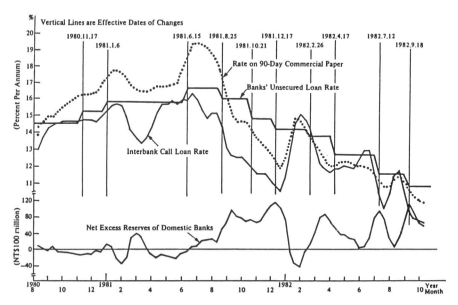

* (1) Rates on 90-day commercial paper are the moving average of three end-of-10-day-period figures. (2) Banks' unsecured loan rates are the average of maximum and minimum rates. (3) Interbank call loan rates and net excess reserves of domestic banks are the moving average of means of three 10-day periods.

Figure 3.9.1   Changes in Interest Rates on Commercial Paper, Interbank Call Loans, Bank Loans, and Net Excess Reserves of Domestic Banks* (August 1980–October 1982)

was rather close to the movement of money market rates and interbank call rates. The movement of official interest rates drew even closer to the money market rate and the call rate after January, 1982.

The first stage of interest rate liberalization failed to widen the range of loan rates, however, due to the existence of the "Regulations for Interest Rate Management," which stipulated that the maximum deposit rate should not exceed the minimum loan rate. Nevertheless, the success of the liberalization at this stage can be seen in two points. First, from then on the Central Bank frequently adjusted interest rates by very small amounts. Second, the interest rate adjustments were guided by money market rates, which were allowed to move freely.

(B) The Second Stage Interest Rate Liberalization. The second stage of liberalization was relatively successful. This time, the planning of the Central Bank was done much more carefully and the timing was much more appropriate. The main Central Bank actions toward interest rate liberalization are described below.

First, the range between maximum and minimum loan rates approved by the Central Bank was widened again beginning in November 1984. Second, starting in March 1985, each depository bank was asked to announce every day its "prime rate" as its own minimum loan rate; the difference in prime rates among banks was not only officially recognized, but even encouraged. Third, in September 1985 the "Regulations for Interest Rate Management," which prohibited the maximum deposit rate from exceeding the minimum loan rate and thus was an obstacle to the widening of the range of loan rates, was abolished. Fourth, in January 1986 deposit categories were reduced from 13 to four. (Since according to the Banking Law the Central Bank determines the maximum interest rate for each kind of deposit, the 13 different categories of deposits lead to 13 different maximum rates). The classifying of deposits into only four categories greatly expanded the free zone of bank activity. Fifth, the range of interbank call rates was gradually allowed to widen from the previous 1.25 percentage points to a 6-percentage-point spread by November 1985. At the same time, the "central interbank call rate system" was abolished to give each bank complete freedom in the determination of its own call rate.

It can be easily seen from Figures 3.9.2 and 3.9.3 that the upper limit set by the Central Bank has not been a binding constraint since 1984. On the contrary, the market interest rate has been moving further and further away from the regulated upper limit. Both loan and deposit rates went down under the pressure of excess liquidity caused by the huge trade surplus. The gap between realized loan rates and the maximum loan rate approved by the Central Bank, therefore, widened accordingly. For example, for all 16 domestic banks in existence at the time, this gap expanded from 0.86 percentage points at the end of 1984 to 3.38 percentage points in December 1988. On the other hand, the gap between average loan rates and average deposit rates narrowed from 3.56 percentage points at the end of 1984 to 2.68 percentage points in December 1988. These figures indicate that neither loan rates nor deposit rates are repressed. They also show more competitive behavior and more efficient management in the banking business. Interest rate liberalization in this second stage, therefore, was successfully achieving its goal by 1988.

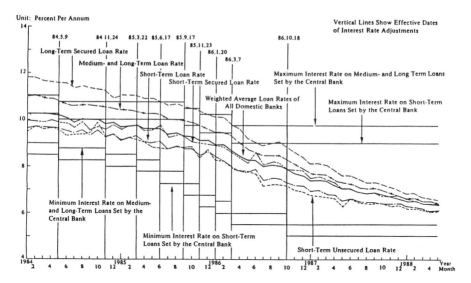

Figure 3.9.2   Average Loan Rates of Domestic Banks

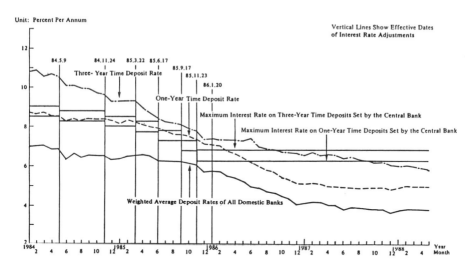

Figure 3.9.3   Average Deposit Rates of All Domestic Banks

In sum, the timing of the second period of interest rate liberalization was very favorable. With stable prices and a balanced budget as preconditions, and with a huge trade surplus that was generating excess liquidity, interest rate liberalization was implemented very smoothly and successfully. It laid down a sound foundation for further liberalization: a removal of the regulations controlling maximum deposit rates and maximum and minimum loan rates. The monetary authority had worked on this for more than seven years, and its success led to the revision of the Banking Law in 1989.

The revision of the Banking Law removed all controls on both deposit and lending interest rates. It permitted foreign bank branches to accept long-term saving accounts. It opened up the establishment of new private banks. As a result, 15 new private banks were approved in 1991, and approval was granted in 1992 for the conversion of the China Trust and Investment Company into a commercial bank. The interest rate liberalization that took place in the 1980s served well to make these substantial amendments to the Banking Law possible.

3.9.3 Foreign Exchange Rate Liberalization

The foreign exchange system was converted from a fixed rate system to a floating rate system in February 1979, and the value of the New Taiwan dollar has fluctuated since then. Both the current account and basic balance were continuously in surplus in the 1980s. After 1985, in particular, the current account balance increased drastically. It equaled 14.8 percent of the GNP in 1985 and then increased to 21.4 percent and 18.3 percent of the GNP in 1986 and 1987, respectively. In addition, the U.S. dollar has continuously depreciated since the "G5" meeting in September 1985, creating a natural tendency toward appreciation of the N.T. dollar against the U.S. dollar. These two basic phenomena led the Taiwan foreign exchange market operation in two directions. One was that the Central Bank of China had to buy up some of the excess supply of foreign exchange. The other was that the N.T. dollar had to appreciate to some extent. That was what actually happened from late 1985 to the middle of 1988 (Table 3.9.1).

(A) Appreciation of the N.T. Dollar. During the period of 1985 to 1987, the nation's foreign exchange reserves increased by US$59.3 billion, while the N.T. dollar appreciated by about 40 percent against the U.S. dollar. The basic philosophy generally held in the community and most of the government sector is that any drastic appreciation of the domestic currency usually involves high adjustment costs in both the export and import-competing sectors, and that the Central Bank must let the N.T. dollar appreciate "gradually" and "smoothly." The Central Bank therefore intervened and sterilized frequently in the foreign exchange market to absorb part of the excess supply of foreign exchange. It was beyond the Central Bank's ability to prevent the appreciation of the N.T. dollar against the U.S. dollar completely, however. Also, it was felt that the undervaluation of the domestic currency would not be beneficial to the adjustment of the serious imbalance in trade. Therefore, the N.T. dollar was allowed to appreciate (See Fig. 3.9.4).

(B) Capital Movement. Long before foreign exchange controls were largely deregulated in July 1987, there were actually official channels for capital flow through the banking system. That is, an importer was eligible to borrow in foreign currency through commercial banks, and was eligible to sell his borrowings in the foreign exchange market for N.T. dollars at any time. Furthermore, in order to make loans to importers, commercial banks were allowed to borrow foreign exchange from abroad.

During the period from 1985 to 1987, the N.T. dollar appreciated tremendously against the U.S. dollar, with the accumulated appreciation amounting to as much as 45 percent. However, in order to avoid a drastic impact on exporters, the Central Bank adopted "a gradual appreciation policy." That is, the appreciation of the N.T.

Table 3.9.1   Current Account Balance and Excess Savings as Percentage of GNP

Year	Gross National Product GNP	Exports of Goods and Services X	Imports of Goods and Services M	Current Account Balance X–M	Gross Savings S	Gross Investment I	Excess Savings S–I
1971	100.0	37.3	34.7	2.6	28.8	26.2	2.6
1972	100.0	43.9	37.4	6.5	32.1	25.6	6.5
1973	100.0	48.9	43.6	5.3	34.4	29.1	5.3
1974	100.0	45.7	53.4	–7.7	31.5	39.2	–7.7
1975	100.0	41.6	45.4	–3.8	26.7	30.5	–3.8
1976	100.0	49.4	47.8	1.6	32.4	30.8	1.6
1977	100.0	50.9	46.6	4.3	32.6	28.3	4.3
1978	100.0	54.6	48.5	6.1	34.4	28.3	6.1
1979	100.0	56.1	55.6	0.5	33.4	32.9	0.5
1980	100.0	55.3	56.8	–1.5	32.3	33.8	–1.5
1981	100.0	55.0	53.7	1.3	31.3	30.0	1.3
1982	100.0	53.5	48.6	4.9	30.1	25.2	4.9
1983	100.0	55.9	47.2	8.7	32.1	23.4	8.7
1984	100.0	59.0	47.1	11.9	33.8	21.9	11.9
1985	100.0	57.0	42.2	14.8	33.6	18.8	14.8
1986	100.0	60.8	39.4	21.4	38.5	17.1	21.4
1987	100.0	60.4	42.1	18.3	38.5	20.2	18.3
1988	100.0	58.0	46.6	11.4	34.5	23.1	11.4
1989	100.0	54.0	45.8	8.2	31.1	22.9	8.2
1990	100.0	50.9	44.1	6.8	29.3	22.5	6.8
1991	100.0	51.5	44.8	6.7	29.4	22.7	6.7
1992	100.0	47.2	43.3	3.9	28.3	24.4	3.9
1993	100.0	47.5	44.5	3.0	27.8	24.8	3.0
1994	100.0	47.5	45.0	2.5	26.1	23.6	2.5

Source: Directorate-General of Budget, Accounting and Statistics, Executive Yuan, *National Income in Taiwan Area, Republic of China, 1995*, pp.22, 26, 176-181.

dollar was limited to one cent a day. This systematic gradual appreciation created a massive inflow of foreign exchange. The mechanism was as follows: with the expectation of further appreciation of the N.T. dollar, importers borrowed foreign exchange from banks in order to earn the appreciation margin. (They could sell this foreign currency at market for N.T. dollars, and six month later they could buy it back at much cheaper price for repayment.) Commercial banks borrowed foreign exchange from abroad both for relending to importers and for earning appreciation margin themselves. Since the N.T. dollar was not an international currency, no arbitrage could have taken place. The Central Bank continued the gradual appreciation policy for almost two years, and became the sole loser of it. Finally, the discovery of the above operation led to the Central Bank's freeze on the outstanding amount of commercial banks' foreign liabilities at the level of May 31, 1987, which was US$13.8 billion.

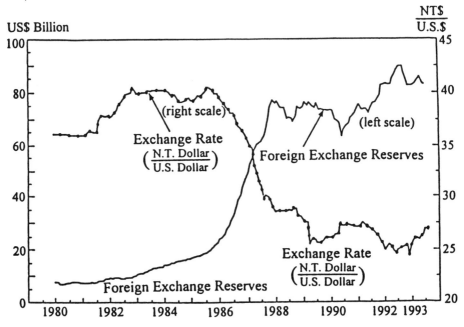

Figure 3.9.4   **Foreign Exchange Reserves and Exchange Rate of the N.T. Dollar Against the U.S. Dollar**

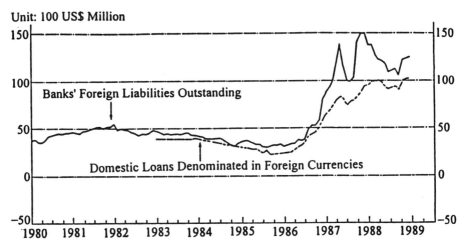

Figure 3.9.5   **Banks' Foreign Liabilities Outstanding and Domestic Loans Denominated in Foreign Currencies**

A significant step toward liberalization, in the direction of capital outflow, was taken in July 1987. Foreign exchange controls were greatly relaxed to allow direct capital outflow by the non-bank private sector; the amount of purchasing of foreign exchange for outward remittance was expanded to a maximum of US$5 million per adult per year, while the maximum amount of inward remittances was increased to a maximum of only US$50,000 per adult per year. However, no immediate net capital outflow was observed in the wake of this relaxation because of the expectation of appreciation of the N.T. dollar. (After a series of adjustments, current regulations allow each adult to remit up to US$5 million in or out of the country annually.)

When the foreign debt of the commercial banks was frozen, the link between capital inflow and the expectation of currency appreciation was broken. Specifically, the termination of the huge and continuous capital inflow helped to moderate further appreciation. The Central Bank tried to lift the ban on October 1, 1987; however, the amount of capital inflow on that day exceeded 3 billion U.S. dollars, and this prompted the Central Bank to reimpose the freeze the next day. This time the freeze was set at the level of October 2, 1987, which was 16.2 billion U.S. dollars. Since that time, the N.T. dollar has been relatively stable.

It is shown elsewhere that the banks' borrowing of foreign exchange was closely tied to the expectation of currency appreciation prior to May 31, 1987, the date of the first freeze, and that the link was much looser after that date (Liu and Kuo, 1990). However, the borrowing of foreign exchange from domestic banks by the non-bank private sector after May 31, 1987 was not yet bound by the freeze on the outstanding amount of borrowing by commercial banks. This activity continued to show a close relationship between the borrowing of foreign exchange and the expected exchange rate (Kuo, 1989).

We may note first that market expectation of N.T. dollar appreciation (i.e., a lower exchange rate) led to an increase in the borrowing of foreign exchange by the non-bank private sector long before the capital account was officially partially liberalized; and second that even though foreign debt by commercial banks was frozen by the Central Bank, the limitation did not hinder borrowing from banks by the non-bank private sector. As a result, people continued to behave as they had before May 1987. The gradual decline in the outstanding amount of foreign exchange borrowing by the non-bank private sector that had set in by July 1988 was thus due largely to the relative stability of the N.T. dollar rather than to the freeze imposed by the Central Bank.

3.9.4 Liberalization of the Securities and Insurance Markets

Liberalization and internationalization of the securities market in Taiwan are characterized by the following government policies and measures:

First, the basic idea is to increase participation by foreign nationals in the Taiwan securities market gradually, in three phases. The first phase allowed foreign investors to make indirect investment through the purchase of mutual funds. Phase two permitted direct investment in the market by foreign institutional investors. And phase three allows overseas Chinese and foreign individuals to invest in the market directly. We have just moved into the third phase this year (1996).

Second, the revision of the Securities and Exchange Law in January 1988 was a major event. The amendment covered a broad range, including the lifting of the restriction on the establishment of new securities companies. Securities firm licenses are now made available to any firm which meets a basic set of financial and operating requirements.

The revised Securities and Exchange Law, and its accompanying administrative law, allow securities companies more leeway to operate. They permit the establishment of integrated securities firms, which can concurrently engage in trading for customers, namely as brokers; trading on their own account, namely as dealers; and underwriting for issuing companies, namely as underwriters.

The 1988 Securities and Exchange Law also permits qualified integrated securities firms to provide margin financing directly to their customers. However, detailed regulations governing margin financing are still in the drafting stage. Until this change in the law, only a securities finance company was permitted to do margin financing.

Also, the SEC has significantly strengthened disclosure requirements for corporate directors, officers, and shareholders, and has introduced much tighter insider trading regulations.

The liberalization of Taiwan's insurance market has proceeded at a good pace in recent years. The total assets of the island's life insurance companies increased at an annual rate of 29 percent over the past 10 years to reach NT$663 billion in August 1993. In 1991 the total assets of property insurance firms were up 31 percent over the previous year, to NT$56.7 billion. Entry into the insurance market was reopened to domestic private companies in 1992. Up to 49 percent of any private insurance company may now be invested by foreign nationals, according to the revised Insurance Law that became effective in August 1991.

In conclusion, financial liberalization in Taiwan seems to be on the right track in terms of order, speed, and coverage. However, since economic liberalization is not only an economic event but also an institutional, political, and social change, careful design and smooth implementation are of great importance.[4] If the ROC is to achieve the national goals of a suitable rate of growth, stable prices, and improved welfare, it is obvious that much remains to be done.

3.10 Policies for High-Tech Industries

Since the early 1970s, high-tech industries have been the driving force for transition and growth in the manufacturing sector. In order to mold an environment more conducive to the development of industrial technology, the government established the Hsinchu Science-based Industrial Park in 1980.

Numerous incentives offered to Park enterprises provided powerful inducements to locate there. The arrangement for leasing land and factories instead of selling them lowered the costs of Park enterprises. R & D grants for innovative technological research helped encourage and reward manufacturers for their commitment to research and their efforts toward constant innovation. Administrative measures, such as tax incentives and one-stop services, also helped to nurture an environment conducive to growth. Bilingual schools and other educational facilities were provided for returning overseas Chinese and other people working in the Park.

Great achievements have been recorded by the Park over the past 15 years. Total sales of Park enterprises exceeded NT$280 billion (US$10.3 billion) in 1995, marking a new high and a 60 percent increase over total sales in 1994.

The Republic of China became the world's third largest producer of information products in 1995. The Hsinchu Science-based Industrial Park has performed a remarkable part in this achievement. Some information products which come mostly from the Park occupied the largest share of the world market in 1995. These products were network interface cards (world share of 35 percent), computer mice (world share of 80 percent), and scanners (world share of 60 percent). Terminals made in Taiwan occupied the second largest share of the world market.

To expand and extend the successful experience of the Hsinchu Science-based Industrial Park, the government has chosen Tainan (in the southern part of Taiwan) as the site of a second science park. The development plan was approved by the Executive Yuan (cabinet) in May of 1995, and implementation has been proceeding smoothly since then.

3.11 Policies on Infrastructure

Infrastructural construction was emphasized from time to time in the past, especially in periods of serious shortage. Ten major construction projects, which included six major transportation projects encompassing an international airport, Taiwan's first freeway, and Taichung harbor, among others, were completed from 1973 to 1980. The completion of these ten major projects greatly alleviated the transportation congestion which had become very serious in the early 1970s.

Table 3.11.1 Real Annual Growth of Investment and the Government's Current Surplus (1956–1995)

(at 1991 constant price, %)

Period	Government Investment	Public Enterprise Investment	Private Enterprise Investment	Total Investment	Pct. of Government's Current Surplus in Gov't Current Expenditure
1956-60	15.1	15.9	17.8	15.9	13.9
1961-70	13.5	15.0	16.3	15.1	12.2
1971-80	14.9	17.6	12.5	13.7	42.0
1981-87	**6.7**	**–1.7**	**6.9**	**4.3**	**29.5**
1988-90	22.4	19.2	6.9	12.4	37.7
1991-94	17.1	–2.9	10.3	9.3	21.7

Source: Directorate-General of Budget, Accounting and Statistics, Executive Yuan, *National Income of the Republic of China*, 1995.

After the ten major projects were completed, however, the emphasis on infrastructural construction paused for nearly a decade during the 1980s. As can be seen in Table 3.11.1, during the period of 1981-87, the growth rate of government investment registered its lowest level at 6.7 percent. Investment by public enterprises, dominated by the Taiwan Power Company and Chinese Petroleum Corporation, even registered negative growth during this period. This was very conservative spending on public construction. It is especially notable that during this period, the general environment was such that the government was saving a huge proportion of the current account surplus (which equaled 29.5 percent of the government budget), and the economy was generating a large savings-investment surplus (as high as 21.4 percent of GNP in 1986), as can be seen in Table 3.11.2.

Table 3.11.2 Investment and Savings as % of GNP

(%)

Year	Domestic Investment	Public Investment by Government and Public Enterprises	Private Investment	Savings	Savings-Investment Surplus
1973	29.1	10.6	18.5	34.4	5.3
1974	39.2	14.8	24.4	31.5	−7.7
1975	30.5	17.6	12.9	26.7	−3.8
1976	30.8	16.7	14.1	32.3	1.5
1977	28.3	14.3	14.0	32.6	4.3
1978	28.3	12.9	15.4	34.4	6.1
1979	32.9	13.3	19.6	33.4	0.5
1980	33.8	16.5	17.3	32.3	−1.5
1981	30.0	15.0	15.0	31.3	1.3
1982	25.2	13.2	12.0	30.1	4.9
1983	23.4	10.9	12.5	32.1	8.7
1984	21.9	8.8	13.1	33.8	11.9
1985	18.7	7.9	10.8	33.6	14.9
1986	17.1	6.7	10.4	38.5	21.4
1987	20.2	7.6	12.6	38.5	18.3
1988	23.1	7.7	15.4	34.5	11.4
1989	22.9	9.0	13.9	31.1	8.2
1990	22.5	11.1	11.4	29.3	6.8
1991	22.7	11.2	11.5	29.4	6.7
1992	24.4	11.4	13.0	28.3	3.9
1993	24.8	11.3	13.5	27.8	3.0
1994	23.6	11.0	12.6	26.1	2.5

Source: Directorate-General of Budget, Accounting and Statistics, Executive Yuan, National Income of the Republic of China, 1995, p.22, and Statistical Abstract of National Income in Taiwan Area, Republic of China, 1951-1996, March 1996, p.42.

During the period 1984-87, public investment constituted a record low share of GNP, while the investment-saving gap grew to a record high share of GNP, soaring from 11.9 percent to 21.4 percent (Table 3.11.2). This was due to a too-conservative public investment policy.

The conservative public investment policy during this period naturally reduced the share of total domestic investment by a significant amount. When we compare the share of investment in the GNPs of neighboring countries for this period, we find that Taiwan's investment share was much lower than that of Korea, Singapore and even Japan, as can be seen in Table 3.11.3. A result of this conservative public investment was, needless to say, a shortage of infrastructure.

Table 3.11.3 Comparison of Investment Rate with ROC, Japan, Korea and Singapore

				(%)
Year	Republic of China	Japan	Korea	Singapore
1981	30.0	31.2	30.7	–
1982	25.2	29.9	29.8	–
1983	23.4	28.0	29.7	47.3
1984	21.9	28.0	30.9	48.2
1985	18.7	28.1	30.3	41.0
1986	17.1	27.7	29.2	36.8
1987	20.1	28.5	30.1	38.5
1988	22.8	30.4	31.1	36.1
1989	22.3	31.5	33.6	34.7
1990	21.9	33.0	37.2	–
1991	22.4	31.9*	39.4	–

Sources: ROC: DGBAS, National Income of the Republic of China, 1991. Japan: Research and Statistics Department, Bank of Japan, Economic Statistics Annual, 1992. Korea: The Bank of Korea, National Accounts, 1991. Singapore: Ministry of Trade and Industry, Republic of Singapore, Economic Survey of Singapore.

Note: * First three quarters.

The shortage of infrastructure had become very evident by the mid-1980s. Shortages and inadequacies were especially serious in electricity, water supply, quality of drinking water, transportation, environmental pollution, residential quality, noise, garbage and recreational facilities. In view of this, the emphasis on infrastructural construction and environmental improvement was brought back again and adopted as the main theme of the Ninth Four-year Economic Plan (1986-1989) and Tenth Four-year Economic Plan (1990-1993). This theme was continued in the Six-year National Development Plan (1991-1996). The result of this emphasis was the undertaking of 14 major projects in recent years, and 12 major projects at the present time. The growth rate of government investment surged to 22.4 percent annually during 1988-90, just before the start of the Six-year National Development Plan. During the period 1991-94, government investment expanded at an annual rate of 17.1 percent (Table 3.11.1).

The government's current surplus, which was the main source of funding for infrastructural construction, made up a high ratio of the government budget every year until 1990. The current surplus started to deteriorate in 1991, however, mainly due to the negative growth of central government revenue that year. One of the reasons for the negative growth in government revenue was a negative growth of revenue from the business income tax. Revenue from the individual income tax, however, experienced normal growth. Another reason was the negative growth of revenue turned over to the government by state-owned enterprises in 1991. At the same time, a much larger proportion of the budget has been spent on social welfare in the past few years due to the intensive demands of legislators and society in general. These two factors together were enough to reduce the government's current surplus from the previous 37.7 percent to just 21.7 percent in 1991-94 and further to 8.4 percent in 1995 (see Table 3.11.1).

In Taiwan, public bonds are prohibited by law from being issued for current expenditure; they can be issued only for public construction. In the three decades up to 1990, public construction was financed almost solely by the government's current surplus (which constituted about 30 percent of the government budget), and only a negligible amount of public bonds were issued. Due to the deterioration of government revenue on the one hand and the expansion of current expenditure on the other, the government's current surplus declined tremendously during 1991 and 1992. Since those years the government began issuing a significant amount of public bonds. After the government's tax revenue returned to positive growth in 1993, the amount of bond issuance has declined every year. As of April 1996 the outstanding value of public bonds issued by the central government was NT$7,240 billion, equivalent to 13.3 percent of GDP, which was still much lower than some other countries. The comparable figures are 60.2 percent for the U.S., 57.7 percent for Japan, 43.7 percent for the U.K., 18.2 percent for France, 23.4 percent for Germany, and 74.7 percent for Singapore (IMF, 1995).

In response to the decrease in the government's current account surplus, and in order to improve the efficiency of public construction, the government has begun planning to adopt a BOT mechanism for infrastructural construction. That is, a project will be built and operated for a certain period by private business, and then, after a certain number of years, it will be transferred to the government. At the same time, the privatization of some government-owned enterprises has been carried out (although the implementation of privatization has not proceeded very rapidly.) The power generation industry, which was until recently a government monopoly, is now open to the private sector. There is also a movement toward privatization and deregulation in the telecommunications field.

The government's major objective with respect to infrastructural construction is to provide enough resources to support future production, as well as to improve the environment. A continuous emphasis on, and efficient and timely implementation of, infrastructural construction is thus a vital factor in future economic growth.

3.12 Current Issues

The general environment in Taiwan has changed significantly since the early 1980s, and the pace of change is expected to intensify in the remainder of the 1990s. Internationally, the new environment is characterized by the expansion of international cooperation, financial innovation, and keen competition from newcomers. Domestically, we have to deal with several basic issues, such as a labor shortage, rising wages, advancement of technology, upgrading of production, diversification of trade, construction of infrastructure, and improvement of environmental conditions. Some of the current issues we face will be elaborated below.

3.12.1 Increasing International Ties

The future development of Taiwan is closely interrelated with the world economy. Recently, the ROC government has been taking part aggressively in international economic affairs so as to better fulfill its international obligations. The ROC became a member of APEC in October of 1991 and an observer of GATT in September of 1992. Once we become a member of the WTO, we will have access to better channels for working with the international community on matters of trade in the interest of the world economy.

3.12.2 Advancement of Technology

In the new world of high technology, manufactured goods will have the characteristics of "lighter, thinner, shorter, and smaller." Also, a manufactured product will compete by how much service it can provide. This will mean competition through intellectual ability and precision. The most obvious advantage brought by competition is greater efficiency. Competition rewards innovation and efficiency, while monopoly stifles innovation and efficiency. In this sense, the speed of privatization should receive greater attention.

3.12.3 Diversification of Exports

The Taiwan economy has long been heavily dependent on exports to the U.S., but it has become less so in recent years. Exports to the U.S. comprised 48 percent of Taiwan's total exports in 1984, but this share declined to 24 percent in 1995.

As the main source of our trade surplus, the United States has been replaced by Hong Kong and mainland China in recent years. With mainland China, only indirect trade and investment are allowed at the present time. Due to a lack of adequate statistics, we cannot gain a clear picture of this situation; however, we note that the trade surplus with Hong Kong amounted to US$24.2 billion in 1995. This was not only much greater than the trade surplus with the U.S., which was US$5.6 billion, but was also greater than our total trade surplus, which was US$8.1 billion. To avoid being affected too heavily by economic fluctuations in any single area in the future, we have to continue striving for further trade diversification.

3.12.4 The Work Ethic and Political Mechanisms

The old ethic of hard work and austerity has somehow given way to a new ethic of instant gratification. In an age when change comes with frightening rapidity, future blindness is a deadly flaw. We need a collective vision of the future. A new value pattern has placed increasing reliance on public opinion as a source of guidance in social and governmental behavior. However, the political decision-maker today faces a clamor of often contradictory demands from individual interest groups. We need political mechanisms capable of shifting through this noise to find the common interest of society as a whole.

3.12.5 Regional Operations Center

In order to ensure our central role in the region's commercial vitality in the future, the government is carrying out a comprehensive, future-oriented Asia-Pacific regional operations center plan. This plan encompasses six centers: manufacturing, air transportation, sea transportation, finance, telecommunications, and media.

The government has announced the following five principles to be followed in the implementation of its new economic strategies. Competition policy will be the core of our policy menu, while secondary consideration will be given to industrial policy. The main concern will be improving the nation's well-being. The government's role will be redefined as that of an administrator only; it will no longer play the dual roles of both business operator and regulator. Administrative efficiency will be enhanced by adopting a filing and reporting system instead of the existing approval system. The principle of maximum transparency will be applied in all policy-making, and the government's authority will be clearly defined. We believe that the clear announcement of these principles has ushered in a new era of economic policy-making and global economic strategy for Taiwan.

In achieving their present success, the government and the people of the Republic of China on Taiwan have overcome many difficulties during the past five decades. I would like to conclude by saying that if we can make quick responses to new problems and timely adjustments to new circumstances in the challenging 21st century, we can look forward to a bright future with growing prosperity.

3.13 Appendix

Table 3.A.1   Characteristics of the Taiwan Economy (1961-94)

Item	1961-71	1971-81	1981-91	1992	1993	1994
Production						
1. GDP (% real change)	10.0	9.5	7.9	6.8	6.3	6.5
2. Unemployment Rate (%)	2.9	1.6	2.1	1.5	1.5	1.6
3. Gross Domestic Investment Rate (% GNP)	22.3	30.4	22.5	24.4	24.8	23.6
4. Gross National Savings Rate (% GNP)	21.8	31.8	32.9	28.3	27.8	26.1
Balance of Payments						
5. Exports (% GNP)	18.4	42.0	47.0	37.6	37.5	38.1
6. Imports (% GNP)	21.0	40.0	36.1	33.4	34.1	35.0
7. Current Account Balance (% GNP)	−0.5	1.4	10.4	3.9	3.0	2.5
8. Debt Service Ratio	–	3.8[*]	2.9	0.3	0.1	0.1
Fiscal						
9. Public Sector Expenditures (% GNP)	23.6	24.1	25.6	30.1	30.0	30.1
10. Fiscal Surplus (% GDP)	2.4	6.6	5.1	4.5	5.0	4.6
11. Total Change in Monetary Base (% GDP)	1.4[‡]	2.6	2.8	2.3	1.5	2.4
Money and Prices						
12. M_2/GDP (%)	34.1	57.9	113.4	166.1	173.7	182.5
13. Annual Change in CPI (%)	3.3	11.6	3.2	4.5	2.9	4.1
14. Annual Change in WPI (%)	1.8	10.4	−0.4	−3.7	2.5	2.2
15. Annual Change in Real Wage Rate of Manufacturing	6.2	8.0	7.4	5.6	3.8	1.8
Staff	1.3[§]	5.6	7.2	4.9	2.7	1.6
Worker	11.9[§]	9.7	6.9	5.2	3.9	1.5
16. Exchange Rate (NT$=US$1)	40.0	37.8	34.0	25.2	26.4	26.4
17. Real Effective Exchange Rate Index (Trade weighted, 1979=100)	108.9	104.0	99.7	95.8	89.7	86.7

[*]: 1974-81, [‡]: 1962-71, [§]: 1969-71.   Note: Figures are period averages.

Source: DGBAS, *National Income of the Republic of China*, 1995; *Quarterly National Economic Trends, Taiwan Area, The Republic of China*, Nov. 1995; *Yearbook of Labor Statistics, Republic of China*, 1981, 1986, 1987, 1990, 1993, 1994; MOF, *Monthly Statistics of Exports and Imports, The Republic of China*, Nov. 1995; CBC, *Financial Statistics Monthly, Taiwan District, Republic of China*, Nov. 1995.

Table 3.A.2   Quality of Life Indicators

Item		
1. Education	**1966**	**1994**
Literacy rate (of population 6 years old and older) (%)	45.0 (1946)	94.0 (1993)
Percentage of school-age children (6–11) in primary school	78.6 (1946)	98.4
Percentage of junior high-age youths (12–14) in junior high school	48.3	99.5
Percentage of senior high-age youths (15–17) in senior high and vocational school	28.3	92.4
Percentage of junior college- and university-age youths (18–21) in junior college and university	11.3	45.3
2. Health	**1952**	**1994**
Crude death rate (per 1,000)	9.9	5.4
Life expectancy (years)	58.6	74.5
Per capita daily calorie intake	2,078	3,090
Per capita daily protein intake (grams)	49	96
3. Transportation and Communications	**1952**	**1994**
Automobiles (per 1,000 population)	1	206
Motorcycles (per 1,000 population)	0.2	382
Correspondence posted (per capita)	7	96
4. Housing	**1952**	**1994**
Percentage of households with electric lighting	33.0 (1949)	99.7
Percentage of population with piped water	28.8	87.4
Living space per head (square meters)	4.6 (1949)	30.4
Dwelling investment/GNP (%)	1.0	2.7

Source: Ministry of Education, Education Statistics of the Republic of China, 1995; DGBAS, Social Indicators in Taiwan Area of the Republic of China, 1994; DGBAS, National Income of the Republic of China, 1995.

Table 3.A.3 A Comparison of Consumer Durables Among Different Urban Areas in Taiwan, 1994

(per 1,000 households)

Item	Most Urbanized Area	2nd Urbanized Area	3rd Urbanized Area	4th Urbanized Area	Average for the Economy
1. Color T.V. Sets	1,388	1,245	1,239	1,220	1,255
2. Refrigerators	1,067	1,035	1,036	1,034	1,039
3. Air conditioners	1,761	1,184	949	733	1,022
4. Gas geysers	960	924	965	912	936
5. Washing machines	993	951	951	903	938
6. Telephones	1,134	1,012	1,021	981	1,020
7. Driers	371	96	220	108	176
8. Dehumidifiers	429	107	186	65	160
9. Smoke-exhaust machines	948	912	903	825	880
10. Vacuum cleaners	544	357	270	229	309
11. Microwave ovens	622	381	289	216	324
12. Electric geysers	88	74	68	79	76
13. Mixers	621	475	389	389	438
14. Electronic games	307	193	185	119	178
15. Home computers	353	166	161	88	161
16. Cameras	1,005	682	665	516	658
17. Cine cameras	148	65	53	27	58
18. Laser-disk players	98	44	37	22	41
19. Video recorders	876	706	738	599	697
20. Pianos	252	148	77	81	117
21. Hi-Fi stereo sets	523	406	396	349	397
22. Recorders	1,225	974	842	783	897
23. Sedan Vehicles	531	502	470	479	488
24. Motor bicycles	744	1,450	1,162	1,459	1,268
25. Newspapers	801	685	643	573	645
26. Magazines	336	185	135	123	168

Source: Department of Budget, Accounting and Statistics, Taiwan Provincial Government, *Report on the Survey of Family Income and Expenditure, Taiwan Province*, 1994; Bureau of Budget, Accounting and Statistics, Taipei Municipal Government, *Report on the Survey of Family Income and Expenditure and Personal Income Distribution of Taipei Municipality*, 1994; Bureau of Budget, Accounting and Statistics, Kaohsiung Municipal Government, *Report on the Survey of Family Income and Expenditure of Kaohsiung Municipality*, 1994.

3.14 Notes

1   Scholars and policy makers share this view. See, e.g., Ranis (1988), Fei (1988), Li (1988 and 1995).

2   Virtually observers of this early period seem to be in agreement in this case. See, for example, Lundberg (1979).

3   Fig. 3.8.1 is comparable to figures used by Professor Milton Friedman (1981).

4   See, e.g., Edwards (1984 and 1986), Harberger (1982), Kapur (1983), Krueger (1984), McKinnon (1982), Frenkel (1982).

3.15 References

Chang, Kowie, Ming-jen Lu, and Teh-an Hsu, 1968. "Fiscal Operations," in Kowie Chang (ed.), *Economic Development in Taiwan*. Taipei: Cheng Chung Book Company.

Chang, Yen-tien, 1965. *Land Reform and Its Impact on Economic and Social Progress in Taiwan*. Taipei: National Taiwan University.

Edwards, S., 1984. *The Order of Liberalization of the External Sector in Developing Countries*, Princeton University, Essays in International Finance, No. 156.

Edwards, S., 1986. "The Order of Liberalization of the Current and Capital Accounts of the Balance of Payments," in A.M. Choksi and D. Papageorgiou (eds.), *Economic Liberalization in Developing Countries*. Oxford: Basil Blackwell.

Fei, John C.H., 1988. "A Bird's Eye View of Policy Evolution on Taiwan: An Introductory Essay," in K.T. Li, *The Evolution of Policy behind Taiwan's Development Success*. New Haven: Yale University Press.

Frenkel, J., 1982. "The Order of Economic Liberalization: Discussion," in K. Brunner and A.H. Meltzer (eds.), *Economic Policy in a World of Change*. Amsterdam: North-Holland.

Friedman, Milton, 1981. "Money and Inflation." Taipei: Academia Sinica, The Institute of Economics.

Harberger, A.C., 1982. "The Chilean Economy in the 1970s: Crisis Stabilization, Liberalization, Reform," in K. Brunner and A.H. Meltzer (eds.), *Economic Policy in a World of Change*. Amsterdam: North-Holland.

Ho, T.F., 1965. *A Biography of Mr.Chen Chen*. Taipei: Anti-Communist Publisher.

IMF, 1995. *Government Financial Statistics Yearbook*. Washington, DC: IMF.

Jacoby, Neil H., 1966. U.S. Aid to Taiwan: A Study of Foreign Aid, Self-Help, and Development. New York: Frederick A. Praeger Publishers.

Kapur, B.K., 1983. "Optimal Financial and Foreign-Exchange Liberalization of Less Developed Economies," Quarterly Journal of Economics, XCVIII (1): 41-62.

Krueger, A.O., 1984. "Problems of Liberalization," in A.C. Harberger (ed.), World Economic Growth. San Francisco: Institute for Contemporary Studies: 403-423.

Kuo, Shirley W.Y., 1983a. The Taiwan Economy in Transition. Boulder: Westview Press.

Kuo, Shirley W.Y, 1983b. "Cost-Price Changes Caused by External Shocks — The Case of 1973 Inflation," in Shirley W.Y. Kuo, The Taiwan Economy in Transition. Boulder: Westview Press.

Kuo, Shirley W.Y., 1989. "Liberalization of the Financial Market in Taiwan in the 1980s," Keynote Address at the First Annual Pacific-Basin Finance Conference, in Taipei on March 14, 1989.

Lee, T.H., 1969. "Impact of Land Reform on the Farm Economy Structure." Taipei: Joint Commission on Rural Reconstruction, March (mimeo).

Lee, T.H., 1971a. "Government Interference in the Rice Market," Economic Essays, Vol. 2. Taipei: National Taiwan University, Graduate Institute of Economics.

Lee, T.H., 1971b. Intersectoral Capital Flows in the Economic Development of Taiwan, 1895-1960. Ithaca, N.Y.: Cornell University Press.

Li, K.T., 1988. "Final Reflections," in K.T. Li, The Evolution of Policy behind Taiwan's Development Success. New Haven: Yale University Press.

Li, K.T., 1995. *The Evolution of Policy behind Taiwan's Development Success*, 2nd edition, Singapore: World Scientific Publishing Co. Pte. Ltd.

Lin, C.Y., 1973. *Industrialization in Taiwan, 1946-72*. New York: Praeger Publishers.

Liu, Christina Y. and Shirley W.Y. Kuo, 1990, "Interest Rate and Foreign Exchange Liberalization in Taiwan in the 1980s," in *Economic Development in East and Southeast Asia: Essays in Honor of Professor Shinichi Ichimura.* Singapore: Institute of Southeast Asian Studies, and Honolulu: East-West Center: 242-255.

Lundberg, Erik, 1979. "Fiscal and Monetary Policies," in Walter Galenson (ed.), *Economic Growth and Structural Change in Taiwan, The Postwar Experience of the Republic of China.* Ithaca, NY: Cornell University Press.

McKinnon, R.I., 1982. "The Order of Economic Liberalization: Lessons from Chile and Argentina," in K. Brunner and A.H. Meltzer (eds.), *Economic Policy in a World of Change* Amsterdam: North-Holland: 159-186.

Pan, Chih-chi, Jen-ming Chang, and Yin-sheng Yuan, 1968. "Monetary Situation and Price Movements," in Kowie Chang (ed.), *Economic Development in Taiwan.* Taipei: Cheng Chung Book Company: 201-205.

Ranis, Gustav, 1988. "The Evolution of Policy in a Comparative Perspective: An Introductory Essay," in K. T. Li, *The Evolution of Policy behind Taiwan's Development Success.* New Haven: Yale University Press: 1-20.

4 TAIWAN'S INDUSTRIALIZATION POLICIES: TWO VIEWS, TWO TYPES OF SUBSIDY

Alice H. Amsden

This paper explains why the Taiwan government, hostile politically to meddling in markets, nonetheless intervened extensively in the economy both before and after "pseudo-liberalization" in 1958-61.[1] We illustrate such market interference ("getting the prices wrong") in Taiwan's early postwar history with an example from a leading sector, cotton textiles. We show that Taiwan's greater export orientation after 1961 cannot be equated with a lesser governmental role, although the nature of that role changed in the direction of more targeting of strategic industries and "selective seclusion" of the economy.[2]

The government's economic role in Taiwan's industrialization has been misunderstood partially due to a misunderstanding of the distinction between relative price subsidies and investment (production) subsidies. Relative price measures of "trade bias" (favoring or disfavoring export activity over import substitution activity) are calculated after firms' productive capacity has been put in place, and thus exclude subsidies to capital formation, such as long-term investment credit. This exclusion necessarily arises because, analytically, investment subsidies cannot be allocated unambiguously to either export activity or domestic sales. Therefore, to look only at relative price measures of trade bias understates and distorts the government's true role in the economy (for an example of such confusion, see the review essay by Rodrik 1995). After 1961 Taiwan certainly became more "export-oriented," measured by the export share in GNP, but the dynamic support by government of business inextricably combined import substitution and export promotion, and overall support was much greater quantitatively than mere "export bias" calculations suggest. The government supplied long-term subsidized capital to specific firms (especially state-owned firms) in particular industries in order to create productive capacity for both the domestic and export markets. It did so because to achieve international cost competitiveness at market prices without such support, either industrialization would have had to be delayed or wages would have had to fall below their already-depressed level associated with the 1957/58 devaluations (for the theoretical equivalence of exchange rate devaluation and real wage reduction under reasonable assumptions, see Krugman and Taylor, 1978). As expected, during this devaluation period (1955-1960) real manufacturing wages *fell* at a compound annual rate of -0.1 percent compared to 5.6 percent growth in 1952-55 and 5.5 percent growth in 1960-65 (Lee, 1982).

Government intervention worked better in Taiwan than in many other late-industrializing countries because of the principle governing subsidy allocation: "giveaway" in India, Turkey, and most Latin American economies; "reciprocity" in Japan, South Korea, Taiwan and elsewhere in East Asia (Hikino and Amsden, 1994; Amsden,1996). The reciprocity principle — buttressed by Taiwan's relatively equal income distribution — was such that little was given away by government to business for free, without a transparent performance standard for which the government itself was also held accountable. The tight ownership and control by government of all financial institutions facilitated such discipline of business.[3] Investments in a competent bureaucracy enabled performance standards to be monitored.[4]

Finally, the paper presents a schematic outline of a *learning-based approach* to analyzing late industrialization compared to a market failure approach (for the former, see Amsden, 1996). In the market failure analysis, backwardness is defined in terms of market "distortions" (P MC at international prices)[5] and the process of catching up is conceptualized as a movement towards freer, more perfect markets. In the learning approach, exemplified by Taiwan, backwardness is defined as an absence of "competitive assets" (resources and institutions that raise value added per worker), and catching up is conceptualized as a process of socially constructing such assets, many of which embody what in neoclassical theory are considered distortions from Pareto optimality, such as differentiated products and knowledge-based monopolies. The deliberate objective of the firm is to create market power such that $P > MC$, and government policy seeks to reinforce these firm-level advantages internationally.

In the 1980s a renewed role for the government in promoting high-technology sectors arose due to the failure of Taiwan's ubiquitous small- and medium-sized enterprises (SMEs) to invest in research and development (the position of SMEs in the economy weakened in other respects: their share in total exports fell from 73.5 percent in 1981 to 60.5 percent in 1992 although their share of total sales in the same period declined only slightly (Schive, 1995)).[6] The government's position in the economy as major investor also remained large: in 1994 state-owned enterprises and other public entities still accounted for 46.1 percent of gross capital formation, up from 33.3 percent in 1988 (CEPD, various years). Although markets may become more "perfect" in the future as a consequence of additional pressures to liberalize from Washington and the new World Trade Organization, the govern-ment's promotional role is likely to advance rather than retreat if Taiwan's private firms respond to domestic political instability (occasioned again by Mainland policies) by shifting a rising proportion of their investments abroad (Chen, 1995).

4.1 Pseudo-Liberalization (1958-61)

The Taiwan government continued to interfere in markets in order to support business after 1961 notwithstanding a decisive real effective exchange rate devaluation and the introduction of a duty-drawback system for exporters which, in theory, ought to have made labor-intensive industries cost effective in world markets without any government support.[7] The government continued to intervene because domestic producers, even in the bottom end of the cotton spinning and weaving industry ("textiles"), could still not compete at market-determined production costs against its neighbor Japan, which had the most efficient textile industry in the world, with higher wages but also higher productivity, lower capital (and maybe electricity) costs, and more developed distribution channels. The inability of Taiwan textile companies to compete at world prices persisted despite relatively good physical infrastructure and education (by virtue of US. foreign aid in the 1950s) and a long history of accumulating experience in textile manufacture (both on the mainland, by Chinese entrepreneurs who later fled to Taiwan, and on Taiwan proper, as a by-product of Japanese colonialism). Pressure on the government to support the textile industry was exerted by a powerful lobby, consisting of a business association of spinners and weavers (modeled on Japanese lines), and by the fact that the manufacture of textiles in Taiwan had already become a leading sector and major employer. As Table 4.1 indicates, by 1960 the manufacture of textiles alone (excluding apparel) accounted for as much as 20 percent of total manufacturing output. Although the textile industry is considered the premier "comparative advantage" of backward countries, the interventionist policies of the Taiwan government starting in the 1960s arose in response to the competitive needs of this low-wage, relatively labor-intensive sector.

Table 4.1   Share of Total Manufacturing Output of Textile and Garment Industries

Period	Textiles (Spinning and Weaving) (%)	Garments (%)
1951	18.3	na
1955	23.1	na
1960	20.7	2.0
1965	16.7	2.2
1970	18.7	3.1
1975	18.3	3.3

na = not available.

Source: 1951-75: Adapted from *Industry of Free China,* 1955, 1966, 1981, and 1982.

The government's role in promoting textiles and later, a wide range of other industries, was not restricted to "planning for free enterprise."[8] That is, interventionism was not confined merely to removing distortions. Some distortions were, in fact, removed: deposit interest rates were raised in an attempt to increase savings (although later evidence suggests that saving is not interest-rate sensitive in Taiwan); the Taiwan currency was devalued; exporters could purchase inputs at world prices (thanks to a duty drawback system); and investors were given tax breaks (assuming taxes are "distortions"). But these measures were only a small part of the story. In addition, in order to create the competitive assets that were necessary for Taiwan-owned light (and then skilled and heavy) industries to compete profitably at home and abroad, the government *created new "distortions."* It did the following:

(1) allocated long-run credit selectively to targeted industries and firms (private as well as state-owned) at far below-market interest rates (in comparison with competitive curb market rates);[9]

(2) provided exporters with working capital also at preferential prices;

(3) raised or maintained rates of protection and other import barriers for certain domestic industries;

(4) imposed controls on inward foreign investment such as local content requirements;[10]

(5) subsidized inward foreign investment by assuming the costs of building infrastructure and factory dwellings for export-processing zones;

(6) restricted market entry through industrial licensing;[11]

(7) encouraged the formation of cartels which then subsidized export sales with the proceeds from sales in the protected domestic market;

(8) intervened in the labor market to prevent strikes and trade union organization (until the late 1980s);[12]

(9) created model factories, as in many industries with a large component of advanced technology, such as the integrated circuit industry (Wu, 1992); and

(10) established state-owned enterprises and undertook public research and development (R&D), the results of which were then diffused to private firms at below-market costs.

These are ten forms of government intervention that create "distortions" according to neoclassical theory (i.e., they create a discrepancy between P and MC). They conflict with the view of the "liberal camp," which sees Taiwan as "a triumph of the free market system" by myopically focusing only on the reduction of some distortions and not on the creation of others.[13] But because various combinations and permutations of the above-noted interventions were all used extensively by the Taiwan government since sustained growth began in the 1960s, "liberalization" through the mid-1960s is better described as "pseudo-liberalization": the policy changes of the period apparently satisfied the Washington/"liberal camp" lobby, but represented only a very selective return to market forces (exchange rate devaluation, a rise is certain deposit rates, and a strengthening of duty drawbacks). Rather than economic openness or liberalism, the new policy regime that took root after 1961 is better characterized as "selective seclusion," involving more vigorous industrial targeting than previously and an effort on the government's part to encourage import substitution-cum-export activity.

4.2   Why More Intervention in Taiwan than Hong Kong?

Tariffs illustrate one set of measures that was relied on to promote the textile industry both before *and after* pseudo-liberalization. As indicated in Table 4.2, protection of cotton yarn and piece goods (fabrics) tended to increase or at least remain stable over time, whether measured in nominal or actual terms.[14] There is no indication of any tariff liberalization for Taiwan's most important export industry (in 1968 both cotton yarns and fabrics also remained "controlled"). No systematic estimates to compare effective protection rates immediately before and after pseudo-liberalization exist, but approximate rates of effective protection for cotton yarn and cotton piece goods suggest no liberalization either: in the case of yarn, "effective" protection rose from 8.4 percent in 1955 to 19.5 percent in 1968, and in the case of cotton piece goods, remained at approximately 27 percent in both years (Lin, 1973).[15]

Table 4.2   Taiwan's tariffs on cotton yarn and cloth

Year	Nominal Tariff		Actual Tariff	
	Cotton Yarn	Cotton Cloth	Cotton Yarn	Cotton Cloth
1949	5.0	20-30	8.4	26.4 - 38.4
1955	17.0	40.0	44.8	70.4
1959	25.0	42.5 - 45	39.6	64.8 - 68.4
1968	25.0	42.5 - 45	43.5	70.8 - 74.7

Notes: Nominal tariffs are marginally different in Scott (1979), which also shows a small increase in tariffs between the 1960s and 1970s. See footnote 14 in text for a discussion of the difference between nominal and actual tariffs.

Source: Taiwan Custom Import Tariff Schedules, adapted from B-C Lin (1969).

Protection of the domestic market for textiles operated in conjunction with export incentives and discipline of business. All together, these entangled measures drove the dynamic growth of the textile sector. Generally the chronological sequence of incentives and institutional pressures worked as follows: protection of the domestic market plus subsidized long-term investment credit provided the super-profits that were necessary for firms to invest in learning and modern production facilities.[16] Then, given their acquisition of skills and modern production capacity, firms' export activity was induced by performance standards and relative price subsidies. Discipline in the 1960s took the form of subsidies being tied to export targets administered by industry associations that were overseen by government agencies. These associations acted as cartels that collected dues from members out of which bonuses to exporters were paid. Firms were allocated export targets and were penalized if they fell short of their targets (Haggard, 1990). This system was similar to Korea's export targeting system except that targets were set by a quasi-private cartel instead of by negotiations between business and government. In both cases protection from foreign (Japanese) competition in the home market went hand-in-hand with export promotion. Other export incentives included provisions for the retention of foreign exchange earnings to import raw materials and machinery, together with the privilege of selling such rights to other firms, special low-interest loans for working capital, export insurance (from a government-owned organization), and so forth. All such incentives allowed textile firms to sell profitably abroad and at home while raising their productivity and lowering their costs to reach world competitive levels.

There are no available data (to my knowledge) for the early 1960s on the cost disadvantages of Taiwan textile firms vis-à-vis Japanese textile firms, but these disadvantages may be inferred from data available for Hong Kong. Table 4.3 presents a comparison for the early 1960s of production costs of unbleached cotton sheeting (the bottom, least-skilled segment of the market) in the United States, Japan, and Hong Kong. It indicates that total costs per yard were *higher* in Hong Kong than in Japan by a factor of 1.3: $0.14 per linear yard in Hong Kong versus $.0.11 in Japan. The unit cost of raw cotton was slightly lower in Hong Kong than in Japan (possibly a function of the age of equipment in use) whereas labor and all other costs (capital, rent, electricity and distribution combined) were higher.

Table 4.3   Production Cost of Unbleached Cotton Sheeting in the United States, Japan and Hong Kong (U.S. Cents per Linear Yard)

	United States, 1960		Japan, 1960		Hong Kong, 1963	
	Costs Per Yard	% of Total Costs	Costs Per Yard	% of Total Costs	Costs Per Yard	% of Total Costs
Total Costs	14.6	100	11.4	100	14	100
Cotton Cost	8.4	57.5	7.8	68.6	7	50
Labor Cost	3.9	26.8	1.7	15.1	2.1	15
All Other Cost	2.3	15.7	1.9	26.3	4.9	35

Source: U.S. Department of Commerce, *Comparative Fabric Production Costs in the United States and Four Other Countries* (Washington: Government Printing Office, 1961), Table 8, p. 21; and GATT, *A Study on Cotton Textiles* (Geneva: GATT, 1966), p. 69, as cited in Young (1969).

The Taiwan textile industry in the same time period is likely to have been as uncompetitive vis-à-vis Japan as the Hong Kong textile industry. Wages (and rent) were possibly slightly higher in Hong Kong than in Taiwan. But capital and distribution costs in Hong Kong are all likely to have been lower: capital costs in Hong Kong benefited from a parallel dollar-denominated free exchange market (Schenk, 1994) and distribution costs benefited from a long-standing re-export trade. Productivity was also lower in Taiwan than in Hong Kong: in 1962 the ratio of kilograms of yarn production per spindle hour worked was .0237 in Hong Kong and only .0192 in Taiwan; the ratio of kilograms of cloth production per loom in place was 2,901 in Hong Kong compared to only 1,593 in Taiwan (GATT, 1966: pp. 203 and 209).[17] Independent estimates that compare labor productivity in textiles in the early 1960s in Taiwan and Japan indicate a large gap in Japan's favor. In terms of units monitored per worker, labor productivity was roughly 3.3 times greater in Japan than in Taiwan. Measured as machines tended per worker, it was roughly seven times greater (Lin, 1969). The textile industries of Japan and Taiwan employed a predominantly female labor force who earned below-average wages, so textile wages in both countries may not have been all that different, while Japan's productivity, as just suggested, was far higher.

Assuming that as late as the early 1960s neither Hong Kong nor Taiwan could compete against Japan at home or abroad at market determined prices even in the bottom, least skill-intensive segment of the textile industry, the question arises of how Hong Kong managed to export textiles without government support whereas Taiwan allegedly required it. Assuming a similar cost/quality competitive deficit in both countries, was Taiwan's interventionism unnecessary given Hong Kong's supposed success at laissez-faire?

Hong Kong was able to compete internationally without domestic government support because it had more "competitive assets" and market-enhancing constraints than Taiwan. First, Hong Kong was a member of the British Commonwealth and hence, enjoyed Commonwealth trade preferences. This enabled it to export without competing directly against Japan. Second, because it entered export markets in textiles (and garments) before Taiwan or Korea (which suffered from political turmoil in the 1950s), Hong Kong was accorded larger quotas under a 1962 textile agreement that cartelized access to the textile markets of advanced countries.[18] Ironically, then, Hong Kong prospered as a consequence of the very market imperfections (cartels and quotas) that its economic philosophy deplored. Moreover, Hong Kong's policies were not strictly laissez-faire. Land was Hong Kong's most scarce resource, and the government controlled its usage and subsidized its price: to keep production costs down, it provided subsidized housing for an estimated 50 percent of the workforce (Stiglitz, 1991).

Without Hong Kong's competitive assets, and with the marginal costs of Taiwan producers exceeding international prices despite devaluation and other "liberalization" measures, Taiwan faced a strategic policy choice. Realistically, it could either create international competitiveness in textiles (and later in other industries) by subsidizing "learning" and modernization until unit costs equaled world levels due to increases in productivity (as advocated by the "official camp"); or it could reduce the largest variable cost of producers, wages, by further exchange rate devaluation (Krugman and Taylor, 1978). The "liberal camp" proselytizes the exchange devaluation-wage reduction option, although there is no evidence to suggest an awareness on its part of the need for *any* trade-off to achieve international competitiveness.[19]

The Taiwan government intervened to lower marginal costs and raise long-term productivity both directly and indirectly. Given freely-determined curb market interest rates that were far above the capital costs of international competitors (see footnote 9), the Taiwan government subsidized the learning and equipment modernization costs of firms directly. This was a necessary first step for the textile industry to begin even to think about exporting. The government also invested heavily in infrastructure (physical and human) and in secondary import substitution industries. In the case of textiles, it created a domestic capacity in synthetic fibers, which helped improve fabric quality and circumvent transaction costs related to imported inputs (Chu and Tsai, 1992). Locally-supplied inputs enabled apparel manufacturers and fabric suppliers to respond together to international fashion changes more quickly and effectively.

Thus, in answer to the question of why the Taiwan government created distortions after "liberalization," the answer is because the alternatives — either of waiting for spontaneous industrialization to occur or of further lowering real wages — were considered by the government to be even worse. Nor should the "seclusion" aspects of Taiwan's selective policies be minimized; the textile industry, the trailblazer of Taiwan's export drive, was no outlier. Despite South Korea's reputation for more interventionism, even after pseudo-liberalization effective protection and incentives in the manufacturing sector in Taiwan were *higher* than in Korea (see Table 4.4).

Table 4.4   Incentives to Manufacturing Industry, 1969

	Total Effective Incentives		
Country	Effective Protection	Domestic Sales	Foreign Sales
Taiwan	19	24	23
So. Korea	−1	−9	12
Argentina	97	110	31

The effective rate of protection relates the joint effects of protective measures on the price of the product and the prices of its inputs to value added in the production process. The Balassa method of estimation has been used.

Total effective incentives relate the combined effects of protective measures and credit and tax preferences to value added. Credit relates to working capital only and not to long-term investment capital.
Source: Bela Belassa and Associates (1983).

4.3   Relative Price Incentives

It is a truism that in order for a firm to export it must first have the capacity (physical and human) to produce a product "competitively" — at world prices for normal profit. But in analyzing Taiwan's economic development, *the "liberal camp" merely assumes that such a capacity has always existed.* Then it takes this capacity as given and examines only relative price incentives (short-term subsidies such as working capital plus taxes) to see if there is a bias in selling at home or abroad.[20] In keeping with this line of reasoning the "liberal camp" attributes Taiwan's industrial success to the fact that Taiwan's "total effective incentives" were low relative to those of other countries (an extreme comparison is Argentina, as shown in Table 4.4) and "neutral" with respect to where a firm sold its output (at least in 1969). This neutrality (and later possibly a pro-export bias) is regarded as central to Taiwan's export success, and its export success is regarded as central to its overall economic success.

This line of reasoning about minimalist state intervention in the economy, however, is fallacious to the extent that it takes a competitive export capacity for granted. Such a capacity cannot be taken for granted, as just analyzed in the case of Taiwan's leading sector, spinning and weaving. The creation of such a capacity has involved the Taiwan government in the allocation of more incentives than are included in the estimates of Table 4.4; the heading "**total** effective incentives" is misleading because the incentives in question are partial, not total. They do not include subsidies to create capacity. They include only relative price subsidies, or subsidies to influence in which direction a firm will dispose of its output. In terms of the ten "distortions" discussed earlier which the Taiwan government deliberately introduced in order to promote industrialization, relative price incentives exclude eight, including long-term subsidized investment credits.

4.4   Subsidization of Capital Formation: India vs. Taiwan

The importance of the government's role in capacity creation, as a prerequisite for (or at least as a complement of) export activity, is illustrated by the postwar experience of the Indian textile industry. The Indian textile industry required modernization in order to become internationally competitive, but neither the government nor the private sector was willing to undertake such modernization:

> For quite some time, both the government and the exporters of Indian textiles have been fully aware of the competitive disadvantage arising from the use of relatively old and outmoded capital equipment. Despite this knowledge, very little has been done towards a rationalisation of India's cotton textile industry (Nayyar, 1973: 9).

The explanation for this, according to Nayyar (1973), "is quite straightforward." The government was reluctant "to allow a full-scale complete mechanisation" because the installation of automatic looms "would reduce employment in cotton mills by half," and the replacement of old machinery by new "requires considerable amounts of foreign exchange."

In fact, in 1962 the Indian government consented to modernization by the mills on the condition (performance standard) that they "undertook to export 50 per cent of such production and gave a guarantee towards this obligation."[21] The mill owners refused:

> The response of the textile industry to this incentive was quite marginal because: (1) producers were not willing to guarantee such a high proportion of exports, and (2) they could not raise adequate financial resources necessary for the replacement of old machinery. Apart from the intensely competitive nature of the world market, the incentive to export was impaired by the relative attractiveness of the home market (Nayyar, 1973: 10).

Without modern facilities, exporting was an irrelevant consideration. Alternatively, one could argue that if the home market had not been so attractive (due to the exchange rate, protection, or simply huge size), domestic sales would not have been so profitable and the Indian textile industry would have been forced to modernize in order to survive. It is worth remembering, however, that the experience of the Indian textile industry under free market conditions for most of the nineteenth century does not support this speculation. Free trade, before a modern textile industry emerged starting in the 1850s, gave a large share of the domestic market to foreign imports of yarn and cloth, thereby reducing incentives to Indian textile manufacturers to invest in capital equipment and associated learning; free trade did not stimulate modernization.[22] Certainly the Taiwan textile industry was highly protected, as we have just seen. The key *initial* difference between the Indian and Taiwan textile industries lies in the fact that the Taiwan government (and USAID before it) was willing and able to subsidize the rise of a modern textile production capacity whereas the Indian government was not.

The exclusion by the "liberal camp" of subsidies to capacity creation introduces a biased picture of Taiwan's industrial development and of the role that the state has played in that development. Although case-by-case evidence of that role cannot be given here, not just the textile industry but more capital- and skill-intensive industries witnessed orchestration by the state in their early days. The example of petrochemicals is illustrative:

> The state played the role of entrepreneur, investor, and organizer in the initial stage of development. Other policy tools were used, such as trade controls, selective credit allocation, tax incentives, and land allocation. When the whole industry was almost nonexistent, when private capital was weak and unable and unwilling to undertake the project and bear the risk, the state planned the project, built and operated the naphtha cracker itself, organized (downstream) operation, and groomed a group of private capital investors for the task (Chu, 1994: 785).[23]

Of course, not all industries required or received support (see Amsden (1977) for the example of machine tools). The government also made mistakes when it did intervene, as in the case of shipbuilding. But the overall growth rate of industry strongly suggests that government failures were far outnumbered by successes (for the high scorecard for "secondary import substitution industries," see Schive,1990). Moreover, the principle of reciprocity persisted, with increasingly sophisticated performance criteria in exchange for government support, such as environmental standards and R&D expenditure targets as a percent of sales revenues.

All this is a far cry from "a triumph of the free market system," as the "liberal camp" contends (Fei,1982) and as "free markets" are conventionally defined (P = MC).

4.5   Conclusion: A Market Failure Vs. A Learning-Based Approach

We have contrasted a "liberal camp" and an "official camp" approach to Taiwan's industrial development and have contended that the former may have won the battle in the academic presses, but the latter has prevailed in actual policy making. That is, government economic policy in Taiwan has involved much more than merely removing distortions; the government has had to introduce distortions deliberately ("get the prices wrong") in order to create the production capacity necessary for either export or import substitution activity. The economy has been selectively secluded rather than indiscriminately opened, with devaluation in 1957/58 operating hand in hand with both export incentives above duty drawbacks and higher tariffs in certain industries. The alternatives to government intervention, delayed industrialization or further real wage reductions, were judged by policy makers to be worse than government interference — a sensible judgment, in my opinion.

Different perceptions among economists about the role of the government in Taiwan have partially hinged on the nature of subsidies. Market theories emphasize the importance in economic development of *relative price subsidies* that influence whether a firm finds it more profitable to sell at home or abroad. The learning-based approach emphasizes *investment (production) subsidies* that influence whether a firm finds it profitable at all to invest in new productive capacity. The question of profitability arises because even in allocatively-appropriate labor-intensive industries the low-wage advantage of an underdeveloped country tends to be offset by a low-productivity disadvantage such that units costs are above those of more economically-advanced, higher-wage countries. The market approach takes the world-price competitiveness of such productive capacity for granted, given sufficient domestic wage (exchange rate) reductions. The learning-based approach acknowledges a government policy choice to make such productive capacity profitable for the private investor to undertake. Either real wages can be reduced through devaluation or other means (a short-run option) or productivity can be increased (a long-run option that typically requires subsidizing capital investment-cum-learning). Investment subsidies (for instance, long-term preferential credit) "distort" both export and import substitution activity because they reduce production costs *for either type of transaction* below what the market would otherwise determine.[24] Production subsidies cannot be "allocated" to either export activity or import substitution, and to the extent that they are omitted in calculating pro-trade and anti-trade bias (relative price subsidies), they understate the true extent of the government's support to business. Misunderstanding of the government's role in Taiwan's economy partially arises from a failure to appreciate the role of investment subsidies.

The "wrong" prices were right in Taiwan's case because key distortions related to the exchange rate were, in fact, removed early on (although the actual exchange rate faced by importers and exporters deviated from that rate), and subsidies were allocated according to a principle of reciprocity, in exchange for monitorable performance standards to which both entrepreneurs and bureaucrats could be held accountable. An analysis of the socio-political conditions that enabled the government to devalue the currency in 1957/58 and to impose reciprocal obligations are beyond the scope of this paper, but include government control over finance and its concomitant, an equal income distribution. Government interference operated under conditions of political authoritarianism as well as established bureaucratic norms of behavior (inherited from China) that guided business-government relations.

The economic ideas of the "liberal camp" conform generally with *market failure theories* of development, and may be contrasted with the ideas of the "official camp," which are complementary with what I have called a *learning-based approach* to industrialization (Amsden in process). Table 4.5 summarizes the major differences.

In terms of *initial conditions*, the market approach regards market failures as government-induced: a representative firm's price is higher than its marginal costs (and international prices) because of protection, monopoly power, and other man-made distortions. By contrast, the initial conditions envisioned in the learning-based model start with a situation in which domestic firms cannot compete internationally because of low productivity. Domestic and international prices may be equal, but do not cover domestic marginal costs (low wages notwithstanding) because of the unproductive equipment and scant skills characteristic of underdevelopment.

Table 4.5   Market Failure Vs. Learning-Based Models of Industrialization

Market	Learning
1. **Initial conditions** (i-type industry):	
$P_D > MC_D = MC_I = P_I$	$P_I < MC_D$
.... domestic distortion	.... low productivity
.... same technology	If $P_I = P_D$ no production
.............competitive equilibrium	
2. **Catch-up process** (m-type industry):	
$P_D = MC_D = MC_I = P_I$	MC_D MC_I; P_D P_I
Removing distortions	Subsidizing learning
3. **Technological frontier** (h-type industry):	
$P_D = MC_D = MC_I = P_I$	$MC_D < MC_I$
Absence of distortions	First Mover D's advantage
	If $P_I > P_D$, world market control
	If $P_I = P_D$, extra surplus

P_D Domestic price;
P_I International price;
MC_D Domestic marginal (unit) cost;
MC_I International marginal (unit) cost.
Industry types: i = low-skill, labor-intensive; m = mid technology; h = high technology. (Amsden, 1996)

Given these different conceptions of initial conditions — high prices in one case, high costs in another — the role of government in the *catch-up process* is also different. In the market failure model the prescribed role for the government is to get out of the economy and reduce distortions (including "too-high" wages) through liberalization, deregulation, and privatization such that prices are free to equal marginal costs (distortions are zero). In the learning-based model, the government must intervene in order to raise productivity and reduce marginal costs by means of subsidizing capital formation and building technological capabilities generally. During this catch-up process domestic and international prices may deliberately deviate and domestic prices may exceed marginal costs.

At a later stage, when leading firms in an economy begin to approach the *world technological frontier*, the behavior of the two models is also different. In the market failure case, the more advanced the economy, the more perfect its markets and the more minimalist the role of its government can be. In the learning-based case, the firm creates competitive assets in Schumpeterian fashion. These assets raise value added per worker and give rise to international monopolistic advantages ($P > MC$) owing to product differentiation, innovation, distributional advantages, and so forth. The government's role is to strengthen these competitive assets on a national scale using procurement policies, subsidies to R&D, regional incentives, and other measures.

We have tried to suggest in the foregoing that given Taiwan's initial conditions, the role that its government has played during the catch-up phase has been closer to the learning-based model than to the market failure model. We would also venture to guess, based on existing evidence for certain of Taiwan's high-tech industries (such as integrated circuits)[25] and examples from Japan, Korea, and even the United States (whose R&D is heavily state-subsidized), that as the Taiwan economy approaches the world technological frontier, the role of its government will change but will hardly approach the minimalism idealized by the "liberal camp."

4.6 Notes

1   Philosophically, only one influence on the government, the Von Hayek tradition assimilated through USAID and US-educated Taiwan-based economists, was typically hostile; another influence, exemplified by the ideas of Sun Yat Sen and over 1,000 years of Chinese bureaucracy, appears to have been more tolerant of an activist economic role for the government in the development process. Fei (1982) distinguishes these two thrusts in terms of two pressure groups, a "liberal camp," which has dominated the academic literature on Taiwan's economy, and an "official camp," which has dominated the state's economic bureaucracy. For the planned interventionism of Taiwan by the Chiang Kai-shek government in the period 1943-1947, see Kirby (1995).

2   The term "selective seclusion" was coined by Henry Rosovsky with respect to Japan's economic development.

3   Financial reforms were supposedly part of the late-fifties "liberalization" package, but Taiwan's financial markets remained tightly under government ownership and control and credit was (and continues to be) preferentially allocated, as discussed later. In 1982 S.C. Tsiang conceded: "The actual fact, however, remains that not only do the commercial banks have their interest rates fixed for them by the Central Bank but they are mostly owned by the government and have their top officers appointed by the government" (Tsiang, 1982: 182). As late as 1988 K.T. Li wrote: "The liberalization of the foreign exchange rate and the interest rate was officially announced by the Central Bank to convey to the public the idea that these rates would no longer be used as policy instruments [to support industrialization] and manipulated by political forces. This is not to deny the fact that, in practice, there has still been interference with the market mechanism in these areas" (Li, 1988: 110).

4   Taiwan's banker-bureaucrats, for instance, were held personally responsible in terms of their salaries and promotions for the soundness of their loans. See Wade (1990) on Taiwan's economic bureaucracy.

5   Where P refers to a firm's product price and MC refers to its marginal production costs.

6   Schive's data are from the Ministry of Economic Affairs, *Small and Medium Enterprises White Paper*, 1991.

7   Multiple exchange rates were consolidated and the purchasing-power- parity effective exchange rate on exports (NT dollar per US dollar) rose from 34.4 in 1957 to 43.7 in 1958 (the official exchange rate for exports rose from 25.5 to 34.1) (Liang, 1982 #698, p. 224).

8   This term was used in a "manifesto" supported by 20 economists at the Taiwan Economic Research Institute on August 4, 1981, as cited by Fei (1982: 96): "Our unanimous conclusion is that a 'planned free economy' is the best institution for the eighties (1980-1990). The complexities of the issues due to the metamorphism of the industrial structure cannot be dealt with effectively by government control. The essence of a 'planned free economy' is the construction of the free market system through the adoption of long and short run measures to decontrol."

9   Repression in Taiwan's financial markets is analyzed in Lee (1990), Shea (1994), and Yang (1994). The discrepancy between curb market and preferential interest rates sometimes exceeded 20 percentage points, indicating that repression was severe rather than mild.

10   According to Schive (1995: 16): "Local content requirements were adopted in Taiwan in 1962 when Japanese companies came to Taiwan to the highly protected domestic markets and concentrated on final assembly. A minimum 40 percent local content rate was set up for 9 products for foreign firms first, then to all producers (foreign and local)." Initially these requirements were designed to prevent Japanese-owned enterprises from dominating certain Taiwan industries. Later they helped in the formation of secondary import substitution industries, as discussed below.

11   For the case of the petrochemical industry, see Chu (1994) and Chu (1996); for a business history of Formosa Plastics, see Takao (1989). Given the government's control over entry into specific industries, and its fear in the early postwar period of the emergence of Taiwanese (as opposed to Mandarin) business elites, it is likely that the (stunted) growth of Taiwan's big business groups and its plethora of small- and medium-size firms have more to do causally with deliberate government policy than free market forces. For more on this proposition, see Amsden (1991).

12   If, prior to this, P > MC because labor's bargaining power was weak (in fact, labor productivity has tended to rise faster than wages in Taiwan), then government intervention that prevented labor costs from rising may be considered to have been a distortionary measure.

     13Fei (1982: 98), for instance, writes: "I am inclined to agree with an opinion expressed on many occasions by Professor Milton Friedman that, for the contemporary mixed economies, development performance is commensurate with the extent to which free market forces prevail....The liberalization reform in the early sixties (i.e., devaluation and interest reform) furthered the rationalization of the price system domestically. With the tariff rebate system, nearly all artificial price differentials were eliminated, and with the establishment of an export processing zone, all other man-made barriers to exports crumbled. These pragmatic schemes were used to get around the controls that otherwise permeated the economy so that the flourishing of manufactured exports was basically *a triumph of the free market system*. The only regret of the liberal camp is that this experience has not been learned as an abstract lesson" (emphasis added).

14   The difference between nominal and actual tariffs arose for two reasons: many manufactures were protected not only by tariffs but also by quantitative restrictions; duties other than tariffs had to be paid on imports. Thus, with a mark-up of 10 percent, the adjusted tariff rate for a "controlled" commodity with a legal tariff rate of 40 percent was estimated to be 68.1 percent (Lee and Liang,1982).

15   Lin (1973) measures effective protection approximately as the differential of permissible excess of domestic prices over CIF import costs on one product and that of one of its principal raw materials or manufactured inputs at the immediate preceding stage of production.

16   Protection also aided the balance of payments: in 1960 and 1965, imports of cotton textile products accounted for as much as 7 percent of total imports, and in these years Taiwan's aggregate trade balance was negative (Taiwan's trade balance in cotton textile products only was negative until 1963). For trade in textiles, see Lin (1969); for overall trade balance, see Economic Research Department, Central Bank of China, *Balance of Payments, the Republic of China*, Taipei, various years.

17 These productivity differences may have been due to the relative inexperience of Taiwanese (as opposed to overseas Chinese) producers. In 1976, overseas Chinese firms accounted for 6.7 percent of Taiwan's textile exports and foreign-owned firms accounted for 11.8 percent (Lee and Liang,1982: 337). These percentages may be expected to have been much lower in the early 1960s. The incidence of overseas Chinese is also likely to have been higher in Hong Kong than in Taiwan.

18 According to Ho and Lin (1991: 277), "Hong Kong possessed larger export quotas than Taiwan and South Korea, and especially other LDCs."

19 For a further exposition of this trade off, see Amsden (1994).

20 (Krueger, 1984) exemplifies this approach. For a critique, see Helleiner (1990). In his synthesis of other people's research on trade and development, Rodrik (1995) seems to think that a "neutral" trade regime implies an absence of distortions (P = MC), although neutrality may involve distortions in two directions, subsidies and taxes on both imports and exports. Neutrality simply means that such biases are of equal magnitude.

21 After pseudo-liberalization, Taiwan offered a 10 percent tax reduction to any firm that exported more than 50 percent of its output. In 1973 the Board of Investment in Thailand also made a 50 percent export target a condition for textile companies to receive incentives.

22 For the Bombay textile industry, see Chandarvarkar (1994). For overviews of the controversy about free trade and the role of the British Raj in Indian industrial development, see Maddison (1971), Robb (1981) and Tomlinson (1993).

23 Chu (1996) answers some neoclassical speculations about what might have happened in this sector if the state had not intervened, although she does not challenge the assumptions that underlie the presumption that free market forces will create faster economic growth than interventionism; for the sake of argument she accepts that if markets are free, they will behave in practice the way theory predicts, although theory is based on many unrealistic assumptions.

24 Rodrik (1995: 24) incorrectly imagines that Walras' Law and Lerner's symmetry theorem are violated if "prices are distorted in all directions" (for domestic and foreign sales), but investment subsidies simultaneously "distort" a single industry's economic activity for both types of exchange (p mc at international prices) .

25 See Wu (1992).

4.7 References

Amsden, A. H., 1977. "The Division of Labor is Limited by the 'Type' of Market: The Taiwanese Machine Tool Industry." *World Development* (5): 217-34.

Amsden, A. H., 1991. "Big Business and Urban Congestion in Taiwan: The Origins of Small Enterprise and Regionally-Decentralized Industry (Respectively)." *World Development* 19(9): 1121-1135.

Amsden, A. H., 1994. "Why Isn't the Whole World Experimenting With The East Asian Model to Develop?" *World Development* 22 (4).

Amsden, A. H., 1996. "Korea: Industrialization Through Learning and the Chaebol," in Alfred D. Chandler, Jr., F. Amatori and T. Hikino (eds.), *Big Business and the Wealth of Nations*. New York: Cambridge University Press.

Amsden, A. H., in process. *The Rise of the Rest: Late Industrialization Outside the North Atlantic Region*.

Belassa, Bela and Associates, 1983. *Development Strategies in Semi-Industrial Economies* Baltimore: Johns Hopkins University Press.

Chandarvarkar, R., 1994. *The Bombay Textile Industry, 1900-1940*. Cambridge, UK: Cambridge University Press.

Chen, T.-J. a. Y.-P. C., 1995. "Taiwanese Foreign Direct Investment: The Risks of De-Industrialisation." *Journal of Industry Studies* 2(1): 57-68.

Chu, W.-W., 1994. "Import Substitution and Export-led Growth: A Study of Taiwan's Petrochemical Industry." *World Development* 22(5): 781-94.

Chu, W.-W., 1996. "Demonstration Effects and Industrial Policy: the Birth of Taiwan's Petrochemical Industry." Taipei: Acadmia Sinica.

Chu, W.-W. and M. C. Tsai, 1992. "Linkage and Uneven Growth: A Study of Taiwan's Man-Made Fiber Industry." Taipei: Academia Sinica.

Fei, J. C. H., 1982. "Ideology of Economic Development in Taiwan," in K.-T. Li and. T.-S. Yu (eds.), *Trade and Incentive Policies in Taiwan*. Taipei: Academia Sinica, 83-99.

GATT (General Agreement on Tariffs and Trade), 1966. *A Study on Cotton Textiles*. Geneva: General Agreement on Tariffs and Trade.

Haggard, S., 1990. *Pathways From the Periphery: The Politics of Growth in Newly Industrializing Countries*. Ithaca, Cornell University Press.

Helleiner, G., 1990. "Trade Strategy in Medium-Term Adjustment." *World Development* 6 (June)).

Hikino, Takashi and Alice H. Amsden, 1994. "Staying Behind, Stumbling Back, Sneaking Up, Soaring Ahead: Late Industrialization in Historical Perspective," in R. R. Nelson, William J. Baumol, and Edward N. Wolff (eds.), *Convergence of Productivity: Cross-National Studies and Historical Evidence*. New York and Oxford: Oxford University Press: 285-315.

Ho, Y.-P. and T.-B. Lin, 1991. "Structural Adjustment in a Free-Trade, Free Market Economy," in Hugh Patrick (ed.), *Pacific Basin Industries in Distress: Structural Adjustment and Trade Policy in the Nine Industrialized Economies*. New York: Columbia University Press.

Kirby, W. C., 1995. "Industrial Policy and the Nationalist Takeover, 1943-1947." *Harvard Studies on Taiwan: Papers of the Taiwan Studies Workshop, Fairbank Center for East Asian Research* 1.

Krueger, A. O., 1984. "Trade Policies in Developing Countries," in R. W. Jones and P. B. Kenan (eds.), *Handbook of International Economics*. Amsterdam: North-Holland.

Krugman, Paul and Lance Taylor, 1978. "Contractionary Effects of Devaluation." *Journal of International Economics* 8: 445-56.

Lee, S.-Y., 1990. *Money and Finance in the Economic Development of Taiwan*. Houndmills: Macmillan.

Lee, T. H. and K.-S Liang, 1982. "Taiwan," in Bela Balasaa and Associates (eds.), *Development Strategies in Semi-Industrial Economies*. Baltimore: The Johns Hopkins University Press for the World Bank: 310-350.

Li, K. T., 1988. *The Evolution of Policy Behind Taiwan's Development Success*. New Haven: Yale University Press.

Liang, 1982 [fn7]

Lin, B.-C., 1969. "The Study of Taiwan's Textile Industry Development". (ed.) ADD *On Taiwans Industrial Development* (in Chinese).

Lin, C.-Y., 1973. Industrialization in Taiwan, 1946-72. New York: Praeger.

Maddison, A., 1971. Class Structure and Economic Growth: India and Pakistan since the Moghuls. New York: Norton.

Morris, D. Morris, 1983. "The Growth of Large-Scale Industry to 1947." The Cambridge Economic History of India, Vol. 2: c. 1757-1970. Meghnad Desai (ed.). Cambridge, UK: Cambridge University Press: 553-676.

Nayyar, D., 1973. "An Analysis of the Stagnation in India's Cotton Textile Exports During the 1960s." Oxford Bulletin of Economics and Statistics 35(1): 1-19.

Robb, Peter, 1981. "British Rule and Indian 'Improvement'." Economic History Review XXXIV (4): 507-523.

Rodrik, Dani, 1995. "Trade and Industrial Policy Reform," in J. R. Behrman and T. N. Srinivasan (eds.) Handbook of Development Economics, vol. IIIB. Amsterdam: North Holland.

Schenk, C. R., 1994. "Closing the Hong Kong Gap: The Hong Kong Free Dollar Market in the 1950s." Economic History Review **XLVII**(2): 335-353.

Schive, C., 1990. "The Next Stage of Industrialization in Taiwan and Korea," in D. L. Wyman and G. Gereffi, Manufacturing Miracle. Princeton, NJ: Princeton University Press.

Schive, C., 1995. "Industrial Policies in a Maturing Taiwan Economy." *Journal of Industry Studies* 2(1).

Scott, Maurice, 1979. "Foreign Trade," in W. Galenson (ed.), *Economic Growth and Structural Change in Taiwan*. Ithaca: Cornell University Press.

Shea, J.-D., 1994. "Taiwan: Development and Structural Change of the Financial System," in Hugh T. Patrick and Yung Chul Park (eds.), *The Financial Development of Japan, Korea, and Taiwan: Growth, Repression and Liberalization*. New York and Oxford: Oxford University Press: 222-287.

Stiglitz, J., 1991. "East Asia's Financial Systems." Washington, DC: World Bank, mimeo.

Takao, T., 1989. "Management in Taiwan: The Case of the Formosa Plastics Group." *East Asian Cultural Studies* **28**(1-4).

Tomlinson, B.R., 1993. *The Economy of Modern India, 1860-1970. The New Cambridge History of India*, III.3. Cambridge: Cambridge University Press.

Tsiang, S. C., 1982. "Monetary Policy of Taiwan," in K.-T. Li and T.-S. Yu (eds.), *Experiences and Lessons of Economic Development in Taiwan*. Taipei: Academia Sinica: 165-185.

Wade, R., 1990. Governing the Market: Economic Theory and the Role of the Government in East Asian Industrialization. Princeton, NJ: Princeton University Press.

Wu, S.-H., 1992. "The Dynamic Cooperation Between Government and Enterprise: The Development of Taiwan's Integrated Circuit Industry," in N. T. Wang (ed.), *Taiwan's Enterprises in Global Perspective*. Armonk, N.Y: M.E. Sharpe: 171-192.

Yang, Y.-H., 1994. "Taiwan: Development and Structural Change of the Banking System," in Hugh T. Patrick and Yung Chul Park (eds.), *The Financial Development of Japan, Korea, and Taiwan: Growth, Repression and Liberalization*. New York and Oxford: Oxford University Press: 288-324.

Young, Shik Chun, 1969. "The Gatt's Long-Term Cotton Textile Arrangement and Hong Kong's Cotton Textile Trade." Ph.D. dissertation, Washington State University.

5 THE TRADE–GROWTH NEXUS IN TAIWAN'S DEVELOPMENT[1]

Gustav Ranis

5.1 Introduction

There are many convincing arguments in the development literature as to why trade is important for growth. These range from the well-known static gains from trade — which Samuelson acknowledged to hold as possibly the only proposition in economics both non-trivial and true — to such dynamic elements as accommodating the vent for surplus of previously idle resources (including labor) and to trade as the critical carrier of both the Smithian and Schumpeterian types of technology change.

But there are equally convincing arguments to be made as to why growth — more specifically, differences in the type of growth — are critical for trade. These range from such obvious elements as reductions in transport costs, changes in the distribution of income, and breakthroughs in communication and information technology — all of which are likely to stimulate previously dormant demands for goods and services — to internal human capital and R&D accumulations, which, along with policy change, macro and micro, are likely to enhance the response capability of the domestic economy to growing trade opportunities.

It is for this reason — i.e. the two-way linkage between growth and trade — that we view the concept of trade as a "leading sector" or the concept of "trade-led growth" to be wide of the mark, even in the case of a relatively small country such as Taiwan. We find ourselves much more comfortable with the Kravis view of trade as a hand-maiden of growth, but would add that we also see growth as a hand-maiden of trade. It is useful to recall that the initial stimulus for the remarkable global trade/growth interactions of the 19th century was undoubtedly provided by the transport revolution of the post-1830s — and that it was the good performance of British agricultural productivity, plus domestically generated commercial surpluses, which provided the initial wherewithal for the required infrastructural and industrial expansion. The remarkable post-World War II experience of Taiwan should, we believe, be similarly viewed as the consequence of mutually beneficial trade-growth interactions. As Arthur Lewis has aptly put it, exports should be seen as a lubricant for growth — and vice versa.

Such mutual interaction, with ill-defined lags, provides a challenge to any Granger causality test. The causal chain which runs from growth to exports must be examined in terms of the overall macro and micro-economic policy environment within which output is being generated, as well as the direct actions, public and private, affecting the international competitiveness of that output via public and private investments in human capital, R&D, institutions, etc. The causal chain which runs from exports to growth must be examined in terms of the contribution of an overall enhanced level of discipline and competitiveness, as well as the direct contributions of imported human capital and of imported technology embodied in the machines, licenses and blueprints often associated with the direct foreign investment activities of multinational corporations.

The precise nature and impact of these two-way relationships is, moreover, bound to undergo substantial change over time. Section 5.2 of the paper is focused on the 1950s and early 1960s when the Taiwan economy was still dominated by agricultural productivity growth, and when a shift occurred from traditional to non-traditional crops and policy changes yielded a boom in processed food exports. Section 5.3 focuses on the two-way relationship between total factor productivity (TFP) change, a function largely of domestic macro as well as structural policy change, and the labor intensive manufactured export boom of the 1960s and early 1970s. Section 5.4 demonstrates the growing importance, in recent decades, of foreign technology imports and foreign capital, physical and human, along with domestic R&D and further changes in the micro-economic policy mix, in shaping the quantity and quality of growth and trade. Section 5.5 briefly sums up.

5.2   The Agricultural Growth/Export Nexus

As is well-known, Taiwan was a major exporter of agricultural produce to the Japanese motherland in the pre-war or colonial period. Indeed, until the 1930s, when Japan, given its increasing domination by the military, came to view Taiwan as a potential secondary industrial base, colonial policy was focused almost entirely on helping assure Japan of an adequate supply of rice and sugar. Nor did the agricultural revolution on Taiwan begin with post-war land reform and technology change; it had its institutional roots in the earlier (1905) redistribution of land and its technological roots in the continuing improvements in agricultural inputs and practices, yielding, for example, the Ponlai variety of rice during the pre-war period. Moreover, contrary to many other colonial experiences, agriculture and rural non-agriculture reinforced each other within a setting in which agricultural technology change and exports were interacting in a symbiotic fashion. Especially relevant here were the modernizing elements within rural non-agricultural activities, or so-called

Z-goods, which permitted an almost 7 percent annual growth of industrial output between 1902 and 1938.[2] This performance stands in marked contrast to the more "typical" LDC colonial experience under export expansion modeled by Hymer and Resnick (1969) and documented by Resnick (1970). In Taiwan, colonial demands for agricultural exports led to policy changes that induced the desired supply response.

As Thorbecke (1979) and Ho (1977) have pointed out, the stage for further substantial agricultural productivity increase in the post-war period was set by the prior Japanese colonial regime's attention to both physical infrastructure, — roads, irrigation and drainage — and institutional infrastructure — primary education and the farmers' associations — as mutually reinforcing instruments for generating and disseminating new techniques, as well as for providing credit services. A literacy rate as high as 56 percent as early as 1950 (see Table 5.1) is an indication of substantial human capital input into agriculture, which at that time still comprised 48 percent of national product and engaged more than 50 percent of the working population. While there persists a good deal of controversy in the literature concerning overall TFP growth in Taiwan, most observers will agree that technology change in agriculture during the 1950s and early 1960s was little short of dramatic by international standards. Indeed, levels of total agricultural productivity rose steadily until 1966 (see Figure 5.1). Here the argument for the causation running mainly from domestically generated productivity change to agricultural export opportunities is unmistakably strong. Agricultural exports, including of the processed variety, grew from $114 million in 1952, comprising about 95 percent of total exports, to $289 million in 1966 (see Tables 5.2 and 5.3). Moreover, it should be noted that the composition of agricultural output and exports changed dramatically over the years (see Table 5.4 and Figures 5.2.1, 5.2.2 and 5.2.3), a clear indication of high rates of technology change. We may note a relative decline in the importance of traditional commodities such as rice, tea and sugar, with an expansion of such non-traditional crops as bananas, pineapples, and later mushrooms, asparagus and timber (see Table 5.4). Taiwan was clearly a price taker in all of these items and the sources of productivity

Table 5.1   Literacy Rates, Age 6 and Over, Taiwan, 1950–1993

					% of Population, Age 6 and Over
Year	Literacy Rate	Year	Literacy Rate	Year	Literacy Rate
1950	56.01	1979	89.26	1987	92.21
1956	62.88	1980	89.66	1988	92.57
1961	74.13	1981	90.12	1989	92.90
1966	76.84	1982	90.39	1990	93.22
1971	83.17	1983	90.85	1991	93.59
1976	87.84	1984	91.16	1992	93.85
1977	88.29	1985	91.54	1993	94.02
1978	88.76	1986	91.92		

Source: Ministry of Education, ROC. *Educational Statistics, 1995*, p. 29.

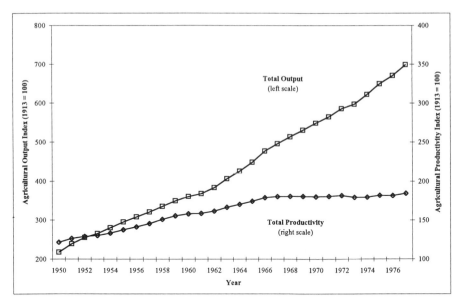

Figure 5.1   Agricultural Output and Productivity Indexes, Taiwan, 1950–1977

Source: *Taiwan Agricultural Statistics, 1901–1965,* JCRR, 1966. *Taiwan Agricultural Yearbook,* Taiwan
    Provincial Dept. of Agriculture and Forestry, annual, as found in Chen, Yueh-eh, and You-tsao
    Wang, "Secular Trends of Output, Inputs, and Productivity" A Quantitative Analysis of Agricultural
    Development in Taiwan." Conference on Agricultural Development in China, Japan and Korea, Dec.
    1980, pp. 657–8.

change were almost entirely domestic in origin. Between 1954 and 1967,
agricultural output grew at 4.4 percent annually, agricultural exports made up in
excess of 70 percent of total exports, and inorganic and organic fertilizer inputs,
associated with technology change, rose at annual rates of 5.7 percent and 3.3
percent, respectively (Thorbecke, 1979). The rapidly increasing ability to capture
foreign markets was clearly a function of increased international competitiveness
occasioned by domestic productivity increase.

5.3   The Labor Intensive Industrial Growth/Export Nexus

There is no need to detail the well-known major macro policy changes of the late
1950s and early 1960s, which permitted Taiwan to shift from import substitution
towards an export oriented production and export regime. It is, however, particularly appropriate on this occasion to quote Ian Little: "Much credit must go to T.C.
Liu and S.C. Tsiang who first advocated in 1954 and continued to advocate. . .the
policies that were at last largely put into effect in 1959" (Little, 1979: 475).
Actually, as early as 1955 the system of rebates of indirect taxes for exports was put
in place, followed by exchange rate unification and a series of devaluations in the
1958 to 1960 period, accompanied by the elimination of direct controls on trade,

Table 5.2 Composition of Exports, Taiwan, 1952–1971, in US$ Millions

A. In US$ Millions

	1952	1953	1954	1955	1956	1957	1958	1959	1960	1961	1962	1963	1964	1965	1966	1967	1968	1969	1970	1971
Total Exports	119.5	129.8	97.8	133.4	130.1	168.5	164.4	160.5	169.9	214.0	238.6	357.5	463.1	487.9	569.4	649.9	841.8	1110.6	1561.7	2135.5
Total Non-Agric. Exports	5.3	8.6	7.0	9.0	15.2	13.1	18.8	32.1	48.9	82.1	109.2	139.3	185.5	201.9	280.4	353.0	526.2	768.4	1169.5	1655.4
Total Agric. Exports	114.2	121.2	90.8	124.4	114.9	155.4	145.6	128.4	121.0	131.9	129.4	218.2	277.6	286.0	289.0	296.9	315.6	342.2	392.2	480.1
Primary Agric. Exports	33.7	17.7	15.1	40.2	20.1	29.0	40.1	39.5	21.4	34.8	35.5	53.4	75.9	125.0	121.0	125.3	129.6	137.5	168.1	203.1
Rice	23.3	11.4	7.9	32.8	12.8	21.2	28.6	23.5	4.3	10.1	18.0	23.3	18.0	42.9	33.0	19.7	13.9	4.2	2.6	2.9
Banana	6.6	3.4	4.7	4.0	3.2	3.8	6.2	6.6	6.9	10.6	8.0	8.6	33.3	55.3	52.6	62.0	57.2	59.2	38.1	44.2
Vegetables	0.8	1.1	0.8	0.8	1.3	1.2	1.1	1.6	2.5	4.4	5.7	8.7	9.0	9.2	10.8	16.7	23.6	20.5	31.4	37.2
Sea Products	0.0	0.3	0.3	0.3	0.3	0.2	0.2	0.3	0.4	0.4	0.7	1.5	2.2	2.0	7.4	8.7	13.1	24.8	61.4	81.2
Other Primary	3.0	1.5	1.4	2.3	2.5	2.6	4.0	7.5	7.3	9.3	13.7	11.3	13.4	15.6	17.2	18.2	21.8	28.8	34.6	37.6
Processed Agric. Exports	80.5	103.5	75.7	84.2	94.8	126.4	105.5	88.9	99.6	97.1	93.9	164.8	201.7	161.0	168.0	171.6	186.0	204.7	224.1	277.0
Sugar	69.7	90.3	58.6	67.9	76.1	110.8	84.7	65.9	74.4	61.1	49.6	106.0	135.4	68.0	61.7	43.7	50.8	48.0	47.5	67.3
Tea	5.8	6.9	9.4	5.6	5.1	5.8	6.8	7.1	6.3	8.9	7.9	8.1	8.4	9.7	11.1	12.4	11.7	13.6	14.3	14.2
Pineapples, canned	2.0	2.6	4.0	5.6	6.1	4.4	7.5	8.4	8.5	12.1	10.9	11.6	13.9	19.4	19.3	19.3	19.0	20.7	20.2	22.2
Mushrooms, canned									0.2	1.8	8.5	16.2	15.8	20.8	25.2	32.7	32.3	32.3	33.6	47.1
Asparagus, canned											0.0	0.0	0.4	11.1	14.2	24.0	25.4	31.6	33.3	35.0
Fruits, preserved	0.2	0.3	0.0	0.2	0.2	0.1	0.1	0.3	0.9	2.2	2.0	3.3	6.2	7.4	6.4	9.7	9.1	12.1	13.6	16.2
Timber & Lumber	0.0	0.3	0.2	0.7	0.6	0.5	1.9	2.8	2.8	3.7	5.6	9.3	13.6	15.6	23.7	25.2	30.6	42.3	53.9	63.0
Other Processed	2.8	2.8	3.5	4.2	6.7	4.8	4.5	4.4	6.5	7.3	9.4	10.3	8.0	9.0	6.4	4.6	7.1	4.1	7.7	12.0

B. Using Modified Categories, In US$ Millions

	1952	1953	1954	1955	1956	1957	1958	1959	1960	1961	1962	1963	1964	1965	1966	1967	1968	1969	1970	1971
Total Exports	119.5	129.8	97.8	133.4	130.1	168.5	164.4	160.5	169.9	214.0	238.6	357.5	463.1	487.9	569.4	649.9	841.8	1110.6	1561.7	2135.5
Total Non-Agric. Exports	5.3	8.6	7.0	9.0	15.2	13.1	18.8	32.1	48.9	82.1	109.2	139.3	185.5	201.9	280.4	353.0	526.2	768.4	1169.5	1655.4
Total Agric. Exports	114.2	121.2	90.8	124.4	114.9	155.4	145.6	128.4	121.0	131.9	129.4	218.2	277.6	286.0	289.0	296.9	315.6	342.2	392.2	480.1
Traditional Agric. Exports	93.0	101.7	66.5	100.7	88.9	132.0	113.3	89.4	78.7	71.2	57.0	129.3	153.4	110.9	94.7	63.4	64.7	52.2	50.1	70.2
Rice	23.3	11.4	7.9	32.8	12.8	21.2	28.6	23.5	4.3	10.1	18.0	23.3	18.0	42.9	33.0	19.7	13.9	4.2	2.6	2.9
Sugar	69.7	90.3	58.6	67.9	76.1	110.8	84.7	65.9	74.4	61.1	49.6	106.0	135.4	68.0	61.7	43.7	50.8	48.0	47.5	67.3
Non-Traditional Agric. Exports	21.2	19.5	24.3	23.7	26.0	23.4	32.3	39.0	42.3	60.7	72.4	88.9	124.2	175.1	194.3	233.5	250.9	290.0	342.1	409.9
Banana	6.6	3.4	4.7	4.0	3.2	3.8	6.2	6.6	6.9	10.6	8.0	8.6	33.3	55.3	52.6	62.0	57.2	59.2	38.1	44.2
Vegetables	0.8	1.1	0.8	0.8	1.3	1.2	1.1	1.6	2.5	4.4	5.7	8.7	9.0	9.2	10.8	16.7	23.6	20.5	31.4	37.2
Sea Products	0.0	0.3	0.3	0.3	0.3	0.2	0.2	0.3	0.4	0.4	0.7	1.5	2.2	2.0	7.4	8.7	13.1	24.8	61.4	81.2
Tea	5.8	6.9	9.4	5.6	5.1	5.8	6.8	7.1	6.3	8.9	7.9	8.1	8.4	9.7	11.1	12.4	11.7	13.6	14.3	14.2
Pineapples, canned	2.0	2.6	4.0	5.6	6.1	4.4	7.5	8.4	8.5	12.1	10.9	11.6	13.9	19.4	19.3	19.3	19.0	20.7	20.2	22.2
Mushrooms, canned									0.2	1.8	8.5	16.2	15.8	20.8	25.2	32.7	32.3	32.3	33.6	47.1
Asparagus, canned											0.0	0.0	0.4	11.1	14.2	24.0	25.4	31.6	33.3	35.0
Fruits, preserved	0.2	0.3	0.0	0.2	0.2	0.1	0.1	0.3	0.9	2.2	2.0	3.3	6.2	7.4	6.4	9.7	9.1	12.1	13.6	16.2
Timber & Lumber	0.0	0.3	0.2	0.7	0.6	0.5	1.9	2.8	2.8	3.7	5.6	9.3	13.6	15.6	23.7	25.2	30.6	42.3	53.9	63.0
Other Non-Traditional	5.8	4.3	4.9	6.5	9.2	7.4	8.5	11.9	13.8	16.6	23.1	21.6	21.4	24.6	23.6	22.8	28.9	32.9	42.3	49.6

Source: Compiled from Bank of Taiwan and the Central Bank of China; found in Lee, The. H. and Yueh-eh Chen, "Diversification of Agricultural Exports," *Agriculture's Place in the Strategy of Development: The Taiwan Experience*. The. H. Shen, ed. Taipei, Taiwan: JCRR, 1974, p. 339, Table 1.

Table 5.3   Composition of Exports, Taiwan, 1952–1971, as % of Total Exports

A. Non-Agricultural versus Agricultural Exports, as % of Total Exports

	1952	1953	1954	1955	1956	1957	1958	1959	1960	1961	1962	1963	1964	1965	1966	1967	1968	1969	1970	1971
Total Exports	100.0%	100.0%	100.0%	100.0%	100.0%	100.0%	100.0%	100.0%	100.0%	100.0%	100.0%	100.0%	100.0%	100.0%	100.0%	100.0%	100.0%	100.0%	100.0%	100.0%
Total Non-Agric. Exports	4.4	6.6	7.2	6.7	11.7	7.8	11.4	20.0	28.8	38.4	45.8	39.0	40.1	41.4	49.2	54.3	62.5	69.2	74.9	77.5
Total Agric. Exports	95.6	93.4	92.8	93.3	88.3	92.2	88.6	80.0	71.2	61.6	54.2	61.0	59.9	58.6	50.8	45.7	37.5	30.8	25.1	22.5

B. Primary versus Processed Agricultural Exports, as % of Total Exports

	1952	1953	1954	1955	1956	1957	1958	1959	1960	1961	1962	1963	1964	1965	1966	1967	1968	1969	1970	1971
Primary Agric. Exports	28.2	13.6	15.4	30.1	15.4	17.2	24.4	24.6	12.6	16.3	14.9	14.9	16.4	25.6	21.3	19.3	15.4	12.4	10.8	9.5
Rice	19.5	8.8	8.1	24.6	9.8	12.6	17.4	14.6	2.5	4.7	3.1	6.5	3.9	8.8	5.8	3.0	1.7	0.4	0.2	0.1
Banana	5.5	2.6	4.8	3.0	2.5	2.3	3.8	4.1	4.1	5.0	3.4	2.4	7.2	11.3	9.2	9.5	6.8	5.3	2.4	2.1
Vegatables	0.7	0.8	0.8	0.6	1.0	0.7	0.7	1.0	1.5	2.1	2.4	2.4	1.9	1.9	1.9	2.6	2.8	1.8	2.0	1.7
Sea Products	0.0	0.2	0.3	0.2	0.2	0.1	0.1	0.2	0.2	0.2	0.3	0.4	0.5	0.4	1.3	1.3	1.6	2.2	3.9	3.8
Other Primary	2.5	1.2	1.4	1.7	1.9	1.5	2.4	4.7	4.3	4.3	5.7	3.2	2.9	3.2	3.0	2.8	2.6	2.6	2.2	1.8
Processed Agric. Exports	67.4	79.7	77.4	63.1	72.9	75.0	64.2	55.4	58.6	45.4	39.4	46.1	43.6	33.0	29.5	26.4	22.1	18.4	14.3	13.0
Sugar	58.3	69.6	59.9	50.9	58.5	65.8	51.5	41.1	43.8	28.6	20.8	29.7	29.2	13.9	10.8	6.7	6.0	4.3	3.0	3.2
Tea	4.9	5.3	9.6	4.2	3.9	3.4	4.1	4.4	3.7	4.2	3.3	2.3	1.8	2.0	1.9	1.9	1.4	1.2	0.9	0.7
Pineapples, canned	1.7	2.0	4.1	4.2	4.7	2.6	4.6	5.2	5.0	5.7	4.6	3.2	3.0	4.0	3.4	3.0	2.3	1.9	1.3	1.0
Mushrooms, canned	0.0	0.0	0.0	0.0	0.0	0.0	0.0	0.0	0.0	0.0	0.0	0.0	3.4	4.3	4.4	5.0	3.8	2.9	2.2	2.2
Asparagus, canned	0.0	0.0	0.0	0.0	0.0	0.0	0.0	0.0	0.0	1.0	0.8	0.9	0.1	2.3	2.5	3.7	3.0	2.8	2.1	1.6
Fruits, preserved	0.2	0.5	0.0	0.1	0.2	0.1	0.1	0.2	0.5	1.0	0.8	0.9	1.3	1.5	1.1	1.5	1.1	1.1	0.9	0.8
Timber & Lumber	0.0	0.2	0.2	0.5	0.5	0.3	1.2	1.7	1.6	1.7	2.3	2.6	2.9	3.2	4.2	3.9	3.6	3.8	3.5	3.0
Other Processed	2.3	2.2	3.6	3.1	5.1	2.8	2.7	2.7	3.8	3.4	3.9	2.9	1.7	1.8	1.1	0.7	0.8	0.4	0.5	0.6

C. Traditional versus Non-Traditional Agricultural Exports, as % of Total Exports

	1952	1953	1954	1955	1956	1957	1958	1959	1960	1961	1962	1963	1964	1965	1966	1967	1968	1969	1970	1971
Traditional Agric. Exports	77.8	78.4	68.0	75.5	68.3	78.3	68.9	55.7	46.3	33.3	23.9	36.2	33.1	22.7	16.6	9.8	7.7	4.7	3.2	3.3
Rice	19.5	8.8	8.1	24.6	9.8	12.6	17.4	14.6	2.5	4.7	3.1	6.5	3.9	8.8	5.8	3.0	1.7	0.4	0.2	0.1
Sugar	58.3	69.6	59.9	50.9	58.5	65.8	51.5	41.1	43.8	28.6	20.8	29.7	29.2	13.9	10.8	6.7	6.0	4.3	3.0	3.2
Non-Traditional Agric. Exports	17.7	15.0	24.8	17.8	20.0	13.9	19.6	24.3	24.9	28.4	30.3	24.9	26.8	35.9	34.1	35.9	29.8	26.1	21.9	19.2
Banana	5.5	2.6	4.8	3.0	2.5	2.3	3.8	4.1	4.1	5.0	3.4	2.4	7.2	11.3	9.2	9.5	6.8	5.3	2.4	2.1
Vegatables	0.7	0.8	0.8	0.6	1.0	0.7	0.7	1.0	1.5	2.1	2.4	2.4	1.9	1.9	1.9	2.6	2.8	1.8	2.0	1.7
Sea Products	0.0	0.2	0.3	0.2	0.2	0.1	0.1	0.2	0.2	0.2	0.3	0.4	0.5	0.4	1.3	1.3	1.6	2.2	3.9	3.8
Tea	4.9	5.3	9.6	4.2	3.9	3.4	4.1	4.4	3.7	4.2	3.3	2.3	1.8	2.0	1.9	1.9	1.4	1.2	0.9	0.7
Pineapples, canned	1.7	2.0	4.1	4.2	4.7	2.6	4.6	5.2	5.0	5.7	4.6	3.2	3.0	4.0	3.4	3.0	2.3	1.9	1.3	1.0
Mushrooms, canned	0.0	0.0	0.0	0.0	0.0	0.0	0.0	0.0	0.0	0.0	0.0	0.0	3.4	4.3	4.4	5.0	3.8	2.9	2.2	2.2
Asparagus, canned	0.0	0.0	0.0	0.0	0.0	0.0	0.0	0.0	0.0	0.0	0.0	0.0	0.1	2.3	2.5	3.7	3.0	2.8	2.1	1.6
Fruits, preserved	0.2	0.5	0.0	0.1	0.2	0.1	0.1	0.2	0.5	1.0	0.8	0.9	1.3	1.5	1.1	1.5	1.1	1.1	0.9	0.8
Timber & Lumber	0.0	0.2	0.2	0.5	0.5	0.3	1.2	1.7	1.6	1.7	2.3	2.6	2.9	3.2	4.2	3.9	3.6	3.8	3.5	3.0
Other Non-Traditional	4.9	3.3	5.0	4.9	7.1	4.4	5.2	7.4	8.1	7.8	9.7	4.6	4.6	5.0	4.1	3.5	3.4	3.0	2.7	2.3

Source: Compiled from Bank of Taiwan and the Central Bank of China; found in Lee, The. H. and Yueh-eh Chen, "Diversification of Agricultural Exports," *Agriculture's Place in the Strategy of Development: The Taiwan Experience.* The. H. Shen, ed. Taipei, Taiwan: JCRR, 1974, p. 339, Table 1.

Table 5.4   Composition of Exports, Taiwan, 1952–1971, as % of Total Agricultural Exports

	1952	1953	1954	1955	1956	1957	1958	1959	1960	1961	1962	1963	1964	1965	1966	1967	1968	1969	1970	1971
Total Agric. Exports	100.0%	100.0%	100.0%	100.0%	100.0%	100.0%	100.0%	100.0%	100.0%	100.0%	100.0%	100.0%	100.0%	100.0%	100.0%	100.0%	100.0%	100.0%	100.0%	100.0%
A. Primary versus Processed Agricultural Exports, as % of Total Annual Agricultural Exports																				
Primary Agric. Exports	29.5	14.6	16.6	32.3	17.5	18.7	27.5	30.8	17.7	26.4	27.4	24.5	27.3	43.7	41.9	42.2	41.1	40.2	42.9	42.3
Rice	20.4	9.4	8.7	26.4	11.1	13.6	19.6	18.3	3.6	7.7	5.7	10.7	6.5	15.0	11.4	6.6	4.4	1.2	0.7	0.6
Bananas	5.8	2.8	5.2	3.2	2.8	2.4	4.3	5.1	5.7	8.0	6.2	3.9	12.0	19.3	18.2	20.9	18.1	17.3	9.7	9.2
Vegetables	0.7	0.9	0.9	0.6	1.1	0.8	0.8	1.2	2.1	3.3	4.4	4.0	0.8	3.2	2.6	5.6	7.5	6.0	8.0	7.7
Sea Products	0.0	0.2	0.3	0.2	0.3	0.1	0.1	0.2	0.3	0.3	0.5	0.7	0.8	0.7	6.0	2.9	4.2	7.2	15.7	16.9
Other Primary	2.6	1.2	1.5	1.8	2.2	1.7	2.7	5.8	6.0	7.1	10.6	5.2	4.8	5.5	6.0	6.1	6.9	8.4	8.8	7.8
Processed Agric. Exports	70.5	85.4	83.4	67.7	82.5	81.3	72.5	69.2	82.3	73.6	72.6	75.5	72.7	56.3	58.1	57.8	58.9	59.8	57.1	57.7
Sugar	61.0	74.5	64.5	54.6	66.2	71.3	58.2	51.3	61.5	46.3	38.3	48.6	48.8	23.8	21.3	14.7	16.1	14.0	12.1	14.0
Tea	5.1	5.7	10.4	4.5	4.4	3.7	4.7	5.5	5.2	6.7	6.1	3.7	3.0	3.4	3.8	4.2	3.7	4.0	3.6	3.0
Pineapples, canned	1.8	2.1	4.4	4.5	5.3	2.8	5.2	6.5	7.0	9.2	8.4	5.3	5.0	6.8	6.7	6.5	6.0	6.0	5.2	4.6
Mushrooms, canned	0.0	0.0	0.0	0.0	0.0	0.0	0.0	0.0	0.2	1.4	6.6	7.4	5.7	7.3	8.7	11.0	10.2	9.4	8.6	9.8
Asparagus, canned	0.0	0.0	0.0	0.0	0.0	0.0	0.0	0.0	0.0	0.0	0.0	0.0	0.1	3.9	4.9	8.1	8.0	9.2	8.5	7.3
Fruits, preserved	0.2	0.5	0.0	0.2	0.2	0.1	0.1	0.2	0.7	1.7	1.5	1.5	2.2	2.6	2.2	3.3	2.9	3.5	3.5	3.4
Timber & Lumber	0.0	0.2	0.2	0.6	0.5	0.3	1.3	2.2	2.3	2.8	4.3	4.3	4.9	5.5	8.2	8.5	9.7	12.4	13.7	13.1
Other Processed	2.5	2.3	3.9	3.4	5.8	3.1	3.1	3.4	5.4	5.5	7.3	4.7	2.9	3.1	2.2	1.5	2.2	1.2	2.0	2.5
B. Traditional versus Non-Traditional Agricultural Exports, as % of Total Annual Agricultural Exports																				
Traditional Agric. Exports	81.4	83.9	73.2	80.9	77.4	84.9	77.8	69.6	65.0	54.0	44.0	59.3	55.3	38.8	32.8	21.4	20.5	15.3	12.8	14.6
Rice	20.4	9.4	8.7	26.4	11.1	13.6	19.6	18.3	3.6	7.7	5.7	10.7	6.5	15.0	11.4	6.6	4.4	1.2	0.7	0.6
Sugar	61.0	74.5	64.5	54.6	66.2	71.3	58.2	51.3	61.5	46.3	38.3	48.6	48.8	23.8	21.3	14.7	16.1	14.0	12.1	14.0
Non-Traditional Agric. Exports	18.6	16.1	26.8	19.1	22.6	15.1	22.2	30.4	35.0	46.0	56.0	40.7	44.7	61.2	67.2	78.6	79.5	84.7	87.2	85.4
Bananas	5.8	2.8	5.2	3.2	2.8	2.4	4.3	5.1	5.7	8.0	6.2	3.9	12.0	19.3	18.2	20.9	18.1	17.3	9.7	9.2
Vegetables	0.7	0.9	0.9	0.6	1.1	0.8	0.8	1.2	2.1	3.3	4.4	4.0	3.2	3.2	3.7	5.6	7.5	6.0	8.0	7.7
Sea Products	0.0	0.2	0.3	0.2	0.3	0.1	0.1	0.2	0.3	0.3	0.5	0.7	0.8	0.7	2.6	2.9	4.2	7.2	8.0	7.7
Tea	5.1	5.7	10.4	4.5	4.4	3.7	4.7	5.5	5.2	6.7	6.1	3.7	3.0	3.4	3.8	4.2	3.7	4.0	3.6	3.0
Pineapples, canned	1.8	2.1	4.4	4.5	5.3	2.8	5.2	6.5	7.0	9.2	8.4	5.3	5.0	6.8	6.7	6.5	6.0	6.0	5.2	4.6
Mushrooms, canned	0.0	0.0	0.0	0.0	0.0	0.0	0.0	0.0	0.2	1.4	6.6	7.4	5.7	7.3	8.7	11.0	10.2	9.4	8.6	9.8
Asparagus, canned	0.0	0.0	0.0	0.0	0.0	0.0	0.0	0.0	0.0	0.0	0.0	0.0	0.1	3.9	4.9	8.1	8.0	9.2	8.5	7.3
Fruits, preserved	0.2	0.5	0.0	0.2	0.2	0.1	0.1	0.2	0.7	1.7	1.5	1.5	2.2	2.6	2.2	3.3	2.9	3.5	3.5	3.4
Timber & Lumber	0.0	0.2	0.2	0.6	0.5	0.3	1.3	2.2	2.3	2.8	4.3	4.3	4.9	5.5	8.2	8.5	9.7	12.4	13.7	13.1
Other Non-Traditional	5.1	3.5	5.4	5.2	8.0	4.8	5.8	9.3	11.4	12.6	17.9	9.9	7.7	8.6	8.2	7.7	9.2	9.6	10.8	10.3

Source: Compiled from Bank of Taiwan and the Central Bank of China; found in Lee, The. H. and Yueh-eh Chen, Diversification of Agricultural Exports," *Agriculture's Place in the Strategy of Development: The Taiwan Experience.* The. H. Shen, ed. Taipei, Taiwan: JCRR, 1974, p. 339, Table 1.

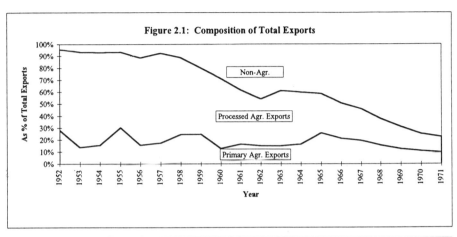

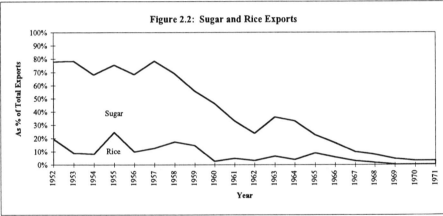

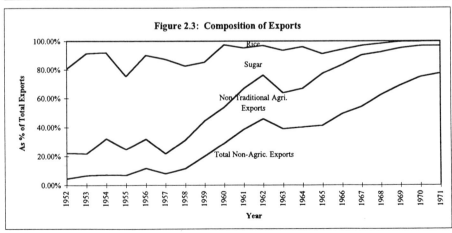

Figure 5.2   Export Composition, Taiwan, 1952–1971
Source: Table 5.3.

and a bit later by the establishment of export processing zones and bonded factories. Thus, while the rest of the Taiwan economy remained protected for some time to come — tariffs were not radically lowered until much later — the incentives for import substitutes and exports were more or less equalized on average, even if not for every industrial activity. Accompanied by approximate budgetary balance and a fairly restrictive monetary policy, these changes provided the backdrop for a dramatic shift in both output and export mixes accompanying an equally dramatic increase in the relative importance of exports relative to GDP. During the 1960s and early 1970s, total exports grew almost 30 percent a year, compared to about 12 percent a year in the 1950s. Most pronounced was the shift from agricultural or land-based to industrial or labor-based exports, concentrated initially in textiles, synthetic fiber, apparel, wood, and leather products (see Table 5.5).

During this sub-phase of transition growth we undoubtedly witnessed the emergence of a genuinely two-way nexus between the two mutual handmaidens of domestic growth and export performance. As Riedel (1984) emphasizes, both growth and exports depend on investment and technology change, with the proportions, of course, debatable. In the case of Taiwan there clearly existed an initial vent for surplus in the form of labor which permitted unit labor costs in food processing, an initially important export industry, to lag behind the trend in manufacturing until the late 1970s, when this relative advantage shifted to apparel and textiles and electronics, as well as, somewhat surprisingly, to industrial chemicals (which are, however, not significant). Unfortunately unit labor cost data for the earlier period were not available (see Table 5.6 and Figure 5.3).

A shift in educational priorities over time should be noted here, with emphasis on primary education giving way to emphasis on secondary, including vocational education, in the mid-1960s. Indeed, compulsory education was raised from 6 to 9 years, with the first harbingers of unskilled labor shortage being experienced at the end of the 1960s. Overall, expenditures on education rose from 2.1 percent of GNP and 11 percent of the budget in 1955 to 4.6 percent of GNP and 20 percent of the budget by 1970. We may note the decline in the share of primary in total education expenditures from the outset, although the rise in the share of higher education was postponed until the 1980s (see Table 5.7). Expenditures on education per student increased six-fold between 1960 and 1975. The early signs of labor shortage also led to a much increased emphasis being given to vocational, as opposed to academic, training at the secondary level. Between 1966 and 1974, during a period when the non-agricultural labor force increased by 80 percent, vocational training increased six-fold. Only 40 percent of high school students were in the vocational track in 1963; this percentage was 52 percent in 1972, and almost 70 percent by 1980. Approximately half of the vocational education was administered by private enterprises, and the other half by government agencies. The government influenced this changing mix of academic and vocational or technical high school education by using differential tuitions as a carrot. Most important to the success of the educational system was the fact that vocational education was highly diversified, flexible and continuously responsive to changing market demands.

It is, moreover, noteworthy (see Table 5.8) that the educational expenditures per student became as high for vocational as for academic secondary schools. At

Table 5.5   Export Composition by Commodity Classification, Taiwan, 1952–1994

As % of Total Annual Exports

Year	Total	Food, Beverage, & Tobacco Preparations	Textile, Leather, Wood, Paper & Related Products	Non-metallic Mineral Products	Chemical & Pharmaceutical Products	Basic Metals	Metal Products	Machinery	Electrical Machinery & Apparatus	Transportation Equipment	Others
1952	100.00	83.62	0.86	0.00	3.45	0.86	0.00	0.00	0.00	0.00	11.21
1955	100.00	84.55	2.44	0.00	3.25	1.63	0.00	0.00	0.00	0.00	8.13
1960	100.00	58.54	17.07	1.83	4.88	3.66	0.61	0.00	0.61	0.00	12.80
1965	100.00	39.11	26.22	3.11	4.44	3.56	1.11	1.33	2.67	0.44	18.00
1966	100.00	30.22	29.66	4.85	4.10	3.92	1.68	2.24	4.85	0.37	18.10
1967	100.00	25.90	34.17	4.99	4.37	3.43	1.56	2.34	6.08	0.62	16.54
1968	100.00	16.49	29.08	2.76	2.29	1.72	1.14	2.10	7.34	0.57	36.51
1969	100.00	12.56	28.83	1.89	2.03	2.09	1.15	2.23	7.97	0.74	40.51
1970	100.00	9.37	30.34	2.48	1.75	3.16	1.36	2.33	8.83	0.63	39.76
1971	100.00	7.86	31.12	2.14	1.27	1.97	1.31	2.21	8.90	0.77	42.44
1972	100.00	7.03	24.49	0.80	1.29	2.21	1.25	1.18	11.84	1.41	48.49
1973	100.00	7.75	31.48	0.89	1.38	1.40	1.61	2.31	13.97	1.86	37.35
1974	100.00	12.02	37.80	1.26	2.83	2.56	2.73	4.39	14.24	2.49	19.68
1975	100.00	7.30	24.44	0.62	1.98	1.49	1.62	2.35	9.58	1.40	49.22
1976	100.00	7.26	33.21	1.07	2.98	1.43	2.60	3.11	13.64	2.12	32.58
1977	100.00	6.00	24.02	1.22	2.90	1.02	2.55	2.65	11.74	2.59	45.31
1978	100.00	6.05	25.90	1.34	3.45	2.00	3.13	2.79	13.10	2.65	39.58
1979	100.00	5.59	26.38	1.37	3.34	2.95	3.51	3.07	14.01	2.25	37.53
1980	100.00	5.90	27.21	1.69	3.59	1.76	3.81	3.29	15.92	2.84	33.99
1981	100.00	5.30	30.65	2.07	4.42	2.27	4.74	4.24	18.78	3.89	23.64
1982	100.00	4.83	26.20	1.92	4.03	2.64	4.06	3.36	15.57	4.33	33.07
1983	100.00	4.03	23.71	2.00	3.43	2.29	4.45	3.17	15.93	3.36	37.64
1984	100.00	4.23	27.55	2.30	4.05	2.40	5.66	3.72	21.42	3.93	24.74
1985	100.00	4.49	27.57	2.14	4.36	2.48	5.79	4.00	20.99	4.10	24.07
1986	100.00	4.89	26.58	1.98	3.71	1.76	5.92	4.01	22.35	4.39	24.40
1987	100.00	4.68	24.55	2.15	3.28	1.40	6.01	4.43	25.14	4.42	23.94
1988	100.00	3.88	22.32	2.06	4.04	2.17	5.75	5.26	27.44	4.16	22.94
1989	100.00	3.61	22.29	1.81	4.17	2.26	5.98	5.81	27.32	4.56	22.21
1990	100.00	3.46	20.59	1.66	4.46	2.03	6.02	6.30	26.61	5.11	23.76
1991	100.00	3.63	20.45	1.53	4.72	1.83	6.25	6.44	26.60	5.07	23.49
1992	100.00	3.26	17.52	1.49	4.84	1.78	6.51	7.03	27.28	4.97	25.31
1993	100.00	3.16	16.15	1.26	5.20	2.08	6.65	7.31	22.46	5.16	30.57
1994	100.00	3.05	16.18	1.09	5.78	2.17	6.67	6.97	22.49	4.16	31.44

Source: OECD, *Taiwan Statistical Data Book 1995*, pp. 194–195.

Table 5.6   Indexes of Unit Labor Costs of Manufacturing Establishments in Taiwan, 1974–1994

Year	Manufacturing	Food Manufacturing	Textile Mill Products	Apparel & Textile Products	Industrial Chemicals	Chemical Products	Rubber Products	Electrical & Electronic Equip.	Inflation Figures * Consumer Prices	(1974 = 100) Wholesale Prices
1974	100.00	100.00	100.00	100.00	100.00	100.00	100.00	100.00	100.0	100.0
1975	105.01	102.31	93.23	114.11	94.85	106.18	131.23	112.25	105.1	95.0
1976	110.62	94.39	111.94	94.66	83.67	111.06	139.97	130.23	107.8	97.5
1977	127.05	111.08	127.68	114.11	83.87	128.52	180.39	141.37	115.4	100.3
1978	123.83	115.82	114.04	102.81	88.93	128.40	203.38	118.04	122.1	103.8
1979	146.60	125.99	141.20	110.33	99.30	153.80	227.90	143.14	133.9	118.1
1980	177.26	171.24	153.81	118.35	108.24	220.74	272.59	167.16	159.6	143.6
1981	203.60	190.18	187.12	143.96	113.31	249.23	329.59	168.63	185.5	154.6
1982	224.75	201.61	223.33	167.05	122.73	258.90	357.20	176.46	191.1	154.4
1983	222.20	194.28	227.45	186.36	105.96	260.57	368.22	167.47	193.5	152.5
1984	240.61	228.55	244.50	204.70	119.52	251.08	394.49	176.80	193.5	153.1
1985	253.05	228.34	258.57	202.57	124.71	258.71	381.83	191.33	193.3	149.2
1986	253.88	250.79	258.83	218.06	117.66	255.19	417.08	178.32	194.6	144.3
1987	257.80	253.77	268.64	224.19	128.08	243.36	410.33	171.77	195.5	139.5
1988	277.13	263.14	313.99	272.39	144.69	262.92	456.41	182.08	198.2	137.3
1989	293.68	306.31	306.95	282.69	155.04	281.83	487.98	197.87	206.9	136.9
1990	311.64	339.78	293.87	329.96	157.33	298.89	465.54	208.76	215.4	136.0
1991	318.98	350.75	291.97	356.25	158.81	309.02	496.52	210.53	223.2	136.2
1992	334.58	373.80	306.92	405.20	147.53	314.15	484.91	218.65	233.3	131.2
1993	348.96	391.20	334.60	479.30	155.22	331.15	541.46	219.54	240.0	134.6
1994	357.89	399.61	329.08	598.54	125.15	340.88	587.44	221.62	249.8	137.5

*Source: CEPD, *Taiwan Statistical Data Book 1995*, p. 3.

Source: DGBAS, Executive Yuan, ROC. *Monthly Bulletin of Earnings and Productivity Statistics, Taiwan Area, Republic of China*, June 1995, pp. 132–133. Seasonally adjusted, 1974 = 100.

Figure 5.3   Labor Costs and Labor Productivity in Manufacturing,
Taiwan, 1974–1994

Source: Table 5.5.

Table 5.7   Educational Expenditure at All Levels, 1964–1994

Fiscal Year	Preschool Education	Primary Education	Secondary Education	Higher Education	Social Education	Other	Total
1964	0.78	39.43	32.26	14.70	2.79	10.04	100.00
1965	0.80	35.98	32.43	18.28	3.09	9.42	100.00
1966	0.80	32.72	35.09	19.63	3.90	7.86	100.00
1967	0.69	32.54	35.87	19.63	3.13	8.14	100.00
1968	0.64	31.72	35.45	22.45	3.32	6.42	100.00
1969	0.29	26.66	40.15	22.53	2.88	7.49	100.00
1970	0.53	27.28	37.69	24.53	4.33	5.64	100.00
1971	0.42	25.13	37.29	27.32	4.29	5.55	100.00
1972	1.10	27.12	40.26	21.72	4.21	5.59	100.00
1973	1.04	28.23	40.63	21.81	3.73	4.56	100.00
1974	1.21	27.79	39.26	21.89	3.39	6.46	100.00
1975	1.09	28.87	36.40	19.97	3.23	10.44	100.00
1976	0.91	28.20	37.76	20.75	3.21	9.17	100.00
1977	1.14	27.78	35.40	20.35	3.15	12.18	100.00
1978	0.94	27.50	33.62	19.98	2.30	15.66	100.00
1979	1.03	29.48	37.43	19.23	3.15	9.68	100.00
1980	1.42	28.41	35.53	19.57	3.79	11.28	100.00
1981	1.64	25.64	34.98	21.46	4.37	11.91	100.00
1982	1.73	23.55	34.10	22.34	3.23	15.05	100.00
1983	1.64	24.51	31.46	23.68	3.39	15.32	100.00
1984	2.32	24.31	33.23	22.12	3.21	14.81	100.00
1985	3.23	22.91	32.35	21.79	3.75	15.97	100.00
1986	3.21	22.48	31.36	21.51	3.85	17.59	100.00
1987	3.10	21.98	31.63	24.70	3.28	15.31	100.00
1988	3.12	23.42	30.32	25.64	4.56	12.94	100.00
1989	3.33	24.59	30.15	23.67	4.45	13.81	100.00
1990	3.20	23.74	31.35	23.85	6.33	11.53	100.00
1991	2.74	23.58	32.70	23.94	5.74	11.30	100.00
1992	2.90	22.72	29.10	23.80	5.94	15.54	100.00
1993	2.72	24.37	29.53	22.82	6.66	13.90	100.00
1994	2.45	23.52	29.71	22.25	5.75	16.32	100.00

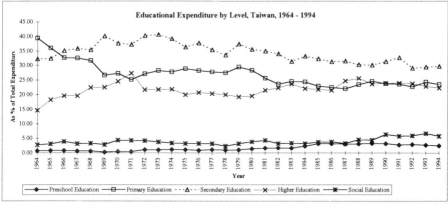

Source: DGBAS, *Social Indicators in Taiwan Area of the ROC, 1994.*

Table 5.8   Educational Expenditure Per Student at All Levels, Taiwan, 1976–1995

I. In NT$/Student

Period	Pre-School Education	Elementary School	Jr. High School	Sr. High School	Sr. Vocational School	Junior College	Univ. & College
1976-77	2,899	3,660	5,728	8,860	10,480	11,645	30,734
1977-78	2,557	4,351	6,066	10,652	11,902	16,939	30,965
1978-79	2,953	5,597	8,014	13,557	16,254	23,176	33,551
1979-80	4,889	7,164	9,770	16,612	20,093	24,289	48,453
1980-81	6,821	8,506	12,855	30,190	24,276	39,573	61,006
1981-82	8,549	10,075	15,594	25,085	29,216	48,316	79,889
1982-83	9,412	12,213	17,461	25,043	28,590	54,622	95,632
1983-84	12,058	12,044	18,413	25,530	29,916	54,124	83,256
1984-85	17,092	12,487	19,869	28,073	32,574	56,260	89,704
1985-86	18,878	13,354	21,230	29,869	34,342	56,888	97,666
1986-87	19,241	13,765	22,225	31,606	39,356	64,689	119,285
1987-88	21,022	16,424	23,854	34,602	47,247	48,187	141,891
1988-89	26,840	20,489	27,900	41,332	47,958	55,549	140,782
1989-90	32,296	24,416	32,921	55,041	64,105	64,215	161,547
1990-91	34,788	30,412	42,104	66,691	78,092	67,022	190,402
1991-92	43,548	34,991	49,685	59,417	66,025	79,386	198,769
1992-93	47,530	44,665	58,397	65,978	69,839	83,224	203,121
1993-94	45,324	49,058	62,366	70,013	78,497	87,174	204,795
1994-95	53,620	54,804	67,880	69,349	81,232	81,978	200,344

II. Indexes (1977 = 100)

Period	Pre-School Education	Elementary School	Jr. High School	Sr. High School	Sr. Vocational School	Junior College	Univ. & College
1976-77	100.00	100.00	100.00	100.00	100.00	100.00	100.00
1977-78	88.20	118.88	105.90	120.23	113.57	145.46	100.75
1978-79	101.86	152.92	139.91	153.01	155.10	199.02	109.17
1979-80	168.64	195.74	170.57	187.49	191.73	208.58	157.65
1980-81	235.29	232.40	224.42	340.74	231.64	339.83	198.50
1981-82	294.89	275.27	272.24	283.13	278.78	414.91	259.94
1982-83	324.66	333.69	304.84	282.65	272.81	469.06	311.16
1983-84	415.94	329.07	321.46	288.15	285.46	464.78	270.89
1984-85	589.58	341.17	346.88	316.85	310.82	483.13	291.87
1985-86	651.19	364.86	370.64	337.12	327.69	488.52	317.78
1986-87	663.71	376.09	388.01	356.73	375.53	555.51	388.12
1987-88	725.15	448.74	416.45	390.54	450.83	413.80	461.67
1988-89	925.84	559.81	487.08	466.39	457.61	477.02	458.07
1989-90	1114.04	667.10	574.74	621.23	611.69	551.44	525.63
1990-91	1200.00	830.93	735.06	752.72	745.15	575.54	619.52
1991-92	1502.17	956.04	867.41	670.62	630.01	681.72	646.74
1992-93	1639.53	1220.36	1019.50	744.67	666.40	714.68	660.90
1993-94	1563.44	1340.38	1088.79	790.21	749.02	748.60	666.35
1994-95	1849.60	1497.38	1185.06	782.72	775.11	703.98	651.86

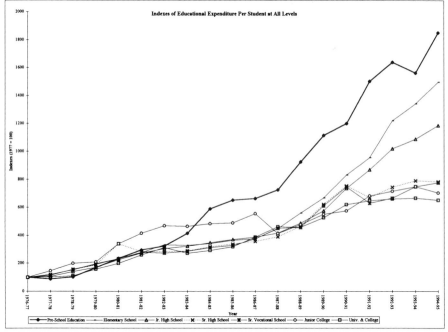

Source: CEPD, *Taiwan Statistical Data Book 1996,* p. 268.

least half of the national vocational and training fund resources went to private enterprises for improved training programs, often in cooperation with vocational high schools; and, as Galenson (1979) has pointed out, these non-academic education figures do not even include on-the-job training or learning by doing.

By the early 1970s, the share of industry in GDP had risen to more than one-third, and the sector provided more than 24 percent of employment. Annual industrial growth rates, which had faltered a bit by the end of the import substitution era in the early 1960s, now climbed again into the range of 16 percent to 20 percent during the late 1960s and early 1970s, while the share of industrial exports in GDP continued to rise and stood close to 50 percent percent by 1973.

Additional important direct government actions were crucial to the emerging role of industrial growth and exports. The most important of these undoubtedly were the provision of rural transportation and power, which permitted a markedly decentralized industrialization effort to develop, and thus continued policies pursued by the Japanese colonial government. Indeed Taiwan's railway system density was second only to Japan's in all of Asia. Power capacity was maintained well ahead of demand and distributed relatively equally throughout the island, and a uniform set of electricity rates between rural and urban locations was established. The government also established a number of industry-oriented technology and investment institutes quite early, including the China Productivity and Trade Center, the Food Industry Research and Development Institute, the China Development Corporation, and the Industrial Development and Investment Center, most of which provided management, training and technical assistance, along with credit, for relatively small industrial entrepreneurs. Throughout the 1960s the government also set up a substantial number of rural industrial estates, providing the essential physical overheads for private industry.

While such efforts are often accompanied by less than full success in many developing countries, in Taiwan they seemed to be particularly focused on providing services to the preponderant group of medium and small scale firms, many of which had moved out from earlier, primarily agricultural processing, pursuits. The early support for food processing technology was channeled through the same Joint Commission on Rural Reconstruction (JCRR)/farmers' association structure that had served agriculture so well in the earlier period. Industrial activity shifted from food processing to textiles, garments, leather goods, wood products, etc., which, together, amounted to 66 percent of total manufacturing production by the late 1950s. Imported raw materials-based industries gradually took over from the agricultural-based exports, but with both still relying heavily on the absorption of unskilled labor. Indeed, the rate of growth of industrial employment, roughly 3 percent to 4 percent in the import substituting 1950s, rose to 6-8 percent in the 1960s. The unusually dispersed rural character of Taiwan's industrialization effort undoubtedly helped keep labor costs down, reduced the social costs of urbanization, and permitted an improvement in the distribution of income during this period of accelerated growth.

It should also be noted that the internal transport network was extremely well articulated with respect to the main ports and export processing zones, starting with Kaohsiung. This not only facilitated the export of domestic raw materials-intensive products, but was also of substantial importance in enhancing the system's export potential, once the overall policy environment had shifted in a favorable direction. With industrial output becoming increasingly oriented towards unskilled labor and imported raw materials, the ability to attract labor to the proximity of the port cities and to locate industries rurally, either the entire operation or subcontracted units, became increasingly important. It was possible for industrial laborers to bicycle in for the day, returning to their rural households at night, and thus transport and transaction costs were minimized.

Institutions which had served agriculture earlier on now provided assistance to agriculture-linked industry and exports. The Joint Commission on Rural Reconstruction, for example, financed research and development efforts in support of fish canning at Kaohsiung. Farmers' associations now included rural transport and the promotion of rural industries among the various services offered. Institutions such as the Forestry Research Institute, agricultural experimental stations and the Food Industries Research and Development Institute provided for a further strengthening of the linkages between agriculture and non-agricultural activities in the rural areas.

As Liang and Liang (1976) reported, using the Chenery decomposition technique, non-durable consumer goods exports accounted for almost 75 percent of total demand sources for manufacturing output growth from 1965 to 1970. Along with the shift from domestic raw materials-based to imported raw materials-based industries came a shift from domestic markets to exports as a source of demand for industrial output. Here again we should note, however, that the domestic market continued to grow vigorously, even while diminishing in relative importance. Domestic industrialization of a decentralized type and of an increasingly high labor intensity were crucially tied up with the achievement of increased international competitiveness. Ho (1977) indeed reports a remarkable relative decline in the urban proportion of total industrial manufacturing employment between 1956 and 1966.

In the case of some industries, such as food processing, this pronouncedly rural location of industry was dictated in large part by the location of the domestic raw material; for others, like textiles and electronics, which imported their raw materials, the export processing zone device, plus access to cheap rural labor, played an important role. In all such cases, adoption of unskilled labor intensive production processes, plus the relative absence of economies of scale, induced a predominance of low cost medium and small-scale firms, yielding international competitiveness.

As we would expect, industries with the highest employment growth registered the highest output and export growth. Liang and Liang (1976), using 1966 and 1971 input/output tables, found export industries had weighted capital-labor ratios substantially below those of import competing industries, as we would expect from Hecksher/Ohlin trade theory. Taiwan's main comparative advantage clearly resided in the abundance of her relatively cheap but efficient supply of labor. It should be no surprise that the system's labor intensive industrial consumer goods exports grew fastest during most of the 1960s. Examining the industrial censuses of 1954, 1961, and 1971, and ranking industries by their total capital-labor ratios, we find that the changes in output mix developed about as expected over time, gradually moving from non-durables to durables and intermediate goods.

While the center of gravity was thus clearly shifting to the industrial sector during the 1960s and early 1970s, it should not be forgotten that sustained steady advances in agricultural output continued to be important for avoiding the premature rises in wage good prices and in industrial real wages that so often prevent countries from taking full advantage of their unskilled labor-based export capacity. Quite the contrary, domestic agricultural output and agricultural exports continued to support rather than to hinder sustained growth of the non-agricultural sector. As C.Y. Lin put it, "the competitiveness of Taiwan's labor supply is the ... result largely of successful agricultural development, which made the 'unlimited' supply of labor a reality" (Lin, 1973: 158). The unusual constancy of the domestic terms of trade in Taiwan, and the fact that until the 1970s a positive international trade balance in basic foods continued to obtain, is evidence of this continued importance of the agricultural sector in facilitating the successful interaction between an increasingly industry-focused growth and export performance.

It should also be noted that the liberalization packages of the late 1950s and early 1960s, combined with the aforementioned success in domestic balanced growth, made the participation of foreign private capital increasingly attractive. Rapid wage increases in the United States, Europe, and especially in Japan, Hong Kong and Singapore during the 1960s, induced increasing numbers of multinationals to take advantage of Taiwan's abundant labor supply, virtually free of union activities, disputes, and strikes. Good levels of health and education, adequate transportation and cheap electric power were the advantages most often noted by foreign investors, initially mainly overseas Chinese and later U.S. and Japanese in origin, who entered in increasing numbers during the 1970s and 1980s.

Taiwan's export processing zones not only helped to attract foreign investment but also provided important technological spillovers as a byproduct of the export generation process. For example, Kaohsiung attracted 30 percent of Taiwan's total direct foreign investment in 1966 and 39 percent in 1972, even as its share of total exports rose from 1.3 percent to 8 percent. It should, moreover, be noted that the export processing zones' procurement of domestic raw materials comprised only 8 percent of the total in 1970 but reached 40 percent by 1979, indicating increased spillover effects, even as, with continued overall liberalization, the relative importance of export processing zones began to diminish.

There can be little doubt that during the 1960s and early 1970s Taiwan's exports were substantially enhanced by the actions of her domestic entrepreneurs, supported by the increasing participation of foreign investors in the export processing zones and bonded factories throughout the island. TFP change in manufacturing remained substantial (see Figure 5.4), even if it was not as high as in the earlier period when the economy was still dominated by agriculture. This helps to explain why the production of exportables, along with the industrial sector as a whole, was able to avoid diminishing returns in the face of high and rising rates of investment. Those who claim that high savings rates are sufficient to explain the Taiwan "Miracle" need to be able to explain why these high rates of investment continued to be accompanied by such still respectable levels of productivity changes. While

Period	Total	Basic Needs	Chemicals	Machinery	Electronics
1952 - 56	36.5%	37.5%	27.5%	56.2%	56.8%
1956 - 61	17.5%	16.0%	19.1%	27.9%	12.2%
1961 - 66	10.7%	8.1%	12.3%	12.9%	32.1%
1966 - 71	7.7%	7.1%	5.2%	9.0%	6.5%
1971 - 76	-0.5%	0.1%	1.7%	-2.7%	-8.7%
1976 - 81	5.1%	7.0%	4.8%	2.0%	3.5%
1981 - 86	5.2%	4.8%	4.6%	5.2%	7.5%
1986 - 90	1.2%	-2.0%	-0.4%	5.8%	5.7%

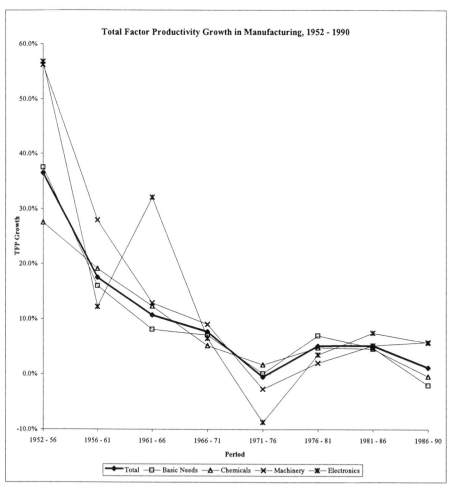

Figure 5.4   Total Factor Productivity Growth in Manufacturing, 1952–1990
Source: Liu, Paul K. C., Ying-Chuan Liu, and Hui-Lin Wu, "Emergence of New Business Organization
and Management in Taiwan," *Industry of Free China,* Vol. 82, No. 11. Nov. 1994. p. 40.

we could encounter equally high or even higher investment rates elsewhere — for example, in Scandinavia and, earlier, in the Soviet Union — these were associated with much higher capital-output ratios and much lower export performance. As Pack (1992) points out, the level of TFP in the export industries of Taiwan was certainly higher than in the domestically oriented industries, even if it was not remarkable by international standards.

5.4 The Science and Technology Dominated Growth/Export Nexus

There can be little doubt that the mutual support of exports and growth in Taiwan has become most pronounced during the period between 1976 and the present. Once labor surplus had been exhausted, Taiwan's output and export mixes became increasingly skilled labor, capital and, ultimately, technology intensive, as one would expect, once again, from the application of dynamic comparative advantage theory. We may note the advent of an increasing labor shortage from rising wages (see Figure 5.5) and rising female participation rates (from 33 percent in 1965 to 35 percent in 1969 to 39 percent by 1975 and 45 percent by 1994). As a consequence, there was a gradual increase in the relative size of intermediate and capital goods industries, including the shifting of electronics assembly processes both forward and backward. Such shifts entailed a substantial change in the industrial output and export mixes, along with an enhanced demand for embodied education and capital, i.e. increasing skilled labor requirements and industrial capital-labor ratios.

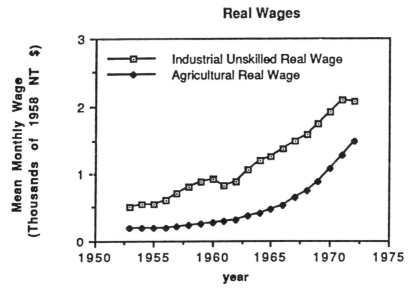

Figure 5.5   Evolution of real wages

Sources: Kuo, S., *The Taiwan Economy in Transition,* Westview Press, Boulder, CO. *Taiwan Statistical Data Book,* Council for Economic Planning and Development, Republic of China, 1990.

During these last two decades a number of additional government actions can be cited that enhanced the flexibility and adjustment capacity of the domestic production structure in terms of continuing the aforementioned shift in product cycle terms. For example, the ten major public sector projects of the early 1970s and those included in the current six year plan were partly designed to address emerging transportation bottlenecks, and partly to circumvent the still inadequate financial intermediation sector by linking small savers to large project investment requirements. Probably even more important were the further shifts in educational policy. In the 1980s Taiwan began to increasingly emphasize tertiary education (see Table 5.9) and, within tertiary education, to move resources towards science and technology oriented fields. Overall, education expenditures as a percentage of GNP began to rise to the vicinity of 5 percent (see Table 5.10).

Another important contribution to the maintenance of international competitiveness in Taiwan was, of course, the increasing impact of domestic R&D expenditures. We may note the substantial increases in R&D as a percentage of both GNP and of total government expenditures (see Table 5.10). Note also that these numbers do not include military or defense-related R&D spillovers, nor the important informal R&D efforts of small firms, the so-called blue-collar R&D, not at all captured in the official statistics. In 1984, tax incentives were provided for manufacturers to allocate a larger percentage of their revenues to R&D. But the bulk of the innovative activities undoubtedly took place unrecorded in the repair shops and floors of Taiwan's thousands of decentralized medium and small-scale firms.

While, as Wang (1994) points out, in-house research continued to be much more important, the government also attempted to assist Taiwan's predominantly medium and small-scale firms by establishing a number of research institutes, science parks, etc. Government's involvement in creating such complementary science and technology institutional infrastructure included the establishment of the National Science Council in 1967, the Chung Shan Institute of Science and Technology in 1965, the Industrial Training and Research Institute (ITRI) in 1973, and the Hsin Chu Science-Based Industrial Park, and the Information Industry Institute, both in 1979. ITRI, initially fully funded by the government, increasingly received private contracts from local enterprises and is generally considered responsible for developing many key technologies ultimately transferred to private local industry, thus facilitating Taiwan's technological development. The Hsin Chu Science-Based Industrial Park has been responsible for a succession of new ventures in high-tech export-oriented areas by providing public facilities to small and medium-sized firms on favorable terms, including five year tax exemptions, a ceiling on taxes thereafter, subsidized rent, credit facilities and other amenities. It also guaranteed close physical and intellectual contact with academic and private commercial interests. As shown in Table 5.11, total R&D expenditures increased in virtually every industry group between 1986 and 1992, but most markedly in those high tech areas assuming an increasing role in Taiwan's exports, e.g. machinery and equipment, electric and electronic machinery, chemical materials and, most pronouncedly, precision instruments. As Table 5.12 indicates, these industries also had the highest R&D expenditures per unit of total sales, which were increasingly export-oriented. Another way of making the point, whichever way the causation

Table 5.9   Net Enrollment Ratios, Taiwan, 1980–1994

School Year	First Level (6 - 11 Years)	Second Level (12 - 17 Years)	Third Level (18 - 21 Years)	Combined First, Second and Third Level
1980	97.56	70.98	11.07	54.69
1981	97.59	72.96	11.47	55.08
1982	96.42	75.40	11.80	55.41
1983	96.70	76.14	12.40	55.99
1984	96.29	78.11	12.57	56.02
1985	96.30	78.29	13.88	57.95
1986	96.75	81.50	14.23	58.96
1987	96.97	82.39	14.82	59.51
1988	97.92	82.88	15.95	60.55
1989	97.74	83.88	17.18	61.18
1990	98.04	85.44	18.93	62.69
1991	98.70	86.19	21.01	64.47
1992	98.92	86.46	23.47	66.01
1993	99.31	84.61	25.61	66.67
1994	98.36	88.59	26.26	67.07

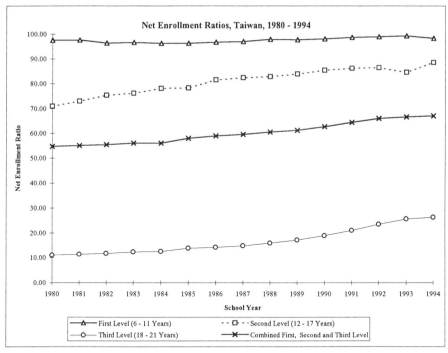

Net Enrollment Ratio: The number of students enrolled in a level of education
who belong in the relevant age group, as a percentage of the population in
that age group.

Source: *Monthly Bulletin of Statistics of the Republic of China,* DGBAS, Sept. 1995, p. 13.

Table 5.10   Expenditures on Education, Social Welfare, and R&D, Taiwan, 1964–1993

| | Ratios to GNP | | | | Ratios to Net Government Expenditure | | | |
Year	Ratio of Educational Expenditure to GNP	Ratio of R&D Expenditure to GNP *	Ratio of Net Social Welfare Expenditure to GNP	Real Growth Rate of GNP	Net Gov't Expenditure/GNP	Education to Gov't Expend.	R&D to Gov't Expend	Social Welfare to Gov't Expend
1964	2.94		1.57	12.3	19.4	15.15		8.09
1965	2.96		1.59	11.0	21.0	14.10		7.57
1966	3.38		0.96	9.0	20.3	16.65		4.73
1967	3.40		1.63	10.6	22.8	14.91		7.15
1968	3.56		1.66	9.1	21.1	16.87		7.87
1969	3.99		2.02	11.3	22.7	17.58		8.90
1970	4.14		2.24	13.0	23.4	17.69		9.57
1971	4.58		2.32	13.4	22.3	20.54		10.40
1972	4.10		2.80	12.8	22.0	18.64		12.73
1973	3.57		2.48	1.2	22.8	15.66		10.88
1974	2.95		1.95	4.4	18.0	16.39		10.83
1975	3.87		2.33	13.7	22.8	16.97		10.22
1976	2.95		2.64	10.3	23.3	12.66		11.33
1977	4.06		2.69	14.0	25.3	16.05		10.63
1978	4.09	0.61	2.73	8.5	25.3	16.17	2.41	10.79
1979	3.96	0.83	2.66	7.1	23.3	17.00	3.56	11.42
1980	4.27	0.71	2.86	5.8	25.9	16.49	2.74	11.04
1981	4.54	0.93	3.13	4.1	26.5	17.13	3.51	11.81
1982	5.15	0.89	3.89	8.7	26.9	19.14	3.31	14.46
1983	5.58	0.91	3.80	11.6	25.1	22.23	3.63	15.14
1984 **	4.95	0.95	3.64	5.6	23.1	21.43	4.11	15.76
1985	5.06	1.01	3.61	12.6	23.0	22.00	4.39	15.70
1986	5.14	0.98	3.68	12.3	23.6	21.78	4.15	15.59
1987	4.73	1.12	3.27	8.3	21.2	22.31	5.28	15.42
1988	4.92	1.22	3.82	8.0	21.8	22.57	5.60	17.52
1989	5.35	1.38	3.99	5.5	32.6	16.41	4.23	12.24
1990	5.90	1.65	2.28	7.6	27.6	21.38	5.98	8.26
1991	6.63	1.70	2.54	6.2	30.6	21.67	5.56	8.30
1992	6.96	1.79	2.60	6.0	32.7	21.28	5.47	7.95
1993	7.24		2.55	6.1	32.6	22.21		7.82
Mean	4.50	1.11	2.66	9.0				

* These statistics exclude information on defense-related science and technology.
** Beginning in 1984, the R&D in humanities and social sciences was included.

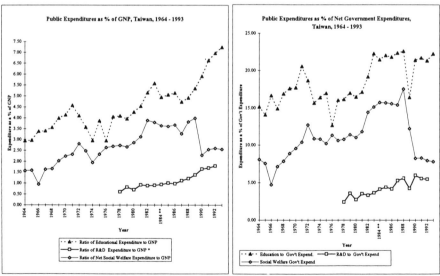

Source: *Social Indicators in Taiwan Area of the Republic of China 1993*, DGBAS, Executive Yuan, Republic of China, pp. 112–113. *Statistical Yearbook of the Republic of China 1994*, DGBAS, Executive Yuan, Republic of China, p. 156. *Taiwan Statistical Yearbook*, CEPD, Republic of China, pp. 27, 30–31.

Table 5.11   Indexes of All R&D Expenditures, by Industry, Taiwan, 1986–1992

Index (1986 = 100)

Industry \ Year	1992	1991	1990	1989	1988	1987	1986
Food	116.14	113.01	135.23	124.03	162.11	120.23	100.00
Beverage & Tobacco	71.43	74.18	153.30	47.80	37.91	63.19	100.00
Textiles	238.96	292.05	271.92	65.75	124.68	308.77	100.00
Wearing Apparel & Accessories	58.72	169.72	160.55	53.21	92.66	221.10	100.00
Leather, Fur, & Products	113.29	197.47	24.05	132.91	9.49	29.75	100.00
Wood & Bamboo Products	189.80	51.02	73.47	159.18	122.45	361.22	100.00
Paper, Pulp & Print	115.54	225.68	215.54	184.46	129.73	201.35	100.00
Chemical Materials	446.96	341.74	352.03	263.77	171.88	51.88	100.00
Chemical Products	119.67	66.74	62.83	52.30	67.78	147.49	100.00
Petroleum & Coal Products	207.72	154.74	125.96	92.28	185.03	89.82	100.00
Rubber Products	219.49	146.67	73.33	275.38	87.69	109.23	100.00
Plastic Products	345.79	224.91	75.32	114.54	23.79	115.81	100.00
Non-Metallic Mineral Products	114.19	61.94	111.07	565.40	272.66	240.83	100.00
Basic Metals	351.83	242.43	250.69	185.78	196.33	118.58	100.00
Fabricated Metal Products	212.78	139.38	157.32	156.29	137.32	130.93	100.00
Machinery & Equipment	475.08	337.08	268.39	388.15	251.06	209.73	100.00
Electric & Electronic Machinery	553.45	551.76	561.08	339.71	206.53	158.03	100.00
Transport Equipment	498.59	428.30	409.99	462.61	211.78	216.77	100.00
Precision Instruments	922.47	339.33	191.01	198.88	432.58	342.70	100.00
Miscellaneous Industry	206.49	129.46	298.92	306.22	121.08	30.54	100.00
Manufacturing Subtotal	344.23	300.49	288.21	225.80	154.13	147.05	100.00
Non-Manufacturing Information Services	6.69	19.90	2.78	7.69	35.02	78.52	100.00
Total R&D Expenditures	312.99	258.73	265.41	192.82	136.12	136.69	100.00

Source: *Indicators of Science and Technology in the ROC,* National Science Council, Taiwan, pp. 108–109.

runs, is illustrated in Table 5.13. When we separate industries by the destination of their output we may note the clearly higher levels of TFP for those with higher export shares.

The break-down between R&D carried on within industry, in S&T institutes and in the universities by major field (see Table 5.14) shows a surprisingly large role for the S&T institutes; these served mainly the medium and small-scale industries, especially in the critical engineering area, where they comprised approximately 25 percent of the total. If we were able to add R&D of the private blue-collar variety, Taiwan's total R&D levels as a percent of sales or GDP would probably begin to approach DC standards. It should be noted that official R&D normally runs below the .5 percent of GNP level in LDCs, in contrast to 5 percent of GNP for developed countries.

It is in this most recent period that the causal chain running from exports to domestic competitiveness is probably most pronounced. As the *East Asian Miracle* authors point out "we believe that rapid growth of exports, as a result of the export push policies. . ., combined with the superior performance of the East Asian economies in creating and allocating human capital, provided the means by which they obtained high rates of ... total factor productivity growth" (World Bank, 1993:

Table 5.12   R&D Expenditures, as Percentage of Annual Sales, by Industry, Taiwan, 1986–1992

A. As a % of Annual Sales

Industry	1992 Total	1992 Private	1991 Total	1991 Private	1990 Total	1990 Private	1989 Total	1989 Private	1988 Total	1988 Private	1987 Total	1987 Private	1986 Total	1986 Private	1986–1992 Ave Total	1986–1992 Ave Private
Food	0.38	0.25	0.43	0.27	0.53	0.38	0.50	0.35	0.69	0.74	0.44	0.32	0.48	0.32	0.49	0.40
Beverage & Tobacco	0.10	0.37	0.13	0.50	0.28	0.94	0.08	0.30	0.07	0.03	0.21	0.56	0.23	0.22	0.16	0.40
Textiles	0.40	0.40	0.55	0.55	0.52	0.52	0.13	0.13	0.24	0.24	0.34	0.31	0.16	0.15	0.33	0.35
Wearing Apparel & Accessories	0.08	0.08	0.24	0.24	0.24	0.24	0.07	0.07	0.12	0.12	0.35	0.33	0.12	0.11	0.17	0.18
Leather, Fur, & Products	0.26	0.25	0.45	0.46	0.06	0.06	0.34	0.34	0.03	0.02	0.20	0.19	0.24	0.22	0.23	0.20
Wood & Bamboo Products	0.10	0.10	0.03	0.03	0.04	0.04	0.08	0.08	0.06	0.06	0.26	0.22	0.11	0.08	0.10	0.08
Paper, Pulp & Print	0.10	0.10	0.21	0.22	0.20	0.21	0.19	0.19	0.14	0.14	0.42	0.40	0.16	0.15	0.20	0.20
Chemical Materials	1.08	1.11	0.84	0.87	0.88	0.90	0.53	0.66	0.40	0.29	0.46	0.43	1.07	0.99	0.75	0.77
Chemical Products	1.24	1.22	0.89	0.87	0.86	0.86	0.78	0.79	1.06	1.03	1.10	0.97	0.80	0.74	0.96	0.92
Petroleum & Coal Products	1.13	0.00	0.86	0.06	0.73	0.06	0.48	0.02	0.77	0.01	0.39	0.52	0.41	0.43	0.68	0.23
Rubber Products	0.75	0.72	0.52	0.53	0.27	0.27	0.96	0.96	0.30	0.30	0.92	0.86	0.51	0.47	0.60	0.55
Plastic Products	1.57	1.56	1.12	1.13	0.39	0.38	0.55	0.55	0.11	0.11	0.68	0.64	0.72	0.66	0.73	0.68
Non-Metallic Mineral Products	0.15	0.15	0.11	0.12	0.21	0.21	1.15	1.16	0.62	0.62	1.00	0.94	0.27	0.25	0.50	0.46
Basic Metals	0.37	0.05	0.32	0.01	0.33	0.13	0.27	0.08	0.32	0.05	0.47	0.07	0.29	0.03	0.34	0.09
Fabricated Metal Products	0.30	0.30	0.25	0.25	0.29	0.30	0.32	0.32	0.30	0.27	0.44	0.40	0.36	0.34	0.32	0.31
Machinery & Equipment	0.60	0.60	0.55	0.55	0.44	0.44	0.66	0.66	0.47	0.46	1.56	1.55	0.86	0.87	0.73	0.70
Electric & Electronic Machinery	2.05	1.89	2.41	2.20	2.53	2.29	1.59	1.35	1.04	0.98	1.00	0.94	0.65	0.60	1.61	1.60
Transport Equipment	0.93	0.96	1.01	1.07	0.99	1.05	1.18	1.24	0.62	0.61	1.17	1.16	0.48	0.46	0.91	0.94
Precision Instruments	1.27	1.27	0.68	0.69	0.39	0.40	0.43	0.43	0.91	0.91	2.09	1.96	0.48	0.44	0.89	0.81
Miscellaneous Industry	0.53	0.53	0.35	0.35	0.82	0.82	0.73	0.87	0.33	0.33	0.31	0.29	0.74	0.68	0.54	0.59
Manufacturing Subtotal	0.92	0.87	0.94	0.91	0.92	0.89	0.86	0.71	0.52	0.68	0.64	0.62	0.47	0.42	0.75	0.75
Non-Manufacturing	0.37	0.15	0.17	0.01	0.19	0.09	0.59	0.15	0.51	0.74	0.20	0.11	0.20	0.09	0.32	0.19
Information Services	3.26	3.26	4.21	4.21	4.00	4.00	0.00	0.00	0.00	0.00	0.00	0.00	0.00	0.00		

Source: *Indicators of Science and Technology in the ROC,* National Science Council, Taiwan, pp. 118–119.

Table 5.13   Export Share and TFP by Industry, 1986

2-Digit Industries	Export Share	TFP Exporting Industry	TFP Import-Competing Industry
20 Food	21.47		2.58 (23.81)
21 Beverages & Tobacco	0.74		2.84 (9.92)
22 Textile	61.64	7.53 (12.65)[1]	
23 Wearing Apparel	79.53	13.96 (18.93)	
24 Leather	72.48	11.79 (16.00)	
25 Lumber & Furniture	62.65	10.46 (17.32)	
26 Paper & Printing	9.85		11.51 (22.96)
27 Chemical Materials	20.30		2.48 (3.38)
28 Chemical Products	11.08		4.12 (7.85)
29 Petroleum & Coal Products	7.91		2.17 (3.60)
30 Rubber Products	50.72	9.82 (16.46)	
31 Plastic Products	57.07	8.80 (13.50)	
32 Nonmetallic Mineral Products	19.54		6.90 (12.50)
33 Basic Metal	15.35		6.27 (11.68)
34 Metal Products	44.79		9.41 (17.44)
35 Machinery	38.19		8.02 (13.22)
36 Electrical Machinery & Appliances	74.80	10.74 (20.61)	
37 Transport Equipment	27.96		7.45 (15.83)
38 Precision Instruments	74.82	12.38 (18.80)	
39 Miscellaneous Industries	75.15	14.54 (110.22)	

[1]The numbers in parentheses are the standard errors.

Source: Calculated by Hwang (1994) "Exports, Returns to Scale, andTotal Factor Productivity: The Case of Manufacturing Industries in Taiwan."

Table 5.14   R&D Expenditures by Sector of Performance and Field of Research, Taiwan, 1992

A. Allocation of R&D Expenditures, As % of *Sector* Totals

Sector	Natural Sciences	Engineering	Medical Sciences	Argicultural Sciences	Humanities & Social Sci.	Totals
Industry						
Subtotal	1.5	94.8	1.1	2.6		100.0
Public	7.1	85.3	0.5	7.1		100.0
Private	0.7	96.1	1.2	2.0		100.0
S&T Research Institute						
Subtotal	14.6	57.4	4.3	17.7	6.0	100.0
Public	33.2	11.9	7.5	41.3	6.1	100.0
Private	0.0	0.0	95.1	0.8	4.1	100.0
Non-Profit	4.5	82.4	2.1	5.0	6.0	100.0
University and Colleges						
Subtotal	18.0	39.7	19.1	16.3	6.9	100.0
Public	20.7	41.7	11.5	19.1	7.0	100.0
Private	8.3	32.5	46.7	5.9	6.6	100.0
Total	8.2	**74.5**	4.8	9.5	3.0	100.0

B. Allocation of R&D Expenditures, As % of *Field* Totals

Sector	Natural Sciences	Engineering	Medical Sciences	Argicultural Sciences	Humanities & Social Sci.	Totals
Industry						
Subtotal	52.5	66.9	12.5	14.2	0.0	52.5
Public	6.1	6.9	0.7	4.5	0.0	6.1
Private	46.5	59.9	11.8	9.7	0.0	46.5
S&T Research Institute						
Subtotal	33.0	**25.4**	30.1	61.2	66.7	33.0
Public	11.5	1.8	18.1	50.0	23.5	11.5
Private	0.1	0.0	2.6	0.0	0.2	0.1
Non-Profit	21.3	23.6	9.5	11.2	43.1	21.3
University and Colleges						
Subtotal	14.4	7.7	57.4	24.6	33.3	14.4
Public	11.3	6.3	27.2	22.7	26.4	11.3
Private	3.1	1.4	30.3	1.9	6.9	3.1
Total	100.0	100.0	100.0	100.0	100.0	100.0

Source: *Indicators of Science and Technology in the ROC,* National Science Council, Taiwan, pp. 80–81.

316). Whether or not we believe in these high rates of TFP growth or something more modest, a subject of substantial current controversy, it is clear that the impact of exports on domestic productivity via associated equipment imports, technological licensing, and the enhanced flow of DFI, became increasingly important and facilitated an accelerated move up the product cycle quality ladder. To this should be added the substantial volume of advice proffered by customers abroad concerning desirable design, quality and product modifications, already a feature in the earlier, labor intensive period. These opportunities for both product and process innovation were additionally enhanced by the concerted effort to attract previously "brain-drained" Taiwanese engineers and scientists from Silicon Valley and elsewhere to participate in the domestic production and export drive. Fully 70 percent of the companies in the Hsin Chu Science-Based Industrial Park have in recent years been led by returned overseas Chinese. It is estimated that almost 10,000 Taiwanese graduates of U.S. universities have returned in recent years, the vast majority taking up positions in high tech export-oriented industries. It should be clear that the combination of an increasingly highly skilled labor force and R&D investments became the dominant component of the interaction between productivity change and exports in recent years.

5.5 Conclusion

Trade and growth are seen to be mutually supportive throughout Taiwan's highly successful transition growth effort. The tendency in the recent literature to ascribe a "leading sector" role to trade is as misleading as earlier tendencies to focus exclusively on domestic development patterns. Early on, technology change and the mobilization of agriculture were at center stage, enabling agricultural and processed agricultural exports to expand rapidly and change their composition radically. Later on, as the economy's center of gravity shifted to an unskilled but literate labor-based output mix, the mutual reinforcements between domestic productivity increase and rapidly expanding light industry exports took over. Policy changes freeing up exports from import substitution regime controls and an extremely flexible labor market permitted Taiwan to utilize its low labor costs, combined with adaptations of imported technology, to take advantage of an expanding world economy. Technology imports were mainly of the simple non-proprietary and easily adaptable variety. Subsequently, Taiwan responded promptly to the early harbingers of labor shortage by shifting emphasis from primary to secondary, especially vocational, education, as well as to science and technology infrastructure, including the encouragement of private and public sector R&D. In recent years Taiwan has tried to prolong the life of her labor intensive exports by investing in neighboring countries, including Mainland China; at home she moved upstream and began to export increasingly high tech commodities. Increasingly, technology imports consisted of machines and multinational company patents and licenses of a proprietary character, inducing substantial "reverse engineering" or "pirating" among Taiwan's many medium and small-scale firms. Exports continued to grow and export composition to change. But persistent domestic learning by doing processes, relatively neglected by the authors of the East Asian Miracle volume, continued to induce exports — as much as exports induced further domestic productivity change.

5.6 Notes

1   The help of Amy Hwang of the Economics Institute, Academia Sinica, Taiwan, as well as the research assistance of Paul Hsu, Yale University, are gratefully acknowledged.

2   See Ranis and Stewart (1993).

5.7 References

Galenson, W. (ed.), 1979. *Economic Growth and Structural Change in Taiwan: The Postwar Experience of the Republic of China*. Ithaca, NY.: Cornell University Press.

Ho, Samuel P.S., 1977. Economic Development of Taiwan, 1860-1970, New Haven, CT.: Yale University Press,

Hymer, S. and S. Resnick, 1969. "A Model of An Agrarian Economy with Nonagricultural Activities," The American Economic Review, 59: 493-506.

Liang, Kuo-shu and Ching-ing Hou Liang, 1976. "Exports and Employment in Taiwan," in Institute of Economics, Academia Sinica, Conference on Population and Economic Development in Taiwan, Taipei, 1976: 192-246.

Lin, C.-Y., 1973. Industrialization in Taiwan, 1946-72: Trade and Import-Substituting Policies for Developing Countries. New York: Praeger.

Little, Ian M. D., 1979. "An Economic Reconnaissance," in W. Galenson (ed.), op. cit, Chapter 7. Ithaca, NY.: Cornell University Press: 448-507.

Pack, H., 1992, "New Perspectives on Industrial Growth in Taiwan," in G. Ranis (ed.), Taiwan: From Developing to Mature Economy. Boulder, CO: Westview Press.

Ranis, G. and F. Stewart, 1993. "Rural Nonagricultural Activities in Development: Theory and Application," Journal of Development Economics, 40: 75-101.

Resnick, S., 1970. "The Decline of Rural Industry under Export Expansion: A Comparison Among Burma, Philippines and Thailand, 1870-1938," Journal of Economic History 30: 51-73.

Riedel, J., 1984. "Trade as the Engine of Growth in Developing Countries, Revisited," Economic Journal, 94: 56-73.

Thorbecke, E., 1979. "Agricultural Development," in W. Galenson (ed.), op. cit., Chapter 2. Ithaca, N.Y.: Cornell University Press: 132-205.

Wang, J.C., 1994, "Cooperative Research in a Newly Industrialized Country: Taiwan," Research Policy 23: 697-774.

World Bank, 1993, The East Asian Miracle: Economic Growth and Public Policy. New York: Oxford University Press.

6 A BALANCED BUDGET, STABLE PRICES AND FULL EMPLOYMENT: THE MACROECONOMIC ENVIRONMENT FOR TAIWAN'S GROWTH

Tzong-shian Yu

6.1 Introduction

During the last four decades, many developing countries have suffered enormous foreign debts, growing fiscal deficits, high inflation, serious unemployment, and chronic balance of payments problems. Although it has been a developing country for these 40 years, Taiwan, the Republic of China, overcame these economic pains before the 1990s and has experienced high economic growth. Generally speaking, since the 1980s, Taiwan has had no foreign debts;[1] prior to 1990, Taiwan enjoyed a fiscal surplus; and since 1954, except during the two oil crises of 1974 and 1980, Taiwan has not suffered from high inflation. Unemployment has not been a problem for Taiwan since 1970. But since 1980, Taiwan has been bothered by a shortage of labor instead. Finally, also since 1980, Taiwan has had no chronic balance of payments problems. These facts have all helped Taiwan to sustain its economic growth.

In this paper, I would like to explore three important economic conditions which have provided a healthy macroeconomic environment for Taiwan's economic growth. These three conditions are balanced budgets, stable prices, and full employment. I will first examine how these conditions influence economic growth and then analyze the role of the government in achieving a favorable macro-economic environment.

6.2 Taiwan's Economic Achievements

The initial conditions for Taiwan's economic development in the 1950s were unfavorable; Taiwan was hampered by political instability, military threats from the Chinese communist regime, high inflation, insufficient employment opportunities, and limited natural resources with high population density. Taiwan has gradually overcome these difficulties, and achieved spectacularly successful economic development with high economic growth, more equitable income distribution, mild inflation, a low unemployment rate, sound public finance and huge foreign exchange reserves. Taiwan has transformed itself from a developing to a mature economy.

6.2.1 Economic Growth

From 1952 through 1995, the average growth rate of Taiwan's GDP was 8.7 percent, the highest in the world. From 1952 to 1962, Taiwan's economy was dominated by the agricultural sector, and the average growth rate of GDP was 7.93 percent. Though the agricultural sector accounted for a large proportion of GDP, its contribution to the GDP growth rate was only 1.74 percent, while the industrial sector had a higher growth rate and made a larger contribution to economic growth, at 2.17 percent. This rapid economic growth was partly attributable to the expansion of the export of agricultural products, processed agricultural products, and textiles.

From 1963 to 1980, the average growth rate of GDP in Taiwan was 10 percent. The contribution rate of the agricultural sector fell to 0.55 percent, while that of the industrial sector increased to 4.75 percent, making it the greatest contributor to economic growth. During this period, agricultural product exports declined, while the export of manufactured products became very important. From 1981 to 1995, Taiwan's average growth rate slowed to 7.52 percent. The industrial sector's contribution was still large, but it declined somewhat because of the rapid appreciation of the NT dollar against the US dollar and because increases in production costs led to a deterioration in the international competitiveness of Taiwan's products.[2] The most significant change is that since 1981 the service sector has come to dominate the economy (see Table 6.1).

6.2.2 Stable Prices

From 1952 through 1995, except for 1974 and 1980, the inflation rate, in terms of the rate of change in the consumer price index, was very low. From 1952 to 1962, the average annual inflation rate was 8.9 percent, while from 1963 to 1980, the average inflation rate was 7.48 percent (if 1974 and 1980 are excluded, the average inflation rate was 4.89 percent). From 1981 to 1995, the average inflation rate was 3.32 percent per annum. The decreasing trend in the inflation rate has been mainly attributable to stable import prices. Sometimes consumer prices were subject to fluctuations in the price of domestically produced food, caused by natural disasters. Since 1981, as the importance of the industrial sector has gradually declined and the service sector has started to dominate the economy, the increase in wage rates in the service sector has played an important role in determining consumer prices.

Table 6.1. Structural Change in Sectors of Taiwan, R.O.C. (at 1991 Prices)

Year	Growth Rate of GDP	Agricultural Sector			Industrial Sector			Service Sector		
		Percentage	Growth Rate	Contribution	Percentage	Growth Rate	Contribution	Percentage	Growth Rate	Contribution
1952	11.98	32.22	11.75	3.79	19.69	3.33	0.71	48.10	16.11	7.47
1953	9.33	34.45	16.92	5.45	19.39	7.71	1.52	46.15	4.91	2.36
1954	9.54	28.03	-10.89	-3.75	23.92	35.13	6.81	48.05	14.04	6.48
1955	8.11	29.09	12.09	3.42	23.23	4.99	1.19	47.68	7.28	3.50
1956	5.50	27.45	-0.42	-0.12	24.41	10.86	2.52	48.13	6.51	3.10
1957	7.36	27.32	6.86	1.88	25.26	11.07	2.70	47.42	5.76	2.77
1958	6.71	27.76	4.52	1.24	24.83	4.88	1.23	48.41	8.94	4.24
1959	7.65	26.35	5.97	1.60	27.10	17.50	4.34	46.56	3.53	1.71
1960	6.31	28.54	15.14	3.99	26.87	5.42	1.47	44.59	1.83	0.85
1961	6.88	24.95	3.00	0.85	23.70	-3.70	-0.99	51.35	15.74	7.02
1962	7.90	23.81	2.95	0.74	24.19	10.15	2.41	52.00	9.27	4.76
1963	9.35	22.29	2.40	0.57	24.88	12.46	3.01	52.83	11.09	5.77
1964	12.20	22.48	13.15	2.93	26.01	17.27	4.30	51.51	9.41	4.97
1965	11.13	21.81	7.83	1.76	26.50	13.23	3.44	51.69	11.52	5.94
1966	8.91	20.56	2.66	0.58	27.76	14.13	3.74	51.67	8.88	4.59
1967	10.71	19.53	5.18	1.06	28.92	15.34	4.26	51.54	10.43	5.39
1968	9.17	18.77	4.93	0.96	30.57	15.36	4.44	50.66	7.30	3.76
1969	8.95	16.55	-3.97	-0.75	33.01	17.65	5.39	50.45	8.49	4.30
1970	11.37	15.49	4.27	0.71	34.71	17.12	5.65	49.80	9.94	5.01
1971	12.90	13.84	0.84	0.13	36.84	19.84	6.89	49.32	11.81	5.88
1972	13.32	12.58	3.00	0.42	38.92	19.71	7.26	48.50	11.43	5.64
1973	12.83	11.50	3.11	0.39	40.07	16.15	6.29	48.44	12.69	6.15
1974	1.16	11.61	2.19	0.25	38.96	-1.65	-0.66	49.43	3.24	1.57
1975	4.93	10.61	-4.09	-0.47	39.44	6.24	2.43	49.94	6.01	2.97
1976	13.86	10.09	8.26	0.88	42.13	21.60	8.52	47.78	8.94	4.46
1977	10.19	9.51	3.79	0.38	42.97	12.41	5.23	47.52	9.59	4.58
1978	13.59	8.28	-1.04	-0.10	44.78	18.36	7.89	46.94	12.21	5.80
1979	8.17	8.01	4.64	0.38	44.50	7.51	3.36	47.49	9.43	4.43
1980	7.30	7.32	-2.00	-0.16	45.33	9.28	4.13	47.36	7.01	3.33
1981	6.16	7.30	-0.38	-0.03	45.38	6.30	2.85	47.32	7.04	3.34
1982	3.55	7.73	2.45	0.18	44.40	1.30	0.59	48.87	5.85	2.77
1983	8.45	7.30	1.78	0.14	44.95	9.80	4.35	47.75	8.15	3.98
1984	10.60	6.33	1.80	0.13	46.16	12.69	5.71	45.22	9.82	4.69
1985	4.95	5.78	2.22	0.14	46.27	3.66	1.68	47.95	6.51	2.94
1986	11.64	5.54	-0.04	-0.02	47.11	13.30	6.02	47.35	11.48	5.50
1987	12.74	5.30	5.86	0.32	46.45	12.43	5.71	48.05	13.75	6.51
1988	7.84	5.03	1.05	0.06	44.83	5.18	2.37	50.14	10.97	5.27
1989	8.23	4.90	-0.55	-0.03	42.31	4.50	2.01	52.79	12.28	6.25
1990	5.39	4.17	2.08	0.10	41.35	1.09	0.47	54.60	9.17	4.84
1991	7.55	3.79	1.76	0.08	41.07	6.82	2.82	55.14	8.54	4.66
1992	6.76	3.45	-2.87	-0.11	40.11	4.28	1.76	56.44	9.27	5.11
1993	6.32	3.42	5.44	0.19	39.29	4.12	1.65	57.29	7.93	4.48
1994	6.54	3.07	-4.37	-0.15	38.97	5.69	2.24	57.96	7.77	4.45
1995	6.06	2.96	2.40	0.07	38.88	5.79	2.26	58.16	6.43	3.73
Average										
1952-62	7.93	28.18	6.17	1.74	23.87	9.76	2.17	48.04	8.54	4.02
1963-80	10.00	14.49	3.06	0.55	35.91	14.00	4.75	49.60	9.41	4.70
1981-95	7.52	4.74	1.24	0.06	43.16	6.46	2.85	51.67	9.00	4.57

Note: (Rate of contribution)i = (growth rate)$_i$ x(percentage distribution)$_{i-1}$

Source: The National Income of the Republic of China, Prepared by the Directorate-General of Budget, Accounting and Statistics.

Taiwan does not have rich natural resources, so external factors are very important in determining prices. Fluctuations in import prices, and changes in tariffs and foreign exchange rates have had substantial impacts on domestic prices. In fact, from 1961 to 1995, import prices remained stable, tariff rates tended to decline, and the New Taiwan dollar appreciated against the US dollar from 40:1 to 27:1, which was helpful in reducing import prices to some extent.

6.2.3   Full Employment
It is rather difficult to define "full employment." According to the American standard,[3] Taiwan has had no unemployment problems since 1964. Statistics indicate that Taiwan's average unemployment rate was 3.95 percent from 1952 to 1962, 2.14 percent from 1963 to 1980, and 1.93 percent from 1981 to 1995. Since the 1980s, Taiwan has had a shortage of labor; guest workers have been imported from the Philippines, Thailand, and Malaysia. The shortage of labor has mainly been felt in construction, labor-intensive manufacturing, and domestic service. Although Taiwanese overseas investment has substantially increased during the last ten years, it has not obviously caused corresponding unemployment problems (see Table 6.2).

6.2.4   A Balanced Budget
For most of the past four decades, the ROC government maintained a sound public finance system. Budget deficits occurred during only seven of the 36 years from 1952 to 1988, and these were mostly in the period before 1963. Until 1988 the government maintained a fiscal surplus, which was used in the 1970s to finance the completion of public works projects. Strict controls on spending and conservative estimates of revenues are important aspects of maintaining sound public finance. Among Chinese policy-makers, maintaining a surplus budget is regarded as sound public finance.

However, since 1989, the government has spent NT$287.5 billion purchasing land for planned but not realized projects from private landlords, and then supporting a six-year national development plan and the National Health Insurance system. This spending has turned the fiscal surplus into a fiscal deficit. To cope with this problem, the government has tried to maintain a zero growth level in government consumption expenditure so as to reestablish a balanced budget.[4]

6.3   The Relevance of Each Factor to Economic Growth

When dealing with economic growth in a developed economy, we can only take its macroeconomic environment into consideration. For a developing economy, on the other hand, the non-macroeconomic environment is equally important.[5] As Taiwan is a newly industrializing economy, when we discuss its economic growth, we should assume "other things being equal" so as to simplify our analysis.

6.3.1   Stable Prices and Economic Growth
Generally speaking, economic growth is based on macroeconomic stability. In a narrow sense, economic stability means stable prices. Mild inflation is tolerable, but

Table 6.2   Main Economic Indicators of Taiwan

Year	Growth Rate of GDP	Inflation Rate*	Unemployment Rate	Gini Coefficient
1952	11.98	4.36		
1953	9.33	18.80	4.13	
1954	9.54	1.70	4.02	
1955	8.11	9.90	3.73	
1956	5.50	10.50	3.65	
1957	7.36	7.50	3.66	
1958	6.71	1.30	3.80	
1959	7.65	10.60	3.82	
1960	6.31	18.50	4.01	
1961	6.88	7.80	4.21	
1962	7.90	2.40	4.11	
Average	7.93	8.90	3.95	
1963	9.35	2.20	4.33	
1964	12.20	-0.20	4.22	0.321
1965	11.13	-0.10	3.30	
1966	8.91	2.00	3.00	0.323
1967	10.71	3.40	2.29	
1968	9.17	7.93	1.72	0.326
1969	8.95	5.05	1.88	
1970	11.37	3.55	1.70	0.294
1971	12.90	2.83	1.66	
1972	13.32	3.01	1.49	0.291
1973	12.83	8.19	1.26	
1974	1.16	47.47	1.53	0.287
1975	4.93	5.22	2.40	
1976	13.86	2.50	1.78	0.280
1977	10.19	7.04	1.76	0.284
1978	13.59	5.76	1.67	0.287
1979	8.17	9.76	1.28	0.285
1980	7.30	19.00	1.23	0.277
Average	10.00	7.48	2.14	
1981	6.16	16.33	1.36	0.281
1982	3.55	2.72	2.14	0.283
1983	8.45	1.59	2.71	0.287
1984	10.60	-0.22	2.44	0.287
1985	4.95	-0.40	2.91	0.290
1986	11.64	0.70	2.66	0.296
1987	12.74	0.52	1.97	0.299
1988	7.84	1.29	1.69	0.303
1989	8.23	4.40	1.57	0.303
1990	5.39	4.13	1.67	0.312
1991	7.55	3.62	1.51	0.308
1992	6.76	4.47	1.51	0.312
1993	6.32	2.94	1.45	0.316
1994	6.54	4.09	1.56	0.318
1995	6.06	3.68	1.79	
Average	7.52	3.32	1.93	

*The Rate of Change in Consumer Price Index.

Sources: 1. Statistical Abstract of National Income, Taiwan Area, Republic of China, 1951-1992, Directorate-General of Budget, Accounting and Statistics, Executive Yuan. 2. Report on the Survey of Personal Income Distribution in Taiwan Area, R.O.C.

hyperinflation has numerous detrimental effects, including the disruption of efficient allocation of resources, and the creation of distortions in investment. Hyperinflation is no different from a tax levied more on the poor than on the rich, which in turn is unfavorable to income distribution. Particularly for a trade-oriented economy such as Taiwan, hyperinflation tends to hamper the expansion of exports and to retard their diversification because it causes prices to rise relative to those in competing countries. Once a country's exports lose their competitiveness in the world market, exports plummet immediately.

High inflation rates are usually coupled with low growth rates, as can be verified by the Taiwan case. For instance, in 1973 and 1974, when there was hyperinflation caused by the oil crisis, the wholesale price index increased by 22.8 percent and 40.6 percent, and the consumer price index increased by 8.2 percent and 47.5 percent, respectively. At the same time, the growth rate was 1.16 percent and 4.93 percent, with a one-year lag. Another oil crisis took place in 1979 and 1980. This time the wholesale price index increased by 13.8 percent and 21.6 percent in 1979 and 1980 and the consumer price index increased by 9.76 percent in 1979, 19 percent in 1980, and 16.33 percent in 1981, while the growth rate was 7.3 percent, 6.16 percent and 3.55 percent with a one-year lag.

Table 6.3 provides an estimate of the relation between inflation and growth by a simple regression. In equations 1 to 3, growth is negatively related to inflation at a statistically significant level in the periods 1960 to 1995 and 1960 to 1980; but negatively and insignificantly related to inflation in the period 1981 to 1995.

Table 6.3   Relationship between Growth and Inflation in Taiwan

Equation Number	Observation Period	Dependent Variable	Constant	Independent Variable P_c	$\overline{R}^2$
1	1960-1980	y	11.280 (17.979)	-0.220 (4.483)	0.488
2	1981-1995	y	8.273 (9.935)	-0.217 (1.323)	0.0508
3	1960-1995	y	9.761 (17.709)	-0.174 (3.259)	0.216
				P_w	
4	1953-1980	e	19.745 (5.882)	-0.342 (1.172)	0.0136
5	1981-1995	e	10.148 (4.944)	-0.394 (0.645)	-0.0435
6	1953-1995	e	15.381 (6.866)	-0.126 (0.535)	-0.0175

Where   y :   the growth rate of GDP
        Pc: inflation rate in terms of the rate of change in consumer price index
        e :   the growth rate of exports
        Pw: the rate of change in wholesale price index
        $\overline{R}^2$:   corrected coefficient of determination

Table 6.3 also indicates that the growth rate of exports is negatively but not significantly related to the rate of change in the wholesale price index, which resulted from the fact that during the period of observation, exports in Taiwan maintained rapid growth almost every year while the wholesale price index remained rather stable. In other words, mild inflation was not harmful to the expansion of exports. If we check the period of the oil crisis, however, we find that inflation and exports were closely related. In 1974-75, exports declined by 5.7 percent (in New Taiwan dollars) and by 5.8 percent (in US dollars), and imports declined by 14.7 percent (in NT dollars) and by 14.6 percent (in US dollars). In 1981-82, exports increased by 4.2 percent (in NT dollars) and by 1.8 percent (in US dollars), and imports decreased by 5.5 percent (in NT dollars) and by 10.9 percent (in US dollars).

Since foreign trade is a leading sector in Taiwan's economy, changes in foreign trade are closely related to economic growth. The historical record reveals that without the growth of foreign trade, it would have been impossible to have had rapid economic growth in Taiwan. Obviously, serious inflation is detrimental to economic growth.

6.3.2   Full Employment and Economic Growth

Employment and economic growth also are closely related, but it is hard to say which one is cause and which is effect. Economic growth is helpful for reducing or eliminating unemployment, while during recessions many factories go bankrupt, and layoff problems occur. Furthermore, unemployment is detrimental to income distribution and social stability. Consequently, full employment is a goal of economic development in all countries.

Economic growth may be defined as the growth of production. In the production function, labor, capital, technology and management are the most important factors. Among them, labor, including both blue and white collar labor, is the soul of economic activities. Increases in labor productivity depend mainly on the ethics and skill of labor. However, without effective demand for products, recession and unemployment will still result.

In Taiwan's case, if foreign markets had not absorbed its products during the last forty years, it would have been impossible to achieve such high economic growth. From the 1950s to the 1970s, in particular, Taiwan developed the labor-intensive industries that created many job opportunities for people and increased their income. If this had not happened, Taiwan would still be a poor country. So the outward-looking development strategy and the policy of promoting the development of labor-intensive industries were both no doubt effective for Taiwan.

The strategy of outward-looking development meant that the government encouraged investment in production for export, and encouraged export to pay for import of items which could support further production, which in turn was for domestic demand and export. In the period from 1950 to 1965, Taiwan's main exports were agricultural products and processed agricultural products, which absorbed underemployed and unemployed farmers. Then, in the period from 1966 to 1985, the main exports were labor-intensive manufactured products, which created many job opportunities for the people who were moving at that time from rural to urban areas. Because appropriate employment was readily available for all these people, national income, living standards, and educational levels could all be raised and social problems avoided.

In 1952, the agricultural sector accounted for 56.1 percent of total employment, the industrial sector for 16.9 percent and the service sector for 27 percent. This indicates that the agricultural sector was extremely important to employment. However, from 1952 on, employment in the agricultural sector started to gradually decline, while the industrial sector absorbed most of the labor thus released. In 1973, employment in the industrial sector first exceeded that in the agricultural sector, with the former accounting for 33.7 percent of total employment while the latter was 30.49 percent. In the same year, the former's production accounted for 40.07 percent of GDP while the latter's production was only 11.50 percent. From 1973 until 1987, the industrial sector kept growing rapidly, not only in its production but in its employment, and since then, both have tended to decline because of the increasing sluggishness of labor-intensive industries in Taiwan.

Manufacturing is the major type of industry in the industrial sector.[6] It can be roughly divided into light industry and heavy industry. In Taiwan, the former is usually characterized by labor-intensive production processes while the latter uses capital- and technology-intensive production processes. From the late 1970s, the proportion of light industry in manufacturing tended to decline while that of heavy industry increased substantially. For instance, in 1976, light industry accounted for 59.71 percent of manufacturing while heavy industry accounted for 40.29 percent. By 1987, the former was exceeded by the latter. By the end of 1995, heavy industry accounted for 63.71 percent of the total.

An empirical estimate of the relationship between economic growth and the unemployment rate indicates that from 1952 to 1980 they were negatively related but at a statistically insignificant level. From 1981 to 1995, and from 1952 to 1995, they were positively related, but again at a statistically insignificant level. This finding is inconsistent with prior expectations, but can be explained by the fact that during the period of time, both tended to decline slightly.[7]

6.3.3   Balanced Budgets and Economic Growth

Many governments want to have a balanced budget. But, for many countries, public debt seems to be inevitable. So far, there is no theory to provide a debt ratio critical for solvency. For instance, in some developed countries — Belgium, Ireland, and Italy — public debt relative to GDP is considerably higher than in prominent developing debtor countries, yet there is no debt crisis. In many developing countries, such as Brazil and Mexico, the share of their public debts in GDP is lower than the developed countries mentioned above, but they have serious debt crises. Brazil and Mexico had debt crises; but Indonesia and Korea had no insolvency problems. This difference may depend on how these governments made use of their foreign debt (See Table 6.4) In effect, foreign loans used for the set-up of factories are quite different from those used for poorly planned infrastructure.[8]

The relation between balanced budgets and economic growth can be analyzed by the following equation:

Table 6.4   Net public debt as a percentage of GDP (1986–87)

Country	Domestic	Foreign	Total
Brazil	20.5	26.1	46.6
Mexico	40.4	53.4	93.8
Indonesia	n.a	53.0	14.4
Korea	6.1	8.3	113.9
Belgium	92.6	21.3	129.3
Ireland	78.3	51.0	76.8
Italy	74.8	2.0	

Source: refer to Reison, 1994.

$$R - (CG+IG) \quad = \quad 0 \quad \text{Balanced budget}$$
$$> \quad 0 \quad \text{Surplus budget}$$
$$< \quad 0 \quad \text{Deficit budget}$$

where   R: government revenue, including taxes and other revenues

CG: government consumption expenditure

IG: government investment

CG +IG: total government expenditure

Balanced Budgets. When total government revenue equals total government expenditure, the government budget is balanced. Under this condition, the government does not waste its resources nor does the government become a source of inflation. So a balanced budget has become a goal for many governments. Actually, balanced budgets rarely exist because government revenues cannot be totally controlled, even if government expenditure can be managed exactly as planned.[9]

Surplus Budgets. A surplus budget is when total government revenue exceeds total government expenditure. If the surplus is very large, theoretically it is a waste of resources since the government did not make effective use of resources which could have been used by the private sector. In Taiwan, prior to 1988, the government maintained a budget surplus in most years (See Table 6.5). In the 1970s, the government used the accumulated surplus to fund 22 major development projects without issuing bonds to the public.[10] These projects have made great contributions to Taiwan's rapid economic growth in later years, on the one hand, and helped Taiwan avoid recession during the two oil crises, on the other. Consequently, from 1973 to 1980 the average growth rate was still high, say 9 percent.

A simple regression estimating the relationship between budget balances and economic growth shows a positive, though not statistically significant, relationship.[11]

Deficit Budgets. When total government expenditure exceeds total government revenue, a deficit budget results. A deficit can be financed by several approaches. The first one is to increase taxes. However, in a democratic society, it is difficult to raise tax rates or to introduce new taxes, because doing so may cause the ruling party to lose in the next election. Another approach is to issue public bonds; this is, however, a measure that feeds debt with debt, and the public may have no desire or no ability to buy public bonds. A third way is to sell public property. This possibility is strictly limited by the amount of public property available. Once all the public properties are sold off, the government has new trouble to overcome. A last option is to issue currency. This, of course, increases the money supply, and has inflationary effects.

Table 6.5   Surplus and Deficit of General Government

(in Current Value)

Unit: NT$ Million

Year	Savings* (1)	Real Surplus** (2)	Real Surplus as Pct. of Current Revenue (3)	External Public Debt (US$ Million)
1971	7,590	1,317	2.38	.
1972	16,355	6,295	9.04	.
1973	20,217	8,926	10.45	.
1974	38,365	14,648	12.27	.
1975	32,395	−2,207	−1.70	.
1976	47,393	−2,198	1.38	.
1977	50,440	−7,169	3.90	.
1978	69,695	12,340	5.50	.
1979	93,813	21,722	7.65	.
1980	95,565	16,633	4.90	.
1981	92,928	6,141	1.52	4,796
1982	69,375	−41,168	−9.91	5,661
1983	88,633	−3,487	−6.54	6,290
1984	103,732	−1,273	−0.26	5,535
1985	97,063	−28,711	−5.53	4,763
1986	90,563	−37,655	−6.97	3,236
1987	161,823	23,979	3.67	1,660
1988	210,490	25,954	3.34	1,529
1989	256,374	−288,578	−31.40	1,146
1990	204,019	−94,269	−9.32	898
1991	85,184	−288,364	−27.64	714
1992	197,695	−198,980	−15.90	455
1993	236,385	−194,119	−14.37	395
1994	231,786	−301,031	−21.20	360
1995	161,051	−406,252	−28.45	305

*Current Government Revenue − Current Government Expenditure = Savings
**Real Surplus = Savings + Capital revenue − Capital expenditure
Source: Annual Report of Fiscal Statistics, ROC.

In Taiwan, the government started to run large deficits only since 1989, but they have been increasing with time. Before 1989, when Taiwan maintained a budget surplus, the relationship between inflation rate and money supply (M2) was rather negatively related, but not at a statistically significant level. We have related inflation rate to the difference between money supply (M2) and economic growth, and found that they are positively related, but again not at a level which is statistically significant.[12] These results also reflect the fact that during the last forty years, Taiwan achieved high economic growth with low inflation and no fiscal deficit.[13]

6.4 Government's Role in Achieving a Favorable Macroeconomic Environment

The government plays a very important role in the achievement of a favorable macroeconomic environment, particularly in developing countries. First of all, the government must have strong leadership to maintain social and political stability, which are essential to stimulate saving and investment. In an unstable society, it is almost impossible to avoid serious inflation and unemployment. In the 1980s, many countries in Latin America suffered from serious inflation and unemployment because of their social and political instability. However, the government in Taiwan has always stood firm against activities that threaten to destabilize Taiwan socially and politically, and maintained a healthy and growing society.

6.4.1 *Making Effective Use of US Aid*
After World War II, many developing countries received aid from the United States, but Taiwan today is one of the most successful of these countries. At the early stage of Taiwan's economic development, Taiwan needed money to improve its infrastructure and to develop new industries, and the US aid gave Taiwan a big boost for its take-off. For instance, Taiwan used imported cotton to establish its textile industry, imported wheat to set up a flour milling industry, and imported machinery to establish a plastic industry. The textile industry became the major industry in the early industrial period in Taiwan and made the greatest contribution to the expansion of foreign trade. The flour milling industry has enriched the Taiwanese people's food, and the plastic industry has also become an important export industry.

6.4.2 *Adopting Appropriate Economic Strategies*
For any developing country, the choice of economic strategies is closely related to its economic development. Appropriate economic strategies can help achieve the goal of economic growth while inappropriate economic strategies waste resources and retard economic development. Taiwan's choice of an outward-looking strategy helped Taiwan overcome a scarcity of natural resources and promote industrial growth. Giving priority to developing the agricultural sector laid a strong foundation for the development of the industrial sector. Giving priority to developing labor-intensive industry created a comparative advantage which not only helped raise

Taiwan's competitiveness but also absorbed surplus labor released from the agricultural sector, which was helpful for the elimination of unemployment. Giving priority to developing small- and medium-sized enterprises was also helpful for the creation of job opportunities.

6.4.3   Establishing Special Zones for Industrial Development

In a society with a strong sense of protectionism and out-of-date regulations and laws, like early postwar Taiwan, it is very difficult for the government to undertake radical policies. So, in order to attract investment and encourage export, the government in Taiwan had to take some roundabout measures, including, for instance, the establishment of the export-processing zones in the 1960s and the Hsinchu Science-based Industrial Park in the 1980s. In the zones and park, the government provided better infrastructure, simplified administrative procedures and offered businesses preferential treatment. The export processing zones helped create many job opportunities and introduced some management skills, while the industrial park has introduced many new technologies and helped promote industrial transformation from labor-intensive to technology-intensive production.

6.4.4   Making Use of Incentives

In order to assist the development of export-oriented industries, the government of Taiwan employed fiscal and financial measures. These included the epoch-making "19-point Financial and Economic Reform" (1959), and the "Statute for Encouragement of Investment" (1960), both of which made substantial contributions to the development of Taiwan's industries in the 1960s and the 1970s. In 1991, the government discarded the latter statute and promulgated the "Statute for Upgrading Industries" instead. This new statute is designed to encourage industries to enhance their R&D programs and reduce their emissions of pollution.[14]

The above strategies and policy measures have made great contributions to economic growth and full employment in Taiwan. The expansion of foreign trade has helped accumulate foreign exchange reserves which have contributed indirectly to price stability through the import of agricultural products and raw materials for industrial use. As for a balanced budget, before 1989, the government had strict control over government expenditure, so there was no fiscal deficit. Unfortunately, since 1991, the political environment in Taiwan has dramatically changed, with social welfare programs becoming a hot issue in elections. The ruling party has chosen to adopt these programs in order to win elections, thus the government no longer strictly controls the budget.[15]

6.5   Concluding Remarks

Roughly speaking, before 1990, Taiwan had very mild inflation, a low unemployment rate and sound public finance, all of which constituted favorable conditions for economic growth. The average growth rate during the period 1952-1990 was 8.7 percent, the highest in the world. This wonderful achievement was made under stable, harmonious social and political conditions, provided by an effective and strong government.

Since the late 1980s, when martial law was discarded, various social movements (including labor-management disputes, the environmental movement, farmer protests, etc.) and the democratization movement have taken place simultaneously. These movements have eroded the government's authority and the investment climate has deteriorated as well. Some people are now wondering whether the process of democratization is unfavorable to economic growth. During the last six years (1990-1995), the average growth rate in Taiwan declined to about 6.4 percent, much lower than that achieved during the period from 1952 to 1990.

It is expected that in the next decade the average growth rate will be moderate, say 6 percent, with mild inflation and low unemployment. But a balanced budget will no longer exist since it will take time to learn to fine-tune our democracy and to mediate the competing interests of pressure groups. This will slow policy-making and reduce the administrative efficiency of Taiwan's government.

6.6 Notes

1. See Table 6.5.

2. Due to the increasing trade surplus and huge foreign exchange reserves, the New Taiwan dollar appreciated rapidly against the US dollar, by 53 percent between January 1986 and January 1989. In other words, the price of exports increased substantially. At the same time, social movements such as the environmental protection movement and political confrontation reduced productivity and increased production costs.

3. In the United States, when the unemployment rate falls to 4 percent, this means full employment. It is impossible for any country to achieve zero unemployment because of frictional unemployment.

4. From 1993 to 1996, the annual growth rates of government consumption expenditure were 0.56 percent, -1.19 percent, 0.35 percent and 1.67 percent, respectively. However, this did not help substantially to reduce the fiscal deficit.

5. Generally speaking, all developed economies are market economies with democratic systems. When dealing with economic development, we may assume "other things being equal," which is a conventional assumption in economic analysis.

6. The manufacturing sector includes mining, manufacturing, construction, and utilities.

7. See the following table.

Equation Number	Observation Period	Dependent Variable	Constant	Independent Variable, y	$\overline{R}^2$
(i)	1952-1980	u	3.568 (4.878)	-0.079 (1.041)	0.0030
(ii)	1981-1995	u	1.472 (3.369)	0.061 (1.110)	0.0163

where   u: unemployment rate
        y: growth rate of GDP
        $\overline{R}^2$ corrected coefficient of determination

8. In many developing countries in Latin America, governments took on numerous foreign loans, but then used them to build highways unnecessary for economic development.

9. It is very difficult to forecast total government revenue. It mainly depends on aggregate economic conditions, such as prosperity or recession, and also on the efficiency of tax collection.

10. Including Ten Major Development projects and Twelve Development projects.

11. The estimates, made by simple regression, are in the following table.
    Relationship Between Budget Balance and Economic Growth (1971–1995)
    y=f(BB)

Equation	Observation Period	Dependent Variable	Constant	Independent Variable BB	$\overline{R}^2$
	1971-1995	y	8.3750 (7.477)	0.1807 (1.065)	0.0095

Where   Y: growth rate of GDP,
        BB: budget balance as percent of current government revenue.
        $\overline{R}^2$:   Corrected coefficient of determination

12. The estimates, made by simple regression, are in the following table.
    Relationship Between Money Supply and Inflation

Equation	Observation Period	Dependent Variable	Constant	Independent Variables, m_2	$\overline{R}^2$
	1962-1995	CPI	7.272 (1.409)	-0.081 (0.357)	-0.0272
	1962-1995	CPI	2.071 (0.571)	(m_2-y) 0.265 (1.036)	0.0022

where   CPI: inflation rate
        m_2:   rate of change in money supply, m_2
        y: growth rate of GDP
        $\overline{R}^2$:   corrected coefficient of determination

13. From the 1960s to the 1980s, Taiwan had no fiscal deficit.

14. The tax reductions and exemptions used for encouraging exports in the Statute for Encouragement of Investment were considered a kind of subsidy on exports to the United States, so the US government opposed it as unfair trade, while in the Statute for Upgrading Industries, the tax reductions and exemptions are mainly for encouraging investment in R&D. Therefore, they are not considered a subsidy to exports.

15. In elections, candidates promise to accept the suggestions of voters in order to win, without thinking about whether these suggestions are realistic or not. As soon as they win the elections, they try to do what they have promised so as to gain support for the next round of elections.

6.7 References

Barro, Robert, 1986a. "U.S. Deficits Since World War I," *Scandinavian Journal of Economics*, 88: 195-222.

Barro, Robert, 1986b. "The Behavior of United States Deficit," in R.J. Gordon (ed.), *The American Business Cycle: Continuity and Change*. Chicago: University of Chicago Press.

Chao-Hsi Huang and Kenneth S. Lin, 1991. "An Empirical Study on Taiwan's Tax Policy: 1966-1988," *Asian Economic Journal*, 5(3) (Nov): 323-338

Meier, Gerald M., 1964. *Leading Issues in Development Economics: Selected Materials and Commentary*. New York: Oxford University Press.

Reison, Helmut, 1994. *Debt, Deficits and Exchange Rates: Essays on Financial Interdependence and Development*. Aldershot, Hants, England: Edward Elgar Publishing Ltd., OECD.

Seiji Naya and Robert McCleery, 1994. "Relevence of Asian Development Experiences to African Problems," *Occasional Papers*, No. 39. San Francisco: International Center for Economic Growth.

Todaro, Michael P, 1994. *Economic Development*, 5th ed., London: Longman.

Yu, Tzong-shian, 1993. "Challenge and Responses: An Overview of Taiwan's Economic Development," *Industry of Free China*, (March): 19-27.

Yu, Tzong-shian, 1995. "The Role of Government in Economic Planning and Development: The Case of the ROC on Taiwan," *Occasional Paper Series*, No. 9503. Taipei: Chung-Hua Institution for Economic Research.

7 COMPARATIVE ADVANTAGE DEVELOPMENT STRATEGY AND THE ECONOMIC DEVELOPMENT OF TAIWAN

Justin Yifu Lin

After the industrial revolution in the 18th century, countries in the world could be divided into two groups. The first group can be termed the developed countries (DCs), Their economies are characterized by high per capita income, industrialization, and extensive use of capital-intensive technology. The second group is less-developed countries (LDCs) which are poor, agrarian, and use predominantly traditional technology in their production. The wealth of DCs is based on their industrial and technological advantages. Therefore, the question of how to industrialize the economy and catch up with the DCs has interested not only political leaders in the LDCs but also many intellectuals in the world since the 19th century (Gerschenkron, 1962; Lal, 1985).

Early work on the industrial gap between DCs and LDCs focused on the cultural differences in these two groups of countries. It was argued that a necessary condition for the industrial revolution in a country is a Protestant work ethic (Weber 1930). When development economics started to take shape in the post-war period, the focus changed to the importance of savings/investment (Harrod, 1939; Domar, 1946; Solow, 1988) and the potential role that the government can play in overcoming the defects of the market during development. These ideas were strongly influenced by the Soviet Union's initial success in nation building and the export pessimism about primary products formed during the Great Depression (Rosenstein-Rodan, 1943; Prebisch, 1959). The dominant view of development economics at that time advised LDC governments to ignore their own comparative advantages and to adopt an "inward-looking" capital-intensive, heavy-industry-oriented or import-substitution strategy that directly aimed to close their industrial/technological gap with the DCs as soon as possible (Chenery, 1961; Warr, 1994). Most LDCs, in both the socialist and capitalist camps, followed that advice. However, these economies were capital-scarce. To make the priority development of capital-intensive industries feasible in a capital-scarce economy, the government became "dirigiste" (Lal, 1983), intentionally distorting interest rates, foreign exchange rates and other price signals, and adopting planning mechanisms and administrative controls to allocate scarce resources to priority sectors (Lin et al., 1994). However, instead of accelerating growth, in many LDCs the adoption of this development strategy slowed economic development and caused the income and industrial/technological gaps between them and the DCs to become even larger.

Taiwan and other successful East Asian economies, except for Hong Kong, also followed the anti-comparative advantage development strategy initially, but soon abandoned it and switched to a strategy that was often referred to as "outward-oriented." Within less than three decades they have become known as the newly industrialized economies (NIES) (World Bank, 1993). Many LDCs are now attempting to reform their economies and adopt the policies that brought about the East Asian miracles (Perkins and Roemer, 1991; Krueger 1992).

The remarkable economic development in Taiwan and other East Asian economies and the relative stagnation of LDCs in other parts of the world have attracted much attention (Balassa, 1982; Harberger, 1985; Hughes, 1988; Lau, 1990; James, Naya, and Meier, 1987; World Bank, 1985; Ranis and Mahmood, 1992). Economists working on comparative studies have produced many stylized facts — such as the investment in human capital, the high saving propensity, the outward-looking policies, and so on — about the East Asian economies. There are two competing and contradictory generalizations about the experiences of these economies. One school argues that their success was due to the fact that governments in these countries got the relative prices right and allowed markets to function well (World Bank, 1985 and 1993; James, Naya, and Meier, 1987). The other school attributes their success to just the opposite (Johnson, 1982; Amsden, 1989; Wade, 1990).

The first school's position is too idealized. Taiwanese, Korean, and Japanese governments all actively used import quotas and licenses, credit subsidies, tax exemptions, public ownership, etc. to nurture and protect infant industry. Therefore, Amsden claims Taiwan and Korea are cases in which "wrong prices yield the right outcome" (see Amsden's paper in this Conference). However, the second school cannot explain why similar governmental interventions in Latin America, Africa, and the rest of Asia failed miserably (Rodrik, 1995). In these remarks, I would like to attempt a new interpretation which can reconcile the conflicts between the above two schools and tell us why government interventions brought in rapid industrialization and development in East Asian economies but causes miserable failures in other economies.

My argument in a nutshell is as follows: An economy's industrial/technological structure reflects the endowment structure — i.e., the relative abundance of labor, capital, and natural resources — of the economy. The attempt to upgrade a country's overall industrial/technological structure can succeed only when the country increases both human and physical capital in its overall endowment structure. If the government adopts a policy framework that provides economic agents with incentives to exploit the economy's existing comparative advantage, the economy will be competitive, will have large profits, and can achieve rapid accumulation of physical as well as human capital. As such, the economy's dynamic change in comparative advantage will be fast and can support a quick upgrading of its industrial/technological structure. The incentives to use and to exploit an economy's comparative advantage depends on the relative prices in the economy. If the relative prices reflect the relative scarcities of factors and commodities in the economy, which occurs only through market competition, then economic agents will make their industrial/technological choice in accordance with the economy's comparative advantage. Therefore, it is essential for a country's development to rely on market mechanisms to get the relative prices right.

An economy's endowment structure is not stationary. During the development process, an economy's technological/industrial structure needs to adjust continuously in response to changes in the endowment structure. Innovation involves risk and positive externality. Therefore, it is also desirable for the government to provide a limited scope of credit, tax or other forms of subsidies for the infant industries, consistent with the emerging comparative advantage of the economy, to compensate for the externality of innovation. On the other hand, if a government ignores the comparative advantage of its endowments and attempts to induce a "leap forward" in its industrial/technological structure — that is, to foster the development of industries which are too far away from the economy's comparative advantage — the government will have to institute a whole set of policy distortions in credit, foreign exchange, and other factors as well as product markets, and, in turn, use administrative means to direct the allocation of those resources. The economy will then become very inefficient, the changes in endowment structure will be very slow, and the attempt to upgrade the overall production/technological structure of the economy will eventually fail.

Taiwan's experience can be reconsidered in light of the above interpretation. In the early 1950s, Taiwan was poorly endowed with capital and its per capita GNP was only US$144. From this starting point, Taiwan did not adopt the heavy industry-oriented development strategy or a full-scale import-substitution strategy. Instead, in line with the capital-scarce and labor-abundant characteristics of her resource endowments, Taiwan relied on the development of labor-intensive and low-technology industries to push forward the industrialization of the whole economy. For example, in 1953-1960, the average annual growth rate of industrial output was 11 percent, and the fastest growing industries were agricultural product processing, foodstuffs, textile, plywood, cement, glass, etc. Because of the development of labor-intensive industries, the industrial share of the economic structure rose from 17.7 percent to 24.9 percent in this period, and the share of industrial products in total exports increased from 8.4 percent to 32.2 percent. The development laid a solid foundation for the subsequent economic takeoff.

Taiwan's rate of economic development was not hampered by its initial choice of labor-intensive light industry as the key sector. On the contrary, because its industrial structure reflected the comparative advantage of its resource endowment,

Taiwan's economy was very competitive in the world economy. Capital, both human and physical, was accumulated in the process. As Japan and other developed capitalist countries upgraded their economic structures to include more capital- and technology-intensive industries along with their accumulation of capital and technology, they gradually relocated their more labor-intensive manufacturing industries to developing economies. Taiwan's endowment structure at that time was in a good position to take advantage of this opportunity for relocated industries, through which it greatly developed its labor-intensive export-oriented processing industries, expanded its export of labor-intensive products, and further speeded up economic growth. Through the development of industries that captured the economy's comparative advantage, industrialization and upgrading of the economic structure accelerated. Between 1961 and 1973, the average annual growth rate of the GNP in Taiwan exceeded ten percent, and the average annual growth rate of industrial products was more than eighteen percent. The share of industry in the economy increased to 43.8 percent and the share of industrial products in exports reached 84.6 percent.

Along with the economic development and the increase of per capita GNP, Taiwan's labor costs gradually rose, and the level of capital accumulation also greatly increased. The country's comparative advantage started to change from the more labor-intensive industries to the more capital-intensive and technology-intensive ones. In line with the changes in comparative advantage, the industrial structure in Taiwan also adjusted accordingly. The economy's dominant industries shifted gradually from light industries, which depend on a cheap labor force, to more capital-intensive and technology-intensive new industries. For example, according to the classification of light industry and heavy industry, light industry made up 75.20 percent of total manufactured products in Taiwan in 1952, but dropped to 44.25 percent in 1990. Correspondingly, heavy industry increased from 24.80 percent to 55.75 percent.

According to the classification of factor intensity, from 1981 to 1990 the share of labor-intensive industry dropped from 50.0 percent to 43.8 percent. It is predicted that the percentage will be further reduced to 37.9 percent in 1996 and the capital- and technology-intensive industry will increase their share from 50.0 percent to 56.2 percent and 62.1 percent, respectively.

During the above development process, the Taiwanese government actively managed its trade. As Wade noted, Taiwan's success is not because the government manages its trade less than other developing economies but "Taiwan manages its trade differently from many other developing countries" (Wade 1990, p. 113). The difference is that the Taiwanese government's intervention has consistently acted in "anticipation of comparative advantage in such sectors as cotton textiles, plastics, basic metals, shipbuilding, automobiles, and industrial electronics" (Rodrik 1995). The industries that the Taiwanese government's industrial policy attempts to foster are in line with the change in her comparative advantage due to dynamic changes in the relative abundance of capital and labor. Therefore, despite the fact that the policy instruments used in Taiwan are similar to those used in countries adopting the anti- comparative advantage, leap-forward strategy, the subsidies and protection are less than elsewhere and more effective.

Finally, just like many other developing economies, Taiwan and the other miraculous East Asian economies, except for Hong Kong, also adopted an anti-comparative advantage, inward-looking, import-substitution strategy in the early 1950s (Tsiang, 1984). However, despite the fact that an import-substitution strategy has always been quite appealing to many intellectuals, economists, and policy makers in Taiwan and other East Asian economies, these economies soon gave up that strategy and switched to a policy framework that allowed their economies to develop along the line of comparative advantages. The contribution by brilliant economists, such as Professors Ta-Chung Liu and Sho-Chieh Tsiang, to the economic policy thinking in those economies was inarguably an important factor behind such policy changes. In addition, I would like to propose a yet to be tested hypothesis: The anti-comparative advantage, inward-looking, import-substitution strategy is very inefficient. The cost of following that strategy is very high to an economy. Therefore, how long an economy can sustain that strategy depends on 1) how rich the per capita natural endowment is in the economy, and 2) how large the economy's population is. The higher the per capita natural endowment in an economy, the more resources the government can mobilize to support the inefficient strategy, and therefore, the longer the strategy can be sustained. Similarly, the larger the population in an economy, the less each individual citizen needs to pay for the adoption of that strategy, and therefore, the longer the strategy can be tolerated. I propose that it was because the poor per capita natural endowment and the small population size that Taiwan and other East Asian economies gave up the inefficient import-substitution strategy earlier than other economies.

Taiwan and the miraculous East Asian economies unintentionally or even unwillingly adopted the policy framework that allowed their economies to foster changes in their endowment structure and to upgrade their industrial structure as their comparative advantage changed. It may be time to switch development policy thinking from focusing on changing an economy's industrial structure to changing its endowment structure, to call the policy framework that has been followed in Taiwan and other East Asian economies the "comparative advantage development strategy," and to encourage other LDCs to adopt that unintentional policy framework intentionally.

7.1 References

Amsden, Alice H., 1989. *Asia's Next Giant: South Korea and Late Industrialization.* Oxford: Oxford University Press.

Balassa, B. et al, 1982. *Development Strategies in Semi-industrial Economies*, Baltimore: Johns Hopkins University Press.

Chenery, Hollis B., 1961. "Comparative Advantage and Development Policy." *American Economic Review*, 51 (1): 18-51.

Domar, Evsey, 1946. "Capital Expansion, Rate of Growth, and Employment." *Econometrica*, pp. 137-47.

Gerschenkron, A.,1962. *Economic Backwardness in Historical Perspective.* Cambridge, Mass.: Harvard University Press.

Harberger, Arnold C. (ed.), 1985. *World Economic Growth*. San Francisco: ICS Press.

Harrod, Roy F., 1939. "An Essay in Dynamic Theory." *Economic Journal*, pp. 1433.

Hughes, Helen (ed.), 1988. *Achieving Industrialization in East Asia*. Cambridge: Cambridge University Press.

Ikeda and Hu Xin, 1993. *The Reconstruction of Economic Structure in Taiwan and Its Prospect for Development*, Beijing: China Economics Press.

James, William E., Seiji Naya, and Gerald M Meier, 1987. *Asian Development: Economic Success and Policy Lessons*. San Francisco: ICS Press.

Johnson, C. 1982. *MITI and the Japanese Miracle*. Stanford: Stanford University Press,.

Kruger, A.O., 1992. *Economic Policy Reform in Developing Countries*. Oxford: Basil Blackwell.

Lal, Deepak, 1983. *The Poverty of Development Economics*. London: IEA, Hobart Paperback 16.

Lal, Deepak, 1985. "Nationalism, Socialism and Planning: Influential Ideas in the South," *World Development*, 13, (6): 749-59.

Lau, Lawrence J., 1990. *Models of Development. (Revised and Expanded)* San Francisco: ICS Press.

Lin, Justin Yifu, Fan Cai, and Zhou Li, 1994. *The China Miracle: Development Strategy and Economic Reform*. Shanghai: People's Press and Sanlian Press, (simplified Chinese character edition); Hong Kong: the Chinese University of Hong Kong Press, 1995 (unsimplified Chinese character edition), 1996 (English Edition); Tokyo: Nihon

Perkins, D.H. and M. Roemer (eds.), 1991. *Reforming Economic System in Developing Countries*. Cambridge: Harvard University Press.

Prebisch, Raul, 1959. "Commercial Policy in the Underdeveloped Countries." *American Economic Review, Papers and Proceedings*, 49 (2): 251-73.

Ranis, Gustav, and Mahmood Syed, 1992. *The Political Economy of Development Policy Change.*, Cambridge, MA: Blackwell.

Rodrik, Dani, 1995. "Trade and Industrial Policy Reform," in J. Behrman and T.N. Srinivasan (eds.), *Handbook of Development Economics, Vol. 3*, Amsterdam: Elsevier.

Rosenstein-Rodan, P.,1943. "Problems of Industrialization of Eastern and Southeastern Europe." *Economic Journal*, June-September.

Solow, Robert M., 1988. *Growth Theory: An Exposition*. Oxford: Oxford University Press.

Tsiang, Sho-chieh, 1984. "Taiwan's Economic Miracle: Lessons in Economic Development." In Arnold C. Harberger (ed.), *World Economic Growth: Case Studies of Developed and Developing Nations*. San Francisco: ICS Press.

Wade, Robert., 1990. *Governing the Market: Economic Theory and the Role of Government in East Asian Industrialization*. Princeton: Princeton University Press.

Warr, Peter G., 1994. "Comparative and Competitive Advantage." *Asian Pacific Economic Literature*, 8 (2): 1-14.

Weber, Max, 1991. *The Protestant Ethic and the Spirit of Capitalism*, London: Harper, 1991 (First translation published in 1930).

World Bank, 1993. *The East Asian Miracle: Economic Growth and Public Policy*. Oxford: Oxford University Press.

World Bank, 1985. *World Development Report, 1985*. Oxford: Oxford University Press.

World Bank, 1993. *World Development Report, 1993*, Oxford: Oxford University Press.

PART III
THE LIU-TSIANG
POLICY PROPOSALS

8 THE LIU-TSIANG PROPOSALS FOR ECONOMIC REFORM IN TAIWAN: A RETROSPECTIVE

Jia-Dong Shea

8.1 Introduction

Professor T.C. Liu and Professor S.C. Tsiang, the two most well-known Chinese economists of their generation, have contributed to the economic development of Taiwan in many aspects. Professor Liu was in charge of the Tax Reform Commission from 1968 to 1970, in which Professor Tsiang was also actively involved. They advised on and/or made policy recommendations, sometimes jointly with Professors M.H. Hsing, John C. Fei, Anthony Y. Koo and Gregory C. Chow. Many of their suggestions materialized into actual policies implemented by the Taiwan authorities. Also, under Liu's suggestion, a macrocconometric model was used in the preparation of the government budget, the technique of national income accounting was improved, and input-output tables were compiled and put to use in decision making. In addition, they contributed to the promotion of economics research and Ph.D. student training by inviting many famous foreign scholars to either participate in international conferences or teach at the Ph.D. program of economics at National Taiwan University, and by setting up the Taiwan Institute of Economic Research and the Chung-Hua Institution for Economic Research.

Liu and Tsiang met each other for the first time in 1947 in Beijing. Since then, they often criticized economic policies and made policy suggestions together. The two of them formed a rare pair. Liu was an able speaker, very eloquent and energetic. Tsiang was a literary talent, very gentle and elegant. Usually, Tsiang was the one who wrote policy recommendation reports, whereas Liu was responsible for marketing the idea or persuading authorities to accept their suggestions.

Liu and Tsiang's economics knowledge and renowned reputation were the key factors that caught the attention of authorities. The recognition and trust they received from Chiang Kai-Shek and a technocratic cast such as K.Y. Yin, K.T. Li and K.H. Yu, who were willing to employ Liu and Tsiang to the best of their advantage, conferred upon Liu and Tsiang the ability to influence economic policies. However, after Yin, Liu and Chiang Kai-Shek passed away one after another, the support Tsiang received from the succeeding President Chiang Ching-Kuo was much weaker than from Chiang Kai-Shek. Tsiang's influence, and even the whole economics profession's influence, on economic policies in Taiwan went on a decline.

The Liu-Tsiang proposal of economic reform in Taiwan focused mostly on financial reform and tax reform. Their contributions to interest rate policy and foreign exchange reform are discussed respectively in Section II and III. Their tax reform proposals are reviewed in Section IV. The last section concludes with some final remarks.

8.2   Interest Rate Policy[1]

Partly influenced by the effective demand theory and the cost-push inflation theory of Keynesian macroeconomics, most developing countries in the early postwar period adopted a low interest rate policy by arbitrarily controlling bank interest rates at an artificially low level, in the mistaken belief that this would stimulate investment, facilitate growth, lower the price level, and thus curb domestic inflation. Tsiang strongly opposed this erroneous but popular belief by arguing that bank interest rates should be determined by market forces. Tsiang summarized his theoretical argument against the low interest rate policy in Tsiang (1979). Also, as early as 1947, when Tsiang was teaching at Beijing University, he wrote an article which urged the authorities to adopt a system of price-index-escalated savings certificates as a policy measure to curb the deteriorating inflation in China. Tsiang argued that this system, by paying savings deposits an interest rate on the basis of the price index, would effectively stimulate private savings and attract savings into banks to finance investments, which hitherto banks were obliged to finance through monetary expansion.

Although his suggestion of price-index-escalated savings certificates was not adopted by the authorities in 1947, it might have given the authorities the idea to introduce a special deposit facility, called the Preferential Interest Rate (PIR) Savings Deposits, in March 1950 to combat inflation in Taiwan. The PIR Deposits offered an extraordinary nominal interest rate of 7 percent per month for one-month savings deposits to attract funds to the savings accounts and absorb the excessive liquidity created by the budget deficit. The impact of these PIR Deposits was quick and effective. Total time and savings deposits rose rapidly, and the rising trend of prices was soon checked. Wholesale prices increased by only 0.4 percent per month from April to the end of June, compared to 10.3 percent during the first quarter of 1950.

The immediate success of the PIR Deposits, the resumption of U.S. aid in July 1950 after the outbreak of the Korean War, and fears that the 7 percent per month interest rate would be unsustainable with stable prices, induced the government to make sharp cuts to the PIR on one-month deposits — to 3.5 percent per month in July and to only 3 percent in October. The public's reaction was to stop depositing savings into banks, and even to withdraw savings. Prices resumed their rapid rise. This renewed inflation forced the monetary authorities to raise the PIR on one-month deposits from 3 percent to 4.2 percent in March 1951, leading to a resumption of savings into banks. Assisted by U.S. aid to the economy, and thus an improved budget, this latest PIR policy gradually led to a stabilization of prices in 1952. Thereafter, the authorities lowered the interest rate step by step whenever the stability of prices seemed to warrant it, with the PIR Deposits schemes being finally phased out in March 1955. Table 8.1 shows money supply, deposits, interest rates and wholesale prices for the period 1950-55.

This PIR Deposits experiment in Taiwan indicated that raising the controlled bank rates seemed to be an effective anti-inflationary measure. Liu and Tsiang in later years often advised authorities in Taiwan to adopt this policy to fight inflation, and repeatedly urged authorities to deregulate bank interest rates. In 1974, 1979 and 1980, when Taiwan faced the threat of inflation caused by energy crises, the Central Bank did raise bank interest rates as part of its stabilization package.[2] In the 1980s, the authorities in Taiwan also gradually liberalized bank interest rates.

The early successful experiment in Taiwan has been illustrated by McKinnon (1973) as empirical evidence supporting his proposal for developing countries to curb inflation by raising repressed bank rates. Establishing high time deposit rates has even become a standard part of policy advice given to developing countries by external economists, including experts of the World Bank and IMF in the 1980s (Van Wijnbergen, 1983: 433).

However, there were also cons to this policy recommendation of raising bank rates to curb inflation. Strong criticism came from some local economists such as Professor Tso-Yung Wang in Taiwan, and from structuralists including Van Wijnbergen (1983), Taylor (1983) and others. Their arguments can be summarized as follows: a) rapid recovery of production capacity and U.S. aid played much more important roles than the PIR Deposits policy in ending inflation in Taiwan;. b) raising the bank deposit rate will cause loanable funds to shift from the curb market to banks. Since banks are required to hold reserves against deposits, the increment of loanable funds of banks is less than the decrement in the curb market. Thus, the total amount of loanable funds decreases, and the curb market interest rate will be pushed up. A higher curb market rate as well as bank loan rate will then lead to a higher financing cost for working capital and hence a higher price level through cost-push.

One of the main reasons for Tsiang to argue for raising repressed bank rates is the adverse impact of a negative real interest rate on financial development. He also pointed out that, theoretically, raising repressed bank rates can lower the price level through at least three channels: a) a higher deposit rate can stimulate more savings, thus relaxing demand pressure on prices; b) after the bank deposit rate is raised, savers will shift their portfolio from unproductive or low productive assets like gold, jewelry, foreign exchange, commodity stock and real estate into bank deposits,

**Table 8.1   Money Supply; Savings, Time and PIR Deposits; Interest Rates;
Wholesale Prices, 1950–55**

		Money Supply (1)[a]	Savings, time & PIR deposits (2)[a]	(2)/(1) × 100%	Monthly interest rate on one-month PIR deposits	Monthly rate of price inflation during the quarter just ended
1950	Mar.	348	6	1.7	7.00	10.3
	June	401	28	7.0	7.00 (from 25 Mar.)	0.4
	Sept.	595	36	6.1	3.50 (from 1 July)	6.0
	Dec.	584	26	4.5	3.00 (from 1 Oct.)	5.4
1951	Mar.	732	30	4.1	4.20 (from 26 Mar.)	4.8
	June	942	59	6.3	4.20	3.9
	Sept.	687	164	23.9	4.20	1.8
	Dec.	940	163	17.3	4.20	3.9
1952	Mar.	867	271	31.2	4.20	2.6
	June	942	494	52.4	3.80 (from 29 Apr.) 3.30 (from 2 June)	−1.0
	Sep.	959	541	56.4	3.00 (from 7 July) 2.40 (from 8 Sept.)	−0.4
	Dec.	1,336	467	34.9	2.00 (from 30 Nov.)	0
1953	Mar.	1,074	499	46.5	2.00	1.5
	June	1,198	640	53.4	2.00	1.4
	Sept.	1,292	671	51.9	1.50 (from 16 July)	1.6
	Dec.	1,683	599	35.6	1.20 (from 10 Oct.)	0.5
1954	Mar.	1,622	667	41.1	1.20	0
	June	1,809	747	41.3	1.20	−1.4
	Sept.	1,923	782	40.6	1.00 (from 1July)	−0.6
	Dec.	2,128	765	35.9	1.00	1.3
1955	Mar.	2,300	816	35.5	1.00	2.7

Note: a. In millions of NT dollars.
Source: Adapted from Tsiang (1982, P.171), which was compiled from the Central Bank of China,
Taiwan Financial Statistics Monthly, and Bureau of Accounting and Statistics, *Taiwan Commodity
Prices Statistics Monthly*.

which can be used as a non-inflationary source to finance investment; c) a higher bank loan rate will improve the allocative efficiency of bank loans. However, as argued above, a higher deposit rate may result in a portfolio shift from curb market loans into bank deposits, and hence probably cause the curb market interest rate to rise. Moreover, the curb market interest rate is market determined and usually much higher than the bank loan rate. If bank loans are not efficiently rationed to those users with higher productivity, then the shift of loanable funds from the curb market to banks also implies that the overall allocative efficiency of total loanable funds in the whole society will deteriorate.[3] Thus, the result will probably be a higher price level rather than a lower one. Consequently, whether raising the repressed bank rates will curb or enhance inflation is basically an empirical question. It cannot be answered easily by any theoretical analysis. As an illustration, Shea (1992) analyzed the effect of raising bank interest rates in a theoretical framework which considers the phenomena of financial dualism and financial market segmentation. His results show that raising the bank deposit rate will push up the curb market interest rate and cause net national product to fall in the short run, but lower the curb market interest rate and raise social welfare in the long run through the encouragement of savings and capital accumulation. Nevertheless, empirically Taiwan seems to have always been successful in curbing inflation by raising the bank interest rates.

Liu and Tsiang also advocated interest rate deregulation forcefully. They and other members of Academia Sinica continuously urged the authorities to first set up a well-organized money market, so that the market determined money-market interest rate can be used as a guidepost or reference for banks to determine their interest rates. The money market was established in 1976, and functioned reasonably well. In 1978, the authorities started to relax bank interest rate control step by step, and finally achieved complete interest rate liberalization in 1989.

Their advocacy of interest rate liberalization, of course, also encountered strong opposition. Liberalizing the interest rate from its repressed level means a higher interest rate. Thus, they were labeled as "high interest rate scholars," which intensified the pressure of opposition. Moreover, the entry of new financial institutions had been tightly restricted for many years. The market structure of financial intermediaries was far away from perfect competition. Opponents hence were worried that banks would apply their monopoly power to raise loan rates and lower deposit rates when they were given the freedom to set up interest rates.

Tsiang in fact shared this viewpoint, and advocated the policy of market openness together with interest rate liberalization. Unfortunately, the authorities delayed the market-entry deregulation policy until the early 1990s, so that the above worries became a fact in the 1980s. After interest rate deregulation, the banks were usually sluggish to lower the loan rate or raise the deposit rate, but were quick to lower the deposit rate or raise the loan rate.[4] As a result, the differential between the prime loan rate and the one-year savings deposit rate, taking First Commercial Bank as an example, widened steadily from 0.75 percent per annum when the prime rate system was first established in March 1985 to 1.75 percent in March 1986, and maintained that level for three years. Only after April 1989 did this interest rate differential start to narrow down. At the year-end of 1989, it had been reduced to 0.875 percent.

8.3   Foreign Exchange Reform[5]

Another area in which Liu and Tsiang made a major contribution is foreign exchange reform. In the late 1940s, Taiwan experienced hyper-inflation as a consequence of several factors, including heavy infrastructure damage during the Second World War, political and military deterioration in mainland China in 1947, the retreat of the Central Government from the mainland to Taiwan in 1948, and the heavy burden of defense expenditure from 1948 onwards. In the course of inflation, the external value of the NT dollar depreciated very rapidly, and the economy suffered from a severe foreign exchange shortage. To overcome these problems, in April 1951 the government introduced stringent foreign exchange control, devalued the currency, and applied multiple exchange rates. Strict quota restrictions on imports and heavy tariffs were also imposed. However, under the belief that a overvalued domestic currency would lower the cost of imported goods and domestic prices, the NT dollar was still overvalued at the new exchange rate. Multiple exchange rates were then imposed discriminatively on various import and export activities, based on the subjective judgment of government officials as to the relative importance of imported goods and the relative competitive abilities of exported goods (Hsing, 1994: 61). Although these policies barely managed to retain a tolerable balance of payments situation, they also hindered the growth of exports and seriously distorted resource allocation.

In 1954, Liu and Tsiang were invited by K.Y.Yin to give advice on economic policies to the government. They wrote a report which suggested that the government should raise the interest rate, as well as modify the foreign exchange certificates system and eventually unify the exchange rate.

The foreign exchange certificates system was originally established in Taiwan in 1949. According to this system, 20 percent of the proceeds from exports had to be settled in NT dollars at the Bank of Taiwan, while 80 percent was paid using foreign exchange certificates, which could be sold in the market or used for import. As a result of inflation, a gap existed between the official exchange rate and the market price of foreign exchange certificates.

In February 1955, partly through the recommendation of Liu and Tsiang, the government modified the system by giving exporters, in addition to the government buying rate, foreign exchange certificates representing 50 or 80 percent (depending on the type of goods exported) of the exchange earnings surrendered to the exchange authorities. Importers were required to obtain the certificates from the free market to be eligible to purchase the same amount of foreign exchange in accordance with the selling rate from the Bank of Taiwan for their imports. This amounted to an effective devaluation of the NT dollar. The market price of foreign exchange certificates was a measure of the gap between the official exchange rate and equilibrium market valuation of foreign exchange.

Liu and Tsiang's recommendation to unify the exchange rate at a equilibrium level, however, was not accepted at the beginning by the authorities, who were trapped by worries that a unified exchange rate would mean a depreciated NT dollar, which would cause inflation and increase government import expenditure. In 1958, K.Y. Yin was appointed to be in charge of foreign trade and exchange. Yin adopted Liu and Tsiang's suggestion to unify the exchange rate in two steps. In April 1958, the multiple exchange rate system was replaced by a dual exchange rate system. Except for some exports and imports which could sell and buy foreign exchange at the official exchange rate, all other exporters were awarded, on top of the official exchange rate, foreign exchange certificates representing the full amount of the exchange proceeds surrendered to the authorities; and other importers were required to obtain the certificates to buy foreign exchange at the official rate. In November of the same year, Yin further replaced the dual exchange rate system by a unitary exchange rate system, by requiring all foreign exchange transactions to be applicable to the official rate and the foreign exchange certificates. Afterwards, the official exchange rate plus the market price of the certificates together roughly reflected the equilibrium market valuation of foreign exchange. In July 1960 this market valuation was used to fix a new and uniform exchange rate of NT$ 40 to the US dollar, which remained unchanged until 1973, and the foreign exchange certificates system was abolished.

This unification of exchange rates had in fact devalued the NT dollar towards its equilibrium exchange value. It permitted a considerable degree of trade liberalization and export expansion. This policy, coupled by export promotion policies such as a preferential interest rate for export loans and tax rebates on exports, marked the beginning of the export-promotion era in Taiwan.

The rapid expansion of exports in the following twenty years supplied the main impetus for the take-off of Taiwan's economy. However, it also increased the openness of the economy, such that any fluctuation in the world market could disturb Taiwan's economic stability on both the real side and the monetary side. From the experience in the 1960s and 1970s that fluctuations in the world economy and Taiwan's balance of payment had seriously disturbed foreign trade, economic growth, money supply and price stability, Liu, Tsiang, and four other members of Academia Sinica jointly recommended to the Taiwan authorities in 1974 to make flexible the exchange rate of the NT dollar, so as to exempt Taiwan's economy from the disturbances of external shocks.

The authorities accepted this policy recommendation, and replaced the fixed exchange rate system by a flexible exchange rate system in July 1978. However, the success of export promotion and the contribution of export expansion to economic growth led to a popular ideology of "export first" or "all out for export" in the society. As a consequence, the exchange rate was used as a key instrument to help exporters make profits and keep exports profitable. After the flexible exchange rate system was officially announced in July 1978, the authorities for many years had no intention at all of letting the NT dollar appreciate when there was a balance of payment surplus, or would only let the NT dollar appreciate as little as possible when appreciation was a must. Even when the economy was troubled by a huge trade surplus and a rapid increase in the money supply in the mid-1980s, the Central Bank still intervened heavily in the foreign exchange market to slow down or minimize the appreciation of the NT dollar. Huge foreign exchange reserves approaching US$ 100 billion were thus accumulated, and the society was swamped by too much excess liquidity. As a result, speculation in stocks and real estate, as well as other gambling activities such as the "everybody-happy lotto" *(ta-chia-lo)* and the "six-combination lotto" *(liou-her-tsai)*, became almost a national movement in the latter half of the 1980s. Even in the 1990s, when the exchange rate of the NT dollar was very flexible and fluctuated more often than before, the shadow of the export-first ideology was still there , with industrial enterprises and even the press arguing frequently for a slow appreciation or a rapid depreciation of the NT dollar.

8.4   Tax Reform[6]

Recognized and trusted by Chiang Kai-Shek, Liu was assigned to be Chairman of the Tax Reform Commission in 1968. Before 1971, the government budget was in deficit for most years, and the deficit was financed by bank loans, government bonds, or from appropriation from the Counterpart Fund generated from U.S. aid. In 1968, the compulsory education system was about to be extended from six years to nine years, which required a prodigious government expenditure. The Tax Reform Commission was therefore set up in March 1968, and charged with increasing total tax revenue and adjusting the tax structure. In two years and four months, before the Commission adjourned in July 1970, it had proposed 25 tax reform programs and published 19 research reports. Tsiang had also served as a member of the Commission for about one year.

One of the main proposals of the Commission was to raise the share of income tax in government tax revenues. In 1968, the share of income tax, including individual income tax and business income tax, was merely 7 percent, much lower than that of South Korea (30 percent), the Philippines (27 percent) and India (18 percent). The Commission modified the range of progressive individual income tax rates from 3-54 percent to 6-60 percent. A minimum amount of standard deductions of income tax was also proposed to lower the tax burden of low income families.

The Commission, especially Tsiang, also made substantial modifications to the Statute for Encouragement of Investment, which was introduced in September 1960. Tax-exemption provisions which led to double encouragement or favored gaining without effort were abolished. Provisions encouraging new investment, such as accelerated depreciation, were introduced.

A flexible import tariff rate system was also proposed by the Commission. This system allowed the government to adjust upward or downward the import tariff rate by 50 percent when there were dramatic changes in the world economy. The Ministry of Finance applied this system effectively in 1972-73 to stabilize the domestic prices of imported goods (Wang, 1993: 203).

Furthermore, a value-added tax (VAT) was advocated by Liu and Tsiang to replace the business tax, stamp tax and some commodity taxes, which resulted in double taxation and hindered optimal allocation of resources. However, the authorities were hesitant to adopt this recommendation of a VAT, because of the concern that the cost-push effect of a VAT might lead to inflation. The poor condition of the accounting system and transaction records in the business community were also considered a major obstacle to a VAT. The implementation of a VAT was put off until April 1986. The result showed that concern for cost-push inflation was in fact completely groundless.

In addition to reform of the tax system, the Commission made great efforts to improve the taxation administration. The Taxation Information Handling and Examination Center was established in May 1968. Taxation information was put together and computerized in the Center. An inspection and auditing system was also set up. All these changes greatly improved the efficiency of auditing and levying taxes and the customs of honest tax reporting.

Under strong support from K.T. Li and K.H. Yu, many of the tax reform proposals were adopted and implemented by the government. Because of the tax reform, the share of income tax increased, and the government budget situation improved significantly after 1971, so that the government was capable of implementing major infrastructure investment projects in latter years.

Nevertheless, there were at least two major critiques of this tax reform. One was that the double taxation problem caused by the coexistence of an individual income tax and a business income tax was ignored. Another was that a highly progressive income tax system, although beneficial to the redistribution of income, was harmful to working, saving and investment incentives.

8.5 Conclusion

Liu and Tsiang distinguished themselves from other contemporary economists by their unselfish contribution of their economics knowledge to policy making in Taiwan. Their proposals for economic reform paved the way for Taiwan's spectacular economic growth starting from the early 1960s.

Without their remarkable academic achievements, Liu and Tsiang might not have been recognized and relied upon by the ruling elites to make economic reform. Equally important, without the recognition and trust of the ruling elites, including Chiang Kai-Shek, K.Y. Yin, K.T. Li and K.H. Yu, Liu and Tsiang's intelligence might not have been able to contribute much to Taiwan's economic development either. When one appreciates Liu and Tsiang's contributions, one should not ignore the role played by this technocratic cast. It is usually said that, if K.Y. Yin, the herald of Taiwan's economic development in 1950s through the early 1960s, had lived longer, the economic liberalization process might have moved much faster. This compliment to Yin should be equally applicable to Liu: If Liu had lived longer to devote more time together with Tsiang, their contribution to Taiwan's economic reform would certainly have been much bigger.

The realization of Liu and Tsiang's reform proposals also benefited from the authoritarian political system during that period. This authoritarian system, together with the competent technocratic elites, provided the basis for Taiwan's government to become a development state, which promoted economic growth effectively. This advantage for Taiwan's economic growth has now gradually disappeared. In recent years, Taiwan's society has became more pluralized and democratic. It is now very difficult, or takes a very long time, for any policy which involves conflict of interest among groups to be implemented. The influences of pressure and interest groups are also getting stronger and stronger. To attract support and votes for election, the political parties, legislators and politicians often compete to please the constituents by their decision making. Meanwhile, there are still no appropriate laws to govern lobbying activities and political donations. Thus, the technocratic cast, experts and scholars are losing their influence on the decision making of economic affairs, and the quality of economic policies is deteriorating. When one now recalls Liu and Tsiang's contribution to Taiwan's economic growth, one may need to urge the authorities in Taiwan to set up as soon as possible an efficient system to settle disputes and reconcile opinions on controversial issues, and to safeguard the quality of decision making.

8.6 Notes

1   A major part of this section is based on Tsiang (1982) and Chen and Mo (1992).

2   The details and the impacts of these interest rate rises have been explained inTsiang (1982).

3   This point was emphasized by Shea (1994) in the discussion of the contribution of the curb market. The empirical results of both Shea (1994) and Shea and Kuo (1984) show that banks in Taiwan emphasized collateral more than the productivity of borrowers when rationing loans. Hence, the shift of loanable funds from the curb market to banks after the deposit rate hike may deteriorate the overall allocative efficiency of loanable funds in Taiwan.

4   Another factor causing these behaviors was that government-owned banks, the dominant players in the market, were required to meet the profit target set by the government.

5   This section is mostly based on Tsiang (1982), Shen (1988), Chen and Mo (1992), Wang (1993), and Hsing (1994).

6   The main references of this section are Editorial Committee (1975) and Wang (1993).

8.7 References

Chen, Tsu-Yu and Chi-Ping Mo (interviewers), 1992. *The Reminiscences of Dr. S. C. Tsiang*. Taipei: Institute of Modern History, Academia Sinica. (in Chinese).

Editorial Committee, 1975. *Remembrances of Mr. and Mrs. Ta-Chung Liu*. Taipei (mimeo, in Chinese).

Hsing, Mo-Huan, 1994. "Professor S.C. Tsiang's View on Economic Policies in Taiwan," in Tzong-Shian Yu and Joseph S. Lee (eds.), *S.C. Tsiang: His Contribution to Economic Theory*. Taipei: Chung-Hua Institution for Economic Research: 59-82 (June).

McKinnon, Ronald I., 1973. *Money and Capital in Economic Development*. Washington, D.C.: Brookings Institution.

Shea, Jia-Dong, 1992. "The Welfare Effects of Economic Liberalization under Financial Market Segmentation: with Special Reference to Taiwan," *Academia Economic Papers*, September: 697-716. Taipei: Institute of Economics, Academia Sinica.

Shea, Jia-Dong, 1994. "Taiwan: Development and Structural Change of the Financial System," in Hugh T. Patrick and Yung-Chul Park (eds.), *The Financial Development of Japan, Korea, and Taiwan: Growth, Repression, and Liberalization*. New York: Oxford: 222-87.

Shea, Jia-Dong and Ping-Sing Kuo, 1984. "The Allocative Efficiency of Bank's Loanable Funds in Taiwan," in *Proceedings of the Conference on Financial Development in Taiwan*, December. Taipei: Institute of Economics, Academia Sinica. (in Chinese).

Shen, Yun-Lung (ed.), 1988. *Manuscript of K.Y. Yin's Biography*, 2nd edition. Taipei: Biography Literature (in Chinese).

Taylor, Lance, 1983. *Structuralist Macroeconomics*. New York: Basic.

Tsiang, Shoh-Chieh, 1979. "Fashions and Misconception in Monetary Theory and Their Influences on Financial and Banking Policies," *Zeitschrift fur die gesamte Staatwissenschaft*, December: 583-604.

Tsiang, Shoh-Chieh, 1982. "Monetary Policy of Taiwan," in Kwoh-Ting Li and Tzong-Shian Yu (eds.), *Experiences and Lessons of Economic Development in Taiwan*. Taipei: Institute of Economics, Academia Sinica: 165-85.

Tsiang, Shoh-Chieh, 1985. *Lessons from the Economic Development of Taiwan: Growth Amidst Stability*. Taipei: Commonwealth. (in Chinese).

Van Wijnbergen, Sweder, 1983. "Interest Rate Management in LDCs," *Journal of Monetary Economics*, September: 433-52.

Wang, L. Sophia, 1993. *K.T. Li's Oral History*. Taipei: Excellence (in Chinese).

9 LIBERALIZATION PROMOTES DEVELOPMENT: EVIDENCE FROM TAIWAN[1]

John C. H. Fei and Yun-Peng Chu

From a long run historical perspective, postwar economic development in Taiwan, like that in many other contemporary LDCs (less developed countries), has been a *transition process* that terminated centuries of agrarianism and initiated what was referred to by the late Professor Kuznets as the EMG (epoch of modern economic growth) (Kuznets, 1966). With its well-known economic miracle (1950-1990) now in the past, Taiwan will soon join the ranks of the DCs (the "developed" countries such as the U.S., Japan and countries in Western Europe) which have gone through similar transition processes since the EMG was first ushered in by the industrial revolution in England toward the end of the 18th century.

With the death of President Chiang Ching-Kuo in 1988, the economic miracle of Taiwan was followed by a political miracle, *democratization.* From a historical perspective, transition to the "modern" epoch suggests that the "development" of Taiwan (in the title of this paper) can, and will, be interpreted broadly as a process of *modernization.* This modernization is occurring in Taiwan's

a) *political institutions* through *democratization*, i.e., an evolutionary replacement of a "paternalistic polity" by *pluralism*, defined as a harmonious coexistence of possibly conflicting ideas and interests in the society, and

b) *economic institutions* through *marketization* i.e., an evolutionary replacement of the "centralism of political command" by the competitive market mechanism which automatically coordinates privatized decisions of families and firms in the society.

We shall argue that what is central to both a) and b) is *liberalization*, i.e., a rearrangement of the *government-society relationship*, characterized by an atrophying of the power of the former as well as an enrichment of the lifestyle of the latter by the non-homogeneity of pluralism. In this paper we shall use four capital letters to denote certain key concepts: democratization (D), marketization (M), government (G), and society (S). These concepts of political economy are used to remind the readers that this paper is interdisciplinary in scope and evolutionary in intention.

Is the democratization, or D, that is observable in Taiwan an inevitable consequence of marketization, or M? This issue of the relationship between *D and M* is of paramount importance for the political unification of China and world peace in the years ahead. The two political entities of the currently divided China (the ROC and the PRC) shared the common experience of a long run marketization during the postwar transition period. If democratization follows marketization inevitably, an *evolutionary institutional convergence* across the Taiwan Strait will certainly pave the way for a smooth political unification in the early part of the 21st century. This is, indeed, the optimistic conclusion of this paper.

Academically, the D-M relation is a question of the evolution of human institutions, i.e., changes in social organizations accompanied by changes in cultural values (ideas, beliefs and moral principles) that sustain all human institutions. The issue of social organizational change has been studied by sociologists and political scientists such as Huber et al. (1993), Lipset (1995), and Moore (1966). However, the role of cultural values, which have the power to cut across the disciplinary boundaries of economics, sociology and political science, has not been sufficiently emphasized.

This paper represents a historical approach by an economist that stresses the role of *cultural values* (traditional Chinese cultural values in particular) in the modernization process. In emphasizing cultural values, our methodology is consistent with recent trends in historiography (Yu, 1991). The optimistic conclusion (i.e., "liberalization has promoted modernization" in Taiwan) can be explained by the fact that the traditional Eastern (Chinese) cultural values are consistent with the requirements of modernization, which has a Western origin.

In the analytical framework of this paper (see Figure 9.1) the *evolutionary perspective* is brought out by the contrast between the "traditional" and the "modern system" indicated at the top. D-M relatedness will be analyzed as a facet of changes in government-society relations (G-S) shown by the dichotomy of G (shown as a triangle to represent a "power focus" on top) and S (shown as an ellipse S) that contains individual *families* (F_i) and *firms* (f_i) as the decentralized decision-making entities. Traditional and modern government and society will be denoted by {Gt,St} (reads: traditional government-society relation or interaction) and {Gm,Sm} (the modern counterpart) respectively. The use of {G,S} (without a subscript) is an abstract *government-society relation* or *interaction.*

The notion {G,S} is central to our analysis of both democracy (in the political arena) and markets (in the economic arena) because "what government can do to society operationally" is the key issue in both arenas. The analytical framework of Figure 9.1 emphasizes a *double dichotomy* of two separate analytical issues that should not be confused. On the one hand, there is a problem of comparative economic systems, i.e., the comparison of {Gt,St} and (Gm,Sm} where institution transformation is *not* involved. On the other hand, there is a more difficult issue of the evolution from the former to the latter that usually involves imagination, agitation,

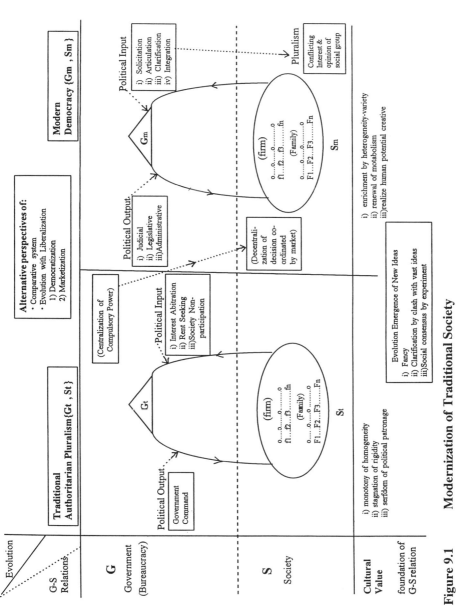

Figure 9.1   **Modernization of Traditional Society**

and experiments, a time of turbulence when the "vested ideas" are challenged to form a new societal consensus that is "epochal."

As a point of departure, features of "modern" democracy in the political arena will be sketched to highlight the contrast with the traditional "paternalistic" polity (Section 9.1). The essence of a cultural approach to the modernization of political institutions will be sketched in Section 9.2. Features of the automatic market mechanism will be analyzed to show their dynamic efficiency, i.e., their ability to accommodate rapid growth with structural flexibility in a modern economy (Section 9.3). The traditional economic institutions of Taiwan will then be examined in an evolutionary perspective (Section 9.4).

In our cultural approach, *D-M relatedness will be viewed in terms of a "human quest for the (higher) cultural value of creativity."* The optimistic conclusion of this paper is that, with time, democratization is an inevitable evolutionary consequence of marketization (Section 9.5). In the postwar transition process, modernization in the economic and political senses has taken place rather smoothly in Taiwan as compared with other contemporary LDCs — a difference that can be explained culturally as being due to the compatibility of traditional Chinese (Eastern) cultural values with the requirements of a modern lifestyle, which have a decidedly Western origin (Section 9.6).

While we build an abstract framework for the analysis of {G,S} in the text, in Appendix One we will apply this framework for the analysis of the case of the modernization of Taiwan, the inductive evidence of which will be processed to become an *economic policy matrix* (EPM), periodized into the subphases of

      (i) Import Substitution (1950-62)

      (ii) Export Orientation (1962-80)

      (iii) Science and Technology Orientation (1980-96)

and a *political event matrix* (PEM), periodized into the subphases of

      (i) Embryonic Democratization (1970-87)

      (ii) Intensive Democratization (1987-96)

We shall experiment with a methodology for an interdisciplinary approach for the analysis of the interaction of the evolution of political and economic institutions simultaneously through the subphases identified above. The major conclusions ((C1)-(C4)) will be given. This method can be extended for future research on Taiwan and/or for other countries.

The following outline guides our discussion:

1. Modern and Traditional Political Institutions Contrasted

2. Contrasting Political Cultural Values

3. Modern and Traditional Economic Institutions

4. Transformation of the Traditional Economic System

5. Cultural Approach to Political and Economic Evolution

6. Chinese Cultural Foundations of Democratization and Marketization

Sections 9.1 and 9.2 deal with the political aspect, Sections 9.3 and 9.4 deal with the economic aspect. The interaction of the two is treated in Section 9.5, with references to Chinese cultural values postponed to Section 9.6.

9.1   Modern and Traditional Political Institutions Contrasted

9.1.1   Democracy: the Modern Political Institution

A key feature of modern society is *pluralism*, defined as a coexistence of opinionated and vested interest groups having conflicts that must be resolved and harmonized to maintain the orderliness of social life. In a modern society, conflicts are blessings in disguise, provided they can be integrated into the political process of {Gm,Sm} interaction.

According to the pluralistic approach (Easton, 1953; Almond, 1960) the integration of conflict is the key feature of democracy. This is shown by the political input-output relation of {Gm Sm} interaction (Figure 9.1 on the right-hand side).

Information on conflicting opinions about an issue (e.g., "prolife" v.s. "prochoice" in the abortion conflict) and/or economic interests (e.g., supporters of universal health insurance vs. supporters of a balanced budget) must be solicited, articulated, clarified and integrated — by elites in a process of persuasion and debate (e.g., in Congress and/or the mass media) — to provide the *political input* from the modern society into the modern government to let government know what the society wants.

The political output includes administrative, judicial and legislative services "produced" by the sovereign government that exercises vast compulsory power. The airing and resolution of conflicts through pluralism is the heart of democracy, whereby power is constrained by "input" from below. This is the essence of "power to the people," which is the political slogan of the 1996 presidential election in Taiwan.

9.1.2   The Traditional Autocratic Polity

Under the alleged historical tradition of oriental despotism, the paternalistic polity in Taiwan — i.e., authoritative rule by a "fatherly" strongman — was referred to by political scientists as *authoritative pluralism* (see {Gt,St} in Figure 9.1, left-hand side). (As a political institution, it has a closer affinity with democratic pluralism {Gm,Sm} than the *totalitarianism* of the party state of the PRC on the mainland, where the lifestyle before 1978 was characterized by *homogeneity* (an antithesis of pluralism) after private society was wiped out by brutal political force.)

Anti-colonial sentiments account for the fact that the vast majority of non-communistic LDCs (including Taiwan) initiated their postwar transition process with an "authoritative pluralism." For the young sovereign states (i.e., the ex-colonies) obsessed with an intense xenophobia, the solidification of the government's power was a purpose in itself — not necessarily a means to promote something else (e.g., economic development via central planning) (see Section 9.4.1).

As compared with a democratic government, Gm, the traditional governments, Gt, of LDCs wield political power in a vastly more pervasive and arbitrary way. On the political "input" side, members of the traditional society, St, are "ideologically" discouraged from forming special interest groups by slogans of political values ("united we stand," "out of many rise one," "the sharing of wealth," or even "non-differentiation of human beings"). In the place of pluralism, the traditional governmental "authority" serves as the final arbitrator for all conflicts of societal interests.

On the "output" side, the arbitrariness of government decrees obviates the necessity for a legislative branch (or, under totalitarianism, even a judicial branch), when these do exist they are largely window-dressing. According to the "state-centric approach" (Skocpol, 1985; Krasner 1985; Stepan 1985), the *authoritative pluralistic state* becomes autonomous and can interfere arbitrarily (e.g., in hair styling and cutting prices in Taiwan in the 1950s) demanding homogeneity and standardization.

9.2 Contrasting Political Cultural Values

9.2.1   Historical Approach to the Cultural Values of Modern Government and Society

One can reasonably argue that it took almost all the well-known cultural values developed in Western history since the 14th century — e.g., nationalism, egalitarianism, secularism, and rationalism, just to name a few — to create a foundation for the *political* institution of democracy. Professor Kuznets believed that the same set of cultural values also sustains the *economic* institutions essential for modern economic growth: "The broad views associated with modern economic epoch can be suggested by three terms: *secularism* (or "assignment of high rank to *economic attainment*"), *egalitarianism* and *nationalism*" (Kuznets, 1966:12).

To economists, it is well known that market institutions presume *freedom of choice*, the *rationalism* of utility maximization, *decentralization of power* (i.e., aversion to monopolistic collusion in "atomistic competition"), etc. These remarks serve to remind the readers that the cultural values approach, as a conceptual tool, can, indeed, cut across disciplinary boundaries.

9.2.2   Cultural Approach to the Contrast between {Gt,St} and {Gm,Sm} in the 20th Century

In the 20th century, the contrast between traditional forms of government and society and modern forms, shown in Figure 9.1, reveals a fundamental organizational difference. The concentrated political power of the traditional government, Gt, is replaced by decentralized decision-making (i.e., by families and firms) in the modern society, Sm. Consequently, there is a difference in the *values* placed on pluralism. This difference can be stated in a juxtaposition as follows:

	Modern Society		*Traditional Society*
i)	enrichment of lifestyle by variety and non-homogeneity	i)	monotony of standardization conformity and homogeneity
ii)	vitality of a healthy social metabolism ensured by perpetual self-renewal	ii)	stagnation and rigidity
iii)	progress through full use of human creative potential	iii)	security of serfdom through government patronage

A basic difference between democracy and autocracy is that pluralism (i.e. of opinions, ideas and interests) is preserved and encouraged in the former and suppressed in the latter. Pluralization is more than a static "preservation of non-homogeneity," as the very respect for non-homogeneity encourages the *dynamics of human creativity* — or destructive challenges to vested ideas. For this reason, "conflicts and chaos" can be a blessing in disguise — a necessary cost of progress. That this spells the difference between what is "traditional" and what is "modern" will be analyzed further (see Section 9.5.1).

In an evolutionary perspective, liberalization is a process usually defined as the shift of the balance of power from the government to the society. When the decision-making process is thus privatized and transferred from the political center, G, to the multitude of decision-makers in the society, S, *pluralization* is only the natural outcome. That this will confirm all the advantages of variety, vitality, and creativity constitutes the primary defense, on cultural grounds, of the thesis that democratization will follow as a natural consequence of marketization.

In the 20th century and beyond, modern cultural values (identified in this section) are clearly elevated to a higher "transcendental level" (as suggested by the explosion of creativity in fine arts and music) as a natural outgrowth of those (e.g., nationalism, egalitarianism, secularism) identified in the previous subsection (9.2.1).

9.3 Modern and Traditional Economic Institutions

Historically speaking, modern economic institutions originated from the *industrial capitalism* that accompanied the arrival of the EMG (Section 9.3.1). We will present a macro-economic framework to portray industrial capitalism operationally in two steps. First, the automatically adjusting market mechanism compatible with the requirement of *rapid growth with structural flexibility* will be sketched (Section 9.3.2). Next, the role of modern government and society, {Gm,Sm}, in the economic arena will be analyzed in terms of the *policy instruments* that supplement and/or protect competitive markets (Section 9.3.3).

9.3.1 Modern Economic Growth with Structural Flexibility

The primary force promoting growth in the EMG is the routinized devotion of human time and energy to exploration of the frontier of *science and technology* to accumulate knowledge, as an essential part of the art of production that benefits humanity (Kuznets, 1966). Unlike the creative endeavors in fine arts and science that are restricted to a small minority (i.e., artists and scientists), the industrial revolution ushered in a lifestyle where innovative creation, guided by pecuniary motives, became a popular phenomenon.

The modern lifestyle can be described in terms of a macro-economic system formed of a "dualistic production sector" (agricultural and non-agricultural) on top and a "household sector" at the bottom (see Figure 9.2). Conceptually, the aggregate non-agricultural sector contains a number of firms (f_1, f_2,...,f_m), producing a vector of output ($Q_1,Q_2,...,Q_n$) by managing a vector of capital stock ($K_1,K_2,...,K_n$), and hiring a structure of labor force. The characteristics of a *modern* economy are definable primarily in terms of the "macro-*dualism*" (i.e., the coexistence of agricultural and non-agricultural sectors) as well as a multitude of products produced by the *microscopic firms in the industrial structure.*

Money Flow →

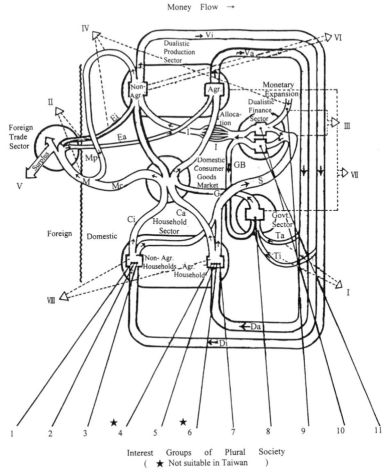

Interest   Groups   of   Plural   Society
(★ Not suitable in Taiwan   )

Legends:

I: Fiscal - Taxation Policies: Domestic Taxes
II: Fiscal - Taxation Policies: External Taxes
III: Interests Rate Policies
IV: Foreign Exchange Rate Policies
V: Policies of International Capital Movement
VI: Public Enterprises & National Construction
VII: Agriculture Policies
VIII: Manpower and Labor Policies
 1. Workers
 2. Medium Scale Entrepreneurs
 3. Large Scale Entrepreneurs
 4. Agr. Export Production Entrepreneurs
 5. Landlords
 6. Primary Product Exporter Workers
 7. Farmers for Domestic Market
 8. Government Bureaucrats
 9. Monetary Authority
10. Private Bankers
11. Private Lenders

Ca: Consumption by Agricultural Households
Ci: Consumption by Non-agricultural
        Households
Da: Disposable Income of Agricultural Hhlds.
Di: Disposable Income of Non-agricultural
        Households
Ea: Exports of Agricultural Products
Ei: Exports of Non-agricultural Products
G: Government Expenditure
GB: Government Bonds
I: Investment
M: Total Imports
Mc: Imports of Consumer Goods
Mp: Imports of Producer Goods
S :   Savings
Ta: Taxes Paid by Agricultural Sector
Ti: Taxes Paid by Non-agricultural Sector
Va: Agricultural Value-added
Vi: Non-agricultural Value-added

Figure 9.2   Policy Formation in an Open Dualistic Economy

According to Kuznets, an essential feature of the EMG is *rapid growth* accompanied by a *dualistic structural change* (i.e., the decline of the relative weight of the agricultural sector). This macroscopic structural change really hides the true spirit of economic creativity of a modern society, which can only be sensed from the *microscopic structural flexibility*. Routinized innovations in products and processes (Schumpeter, 1939) necessitates a *healthy metabolism* — i.e., the timely birth of new firms and products and the timely death of those which have become obsolete — as visible in the fate of most popular music or female fashions that are constantly created but enjoy only a short-lived popularity. Creation is a meaningful end in itself in the modern society, much more important than the static resource allocation efficiency of the Pareto variety.

Modern growth with structural flexibility is brought about by the timely allocation of the total volume of investment (I) as investment goods (I1,I2,...,In) = (dK1/dt,dK2/dt,...,dKn/dt) for capital accumulation at the level of individual firms — these are analogous to biological entities whose life cycle is punctuated by birth (incorporation), growth (expansion), and death (bankruptcy). In a technologically dynamic society, rapid growth for the whole economy is impossible without microscopic structural flexibility.

9.3.2 *Capitalistic Markets and Decentralized Growth*

With the arrival of the EMG, commercial capitalism (1500-1750) evolved into industrial capitalism, with its automatically adjusted commodity, labor and, above all, finance markets, to accommodate the requirements of decentralized growth with structural flexibility (see Figure 9.2):

a) the *domestic consumer goods market* clears the demand and supply of consumer goods, while the structure of investment goods (I1,I2,...,In) is related to the dualistic financial market as regulated by a price system (p1,p2,...,pn);

b) the labor market regulates the allocation of labor (L1,L2,...,Ln) to firms by the wage rate (w);

c) financial institutions (banks, money and stock markets) specialize in clearing the *finance market* (i.e., loanable funds) by the interest rate. Through *credit rationing* they act to

   i) allocate monetary purchasing power S (provided by saving families) to borrowing entrepreneurs who must prepare investment plans for individual firms to buy "planned" investment goods (I1,I2,...,In) in the commodity market and to

   ii) award the "title to capital wealth" to families that save — to enhance their social status, material affluence and political power. They are allowed to swap their entitlements (i.e., in the stock market).

Thus, under industrial capitalism, rapid growth with structural flexibility is assured by the *marketized regulation of decentralized growth* of the microscopic units, i.e., the firms and families that originate new innovative ideas.

Since all innovative investment plans are adventurous, purchasing power is granted *on credit terms* in the financial market and must be repaid within a specified period of grace during which its viability is "tested" pragmatically (i.e., experimentally) in the market. In a technologically dynamic economy, growth with structural flexibility always involves "freedom of choice," "imagination," and "experiments," as the human race sails into an unknown future through a perpetual process of renewal as they search for a form of "collectivism" of human relations (i.e., of *confidence and trust* in the financial world) which is not at variance with individual private property ownership. The economic institution of private property ownership is sustained by the cultural value of human creativity (rather than static efficiency) in the 20th century.

9.3.3   The Role of the State in Modern Capitalism

The above economic system is enlarged in Figure 9.2 to show economic policy instruments as it is imbedded conceptually in the political input-output system. The government, as an economic agent, purchases a part of Q by government expenditures (g) financed by taxation (T) and/or borrowing from the financial market (G_B) to cover a budget deficit. In addition to *fiscal instruments*, the *monetary instrument* centers on expansion of the monetary supply (dm/dt) that amounts to an injection of artificially created purchasing power into the loanable funds market.

All capitalistic governments produce a political "output service" that protects property rights and settles contract disputes (by the judicial branch) and that maintains law and order and national defense (by the administrative branch). Whether or not a particular government/society relation is *modern* should be gauged primarily by its *problem sensitivity*, as in a modern government the conflicting interests of the pluralistic modern society are integrated in the political input process (as discussed in Section 9.1.1).

Even in a modern society, government will have to play important roles in the economic arena. However, ideally the government output (g in Figure 9.2) should aim primarily at remedial measures to deal with various well-known areas of market failure such as

a) the deployment of resources for collective functions:
　　1)　for internal security, national defense
　　2)　to protect capitalistic legality (enforcement of contracts, protection of property rights)
　　3)　to external diseconomies (roads, transportation, communication, environmental protection)
b) the protection of competitiveness
　　1)　to enforce anti-trust laws
　　2)　to regulate pricing of natural monopolies
c) the enforcement of standardization of measurement, and a monetary standard
d) macro economic management due to market failure (Tobin, 1993)
e) the creation of more *equitable income distribution* (by social consensus) than that warranted by the competitive market forces (for the social sharing of privatized insurance cost of old age, health, unemployment, etc.)

Thus the Gm-Sm relation in a capitalistic society exhibits the principle of maintenance of *competition*. Government action is called for only when there is social consensus revealing a sensitivity to problems that emerge due to market failure.

9.4   Transformation of the Traditional Economic System

The traditional economic system that prevailed in LDCs differs from the modern system primarily because the policy instruments were used with a sensitivity to a different set of problems. In the traditional government-society interaction in LDCs, the government plays a much more active role than simply compensating for market failure (as is the case for DCs). For LDCs the problem that occupies the government in the earlier transition phase is more likely to be one of *market construction* in an evolutionary process so that these markets can eventually take over some of the roles of the government in the later phase. (In the case of Taiwan, this later phase occurred after 1970 as will be discussed in sections A5 and A6 of Appendix One.) It will be also be clear there that in order to let markets take over, the process of market construction in the earlier period was a sequential one, albeit all steps were directed toward the same final goal. Taking interest rate liberalization as an example, the government first determined the rates for the banks, then the association of banks was asked to draft a rate proposal which would be reviewed by the government, finally the government asked all banks to establish their own prime-rate system and completely liberalized interest rates.)

9.4.1   Contrasts between Traditional and Modern Economic Problem Sensitivity

The contrast of the problem sensitivity of economic policies between LDCs and DCs may be succinctly summarized as follows:

DCs (developed countries)	LDCs (less developed countries)
a) Growth avoiding	growth-centric
i) market reliant.....................................	bureaucratic planning
ii) stability sensitive	
iii) equity orientation	
b) Direction neutrality....................................	direction specificity
i) matured loanable fund market...........	primitive private finance
ii) advanced stage of capitalism	
1) product multiplicity.	lack of variety
2) routinized innovation...................	deficient innovative capacity
iii) flexible-structural sensitivity.............	accomplishment orientation
c) Overt income transfer	covert income transfers
i) welfare program proliferation.	welfare slogan proliferation
ii) aversion to transfer payment to	windfall profit manufacture (rent-
business	seeking)
d) Open to foreign competition.......................	fearful of foreign competition
i) open trade and foreign investment	markets closed to competition
ii) temporary protection to ease	permanent prohibition of free entry
structural adjustment	
e) Existence of efficient government...............	construction of government
	administrative capacity

     The above contrast of the problem sensitivity of traditional government and societies of LDCs and modern governments of DCs (in the spirit of "comparative economic systems") immediately suggests an evolutionary approach that may be briefly outlined both in theory (Section 9.4.2) and in terms of its empirical verification (Section 9.4.3).

9.4.2   An Evolutionary "Theory" of Economic Modernization

An evolutionary theory of the *modernization of economic institutions* centers on the *liberalization of government-society relations* from {Gt,St} to {Gm,Sm}. This liberalization involves the replacement of centralized government power (Gt) by the decentralized decision-making power of families and firms within a society (Sm):

I) Management of Growth and Investment
   a) From growth-centric to growth avoidance
   b) From direction specificity to direction neutrality
   c) From covert to overt income transfers in the political process
II) Management of International Economic Relations
   d) From closed markets to markets open to international competition
      i) in trade
      ii) in investment
III) Central Bank Management of the Money Supply
   e) From monetary activism to monetary conservatism: the abandonment of an expansionary monetary policy
      i) to plug the government budget gap (taxation without consent)
      ii) to achieve covert income transfer in investment financed by artificially low interest rates accompanied by insufficient discounting of price inflation via "indexing" and/or "rational expectation"
      iii) to stockpile official foreign exchange reserves in the central bank
   f) From monetary nationalism to monetary internationalism: the abandonment of central bank regulation of
      i) government monopoly in the holding of foreign exchange reserves
      ii) the effective control of all economic contacts between the citizens of a nation state and all foreign nationals by the requirement that all spending of foreign exchange must be approved by the central bank
      iii) the exploitation (or subsidy) of the exporter by an artificial over (or under) valuation of the domestic currency in the official exchange rate to implement growth centric policies
IV) From Bureaucratism to "Market with Efficient Government"
   g) Functional specialization between market and government

While there are many dimensions (from (a) to (g)) in this institutional transformation process, an evolutionary "theory" stresses their relatedness as unified by a central theme, namely, the requirement of growth with structural flexibility — with an international (d,f) as well as a domestic dimension (a,b,c,e,g). The domestic dimension centers on the advantages of decentralized management of investment in the capital accumulation process (a,b,c,e(ii)) while the international dimension stresses the advantages of human interaction across national frontiers (d(i),(ii), e(iii), f(i)-(iii)). The feasibility of their empirical verification will be examined in Appendix One.

9.4.3 Empirical Verification of the Evolution Thesis
The economic modernization of Taiwan has been studied statistically (in terms of output, trade, labor productivity, etc.) (Kuo, 1983). However, according to the evolutionary theory outlined above, liberalization is really a process of *transformation of the political and economic institutions* (i.e., of the mode of organizing {G,S}), supported by cultural values, that defies the use of statistics for its empirical verification. The primary data used for verification should be a *policy matrix* that describes the contour of all major economic policy events in chronological order during the transition process. The evolution of economic policies not only reveals a changing pattern of government-society relations, but also demonstrates the birth of new political and economic ideas generated by deliberations and debates in the process of policy formation (see Table A1 in Appendix One).

9.5 Cultural Approach to Political and Economic Evolution

9.5.1 Quest for Creativity Through Marketization and Democratization
While some Western intellectuals, disillusioned by the Great Depression in the 1930s, turned to communists for salvation, Keynes made a forceful defense of industrial capitalism by identifying the "advantages of private initiative and responsibility" propagated by *individualism* — i.e., the cultural value that emerged in the 19th century to support the market system after the arrival of the epoch of modern growth (EMG). In the concluding chapter of the General Theory, Keynes wrote:

> Let us stop for a moment to remind ourselves what these advantages are. They are partly advantages of *efficiency* —the advantages of decentralization and of the play of self-interest. The advantages to efficiency of the decentralization of decision and of individual responsibility [i.e., the exercise of *free choice*] is even greater, perhaps, than the nineteenth century [*Marxists*] supposed; and the reaction against the appeal to self-interest [by the *socialistic experiment*] may have gone too far..." (Keynes, 1936: 380, bracketed text added).

Keynes had already sensed the enhanced importance of "efficiency" in the 20th century, even before the world was inundated by the stream of new products (TVs, copiers, atomic energy, commercial air travel, transistors, computers, glass fiber, space travel, material science, genetic engineering, super conductivity...) which were developed during the "second industrial revolution" after the Second World War (1950-75) with a "rapidity of metabolism" unequaled in human history.

However, Keynes lived at a time before a whole generation of postwar economists became fascinated by the "efficiency of Pareto optimality." What Keynes saw in individualism was a human creativity conducive to the "variety" of life when he wrote:

> But, above all, individualism ...is the best safeguard of personal liberty in the sense that, as compared with other systems, it greatly *widens the field of exercise of personal choices*. It is also the best safeguard of the *variety of life* which emerges precisely from this extended field of personal choice and the

loss of which is the greatest of all the losses of the homogeneous totalitarian state. (Keynes, 1936, p.380)

Keynes clearly believed that "variety" and "non-homogeneity" (i.e., multiplicity of opinions and their expression) in a modern plural society are major cultural values, the suppression of which is to be lamented. It is well known that Keynes believed that new ideas must overcome the resistance of prejudices of the "vested ideas" before they can be established firmly as a secure part of the cultural values that "rule the world" (Keynes, 1936: 383). To Keynes, the "freedom of choice" has a *creative connotation* — a far cry from the "consumer" choice of Pareto optimality:

> . . .for this variety preserves the traditions which embody the most *secure and successful* choices of former generation; it colors the present with the diversification of its *fancy*; and being the handmaid of *experiment* as well as of tradition and fancy, it is the most powerful instrument to better the future.

References to imagination (fancy) and experiment can only mean a *pragmatic creative process* where new ideas must be tested — i.e., proved "secure and successful" — before being handed down to the next generation.

The common denominator of both democratization and marketization is a *human quest for unfettered creativity* that leads unfailingly to a healthy metabolism (i.e., to product multiplicity and structural flexibility) in the economic arena (see Section 9.3.1) as well as to pluralism (i.e., the perpetual regeneration and harmonization of conflicting opinions and interests) in the political arena (see Section 9.1.1). In the 20th and 21st centuries, the evolution from (Gt,St) to (Gm,Sm) primarily reflects a quest for an institutional environment in which the full human creative potential can be explored (see Section 9.2.2 and the bottom of Figure 9.1).

A cultural approach leads to the conclusion that democratization always follows marketization, possibly with a time lag, because the human race is ruled by cultural values and little else!

9.5.2   Cultural Values Consistent with Human Creativity

If we believe in "humanism" — i.e., the cultural value that attaches a high priority to the exploration of the *human potential* to the fullest extent — then creativity (which reminds us of the supreme power of deity) should, indeed, be regarded as a supreme cultural value. However, if we take an analytic approach, we can see that human creativity, as a social phenomenon, is really grounded on belief in other values such as:

a) a disciplined cultivation of human potential through *education*

b) *pragmatism*, where "fancies" are practically tested by experiment

c) an *individualistic* respect for and tolerance of differences of opinion as well as a willingness to engage in social interaction and communication

d) the transcendental value that human beings are an integral part of the universe which is in a *constant state of self-renewal* in an evolutionary process.

That the discipline of education is essential for intelligent economic and political choices in a modern society needs no explanation. Since every instance of creation is unique, pragmatism — defined in Webster's Dictionary as "busy" (pragmatic) and the idea that "truth is to be tested by practical consequence of belief" — implies the use of experiment to differentiate creative imagination from the insecurity of "crackpot" fantasies.

Human creativity suggests an individualistic endeavor with "originality," "uniqueness," "distinction," and "singularity," as well as a willingness to engage in social interaction (e.g., going to the library occasionally in writing a Ph.D. thesis). That human beings should move harmoniously along with the forward-moving world is certainly conducive to human creativity in secular affairs.

9.6. Chinese Cultural Foundations of Democratization and Marketization

9.6.1 Chinese Cultural Values

A cultural approach can explain the political-economic miracle of Taiwan, i.e., the fact that democratization and marketization took place more smoothly in the transformation process than in the vast majority of other contemporary LDCs. Using the criteria for creativity developed in the last section, the positive significance of traditional Chinese cultural values can be readily verified (see Yu, 1984 and Fei, 1985).

The Chinese emphasis on education needs not be elaborated beyond the remark that in the Confucian tradition, education implies a lifelong *cultivation of human potential* (c1, see the definitions in Appendix Two), which is optimistically perceived to be virtually unlimited. With persistence and discipline, human beings can perform miracles reserved for deities (c2) (see 9.5.2 above).

The Confucian bible begins with the line, "To practice what one learns is valuable" (c3). The *pragmatism* of an interaction between "learning" and "practicing" (c4) has been the central philosophical theme of New Confucianism after the 11th century. The Chinese always detest "untestable theory" as hot air (c5), while the huge Chinese population provides a living testimony that living effectively has always been a cardinal Chinese cultural value (see Section 9.5.2).

The dignity of human beings is firmly established in the Confucian tradition (c6) with an *individuality* stressing the value of "harmony of non-conformity" (c7) and that "supreme harmony is the harmony of differentiated human beings" (c8). Since creativity is aproduct of individualistic endeavors that presume an active social interchange of ideas, the non-collusive Chinese social personality (c9) is quite compatible with the requirement of creativity (see Section 9.5.2).

Instead of an anthropomorphic god, the Chinese believe in a cosmos (heaven and earth, c10) with the individual at the center (c11). As the supreme power of the cosmos is ceaseless self-renewal (c12), every individual should make a lifelong effort to renew himself through education (c13) to live harmoniously with "heaven." The procreation process is both adventurous and exciting, full of uncertainties. Chinese are certainly not a risk-averse race, as their willingness to take a chance makes them the best customers in the casinos of Las Vegas and Atlantic City (see Section 9.5.2d).

9.6.2   The Integration of Western and Eastern Culture

In conclusion, it should be pointed out that all the modern cultural values identified in Section 9.1.2 have a Western origin. Professor Huntington of Harvard University believes that Eastern cultural values will rise to challenge the dominance of Western values in the next century (Huntington, 1989). The democratization and marketization of Taiwan in the postwar period represents a successful integration of Western and Eastern traditions, as the Eastern cultural values identified in the previous section have already been blended with those of the Western tradition.

In the final analysis, it is this cultural integration in Taiwan that lies behind its modernization (i.e., Westernization) process. There is a good chance that this integrated system will become a model that can be extended not only to the mainland, but one which will also exercise a reciprocal influence on the Western world in the early part of the 21st century.

9.7   Appendix One: Evolution Matrix of Political Economic Institutions

The modernization of the political and economic institutions in Taiwan via democratization and marketization (1950-1990) is a process of evolutionary change of the {G,S} oriented toward "liberalization" to decentralize the decision-making power of G to the families and firms of S to realize the human creative potential in a plural society with a life style perpetually enriched by heterogeneity and variety. The evolutionary transformation of the {G,S} in the economic arena (i.e. the marketization process) and/or the political arena (i.e. democratization) can be studied with the aid of the conceptual tool of a economic policy matrix (EPM) and/or the political event matrix (PEM) as "primary data."

The use of the pair (EPM and PEM) suggests an experiment in a methodology for the study of an "evolutionary process" of human society in which the simultaneity of {G,S} interaction, indicated by observable events (i.e. as "data"), cuts across the disciplinary boundaries (e.g. of economics, political science, sociology, etc.). This experiment in a methodology for interdisciplinary research will be briefly outlined in this appendix, according to the following order:

(A1) Economic policy matrix (EPM)
(A2) Application of EPM for marketization
(A3) The political event matrix (PEM)
(A4) Periodization of the PEM
(A5) Economic background of the embryonic democratization phase
(A6) Economic background of the intensive democratization phase
(A7) Conclusions
(A8) Future research

A1) Economic Policy Matrix (EPM)

The EPM originally constructed by Li (1988) describes the contour of all major economic policy events in a chronological order during the transition process classified into the following economic areas indicated by subtitles on Table Al. Of the three panels in Li (1988), only panel a is reproduced here:

I.   domestic fiscal
II.   external trade related fiscal
III.   monetary
IV.   foreign exchange rate
V.   international capital movement
VI.   government enterprise and national construction
VII.   agriculture
VIII. manpower and labor
IX.   science and technology
X.   economic development planning

Table A1   Economic Policy Matrix (EPM), 1970–2000 (panel a)

Stage	Year	Policies
I. Fiscal Policy — Domestic		
Export Orientation Period	1974	Bond market established.
		Combating inflation with high interest rates.
	1975	Setting ceiling for bond issues outstanding as percentage of central government budget.
Science and Technology Orientation Period	1982	Small budget deficit.
	1983	Introduction of bill for value-added tax.
	1986	Implementation of value-added tax.
	1987	Ceiling rate raised on government bond issuance.
		Tax reform commission established by Ministry of Finance.
	1988	Amendment of Land Tax Law.
	1990	Statute for the Encouragement of Private Investment in Infrastructure.
II. Fiscal Policy — External Trade		
Export Orientation Period	1971	Liberalization of import controls.
		Tariff rate adjustments within 50% authorized by law.
Science and Technology Orientation Period	1983	Further tariff reduction.
		Further liberalization of import controls.
	1986	New customs valuation system introduced.
	1987	Extensive tariff reduction, top rate reduced from 67.5% to 58%.
	1988	Further tariff reduction, top rate reduced to 50%.
	1990	Foreign Trade Law drafted.

Table A1   (Continued)

Stage	Year	Policies
III. Monetary and Foreign Exchange Policies — Monetary Policy		
Export Orientation Period	1972	Bond market established.
		Combating inflation with high interest rates.
	1974	Bond market established.
	1976	Interest rate liberalization.
		Money market established.
Science and Technology Orientation Period	1985	Interest rate regulations discontinued.
		Prime rate system introduced.
		Issuing of beneficiary certificates approved.
	1986	Structure of interest rates on deposits simplified.
	1987	Insurance market opened to U.S. companies.
		Bank credit rating system established.
	1988	Restriction relaxed on establishment of security brokerage and trading firms.
	1989	Banking Law revised to allow the entry of new private banks.
		Interest rate restrictions relaxed.
	1991	Promoting privatization of state-owned financial institutions.
		Opening of 15 private banks.
	1992	Insurance Law revised.
IV. Monetary and Foreign Exchange Policies — Foreign Exchange Policy		
Export Orientation Period	1973	Appreciation of NT dollar first in 1973 and second in 1978.
	1978	Floating exchange rate introduced.
	1979	Foreign exchange market established.
Science and Technology Orientation Period	1983	Rationalization of foreign exchange regulation.
	1985	Simplifying settlement procedure for trade-related foreign exchange transactions.
	1986	Appreciation of NT dollar.
		Amendment of foreign exchange regulations.
	1987	Relaxing foreign exchange controls and allowing residents to freely hold and use foreign exchange.
	1989	Establishing a new exchange rate system based on free price negotiation.
	1991	Reopening forward foreign exchange market.

Table A1 **(Continued)**

Stage	Year	Policies
V. Monetary and Foreign Exchange Policies — International Capital Movement		
Export Orientation Period	1973	Raising of large loans to support large infrastructure and heavy industrial projects.
Science and Technology Orientation Period	1983	Liberalization of capital market.
		Statute for international financial activities enacted.
	1990	Allowing foreign institutional investors to directly invest in local stock market.

The policy events that took place over a time span of some 50 years (1950-1995) that can be subdivided into three subphases of evolution as indicated on the horizontal axis of each panel:

I) Import Substitution phase (1950-1962) (IS phase)

II) Export Orientation phase (62-80) (EO phase)

III) Science and Technology Oriented Phase (80-2000) (ST phase)

representing a long run trend of liberalization. Well over 200 major policy events (indicated in boxes erected over the horizonal axes I,II,...,X) occurred in the transition process to describe the process of marketization over the period of transition growth of 45 years. A highly controlled economy in the IS phase is transformed into a depoliticized system resembling that of an industrially advanced country toward the end of the ST phase. Fei (1988) and Ranis (1988) proposed that the EPM can be used for the study of the evolutionary transformation of the economic institutions—leading to the construction of the original EPM as a result of the cooperation of Li, Ranis and Fei in Li (1988). Li elongated the EPM for the period after 1985 in Li (1995).

The EPM constructed by Li (1995) described the policy events over the 40-year period (1950-1990). As reproduced in Table A1 in this appendix, the initial 20-year period covering the IS phase (1950-1962) as well of the first 8 years of the EO phase (1962-1970) are *not shown*. Thus Table A1 shows only the process of policy evolution after 1970. The time axes (I,II,...,X) are thus shortened for the purpose of their alignment with that of the political event matrix (PEM) shown as Table A2. Notice that the time axes of the PEM are labeled as number XI (Election), XII (Laws and regulation), XIII (Political movement and party formation), and XIV (Other exogenous historical events) to be explained below (See section A3).

The ten areas of policies (I,II,...,X) are not isolated events. In fact, they exercise their policy impacts on different parts of a highly integrated economic system provided by the holistic operational perspective of a dualistic economy of Figure 9.2 (see Figure 9.2, which links policies I to VIII to the operational perspective). The various economic interest groups of the dualistic economy are listed at the bottom of the diagram. They constitute the conflicting interest groups in the pluralistic society of Taiwan which are to be compromised in the political process after the arrival of the phase of constitution democracy (see below).

Table A2   Political Event Matrix (PEM), 1970–2000

Stage	Year	Policies
XI. Elections		
Embryonic Democratization	1969	Election of "Additional Members" (AMs) of the National Assembly (NA) and Legislative Yuan (LY).
	1972	Election of more AMs of LY.
	1975	Election of AMs of LY.
	1980	Election of AMs of LY and NA.
	1983	Election of AMs of LY.
	1986	Election of AMs of LY and NA.
Intensive Democratization	1989	Election of AMs of LY.
	1990	Lee Tung-Hui elected President by NA.
	1991	Election of the all new 2nd NA.
	1992	Election of the all new 2nd LY.
	1994	Governor of Taiwan Province and City Mayors elected.
	1995	Election of Members of 3rd LY.
	1996	First direct election of the President.
XII. Laws and Regulations		
Embryonic Democratization	1980	The LY passed a law setting specific rules for elections.
Intensive Democratization	1987	People are formally allowed to visit Mainland China.
		Martial law is lifted.
		The National Security Act became effective.
		LY passed the National Security Act resuming people's right to hold meetings and demonstrations and to form political parties.
	1988	Ban on newspapers lifted.
	1989	LY passed Act to retire First-term Senior Representatives.
	1990	KMT decided: KMT Senior Members of the LY should all retire.
	1991	NA annihilated the Temporary Articles of Constitution which did not restrict the terms of presidency.
	1993	LY passed an act permitting cable TV.
XIII. Political Movement and Party Formation		
Embryonic Democratization	1977	The "Chung-Li" incident: riot in reaction to suspected vote tampering.
	1979	The "Formosa Island" incident: parade to promote human rights turned into a riot.

Table A2   (Continued)

Stage	Year	Policies
Intensive Democratization	1986	Establishment of the opposition party, the Democratic Progress Party.

XIV. Other Events

Stage	Year	Policies
Intensive Democratization	1988	President Chiang Ching-Kuo died.
		Lee Tung-Hui became president.
	1991	DPP advocated a referendum on the independence of Taiwan.
		Completion of retirement of all remaining Senior Members of the NA.
		Completion of retirement of all remaining Senior Members of the LY.

A2) Application of EPM for Marketization

The applicability of the EPM as a conceptual tool for the study of the marketization process has certain obvious advantages and inherent weaknesses. Every policy event went through a political process of "enactment" that operationally redefines the {Gt,St} in terms of certain ways that the (originally imperfect) markets (i.e. the commodity, labor, finance and international trade described in Figure 9.2) are being penetrated by the political power of G. In a perspective of comparative economic system (i.e. in comparison with that of {Gm,Sm}), for the transition period as a whole, the EPM of Taiwan reveals the following structural characteristics:

    i) bureaucratically planned and growth centric

    ii) direction specificity in planning for expansion of sectoral outputs

    iii) covert income transfer for specific sectoral expansion

    iv) market closure for fear of international competition

    v) construction of (deficient) government administrative capacity

as discussed in Section 9.4.2. These general characteristics provided the guideline for the study of the process of evolutionary changes in the art of government management of the economy, oriented toward "liberalization" through time — as proxied by the sequentially ordered policy events in the EPM:

    i) Management of growth and investment (a,b,c)

    ii) Management of international economic relations (d)

    iii) Central bank management of money supply (e.f)

    iv) Functional specialization of markets and government (g)

The details of a,b,c,...,g, given in 9.4.2 in the text, provide the guidelines according to which the individual policy events should be interpreted. In this regard, the fact that the time axes I,II,...,X (i.e. for the ten policy areas) are perfectly aligned is highly significant in that all economic policies are somewhat related in a holistic operational perspective. A typical example is the allocation of loanable fund for investment finance that involves not only the finance market but also the wage "price information" from all the other markets to determine the viability of a particular investment project. Thus a direction specific policy (Ib) is usually implemented in many policy areas simultaneously. For example, the bureaucrats can foster the expansion of the industry of video-tape recorders by

   i) granting it a tax holiday (Domestic Fiscal Ax.I 60)

   ii) tariff protection and import control (Ax.II 52)

   iii) preferential loan from government banks (Ax.III)

   iv) prohibition of investment by foreign nationals (Ax.V)

It usually takes the adoption of a package of policies to implement a "growth promotion strategy" consistently in order to create profit (covert income transfer) for a particular industry. Generally speaking, it takes a combination of both micro- and macro economic theory (e.g. the loanable fund theory of investment and inflation) to analyze the policy events diagnostically to assess the changing role of the government G as its command is gradually replaced by the functionally specialized markets.

The evolution of human institutions is a complex process involving changes in ideas, ideology and cultural values (see Sections 9.2, 9.5, 9.6) that accompanied the "institutional" (i.e. organizational) change in the process of marketization. The EPM is a useful conceptual tool for the study of "evolution" when, and only when, with the aid of theory, knowledge of the "perfection of markets" and hermeneutical interpretation of human nature can be inferred from the enactment of "policies" in the EPM to reflect the societal consensus on $\{G,S\}$.

A3) The Political Event Matrix (PEM)

The EPM motivated the PEM of Table A2, which is a chronological listing of the "political events" classified into

XI) *Election* of the

   1) National Assembly (NA) (Ax.XI 69,80,86,91)

   2) Legislative Yuan (LY) (Ax.XI 69,72,75,80,83,86,89,92,95)

   3) President (Ax.XI 90,96)

   4) Local: provincial and municipal heads (Ax.XI 94)

XII) *Laws and Regulations* on:

   1) elections (Ax.XII 80,89,90,91)

   2) human rights: to hold meetings, form parties, free press, free travel (Ax.XII 87,88,93)

XIII) *Political Movement and Party Formation*

   1) Protests, riots and other social movements for democracy and/or clean elections (Ax.XIII   77,79)

   2) Establishment of opposition party DPP (Ax.XIII 86)

XIV) *Other Exogenous Historical Events*

   1) President CCK died (Ax.XIV 88)

   2) DPP advocated referendum for Taiwan independence (Ax.XIV 91)

   3) Completion of retirement of senior members of NA and/or LY (Ax.XIV 91)

as indicated by the boxes erected over the time axes XI,XII,XIII and XIV, to represent the four key dimensions in the process of democratization.

The transformation from authoritarian pluralism $\{Gt,St\}$ to the modern polity of constitutional democracy $\{Gm,Sm\}$, as described in Figure 9.1 in the text, clearly has these four dimensions. In addition to the formalism of "election" (Ax.XI) and the "enactment of laws and regulations" (Ax.XII) the democratization process has a "turbulent dimension" of social movements (Ax.XIII) in the forms of protests, street demonstration, marches and rallies that usually accompanies the sprouting of the idea of democracy that is to be entrenched as an integral part of the political cultural value through time.

The democratization process did not occur in the context of a historical vacuum. Since democratization represents a decentralization of compulsory power of Gt, it is inevitable that the process is accompanied by struggle for power inheritance. In the case of Taiwan, this "short run" power struggle was manifested by two exogenous historical events:

  i) the conflict over independence for Taiwan or unification with the mainland
  ii) ethnic conflicts between the Taiwanese and the Mainlanders

that became political issues fully exploited by the politicians. In a historical perspective, turbulence from these sources are clearly short run phenomena and will not enter into our analysis of the democratization process, the contour of which is demonstrated quite clearly by the PEM.

A4) Periodization of the PEM

In our paper the application of the pair EPM and PEM is directed at the key issue of the relatedness of D and M, i.e. *whether D is an inevitable consequence of M* (see introduction). To prepare for the analysis of this issue notice that in the EPM, the year 1980 is a landmark year as it is a turning point marking off the EO phase (1962-80) from the ST (science and technology) phase (after 1980). From the viewpoint of the political transformation we have the following periodization as indicated on the time axis of the PEM of Table A2:

1) The Phase of *Embryonic Democratization*, 1970-87
  i) election of additional members of LY and NA (Ax.XI 69,72,75,8o,83,86)
  ii) social movements for "clean elections" and "human rights" (Ax.XIII 77,79)
2) The Phase of *Intensive Democratization*, 1987-96
  i) initiated by the suspension of the Martial Law (Ax.XII 87)
  ii) terminated with direct presidential election (Ax.XI 96)
3) Post (Presidential) Election, 1996-2006

The historical significance of the D-Embryonic phase (that lasted almost 20 years) is basically the surfacing and the growth of the *ideas of D as well as the demand for D* in social movements as protests against the slow pace in the election of the "additional members" to the legislature (the NA and LY) that have lost their popular "legitimacy" (see (1) above). The major events of the intensification phase of D (87-96) are straddled between the epochal events of the lifting of the Marshall Law (87) and the direct presidential election (96) over a 10-year period (see (2) above).

A5) Economic Background of the Embryonic Democratization Phase

In China the demand for the Western polity of D has had a long history, and can be dated back to the time after the May 4th social movement some 70 years ago after the first World War. That the D-Embryonic phase (70-87) occurred at the "juncture of transition of the export orientation phase (62-80) into the ST phase (after 1980) is highly significant. The ST phase represents the beginning of economic modernization as the creative potential was fully explored in the economic arena as labor intensive exports gave way to the wave after wave of technology intensive exports with a structural flexibility of production that could only be ensured by the system of competitive markets.

The heart of democratization lies in decentralization of the power of the government G to the micro decision-making units to be coordinated by the automatically adjusted market (see Figure 9.1 and discussion in 9.2.2). Thus an economic explanation of the evolutionary emergence of the embryonic democratization phase (70-87) in the PEM can be established by the empirical findings of the following type in the EPM over the period (70-87) as the Taiwan economy evolved from the EO phase (70-80) to the ST phase (80-87). For the EO phase (70-80)

1) *Marketization, i.e. the evolutionary emergence of the markets consisting of*
   i) the finance market regulated by the interest rate, including the
      a) the money market (Ax.III 76)
      b) the loanable fund market (Ax.III 76) for "private" finance
      c) the bond market (Ax.I 74 and Ax.III 74) for public finance
   ii) the foreign exchange market regulated by the exchange rate
      a) the formal establishment (Ax.IV 79) preceded by
      b) commanded (or "dirty") float (Ax.IV 73,78)
2) *Depoliticization, i.e. the withdrawal of arbitrary political force from*
   i) interfering with the market price system by fiscal policies including
      a) liberalization of import controls (Ax.II 71,83,86,88)
      b) self imposed fiscal discipline of the ceiling for government bonds (Ax.I 75) in the finance market
   ii) promoting commercialization of the public enterprises (AX.V 73)
3) *Central Bank autonomy*: the adherence to a high interest policy to combat price inflation á là the loanable fund theory of interests (Ax.III 72)

In an evolutionary perspective, the above marketization process during the first part of the embryonic phase (70-80) paved the way for the emergence of the ST phase when the creative potential of the Chinese was fully accommodated by the market system to build a flexible economic system. The life style of "heterogeneity and variety" in the economic arena (see Section 9.2.2) was accentuated by a continuation of the liberalization process in the ST phase (80-87) as can be seen from a further erosion of the power of the government as the markets are perfected by "functional specialization" and "internationalization."

(1) Functional Specialization and Internationalization of Financial Market
   i) functional specialization (Ax.III 85,86,87)
   ii) internationalization (Ax.V 83)
(2) Rationalization and "clean float" of the foreign exchange rate (AX.III 83,85 86)
(3) Depoliticization by adherence to fiscal conservatism (Ax.I 82,83)

Thus we see that the establishment and perfection of the markets and the withdrawal of political power from the economic arena is conducive to the emergence of the phase of *embryonic democratization* when popular demand for the decentralization of political power arose.

A6) Economic Background of the Intensive Democratization Phase

The policy evolution in the PEM for the intensive democratization phase was merely a continuation of the trends of *privatization, internationalization* and *further market perfection*:

(a) *For privatization*: demand for and granting of human rights in the

   i) economic arena: for owning foreign exchange (Ax.IV 87), for establishment of brokerage firms (Ax.III 88) and banks (Ax.III 89), and participation in infra-structure investment (Ax.1 90) to go along with those in the

   ii) political arena: to hold meetings, form parties, free press, free travel (Ax. XII 87,88) to show the interaction and reenforcement of the economic and political liberalization process.

(b) *For internationalization*: the opening up of insurance markets to foreign firms (Ax.III 87) and that of the stock market to foreign institutional investors (Ax.V 90).

(c) *For further market perfection*: the establishment of a new exchange rate system (Ax.IV 89) and the re-opening of the forward foreign exchange market (Ax.IV 91).

A7) Conclusions

The findings in the above analysis due to use of the PEM and EPM can be succinctly summarized as follows (C1,C2,C3,C4):

C1) *In an evolutionary perspective, the arrival of the "political miracle" of* **Intensive D phase** *over a ten-year period (1987-1996) was herald by a much longer (some 17 years)* **Embryonic D phase** *during which the spreading of the idea of D and demand for D in social movements was grounded on the economic foundation of the* **transition toward the epoch of modern growth** *at a later (terminal) stage.*

We view both D and M as evolutionary processes carrying subphases. Our finding is that the M-process in the later stage gave rise to the emergence of the D-process. The D process is a consequence of economic modernization. Specifically, *without the solid economic foundation*, D as a human institution simply will not materialize. For example, in the case of China, there was no shortage of the "idea" or the "social movements" for D in the period 1920- 1970, and yet D did not arrive due to the absence of the economic modernization emphasized in this paper.

C2) *The* **Embryonic D phase** *occurred as the economy entered into the ST phase when labor intensive manufactured exports gave way to production based on an educated labor force as well as a rapid* **accumulation of capital assets, physical and/or intellectual,** *managed by an* **entrepreneurial class** *that is sensitive to* **technology** *and the* **legality of property rights and contractual disputes** *of a market economy.*

This conclusion gives support to the popular economic thesis on the "sprouting of democracy" as the consequence of the emergence of the *middle class*. D is very much story of the maturity of *economic agents* that can grow (in ideas and cultural values) in an education and learning process. For a more detailed listing of the social groups formed of these agents, see bottom of Figure 9.2.

C3) *In an evolutionary perspective, the economic foundation of (C1) centered on the transformation of the {G,S} characterized by the complementarity of* **"privatization and marketization"** *on the one hand and* **depoliticization** *on the other. The* **substitution** *of the government power (G) by the society power (S) implies the* **evolutionary destruction of the practices of "rent seeking"** *(see 4.1c on the one hand) as well as the* **evolutionary construction** *of an economic system compatible with the requirement of* **structural flexibility** *(see 4.1 b.iii) on the other).*

The construction and the opening up of the domestic markets for international competition implies a change of the focus of economic policies (monetary, fiscal and "economic") from "direction specific and growth centric" to "direction neutral and growth promotion insensitivity" (see (4.1.a and b). The "substitution of power" in the economic arena is the sine qua non of D as demonstrated in this paper.

C4) *The decentralization of the power of G to the microscopic economic agents of decision making units in S implies a process of gradual* **expansion of the political and economic domain** *for the exercise of free choice and experiments in human associations and contacts (see remarks by Keynes in 5.1 and A6.a.i and ii). As the variety of products was multiplied in the ST phase, the society became* **pluralized** *as the integration of conflicting interests on the political stage became easier when the acceptance of the discipline of competition (in both the world and domestic markets) was internalized as the new commercialized cultural value.*

While the party state of the PRC is, perhaps, the most politicized polity ever designed, the institution D, with its automatically adjusted markets, is the least, because it is conducive to human creativity. The resentment of political interference in economic life was indeed the theme of the first folklore ever written in long history of Chinese literature

> "early to rise and work with sun,
> early to bed with sunset is best,
> a well to dig for drink is fun,
> a field to plow for stomach rest
> what use is emperor power to me?" (c14)

where the modern counterpart of emperor power is politics. The folklore provides a testimony that democracy is indeed suitable for a race with the Chinese social personality. (See Section 9.6 in text.)

A8) Future Research

The experiment in methodology of this paper suggests that study of evolution of human institutions (e.g. the polity of democracy and the economic system of markets) calls for an interdisciplinary framework of analysis that can make full use of the wealth of anecdotal information in the archives of public offices. In this appendix, we have illustrated the applicability of this method for the study of the interaction between D and M. However discussion was limited to only the first panel of diagram A1. A similar analysis can be made on the relatedness of D and M by making use of

i) Ax VI — to study atrophy and the changing role for public enterprises that results

ii) Ax VII — to show the relatedness of urbanization and D

iii) Ax VIII — to show the relatedness of D with human agents and resources

iv) Ax IX — to show the profile of the development of science and technology with that of D

v) Ax X — to study the changing art of government management in the process of decentralization of government power.

in the other panels (panels b and c of Table Al). Early work has been done by economists on the early part of the EPM without references to political transformation (see Fei, 1995). In this appendix, we have concentrated on the economic transition at the later stage (i.e. after 1970). The analysis can apparently be extended to the earlier period (1950-1970) by the construction of the PEM for this period to show that it was a tightly controlled society in the economic sense (e.g. controlling the price of a haircut), the political sense(e.g. martial law) as well as the cultural sense (e.g. high school hair style).

9.8 Appendix Two: Glossary of Chinese Characters

c1	培養人性內涵
c2	舜何人也，予何人也，有爲者亦若是
c3	學而時習之，不亦悅乎
c4	知行合一
c5	古者言之不出，恥躬之不逮
c6	人的尊敬在中國自古就建立了
c7	和而不流，群而不黨
c8	同不同，之謂大同
c9	一盤散沙的中國社會人格
c10	天地
c11	人是宇宙的中心；人能弘道非道弘人
c12	天地之大德曰生，生生不息
c13	苟日新，日日新，又日新；天行健君子以自強不息
c14	日出而作，日落而息，鑿井而飲，耕日而食，帝力於我何有哉
c15	從價值系統看中國文化的現代意義

9.9 Note

1 The authors thank Prof. Erik Thorbecke for his helpful comments and suggestions.

9.10 References

Almond, Gabriel A., 1960. "Introduction: A Functional Approach to Comparative politics," in G. A. Almond and James Coleman (eds)., *The Politics of the Developing Areas*. Princeton: Princeton University Press: 3-64.

Easton, David, 1953. *The Political System*. New York: Alfred A. Knopf.

Fei, John C. H., 1986. "Economic Development and Traditional Chinese Cultural Values," *Journal of Chinese Studies*, Published by American Association for Chinese Studies, 3 (1): [pages].

Fei, John C. H., 1988. "Bird's Eye View of Policy Evolution on Taiwan: An Introductory Essay," in Li, *op. cit.*: 26-46.

Fei, John C. H., 1995. "The post-war ROC Economy in Historical Perspective," *Nota Economicas*, [vol?, no?] May: 6-21

Huber, Evelyne, Dietrich Rueschemeyer, and John D. Stephens, 1993. "The Impact of Economic Development on Democracy," *Journal of Economic Perspective*, 7: 71-85.

Huntington, Samuel P., 1989. "The Contest of Democratization in Taiwan." Keynote speech given at *the Conference on Democratization in the Republic of China*, the Institute of International Relations of National Chengchi University, Taipei, Taiwan, R.O.C., January 9-11.

Keynes, John Maynard, 1936. *The General Theory*. London: MacMillan and Co.

Krasner, Stephen, 1985. *Structural Conflicts: The Third World Against Global Liberalism*. Berkeley: University of California Press.

Kuo, Shirley W.Y., 1983. *The Taiwan Economy in Transition*. Boulder: Westview Press.

Kuzuets, Simon, 1966. *Modern Economic Growth*. New Haven: Yale University Press.

Li, Kuo-ting, 1988. *The Evolution of Policy Behind Taiwan's Development Success*. New Haven: Yale University Press.

Li, Kuo-ting, 1995, *The Evolution of Policy Behind Taiwan's Development Success, 2nd Ed.*, Singapore: World Scientific.

Lipset, Seymour Martin, 1995. "Some Social Requisites of Democracy: Economic Development and Political Legitimacy," *American Political Science Review*, 53: 69-105.

Moore, Barrington, Jr., 1966. *The Social Origins of Dictatorship and Democracy*. Boston: Beacon Press.

Ranis, Gustav, 1988. "The Evolution of Policy in a Comparative Perspective: An Introductory Essay," in Li, *op. cit.*: 1-25.

Schumpeter, Joseph A., 1939. *Business Cycles*, 2 vols., New York: McGraw Hill.

Skocpol, Theda, 1985. "Bring the State Back In: Strategies of Analysis in Current Research," in Peter B. Evans, Dietrich Rueschemeyer and Theda Skocpol (eds.), *Bringing the State Back In*. N.Y.: Cambridge University Press: 3-37.

Stepan, Alfred, 1985. "State Power and the Strength of Civil Society in the Southern Cone of Latin America," in In Peter B. Evans, Dietrich Rueschemeyer and Theda Skocpol (eds.), *Bringing the State Back In*. N.Y.: Cambridge University Press: 317-343.

Tobin, James, 1993. "Price Flexibility and Output Stability: An Old Keynesian View," *Journal of Economic Perspective*, 7: 45-65.

Yu, Ying-shih (in Chinese), 1984. *The Modern Meaning of Chinese Culture as a Value System* (c15), [place]: China Times Publishing Co.

Yu, Ying-shih, 1991. "Clio's New Cultural Turn and the Rediscovery of Tradition in Asia," University of Hong Kong: 12th Conference of the International Association of Historians of Asia.

PART IV
THE ROLE OF AGRICULTURE, INDUSTRIAL POLICY, HUMAN CAPITAL AND LABOR INSTITUTIONS IN TAIWAN'S DEVELOPMENT

10 AGRICULTURE AS THE FOUNDATION FOR DEVELOPMENT: THE TAIWANESE STORY

Tsu-tan Fu and Shun-yi Shei

10.1 Introduction

The role of agriculture in the post-colonial Taiwanese economy can be roughly divided into two stages. In the first stage, 1945-1973, agriculture acted as a supporting sector providing vital resources to the rest of the economy. This part of the story is well documented by Professor Thorbecke (1979). In the second stage, 1973-1995, agriculture became a dependent and protected sector, drawing resources from the general economy. As the Taiwanese economy gained maturation, more attention was given to agriculture's role in providing environmental and public services other than the traditional food and agricultural services. How and to what extent should agriculture play its role lies in the social benefits it contributes weighted against the costs the society has to pay for protecting it. This changing role of agriculture simply reflects the requirements of a more mature Taiwanese economy in balancing and achieving its multiple objectives of material well-being as well as quality of life.

Five elements of the Taiwanese rural development strategy were identified as crucial to the success of overall economic growth and development in the years between 1945 and 1973. These elements are: 1) the land reform measures; 2) the integrated functions of the Joint Commission on Rural Reconstruction (JCRR); 3) the set of polices and taxes that were used to squeeze agricultural surplus; 4) a choice of labor intensive technology in agriculture and manufacturing; and finally 5) the regional and rural decentralization of industrial development to absorb rural labor (Thorbecke, 1979: 200). It is generally claimed that the Taiwanese government made wise decisions in carefully designing and implementing these five elements such that a set of favorable incentives and opportunities were created for economic development. However, it is hardly ever mentioned that the Taiwanese government did not interfere in the operation of agricultural agents, where the market was performing more efficiently. This was crucial for the sustained growth of private enterprise and domestic industrialization — the two major factors contributing to the successful transition of the Taiwanese economy from import substitution to export orientation in the 1960s. Therefore, in the first part of this paper, we try to compare the impact of government interventions affecting the agricultural sector with the impact of the market in the process of building the foundation for development. More precisely, we show how the government and the market operated to generate a vast number of entrepreneurs and small business units which were decisive in the industrial development of Taiwan. In the second part of this paper, we will first present an overview of the major supportive government programs with a close examination of their budget allocations and their institutional mechanisms. Four types of representative government policies are discussed. The benefits transferred to farmers, including Direct Benefit as well as Indirect Benefit, are further analyzed. The well-known import regulations are also examined to reveal the level of government transfer due to intervention in Taiwan's agriculture. This is then followed by a discussion of the new role of agriculture and its implication for Taiwan's society. The paper concludes with a discussion of the relevance of Taiwanese lessons in the context of a changing global economy.

10.2 Basic Building Blocks of the Foundation, 1945-1973

From the perspective of agriculture, at least three sets of building blocks could be identified as factors contributing to the foundation of Taiwanese economic development. These are effective institutional mechanisms, agricultural surplus extraction, and integration with the world economy. Both the government and the market exerted their powers either separately or jointly to affect these three sets of contributing factors. Their merits and limitations are the focus of the following discussions.

10.2.1 Effective Institutional Mechanisms

It is generally believed that the productivity growth of a country's agricultural sector depends on its institutional arrangements. The government which provides a set of effective institutional mechanisms such that its farmers can obtain the right technology, the right inputs at the right time and in the right amount should be credited for a sustained growth of its agricultural sector. Hayami and Ruttan (1971) regard the adoption of appropriate technology as being influenced by the profitability of research and development and the initial resource endowment of a country. They recognize that in order to spread technology, it is not only necessary to offer new or modern inputs at attractive prices, but also to have effective institutional mechanisms for the distribution of inputs and outputs.

By the early 1950s, the institutional framework of Taiwanese agriculture was almost complete. Dr. Chan, a former chairman of JCRR, gave a lively description in his memoirs (1990) of how the system worked:

Beginning in 1953, with the assistance of JCRR and Taiwan Provincial Food Bureau, Farmers' Associations (FAs) of Taiwan had expanded their businesses. By the late 1950s, the FA in each county had the capacity to serve as the farmers' supermarket. For example, farmers loaded their rice on an oxcart and walked five kilometers on average to the county's FA and engaged in the following activities:

1) Exchange rice for fertilizers, conducted under the rice-fertilizer barter program, and apply 70 percent of fertilizer loan, and load fertilizers on oxcart again.
2) Pay land tax in kind (rice), keep it in the FA's storage silo.
3) Sell part of their rice to FA.
4) Deliver the rest of their rice to FA's miller and load the husked rice on the oxcart.
5) Deposit their cash revenue from rice and sugar in the credit section of FA.
6) Draw cash to purchase soybean cake, sliced sweet potatoes for pig feed and home necessities from the supplies section of FA.
7) Go to the extension section to chat with extension personnel about new rice species and pig breeds and so on.
8) Others.

When all things were done, the farmer would join other farmers in the FA's open space to have snacks, to smoke, to talk and laugh and then go home with their oxcart. When I visited south and southeastern Asian countries, the sight of loneliness of the local farmers was in sharp contrast with Taiwanese farmers. This inspired me to assert that the scene of Taiwanese FAs should be the most lively description of Taiwanese development experience.

A more complete and intensive discussion of the institutional framework of Taiwanese agriculture can be found in Thorbecke's papers on "Agricultural Development of Taiwan" (1979) and "The Process of Agricultural Development in Taiwan" (1992). My task here is to show that although government institutional arrangements were important, they certainly were not sufficient to warrant sustained economic growth, which should be the domain of market competition and private entrepreneurs.

The first element of the Taiwanese rural development strategy was the land reform program. Some writers have singled out the successful land reform programs of 1948-1956 as the key to Taiwanese agricultural growth and equal income distribution. However, it is not difficult to see that a one-time distribution of the existing land could not have solved Taiwan's economic problems, and the benefits of the land reform would soon have been eroded without rapid economic growth when Taiwan had a rapidly growing population of very high density in the 1950s. Certain writers claimed that the land reform program served in particular ways to make Taiwan's rapid economic growth sustainable. For example, Jacobs (1984) argued that the compensation to landlords generated a string of payments that converted rural landlords into capitalists. Murphy et al. (1989) concluded that the land reform had a wealth leveling effect, which caused local investors to produce mass consumption goods and discriminate against imports of luxury goods. The increase in the demand and supply of domestic mass consumption goods provided incentives and opportunities for domestic industrialization. Taiwan also inherited the Japanese flair for small scale labor intensive manufacturing industries. Therefore, land reform helped create favorable conditions for the growth of small scale labor intensive business.

It will be very difficult to quantify the impact of land reform on domestic industrialization. However, data on the distribution of manufacturing production by ownership and the numbers of private entrepreneurs and business units will provide us with a feeling of land reform's impact. In 1952, the year before the Tiller Act was enforced, private ownership in manufacturing accounted for 43.8 percent of value added. Three years after the implementation of the Tiller Act, in 1956, this figure jumped to 51.7 percent, with a moderate increase to 54.7 percent in 1961. The industrial and commercial census of Taiwan revealed that between 1954 and 1961, manufacturing enterprises increased from 39,748 units to 51,567 units, while employees increased from 309,887 persons to 445,667 persons. In the next section, we will provide a more general picture by comparing land reform, surplus squeeze and agricultural trade in shaping these changes.

The second element of the rural development strategy was the establishment of the Chinese-American Joint Commission on Rural Reconstruction in 1948. The JCRR was involved in integrated rural development by providing research and extension services, credit, and irrigation, and by strengthening Farmers' Associations and supporting investment in many rural and agricultural projects. Between 1951 (the year U.S. foreign aid was first granted) and 1965 (the termination of aid) the JCRR undertook nearly six thousand projects. Total foreign aid in agriculture represented nearly 59 percent of net domestic capital formation in agriculture. There should be no doubt that the capital resources generated by U.S. foreign aid and administered by JCRR played a key role in building the Taiwan's agricultural foundation.

The third element is the design of mechanisms through which capital resources were transferred from the agricultural sector to the rest of the economy. One major specific mechanism was the rice-fertilizer barter. By setting a distorted ratio of rice and fertilizer exchange, the government was able to transfer a substantial amount of capital resources from agriculture to other sectors.

The fourth element of the Taiwanese rural development strategy was the selection of appropriate technology consistent with the factor endowment of the country. Hence, until the labor constraint became binding in the late 1960s, Taiwan relied on agricultural technology that intensively used its available labor. However, one would suspect that there was significant government role in affecting farmers with respect to the choice of labor intensive farming technology. Because of the constraint of small farms' size, it is rational for farmers to choose labor intensive farming technology in response to market incentives and opportunities.

Rural decentralization of industrial development was identified as the final element of the government's successful strategy. Since this element was not directly under the control of agricultural policy makers, we will not give a detailed discussion of how it worked. We even suspect that rural decentralization of industrial development was shaped by the market forces rather than by a deliberate government strategy.

It will be a difficult task to identify separately these five elements affecting Taiwan's agricultural growth and development. However, their combined effects can be shown in Table 10.1. Rice and sugar were given particular attention because rice was squeezed for food and sugar was mainly squeezed for foreign exchange purposes. Although all crops and livestock were affected in terms of absolute advantage, only rice and sugar were affected by comparative advantage. A comparison of their growth rates may provide some crude observation of the role government and the market had in shaping the outcomes.

Table 10.1   Growth Rates of Agricultural Output by Commodity Groups, 1946–1973

(%)

	1946/1948 ~ 1953/1955	1953/1955 ~ 1961/1963	1961/1963 ~ 1966/1968	1966/1968 ~ 1971/1973
Rice	7.6	2.9	3.2	-0.9
Other food crops	5.8	3.1	3.9	-1.8
Sugarcane	NA	-0.2	3.1	-1.3
Tobacco	NA	5.9	1.6	-0.9
Tea	NA	5.1	3.6	3.1
Peanut	NA	5.3	4.2	-4.2
Bananas	NA	4.7	35.3	-7.2
Pineapples	NA	12.6	10.7	3.1
Citrus fruits	NA	11.0	18.4	13.4
All fruits	1.2	9.3	22.5	3.8
Asparagus	NA	0.0	0.0	20.1
All vegetables	5.0	4.5	8.2	12.8
Mushrooms	NA	0.0	21.2	8.0
Hogs	NA	6.1	7.5	8.2
Chicken	NA	3.0	8.9	11.4
All livestock products	NA	5.7	7.3	7.7

Source: Taiwan Agricultural Production Statistics (1979), Statistics Department, Ministry of Economic Affairs. The growth rates are computed on the basis of the index of agricultural production. NA denotes not available.

There were many market demand and supply forces in the determination of the growth rate of individual crops, fruits, vegetables, and livestock products. Furthermore, the government set up institutional arrangements which introduced technologies and incentives in favor or against the production and marketing of each product. The realized growth rate of each item in Table 10.1 was the result of the interplay of market and government forces. The government intervened in rice production largely through the rice-fertilizer barter by setting unfavorable terms of trade against rice producers. It interfered with sugarcane and tobacco production through the government-owned Taiwan Sugar Corporation and Taiwan Tobacco & Wine Monopoly Bureau. The rest of the items were relatively market oriented.

The growth rate of Taiwan's first stage of agricultural development, 1945-1973, is divided into five subperiods. The average for three years was taken to minimize the yearly variation in production due to weather. The production data beginning in 1946 was compiled by the Department of Agriculture and Forestry and Taiwan Provincial Food Bureau. The year 1953 marked the completion of institutional changes in the land reform processes, that is, the enactment of the Land-to-the-Tiller program. The change from import substitution to export orientation occurred in 1961. The overall agricultural sector experienced a decline in 1969, the first since 1945, and the binding nature of labor and land constraints was identified as the major cause of this event. By the end of 1972, the rice-fertilizer barter was abolished, ending an era of taxing and squeezing agriculture.

One aspect of government intervention is observed by the relative narrow range of variation in the average rates of growth of rice, sugarcane and tobacco. By contrast, if the market forces act alone, then there is a large swing in the average rates of growth. This is especially true for export oriented products such as bananas, mushrooms and asparagus. The table also shows that products with high income elasticities such as fruits, vegetables and livestock products have high rates of growth. This implies that the relatively low growth rates of rice, sugarcane and tobacco might be due largely to the relatively low income elasticities. Government attempts to boost the growth rate of a particular product might fail simply because its income elasticity is too low.

How agriculture was further exploited to provide the foundation for development is another question to be addressed. On the basis of the built foundation of agricultural growth, two major instruments — the developmental squeeze on agriculture and the agricultural export push — were pursued. The roles of government and market in these instruments, and their merits for economic development, will be discussed in the following two sections.

10.2.2 Developmental Squeeze on Agriculture

In the 1950s, it was generally believed that in economically underdeveloped countries any substantial sacrificing of present consumption opportunities for the sake of higher rates of investment and future consumption possibilities must fall on the shoulders of the poor peasants. Therefore, the fundamental questions of development policy in poor countries are twofold: 1) how can a government design a set of effective institutional mechanisms to encourage farmers to produce agricultural surplus over and above their own consumption; 2) how can this surplus be extracted efficiently from agriculture and transferred to the rest of the economy.

The first question was addressed in the previous section. Owen (1966) and Sah and Stigliz (1984) wrote two excellent papers focusing on the second question. Owen stated that the logic of extracting the agricultural surplus can be described in terms of the "double developmental squeeze": the production squeeze and the expenditure squeeze. Most studies focus only on the production squeeze simply because it is easy to estimate empirically. The production squeeze in Taiwan took place largely through the rice-fertilizer barter, similar to the Marxism-Leninist model of compulsory deliveries. If the government can control part of the capital resources from an involuntary squeeze, then it might invest it in public enterprise which would be, in general, less efficient than private enterprise. Data on the distribution of industrial production by ownership showed that the Taiwanese government accounted for 56.6 percent in 1952, and maintained roughly 50 percent until 1961 (see Table 10.2). One would suspect that a substantial amount of squeeze on agriculture was used indirectly in the public enterprise to maintain its operation. The public share started to decline gradually in the 1960s when the capacity to squeeze agriculture dropped.

Table 10.2   Distribution of Industrial Production by Ownership (Based on value added)

	Industrial		Manufacturing	
	Private	Public	Private	Public
1952	43.4	56.6	43.8	56.2
1956	49.0	51.0	51.7	48.3
1961	51.8	48.2	54.7	45.3
1966	61.8	38.2	66.7	33.3
1971	75.0	25.0	82.1	17.9
1972	79.4	20.6	86.9	13.1
1973	77.3	22.7	84.0	16.0

Source: Taiwan Statistical Data Book, Economic Planning Council, 1976.

Sah and Stigliz formalized a simple model from which they derived several interesting propositions. The proposition that is most relevant here is that turning the terms of trade against peasants leads to an increased accumulation of non-agricultural surplus or capital resources. Moreover, if the price response of agricultural production is larger than the price distortion against peasants, this will lead to an increase in capital resources in the non-agricultural sector. This is because in a closed economy, a decrease in the relative price of an agricultural good will cause a decline in agricultural surplus, urban expenditure on the agricultural good will also drop, and this can decrease the urban real wage which, in turn leads to a higher surplus in the urban or non-agricultural sector.

The Taiwanese government's vision of economic development was consistent with the development thought of the 1950s. They believed that an effective institutional mechanism alone simply was not enough to warrant sustained overall economic growth. The government should be involved in extracting agricultural surplus for the sake of capital accumulation and economic growth. The most important extraction mechanism was the rice-fertilizer barter program, which began in 1948 and ended in December 1972. The rice-fertilizer barter ratios were officially set at levels that made chemical fertilizers quite expensive in terms of rice. The differences of actual and efficient rice-fertilizer barter ratios can be shown by comparing columns (1) and (2) of Table 10.3. The actual ratios declined slowly and gradually. However, the efficient ratios of barter were subject to variations in international rice and fertilizer prices. The international rice price, measured as Taiwan's rice export price, was between US $150/mt and US $170/mt in most years. By contrast, the international fertilizer price, measured as Taiwan's fertilizer import price, showed a significant declining trend. By 1972, the price of imported fertilizer was only about one-third of the price level in 1951. These differences reveal the extent to which price distortions against rice crop had increased in the 1960s.

The magnitude of the rice-fertilizer barter squeeze on rice was large. In 1969, the capital resources squeeze on rice alone reached 1.3 billion NT dollars, which accounted for 4.6 percent of the total value of agricultural production. There are many direct and indirect approaches to measuring the magnitude of the squeeze on agriculture. Table 10.3 presents several estimates of the rice-fertilizer barter distortion. Our own calculation, columns (5a) and (5b), reveal that the magnitude of the rice-fertilizer barter's hidden tax as a percentage of the total value of agricultural production was generally lower than the figures of columns (5c) and (5d) of previous studies.

The overall impacts of the governmental squeeze on agriculture can be summarized as follows:

1. Total compensation to landlords amounted to 12 billion NT dollars, which was roughly equal to 25 percent of the total value of agricultural production for 1952 (Ho, 1978).
2. The real capital outflow arising from terms of trade distortion, due largely to the rice-fertilizer barter, amounted to about 6.3 percent of total agricultural production between 1952 and 1955, and 5.8 percent between 1956 and 1960. Between 1961 and 1965, the government could only squeeze 0.6 percent of total agricultural production. Between 1966 and 1970, the terms of trade was in favor of agriculture, and the net inflow of real capital to agriculture amounted to about 0.9 percent of total agricultural production (Lin, 1973).
3. Total real capital outflow from agriculture accounted for 22 percent of agricultural production between 1952 and 1955, 12 percent in 1956-1960, 9.8 percent in 1961-1965, and 6.7 percent in 1966-1970 (Lin, 1973).
4. A transfer of funds through financial institutions grew from 1 to 3 percent in the 1950s to 12.3 percent in 1961-1965, and was over 17 percent of total agricultural production in 1966-1969 (Lee, 1972).
5. Primary and processed agricultural exports accounted for 31 percent of the value of total agricultural production in 1952, 31 percent in 1955, 27 percent in 1960, 39 percent in 1965 and 35 percent in 1970.

Judging from different dimensions, it is quite obvious that the outflow of capital resources from agriculture to the rest of the economy was substantial in the period between 1952 and 1970.

In retrospect, one may ask whether the involuntary squeeze on agriculture through the Tiller Act, rice-fertilizer barter and other schemes was necessary. If the landlords were allowed to keep their land, would the rents be largely consumed or

Table 10.3   Squeeze on Agriculture through the Rice–Fertilizer Barter

	Actual rice-fertilizer barter (1)	Efficient rice-fertilizer barter (2)	Value of extraction (3a)	(3b)	Value of total agricultural production (4)	Value of extraction as percentage of agricultural production (5a)†	(5b)‡	(5c)	(5d)
	(kg rice/ per kg fertilizer)		(million NT dollars)			(%)			
1948	1.5	NA	NA	NA	NA	NA	NA	NA	NA
1949	1.5	NA	NA	NA	NA	NA	NA	NA	NA
1950	1.010	NA	NA	NA	NA	NA	NA	NA	NA
1951	0.959	0.753	80.6	43.9	NA	NA	NA	NA	NA
1952	0.871	0.753	373.7	65.0	5,233	7.2	1.2	1.2	6.5
1953	0.828	0.493	215.8	267.4	7,436	2.9	3.6	5.1	8.0
1954	0.824	0.603	104.4	156.6	6,533	1.6	2.4	5.8	4.2
1955	0.857	0.699	312.4	130.3	8,028	3.9	1.6	0.0	6.7
1956	0.840	0.836	298.5	3.6	8,759	3.4	0.0	4.5	5.6
1957	0.854	0.808	264.1	48.9	10,163	3.6	0.1	3.8	6.0
1958	0.865	0.726	668.7	146.2	11,127	6.0	1.3	4.5	5.1
1959	0.863	0.671	602.4	239.8	12,591	4.8	1.9	6.8	4.7
1960	0.849	0.630	465.3	382.7	16,528	2.8	2.3	4.4	6.0
1961	0.835	0.644	335.2	326.8	17,872	1.9	1.8	4.3	6.5
1962	0.832	0.534	344.5	549.0	17,891	1.9	3.1	4.6	5.2
1963	0.799	0.452	384.0	690.9	18,844	2.0	3.7	5.4	5.1
1964	0.792	0.507	418.5	682.6	23,509	1.8	2.9	5.2	4.4
1965	0.820	0.562	537.6	619.1	24,797	2.2	2.5	4.3	4.4
1966	0.869	0.534	559.0	796.3	26,326	2.1	3.0	4.8	4.2
1967	0.842	0.397	508.1	1,110.3	27,448	1.9	4.0	6.1	4.3
1968	0.833	0.411	261.4	1,026.7	29,363	0.9	3.5	6.2	3.9
1969	0.789	0.342	520.3	1,304.4	28,304	1.8	4.6	3.1	2.3
1970	0.68*	0.370	−39.6	665.9	31,523	−0.1	2.1	0.7	1.8
1971	0.58*	0.288	−50.0	738.2	31,575	−0.2	2.3	0.4	1.4
1972	0.53*	0.260	108.5	547.1	35,884	−0.3	1.5	0.3	NA

Notes: † $(5a) = \frac{(3a)}{(4)} \times 100$; ‡ $(5b) = \frac{(3b)}{(4)} \times 100$.

Source: Column (1) was taken from Taiwan Provincial Food Bureau. * denotes the rice-fertilizer barter was set to per kg rice over per kg ammonium surphate; Column (2) was calculated as the import price of ammonium surphate over the export price of polished rice × (1 + 0.15)/(1 − 0.15)/0.73; Column (3) was calculated as (export price of polished rice × 0.79 × 0.92/(1 + 0.15) × exchange rate of US$/NT$ − government purchase price) × total quantity of rice bartered/0.79; Column (4) was taken from Taiwan Statistical Data Book; Column (5c) and (5d) were reestimated using data from Koo (1995) and Kuo (1983).

invested? Would there be a bias toward consumption of luxury imports? What would happen if a free market were enforced such that a squeeze on agriculture was voluntary in the context of a Mill-Marshallian model? Under a Mill-Marshallian model, the implication of a squeeze on agriculture would be the same as an involuntary squeeze, in which the relative agricultural price would also be depressed by the market forces. However, there would be a larger agricultural surplus in response to the fall of the relative agricultural price by the introduction of new technology. Theoretically, the government then can increase taxes on the wage rate such that a surplus can be squeezed from non-agricultural consumption and be directed towards investment.

10.2.3 Industrialization through Agricultural Integration with the World Economy

Agricultural integration with the rest of the world through the exports and imports of primary and processed agricultural products could act as an engine of economic growth and development. The importance of this integration was well emphasized in two recent World Bank reports (1991, 1993). The mechanisms through which the market was expanded, and how the production feasibility curve was shifted toward a production possibility curve was formalized in Myint's paper (1987). The openness of agricultural trade creates incentives for improvisers to explore new opportunities such that entrepreneurs and new business units can be created at a faster speed.

The story of Taiwan's agricultural trade and its contribution to industrialization can be described as follows. First, between 1952 and 1955, foreign exchange earnings from rice and sugar exports, which accounted for 80 percent of total agricultural exports and 75 percent of total exports was controlled by the government (see Table 10.4). The exchange earnings were able to support the imports of food, feed and industrial raw materials.

Second, the government controlled exchange earnings as the percentage of agricultural exports declined to 54 percent between 1961 and 1963, while market oriented earnings from private enterprises in banana, pineapple and mushroom exports increased gradually. The yearly average of exchange earnings from rice and sugar exports was 79.2 million US dollars between 1961 and 1963. Agricultural imports of raw cotton, wool, logs and lumber amounted to a yearly average of 52 million US dollars during the same period. This was followed by structural changes in employment and business units. Employees in textiles, apparel and leather products (hereafter textiles for short) increased from 67,933 persons in 1954 to 100,906 persons in 1961. Employees in food, beverages and tobacco (food for short) increased from 68,767 to 117,584 persons. Sixty percent of the increase in total manufacturing employment came from food and textile products (See Table 10.5). The total number of manufacturing business units increased 30 percent, from 39,748 units in 1954 to 51,567 units in 1961. The number of business units in food also had a 30 percent increase while business units in textiles increased only 10 percent. The increase in the average number of employees per business unit in food and textiles was a sign of economies of scale and also an indication of industrialization.

Third, the export share from rice and sugar declined to 25 percent of the total value of agricultural exports between 1966 and 1968, while exports from private en-

Table 10.4   Values of Agricultural Trade (Yearly averages)

				(US\$ million)
	1952/1955	1961/1963	1966/1968	1971/1973
Total agricultural exports	112.5	147.3	261.0	516.7
Primary products	26.7	29.6	92.3	177.0
Rice	18.9	11.1	20.7	6.9
Bananas	4.7	7.9	49.0	23.6
Hogs and pork	0.1	1.4	0.8	32.6
Sea products	0.2	0.4	4.4	59.7
Processed products	85.8	117.7	168.7	339.7
Sugar	71.6	68.1	45.7	79.1
Tea	6.9	8.0	10.7	16.1
Pineapples	3.6	10.3	17.5	17.7
Mushrooms	0.0	8.6	28.1	49.6
Asparagus	0.0	0.0	20.5	42.9
Total agricultural imports	69.9	112.2	192.3	633.3
Food and feed	42.8	55.9	107.5	356.7
Wheat	15.8	22.1	24.7	50.6
Corn	0.0	0.2	11.4	82.8
Barley	0.0	0.8	1.6	23.4
Soybeans	20.0	14.2	35.8	109.5
Fish meal	0.0	0.0	2.0	8.5
Dairy products	2.4	3.6	7.5	23.2
Beef	0.0	0.0	0.0	1.3
Fruits and nuts	0.1	0.3	1.6	3.8
Vegetables	1.2	1.2	3.1	4.7
Industrial raw materials	27.1	56.3	84.8	276.6
Raw cotton	18.0	31.9	42.8	102.9
Woll	3.8	11.4	9.0	28.9
Tobacco	1.4	3.3	5.8	14.8
Hides and leather	1.5	1.0	2.2	7.1
Logs and lumber	2.4	8.7	25.0	122.9

Source: Basic Agricultural Statistics, Council of Agriculture, 1985.

Table 10.5   Number of Enterprises and Employees in Manufacturing

	Manufacturing		Food, beverages and tobacco		Textiles, apparel and leather products		Manufacture of metal products, machinery, electronics	
	Units	Employees	Units	Employees	Units	Employees	Units	Employees
1954 Total	39,748	309,887	11,676	68,767	7,043	67,933	4,780	32,559
1961 Total	51,567	445,667	14,827	117,584	7,707	100,906	6,355	49,734
1966 Total	27,709	589,660	16,514	137,767	1,706	117,394	4,360	86,017
Government	63	79,726	6	38,756	5	1,222	1	2,118
Private	27,666	509,934	13,508	99,011	1,701	116,172	4,359	83,899
1971 Total	42,626	1,201,539	12,934	145,576	3,531	310,079	10,272	273,567
Government	44	89,754	4	34,750	3	2,108	5	7,813
Private	42,592	1,111,785	12,930	110,826	3,528	307,971	10,267	265,754

Source: Industrial and Commercial Census of Taiwan, various issues. Census data in 1966 and hereafter included only registered enterprises.

Table 10.6   Sources of Gross Savings

	Gross savings (NT$ million)	Gross savings as percentage of GNP	Gross domestic savings as percentage of gross savings	US aid and foreign loans as percentage of gross savings	Private enterprise savings as percentage of gross savings	Public enterprise savings as percentage of gross savings	Government savings as percentage of gross savings
	(1)	(2)	(3)	(4)	(5)	(6)	(7)
1952	1,586	9.2	60.0	40.4	49.8	13.5	-3.3
1955	2,700	9.0	67.5	32.5	53.7	16.8	-3.1
1961	8,935	12.7	64.3	35.7	53.6	17.6	-6.9
1966	28,009	22.2	95.6	4.4	73.2	13.4	9.0
1971	73,929	30.1	109.4	-9.4	77.4	16.4	15.6
1972	92,626	33.0	127.2	-27.2	82.2	17.5	27.5
1973	128,200	30.1	120.3	-20.3	83.8	12.8	23.7

Source: Taiwan Statistical Data Book, Economic Planning Council, 1976.

terprises in bananas, mushrooms, asparagus and pineapples accounted for 44 percent of the share. The numbers of employees in both food and textiles increased 17 percent between 1961 and 1966. During the same period, the number of employees in machinery, electronics and metal products (machinery for short) experienced a 73 percent increase. The 1966 census also showed that among 27,709 business units, 27,666 units were run by private enterprises. Capital formation was largely generated by private enterprise in the mid-1960s. By 1966, private enterprise savings as a percentage of national gross savings reached 73.2 percent. This was a 20 percentage point increase from 1961; a very significant change since this figure was relatively unchanged since 1952 (see Table 10.6). During this phase, we observe that not only did agricultural export earnings from private enterprise increase but the share of employees in food as a percentage of all manufacturing also increased, from less than 30 percent in 1961 to roughly 50 percent in 1966. By 1966, almost all of the manufacturing units were run by the private sector. One would suspect that this development was related to the increase of export oriented farm products. Foreign exchange earnings from export oriented farm products then supported more industrial raw materials imports, which averaged 84.8 million US dollars between 1966 and 1968.

Fourth, there was a significant increase in the number of employees in textiles and machinery products between 1966 and 1971. A substantial increase in both units and number of employees in the machinery sector in this period suggests that the entrepreneurs involved in the economic transformation had shifted from food in the early 1960, to textiles in the mid-1960s and then to machinery in the early 1970s.

How and to what extent did the agricultural exports interact with the rest of the economy, and how were they linked backward and forward to generate the vast pool of entrepreneurs and the fast speed of Taiwanese industrialization, are very difficult issues to comprehend. Jacobs suggests that "economic improvisation" are the two words most appropriate to characterize the process of industrialization. One would agree that improvisation is the domain of private business. It is the entrepreneurs' ability to copy, imitate, adopt, modify and diffuse new technologies and deliver goods to customers within a given time constraint that makes the difference in business performance. Therefore, we shall conclude that it was the increasing share of market oriented exports of private business in agriculture that fostered the incentives and opportunities for improvisers who sped up the process of Taiwan's industrialization, especially since the mid-1960s, that accounted for a major part of the success story of Taiwanese experience. The effective institutional mechanisms and the squeeze on agriculture all mattered, but they could not provide lasting momentum for industrialization and growth.

One final note on the successful Taiwanese story in industrialization is the significance of U.S. aid. Foreign capital and loans as well as U.S. aid accounted for more than one third of gross domestic capital formation (see Table 10.6) and were crucial in lessening the dollar shortage problem between the 1950s and 1960s. However, some writers cast doubt on the effectiveness of this unearned foreign exchange in the process of economic development. Without U.S. aid, the real exchange rate of NT dollars relative to the US dollar would fall and Taiwanese agricultural exports would benefit from the devaluation of the NT dollar. Agricultural exports might play an even more important role in the process of Taiwanese industrialization under such circumstances. However, without U.S. aid, the general equilibrium outcome of the US dollar shortage problem might have led the government to prolong import substitution and defer export substitution.

10.3 The Transition of Taiwan's Agriculture, 1973-1995

In the second stage of Taiwan's agricultural development (1973 to present), the role of agriculture changed from a resource supporting sector to a dependent and protected sector drawing resources from the general economy. Government agricultural policy switched from a strategy of taxing agriculture to one of supporting it. Such a changing policy environment can be attributed to a marked deceleration of agricultural production growth since the late 1960s, a steady deterioration of farmers' income relative to non-farmers' income, food insufficiency, and high market prices resulting from the world-wide food shortage and energy crisis in 1973. Therefore, starting from 1973 a sequence of agricultural programs was designed to achieve multiple policy goals. While the benefits transferred to producers via these programs were substantial during the whole study period, the policy focuses and program mechanisms varied in each sub-period. In what follows, we shall present an overview of these government policies by examining their budget allocations and their redistributive effects on policy groups.

For analytical purpose, these farm support programs can be classified into four types of policies according to their policy focus. Public investment in infrastructure, price supports for outputs, subsidies on inputs and on farmer's welfare, and import regulation were the major policies undertaken in the 1970s and 1980s. It is also interesting to note that the importance of the environmental functions served by normal agricultural production and activities has been increasingly recognized by the general public recently. Accordingly, this emerging function is shown to be a new role of modern agriculture in Taiwan.

10.3.1 Major Agricultural Policies and Their Income Redistributive Mechanisms

In 1973, the government promulgated the Agricultural Development Statute. This Statute program may be recognized as the milestone that marked the transformation of Taiwan economic development policy from squeezing agriculture to supporting agriculture. This is also the first time in Taiwan's history that the government's support for and protection of agriculture was guaranteed by law. Several features stated in the Statute provide a legal basis for giving more favorable consideration to the agricultural sector. These include: (1) exemption of farmland tax and inheritance tax for those lands continuing farm usage after inheritance; (2) exemption of the land value increment tax if the farmland is sold to another farmer for cultivation; (3) the requirement of approval from the agricultural authority for any importation of agricultural commodity; (4) the increase of public expenditure to strengthen rural infrastructure and to implement farmers' welfare measures (5) the implementation of agricultural insurance programs to enhance farmers' incomes and to maintain rural social order (Mao, 1991). Following this Statute, four types of policies are briefly described respectively.

The Public Investment in Infrastructure. In 1973, the government also launched another monumental program, the Accelerated Rural Development Program. This program was aimed at increasing agricultural production, raising farm incomes, improving the rural environment and accelerating agricultural modernization. In support of this program, the government appropriated NT$ 2 billion in 1973-74. The program was further extended to 1979, with a budget that amounted to NT$ 22.9 billion, including NT$ 13.6 billion set aside for the Food Stabilization Fund.

After the termination of the Accelerated Rural Development Program in 1979, a new set of programs was instituted in 1979-1985. These included: "Program to Enhance Farm Income and to Strengthen Rural Reconstruction" in 1979, "Program for Basic Infrastructural Development" in 1980, "Program to Strengthen Basic Infrastructure and to Enhance Farmers' Income" in 1982, and "Program to Improve the Structure of Agricultural Production and to Enhance Farmers' Income" in 1985.

By the year 1989, government had spent a budget of NT$ 125.7 billion on these programs for the last 11 years (Mao, 1991). We also observe that an average of 34 percent of the government agricultural budget was allocated for public investment in infrastructure in 1983-1987 and 37.2 percent in 1992-1996 (see Table 10.7).

Price Supports for Agricultural Products. Following the abolishment of the rice-fertilizer barter system, the government instituted a guaranteed price program for rice in 1974. This program, based on a similar spirit as the preceding two pro-

Table 10.7   Government Budget Allocations for Agricultural Programs

Fiscal Year	Total agri-cultural budget	Public investment on infrastructure	Price support and subsidy	Others[a]
	NT$ million	%	%	%
1983	8,920	25.57	39.24	35.19
1984	9,030	33.23	33.22	33.55
1985	9,081	36.14	33.04	30.82
1986	10,487	37.05	38.33	24.62
1987	11,548	36.46	40.62	22.92
1992	41,457	37.72	34.30	27.98
1993	48,999	39.81	32.66	27.53
1994	50,105	38.64	31.97	29.39
1995	51,586	38.96	39.93	21.11
1996	77,521	30.99	25.71	43.30[b]

[a]Others include: farmers' organizations & extension, farm management improvement, marketing, processing and trade, rural community improvement, research & experimentation, information service, administrative service, credit loans and other items.

[b]There are two special budgets newly added in 1996: NT 13.2 billion for the Farmer's Pension Program and NT$10 billion for the Trade Loss Compensation Fund.

Data source: Chen (1987) and the Council of Agriculture, Taiwan, R.O.C.

grams, was aimed at providing an incentive for rice farmers to increase rice production and ensuring a reasonable income from farming. The Food Stabilization Fund was established in April 1974 with an initial endowment of NT$ 3 billion. Initially, the government was committed to purchase unlimited amounts of rice at prices higher than the market price. The floor support prices of rice were in principle fixed at the cost of rice production plus a 20 percent profit. Given this favorable incentive, brown rice production reached a record high of 2.7 million metric tons in 1976, a more than 20 percent increase of rice produced over 1973. It was this no-limit mechanism of government purchase that resulted in a heavy financial burden. In 1977, a deficit (Table 10.8) appeared in the Food Stabilization Fund account. This caused the government to overhaul its rice purchase policy. Under the new policy, the committed rice purchase at the guaranteed price was set at a maximum of 970 kilograms per hectare per crop. However, ever since 1989, the amount of purchases

Table 10.8   Food Stabilization Fund Annual Surplus Condition

Fiscal Year	Government purchase		This year's surplus		Cumulative surplus	
	1,000 m.t.	% of total production		NT$ million		NT$ million
1974	187	8		61		61
1975	338	14		—[b]		—
1976	729	27		29		90
1977	636	24	(−)[a]	194	(−)	104
1978	475	19	(−)	3,458	(−)	3,562
1979	620	25	(−)	2,806	(−)	6,368
1980	659	28	(−)	4,558	(−)	10,926
1981	943	40	(−)	782	(−)	11,709
1982	803	32	(−)	5,718	(−)	17,427
1983	1,097	40	(−)	10,717	(−)	28,144
1984	671	30	(−)	12,185	(−)	40,330
1985	805	37	(−)	8,990	(−)	49,320
1986	675	34	(−)	7,876	(−)	57,196
1987	657	36	(−)	7,664	(−)	64,860
1988	497	27	(−)	8,924	(−)	73,784
1989	732	39	(−)	7,150	(−)	80,934
1990	684	38	(−)	6,762	(−)	87,696
1991	533	29	(−)	6,899	(−)	91,593
1992	513	32	(−)	7,678	(−)	102,271
1993	551	30	(−)	7,253	(−)	109,524
1994	633	38	(−)	9,538	(−)	119,062

[a](-) indicating a deficit in that year.
[b]No sales in Fiscal Year 1975.
Data source: The Council of Agriculture, Taiwan, R.O.C.

at the guaranteed price has again increased to 1,400 kilograms per hectare per crop due to the government's favorable political concerns toward farmers. Table 10.8 indicates that the financial cost of this program has been around NT$ 7 billion to NT$ 10 billion annually since 1983. By the end of 1994, the cumulative financial loss of the Food Stabilization Fund amounted to NT$ 119 billion.

It should be noted that the government also instituted guaranteed prices for grains other than rice, including sorghum, soybeans and other export crops, whereas similar stabilization funds were established for sugar, hog, and dairy. However, the total budget for these two classes of products was insignificant relative to rice.

The Subsidies on Inputs and on Farmers' Welfare. In addition to providing price supports, reducing production costs is another effective way to enhance farming profit. The government in Taiwan has allocated a budget to subsidize various farming inputs since 1973. During the period 1973-1990, government subsidies included NT$ 1.76 billion for farm use machinery, NT$ 0.76 billion for interest on loans, NT$ 1.5 billion for agricultural utility use, NT$ 40 billion for fishing boat gas use, NT$13 billion for agricultural water use, and NT$ 2.6 billion on fertilizer use (Chen, 1989).

In addition to direct intervention in the pricing of farm outputs and the costs of farming inputs, the government also allocated a significant budget to enhance farmers' welfare. For example, since the implementation of the Farmers' Health Insurance Program in 1985, the government has subsidized 70 percent of the due premium. Government spending on this program reached NT$ 54 billion by the year 1994. Improving Rural Community is another case of government investment in farmers' welfare. This program amounted to NT$ 12 billion in 1973-1990. Recently, the government allocated NT$ 13.2 billion in 1996 for the newly established Farmers' Pension Program.

Although price supports and input subsidies differ in their designed mechanisms, they all transfer taxpayers' money directly to farmers. Table 10.7 indicates that the total budget allocated for price supports and input subsidies accounted for more than 30 percent of the total agricultural budget for those years in the 1980s and 1990s.

The Import Regulation Measures. The requirement of approval from the agriculture authority for the importation of any agricultural commodity was written in the Agricultural Development Statute in 1973. Since then, import regulations have been imposed on most agricultural products that Taiwan imports. There are several types of indicators that measure the level of protection provided by import regulation. Among them, the nominal tariff rate is the most popular one. In addition to this nominal tariff rate measure, the Producer Subsidy Equivalent (PSE) is widely used in measuring government intervention in agriculture. The PSE measure is especially meaningful if the product's import regulation is a type of non-tariff barrier. Table 10.9 provides figures on level of protection for those imported agricultural products. Since most importation of the products listed in Table 10.9 is somewhat regulated by a non-tariff barrier, the PSE figures would be a better approximation of the true level of protection. However, in line with an agricultural trade policy that leans toward liberalization, both tariff rates and non-tariff barriers have been substantially reduced in recent years.

Table 10.9 Nominal Import Tariff Rates, Import Regulations and Commodity Programs for Agricultural Commodities, 1990

Commodity	Nominal tariff rate	Import regulations	Commodity program	PSE[d] (%)		
				'82–'86	1986	1988
Rice	0%	Permitted/L; subject to approval of admin. dept.	Price support plan conversion soil conservation	28.1	43.4	47.7
Corn	2.0%	Permitted/L	Price support Deficiency payment	70.1	77.4	83.6
Soybeans	1.5%	Permitted/L	Price support Deficiency payment	57.3	66.5	74.7
Sorghum	3.0%	Permitted/L	Price support Deficiency payment	74.3	79.4	82.8
Wheat	6.5%	Permitted/L	Price support (contracted)	64.8	72.4	80.2
Beef	23.5 NT$/kg (prime or choice) 30.0 NT$/kg (medium)	Permitted/RA	Price support	18.4	32.3	28.5
Pork	15.0%	Permitted/F (prime) Permitted/L (medium)	—	1.9	1.4	1.2
Chicken	40.0%	Permitted/L	—	23.4	NA	31.5
Milk, fresh	40.0%	Controlled	Price support (contracted)	NA	53.5	59.9
Milk, powdered	20.0%	Permitted/L	—	NA	NA	NA
Sugar	25–35%[a] 40%[b]	Controlled Permitted/F	Price support (contracted)	29.2	64.1	46.4
Fruits	15–50%[c]	Controlled; permitted/F Permitted/RA; subject to approval of admin. dept.	Price support Marketing order (Selected products)	NA	NA	34.5
			Avg.	19	26.8	29.4

[a]: Cane and raw-cane sugar (25%), rock sugar (35%), cube sugar (35%), maple sugar (40%). [b]: maple sugar (40%). [c]: Grapefruit and citrus have seasonal import tariffs. [d]: Data for '82–'86 average adopted from USDA (1987), and for 1986 and 1988 adopted from Hou and Yu (1993).

Note: Permitted/F: free to import; Permitted/RA: import permitted only from restricted areas or countries; Permitted/L: import permitted with licenses issued by B.O.F.T. Data sources: Woo & Fu, 1990; Hou and Tu, 1993.

10.3.2 The Benefit Transferred to Producers, 1973-1990

A closer examination of mechanisms embodied in the four types of government policies discussed in the previous section makes one aware of their different impacts on income redistribution. The magnitude of benefit transfer is also dependent on the choice of mechanisms. For example, the price support program for rice in Taiwan transfers taxpayers' money to rice producers via government purchases at guaranteed prices. The magnitude of the transfer depends upon the amount and the price of purchase. The more rice being purchased at higher prices, the more benefit is transferred to producers. Moreover, the government is flexible in choosing the level of intervention on the spectrum ranging from free market to government control. Unlike the full government control case as in Japan, the Taiwan government only controls around 30 percent of the rice production via guaranteed price purchases and leaves some room for the market mechanism to come into play. This limited amount of price support reduces the cost of protection borne by taxpayers.

In a comprehensive study of benefits transferred to Taiwanese farmers via government programs of Taiwan in 1989, Chen (1989) found the total benefit that farmers received for 1973-1990was NT$ 331 billion. Table 10.10 also indicates high growth rates of benefit received by producers after 1985. We can further classify government programs into Direct Benefit and Indirect Benefit categories. Direct Benefit includes those benefits resulting from policies of product price supports or deficiency payments, and government input subsidy programs on agricultural water use, fishing boat gas use, agricultural land tax, value increment tax of agricultural land, farmers' health insurance, and so on —benefits paid directly to farmers. The indirect benefits are generated through government investment projects on product technology improvement, rural environment improvement, public investment on infrastructure, research and experimentation, and others. We found that the Direct Benefit dominates the Indirect Benefits for most of these years (Table 10.10).

Among those project items in Direct Benefit, subsidy of rice purchases ranked first in 1977-1988, whereas the subsidy for fishing boat gas use also had a good share of benefit during the whole period of study (Table 10.11). In addition, the benefits of government exemption from agricultural land taxes became significant since the mid-1980s. Subsidy on farmers' health insurance has increased substantially since the late 1980s. However, the structure of Indirect Benefit has shown little change from 1973 to 1990. We also noted that the benefits generated from public investment in infrastructure tend to dominates benefits from other projects.

Another measure of income transfer to producers resulting from government policies is the Producer Subsidy Equivalent (PSE). The PSE, measured as a percentage of total value of production, indicates the excess return to producers above world market prices. This includes direct assistance to farmers via border measures that keep the domestic producer price above the world price, and non-border measures such as government assistance financed through the budget.

The average level of PSE in Taiwan in 1982-1986 estimated by the USDA was 19 percent, which is a figure lower than most developed countries. Similar level of estimates were estimated by Hou and Tu (1993) as shown in Table 10.9. By using these estimates, we conjecture that the income transfer to producers resulting from

Table 10.10 The Direct and Indirect Benefit of Farmers Resulting from Government Programs, 1973–1990

Unit: NT$ million (%)

Fiscal year	Total benefit	Direct benefit	(%)	Indirect benefit	(%)
1973-1974	3,333	1,090	32.70	2,243	67.30
1975	1,833	1,089	59.41	744	40.59
1976	4,409	2,205	50.01	2,204	49.99
	9,575	4,384	45.79	5,191	54.21
1977	7,371	4,414	59.88	2,957	40.12
1978	10,386	7,016	67.55	3,370	32.45
1979	8,811	5,492	62.33	3,319	37.67
1980	13,014	5,463	41.98	7,551	58.03
	39,582	22,385	55.85	17,197	44.15
1981	12,346	6,625	53.66	5,721	46.34
1982	14,083	7,961	56.53	6,122	43.47
1983	17,333	10,767	62.12	6,566	37.88
1984	20,933	12,795	61.12	8,138	38.88
	64,695	38,148	58.97	26,547	41.03
1985	25,456	16,432	64.55	9,024	35.45
1986	30,928	17,870	57.70	13,058	42.30
1987	32,541	18,887	58.04	13,654	41.96
1988	36,601	20,397	55.73	16,204	44.27
	125,526	73,586	58.87	51,940	41.13
1989	40,511	22,805	56.29	17,706	43.71
1990	50,654	28,562	56.39	22,092	43.61
	91,165	51,367	56.35	39,798	43.65
Sum	330,543	189,870	57.44	140,673	42.56

Data source: Compiled from Chen (1989).

government policies in Taiwan was about 20 to 30 percent of the total value of agricultural production in the 1980s. They also showed that in 1988 alone, agricultural policies helped farmers gain 1,477 million US. dollars, whereas consumers lost 1,726 million US dollars and taxpayers lost 297 million US dollars. The net social loss to the whole economy was 556 million US dollars, about 0.45 percent of GDP.

An interesting question one might like to ask is "Did the supportive policies implemented since 1973 effectively improve the status of farmers' income?" It is no doubt that with government supportive policies farm income has increased substantially since 1973. However, it is also observed that farm household income remained at about 74 percent of non-farm household income during the period 1975-1980. After 1984, the ratio declined to less than 70 percent, and fell to 65 per-

Table 10.11 The Changing Structure of Farmers' Benefits Resulting from Government Programs, 1973-1990

					(%)
Item	1973–1976	1977–1980	1981–1984	1985–1988	1989–1990
Direct benefit	100.00	100.00	100.00	100.00	100.00
Government subsidy on:					
Rice purchases	24.55	35.73	40.32	32.12	17.42
Sugar purchases	0.40	23.84	5.61	3.18	0.29
Ag. water use	19.69	8.32	6.41	3.79	10.56
Fishing boat gas use	49.86	17.99	31.03	18.01	14.21
Ag. land tax	0.00	8.87	12.14	30.83	39.32
Farmers' health insurance	—	—	—	1.69	12.70
Others	5.50	5.25	4.49	10.38	5.5
Indirect benefit	100.00	100.00	100.00	100.00	100.00
Government investment projects on:					
Production technology improvement	32.33	12.15	9.28	9.24	9.47
Rural environment improvement	12.70	13.42	3.08	9.32	8.86
Public investment on infrastructure	38.70	65.28	70.94	70.72	71.17
Others	16.27	9.15	16.7	10.72	10.5

Data source: Compiled from Chen (1989).

cent in 1991-94. In addition, the ratios of farm household income to non-farm household income on a per capita basis seem to be relatively static over time, ranging from 65 percent in the 1970s to 70 percent in the late 1980s. The declining trend of these relative income ratios thus casts a doubt on the effectiveness of the income enhancing programs instituted in the 1970s and 1980s. One might argue that the inequality of income distribution between farming and non-farming households might have been worse without various measures of agricultural protection. On the other hand, one would also tend to ask, from an ex post perspective, if such an income enhancement purpose could have been better achieved by a freer market mechanism. A good alternative may be the newly proposed decoupling principle. Under this principle, payment to farmers is decoupled from the production decision, which thus promotes growth with equity.

10.3.3 *Environmental and Social Functions: A New Role for Agriculture in Taiwan*

Agriculture plays an important role as the source of a stable, continuous supply of basic foodstuffs to a nation. However, as described by Nagata (1991), once the society becomes richer and more mature, more people recognize that agriculture is no longer simply a food and raw material industry, but an industry that supplies society with many multilateral benefits. This new role of agriculture lies in the various social benefits it contributes accruing from agricultural land use and normal agricultural production.

Under this new emerging role, social benefits from farming would include the preservation of water resources, flood control, soil erosion prevention, prevention of landslides, soil purification, health and recreation, protection of wildlife, supply of oxygen, and purification of the air. Although the value of these external economic effects of agriculture is difficult to assess through the market mechanism, a rough figure equivalent to about 15 percent of Japan's current GNP and three times the gross product of the agricultural and forestry industries was estimated by the Ministry of Agriculture, Forestry, and Fisheries of Japan (Nagata, 1991). In addition, social stability induced from maintaining agriculture and rural villages is also regarded as an important benefit to Japanese society (Egaitsu, 1991).

This new role for agriculture has been increasingly appreciated by the general public since the late 1980s. This emerging consensus may represent a change toward a more mature society in Taiwan. Recent public attitude on how to resolve environment and development disputes may reflect their expectations of this new role. Three cases are described here to show how the government did accommodate this public need. The first case refers to the changes of farmland and slopeland use policies. Due to land scarcity on the island of Taiwan, government used to encourage land cultivation for agricultural production even in environmental sensitive areas such as slopelands. Scientists in Taiwan often warned that severe degradation of environmental quality such as soil erosion, destruction of scenic amenity, water shortage or water quality degradation may result from continued abuse of slopeland. However, it was not until the late 1980s that such a warning was appreciated by the general public and government authorities. To prevent further deterioration, a stricter slopeland use law was promulgated in 1993. A new forest use policy has also been implemented in the 1990s which converts forestry land from production into conservation and preservation.

Another case representing a conflict of land use between the habitat of an endangered species, the migrating black face crane, and an industrial park is happening in a swamp area of Tainan county. While maintaining the swamp area may provide environmental and educational functions to society, it jeopardizes local society's opportunity to expand its industrial development. The solution to this dilemma depends upon people's expectations of the role of agriculture. The final decision to maintain the swamp for habitat use seems to be compatible with the new role of agriculture.

The last, but not least, case refers to the environmental preservation functions of paddy field farming. Paddy fields are mainly used for rice production. However, due to the high cost of rice production, a tendency of trade liberalization in the rice market, and high demand for agricultural land, the release of paddy fields for non-agricultural use has become a heatedly debated issue in the formulation of future land use policy. If we adopt the concept of agriculture's new role, then the environmental functions of paddy fields may force the government to provide subsidies to slow down the conversion of paddy fields to non-agricultural uses.

10.4 Concluding Remarks

During the past four decades, economic development in Taiwan has been characterized by a successful structural transformation from a predominantly agricultural economy to a newly developed economy. Within this changing development process, agriculture has played different roles in the economy to accommodate changing economic and social environments. In the first stage of this process (1945-1973) agriculture acted as a supporting sector providing vital resources to the rest of the economy. Three sets of building blocks, including effective institutional mechanisms, agricultural surplus extraction, and integration with the world economy, were identified by this paper as factors contributing to·the foundation of Taiwanese economic development in this period. Government policies for agricultural products in this stage were mainly tax measures and programs established to promote agricultural production. However, after 1973 agriculture became a dependent and protected sector drawing resources from the general economy. During 1973-1995, various government programs with huge budget allocations were instituted to support agriculture. The income transfers to farmers from consumers and taxpayers via those supportive government programs have proved to be substantial in the second stage. Additionally, as Taiwan's economy is getting more mature in the 1990s, the provision of environmental and social services to society has become an important part of the role of agriculture in the modern economy.

Although the government has heavily intervened in markets either in the form of implicit taxation of rice production or in the form of direct subsidies, the development of Taiwan agriculture is known to be a successful case. One of the major characteristics of Taiwanese government interventions in agriculture is that they have been carried out within well-defined bounds limiting the implicit or explicit costs (World Bank, 1993). In the first stage, the government restrained its interventions to few selected products such as rice, sugarcane and tobacco, and left other products to the market. Similar phenomena were observed in the second stage of Taiwan's agricultural development, where the limited-quantity rice purchase policy also left some room for market forces to come into play in the rice market. Thus, those price distortions or explicit subsidies were not excessive in the past, and one would expect less government intervention in the world agricultural commodity markets in the future. In Taiwan, it may be difficult or politically infeasible to cut down or abandon existing price supports or subsidy measures without any compensation for income loss. However, in line with the recent free trade atmosphere, the so-called "Decoupling," which subsidizes farmers' income but does not cause any bias in their production decisions, can be a good policy instrument compatible with the free market mechanism. The political and social valuation of the effect of direct income support would be viable if the social value accrued from environmental improvements and social functions provided by agriculture were taken into consideration.

10.5 References

Chan, S.C., 1990. Memoirs of Joint Commission on Rural Reconstruction, Council of Agriculture, Republic of China (in Chinese).

Chen, C.L., 1989. "A Study on Benefit Transferred from Taiwan's Agricultural Policies," *Industry of Free China*, Aug. 1989: 9-29, (in Chinese).

Chen, Wu-sung, 1987. *An Analysis of Agricultural Expenditures for Taiwan and Asian Economies*. Taipei: Council of Agriculture, Executive Yuan, the Republic of China.

Egaitsu, F., 1991. "Income Disparities Between Agricultural and Industrial Workers, and Price-Support Policies for Agricultural Products," in *Agriculture and Agricultural Policy in Japan*, Edited by The Committee for the Japanese Agriculture Session, XXI, IAAE Conference. Tokyo: University of Tokyo Press.

Hayami, Y. and V.W. Ruttan, 1971. *Agricultural Development — An International Perspective*, Baltimore: Johns Hopkins Press.

Hayami, Y. and V. W. Ruttan, 1985. *Agricultural Development: An International Perspective*, Baltimore: Johns Hopkins University Press.

Ho, Samuel P.S., 1978. *Economic Development of Taiwan, 1860-1970*, New Haven and London: Yale University Press.

Hou, C.M. and C.H. Tu, 1993. "The Political Economy of Agricultural policy in Taiwan," in D. Gale Johnson (ed.), *Agricultural Policy and US-Taiwan Trades*. Washington D.C.: AEI Press.

Jacobs, Jane, 1984. *Cities and the Wealth of Nations*. New York: Random House.

Koo, H.W., 1995. *Rice-Fertilizer Barter*. Taipei: National Taiwan University, Department of Economics (in Chinese).

Kuo, Shirley, 1983. *The Taiwan Economy in Transition*. Boulder: Westview Press.

Lee, Teng-hui, 1972. *Inter-Sectional Capital Flows in the Economic Development of Taiwan: 1895-1960*. Ithaca: Cornell University Press.

Lin, W.L., 1973. *Economic Interactions in Taiwan: A Study of Sectoral Flows and Linkages*, Ph.D. dissertation, Stanford University.

Mao, Y.K., 1991. "Agricultural Development and Policy Adjustments in Taiwan," *Industry of Free China*, Sept. 1991: 33-52.

Myint, Hla, 1987. "The Neoclassical Resurgence in Development Economics: Its Strength and Limitations," in Gerald M. Meier, ed., *Pioneers in Development*. Oxford: Oxford University Press: 107-136.

Murphy, Kevin M., Andrei Shleifer and Robert Vishny. 1989. "Income Distribution, Market Size, and Industrialization," *Quarterly Journal of Economics,* 104 (48): 537-564.

Nagata, K., 1991. "The Maturation of the Japanese Economy and the Role of Agriculture," in *Agriculture and Agricultural Policy in Japan*, Edited by The Committee for the Japanese Agriculture Session, XXI, IAAE Conference, Tokyo: University of Tokyo Press.

Owen, W., 1966. "The Double Developmental Squeeze on Agriculture," *American Economic Review*, 56: 43-70.

Sah, Raaj Kumar and Joseph E. Stigliz, 1984. "The Economics of Price Scissors," *American Economic Review*, 74: 125-138.

Taiwan Agricultural Production Statistics, 1979. Statistics Department, Ministry of Economic Affairs, Republic of China.

Taiwan Statistical Data Book, 1976. Economic Planning Council, Republic of China.

Thorbecke, E., 1979. "Agricultural Development," in Walter Galenson (ed.), *Economic Growth and Structural Change in Taiwan*. Ithaca: Cornell University Press: 132-205.

Thorbecke, Erik, 1992. "The Process of Agricultural Development in Taiwan," in Gustav Ranis (ed.), *Taiwan: From Developing to Mature Economy*. Boulder: Westview Press.

Woo, R.J. and T.T. Fu, 1990. "Proposed Approaches to Facilitating Agricultural Trade Liberalization in Taiwan," *Industry of Free China*, Nov. 1990: 13-24.

World Bank, 1991. *World Development Report 1991: The Challenge of Development*. New York: Oxford University Press.

World Bank, 1993. *The East Asia Miracle*. New York: Oxford University Press.

11 THE ROLE OF INDUSTRIAL POLICY IN TAIWAN'S DEVELOPMENT

Pochih Chen

11.1 Introduction

Industrial development in Taiwan has been widely regarded as quite successful. Many scholars attribute this success to the country's policies, especially its industrial policy. However, it is always difficult to verify the contribution of economic policies to the success of industrial development. Many people simply use the coexistence of industrial policies and successful industrial development as evidence of the success of industrial policies, disregarding the fact that such coexistence is at most a necessary condition for the success of industrial policies.

Recently, the argument that Taiwan is an example of successful economic development has also been challenged. If Taiwan did not succeed in economic development or in industrial development, it is almost meaningless to discuss the contribution of Taiwan's industrial policies. Since this kind of debate is too complicated to be addressed here, I will not try to give a definite answer to the questions of whether Taiwan has succeeded in economic development, or whether its industrial policies have been effective. This paper will simply present some data analysis which may be helpful for one to form a judgment or conduct further studies on the above two questions.

The second section of this paper gives a brief description of industrial development in Taiwan, focusing on recent industrial structural changes. The third section analyses the correlation between growth targets of major products in Taiwan's economic plans and actual growth rates of these products in the plan periods. The results imply that either the industrial policies of Taiwan did not accurately focus on the targets of the economic plans or the industrial polices were not successful enough. In the concluding section, some characteristics of Taiwan's industrial policy are raised to explain the possible success of Taiwan's industrial development.

11.2 Industrial Development of Taiwan

Taiwan started its industrial and economic development in the late 19th century. Some light industries were established before World War II, and a few heavy industries were developed during the war period. However, agricultural processing was still the major industrial sector in Taiwan before 1960. In 1952, the manufacturing sector accounted for only 13 percent of Taiwan's economy (Table 11.1). The destruction of war, the separation from the Japanese market, the loss of the Chinese market, and the addition of 1.6 million people from China created difficulties for Taiwan at the beginning of the post-War period. Taiwan thus adopted an import substitution policy to encourage the development of light industries, especially consumer goods industries. With the help of U.S. aid, Taiwan was able to carry out her economic and industrial development in the 1950s without worrying too much about the trade deficit. Consequently, the share of the manufacturing sector in aggregate GDP increased to 19 percent in 1960.

However, the trade deficit was still quite big and many industries that had developed under high trade protection already faced significant excess capacity in the late 1950s. Moreover, U.S. aid was scheduled to end in the early 1960s. Consequently, the Government started to adopt a number of policies by 1958. Foreign exchange control and import restrictions were liberalized to some extent. Savings, investments and exports were actively encouraged by tax, financial, and executive measures.

With these changes in policies and in international conditions, Taiwan started her export led economic growth. The average annual growth rate of exports in real terms was 26 percent from 1963 to 1973. As a result, the average annual growth rate of the manufacturing sector reached 21 percent and that of real GDP exceeded 11 percent during the same period (Table 11.2). The share of the manufacturing sector in GDP also increased from 20 percent in 1962 to 36.8 percent in 1973. The rapid export growth of labor intensive goods in textile, plastic products, plywood, and electronic industries enabled Taiwan to achieve rapid industrialization.

After the development of labor intensive industries, Taiwan started to develop heavy industries such as artificial fiber, plastic, steel, machinery, automobile, and ship building in the late 1960s. The Government tried even harder in the 1970s, especially after the first oil shock, to develop heavy and chemical industries as a second round import substitution. If we classify the manufacturing sector into three groups by capital intensities, the growth rate of the highly capital intensive industries was higher than that of the others in the early 1970s, when the Government made substantial efforts to promote capital intensive industries. The growth rate became lower than the others in the following decade, however, and the average growth rates between 1971 and 1980 were roughly equal for the three groups of industries (Yang, 1993). It should be noted that this result does not imply a failure in developing the capital intensive industries, because the total production of the

Table 11.1 Gross Domestic Product By Kind of Activity

(%)

Year	Total	Agri-culture	Industries				Services				
			Subtotal	Manu-facturing	Construc-tion	Electricity, Gas and Water	Subtotal	Commerce	Transport, Storage and Com-munication	Govern-ment Services	Finance Insurance &Busines Service
1952	100.0	32.2	19.7	12.9	3.9	0.9	48.1	17.9	4.2	9.6	9.6
1953	100.0	34.5	19.4	12.6	4.1	0.9	46.2	18.5	3.8	8.8	9.5
1954	100.0	28.0	23.9	15.8	5.3	0.9	48.1	17.2	3.9	10.3	9.6
1955	100.0	29.1	23.2	15.6	4.9	1.0	47.7	16.6	4.3	11.0	9.5
1956	100.0	27.5	24.4	16.6	4.5	1.1	48.1	17.3	4.2	10.7	9.8
1957	100.0	27.3	25.3	17.4	4.1	1.3	47.4	16.1	4.9	9.9	10.4
1958	100.0	26.8	24.8	16.8	3.8	1.4	48.4	16.6	4.6	10.5	10.4
1959	100.0	26.4	27.1	19.4	3.8	1.5	46.6	15.8	4.5	10.7	9.9
1960	100.0	28.5	26.9	19.1	3.9	1.7	44.6	15.4	4.7	10.7	9.0
1961	100.0	27.5	26.6	18.9	3.9	1.8	46.0	16.0	5.3	11.3	8.8
1962	100.0	25.0	28.2	20.0	3.9	2.0	46.8	16.3	5.3	11.2	9.3
1963	100.0	23.3	30.0	22.0	4.0	1.9	46.8	16.4	5.0	11.0	9.6
1964	100.0	24.5	30.4	22.9	3.7	2.0	45.1	15.6	5.1	10.4	9.1
1965	100.0	23.6	30.2	22.3	4.0	2.1	46.2	15.8	5.4	10.2	9.2
1966	100.0	22.5	30.6	22.5	4.0	2.1	46.9	15.4	5.8	11.0	9.2
1967	100.0	20.6	33.0	25.0	4.2	2.0	46.4	14.5	5.4	11.2	9.3
1968	100.0	19.0	34.4	26.5	4.3	2.1	46.5	14.2	5.8	11.0	9.3
1969	100.0	15.9	36.9	29.1	4.2	2.3	47.3	14.7	5.9	11.0	9.7
1970	100.0	15.5	36.8	29.2	3.9	2.4	47.7	14.5	6.0	11.5	9.8
1971	100.0	13.1	38.9	31.5	3.9	2.3	48.0	14.5	6.2	11.5	9.6
1972	100.0	12.2	41.6	34.3	4.0	2.2	46.2	13.8	6.1	10.4	9.5
1973	100.0	12.1	43.8	36.8	4.0	1.9	44.1	12.3	5.9	9.5	9.6
1974	100.0	12.4	40.7	32.8	4.5	2.2	46.9	13.8	5.8	9.3	10.3

Table 11.1 (Continued)

(%)

Year	Total	Agri-culture	Industries				Services				
			Subtotal	Manu-facturing	Construc-tion	Electricity, Gas and Water	Subtotal	Commerce	Transport, Storage and Com-munication	Govern-ment Services	Finance Insurance &Busines Service
1975	100.0	12.7	39.9	30.9	5.3	2.6	47.4	13.2	6.0	10.5	10.5
1976	100.0	11.4	43.2	33.8	5.7	2.4	45.5	12.5	5.9	9.8	10.5
1977	100.0	10.6	44.0	34.2	6.1	2.5	45.4	12.4	5.9	9.7	10.6
1978	100.0	9.4	45.2	35.6	6.1	2.5	45.4	12.1	6.0	9.6	10.9
1979	100.0	8.6	45.3	35.9	6.2	2.3	46.1	12.3	5.9	9.7	12.1
1980	100.0	7.7	45.8	36.0	6.3	2.5	46.6	13.2	6.0	9.7	12.7
1981	100.0	7.3	45.5	35.6	5.7	3.4	47.2	13.3	6.0	10.4	13.8
1982	100.0	7.7	44.3	35.2	5.0	3.3	47.9	13.3	6.0	11.0	13.7
1983	100.0	7.3	45.0	35.9	4.6	3.7	47.7	13.0	6.0	10.6	13.1
1984	100.0	6.3	46.2	37.5	4.3	3.8	47.5	13.2	6.3	10.2	13.3
1985	100.0	5.8	46.3	37.6	4.1	4.0	47.9	13.3	6.4	10.3	13.8
1986	100.0	5.6	47.1	39.4	3.8	3.5	47.3	13.0	6.2	9.4	13.0
1987	100.0	5.3	46.7	38.9	3.9	3.4	48.0	12.9	6.1	9.0	13.6
1988	100.0	5.0	44.8	37.2	4.2	3.0	50.1	13.3	6.3	9.5	15.1
1989	100.0	4.9	42.3	34.6	4.5	2.9	52.8	13.5	6.2	9.7	17.6
1990	100.0	4.2	41.2	33.3	4.7	2.8	54.6	14.2	6.2	10.6	18.2
1991	100.0	3.8	41.1	33.3	4.7	2.7	55.1	14.6	6.2	11.1	17.9
1992	100.0	3.6	39.9	31.7	5.0	2.7	56.5	15.0	6.3	11.0	18.7
1993	100.0	3.7	39.0	30.5	5.3	2.7	57.4	15.1	6.4	10.8	19.3
1994	100.0	3.6	37.3	29.0	5.3	2.6	59.2	15.4	6.6	10.6	20.9
1995	100.0	3.5	36.3	28.2	5.2	2.5	62.1	16.1	6.6	10.5	19.2

Source: National Income of Taiwan Area, the Republic of China, Taipei, DGBAS, 1995.

Table 11.2   Growth Rates of Real GDP, Production Index of the Manufacturing, and Real Export of Goods and Non-factor Services

%

Year	GDP	Manufacturing Production Index	Export	Year	GDP	Manufacturing Production Index	Export
1952	11.98	32.35	1.39	1974	1.16	-6.33	-7.26
1953	9.33	33.33	20.12	1975	4.93	7.98	0.69
1954	9.54	7.22	-25.29	1976	13.86	25.60	36.26
1955	8.11	10.36	28.03	1977	10.19	13.33	12.83
1956	5.50	5.63	11.69	1978	13.59	24.08	22.70
1957	7.36	14.67	15.74	1979	8.17	5.67	6.01
1958	6.71	7.75	1.46	1980	7.30	6.20	7.99
1959	7.65	13.31	20.94	1981	6.16	3.69	9.42
1960	6.31	14.29	12.94	1982	3.55	0.82	2.21
1961	6.88	12.50	26.01	1983	8.45	13.80	17.15
1962	7.90	8.15	2.16	1984	10.60	12.42	17.92
1963	9.35	9.36	30.74	1985	4.95	2.55	2.45
1964	12.20	23.17	28.12	1986	11.64	15.11	28.22
1965	11.13	16.61	24.93	1987	12.74	11.09	18.85
1966	8.91	16.13	19.32	1988	7.84	3.61	5.01
1967	10.71	17.40	14.70	1989	8.23	3.64	5.05
1968	9.17	24.84	27.82	1990	5.39	-0.74	0.79
1969	8.95	22.72	23.90	1991	7.55	7.50	12.82
1970	11.37	22.20	28.14	1992	6.76	3.95	5.34
1971	12.90	24.09	33.83	1993	6.32	2.34	7.17
1972	13.32	22.72	34.39	1994	6.54	5.85	5.45
1973	12.83	18.14	25.35	1995	6.06	4.46	12.93

Note: 1991 constant price for GDP and Export.
Sources: 1. National Income of Taiwan Area, the Republic of China, Taipei, DGBAS, 1995. 2. Industrial Production Statistics Monthly, Department of Statistics, Ministry of Economic Affairs.

manufacturing sector increased almost five times during this period. All three groups of manufacturing industries were growing quite fast, but the growth rates were fluctuating and showing a tendency of secular decline. However, the share of the manufacturing sector in GDP in 1980 was still 36 percent.

After 1986, because of the appreciation of New Taiwan Dollar, the reduction of import barriers, the competition from other developing countries, and the fast growth of the service sector in Taiwan, the growth rate of the manufacturing sector became smaller than the aggregate growth rate (Table 11.2). The share of the manufacturing sector in GDP started to decline rapidly. The share was 28.2 percent in 1995, much lower than the record high of 39.4 percent in 1986. Despite the lower rate of growth, structural changes in the manufacturing sector became more significant after 1986. The structure of export and production of Taiwan became much closer to that of advanced countries (Chen, 1994).

With the significant rise in Taiwan's labor costs, Taiwan's international comparative advantage and trade structure should have changed. Table 11.3 classifies Taiwan's exports according to the factor input intensities of commodities. The degree of labor intensity of each product is measured by the ratio between the amount of domestic labor utilized by the product and the domestic factor income the product contains. All industries were divided into three groups according to the level of this measure (Chen *et al.*, 1991). Table 11.3 shows that the share of highly labor intensive commodities declined from 47.03 percent in 1986 to 37.25 percent in 1995. On the other hand, the share of commodities with low labor intensities increased from 14.89 percent in1987 to 22.95 percent in 1995.

If we use the ratio of domestic capital to labor used directly and indirectly in the production process as the indicator of capital intensity, the proportion of products with high capital intensities in Taiwan's exports increased from 22.35 percent in 1987 to 31.83 percent in 1995, and that of products with low capital intensities dropped from 27.72 percent in 1986 to 11.39 in 1995.

When commodities were reclassified by the degree of human capital intensity, the speed of adjustment seems to be even faster than in the previous two cases. Here human capital intensity is measured by the relative amount of labor with college or higher education in the directly and indirectly utilized domestic labor of an industry (Chen *et al.*, 1991). Table 11.3 shows that the proportion of products with a high degree of human capital intensity in Taiwan's exports increased from 18.37 percent in 1986 to 36.1 percent in 1995, while the proportion of low human capital intensity products declined from 47.94 percent in 1986 to 21.67 percent in 1995. The direction of adjustment is consistent with what one may expect from economic theories, but the speed of the adjustment in this classification might be a surprise to many people.

Table 11.4 regroups Taiwan's exports into ten categories according to stages of fabrication or use of commodities. The results shown in Table 11.4 indicate further the rapid structural adjustment of Taiwan's exports. The shares of primary products and processed food declined as expected. In the categories with increasing shares in Taiwan's exports, type B intermediate products, which are those intermediate products readily usable as final products, replaced consumer non-durable goods as the biggest category in Taiwan's exports. The share of type B intermediate products was only 25.98 percent in 1986, but increased sharply to 44.4 percent in 1995. The decline of consumer non-durable goods is even more striking. The share of this category dropped from 35.34 percent in 1986 to 12.6 percent in 1995. The primary reason for this drastic change is the change in relative labor costs between Taiwan and its competing countries. However, it is also worthwhile to note that the international investment flowing from Taiwan to her neighboring countries is one of the reasons for this drastic change. Many Taiwanese firms are now using Taiwan's intermediate products and capital goods to produce final products in neighboring developing countries. The share of both types of intermediate products and of capital goods in Taiwan's exports increased, while that of both kinds of consumer goods declined.

Table 11.3 Export Structure of Taiwan by Input Intensities

(%)

Year	Degree of Labor Intensity			Degree of Capital Intensity			Degree of Human Capital Intensity			Degree of Energy Intensity		
	High	Mid	Low	High	Mid	Low	High	Mid	Low	High	Mid	Low
1985	45.93	35.60	18.47	24.48	48.70	26.83	18.75	33.62	47.63	14.14	46.89	38.97
1986	47.03	36.93	16.05	22.91	49.37	27.72	18.37	33.68	47.94	11.82	46.55	41.62
1987	47.93	37.18	14.89	22.35	50.52	27.13	19.30	35.30	45.40	10.84	45.39	43.77
1988	46.27	36.79	16.94	23.49	51.50	25.01	22.55	36.92	40.53	12.37	48.05	44.56
1989	43.44	37.75	18.80	26.59	50.73	22.68	24.25	38.10	37.65	13.07	45.29	41.64
1990	41.02	38.30	20.68	28.95	50.54	20.51	26.73	38.57	34.70	13.78	45.37	40.85
1991	40.10	38.73	21.17	29.82	50.98	19.20	27.23	38.52	34.25	13.89	45.74	40.37
1992	39.57	40.01	20.42	29.12	52.74	18.14	29.36	38.81	31.83	13.57	45.15	41.28
1993	38.95	41.14	19.91	28.99	54.70	16.31	31.33	40.34	28.33	14.23	42.78	42.99
1994	38.68	39.75	21.56	31.13	54.91	13.96	32.49	41.87	25.64	15.80	40.84	43.36
1995	37.25	39.80	22.95	31.83	56.78	11.39	36.10	42.23	21.67	17.55	37.82	44.63

Note: For definitions of measures, see text (also Chen, Schive, and Wu 1991).
Source: Calculated from tapes of trade statistics of Taiwan (Taipei: Ministry of Finance).

Table 11.4   Export Structure of Taiwan by Industry and Use

(%)

Year	Agriculture, Forestry, Livestock and Hunting Products	Processed Food	Beverage and Tobacco Preparation	Energy and Minerals	Construction Materials	Intermediate Products A	Intermediate Products B	Consumer Nondurable Goods	Consumer Durable Goods	Machinery	Transportation Equipment
1985	1.57	4.28	0.04	0.03	0.55	8.66	26.76	35.54	10.34	10.30	1.71
1986	1.67	4.69	0.03	0.06	0.44	7.40	25.98	35.34	11.68	10.84	1.86
1987	1.40	4.51	0.03	0.11	0.35	6.86	26.51	33.29	11.93	13.14	1.86
1988	1.60	3.73	0.04	0.07	0.35	8.74	27.69	29.67	11.20	15.36	1.54
1989	0.96	3.57	0.03	0.06	0.29	8.98	31.02	27.42	10.30	15.47	1.89
1990	0.84	3.51	0.03	0.05	0.22	9.47	34.92	23.67	8.87	16.31	2.11
1991	0.91	3.62	0.05	0.04	0.23	9.45	36.97	22.00	8.51	16.10	2.12
1992	0.86	3.29	0.06	0.04	0.22	9.39	39.05	19.89	8.14	17.13	1.95
1993	0.78	3.22	0.06	0.06	0.16	10.01	41.22	17.06	7.77	17.33	2.33
1994	0.75	3.25	0.07	0.04	0.13	11.38	43.41	14.60	7.31	16.73	2.31
1995	0.63	2.80	0.08	0.04	0.15	13.24	44.40	12.06	5.93	18.57	2.11

Source: Calculated from tapes of trade statistics of Taiwan (Taipei: Ministry of Finance).

The increase in the share of producer goods in Taiwan's exports may be regarded as an indication of the upgrading of Taiwan's economy. The rapidly increasing share of less labor intensive, highly capital intensive, or highly human capital intensive goods also has similar implications. Since Taiwan is a highly open economy, changes in international comparative advantage and trade structure always have important impacts on the structure of production, although the changes in production may not be as significant as the changes in trade.

Manufacturing industries with high capital intensities and with high human capital intensities grew 65 percent and 93 percent, respectively, from 1986 to 1994, but industries with low capital intensities and those with low human capital intensities declined 31 percent and 18 percent, respectively, in the same period. The structure in Taiwan's manufacturing sector was obviously moving toward the structure of advanced countries.

11.3 The Accuracy of Policy Targets

Judging from the growth rate and the structural changes in Taiwan, it seems reasonable to regard Taiwan's economic and industrial development as quite successful. Because this development was accompanied by many government policies, it is easy for people to conclude that active government policies were major factors in Taiwan's successful economic development. One way to reject this proposition is to deny the success of Taiwan's economic growth. For instance, it has been argued that the rapid economic growth of the newly industrializing countries in Asia was achieved in large part through an astonishing mobilization of resources made possible by people's willingness to sacrifice current satisfaction for future gain, but there is little evidence of improvements in efficiency (Krugman, 1994). It has even been implied that these Asian countries can never catch up with the Western advanced countries, and that the Soviet Union is an example for the future of these countries. However, measures of efficiency or technical progress are often controversial, and may simply be a measure of our ignorance. In the case of Taiwan, there are no reliable data for the stock of capital. For instance, the amount of new capital obtained by the manufacturing sector from 1986 to 1988, as indicated by the National Wealth Survey of 1988, is 70 percent higher than the data on gross capital formation in the national income statistics.

The capital stock data of South Korea have similar problems (Kong, 1993). Even if we have reliable data and reliable econometric methods which can prove statistically the absence of improvements in efficiency, we still need to face the real world facts that many firms in these countries really improved their efficiency in the past, that many products they were not able to produce some years ago have become their major exports, and that they can produce many commodities as well and as efficiently as the firms in advanced countries now. Moreover, the current wealth and standard of living in these countries are much higher than in other developing countries. There is also no evidence that people in these countries had a long period of sacrifice with low living standards before they achieved higher levels of income and economic development than other developing countries. Even if economic development in these countries is merely a result of resource accumulation, how to accumulate and mobilize resources is probably an important lesson that other countries would like to learn. Therefore, the policies adopted by these countries may still be attractive to other developing countries.

Nevertheless, even if economic development in Taiwan and other NICs has been as successful or better than other developing countries, one still can not jump to the conclusion that their policies were good. Since many industrial policy measures give benefits to firms directly, the impact of such policies on the level of the firm will be quite obvious. However, in the economy as a whole or even within an industry, policy measures toward different industries and firms may counteract each other. Complicated general equilibrium effects and the strategies of firms could also reverse the effects of industrial policies. These complicated factors and ever changing economic conditions also make it difficult for economists to verify the contribution of policies to industrial development. It is even impossible to quantify the various industrial policies so that economists can use rigorous models to analyze their effects.

If we define industrial policies as those policies which are intended to affect the relative growth rates of industries, and assume that the government could effectively design industrial policies according to the growth targets of each industry, then there should be a high correlation between the growth targets and the realized growth rates of industries when these industrial policies were successful. However, this correlation turns out to be quite low in Taiwan since 1960.

The National Economic Plans of Taiwan announced growth targets for major products in every planning period. Letting X_1 represent the planned annual growth rate and Y_0 the realized growth rate, we can see from Table 11.5 that the correlation coefficient of these two growth rates is not high for the planning period. The highest correlation is only slightly larger than 0.5, while the lowest is only 0.23. Since the number and coverage of products are different in each period, we can neither compare the achievement of different periods, nor analyze the time series of each product. Using the logarithm of these variables (plus one) gives similar results (Table 11.5). However, the correlation coefficients between the planned growth rate (X_1) and the realized growth rate of the four years following the planning period (Y_1) or the realized growth rate from the beginning of the planning period to four years after the planning period (Y_2) are even lower in general, indicating that the low correlation between planned and realized growth rates in the planning period is probably not a result of the time lag in the effects of industrial policies.

However, the correlation between the planned growth rate and the realized growth rate is generally higher than the correlation between the realized growth rate in the four years preceding the planning period (X_2) and the realized growth rate in or after the planning period. Economic plans or industrial policies might have some prediction power on the realized growth that the previous growth rates do not have.

Using simple regression to explain Y_0 by X_1 or by X_1 and X_2 (Table 11.6), the planned growth rate is significant in most of the planning periods, while the growth rate in the previous years is significant in only three periods. Taking the logarithm of these variables (plus one) still gives similar results. The planned growth rate still has higher t values in five of the eight periods analyzed (Table 11.7). However, the

Table 11.5 Correlation Coefficients of Planned and Realized Growth Rates of Major Manufacturing Products

	1960~1964	1964~1968	1968~1972	1972~1976	1975~1981	1981~1985	1985~1989	1989~1993
number of products included	45	34	87	76	85	77	99	82
X_1Y_0	0.54689	0.43432	0.32337	0.30193	0.26818	0.50228	0.42411	0.23995
X_2Y_0	0.25653	-0.08499	0.21590	0.36230	0.40359	0.40079	0.30395	0.08596
X_1Y_1	0.19795	0.09312	0.24229	0.29743	0.08155	0.25973	0.09313	0.12810
X_2Y_1	0.31885	-0.24363	0.27604	0.29375	0.16011	0.25953	-0.05207	0.10901
X_1Y_2	0.50486	0.39578	0.37763	0.35230	0.13632	0.45523	0.33008	0.25601
X_2Y_2	0.33238	-0.22938	0.32789	0.41418	0.33437	0.40318	0.13690	0.09404
X_1X_2	0.41145	-0.13487	0.49370	0.57376	0.20579	0.20918	0.55187	0.03344
$\ln(1+X_1)\ln(1+Y_0)$	0.53893	0.43177	0.38137	0.28964	0.27642	0.42786	0.41511	0.25121
$\ln(1+X_2)\ln(1+Y_0)$	0.26565	-0.06852	0.28069	0.39503	0.45743	0.32529	0.27718	0.06622
$\ln(1+X_1)\ln(1+Y_1)$	0.21033	0.16824	0.22426	0.29993	0.05107	0.24997	0.09991	0.13993
$\ln(1+X_2)\ln(1+Y_1)$	0.34300	-0.23699	0.28017	0.33767	0.18687	0.23917	-0.06822	-0.00852
$\ln(1+X_1)\ln(1+Y_2)$	0.49445	0.40478	0.38462	0.35450	0.13287	0.40002	0.33235	0.25419
$\ln(1+X_2)\ln(1+Y_2)$	0.34638	-0.23127	0.35406	0.46472	0.39919	0.33152	0.09731	0.02900
$\ln(1+X_1)\ln(1+X_2)$	0.42064	-0.14209	0.50480	0.64692	0.22198	0.18835	0.50659	0.04313

Source: Calculated for this paper by TIER. The planned growth rates are taken from the Economic Plan of each period, the realized growth rates are taken from the Industrial Production Statistics Monthly, Ministry of Economic Affairs.

higher correlation coefficients and the higher t values of the planned growth rate may partly come from the fact that the government already knew part of the investment or production plans of these products when the government was making the Economic Plan. Therefore we may conclude that the Economic Plans of Taiwan did not predict the relative growth rate of the major products accurately.

Table 11.6   Regression Results I

	Constant term	X_1	X_2	R^2	Adj,R^2
1960~1964	0.179215	0.873748		0.2991	0.2828
	(0.770)	(4.284)			
	–0.119610	1.149026	–0.019067	0.4230	0.3927
	(–0.443)	(4.850)	(–0.098)		
1964~1968	0.550394	0.569761		0.1886	0.1633
	(2.266)	(2.728)			
	0.573389	0.535681	–0.016830	0.2434	0.1746
	(1.746)	(2.621)	(–0.101)		
1968~1972	0.467668	0.658504		0.1046	0.0940
	(1.978)	(3.151)			
	0.787200	0.216073	0.121136	0.0538	0.0285
	(2.789)	(0.753)	(1.318)		
1972~1976	0.516542	0.509689		0.0912	0.0789
	(2.476)	(2.724)			
	0.651329	0.229488	0.138678	0.1444	0.1192
	(3.057)	(1.022)	(2.059)		
1975~1981	0.699113	0.377196		0.0719	0.0607
	(4.285)	(2.536)			
	0.517560	0.350631	0.185929	0.2199	0.1920
	(3.030)	(2.218)	(3.498)		
1981~1985	0.146553	0.856883		0.2523	0.2423
	(0.798)	(5.030)			
	–0.137656	0.843865	0.264821	0.3658	0.3466
	(–0.694)	(4.621)	(2.725)		
1985~1989	0.162990	0.848037		0.1799	0.1714
	(0.839)	(4.612)			
	0.249474	0.737126	0.026302	0.1869	0.1700
	(1.153)	(3.340)	(0.911)		
1989~1993	0.609785	0.410576		0.0576	0.0458
	(3.043)	(2.211)			
	0.575287	0.406295	0.035394	0.0638	0.0398
	(2.761)	(2.168)	(0.760)		

Source: Calculated for this paper by TIER. The planned growth rates are taken from the Economic Plan of each period, the realized growth rates are taken from the Industrial Production Statistics Monthly, Ministry of Economic Affairs.

Since the R^2 in all these regressions are not high, and the coefficients of X_1 are far from unity, the planned growth rates are probably quite different from the realized growth rate. The average of the absolute values of the difference between the planned and the realized annual growth rates of each product turns out to be quite high for all planning periods. As shown in Table 11.8, the average absolute

Table 11.7   Regression Results II

	Constant term	X_1	X_2	R^2	Adj,R^2
1960~1964	0.171594	0.814739		0.2904	0.2739
	(1.318)	(4.195)			
	0.012152	1.092441	-0.014172	0.4251	0.3948
	(0.087)	(4.841)	(-0.077)		
1964~1968	0.398102	0.570541		0.1864	0.1610
	(2.661)	(2.708)			
	0.304012	0.536158	-0.001884	0.2190	0.1479
	(1.529)	(2.457)	(-0.011)		
1968~1972	0.388715	0.666619		0.1454	0.1354
	(3.644)	(3.804)			
	0.353985	0.272785	0.169978	0.0950	0.0709
	(3.081)	(1.160)	(1.651)		
1972~1976	0.079381	0.515058		0.0839	0.0715
	(0.813)	(2.603)			
	0.048858	0.087256	0.242343	0.1575	0.1327
	(0.520)	(0.341)	(2.485)		
1975~1981	0.388964	0.415378		0.0764	0.0653
	(3.733)	(2.620)			
	0.261235	0.340912	0.381727	0.2506	0.2316
	(2.588)	(2.088)	(4.116)		
1981~1985	0.003990	0.773619		0.1831	0.1722
	(0.049)	(4.100)			
	-0.107114	0.770344	0.248562	0.2603	0.2379
	(-1.140)	(3.713)	(2.072)		
1985~1989	0.015425	0.875339		0.1723	0.1638
	(0.261)	(4.494)			
	0.015407	0.779218	0.045126	0.1783	0.1612
	(0.261)	(3.444)	(0.839)		
1989~1993	0.037036	0.471967		0.0631	0.0514
	(0.469)	(2.321)			
	0.021986	0.468354	0.047015	0.0665	0.0426
	(0.257)	(2.279)	(0.581)		

Source: Calculated for this paper by TIER. The planned growth rates are taken from the Economic Plan of each period, the realized growth rates are taken from the Industrial Production Statistics Monthly, Ministry of Economic Affairs.

Table 11.8   Prediction Errors

	1960~ 1964	1964~ 1968	1968~ 1972	1972~ 1976	1975~ 1981	1981~ 1985	1985~ 1989	1989~ 1993
Absolute Error	0.1186	0.1340	0.1536	0.0989	0.0851	0.2162	0.0761	0.2019
Adjusted Absolute Error	0.1260	0.1369	0.1469	0.0971	0.0844	0.2528	0.0761	0.2269
RMSE	0.2029	0.1883	0.2610	0.1267	0.1140	0.3998	0.1109	0.3637
Theil's U	0.4150	0.3837	0.5214	0.4460	0.4142	0.8007	0.5119	0.7977
Modified Theil's U	0.6982	0.6716	0.7913	0.8478	0.7386	1.0614	0.8228	1.0271

Source: Calculated for this paper by TIER. The planned growth rates are taken from the Economic Plan
of each period, the realized growth rates are taken from the Industrial Production Statistics Monthly,
Ministry of Economic Affairs.

error can be as high as 20 percent. In other words, the realized annual growth rates
of these major products were 20 percent higher or lower than the planned annual
growth rates on average. This seems to be a very high prediction error even though
the growth rates of Taiwan's products were high. If we consider the possible
influence of business cycle and subtract the average planned (realized) growth rate
from the planned (realized) growth rate before calculating the average absolute
error, the adjusted absolute errors in Table 11.8 indicate an even larger average
prediction error. The usual indicators for prediction error such as root mean square
error, Theil's U or Modified Theil's U also indicate a large prediction error (Table
11.8).

Since the planned growth rate of major products in Taiwan's Economic Plans
cannot predict the realized growth rate accurately, we may conclude that either the
industrial policies of Taiwan were not consistent with the targets of the government
or the industrial policies were not successful.

However, one can still find some successful cases of industrial policy in
Taiwan. Since almost all industries in Taiwan received some kind of policy
encouragement in the past, it is quite easy to find some successful industries that
had strong policy supports. The positive correlation between planned and realized
growth rates we found in this section also indicate that some industries with higher
planned growth rate actually had higher realized growth rate. The success of
specific industries and the policies that encouraged them were often mentioned as
evidence of the success of Taiwan's industrial policies. But what we should not
neglect is the other side of the story, namely, there were many other industries that
did not succeed despite the strong policy support they had.

In the manufacturing sector, the automobile industry is the best known counter
example. The import tariff rate for cars has been kept much higher than that of other
industrial products in the past four decades. Imports were prohibited or restricted for
many years. Currently, only cars made in America or Europe can be imported. The
Government also used local content requirements, limitation of new plants, tax

reductions for new design and research and development, assistance with inter firm cooperation, and government procurement to assist the development of the automobile industry. In short, almost all kinds of incentives were applied to this industry, but its development and international competitiveness are still much lower than those of other major industries in Taiwan, and much lower than those of the automobile industry in South Korea.

Shipbuilding is another counter example. The Government invested in a big ship yard as part of the Ten Big Construction Plan in the 1970s. This shipbuilding company would not have survived without government support over the past twenty years, and it has not been able to fulfill its original goal of building ships for national defense. Since the wage rate in Taiwan is now much higher than it was twenty years ago, and since the operation of this company is still unsatisfactory, there is not much hope that it will ultimately make a significant contribution to Taiwan's shipbuilding industry, in spite the huge amount that the Government has been spending on it.

In contrast with the shipbuilding project, an integrated steel mill project in the Ten Big Construction Plan is generally regarded as a successful example of government policy. However, this steel company used to enjoy a number of special privileges compared to other firms and industries, including having the right to issue import permits for some steel products until recent years. The boom in the international steel market just after the completion of this steel mill also gave an excellent opportunity for the success of this company.

Currently, the steel industry is still growing fast, and there are many competing private investment projects in Taiwan. It is fair to say that the integrated steel mill could not have been built in the 1970s or even in the 1980s without government investment. But the linkage effect of the steel mill within the steel industry and toward other industries is not as significant as the government expected it would be in the early 1970s.

The petrochemical industry also expanded successfully in the 1970s with the coordination of investment projects from the government and the private sector. However, some private enterprises had already had the intention of investing in the project that was undertaken by the government at that time, but were prohibited from doing so by government policy and regulations. Therefore, the government investment in the petrochemical industry might have been unnecessary.

The encouragement of technology intensive industries has become the major object of industrial policy in Taiwan since the 1980s. The success of electronic and information industries can be attributed at least in part to government's support for R&D, investment in pioneering projects, extension of education and training, and supply of land and infrastructure. However, it is interesting to note that personal computer manufacturing was not among the targets for government support in the Development Plan for Information Industry (1980–1989) published by the Council for Economic Planning and Development in 1982, but computers soon became the leading product of Taiwan's successfully growing information industry.

Biochemical and medical industries are also among the targeted technology intensive industries. A major policy in this field was to invest in the production of a hepatitis vaccine, but the firm that had been invested in and protected by the government was shut down recently because of its inability to keep up with new technology development.

In the service sector, Taiwan tried in vain over the past thirty years to encourage big general trading companies. The protection and control of government owned banks, in fact, seriously limited the competitiveness and globalization of Taiwan's financial sector.

In short, we observe the industrial policies have failed in many major industries in Taiwan. These counterexamples of unsuccessful industrial policies, and the low correlation we found between the planned and realized growth rates of major products, caution us not to overestimate the role of industrial policy in Taiwan's development.

11.4 Concluding Remarks

In the past half century, Taiwan succeeded in changing her industrial structure from agriculture to manufacturing, from the import substitution of consumer goods to the export expansion of labor intensive products, from the import of producer's goods to second round import substitution, and from the export of labor intensive products to the export of capital and human capital intensive goods or hi-tech products. This process of economic and industrial development has been regarded by many people as a success or even a miracle. Since the government adopted and talked about many policies during this development process, some people quickly jumped to the conclusion that these policies were part of the reason for Taiwan's success in economic and industrial development.

However, with the successful development of many products and the existence of many policies or policy proposals, it is not only easy to find some products that were supported by active government policies and experienced successful development, but it is also easy to find some industries that succeeded with little support from the government or that failed with a lot of government support. Therefore, case studies of only one or a small number of products can be quite misleading.

For instance, the active support for R&D, the privileges of the Hsin Chu Science Based Industrial Park, and the government investment in the semiconductor industry can be used as evidence of the importance or success of Taiwan's industrial policy. On the other hand, the lack of international competitiveness of the auto makers under the protection of very high tariff rate, severe import restrictions, and even government procurement is widely accepted evidence of an industrial policy failure in Taiwan. The government also wasted a lot of money invested in some industries such as ship building, copper and aluminum refinery, and machinery.

Since so many industrial policies invested in certain industries directly or gave direct benefits to particular firms, and since many industrial policies were beneficial to the targeted industries — in theory at least from the partial equilibrium point of view — many industrial policies should have encouraged the development of some targeted industries. The real question about the success or failure of industrial policy should be the proportion of success and the overall effect of these policies on the welfare of the whole country. The analysis in Section III casts a strong doubt on the proportion of success in Taiwan's industrial policies, but the data in Section II seem to imply a satisfactory, if not a very successful, industrial development. If these two guesses are both close to the fact, the remaining question is why industrial development was successful. One logical explanation is that the assumption we made about the consistency between industrial targets and industrial policies is inappropriate. However, it is hard to believe that the actual aims of industrial policies were so much different from the industrial targets in the Economic Plans that we could have such a low correlation between planned and realized growth rates of major products when these industrial policies were successful. In fact, in the Economic Plans of Taiwan, major industrial policies were summarized and linked with the targets of industrial growth. Therefore, it is not possible for industrial policies to have had little connection with the growth targets for industries.

Another possible explanation is that most of the industrial policies in Taiwan were ineffective. However, given the efforts and levels of benefits given to some targeted industries, it is also difficult to believe that most of these policy measures were ineffective in raising the growth rate of their targeted industries.

A more plausible explanation might lie in the nature of Taiwan's industrial policies. Although many policies were aimed at specific industries at the very beginning, many of them were soon extended to other industries that asked for the same privileges. For instance, the government set up a low interest long term loan project for "strategic industries" in 1982 to support the future industries of Taiwan. However, this loan was soon extended to strategic and important industries so that those existing industries could have the same privilege. It turned out that traditional industries such as textile and textile processing obtained even more loans than did the electronic industries in some periods (Chiau Ton Bank, 1990). The industries that were not listed as the beneficiaries of a specific privilege could request the same privilege with high probability of success. Therefore, many industrial policies became so general that the private sector could develop the industries they thought profitable without bothering too much about the industrial targets of the Government.

In addition, the government also had a number of industrial policies aimed at broad industrial sectors such as manufacturing, export industries, or high-tech industries, rather than at specific products. The encouragement of saving, investment, and export were the most important policies in the development process of Taiwan, but these goals are general enough to avoid the possible inadequacy of the growth targets of the economic plans. Many of these general policies, such as the tariff rebate for exports and tax reduction for investments, could also be regarded as a reduction of or compensation for other inadequate policies, rather than as active policies. But this does not mean that all the general policies of Taiwan were adequate. For instance, despite the successful emphasis on education, the suggestion of Mr. K.T. Lee in 1965 to increase the proportion of professional schools over high schools in order to raise the supply of skilled labor probably has restricted the choices of students, and made the competition for entering universities so keen that education in the middle and high schools has been severely distorted. Many people decided to migrate out of Taiwan in order to give their children a better education. When the human capital intensive industries became the major source of industrial development in Taiwan, the past emphasis on professional school rather than high school and university became a hindrance to the supply of qualified human capital.

Besides the practice of making policies more general, the government also set up some rules or slogans to simplify the decision making process and to avoid pressures from interest groups. For instance, the notion of effective protection was introduced into Taiwan quite early (Liang, 1967). The government has insisted that, in principle, the tariff rate of a product should be higher than the tariff rate of its major input. With this principle, it was usually hard for interest groups to ask for significantly unreasonable changes in tariff rates. Therefore, this kind of general rule or principle can prevent or at least reduce the possibility of extremely biased industrial policies. Of course, some such rules may be inadequate or harmful. For instance, the effort to encourage high value-added products was translated into a rule that called for raising the domestic value added of products, so that some people wanted to remove the tariff rebate for exports in order to encourage the use of domestic intermediate products.

If there is something to learn from the industrial policy of Taiwan, these general simplified rules would be better candidates for explaining Taiwan's successful development than would industry-specific policies, but many further studies are needed before one can have a more definite answer.

11.5 References

Chen, Pochih, 1994. "Changing Patterns of Trade in Goods and Services, The Case of Taiwan," in Pacific Economic Cooperation Council, *Changing Patterns of Trade in Goods and Services in Pacific Region*. Osaka: The Japan Committee for Pacific Economic Outlook: 353-408.

Chen, Pochih, Chi Schive, and Chung Chi Wu, 1991. *Report on the Characteristic Classifications of Tradable Commodities*. Taipei: National Taiwan University.

Chiau Tong Bank, 1990. *Illustration and Related Data of the Preferred Loans to Strategic Industries by Chiau Tong Bank*. Taipei: Chiau Tong Bank.

Liang, Kuo-shu, 1967. "Foreign Trade and Balance of Payments," in Kuo-wei Chang (ed.), *The Economic Development of Taiwan*.Taipei: 415-468.

Krugman, Paul, 1994. "The Myth of Asia's Miracle," *Foreign Affairs* 73 (6): 62-78.

Kong, Ming Hsin, 1993. *An Analysis on the Reasons for Lower Fixed Capital Formation Ratio in the Manufacturing Sector of Taiwan Than in the Case of Japan and South Korea*. Taipei: Taiwan Institute of Economic Research.

Yang, Wen-jui, 1993. *Studies on the Manufacturing Sector and Indicators of Industrial Up-grading*. Taipei: Taiwan Institute of Economic Research.

12 HUMAN CAPITAL CREATION AND UTILIZATION IN TAIWAN

Grace Ren-juei Tsiang[1]

12.1 Introduction

This paper reviews some of the measures and sources of the enhancement of human capital in Taiwan over the last forty years. Taiwan's labor productivity went up due to education at home and abroad, and due to efficient utilization of the rising skills of the labor force. Economists have been busy accounting for the sources of Taiwan's sustained output growth of 10 percent in the 1970s and 8 percent in the 1980s. Recent studies by Tallman and Wang (1994) and Young (1995) find the combined effects of thrift and investment created the extraordinary rate of growth in the Pacific rim. Although Taiwan was part of the group of Asian "tigers" which grew rapidly in these decades, there are large differences in the percent of GDP which each of these countries invested (I/GDP). Young points out that Singapore invested an average of 40 percent of GDP over this period, South Korea invested 30 percent in the 1970s and 40 percent by 1991, but Taiwan invested a high of 27 percent in 1975, after which it averaged 22 percent. What has Taiwan done to get more growth per dollar invested? This paper examines Taiwan's education, manpower, and patent office information to assess the strengths of Taiwan's human resources. In addition, significant international differences in education policy are highlighted where they may shed light on the question of how Taiwan's growth came at a lower measured aggregate cost.

Section 12.2 reviews the achievements of Taiwan's education policy. The government made a commitment to literacy through the provision of universal primary schooling in the 1950s, and in 1968 made nine years of schooling mandatory. In international educational comparisons, Taiwan students have done extremely well. A review of expenditures does not show that Taiwan outspent other countries: the effectiveness of the expenditures suggests that students' motivation and cultural preferences must be considered an important factor in their success. The R.O.C. government encouraged students to study abroad. While government scholarships gave large numbers of Taiwan students the opportunity for study, it was individual students' choices that consistently led them into more "applied" fields. Similarly, the recent surge in the number of Chinese students who are returning to Taiwan after completing their studies can also be interpreted as the result of income-maximizing strategies of migration and occupational choice.

A rapidly changing labor force poses problems of efficient utilization. For example, Taiwan is facing labor shortages across the whole economy, with great shortfalls in the supply of low-skilled workers. A recent change in immigration policy allows foreign workers to take temporary jobs in Taiwan: this will ease shortages for many low-skilled jobs as well as spread some wealth to neighboring countries. In order to keep up with the changes in available workers, the product mix of Taiwan's economy has had to shift. The changing factor composition is clear, but what mechanisms have smoothed the structural shifts in employment? Section 12.3 examines the role of entrepreneurship in keeping labor efficiently employed throughout the structural changes in the Taiwan economy.

Taiwan successfully transferred much of its labor force from low-income employment in traditional agriculture into light industry with successively higher levels of capital utilization in the 1950s and 1960s. This transfer is well-documented in the volume edited by Galenson (1979). This paper focuses upon the more recent decades, during which the increased skills of the labor force and rising wages resulted in the shift of resources into more technologically complex production processes. Section 12.3 reviews recent theory relevant to production of complex goods and research on entrepreneurship, and interprets some of the experiences of Taiwan in light of these theories. The investment in the education of the whole cohort of youth in the 1950s and 1960s had a large payoff in productivity, and resulted in simultaneous enhancement of the cohorts that entered the market in the 1970s.

It was S. C. Tsiang's firm belief that the entrepreneur stood at the vanguard of economic development, opening new markets for existing goods and developing new goods and processes to meet demand and lower production costs. In fact, many of the policies which he and T.C. Liu promoted were to aid entrepreneurs and encourage capital to flow freely to the most profitable ventures. He wrote,

> Taiwan was very fortunate to be endowed with an ample supply of capable entrepreneurs, but it should be emphasized that proper incentive afforded by realistic exchange rate, which could reward the exporters with the full market equilibrium value of the export proceeds they earned, was also very important. Furthermore, Taiwan's openness...was useful, for foreign investors would often bring new ideas about products and have new connections in untapped markets as well (Tsiang, 1984).

Section 12.4 concludes with a look at Taiwan's performance as a source of inventions and new designs, given the recent surge in public expenditure on research and development. In the future, Taiwan may become a greater source of innovations, as well as the successful user of new ideas.

12.2 Educational Achievements of Taiwan

In the last four decades the work force of Taiwan has been completely transformed. The rate of illiteracy was 42 percent in 1952, and has now dropped to 6 percent (see Table 12.1). Nearly 50 percent of the population over the age of 6 has completed high school, and 13 percent of the population hold college or higher level degrees. For comparison, the U.S. secondary school completion rate in 1993 was 80 percent and those with college or higher levels of education was 21 percent.

Table 12.1   **Percent of Taiwan Population over Age 6, by Educational Attainment**

Year	Illiterate	Primary	Secondary	Higher
1952	42.1	43.5	8.8	1.4
1960	27.1	54.1	12.4	1.9
1970	14.7	51.8	26.5	3.7
1980	10.3	43.3	36.9	7.1
1990	6.8	35.1	46.1	10.8
1993	6.1	31.1	48.7	13.1

Source: *Taiwan Statistical Data Book 1995.*

The demographics of post-war Taiwan have favored this transformation. Aggregate labor force participation rates have been about 60 percent due to declining birth rates and rising female labor force participation. The age distribution in the postwar era has also been skewed towards the working cohorts: the percent of youth under age 15 has steadily declined from 42 percent in 1952 to 25 percent in 1994 and only since 1989 has the proportion of the population older than 64 exceeded 6 percent.

12.2.1 Primary and Secondary Education

In some developing nations, the percentages of degree holders does not truly represent skill acquisition. I turn now to some hard evidence that degrees in Taiwan represent real achievements in literacy, numeracy, and analytical skills.

Government policy in the 1950s was committed to lowering illiteracy. In the 1960s, the Ministry of Education's Manpower Development Plan made middle school completion (9 years of education) mandatory for both boys and girls. Colleges and higher education, with special attention on applied areas such as engineering and business management were the focus of more recent policies. The cost of addressing increasing higher-level education for the post-war generation of Taiwan has required ever higher expenditures per pupil. Table 12.2 shows expenditures per student have risen to the point where the 1991-92 expenditure per student in Taiwan now approaches those of countries with much higher per capita income. Expenditures on education as a percent of GNP have increased from 2.6 percent in 1960 to 5.5 percent in 1990. Taking into account the high rate of output growth over this period, this amounts to an impressive commitment to education. The lower public expenditure of Japan also emphasizes Taiwan's government policy commitment to provide affordable education even at the college level. The 1991 Taiwan expenditures for higher education reflect an initiative to build domestic colleges and universities.

Table 12.2   **1991 Public Expenditures and Student/Teacher Ratios (1991 U.S. Dollars)**

Country	Public Expenditures per Student (Secondary)	Public Expenditures per Student (Tertiary)	Students/ Teacher (Primary)	Students/ Teacher (Secondary)
Taiwan	1863	7772	28.5	20.3
Japan	2707	2358	19.8	16.6
United States	4909	6984	.	15.9
United Kingdom	3365	9154	20.8	15.2

Sources: *OECD Education at a Glance,* Paris, 1992. ROC, Directorate-General of Budget, Accounting and Statistics, *Statistical Yearbook* [1991, 1994].

Taiwan and South Korea led the world in average proficiency scores in the 1992 Second International Assessment of Educational Progress (IAEP) for 9 and 13 year old students administered by the Educational Testing Service. Taiwan's average scores were 51 and 42 scale points over the corresponding scores for the U.S. The distributions of scores for both mathematics and science show that the lowest scores are roughly equal in Taiwan and the U.S. The distribution of math achievement scores for Taiwan students has a broader range of than that of the U.S. and each decile is higher than that of the U.S. This is not simply a shift in average scores due to a few higher performers at the top end. The results of the second IAEP serve to emphasize that in one generation, Taiwan's work force has been transformed from a half non-reading population to one in which the majority of middle school graduates are not only literate but numerate.

In the light of the IAEP findings the most interesting question is how this was achieved with large class sizes. The cost-effectiveness of Taiwan's expenditures on schooling has been impressive. It calls into question whether the strength of the U.S. teachers' labor unions have brought too much attention to small class sizes as a key measure of the quality of education. Student and parental incentives to invest in early achievement in academics are stronger in Taiwan than they are in the U.S. Schools at the middle and high school level have selective entrance examinations: at each stage, students and parents believe that entrance into the best lower schools secure admission to quality schools at the next level and beyond. The countries which follow such a system appear high on the IAEP scores: Japan, Taiwan, and South Korea. In addition, they support the ideas currently prevalent among educators: that opportunities to learn must be augmented by student and parent motivation. This model for schooling and examination-based entrance to primary and secondary schools has the unfortunate result that competition for entrance to each successive level can lead to unhealthy stresses on youth and overemphasis on easily tested skills, such as rote memorization over creativity or inventiveness. (See

Section 12.4 for information on patent applications.) One might ask why selective admission to lower schooling levels is tolerated in Taiwan and not in the U.S. Historically, scholarship has been part of the traditional route to social advancement in China: a successful youth from a small village is one who studies hard and earns top distinction in civil service examinations, thereby earning himself a job in the government. In the American version of the prototypical success story, schooling is an unattainable luxury for Horatio Alger, who works his way from an errand boy to a successful businessman. Ironically, the myth of an open American society is the basis for the "open" public education system paid for by community property taxes. Yet this system has failed to provide access to consistently high quality education across communities.

12.2.2 Higher education
The increase in public expenditures on education in the 1980s reflects a shift in focus towards higher education, where expenditure per student is high. The expansion of domestic programs has been a recent phenomenon: in earlier decades, the government provided scholarship funds for qualified students wanting to obtain advanced degrees from abroad. The numbers of successful applicants to foreign graduate programs is further evidence of the quality of Taiwan's lower education system. The high quality of Taiwan's primary and secondary education generates a large number of graduates relative to undergraduates in U.S. programs. In recent years Taiwanese graduate students outnumber undergraduates 2:1 (i.e. 33 percent undergraduates). Singapore and Malaysia sent 75 percent and 82 percent undergraduates to the U.S. in 1993, respectively.

Taiwan supplies an extraordinary number of students to the U.S. In 1962, 1972, 1982 and 1992, Taiwan was one of the top 4 sending countries. In 1993-94, the three countries with the most students enrolled in U.S. colleges and universities were China (P.R.C.) with 44,380 , Japan with 43,770, and Taiwan with 37,581. The next two were India and South Korea. Singapore sends far fewer: only 4864 in 1992. Obviously, weighting by home population puts Taiwan far beyond the others. Table 12.3 gives a forty year history for Taiwan, Hong Kong, and Korea as well as approximate population numbers for 1982.

Table 12.3 Asian Students in U.S. Colleges and Universities: Selected Countries

Year	Taiwan (pop: 18 M)	Hong Kong (pop: 5 M)	Korea (pop: 40 M)
1962	5526	1659	2233
1972	9633	10,298	3230
1982	20,770	8610	11,360
1992	37,432	14,020	28,519

Source: Institute of International Education, New York, "Open Doors" annual.

Comparisons with other countries such as Singapore, Malaysia, and Thailand are revealing: historically, these countries did not send large numbers of students to the U.S. Malaysian students often go the Islamic nations for study. Kim (1994) finds that the venue of foreign study affects the value of having foreign-trained workers, measured by aggregate growth rates. Countries which sent students to Western nations have performed better than those sending students to Islamic countries or the Soviet bloc.

Taiwan's policy of unrestricted emigration yielded outflows of foreign trained scholars and scientists in the 1960s. In 1965 returnees were 5 percent of students leaving. However, this "brain drain" has been stemmed in recent years: the flow of students returning has increased dramatically since the late 1980s. Increasing numbers of the accumulated stock of highly-trained students will respond to the expanding employment opportunities in Taiwan, vindicating the open emigration policy: these predictions are based on the following examination of recent information from both Taiwan and U.S. sources.

The enrollment numbers from U.S. programs are taken from the Institute for International Education (I.I.E.)'s survey of U.S. colleges and universities (I.I.E., 1994). An additional source of information is the R.O.C. Ministry of Education (reproduced in R.O.C., 1995) which reports 7122 "Students studying abroad" in 1988. After 1988, the series omits privately funded students and the numbers drop dramatically. The sudden drop is a clear indication that many study abroad without direct government subsidies. This is indicative of both the increased competitiveness of Taiwan students for foreign scholarships as well as increased wealth positions of households. The I.I.E. survey reports four to five times the number of enrollees in the U.S. as the R.O.C. time series. Although the source (ROC, 1995) is unclear, the Taiwan data most likely describe not stocks but flows of new students embarking to study abroad. Figure 12.1 shows a log growth interpolation of data points of I.I.E.'s measure of Taiwanese students enrolled in U.S. programs. The interpolated annual series is used to estimate flows, where all students are assumed to study for exactly four continuous years. That estimated flow is a reasonable approximation to the magnitude of the R.O.C. time series: each year's stock is slightly more than four times the flows, where stocks are growing at 6 percent per annum.

Detailed information on field-of-study is provided by the R.O.C. on both domestic students and those leaving to study abroad. The choice of field of study is influenced by students' self-knowledge regarding talents and tastes as well as information on the market evaluation of various fields. Table 12.4 below shows how choices have changed over the decades, reflecting the economy's structural changes. Engineering has been consistently one of the top two fields. Agriculture, however, falls from the top 5 fields after 1980, matching the decline of employment in that sector. It is surpassed by Mathematics (including Computer Science) and Business, which since the early 1980s has been exceeded only by Engineering.

Examining the job commitments of new Ph.D.'s planning to work in the U.S., the information in Table 12.5 shows that in the U.S., Humanities Ph.D.'s are most likely to stay in academia, Engineers and Science degree holders least likely. The fields chosen by the most Taiwan students are precisely in those fields which are most often used as training for jobs outside of academics. U.S. graduate students are more likely to choose Business, Education, and Health as fields than are foreign students in the U.S. (See National Research Council, Survey of Earned Doctorates.)

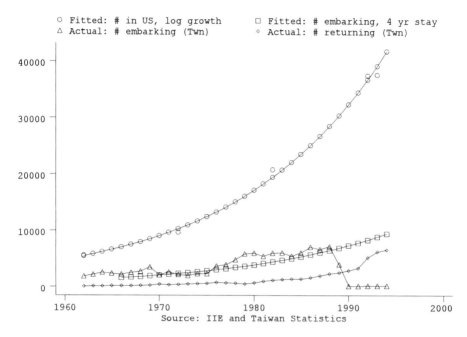

Figure 12.1   R.O.C. Students Abroad: Stocks and Flow

Table 12.4   Changing Fields of Study: Taiwan Students Abroad

1970: From Taiwan	1980: From Taiwan	1988: From Taiwan	1988: All Foreign Students in the U.S.
Engineering	Soc. Sci.	Engineering	Business
Nat'l Sci.	Engineering	Business	Engineering
Soc. Sci	Humanities	Humanities	Nat'l Sci.
Agriculture	Nat'l Sci.	Math/Comp.Sci.	Math/Comp Sci.
Humanities	Agriculture	Nat'l Sci.	Soc. Sci

Source: ROC, *Taiwan Statistical Data Book 1995.*

Table 12.5   Percent of New U.S. Ph.D.'s with Academic Job Commitments on Graduation

Year	Total	Humanities	Soc. Sci.	Nat. Sci.	Engineering	Comp. Sci.
1971	68.1	96.1	80.3	56.5	28.6	.
1980	55.1	82.3	58.2	41.7	26.6	53.2
1990	52.7	83.1	53.2	39.6	30.6	64.9
1994	51.9	86.0	53.4	39.6	23.5	47.2

Source: *Digest of Education Statistics,* U.S. National Center for Education Statistics.

The sharp differences hold whether one compares Taiwan students enrolled in domestic programs or the Taiwan students in the U.S. Indeed, foreign students from all countries are more likely to select the fields which offer non-academic employment after graduation than are U.S. domestic residents. The U.S. enforces student visa restrictions: unless an employer vouches for a change in the visa status, the student must returning to the home country on graduation. For foreign students from many sending countries, this a penalty in foregone wages.

Changing market pressures may push more degree holders to return to Taiwan. A full 43 percent of recent returnees bring back training in engineering and business. The highest wage sectors of the Taiwan economy are currently utilities and financial services. Figure 12.2 gives a comparison of average monthly earnings in the U.S. and Taiwan for these sectors. After using the exchange rates as well as a purchasing power adjustment, as suggested by Summers and Heston (1991 and 1994), to convert the NT$ wages to current international dollars (US $ price deflator =100), it can be seen that the gap is shrinking rapidly. The numbers for the most recent available year are as follows. In Utilities, R.O.C. workers average NT$46,182 (US$1326) and in Financial Services, workers average NT$38,601 (US$1108) in 1990. In the U.S. corresponding monthly earnings are roughly US$1653 and US$1169,respectively. These two sectors require large investments in training, but pay is correspondingly high for these specialties. The shrinking Taiwan-U.S. earnings gap occurring to varying degrees across specializations is now reinforced by an increasingly tight academic job market in the U.S. Two forces will affect the future patterns of study abroad: the increased international markets for Taiwan industry, trade, and , increasingly, services, will push more workers to travel abroad for language training and cultural exchange, but increased government support for colleges and universities may supply more of the required training domestically.

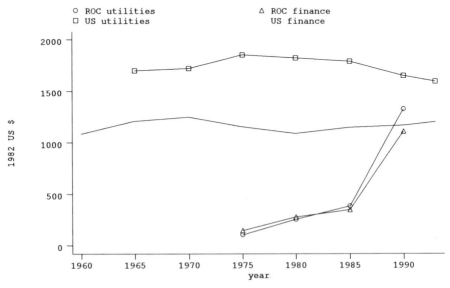

Figure 12.2   **Avg. Monthly Earnings by Industry: US and ROC**

Using the rough calculations on interpolated stocks and estimated flows, two important features are apparent. First, the proportion of returnees to estimated leavers has exceeded 50 percent since 1990. The percent of returnees calculated more realistically on a base of those who left four years preceding is even greater (see Figure 12.3). Second, the total stock of Taiwan students holding degrees from the early 1960s to the present is an estimated 128,000. Of these, 44,905 are recorded as having returned, leaving about 83,255 residing abroad. Given exponential patterns of increase, most of their degrees will have been of recent vintage. This constitutes an impressive supply of high-skilled workers.

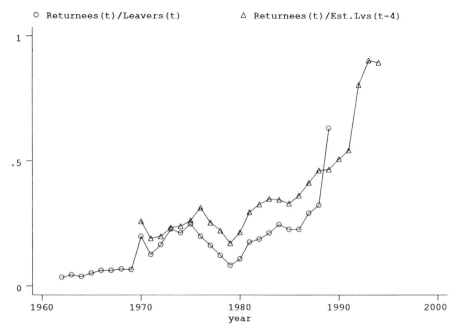

Figure 12.3   Taiwan Student Returnees as Percentage of Flow Abroad

In summary, the fields of study chosen by students from Taiwan reflect an income maximizing strategy: given the problems of changing from their native tongue to English, they are less likely to excel in the U.S. academic labor market. Only in the 1990s has Taiwan substantially expanded academic employment at home with the creation of new colleges and universities. Higher wages and higher premia for mathematical facility were to be found in the private sector, clearly affecting the field choices of these students.

The combined incentives of the competitive entrance system and the policy of open borders for obtaining higher education rewarded students and parents who invested heavily in the effort required to excel in school. In this light, high international rankings of 9 and 13 year olds, successful competition for entrance to foreign schools, comparatively low public schooling expenditures and large class sizes do not appear paradoxical.

12.3 Efficient labor utilization

Thus far, this paper has described only the education choices of the postwar generation in Taiwan. Equally impressive is how this skilled and technically adept work force has been absorbed into the economy. The economy has been booming, with unemployment under 2 percent since 1987 and no higher than 3 percent since 1966. Empirical researchers have tried to describe "product cycles'" of ever more capital-intensive and technologically sophisticated outputs. During the 1950s and 1960s, Taiwan met world demand for a succession of manufactured goods such as textiles, apparel, shoes, umbrellas, transistors, and household electrical appliances. In that period, the structural changes in Taiwan's labor force (well documented in Galenson, 1979) were apparent as shifts of labor out of agriculture into manufacturing. In that volume, Ranis remarks upon the luck of geography that placed almost all the rural labor force in close proximity to rail and highways running from the north to the south of the island. Temporary, even seasonal shifts in employment between light industry and agriculture augmented the income of rural households. Shifting output composition occurred in agriculture as well as manufactures. Instead of having to strive to meet domestic demand for rice, Taiwan began to supply world markets for specialty food items such as citrus fruits, asparagus, mushrooms and melons.

Then as now, the economy exhibited an outstanding nimbleness: as quickly as resources have shifted out of some products (world demand for canned asparagus became inelastic as the U.S. and Europe imposed protectionist measures, other countries have comparative advantage in low-skilled labor-intensive commodities) other ventures have taken their place. The industries that produced Taiwan's major exports of the 1960s — household appliances, radios, and consumer electronics — are now lagging due to rising labor costs. Both product and process innovation have continued to reshape the allocation of resources: Taiwan now exports computer chips and computer monitors. Some goods have remained highly ranked in terms of annual value exported, but have changed in the amount of embodied technology: bicycles today are now eighteen-geared marvels made of lightweight plastic, aluminum, and graphite. Long-standing economic theories of specialization of labor and learning-by-doing capture a part of the productivity gains associated with these anecdotal "product cycles." There has also been a well-documented increase in capital per worker. The continuous shifts in the productive capacity, both human capital and physical capital, were somehow part of the successful growth of Taiwan's economy.

Two necessary elements for generating this resource fluidity are the focus of this section. These are theoretical discussions, not meant to provide conclusive answers, but to provoke further empirical study. First, what motivates the entrepreneurs that yielded this ever-shifting output mix and incorporation of new processes? Is entrepreneurial motivation a resource with which all cultures are equally endowed? Secondly, given Taiwan's general education achievements, which span all members of these recent cohorts, should Taiwan's workforce perform better or worse than other countries in the face of ever-increasing production processes?

12.3.1 The supply of entrepreneurs

Most would agree that if there is a national personality trait in Taiwan, then one of the main characteristics would include a strong entrepreneurial drive. Yet this is one aspect of economic behavior that is rarely made explicit in standard economic models. An exception is a collected volume of studies on entrepreneurship edited by Joshua Ronen. Sherwin Rosen (1983), in his contribution to this volume, attributes this to the mercurial nature of the activity and its rewards. Entrepreneurial activity is distinguished from mere invention as being the creation of a new market by supplying a new good or process. (The Cornell physicist Richard Feynman was a brilliant innovator, but an indifferent entrepreneur. He wrote that while at Los Alamos, he sold the idea for a nuclear submarine, among other things, to the U.S. government for a dollar.) In a competitive economy the monopoly profits of entrepreneurs are quickly dissipated by copycat entrants. Nevertheless, a healthy supply of entrepreneurs in the labor force (too often thought of as composed of "employees") ensures that all factors, human and non-human, are constantly shifted to their most productive activity. Ronen (1983) outlines the personality traits of the entrepreneur. In summary, through interviews with twenty-three chief executive officers of U.S. firms with sales which grew at more than a 10 percent compound rate over the previous 5 years, he found these common traits. These successful entrepreneurs were easily bored and changed primary activity often (each 5 years), disliked routine, were no more risk-loving than average, and sought high profits and personal wealth as outward sign of success and prestige.

Ronen also allows himself a "metaphysical digression" which I note here for obvious cultural reasons:

> . . .I would also assert my strong impression that the entrepreneurially oriented are driven to continue to accumulate wealth (even after securing the consumption needs of themselves and their offspring) so as to gain a measure of *immortality*. . . . The piling up of business triumphs (and thus wealth) demands an ongoing process of creativity, new ideas, continued research. (Ronen, 1983: 150; emphasis in original).

He continues by suggesting that utility functions of entrepreneurs "are better specified throughout the life cycle with wealth surrogating for immortality as an argument in addition to the consumption vector" and adds this cultural speculation.

> . . .One would then expect those whose ethos is manifest in notions of reincarnation (therefore, in due time, infinitely wealthy) to exhibit *ceteris paribus* a much lesser passion for the entrepreneurial attainment of wealth. Consider that for such as the Hindus (as perhaps contrasted with the Jews) the future state of infinite bliss (self-believed) must render far less urgent any entrepreneurial accumulation of worldly wealth. (Ronen, 1983: 151).

In Taiwan, a common practice in graveside rituals is transferring symbolic food and money to the spirit world for one's ancestors. Worldly wealth accumulated by current generations enhances status in this lifetime, and also honors the ancestral family line. The work ethic derived from this Confucian philosophy is at least as strong as the Calvinist strain. In one final observation applicable to Taiwan, Ronen also argues that a sense of displacement or being outside established social networks can add to the push toward entrepreneurship. Historically, the highest social status is not given to the merchant class but to those who rose through the civil examination system to become scholarly officials in government service.

12.3.2 Worker Complementarities

Theoretical attention to models of economic growth was spurred by Lucas (1988) and Romer (1990). Romer discussed how innovations in product or process design work to increase the productivity of each worker. In his example, a design innovation changes the storage capacity of a computer's hard disk ten-fold. This increase costs little in terms raw materials, but the productivity per worker, measured in storage capacity, increases ten-fold. These two papers have generated many theoretical explorations of the role of human capital in growth. Romer proposes that some of the gains to increased general knowledge constitute externalities: the market economy does not adequately compensate those who increase levels of knowledge, and therefore the government ought to subsidize general education and basic research. Others disagree, saying that private research institutes and universities are able to charge for their contributions to knowledge in the form of tuition and royalties on publications. Empirical work has not yet caught up with these speculations but the theories are of interest to Taiwan.

Other economists have tried to describe more explicitly how the increasing complexity of products has changed the nature of the complementarities between workers. Modern business managers have been addressing maintenance of quality in production: for example, in some firms teams of workers compete for prizes awarded for highest non-defective output. Kremer (1983) has an interesting thesis incorporating notions of quality control: instead of writing a production function as $F(L,K)$ an increasing function of capital K, and aggregate labor inputs L = number of worker hours summed over all workers, allowance should be made for the capability of each worker involved to thoroughly destroy the value of the end-product. Although his paper's title refers to the dramatic explosion of the space shuttle Challenger due to the failure of a low-cost rubber "O-ring" gasket, his revised production function is also applicable to complex products like computer panels. These aren't repaired if found defective: they are thrown away. The products themselves involve so many steps that even pin-pointing the problem can be too costly an effort. Thus, the quality of the final good is affected by every worker who touches one small phase of production. The implications of this kind of production technology are that the value of having a team of homogeneous high-skilled workers becomes greatly magnified. He writes that expected output of good y is a function of capital (conventionally Cobb-Douglas form), multiplicative in each worker's skill (or quality) measured by $q(i)$ = the expected percentage of maximum value the output retains after the worker i has completed the task, N= the number of tasks, and B = output per worker with a single unit of capital if all tasks are performed perfectly. Expected production is therefore

$$E(y) = k^\alpha \left(\prod_{i=1}^{N} q(i) \right) N B$$

A product's N is determined by technology. The firm's profit maximization, facing a wage schedule $w(q)$ and rental rate on capital r is

$$\underset{k,\{q\}}{\max} = k^{\alpha} \prod_{i=1}^{N} q(i)NB - \sum_{i=1}^{n} wq(i) - rk$$

This technology implies complementarity between workers: the derivative of the marginal product of skill for the ith worker with respect to the skill of other workers is positive. Firms with n-1 high skilled workers place the highest value of having another high-skilled worker in the nth task. An equilibrium will display positive assortative matching: high skilled workers will be hired to work with each other. The equilibrium capital is

$$k = (\prod_{i=1}^{N} q(i))NB)^{(1/(1-a))}$$

High capital per worker will characterize the high-skill industries: it is less costly to entrust such production to those with lower probability of destroying output.

In expansion of his model, he allows two variations: if workers cannot find exact matches to their own skill levels in a given population, then they will tend to cluster. Regions or cities with certain specialties arise by individuals seeking to find workers similar to them to raise their own productivity. In another variation, Kremer considers a case where one has imperfect information regarding one's skills. One's skill is the sum of some unobservable endowment plus one's education level. A characteristic of a strategic Nash equilibrium is that the marginal payoff to increasing one's own education increases with the rest of the workers' education. Workers in his model increase education in response to education being increased by others. The role of government in investment in general education can have a magnified effect through this strategic decision-making of each student. Kremer points out that the possibility for a bad alternative exists: everyone can choose to invest little in education if each presumes he will be surrounded by low-skilled workers. Strategic complementarity and the possibility of bad equilibria constitute an argument in addition to that of Romer's knowledge externalities in favor of government subsidization of general education.

In the strictest interpretation of Kremer's model, workers with lower skill damage the output of other workers. Obviously, this view of non-complementarity is not an accurate representation of the real world. However, the idea that skilled workers enhance the productivity of others is not unreasonable. The enhancement of productivity through mechanical or physical forms of infrastructure is well-accepted. Many of the recent technological gains from the expanded use of information technologies has been enhancement of infrastructure, allowing more efficient consolidation of the activities of coworkers. One worker's re-organization of scheduling and shipping in a delivery company certainly enhances the productivity of every driver. The productivity enhancement is made possible by information technology and limited by the worker's own training in programming and management, as well as the scale of the operation. As Taiwan continues to produce more complex outputs which embody sophisticated technology and processes relative to the raw materials, the homogeneity of a well-educated, technologically adept work force will give the country a comparative advantage in this area. Having raised the average level of skill through subsidizing education over the past 40 years raises the value to each individual of investing in matching that increased level: an individual is more productive and will command higher wages if her skills are comparable and thus complementary to those around her. If Kremer's articulation of the complementarities across skilled workers is sound, then the clustering of high-skilled workers together occurs in response to market forces. In the U.S., few would consider the presence of an extremely high number of engineers and programmers in northern California's Silicon Valley an imbalance: California will continue to trade with the rest of the country and the world. The continued integration of Taiwan in world markets is of course key to the success of this strategy of specialization in technologically complex industries.

12.3.3 Changing utilization of labor

These theoretical perspectives raise questions that can best be answered by empirical studies of production at the firm level, using worker characteristics measured by education and job tenure. In the hopes of stimulating further research into these questions, here are some observations based on available aggregate statistics. Unfortunately, the aggregate data do not reveal as much information regarding shifts in labor utilization as they once did: large differences in technology exist within sectors which previously described similar industries and big changes are occurring within sectors. The employment shift from agricultural to industrial employment in the 1950s and 1960s was evident: the time series of agriculture employment fell as manufacturing employment rose. There are, however, no time series track the increase of employment in high-technology industries: all sectors have some firms which benefit from recent technological innovations.

Kremer's insights on skill complementarities imply that high labor turnover rates would not be as common in high-skilled industries as low-skilled. The costs of ascertaining a worker's skill and finding a team of employees with matching skill would be higher in high-skilled firms. This augments the standard observation that firm- or job-specific training reduces incentives for rapid job turnover: there is no distinguishing the two theories on the basis of these data. The Taiwan industries with lowest labor turnover (accession and separation rates less than 2 percent in 1993) are Utilities and Financial Services, which are also the industries with the highest capture rate of foreign-educated returnees. The Utilities subsector of Electricity, Gas & Water (shown in the table as "Power") has lower labor turnover than the Utilities subsector Transport, Storage, & Communication. Turnover rates greater than 2 percent are found in Manufacturing, Business Services, Construction, and Commerce. Employees in these high turnover industries have lower average monthly earnings than the low job turnover industries.

Kremer would also predict that establishment size increases as general education level of workers and skill levels used in production increase. Unfortunately, the manufacturing category mixes light industry, heavy industry and high technology firms, obscuring these distinctions. High skilled workers in Utilities work tend to work in larger firms: scale economies of this industry require it. Financial service firms exhibit large establishment size together with high capitalization (reported for newly registered firms) for the decade, though new firms seem to be entering with lower capitalization and number of employees in the 1980s as compared to the 1970s. This coincides with the speculative boom on the new stock exchange. New firms in Commerce (labeled as "trade" in the accompanying figures) and Construction firms tend to be smaller in initial capitalization, number of employees, and skill levels (see ROC, 1995).

Tables 12.6 and 12.7 show cross-industry variation in capital per worker along with the ten-year percentage change in number of workers in the industry. In the 1970s, Manufacturing took the lion's share of new employees but the largest percentage increases in employment were in Business Services, Finance, and Construction. From 1982-1991, the Manufacturing sector again experienced the largest employment increase, (half the size of the 1972-81 increase) and nearly all sectors grew faster in percentage terms.[2]

Table 12.6   Employment Shifts in Taiwan Industries: 1981

Industry	K/L (1981)	ΔL (1971–1981)	%ΔL (1971–1981)
Utilities/Power	.104	6,942	54.7
Construction	.159	236,753	124.3
Mining	.208	–31,393	–41.2
Manufacturing	.347	987,948	83.3
Finance	.478	75,962	14.5
Trade	.496	58,238	58.1
Transport/Comm	.801	121,040	69.8
Services (Busn.)	.848	44,669	206.2

Note: K/L uses initial capitalization of only new firms in the industry. Source: ROC, 1995.

Table 12.7   Employment Shifts in Taiwan Industries: 1991

Industry	K/L (1991)	ΔL (1981–1991)	%ΔL (1981–1991)
Utilities/Power	.244	12,344	62.9
Construction	.766	24,970	5.8
Manufacturing	1.003	448,673	20.6
Finance	1.598	169,354	132.1
Trade	2.274	138,679	87.4
Transport/Comm	8.273	60,434	20.5
Mining	35.6	–27,356	–61.3
Services (Social)	46.7	–230,676	–83.8

Note: K/L uses initial capitalization of only new firms in the industry. Source: ROC, 1995.

Table 12.8 shows industries ranked by 1991 firm size. In keeping with Kremer's hypothesis of worker complementarities, the industries with the highest recent capture rates of foreign trained workers, Finance and Utilities, are also those with highest industry averages of firm size, as measured by workers per establishment. Finally, these employment figures emphasize that Taiwan's labor utilization continues to shift dramatically. The combination of training and individual initiative has enabled the rapid shift of employment across the continually changing economy.

Table 12.8   **Workers per Establishment: 1981 and 1991**

Industry	1971	1981	1991
Utilities/Power	166.8	49.2	78.0
Finance	23.6	62.9	26.1
Construction	32.6	34.0	18.0
Manufacturing	26.9	23.1	18.0
Transport/Comm	31.7	17.4	7.1
Trade	7.0	5.8	6.1
Services (Business)	6.9	5.6	6.0
Mining	83.4	43.4	1.7

Source: ROC, *Taiwan Statistical Data Book 1995.*

12.4 Research and Development

The government initiatives encouraging high technology firms to locate in parks such as the Hsinchu Research Park may be justifiable in the light of work on complementarities among high skilled workers. Given the success of this initial project, in the future, private developers may mimic this innovation in urban design. Real estate may be the only resource which the government may still have a cost advantage over private developers, although auctions may be the right way to ensure that government allocates its acreage efficiently across competing uses. Market forces generated the American high-technology clusters of Silicon Valley and Route 2 outside Boston. In all cases, location near air and ground transportation hubs as well as highly educated local populations (proximity to Stanford University and the University of California, and to M.I.T. and Harvard, respectively) were important preconditions for the subsequent clustering of firms. Justifying subsidization of loans or preferential tax treatment may not be as simple.

In general, the value of R & D expenditures can be hard to measure: as is often the case, costs are easier to quantify than the benefits. In the case of Hsinchu, the number of firms locating there and the number of new products introduced are often listed as the benefits. A fair examination of the "success" of Hsinchu Research Park would have to take into account the full range of costs incurred on both the fair retail value of the land, the expenditure on plant, and the additional subsidies implicit in the tax-advantages and loan discounts which research companies received. To justify these expenditures, the question must be, are subsidized firms producing more efficiently or profitably than similar non-subsidized firms? If so, these companies should be able to pay back any favorable treatment they received out of their increased profits. If not, the companies would fail under standard free-market test of profitability. Taiwan's strength has been in subjecting new enterprises to the cold light of world competition: it would be disappointing to see tax revenues frittered away on protection of a high-technology version of an "infant industry" at this late stage. If skill complementarities exist with imperfectly observable skills, then clustering will emerge due to market forces. Auctions of government land to the highest private bidder would ensure that those developers incorporate the latest concepts in community design to maximize rental values. (Although land is not as scarce a commodity in the U.S. as in Taiwan, an analogous auction strategy has been successful in transferring rights to government-held radio bandwidths to cellular communications companies.)

The government policy of encouraging increasing levels of private investment in R & D must be examined on another basis: that of long-term profitability. If one goal of investment in education is to create and capture the rents from domestic innovation, then it is worth evaluating the rate at which Taiwan innovators have been granted patents. In Table 12.9, data from the National Bureau of Standards of the R.O.C. give some indication that Taiwan is advancing in this regard. It shows patent applications and awards by residency of the applicant. The proportion of domestic applicants shows some increase, but more dramatically, the success rate of Chinese applicants has increased from 50 percent to nearly 70 percent.

Table 12.9   R.O.C. Patent Applications and Successful Award Rate by Residency of Applicant

Year	Total (1000s)	Taiwan (% of Total)	Taiwan Success Rate (%)	R.O.W. Success Rate (%)
1985	23.8	68.4	53.5	46.5
1990	32.3	58.1	49.1	50.9
1993	42.1	69.5	69.1	30.8

Source: ROC, *Taiwan Statistical Data Book 1995.*

the taiwan patent numbers are encouraging, but may not indicate that taiwan has been shifting to greater "inventiveness." the u.s. patent and trademark office provides detail on type of rights granted; for 1) a new invention, 2) a new design of an existing creation, or for 3) a botanical innovation, such as a new hybrid variety of corn. table 12.10 shows that residents of taiwan were granted more design patents relative to other countries with similar numbers of invention patents. taiwan has been a markedly successful learner: new ideas, perhaps borrowed, have been put to productive use. this is in keeping with the discussion in section 12.2 of the competitive examination system's potential for overemphasizing memorization over creativity. it is possible that the government initiative is pushing the labor force into activities in which the work force does not currently have an international competitive advantage. developing strength in basic research may require rethinking education in lower schools as well as large expenditures already begun at the university level.

Ironically, Taiwan's R & D expenditures targeting basic research come at a time when in the U.S., cost-conscious policy makers are reevaluating all expenditures on basic research. It has been quite profitable for many countries to apply ideas generated by the basic research funded by the U.S. The scale required for advancement of basic knowledge, such as that in high-energy physics or space exploration, is beginning to surpass the costs that any individual country is willing to shoulder. Increased international cooperation in basic science will most likely be the most efficient path for the future.

Table 12.10   U.S. Patent Awards to Foreign Recipients; Top 11 Countries

Country	Invention	Design	Botanic + Reissued
Japan	21,925	1149	9077
Germany	7,311	258	36
France	3,029	234	17
U.K.	2,425	194	14
Canada	1,964	240	13
Italy	1,271	172	3
Switzerland	1,196	93	4
Taiwan	**1,000**	**250**	**2**
Netherlands	855	66	52
Sweden	627	98	3
S. Korea	538	48	0
All Non-U.S.	45,189	3256	254

Source: U.S. Bureau of the Census, *Statistical Abstract of the U.S.*, Govt. Printing Office, 1995.

12.5 Conclusion

Many former Chinese citizens who were fortunate enough to have professional or scholarly training before the war used their wealth of experience, training, and skill to the benefit of Taiwan's development. Sho-Chieh Tsiang and Ta-Chung Liu were prime examples but only two of the hundreds of voluntary consultants to Taiwan. The postwar generation is the beneficiary of parental and government policy decisions of those who lived through the war. The government tax reforms generated revenues which funded public education initiatives. The open emigration policy allowed students from Taiwan to choose the training programs that suited their talents and enhanced their own productivity. In addition, these students had exposure to foreign markets and knowledge of the foreign languages which have aided Taiwan's ability to become a major exporter. Whether other countries can reproduce these impressive achievements will depend not only on enlightened policy allowing freedom to choose activities which reap high returns, but also on cultural factors which in the case of Taiwan have provided additional motivation to work hard.

12.6 Notes

1   The author wishes to thank Sherwin Rosen, Gary Becker, James Heckman and Lars Hansen for suggestions and comments.

2   Capital stocks are unavailable so the reported capitalization of newly registered firms in each year is used as a proxy. This proxy capital measure is in nominal millions of nominal national Taiwan dollars (NT$). The change between the 1981 and 1991 numbers surely reflect inflation, but the ordering by increasing capital intensity also changes over this decade. Unfortunately, using capitalization only of new firms will be misleading in cases where the startup firms are using extremely different technology than the old vintage establishments. Employment numbers are from industry census information.

12.7 References

Feynman, R., 1985. *Surely You're Joking, Mr. Feynman; Adventures of a Curious Character as told to R. Leighton.* New York: W.W. Norton.

Galenson, W. (ed.), 1979. *Economic Growth and Structural Change in Taiwan.* Ithaca: Cornell University Press.

Institute of International Exchange, 1994. *Open Doors 1993/94: Report on International Educational Exchange 1994.* Todd Davis, ed. New York: Institute of International Education.

Kim, Jinyoung, 1994. *Knowledge Creation, Human Capital Investment and Economic Growth.* Ph.D Thesis, Chicago: University of Chicago Dept. of Economics

Kremer, M., 1993. "An O-Ring Theory of Labor Productivity." *Quarterly Journal of Economics* 108 (3): 551-575.

Lucas, R.E, Jr., 1988. "On the Mechanics of Economic Development." *Journal of Monetary Economics* 22: 3-42.

Republic of China, Directorate-General of Budget, Accounting and Statistics, 1991,1994. *Statistical Yearbook of the R.O.C.* Taipei: ROC.

Republic of China, Council for Economic Planning & Development, 1995. *Taiwan Statistical Data Book, 1995.* Taipei: ROC

Republic of China, Executive Yuan, 1989. *Yearbook of Manpower Statistics; Taiwan Area.* Taipei: ROC.

Romer, P., 1990. "Endogenous Technical Change." *Journal of Political Economy.* 98 (5): S71-S102.

Ronen, J., 1983. "Some insights into the entrepreneurial process." Chapter 7 in J.Ronen, ed., *Entrepreneurship.* Lexington, Massachusetts: Lexington Books.

Rosen, S., 1983. "Economics and Entrepreneurs." Chapter 13 in J. Ronen, ed., *Entrepreneurship.* Lexington, Massachusetts: Lexington Books.

Summers, R. and A. Heston, 1991 and 1994. "The Penn World Table (Mark 5): An Expanded Set of International Comparisons, 1950-1988." *The Quarterly Journal of Economics.* (1994 Update (Mark 5.6) anonymous ftp from nber.harvard.edu)

Tallman, E.W. and P.Wang, 1994. "Human capital and endogenous growth: Evidence from Taiwan." *Journal of Monetary Economics* 34: 101-124.

Tsiang, S.C., 1984. "Taiwan's Economic Miracle: Lessons in Economic Development," in A. Harberger, ed. *World Economic Growth; Case Studies of Developed and Developing Nations.* San Francisco: Institute for Contemporary Studies: 301-326.

Young, A., 1992. "A Tale of Two Cities; Factor Accumulation and Technical Change in Hong Kong and Singapore." In Olivier Blanchard and Stanley Fisher (eds.), *NBER Macroeconomics Annual 1992* (pp. 13–54). Cambridge: the M.I.T. Press.

Young, A., 1995. "The Tyranny of Numbers." *Quarterly Journal of Economics* 110 (3): 641-680.

13 THE LABOR MARKET IN TAIWAN: MANPOWER, EARNINGS, AND MARKET INSTITUTIONS[1]

Walter Galenson

Development models tend to emphasize capital as the major production factor, with labor a good distance behind. The assumption is that if job opportunities are created, they will be filled without difficulty from the almost unlimited supplies of labor that are believed to exist at early stages of development, and that as economic growth continues, the quantity and quality of labor that a more complex economy requires will be forthcoming. Labor supply will not constitute a bottleneck to the smooth flow of growth.

A half century of development experience has made it clear that this picture is flawed. A well functioning labor market can make a major contribution to growth, while one that is subject to rigidities and imbalances may constitute a source of blockage. A misallocation of labor can lead to low productivity or uneconomic wage levels. Efforts to make rapid adjustments can result in social unrest and inefficiencies. A good current example of this phenomenon is seen in attempts to free the sticky labor markets of the former Soviet Union. The structural adjustment loan policies of the World Bank bear witness to the fact that scarce job opportunities in developing countries create rigidities that can frustrate otherwise sound programs.

The behavior of the labor market in Taiwan has been a major factor in promoting the country's rapid economic development. The massive unemployment that characterizes much of the developing world has never been a problem in Taiwan. Intersectoral shifts of manpower have taken place smoothly in response to economic requirements. The shift from agriculture to manufacturing to services has taken place with remarkably little friction. Where skills were needed, they were provided. And all of this occurred without creating undue hardships for working people. The Taiwan experience can serve as a model of how to handle labor in an environment of economic growth.

13.1 The Labor Force

Data on the labor force covering the period 1975 to 1994 appear in Table 13.1. An increase of over 60 percent was achieved despite a declining rate of male labor force participation. Aside from population growth, what made this possible was the steady rise in participation by women, who were drawn from non-paid occupations on farms by the expansion of industry. Their share of the labor force rose from 32.9 percent in 1975 to 37.2 percent in 1994.

Table 13.1 also shows another aspect of Taiwan's labor force: the rates of unemployment. They are remarkably low and raise the question of whether they represent accurately the real status of the labor market for the years covered. Unemployment is a very difficult concept in developing countries. For Taiwan, however, these unemployment rates appear to be a true representation of the situation. In fact, a tight labor market seems to have prevailed throughout the period, with consequences that are considered below. It was never difficult to find a job, and hidden unemployment in the form of unpaid family workers declined persistently, from 15.9 percent in 1975 to 8.6 percent in 1994. It may be noted, however, that in 1995 unemployment reached 1.79 percent, an eight-year high, as a result of the economic slowdown.[2]

Table 13.1   The Labor Force in Taiwan, 1975-1994

Year	Total number (thousands)	Participation rates (percent) Male	Female	Unemployment rates (percent)
1975	5656	77.6	38.6	2.40
1980	6629	77.1	39.3	1.23
1985	7651	75.5	43.5	2.91
1990	8423	74.0	44.5	1.67
1994	9081	72.4	45.4	1.56

Source: Council of Labor Affairs, *Monthly Bulletin of Labor Statistics*, December 1995, Table 2-1.

Changes in the sectoral distribution of employment, as shown in Table 13.2, were marked. Almost one-third of the labor force was still engaged in agriculture in 1975, with industry the predominant activity. Industrial employment continued to increase, but it was overtaken by the services, with agriculture losing out both relatively and absolutely. From 1990 to 1994, industrial employment rose by 3.5 percent, compared with 18 percent for service employment. Taiwan was rapidly becoming a fully developed industrial nation on the basis of this criterion.

The evolution of the age distribution of the labor force over the last two decades (Table 13.3) was in a direction favorable to productivity. There were fewer young people as a result of longer years of schooling, while the proportion of people of prime working age reached almost 70 percent of the total. The occupational structure has also undergone considerable change, which was to be expected as the economy became more complex. From 1985 to 1994 (consistent data going back to 1975 are not available) the number of professionals and technicians almost doubled, while those engaged in production increased only slightly (Table 13.4). There was a 50 percent increase in the number of high-level executives and managers, many of whom were in the proliferating small business sector.

Table 13.2   Sectoral Distribution of Employment in Taiwan, 1975–1994

(thousands of persons and percentages)

Year	Agriculture	Industry	Services	Agriculture	Industry	Services
1975	1681	2262	1599	30.3	40.8	28.9
1980	1277	3161	2110	19.5	48.3	32.2
1985	1297	3466	2667	17.5	46.6	35.9
1990	1064	3844	3375	12.8	46.4	40.8
1994	976	3979	3983	10.9	44.5	44.6

Source: Council of Labor Affairs, *Monthly Bulletin of Labor Statistics*, December 1995, Table 2-2.

Table 13.3   Age Distribution of the Labor Force in Taiwan, 1975–1994

(percent of total)

Years	Ages 15-24	Ages 25-49	Ages 50-64	65 and over
1975	30.5	55.7	13.1	0.7
1985	22.1	61.1	15.6	1.2
1990	17.2	66.4	15.0	1.4
1994	15.0	68.9	14.5	1.6

Source: Council of Labor Affairs, *Monthly Bulletin of Labor Statistics*, December, 1995, Table 2-1

Table 13.4   Occupational Structure of the Labor Force in Taiwan, 1985–1994

(thousands of persons)

	1985	1990	1994
Legislators, government administrators, business executives and managers	287	391	436
Professionals	308	427	479
Technicians and associate professionals	628	963	1296
Clerks	511	661	839
Service and market sales workers	1225	1383	1438
Agriculture, forestry, fishing workers	1282	1054	965
Production and related workers, plant and machine operators and laborers	3187	3405	3486

Source: Council of Labor Affairs, *Monthly Bulletin of Labor Statistics*, December 1995, Table 2-2.

The changes in the occupational structure imply an improvement in quality of labor, which would not have been possible without a large investment in education. In 1975, some 80 percent of all employees had at most a junior high school education while only 6 percent were college or university graduates (Table 13.5). Twenty years later the percentage in the former group had halved, while the latter had gone up to almost 25 percent. In 1975 a good many young Taiwanese were receiving their higher education in the United States, but by 1994 most of them were attending universities in Taiwan. This record of educational expansion is unmatched by any country at Taiwan's stage of development in the 1970s.[3] The authorities who were guiding Taiwan's development certainly had faith in the returns to education. The same was true of vocational training; in 1994, for example, over 7,000 people were under training in public institutions and 21,500 had completed training in a wide variety of trades. Private industry had its own training programs, and the extent to which skills were upgraded is suggested by the fact that 135,500 individuals were licensed to practice skilled trades in that year.

Table 13.5   Employed Persons in Taiwan by Extent of Education, 1975–1994

(percent of total)

Year	Junior high and less	Senior high and vocational schools	College and graduate schools
1975	79.8	14.2	6.0
1980	70.2	19.6	10.5
1985	54.3	28.9	16.7
1990	44.8	34.2	21.0
1994	39.4	36.0	24.6

Source: Council of Labor Affairs, *Monthly Bulletin of Labor Statistics*, various issues.

13.2 Earnings

The people of Taiwan have profited greatly from the country's economic growth. Real earnings in industry as a whole and in manufacturing have risen by factors of more than 3.5 from 1975 to 1994 (Table 13.6).This amounts to a rate of over 7 percent per annum, and among developing countries is exceeded only by South Korea for a comparable period.[4] This was accomplished, moreover, by maintaining a distribution of income that was among the least concentrated in the world, which meant that all strata of society shared in the growing prosperity.

Bonuses are part of the normal wage structure and are generally equivalent to two month's pay, although they may be adjusted upward or downward depending upon enterprise profits. There may be extra incentive bonuses for individual employees who perform particularly well. Minimum wages are determined by the Basic Wage Commission, consisting of representatives of various government agencies, the Federation of Labor, and employer organizations. They are maintained at roughly half the average wage level, but the tightness of the labor market has minimized the importance of minimum wage setting.

Table 13.6 Indexes of Real Average Monthly Earnings of Employees on Payrolls in Taiwan, 1975–1994 (1975=100)

Year	All industry	Manufacturing
1975	100	100
1980	145.3	154.9
1985	189.3	202.1
1990	295.4	314.6
1994	352.6	378.0

Sources: Directorate-General of Budget, Accounting, and Statistics, *Monthly Bulletin of Earnings and Productivity Statistics*, August, 1995, deflated by official consumer price index.

The length of working hours reflects the fact that Taiwan has not yet reached the welfare state category. In 1994, employees in Taiwan worked an average of 202 hours per month, including overtime. The comparable figure for Japan was 163, where hours worked tend to be higher than in most OECD countries. However, the Taiwan norm in 1975 was 222 hours, so that there has been improvement.

Employees in Taiwan enjoy an extensive menu of fringe benefits in addition to their cash wages. The Labor Insurance Act, last amended in 1988, is financed by a payroll tax of 7 percent of earnings, 80 percent of which is paid by the employer and 20 percent by the employee. This covers what is termed ordinary insurance and occupational hazards. Ordinary insurance includes maternity benefits and life insurance. Lump-sum old age benefits are payable depending on years of service, up to a maximum of 45 months of wages.

Prior to 1995, the Labor Insurance Act covered medical costs for employees. This was replaced by the National Health Insurance Program that includes family members as well as the primary employee. The premium was set at 4.5 percent of an employee's salary for each family member up to a maximum of five members, including the employee. The employee share of the premium was raised to 30 percent, which means that the employee contribution to the insurance and health programs combined have risen considerably. This triggered an hour-long protest called for by the trade unions, the first such action taken in Taiwan on a matter of public policy. The government is considering the possibility of reducing the employee share of the premium.

These benefits are modeled on programs operative in industrial nations, but there is another scheme that is indigenous to Taiwan. Under the Employee Welfare Fund Law, which dates back to 1948, enterprises are required to allocate the following amounts to special welfare funds: one to three percent of the amount of capital investment when a firm is established; 0.05 percent of monthly business income; 0.5 percent of the monthly salary of each employee; and 20 to 40 percent of proceeds from the sale of waste. The welfare funds are devoted to a wide range of activities negotiated with unions or employee committees. Included are educational programs, gifts at the time of marriage or childbirth, recreational activities, and hobbies.

An additional labor cost that might be mentioned is that of severance pay. Under a separate statute an employee dismissed by a manufacturing firm is entitled to a month's wages for each year of unbroken service up to three years, and ten days of wages for each additional year of service.

Employers in Taiwan have complained that wage levels plus fringes have endangered their ability to compete in foreign markets. Indexes of labor productivity and unit labor costs are shown in Table 13.7 for the period 1975 to 1994. The increase in labor productivity is the same as that for Japan and slightly larger than that of Italy for the same period, but exceeds that for the other OECD countries. Rising wage levels in Taiwan pushed unit labor costs beyond productivity, but not as much as in Japan, for example. In any event, Taiwan's export trade does not appear to have been adversely affected, to judge by its record.

Table 13.7   Indexes of Labor Productivity and Unit Labor Costs in Taiwan

(1975=100)

Year	Labor productivity		Unit labor costs	
	Industry	Manufacturing	Industry	Manufacturing
1975	100	100	100	100
1980	141.4	140.4	163.7	168.8
1985	163.9	165.8	236.8	240.6
1990	233.2	234.7	293.2	299.4
1994	286.8	285.9	332.8	342.5

Source: DGBAS, Monthly Bulletin of Earning and Productivity Statistics, August 1995.

13.3 The Employment Service Law

This statute, enacted in 1992, covered both domestic and foreign workers. On the domestic side, it barred discrimination in hiring on the basis of a number of characteristics of the applicant, including sex, physical handicaps, political orientation, or membership in a labor union. The government is enjoined to "specify measures for regulating the supply and demand of manpower and to promote the effective use of manpower resources and national employment." In the event of widespread unemployment, the central authorities are to encourage employers to negotiate with unions or workers on measures to avoid layoffs, including reduced working hours, wage adjustment, or training programs.

Special attention is given to women who are supporting their families, older workers, the handicapped, and the indigenous population of the country. Private employment agencies must be licensed, and the quality of their staff is subject to regulation. The agencies are forbidden to disseminate false information, collect fees beyond those specified by the regulating agency, or engage in other activities that had been the subject of complaints. In sum, the new law was designed to standardize domestic employment practices.

On the foreign side, the growing shortage of labor during the 1980s led to the importation of foreign labor, most of it illegal. The entrants came mainly from Malaysia, Thailand, the Philippines, and Indonesia. There have also been some from

Communist China, but the Taiwanese have been suspicious of this source for security reasons. There has not been an adequate census of the number involved. In 1988, a government agency estimated that there were 35,000 illegal aliens, but higher figures were cited by others. A year later, the estimates ranged from 20,000 to 140,000. Public opinion was generally opposed to the in-migration, but employers insisted that their only alternative to employing immigrants was to move operations offshore.

After some preliminary attempts at regulation, the Employment Service Law established a system for hiring foreign workers legally. All of them must secure work permits — skilled workers and professionals as well as the unskilled. Employers must advertise locally before applying for aliens. They must also pay a stabilization fee into a special fund devoted to the furtherance of national employment, as well as cover any expenses involved in return travel. Regular physical checkups are required of the migrants to prevent the spread of communicable diseases. The maximum duration of permits is two years, but an employer may apply for an extension of one year if necessary.

When the law was passed, several amnesties unearthed 11,000 illegals. Of these, 5,000 were from China, a source for which there is no quota. By June 1995, authorization for the admission of over 325,000 foreign workers had been granted. However, it is probable that there are still many illegals in the country, since the demand for labor, particularly for the unskilled, exceeds the number of permits the authorities have been issuing. As long as the rate of unemployment remains at the levels shown in Table 13.1, the importation of foreign labor will remain an issue.

13.4 The Institutions of the Labor Market

13.4.1 Trade Unions

Trade unions have a long history in Taiwan, but not until 1987 did they begin to operate with some degree of independence. Prior to that year they were able to exercise influence informally, but they were not permitted to bargain about wages. The situation changed in 1987 when martial law was lifted and political democracy expanded.

Trade union membership data from 1988 to 1994 are shown in Table 13.8. The industrial unions are limited to manufacturing and are based on local enterprise-wide units. The craft unions are in fact occupationally oriented, catering to such groups as taxi drivers and food salespeople. Industrial union membership peaked in 1990 and began to decline thereafter, while the craft unions continued to grow. This reflects the shift of employment from manufacturing to services. Surveys of the industrial unions have shown that the degree of organization is positively correlated with firm size, the bulk of their membership being concentrated in large firms.

The membership figures suggest a very high rate of union organization. The non-agricultural labor force in 1994 was 7,986,000, which would mean a density ratio of over 40 percent. However, there are several qualifications that are in order. One involves the question of whether membership in the industrial unions is voluntary, a matter that is dealt with below. Another is the fact that many craft union

Table 13.8   Trade Union Membership in Taiwan, 1988–1994

(number of persons)

Year	Total	Industrial unions	Craft unions
1988	2260585	696515	1564070
1989	2419664	698118	1721546
1990	2756620	699372	2057248
1991	2941766	692579	2249187
1992	3058414	669083	2389331
1993	3172116	651086	2521030
1994	3277833	637095	2640738

Source: Council of Labor Affairs, *Monthly Bulletin of Labor Statistics*, December 1995, Table 3-1.

members are self-employed and join in order to gain coverage under the Labor Insurance Act. Article 6 of that law covers virtually all employed persons as well as "members of an occupational union who have no definite employer or who are self-employed." Individuals are not directly eligible for insurance.

The structure of the Taiwan labor movement is rather complicated. At its head is the China Federation of Labor (CFL), a body that was established on the Mainland and brought to Taiwan in 1950. It was closely intertwined with the Kuomintang from the start. Directly under it are three types of organizations: the Provincial and Municipal General Council, the national federations of industrial and craft unions, and the transport and utility unions. The Provincial Council links city and central general councils with which the craft unions, organized on an area basis, are required to affiliate. Provincial and municipal industrial unions are affiliated with their respective national unions. There can be only one local union at an enterprise or locality level; rival unions are not legally permitted, although in fact some exist. In 1994 there were 20 federations of industrial unions and 42 federations of craft unions with which 3600 local unions were affiliated.

Efforts to establish independent unions have had limited success. For example, in 1988, emboldened by the lifting of martial law, a group of workers at the Chinese Petroleum Company ousted the KMT nominees for union posts and replaced them with independent candidates. Other groups followed, and the movement led to tougher bargaining and some strikes. But the movement declined when both the government and employers took strong action against it. Several independent leaders were imprisoned for alleged union activity and others were disciplined.[5]

Attempts at federating the few independents that survived have also met with limited success. The National Federation of Independent Trade Unions, established in 1988, now claims 20 local union affiliates with 4,000 members. The government permits it to operate, though it has no legal status. Another group, the Taiwan Labor Front, was formed in 1992 and is supported by the Democratic Progressive Party. It has only a handful of union members, but it has been active in protest movements.

The key question is whether the Taiwan trade unions are a genuine vehicle for representing employee interests freely or are dominated by the government, a political party, or employers. A recent article by Joseph S. Lee entitled "Is There a

Bona Fide Labor Movement in Taiwan?" explores this question and comes up with some relevant conclusions (Lee, 1994).

He begins by asking whether workers join unions voluntarily. Surveys made in 1987 indicated that 60 percent of joiners were responding to employer pressure and 25 percent did so of their own free will. Employers were reacting to pressure from foreign unions, particularly the AFL-CIO, that threatened to interfere with their exports. By 1991, however, 66 percent joined voluntarily and only 30 percent in response to employer request. Older workers were more likely to become union members than younger ones because of greater attachment to their jobs and access to higher benefits. Women were less likely to be unionized, blue-collar workers were more prone to join than white-collar, there was a negative correlation between educational attainment and propensity to organize, married workers were more likely to join than unmarried, and there was a positive relationship between the size of the enterprise and unionization. None of this is at variance with the experience of other countries, particularly at early stages of union organization.

Did the unions offer advantages in terms of wages, benefits, and job satisfaction? As for wages, the union premium was only 3.2 percent for males and zero for females, much less than the comparable differential in developed nations. This can be explained, in part, by the fact that many large firms were in the public sector, where wages were set by the Ministry of Economic Affairs. In the private sector, Lee reported that management tended "to use rather sophisticated methods of keeping bona fide unions out of their premises."

The unions have done better with fringe benefits. A greater proportion of workers in organized firms enjoyed profit sharing, stock ownership, and efficiency awards. Another important consideration was that employer violations of government-imposed labor standards were apt to be lower where unions were policing them. Job satisfaction tended to be higher in organized firms, measured, for example, by labor turnover rates. Lee's overall conclusion to the question of whether recent union membership increases mark the birth of a genuinely independent labor movement is a qualified yes.

Continuing close alliance of the Chinese Federation and its constituent organizations with the Kuomintang does call into question the degree of union independence, although the rise of strong opposition parties, the Democratic Progressive Party in particular, may help bring about a less politicized labor movement. Then there is the question of wages: an increase in the union differential would signal growing union power. But there is no doubt that the unions have come a long way since 1987. For example, in the 1994 mayoralty elections in Kaohsiung, the second largest city in Taiwan, they supported the Democratic Progressive Party candidate because of dissatisfaction with the KMT candidate for not opposing the privatization of several large government-owned industries, an issue of concern to the unions.

13.4.2 Labor Relations
The number of collective agreements in force in Taiwan for various years is shown in Table 13.9. Almost all are in the industrial sector and each covers a single enterprise, mainly the largest ones. That there are so few agreements indicates that

this form of labor relations has not yet penetrated far into Taiwan industrial relations.

Table 13.9   Taiwan Enterprises With Collective Agreements, 1988–1994

			(number of enterprises)
Year	Public sector		Private sector
1988	—	281	—
1989	—	346	—
1990	—	289	—
1991	—	302	—
1992	116		190
1993	112		180
1994	117		179

Source: Council of Labor Affairs, *Monthly Bulletin of Labor Statistics*, December 1995, Table 3-5.

There is a comprehensive law on collective agreements that would provide a useful framework for extension of this practice. A union shop is allowed, but not a closed shop, although the unions may make recommendations for hiring. Technological change may not be restricted by contract. The maximum duration of contracts is set at three years. Working conditions stipulated in contracts cannot exceed those provided by law, and many agreements simply repeat legal standards.[6] This law is up for amendment, and the Council of Labor Affairs has recommended that neither employers nor unions can refuse a request to negotiate an agreement.

There is an elaborate procedure for handling labor disputes outside the context of collective agreements. The Law on Labor Disputes, amended in 1988, covers disputes over both rights and interests. The first step involves a tripartite conciliation committee of three to five members, or mediation. If these fail, the parties may apply for arbitration, although arbitration may also be imposed unilaterally by government authorities if the controversy is judged to have serious economic consequences.

Arbitration committees are also tripartite. Awards must be rendered within five days of assumption of jurisdiction by the committee. Awards are binding and may be enforced by the courts. While conciliation and arbitration are taking place, the employer may not shut down or terminate a collective agreement, while the union may not resort to strikes or sabotage.[7]

The Council on Labor Activities has proposed several amendments to refine the procedure for handling labor disputes: private mediation and arbitration agencies could be established; employers would be permitted to counter a strike by various measures, including a shutdown; strikes would be prohibited in essential industries, such as power, gas, and healthcare. The legislature has not yet acted on these proposals.

In general, the existing procedure has been fairly effective in resolving disputes, as indicated by the data in Table 13.10. The number of disputes subject to government intervention has not varied much from year to year. Notable is the predominance of conciliation and mediation. Arbitration was rarely imposed.

Table 13.10   Resolution of Industrial Disputes in Taiwan, 1988–1994

(number of cases)

Year	Conciliation		Mediation	Arbitration	Unresolved
1988	—	1247	—	49	67
1989	1622		275	2	85
1990	1634		245	—	66
1991	1567		231	—	78
1992	1631		216	1	33
1993	1681		189	0	41
1994	1852		244	0	6

Source: Council of Labor Affairs, *Monthly Bulletin of Labor Statistics*, September, 1995, Table 3-6.

The data do not reveal the outcome of the controversies. However, the issues involved in the various forms of government intervention appear in Table 13.11. Labor contracts, wages, retirement, and safety and health were the principal matters in dispute, and all but retirement increased in volume over the period shown. Most involved alleged violation of labor standards (discussed below), rather than the interpretation of collective agreements.

Table 13.11 Subjects of Labor Disputes Referred to the Government, Taiwan, 1989–1994

(number of cases)

Year	Labor contracts	Wages	Retire-ment	Welfare benefits	Hours of work	Insur-ance	Manage-ment	Safety health	Union
1989	710	489	234	64	29	88	67	206	2
1990	788	418	202	29	12	87	55	191	2
1991	836	528	210	51	20	111	58	233	—
1992	848	537	185	55	9	91	68	224	2
1993	852	548	207	61	43	121	73	234	2
1994	931	643	210	55	27	105	64	295	3

Source: Council of Labor Affairs, *Monthly Bulletin of Labor Statistics*, September 1995, Table 3-6.

13.4.3 Strikes and Lockouts

Following are the only published statistics on the number of man-days of work lost due to strikes or lockouts since 1988:

1988	8967
1989	24157
1990	828
1992	13783

These data are not very informative about the tone and trend of labor relations since the lifting of martial law. A brief review of a few of the major labor disputes since 1988 will present more sharply the nature of strike activity during those years.[8]

With the establishment of independent unions in late 1987, the long period during which strikes were forbidden was ended. Wildcat strikes on the railroads were mounted in March and May, 1988, which stopped their operation. This example was followed by organizations of bus drivers, gas station workers, postal workers, telecommunication employees, and dockers. These were all presumably illegal, but the government took no action against them, and all yielded substantial wage gains. The climax to this strike wave came in the form of a stoppage at the Maioli Bus Company, where the workers demanded higher pay, shorter working hours, and back pay for overtime. The company refused these demands and the government called the strike illegal. After staying out for 23 days the drivers returned to work and three strike leaders were convicted of labor law violations. They were given suspended sentences but lost their jobs.

In August, 1988, a shoe factory responded to a strike by discharging all its employees and closing its plant. When the strike was called off the company agreed only to consider the demands that had been raised. This was followed half a year later by strikes at the Taita Chemical Company, the Formosa Plastics Group, and the Hsin Ying Bus Company, but none was productive of employee gains.

In May, 1989, the largest strike in Taiwan up to that date took place at a plant of the Far Eastern Textile Company. The company closed the plant and after several weeks of clashes between workers and the police, the strike collapsed. Far Eastern's lead was followed by several other industrial corporations, all of which refused any compromise and discharged the strikers. However, two other companies, General Plastics and Tai An Textiles, which were in the process of moving offshore, agreed to use the profits from the sale of their land in Taiwan for financing severance pay at a level in excess of that required by law. A threat of strike by the employees of the China Petroleum Corporation, a government-owned enterprise, led the Executive Yuan to warn the employees that they would be arrested if they struck. The union retreated and the company raised its annual bonus.

A recent survey of employer attitudes toward unions elicited the replies shown in Table 13.12. One-third of those responding believed that unions serve as a useful

Table 13.12   Views of Taiwan Management on Establishing Labor Unions, 1993

	(percent of respondents)
Serve as communication vehicle	32.3
Serve as employer's business partner	11.2
Legally required	9.1
Employee demand	0.7
Unnecessary because recruitment and personnel management are satisfactory	23.3
Better not because it may hinder business operation	3.6
Possible trouble by bringing in outside force	12.5
Other	7.3
	100

Source: Council of Labor Affairs, Yearbook of Labor Statistics, 1993, Table 3-21.

means of communicating with their employees, but a larger number found them either unnecessary or a potential source of trouble. In any event, harassment of and even violence against union leaders have served to cool the ardor of unions for direct action. Strikes are not illegal, and have continued, as the statistics cited above indicate, but the returns are apt to be small in the face of strong employer opposition. The unions have tended recently to focus on such wider social issues as the importation of foreign labor, privatization of public enterprises, and discrimination against women, with some success. In sum, the existence of trade unionism in Taiwan is not threatened, but the bargaining power of unions has not risen in step with their membership.

13.4.4 *Workplace Representation*
A statute enacted in 1985 provides for the establishment of labor-management committees at the enterprise level, with equal representation from each side. The worker representatives are selected by the union if there is one, or directly by the workers if there is not. The functions of the committees specified in the legislation are vague. They are supposed to discuss matters relating to the harmonization of labor relations, labor conditions, labor welfare, and the increase of productivity. If suggestions are made they are to be forwarded to the union and to management for implementation, and are returned to the committee if this does not take place. Subcommittees may be appointed to handle special problems or programs.

To what extent does this form of representation provide industrial democracy? The experience of a multinational pharmaceutical company operating in Taiwan throws some light on this question (Frenkel,1995). The company set up two committees with bipartite representation, but in fact they functioned as a single unit.

Both management and employees stated that [the system] was useful but had several shortcomings. Workers argued that by having fewer factory than white-collar representatives the committee tended to be biased against manual workers' interests....The [General Manager] believed that the committee discussed too many trivial issues. By contrast, the human resources director emphasized the usefulness of the committee as a means of communication with employees. Arguably, the worker representatives have been disadvantaged by the structure of the committee meetings, which are designed to foster communication between individuals rather than to facilitate negotiation between groups. (Frenkel, 1995: 29)

More generally, the pattern of consultation that takes place is illustrated by the data in Table 13.13, which are based on a survey of 599 large manufacturing concerns in 1992. A substantial majority of these firms consulted with their employees on working conditions, but fewer on business strategy. Where no decisions were involved, consultation was mainly with individual workers rather than with groups or unions. Approximately one-third of the consultations led to decisions, primarily with respect to working conditions. Strategy discussions yielded relatively few decisions. The authors of the study from which the data were derived remarked: "The findings of prevalence for direct grass roots consultations in corporations with 300 or more workers are interesting. One of the major reasons may be due to the fact that the majority of large corporations are family firms and they tend to inherit Chinese traditions" (Liu et al., 1993: 29).

Table 13.13: Pattern of Labor-Management Consultation in Taiwan, 1992

(percent)

	No consult-ing	Total	Consultation with			Deci-sions reached	Other
			Individ-uals	Groups	Unions		
Work conditions							
Safety & welfare	13.6	86.4	30.9	6.1	5.6	35.6	8.3
Environment	19.4	80.6	26.2	4.1	4.7	36.5	9.2
Education, training	28.2	71.7	19.0	4.5	4.7	32.1	11.4
Personnel change	35.9	64.1	20.7	3.1	5.8	23.0	11.7
Business strategy							
Production	42.4	58.6	12.4	3.1	5.9	29.4	7.9
New machines & technology	49.0	51.0	10.8	1.8	5.9	23.7	8.8
Sales	50.1	49.9	8.8	2.3	5.0	25.5	8.3
Investment	55.1	44.9	8.6	1.1	6.8	21.2	7.2
Mgt. policy	64.8	35.2	6.3	1.1	8.6	14.2	5.0
Mergers	79.9	20.1	3.6	1.3	5.8	4.9	4.7

Source : Liu et al. (1993), Table 21.

That employers in Taiwan enter into discussions with their employees, and with unions where they exist, seems clear. However, this is a long way from codetermination on the German or Scandinavian models. There is no provision for union representation on corporate boards, nor are there works councils with unilateral or joint authority on a variety of issues. The Taiwan system is closer to that of Japan, where the structure of the labor movement and weak unions forestall genuine industrial democracy.

13.3.5 Labor Standards

Taiwan has a comprehensive law on labor standards. Many of its provisions are to be found in collective agreements in developed countries, negotiated through bargaining rather than imposed by statute.

1. An employer may terminate a contract of employment without advance notice if the employee misrepresents important facts when entering employment, commits violence or extends gross insults to the employer, or has been sentenced to temporary imprisonment. Absence without explanation for three consecutive days or six days in a month is another basis for discharge.
2. An employee may terminate a labor contract without advance notice where dangerous working conditions exist, where the employer fails to pay wages

according to the terms of the contract, or if he fails to provide sufficient work for a piece worker.

3. Where an employer legally terminates a contract, a worker with continuous employment of between three months and one year is entitled to ten days of advance notice; twenty days of notice for one to three years of employment; and thirty days beyond that. Having received such notice, the employee is entitled to paid leave of two days a week to look for a new job. If advance notice is not given, the employee is entitled to full pay for the notice period.

4. If a firm changes its structure or ownership, the employees who are retained maintain their seniority,

5. Wages must be paid at least twice a month. Overtime not exceeding two hours a day is paid at 1 1/3 the regularly hourly rate, over two hours at 1 2/3 the rate.

6. If a firm is liquidated or becomes bankrupt, wage claims have priority. Employers must make a monthly payment into a wage arrears fund from which overdue wages may be paid at the direction of a government agency.

7. Regular work time may not be in excess of eight hours a day or 48 hours a week. For seasonal or other special requirements, working hours may be extended with the prior approval of the union or the workers as well as by the local authorities. Leave with pay is set at seven days for employees with one to three years of service, ten days for three to five years, 14 days for five to ten years of service, and one additional day for each year over ten, with a maximum of 30 days.

8. There are a number of special protective provisions for women and children. No person under 15 years of age may be employed unless he or she is a junior high school graduate and the competent authorities find that the employment is not hazardous to physical or mental health. No child may work between the hours of 8 p.m. and 6 a.m. except under specified exceptional circumstances. Women with more than six months of employment are entitled to eight weeks of fully compensated maternity leave, with half pay for less than six months of prior employment. Breast feeding time of 30 minutes twice a day is required as part of regular working time.

9. An employee who has worked for more than 25 years and reaches age 50 may apply for retirement, which may be obligatory at age 60. Employers contribute to a retirement fund out of which benefits are paid on the basis of years of service and wage levels.

These and other provisions of the law are monitored by a labor inspectorate, which was strengthened by a new statute enacted in 1993. It gives the inspectors quasi-judicial powers, requires preexamination for dangerous working places, and raises the penalties for violations. There have been numerous demands by both unions and employers for changes in the law. Unions want maternity leave extended to twelve weeks and reduced working hours. Employers complain that the standards are difficult to comply with. The proposed changes have been under debate in the legislature.

If these standards are in fact enforced, they put Taiwan ahead of almost all recently developed nations in this respect. The Council of Labor Affairs has published relevant statistics going back over the last decade. They reveal a fluctuating rate of violations and penalties varying considerably over time. In 1994, 5,559 establishments were inspected. Of these, penalties were proposed in 30.7 percent of the cases and 63 were sent to the courts for enforcement. But there have been allegations of lax enforcement:

> ...critics point to the failure of the CLA to enforce the labor standards law and other regulations. A June-August 1991 Council of Labor Affairs report noted that at least 59 percent of surveyed firms failed to meet legally mandated labor standards. The most common violations are excessive over-time and inadequate holiday pay (US Dept of Labor 1991-92: 6).

One interesting finding is that compliance with standards is higher in union than in non-union firms.

Ensuring full compliance with mandated labor standards is a tricky affair. In the United States, for example, there has been a long-standing controversy over the enforcement of the Occupational Safety and Health Act, and not all employers pay the minimum wage. What can be said of the situation in Taiwan is that the legislated labor standards are real. They have nothing in common with the fictitious standards adopted by a majority of developing countries, often under pressure from the International Labor Organization. Taiwan was expelled from the ILO when China was admitted, but it needed no prompting from the outside to develop a meaningful body of protective labor legislation.

13.5 Conclusions

Taiwan's labor market has undergone great changes along with the economic growth of the country. Like the rest of the developed world, it is moving out of manufacturing into the provision of services. The kind of informal employment characteristic of developing countries is a thing of the past. It has profited from an educational system that provides the skills needed in a complex economy. Unskilled labor has become scarce and is being provided increasingly by foreign workers. Compensation and other working conditions are beginning to resemble those characteristic of advanced economies.

Room for improvement remains. Employees should be guaranteed the right to select their spokesmen without interference from employers or the government. Trade unions should be freed from political domination if they prefer to be neutral, and should be permitted to determine their own structures. Collective bargaining should be regularized and the strike weapon permitted when critical social services are not involved. The 48-hour week is too long, and will presumably be reduced as manufacturing processes become less labor-intensive. The tightness of the labor market cannot last forever, and there is merit in giving attention to the problems created by unemployment when it arises.

Taiwan has many serious problems, political and economic. Adjusting labor practices and institutions is a relatively minor one. Taiwan is famous as the most successful example of postwar economic development. The rights and privileges of its working people should reflect its present status.

13.6 Notes

1   This paper covers the period since 1975. For earlier years see Galenson (1979), Chapter 6.

2   *The Free China Journal*, January 26, 1996, p. 8.

3   See World Bank, *Workers in an Integrated World*, 1995, Table 28.

4   *Ibid.*, Table 7.

5   U.S. Department of Labor, *Foreign Labor Trends: Taiwan, 1992-93*, p. 5.

6   Labor Laws and Regulations of the Republic of China, Collective Agreements Law, 1994, p. 143.

7   *Ibid.*, Settlement of Labor Disputes Law, p. 159.

8   This account is based largely on the annual reports on labor prepared by the American Institute in Taiwan and published by the U.S. Department of Labor in *Foreign Labor Trends*.

13.7 References

Council of Labor Affairs, 1993. *Yearbook of Labor Statistics, 1993*. Executive Yuan, Republic of China.

Council of Labor Affairs, 1994. *Labor Laws and Regulations of the Republic of China, Collective Agreements Law*. Executive Yuan, Republic of China

Council of Labor Affairs, 1995. *Monthly Bulletin of Labor Statistics,* various issues. Executive Yuan, Republic of China.

Directorate-General of Budget, Accounting, and Statistics, 1995. *Monthly Bulletin of Earnings and Productivity Statistics*, August, 1995. Executive Yuan, Republic of China.

Frenkel, Stephen, 1995. "Workshop Relations in the Global Corporation," in Stephen Frenkel and Jeffrey Harrod (eds.), *Industrialization and Labor Relations*. Ithaca, N.Y.: ILR Press: 179-215.

Galenson, Walter, 1979. *Economic Growth and Structural Change in Taiwan*. Ithaca, NY: Cornell University Press.

Her, Kelly, 1996. "Jobless Rate Reaches 6-Year High," *The Free China Journal*, Taipei, January 26, p.8.

Lee, Joseph S., 1994. "Is There a Bona Fide Labor Movement in Taiwan?" Chung-Hwa Institute for Economic Research, Discussion Paper 9403. Taipei: Chung-Hwa Institute for Economic Research (April).

Liu, Paul C., Ying-Chuan Liu and Hui-Lin Wu, 1993. "The Manufacturing Enterprise and Management in Taiwan," Taipei: The Institute of Economics, Academia Sinica, (February)

Council of Labor Affairs, 1994. *Labor Laws and Regulations of the Republic of China, Collective Agreements Law*. Executive Yuan, Republic of China

U.S. Department of Labor, 1993. *Foreign Labor Trends: Taiwan, 1992-93*. Washington, D.C.: U.S. Department of Labor.

World Bank, 1995. *Workers in an Integrated World*. Washington, D.C.: The World Bank.

PART V
RELEVANCE OF THE TAIWANESE EXPERIENCE TO OTHER THIRD WORLD REGIONS

14 STATE AND MARKET IN THE ECONOMIC DEVELOPMENT OF KOREA AND TAIWAN

Irma Adelman[1]

A country's economic development performance is determined by its: initial conditions — natural resource endowments, human capital, and socio-cultural heritage; institutional structure — economic relations within its agrarian and industrial sectors, the nature of the state, particularly the degree of its autonomy, whose interests the government represents, and the relations between the government and civil society, private enterprise and the citizenry; economic policies with respect to resource allocation and accumulation patterns; and the external economic and political environment within which development takes place. The development process is path dependent, in a pattern of causality that runs from initial conditions to institutional structures and policies that are interdependent within periods and dynamically recursive over time. In what follows, the discussion of similarities and contrasts between South Korea and Taiwan will therefore be subdivided into three sections: initial conditions (part 14.1), development policies (part 14.2) and institutions (part 14.3), taking cognizance of the changing pressures and opportunities afforded by the external environment.

14.1 Initial Conditions

Up to the end of World War II, both Korea and Taiwan were Japanese colonies, whose economies, resources, institutions and social structures were managed so as to complement Japan's economic and political interests. In both Korea and Taiwan development was agrarian, with very limited industrialization, especially in what was to become South Korea; educational opportunities were severely restricted and small servile elites were educated in Japan; and industrial capital and feudal estates were owned primarily by Japanese nationals. On the other hand, a good agricultural extension service and agricultural infrastructure were developed under Japanese rule, especially in Taiwan.

The establishment of both Korea and Taiwan at the end of World War II occurred at the expense of significant turmoil. In the immediate postwar period, both Korea and Taiwan started as wards of the United States, subject to US military influence. The United States took significant steps to influence the reform of their institutional structures, particularly in agriculture, their investment policies, particularly with respect to the amount and content of education, and played an important role in the design and financing of agricultural and industrial infrastructure and development. The development of both countries was thus significantly influenced by World War II and the hot and cold wars between the US and communist China.

Refugee immigration played a significant role in the establishment of both countries. In Taiwan, the defeat of Chiang Kai-Sheck on the Mainland brought an influx of upper echelon military officers, previously landed elites and intellectuals who were superimposed upon a population of Taiwanese farmers. Taiwan's population thus assumed a stratified, heterogeneous ethnic and religious character. In South Korea, the partition in the aftermath of the Korean war resulted in an inflow of 3 million refugees from the North, which increased the population by about 11 percent. But unlike in Taiwan, South Korea's population remained ethnically and religiously homogeneous, and the destruction of capital and de-legitimization of its elites, who had either been Japanese collaborators or war profiteers, and whose real and financial capital was confiscated, left the population base remarkably homogeneous and egalitarian.

Both countries were natural-resource poor, but South Korea was more disadvantaged in this regard. Population density relative to arable land in Korea was the highest in the world; and the mountainous topography and harsh climate were considerably less propitious to the development of agriculture in Korea. There were essentially no mineral resources in either country. Largely as a result the import-content of manufacturing production in South Korea in 1964 was a whopping 60 percent.

In both countries the drive for economic growth was extremely high. The cold war context made the political survival of both countries conditional upon their success in economic development. Leadership commitment to economic development therefore constrained the venality of government, in Taiwan immediately and in South Korea after Syngman Rhee was deposed. The population in both countries felt economic growth to be the primary objective, and they were willing to endure a great deal of personal and political hardship to achieve increases in their standard of living. Abject poverty provided the major motivation in South Korea; per capita GNP in 1953 was about $90, and over 60 percent of its population was living at or below subsistence. While also poor, in Taiwan the need for economic security and the desire of the refugees to reestablish the fortunes they previously possessed in the Mainland provided the main motivational drive.

The elites in both countries shared a Confucian ethic, though this ethic was not universal; there was animism among the Taiwanese, and shamanism and Christianity were practiced in Korea. The primary characteristics of this ethic were a stress upon hierarchy, pragmatism, education, hard work, a long run perspective and egalitarianism. These were to impart a particular flavor to institutional development, development goals and instrumentalities in both countries. The hierarchic values influenced the nature of relationships between government and enterprises, the structure of bureaucracies and internal structure of industry. Pragmatism meant that rational grounds for policy selection and evaluation predominated. Pragmatism also enabled governments to shift policies, strategies and institutional structures in a particularly sensitive, speedy and decisive manner in response to ever changing domestic and international conditions. The Confucian values of education and hard work supported a particularly good and ever improving human resource base, and made education the cornerstone of both countries' economic and social development. Indeed, Taiwan's constitution places explicit emphasis on education, and mandates the proportion of government expenditures that is to be allocated to education. The Confucian long range perspective meant that long run development strategies could be adopted, and that eventually development could be based on high domestic savings rates. Lastly, in both countries Confucian egalitarianism influenced the choice of development strategies, the assessment of development achievements and constrained acceptable corruption levels.

Finally, both countries lacked proven entrepreneurial talent. In both, manufacturing and industrial activity during the colonial period had been the almost exclusive province of the Japanese. Secondary education was severely constrained and college education virtually barred. And, despite adding a great deal of educated manpower, the socio-economic character of immigration from the mainland did little to remedy the deficiency in entrepreneurship in Taiwan.

14.2 Development Strategies

The discussion will be divided into subsections reflecting the primary thrust of economic policy. The dating of each strategy will reflect the dates appropriate to each country; there is some overlap in dates in Taiwan between the reform and reconstruction periods. The sequencing of development strategies is remarkably similar. However, the reconstruction of Korea was delayed by the Korean war, so that the early phases of Korea's development lag behind Taiwan's by about 4 years.

14.2.1 Setting the Stage: Stabilization, Agrarian Reform and Reconstruction Taiwan, 1945–53, and Korea, 1945–61

Both countries were liberated from Japanese control in 1945. After liberation, the development of both countries was heavily influenced by a substantial American presence for a significant part of the period and proceeded with substantial American aid. The US influence was responsible for the large degree of similarity in the design of reform policies in both countries during this period.

Korea was under direct American military control until 1948, when an independent Korea was established under Syngman Rhee. Both Taiwan and Korea experienced a great deal of turbulence during this period. In Taiwan, industrial production in 1945 was less than a third of the pre-World-War II level. Industrial production started a slow recovery, but, in 1949, Taiwan's economy was subjected to a further shock: the Nationalist Government withdrew from the Mainland, the seat of government was shifted to Taipei, and Taiwan absorbed a substantial influx of refugees from the Mainland, leading to a 20 percent increase in its population.

In Korea, the devastating Korean War broke out in 1950 and lasted until 1953. The loss of life and physical destruction during the Korean War were enormous. In 1953, the South was literally in ruins. The war had destroyed a quarter of the real wealth of South Korea and killed over 5 percent of the civilian population. The situation was further exacerbated by an influx of 3 million refugees from the North. Life was grim, with the great majority of Koreans living at or below subsistence. Partially as a result, Korea had neither a viable economy nor a viable polity during the whole period.

The policies adopted in Taiwan during this period were conditioned by the lessons learned by the elites concerning the causes of their expulsion from the Mainland. Ultimately, the reasons for the success of the communist Revolution on the mainland can be attributed to two major causes: oppression of the peasants within the framework of feudal land tenure relations and galloping inflation due to the war with Japan. The two-prong wave of reforms instituted by the government in Taiwan was thus motivated by both objective conditions and a determination to avoid the mistakes made on the Mainland.

Currency Stabilization. The political turbulence gave rise to severe inflation in both countries. In Taiwan, the large migration from the Mainland, due to the loss of the Civil War in China by Chiang Kai-Shek, had increased aggregate demand so much that the price level skyrocketed, rising at an average annual compound rate of 922 percent between 1945 and mid-1949. Since inability to control skyrocketing inflation on the mainland was widely perceived to be one of the major factors responsible for the success of the communists, the newly established government in Taiwan was especially sensitive to the need to control inflation. The Currency System Reform adopted by Taiwan in mid-1949 to restore the population's confidence in the currency consisted of: a currency swap; 100 percent reserves made up of gold, silver, foreign exchange and export goods; a ceiling on credit, which was ultimately exceeded; a pegging of the exchange rate against the dollar; and the establishment of a stabilization fund consisting of gold and foreign exchange. The currency reform stopped the galloping inflation, but, even though by 1951 the inflation rate had dropped to 7 percent of its pre-reform average, it remained at 66 percent annually, necessitating subsequent repeated devaluations.

In Korea, inflation fighting measures, which included conversion of the currency and ceilings on the amounts that could be converted, were introduced to stabilize prices, and the properties of war profiteers were confiscated.

Agrarian Reform: TAIWAN. In Taiwan, prior to land reform, tenant farmers were about 70 percent of the total farming population, and rent payments were between 50 and 70 percent of the annual crop. Thus, with over 55 percent of the total labor force in agriculture, the distribution of income and wealth was quite unequal. The first wave of Agrarian Reform, imposed in 1949, set a ceiling on land rent to no more than 37.5 percent of the annual crop. This rent ceiling redistributed income from landlords to tenant farmers, reducing income disparities.

The second wave of Taiwan's Agrarian Reform, imposed in 1951, resold the land confiscated from Japanese farmers and Japanese corporations to tenant farmers. Over 96,000 hectares were resold. The final wave of Taiwan's Agrarian Reform, implemented in 1953, confiscated holdings in excess of 7.5 acres from landlords and resold them to tenant farmers. Landlords were compensated in a mix of land bonds (70 percent) and stocks of public enterprises. As a result, farm tenancy was cut in half (to 18 percent) and the former landed elite developed a stake in industrial development. But the average farm household operated only slightly over one acre.

Taiwan's Agrarian Reform laid the foundations for its subsequent economic and social development. Since the agrarian reform was of the land-to-the-tiller variety, it left farm sizes unchanged while increasing incentives to farm for the previous tenant farmers. Since the farmers already had managerial know-how, the reform supported rapid productivity growth in the agricultural sector. Multiple cropping expanded and led to a rapid increase in the productivity of land. Farming became diversified and started using new inputs. Farmer incomes rose and the distribution of income within the agricultural sector became much more even. This enabled farmers to manifest their latent demand for increased education and led to a rapid rate of accumulation of human capital, which was subsequently applied not only in manufacturing but also in agriculture. The land reform also contributed to social development: it destroyed the rigid traditional class structure and coopted previous landed elites in support of industrial policies. Thus, the land reform played a critical role in enabling not only subsequent economic development but also egalitarian economic growth.

KOREA. The Korean Land Reform process was quite similar to that in Taiwan. In 1947, the U.S. military government decreed that the land confiscated from Japanese farmers and Japanese corporations should be redistributed to tenants. The next wave of land reform, in 1949, redistributed the holdings of Korean landlords owning more than 7.5 acres to tenant farmers and landless farm workers. About 62 percent of farm families benefited from land reform. Tenancy was virtually abolished, almost one million tenant farmers and landless became land owners, and about 570,000 small farmers were able to expand their holdings. Thus this land reform destroyed much of the wealth of the rich, induced forced savings among the poor and resulted in a very egalitarian distribution of landed assets in the countryside. But farms were extremely small.

Real Asset Redistribution. Not only landed wealth but also much real wealth was redistributed during this period. Both countries confiscated industrial and commercial properties belonging to Japanese individuals and corporations. Formerly Japanese corporations, buildings and mines were confiscated by the Korean and Taiwanese governments, and became public property. Thus, after liberation most real wealth was owned by the government rather than by the private sector.

The formerly Japanese owned vested properties were sold off to the private sector, often much below market value. These discounts amounted to a redistribution of non-landed real wealth to the rich.

Events and policies implemented during this period laid the foundations for the subsequent egalitarian development of both countries during the 1960s (Adelman and Robinson, 1978; Adelman, 1980 and 1984; and H Choo, 1977). A redistribution of financial wealth took place as a byproduct of the inflation fighting measures adopted by both countries. In addition, the land reforms and confiscation of Japanese assets in both countries, and the massive destruction of real wealth during the Korean war, induced a very substantial leveling of real asset ownership. Thus, both Korea and Taiwan started their development process with an initial distribution of real and financial assets which was one of the most even in the capitalist world.

Reconstruction: TAIWAN. After restoring the people's confidence in the currency, the government made a quick start on rebuilding industrial capacity and energy and transportation infrastructure. Emphasis was placed on: electrical capacity to enable subsequent industrialization and rural electrification; upgrading the dense network of feeder roads to link farms with urban centers; fertilizer to serve agricultural development, and textile industries to satisfy consumer demand. By the end of the period, industrial production had regained pre-War levels.

Taiwan had inherited a high-productivity agricultural sector with a good institutional infrastructure from the colonial period. But the harsh procurement policies instituted by Japan during World War II caused a sharp drop in agricultural production during the War. In 1945, agricultural output stood at only 40 percent of its prewar level. A major thrust of policy started during this period was rebuilding Taiwan's agriculture. Indeed, the Taiwan government was required by its constitution to implement agricultural development (Shen, 1964). The first steps were changes in the institutional infrastructure for service delivery to agriculture. A Joint (US-China) Commission for Rural Reconstruction (JCRR) was established in 1948 to provide assistance to the farm sector, stimulate agricultural production, raise farmers' standard of living and develop rural leaders. Farmers' associations were reorganized to provide credit, extension and marketing services as well as to promote rural industry, settle disputes, sell farm tools and consumer goods, and provide facilities for rice milling and warehouses for rice and fertilizer. Agricultural processing plants (for pineapple, sugar, and tea) were also rebuilt, and dikes for irrigation and flood control repaired.

KOREA. Korea's start on reconstruction was delayed and made considerably more daunting by the Korean war and the subsequent partition of the country. The massive loss of life and destruction of physical capital during the Korean War had left the South in ruins. The influx of 3 million refugees from the North further exacerbated the situation. Even in 1961, almost 70 percent of the urban population and a third of the rural population lived below subsistence. Economic recovery was slow; the average growth of per capita GNP was merely 1 percent per year; and the economy was kept from collapse only through massive economic assistance by the United States.[2] The primary policies of the period were aimed at ensuring the population's survival, reconstructing economic and social infrastructure, rebuilding industrial facilities and stabilizing prices.[3] Ninety percent of imports were consumer goods, and constituted emergency relief for the population. Little attention was paid to long-term economic development and the bulk of government investment during this period was on social development.[4] The primary achievement was a dramatic increase in literacy rate, from 30 to over 80 percent over the period, but much more of the cost of education was borne by the private sector.

14.2.2 Import Substitute Industrialization: Taiwan (1949 to 1958) and Korea (1962 to 1966)

Both countries engaged in a short period of classical, import-substitute industrialization effort. In both, the industrialization was implemented through strict and pervasive quantitative restrictions on imports, and benefited from the protection afforded by tariffs and significantly overvalued exchange rates. Industrialization was further promoted by highly subsidized credit and selective foreign exchange licensing and allocations.

In both countries the strategy was successful from both a growth and social development perspective. However, in both countries the newly produced industrial output was not competitive on world markets and, by the end of the period, the opportunities for further industrial output expansion afforded by increases in domestic demand had been exhausted.

But there were also differences among the two countries: In Taiwan, import substitution centered primarily on light consumer-goods industries, while in Korea it focused on inputs — cement, fertilizer and synthetic fibers — and, because of a late start on reconstruction in Korea, the build-up of infrastructure. In Taiwan, the import-substitute industrialization was one of agricultural-development-led-industrialization. Continued high rates of growth of agricultural productivity provided not only cheap food, foreign exchange and labor but also an expanding market for the consumer goods produced by domestic industry. By contrast, in Korea, despite the fact that self-sufficiency in grains was a goal of national development during this period, the agricultural sector did not achieve high levels of productivity growth; PL480 grain imports from the US and rice rationing were used to substitute for deficient domestic agricultural development.

Policy Thrust: KOREA. The accelerated rate of economic growth started with the accession of Major General Park Chung Hee to the Presidency of South Korea, in mid-1961. Part of the explanation lies in his commitment to economic development. (Shortly after taking office, he asked to be tutored in economics!). This commitment had many manifestations, not the least of which was his willingness to allow economic considerations to guide investment, trade and financial policies.

Severe unemployment rates and demonstrations by students and the unemployed provided the primary motivation for the policies and programs formulated during this period. The trade deficit constraint was also very binding.[5] Accordingly, the primary goals of the development strategy followed during this period were to generate rapid increases in efficient employment[6] and to improve the balance of trade. The strategy for employment generation involved applying labor-intensive methods to the construction of certain key types of infrastructure, such as roads, dams, and energy and irrigation projects. The strategy for improving the balance of payments entailed reliance on import-substitution in some key industries — cement, chemical fertilizer, and synthetic fibers — as well as striving to attain self-sufficiency in food grains by the end of the period.

TAIWAN. The success of the land reform made a strategy of agricultural-development-led-industrialization possible. The crux of the strategy was the generation of a high marketable surplus in the agricultural sector. The agricultural sector had to produce not only sufficient food to feed the entire population but also enough exports to exchange for the capital equipment imports required for industrial development while releasing agricultural labor for industrialization. This required the achievement of high productivity levels in agriculture. The attainment of high productivity levels and rapid productivity growth in agriculture was made possible not only by the land reform but also by capitalizing on and expanding the excellent agricultural extension service left over from the Japanese colonial period. As a result, an early start was made on a process of agricultural development which ultimately built up an agricultural sector with the highest productivity levels in the developing world.

The First Five year Plan (1953-56) aimed at attaining economic independence through mutually reinforcing agricultural and industrial development in order to achieve national income growth with a balanced government budget. The growth of the industrial sector was aimed at substituting domestically-produced products for consumer-goods imports. The objectives set for the agricultural segment of the plan were to support the industrialization effort through increased low-price deliveries of food, through increased foreign exchange earnings through exports, and by increased demand for consumer goods manufactures arising from increased farmer incomes.

Implementation Measures: TRADE. In both countries, the import-substitution strategy relied more on quantitative controls than on biased trade incentives for its implementation. Westphal and Kim (1977) estimate that, in Korea, the effective exchange rate for exports was only about 10 percent above that for imports, and that exchange premiums and cash subsidies rather than indirect taxes and tariffs were the main source of the differential between the effective exchange for imports and exports.

Multiple exchange rates, a severely overvalued currency, import controls and high tariffs were the main mechanisms used to protect the domestic market in both countries. In accordance with the major thrust of the import-substitution effort in Korea, the rate of protection for consumer goods was highest, and that on intermediates lowest. By contrast, in Taiwan, the incentive policies applied were aimed at fostering first phase import-substitution. Traditional agricultural exports (sugar and rice) received relatively unattractive exchange rates. Imports of basic raw materials and industrial products and imports by government industrial enterprises received favorable exchange rates. And high tariffs were levied on imports of many finished goods and luxuries.

In both countries, all imports were severely restricted by licensing: quantitative controls were substantial. Imports were subdivided into three categories: prohibited, controlled, and uncontrolled. In Korea, the number of commodities on the list of prohibited imports was over 15,000. In Taiwan, during 1956-61, about 60 percent of items were controlled and only 40 percent were uncontrolled. In Taiwan, the controls on imports were specified not only by import category but also by country of origin. Generally, domestic industry competing imports from other developing countries were prohibited, thus sheltering the "infant" consumer industries from outside competition. In addition, importers in both countries had to deposit 100 percent of the value of their imports in advance in the domestic equivalent of foreign currency.

Exports were both discriminated against and favored through a set of specific measures. On the one hand, in both countries, exporters were allocated import licenses on the basis of their export performance. On the other, in Taiwan, exporters received a relatively unfavorable exchange rate and had to pay a defense tax of 20 percent on foreign exchange settlements.

AGRICULTURAL DEVELOPMENT (TAIWAN). In agriculture, the institutional changes introduced into the organization of the agricultural sector — land reform, JCRR, and farmer organizations — together with repair and buildup of the physical infrastructure serving agriculture, enabled rapid agricultural production and farmer income growth, despite relatively heavy implicit taxation of the agricultural sectors through terms of trade, land taxes, net effective protection and exchange rate policies.

Development Finance: TAIWAN. In monetary policy, a high real interest rate policy was initiated in 1952, first to curb inflation and then continued throughout the next period to stimulate household savings. The government adopted a restrictive public consumption policy; it ran a surplus if US aid to the government is counted as part of government revenue and a deficit if it is not.

Taiwan's development was partially financed through taxes on the agricultural sector, partially through domestic savings, partially through foreign investment and partially through US aid. Foreign aid financed most of the net capital formation that took place during this period. Despite positive, double digit real rates of interest, the share of domestic savings net of foreign aid in the finance of net domestic investment was about 40 percent in 1952 and dropped to 37 percent in 1958. Private savings (exclusive of US aid to the private sector) rose from 17 percent of total savings to 40 percent during this period — an impressive gain in 16 years. The sources of foreign exchange were primary exports, foreign capital inflow and US aid.

KOREA. The ambitious import-substitute industrialization effort required massive amounts of foreign exchange and the mobilization of large amounts of domestic savings. Foreign currency came from US aid, which financed more than twice as much domestic investment as did tax revenues and foreign loans, and which came to finance almost half the trade deficit. The mobilization of domestic savings was facilitated by a tax reform, introduced in 1965, which increased the tax-take of the government by 50 percent, and a doubling of interest rates on bank deposits in 1965, which raised the share of bank loans by deposit money banks from less than 20 percent of loanable funds to over 50 percent.

Policy Results. In both countries, the import-substitution strategy was very successful, from both an economic growth and social development perspective.

KOREA. The rate of growth of per capita GNP rose from about 1 percent in the previous period to about 6.8 percent, leading to an increase in GNP per capita of almost 40 percent over the period. Labor absorption was quite rapid —employment increased by 10 percent and, despite an increase of 12 percent in the economically active population the unemployment rate dropped by 14 percent, from 8.2 percent of the economically active population to 7.1 percent. Import substitution provided the major contribution to economic growth during this period. [7] Nevertheless, the trade deficit remained quite large, as the industrialization effort required a more than 75 percent increase in industrial imports.

There was a substantial improvement in average social welfare. At the beginning of the period, Korea was one of the poorest countries in the world. While still quite poor in 1962, by the end of the period per capita GNP was 39 percent higher. Nutrition had improved and there was a shift towards a more diversified, richer diet. Infant mortality and life expectancy improved somewhat; but the death rate from epidemic diseases increased by 40 percent, due primarily to very rapid immigration into Seoul, a city with poor environmental sanitation, high population densities and a large number of people living in unsanitary, overcrowded shanty towns. In education, by 1966, Korea had achieved universal primary education and the rate of university enrollment was greater than in Great Britain.

Despite the rapid rate of economic growth and substantial labor absorption, poverty remained substantial: about 41 percent of total households were living in absolute poverty in 1965, with almost 55 percent of urban households and 36 percent of rural households below the absolute poverty line.[8] The extensive poverty in Korea was not due to income inequality. While there are no income distribution statistics prior to 1965, there is some indication that income distribution remained very even. Indeed, in 1965, Korea's income distribution was one of the most even in the world.

The evenness of the distribution of income can be attributed to a number of factors. The distribution of wealth from which the growth started was very egalitarian, due to the actions undertaken in the 1945-53 period. Even though 1961-66 was a period of import-substitute industrialization, growth was very labor intensive, partly due to the labor-intensive technology used to construct infrastructure, with capital/output ratios being very low by international standards. In addition, agricultural incomes were high relative to urban wage earner incomes, and agricultural terms of trade improved. And, even though this was a period of selective import substitution, the effective exchange rate for exports was only 11 percent above the effective exchange rate for imports (Westphal, 1978). Thus, the usual reasons why import substitution deteriorates the distribution of income were not operative. The operative consideration was that the growth was labor-intensive. There was massive absorption of labor force from a relatively low productivity sector, agriculture, to a high productivity sector, manufacturing.

TAIWAN. Between 1951 and 1958 real GNP adjusted for terms of trade effects rose by an average rate of 8.3 percent and real per capita income in constant NT$ by 3.5 percent annually. Labor productivity rose by 4.6 percent annually, 1.5 million people were newly absorbed into the labor force, and the unemployment rate decreased from 6.3 percent in 1953 to 5.9 percent in 1958.[9]

There was substantial structural change in the composition of production and trade. Between 1951 and 1958, manufacturing as a percentage of NDP increased from 13 to 16 percent, while the share of the primary sector decreased from 36 to 31 percent. The share of manufactured exports in total exports rose from 2.4 percent in 1952 to 19.3 percent in 1960. In addition, the share of light manufacturing in total manufacturing and in manufactured exports rose to 70 percent by the end of the period. These light industries would become the foundation for the labor-intensive export-expansion strategy that followed in the next period.

Public investment in social development continued to expand. By 1958, the share of education in government expenditures had increased to almost 12 percent — one of the highest in the world. Between 1952 and 1958, enrollment in primary school rose 40 percent, in secondary school 80 percent, and in colleges and universities by a third. Illiteracy dropped by a third, from a high of 42 percent in 1952. Life expectancy at birth rose from 59 to 64; infant mortality dropped by 50 percent; and the incidence of communicable diseases declined by 30 percent .

14.2.3 *Labor-Intensive Export-Oriented Industrialization: Korea (1967– 1972) and Taiwan (1958–1972)*

This period was the golden age of economic development in both countries. It was marked by a significant change in development strategy, from selective import-substitution to export-led growth in labor-intensive consumer goods manufacturing. Exchange rates were significantly devalued, the effective exchange rate favored exports, and market and non-market export incentives were granted to manufacturing exporters in both countries. Thus, though both countries liberalized their trade during this period, in neither country did the export-oriented growth occur within a free trade regime. Rather, both countries pursued mercantilist policies during this period. In both countries, the export-oriented strategy led to rapid growth with equity, substantial employment and wage increases, and substantial industrialization. Both countries started the period with surplus labor and exhausted its supply by the end of the period.

There were also important differences between the two countries: Taiwan was better prepared for the export-led growth effort, in that it had built up experience in consumer goods manufacturing during the prior period. Unlike Korea, Taiwan financed most of its export-led push from internal sources, and relied on small and medium sized firms for the export push.

Strategy Thrust. This period was marked by a significant change in development strategy from import substitution towards export-led growth centering on labor-intensive consumer manufactures. By the end of the import-substitution period, the rate of economic growth decelerated as the process of import-substitution-led growth hit the impasse of deficient rates of increase in domestic demand. During the previous period, the average exchange rate had to be highly overvalued to provide protection to the infant industries and balance the current account, and the inflation rate was running at a two-digit level. Thus, the industrial products were not export-competitive. The governments of both countries therefore instituted major changes in their economic policies designed to promote exports.

Attitudes towards the continuation of import-substitute industrialization differed between Taiwan and Korea during this period. Taiwan abandoned import-substitution entirely, while Korea continued selective import substitution. In Taiwan, starting in 1958, the import quota system on commodities was first gradually liberalized and then abolished.[10] Tariffs were systematically reduced, and customs revenues as a percentage of imports dropped from 28 percent in 1960 to 16 percent in 1973. The cumulative effect of these import liberalization measures was to force the bulk of Taiwan's industries to become export-competitive.[11] By contrast, Korea continued to pursue a significant amount of selective import substitution during its export-led drive. Major import substitution occurred in cement, fertilizer, refined petroleum, textile yarns and fabrics (Hong, 1977: 361) . Both exports and selective import-substitution were subsidized through various specific incentives.[12] While tariffs were reduced[13] and the list of prohibited and restricted imports was shortened, import-restraints continued to be substantial in Korea. Nevertheless, the major thrust of policy was on export-promotion in both countries.

Implementation. EXPORT INCENTIVES. Numerous export incentives were introduced in both countries to enhance the profitability of exports. Both discretionary and non-discretionary export incentives, as well as command and market-oriented incentive-procedures, were used by both countries to increase exports. First, the nominal exchange rate was unified and substantially devalued (by 100 percent). Second, restrictions on imports of raw materials and intermediates for exports were removed entirely and tariffs on these imports were systematically reduced. In addition, exporters were granted rights to retain foreign exchange for imports of raw materials and machinery and to sell the excess rights (known as "wastage allowances" in Korea) to other firms. Third, exporters were granted low-cost credit to finance facility expansion, machinery and intermediate imports, and exports. Fourth, exporters were favored by various tax rebates and exemptions (from customs duties, defense surtax, harbor dues, commodity taxes on imported raw materials, and business taxes). Fifth, there were selective price controls on critical inputs, such as energy and wages.

The successive devaluations undertaken during the previous period, together with the new export incentives, increased the effective exchange rate for exports substantially. The average real effective exchange rate for exports was raised (by about 60 percent in Taiwan (Lee and Liang, 1982) and 20 percent in Korea (Westphal and Kim, 1977)) over that in the previous period, and was maintained stable until the end of the period. In addition, both the effective protection rate and the effective subsidy rate favored exports over domestic sales. In Taiwan, for example, in 1969, the effective protection rate for manufactured exports was -4 percent, while it was 28 percent for domestic sales; and the effective subsidy rate averaged 23 percent for exports and 19 percent for domestic sales. But these effective exchange rate calculations substantially understate the preferences given to exports over production for domestic use. They do not reflect various measures which led to higher domestic prices for the domestic sales of export products. The effective exchange rates do not reflect the value of monopoly profits granted to exporters as a result of protection of the domestic market for their products, the tariff-equivalent of the import quotas, or the value to exporters of the reduction in incentives to import competing production.

It is also noteworthy that, since the numerous export-subsidy measures impacted differently on different commodities, there were multiple, commodity specific, effective exchange rates in force in both countries during this period despite the fact that the *nominal_*exchange rates were unified. The effective government-subsidy rates varied substantially among commodities, ranging, in Korea, from an effective subsidy rate of 125 won per dollar of exports in nylon fabrics to 5 won per dollar of fresh fish exports (Koo, 1977). In Taiwan, the effective exchange rate system favored labor-intensive exports over capital- and skill-intensive exports during this period, and discriminated against primary exports (Lee and Liang, 1982).

The analysis of market incentives also does not tell the whole story of how the export drive was accomplished. A battery of non-market, discretionary incentives was used to stimulate imports. In Korea, export targets were allocated to individual firms by the government. The export performance of individual firms was closely monitored by the President and the Ministry of Commerce and firms exceeding their export quota were rewarded with such incentives as increased subsidized credit and import licenses, while firms falling short of export targets were punished through measures ranging from tax audits to revocation of trading licenses. In addition, in Korea, monthly meetings were held between the President and large exporters, in which those who did best were honored, and through which the President was informed of specific bureaucratic and factor supply bottlenecks to export expansion, which he directed his staff to clear. Thus, direct pressure was exercised on firms to expand exports.

Financing. In Taiwan, monetary management was excellent. Inflation was kept very low: between 1958 and 1972 the average compound annual rate of increase in the wholesale price level was less than 2 percent. To stimulate domestic savings, real interest rates were set at high positive levels, but not above the marginal efficiency of investment throughout the period. As a result, the share of domestic savings in NNP rose from 5 percent in 1958 to above Rostow's takeoff point of 10 percent in 1963. The household savings rate as a percentage of disposable income rose from 4.9 percent in 1958 to 20 percent in 1972. The share of domestic finance of capital formation was accordingly able to increase from 60 percent in 1958 to 86 percent in 1965, and to 124 percent in 1972. U.S. foreign aid was discontinued in 1965, when Taiwan was graduated, although because of prior commitments, aid disbursements continued into 1968. In 1966, Taiwan became a capital exporting country.

In Korea, inflationary finance was a significant source of loanable funds during this period. The average rate of inflation was 8 percent, and the ratio of savings to M2 was only 52 percent. Domestic savings financed about 60 percent of investment during this period and foreign capital inflow, primarily in the form of foreign loans, provided the rest. Domestic finance was available through both heavily subsidized government-directed deposit money bank credit, and through the unorganized money market, which had high real rates of interest. The rationing of this subsidized credit was a major mechanism of industrial policy. Domestic real interest rates, while above world market rates,[14] were substantially below the marginal efficiency of investment.

Results. The strategy was phenomenally successful in both economies, leading to high growth, rapid industrialization, rapid labor absorption, substantial increases in economic welfare and reductions in inequality.

KOREA. The economy grew quite rapidly during this period, at an average annual rate of 9.6 percent. It became considerably more open, with the share of imports plus exports in GNP almost doubling. Structural change accelerated: the share of manufacturing in GNP increased by 50 percent and that of agriculture dropped by a third. Manufactured exports as a share of total exports rose from 60 to 70 percent. The growth was export-led: the annual rate of growth of exports averaged a phenomenal 46 percent, leading to a tenfold increase in exports over the period. Despite this very rapid rise in exports, however, trade deficits continued to be substantial, since exports were import-intensive, with an import-coefficient of 40 percent (Suk, 1977: 405), and substantial imports of machinery were required for the implementation of the export-led industrialization drive.

The exports had substantial favorable effects: the contribution of exports to GNP growth rose from 9.4 percent in 1966-68 to 23.6 percent during 1970-73 (Suk, 1977: 401-403). Manufacturing export industries accounted for 33 percent of total employment (directly and indirectly) in 1973, up by two thirds from 1968, and for 50 percent of the capital stock, up from 14 percent in 1968 (Suk, 1977: 405).

Were the exports dynamically efficient? The answer to this question is not clear, since the overall direct and indirect factor-intensity of exports doubled during this period. Also, the use of labor, the relatively abundant factor, in export production decreased as capital-labor substitution reduced the direct plus indirect labor-intensity of exports by about one third (Hong, 1977: 370). In addition, most of the sectors that experienced rapid export-expansion also experienced significant decreases in backwards import-substitution, indicating that export production became increasingly more import-intensive (Suk, 1977: 412) over the export-led growth period.

This was also a period of very rapid improvement in economic welfare. Per capita GNP increased by a factor of more than two and a half. Labor absorption continued to be quite rapid: employment increased by 25 percent and unemployment rates dropped 45 percent. The labor market became tight and the average wage rates of unskilled workers tripled.

Infant mortality dropped 30 percent. Life expectancy rose by almost four years. Having achieved universal primary education in the previous period, the government increased secondary enrollments to almost 50 percent of the appropriate age cohort. The industrial accident rate dropped dramatically, by almost half. Nevertheless, the negative externalities of economic growth continued to be high: the miracle economic performance was purchased at the cost of long working hours (50 hours per week), high industrial accident rates (almost 10 percent of workers were injured on the job in 1972), and substantial air pollution. By the end of the period some of the planners and economists were starting to wonder whether the rate of growth should not be slowed down.

The distribution of income became even more even than it had been in 1965, the share of income of the poorest decile doubled and absolute poverty declined by over 50 percent. The ratio of farm to non-farm income rose, due to the increase in demand for food by the urban population, which raised the agricultural terms of trade.

TAIWAN. Between 1958 and 1972, total GNP grew at a real rate of 10 percent annually, manufacturing expanded at a rate of 18 percent, exports grew at a rate of 23 percent, and the current balance plus long term capital inflows turned positive after 1970. Labor productivity increased at a very fast annual rate of 6.6 percent; employment rose by 1.4 million people, of which 30 percent were absorbed in manufacturing; and unemployment declined to frictional levels of 2.8 percent. Using a Chenery type decomposition of the total labor absorption achieved between 1961 and 1972, Kuo (1983) concluded that 40 percent was due to export expansion and the development dynamic shifted from agriculture to exports.

Structural change initiated in the previous period accelerated. The manufacturing sector became twice the size of the agricultural sector, the reverse of what it had been just a decade earlier. Exports had shifted from 60 percent agricultural in 1958 to 91 percent manufacturing by 1972. The economy became much more open: between 1961 and 1971, exports plus imports accounted for 30 percent of GNP, as compared to 23 percent in the earlier decade. Chenery-type sources of growth analysis indicated that, on the average, between 1960 and 1970, exports contributed 22.5 percent to the overall expansion of manufacturing, domestic demand 79 percent, and the contribution of import substitution was a negative 2 percent. By the end of the period, the relative weights of the private and government-owned enterprises in the industrial sector, which were fifty-fifty in the earlier period, became 78.9 percent to 21.2 percent, respectively. One can therefore infer that growth had generated significant private wealth.

The gains in welfare achieved with the labor-intensive growth strategy were equally impressive. During this period, real national income per capita rose at an average rate of 7 percent annually, by a factor of 2.5 in constant NT$ and by a factor of 3.4 in US $. Real consumption increased at a rate of 5 percent, and the unemployment rate was halved. There were large gains in education: in 1969, the government increased mandatory education from 6 years of primary schooling to 9 years, an addition of 3 years of secondary schooling. By the end of the period, illiteracy had declined by more than half (to 13 percent), the share of population in secondary schools had tripled, and that in college almost quadrupled. Unlike in Korea, these gains in education were achieved primarily through a large expansion of already high government expenditures on education, to 17 percent of the budget. There were also gains in health, with an increase of five years in life expectancy at birth; a halving of infant mortality, and a virtual disappearance of many communicable diseases. There were significant advances in the quality of medical services.

Income distribution became even more equal during this period: the ratio of income of the richest 20 percent to that of the poorest 20 percent declined half of its 1959 level. By 1972, Taiwan had thus achieved the most even distribution of income among industrial and semi-industrial countries.

Discussion. COMMERCIAL POLICY. A barrage of generalized and selective pressures and incentives was used to promote export expansion. In large part, the stability of the effective exchange rates over the period suggests that the incentives merely overcame the progressive loss of competitiveness in exports over time due to domestic inflation and rising wages. In addition, however, in Korea the real effective exchange rate for exports relative to imports increased by 7 percent over time, and the use of specific incentives allowed the simultaneous promotion of export-expansion and import substitution, and the exercise of suasion for export-promotion. Was this policy preferable to an outright devaluation? Second-best trade theory suggests that unified exchange rate systems are suboptimal in the presence of· factor-market imperfections, externalities, monopoly and "infant industries." Tax or tariff cum subsidy policies are needed to overcome these distortions and move the economy towards optimality (Devarajan, 1990). In addition, calculations undertaken by Adelman with a computable general equilibrium model of Korea which reproduced the trade-incentive systems in place indicated that, in the absence of specific industry-export targets, the exports attained by the model economy averaged only 40 percent of the actual levels achieved.[15] Finally, in the presence of market imperfections and externalities, an exchange rate which is favorable to exports is likely to delay backward and forward import substitution and capital deepening, and delay the expansion of the domestic market for exportables. The last effect is important, since, even in export-industries, the contribution of domestic demand expansion to growth far exceeds that of exports.[16] The primary counterarguments are that the magnitudes of the imperfections and externalities are difficult to estimate in practice, and that the discretionary nature of these subsidies is likely to lead to corruption and rent seeking. Nevertheless, I believe that, on the whole, the positive effects of the mix of discretionary and non-discretionary, market and non-market system of carrots and sticks used by both countries outweighed their negative effects, especially when, as in both countries, distortions from a single uniform effective exchange rate which does not discriminate between exports and production for the domestic market are moderate and the phenomenal export performance of both countries could not have been accomplished without the non-market incentives.

INCOME DISTRIBUTION. Korea's and Taiwan's growth with equity during their take-off period stands in strong contrast to the usual relationship between economic growth and economic equity in developing countries, in which, typically, the takeoff is marked by increases in inequality (Kuznets, 1955; Adelman and Morris, 1973).

As I have indicated elsewhere (Adelman, 1980), an important reason for this was in the "redistribution before growth" strategy adopted in the aftermath of liberation. Starting accelerated growth from an egalitarian distribution of land and real and financial wealth, as both countries did, and adopting a labor-intensive rapid economic growth strategy, meant that there was no conflict between growth and equity. Policies adopted to accelerate economic growth also led to substantial equity improvement, especially reductions in poverty.

Thus, the reasons for the excellent distributional performance of both countries were quite similar: very even distribution of land and physical capital; very rapid labor absorption in the high-productivity manufacturing sector; a tight labor market, especially in the later part of the period, and the eventual disappearance of unemployment; a narrowing in the wage distribution, as unskilled wages rose faster than skilled wages; good agricultural terms of trade; and increasing educational opportunities. Added to these factors in Taiwan were an industrial organization that stressed small and medium sized firms — rather than large firms, as in Korea — and a dramatic increase in the share of non-farm earnings in the total income of farm households.

13.2.4 The Heavy Industry Period: Korea (1973–1981) and Taiwan (1973–1982)

Both Korea and Taiwan feared that Nixon's resumption of diplomatic relations with China in 1971 would mean a diminution of U.S. commitment to their territorial integrity and their defense. Both therefore embarked on the buildup of basic industries critical to the development of their defense potential. In a major shift in development strategy, both economies initiated a second import-substitution drive in heavy and chemical industries. In both economies, however, the drive was accomplished not by changing generalized trade incentives, which continued to favor exports, but rather by adding selective incentives in support of the preferred industries. So, paradoxically, the import-substitution effort took place within an export-oriented commercial environment.

There were also other reasons for changing the overall thrust of development strategies. Developed countries had turned protectionist in the wake of the two oil shocks and had imposed country-and-product-specific quotas on imports of labor-intensive products from developing countries. In addition, because surplus labor had been exhausted, wages in both countries had risen and both started experiencing the effects of competition in labor-intensive commodities from other developing countries with lower wages. Nevertheless, average growth rates in both countries continued to be high.

Korea and Taiwan also differed in some respects. The timing of the shift was more appropriate to Taiwan's changing comparative advantage than to Korea's. Korea implemented the targeted interventions by relying on large firms, while Taiwan continued to rely on medium and small-sized firms and turned to state-owned enterprises for the implementation of the heavy-industry drive. Partly as a result, the distribution of income in Taiwan continued to remain equal, while that in Korea started becoming more unequal. In Korea, the import substitution drive was accomplished by a major buildup of foreign debt, while Taiwan continued to be a net capital exporter. And Korea also implemented a major rural development program during this period to compensate for earlier neglect of agricultural development.

Policy Thrust. KOREA. The shift in policy emphasis away from labor-intensive industries toward heavy and chemical industries (HCI) was undertaken both for security reasons and because of President Park's concept of what a mature industrial economy should look like. The President was personally involved in the HCI drive and is said to have spent between 30 and 40 percent of his time on its implementation.

In addition to the key industries, the third and fourth five year plans, which covered this period, emphasized regional and quality of life objectives. The regional objectives were pursued in part through a rural community development program. Even though farm household incomes had increased slightly relative to urban incomes in the previous period, they were still about 17 percent lower than urban wage earner incomes. Rural social development indicators were considerably lower than urban ones, as well. As a result, there was substantial discontent in the countryside. There was also a desire to slow the rate of rural to urban migration. In 1971, the President initiated a rural animation program, the *Saemul Undong* movement, which provided substantial investment funds and government leadership for village development.

Also, many of the social protection programs were either first introduced or substantially extended during this period: medical insurance for industrial employees was initiated in 1977 and expanded to civil servants and teachers in 1978; pensions were broadened to include private school teachers in 1975; medicaid and public housing assistance to the poor were started in 1977; and the coverage of livelihood protection assistance was increased.

TAIWAN. After a short bout with inflation, combated by vigorous anti-inflation measures undertaken in 1974, the government started its heavy and chemical industry drive by implementing "ten great projects" in 1974-75. These included the construction of state-owned steel and petrochemical complexes and ship-building facilities, and absorbed about 20 percent of total investment in 1975 and 1976. These projects were followed by another set of 12 large scale infrastructure projects in 1978.

Implementation. KOREA. The export oriented emphasis remained, although effective exchange rates for the new key industries were biased against imports. In Korea, six strategic industries were selected — steel, petrochemicals, non-ferrous metals, shipbuilding, electronics and machinery. Promotional laws for each of these industries were promulgated, granting tax subsidies, access to subsidized public services, preferential financing and specifying detailed engineering design. The first four industries were capital intensive and their factor input structure was not in accord with the economy's comparative advantage. The key industries required import of raw materials and absorbed an average of 23 percent of total finance over the period.[17] As a result, labor intensive industries were credit starved. Capital-labor ratios rose faster in the key industries than in the light industries. Also, since, by the very nature of the key industries chosen, small and medium sized firms could not operate the key industries, the new economic direction increased the concentration of economic power in the largest *chaebols*. The relative number of large firms increased from 1.1 percent in 1966 to 4.1 percent in 1976 and their share of value added rose from an already high 50 percent in 1966 to 70 percent in 1976 (Song, 1994). The incentives to key industries benefited large *chaebols* most, thus generating a large transfer to the very rich, and leading to a considerably less equal distribution of assets than was characteristic of the earlier periods. Most economists were opposed to the change in emphasis towards key industries when it was initiated, considering it inappropriate at that time.

The adoption of the import-substitution strategy in HCI industries did not signal a discontinuation of the bias of trade-incentives in favor of exports. The various incentive measures adopted to stimulate exports in the previous period were continued. In addition, generalized trading companies consisting of the huge conglomerates were formed in 1975. These companies were pressured to increase exports by successively raising the minimum export share needed to be designated as a trading company.

The rural development program was implemented through large scale investment in rural development. The *Saemul Undong* program absorbed about one half of total government investment during 1973-78. Of this total, 28 percent was allocated to production infrastructure, 41 percent to income increasing projects, 28 percent to welfare and environment improvement (social development) and 3 percent to rural factories (Whang, 1981). The result was a substantial narrowing of the rural-urban social development gap.

TAIWAN. Three of the ten great projects consisted of direct government investment in heavy industry: an integrated steel mill, a petrochemical complex, and a large shipyard. Seven were in infrastructure: a freeway, two railways, an airport, 2 harbors, and a nuclear power plant. The industrial projects increased domestic backwards integration by providing domestic semi-industrial inputs, and transformed the factor-content of exports from labor-intensive to capital and skill-intensive. The infrastructure projects lowered transport costs, reduced fuel imports and increased regional integration. These large-scale government investments were followed by another set of 12 large projects in 1978, consisting mostly of infrastructure but also including expansion of the integrated steel mill. As a result, direct government ownership of industry increased again, to 19 percent in 1983, after falling from 50 percent in the first import-substitution period to about 15 percent in the export-led-growth era.

The lower export incentives started in 1974 as part of the anti-inflation drive were continued, but they were by no means withdrawn: tax rebates as a percentage of total taxes dropped from a high of 52 percent in 1972 to 37 percent in 1974 and to 25 percent during 1979-81; the share of subsidized export loans in total loans decreased from 6 percent in 1972 to 3.5 percent in 1974 to 2 percent in 1979-81. After dropping 5 percent in 1974, the official exchange rate for exports remained essentially unchanged through 1986.

Results. Unfortunately, the heavy and chemical industry drives were initiated during a particularly inauspicious period, which was marked by significant adverse exogenous shocks from world markets. The HCI industries are energy and import-intensive and the oil shocks, which raised oil prices sixfold, raised the cost of operating these industries substantially. In addition, the two oil shocks induced stagflation in the OECD countries and led them to adopt contractionary policies that halved their rates of growth; the rate of growth of world demand for imports was also halved as a result. Nevertheless, both Korea and Taiwan continued their spectacular growth and export performance.

KOREA. The oil shocks started a construction boom in the Middle East, which led to a withdrawal of about 300,000 workers from Korea's domestic labor force, generating labor shortages and wage increases. The labor migration to the Middle

East raised the construction costs of the HCI industries and exacerbated problems with competitiveness in the labor-intensive export-oriented industries. Partly as a result of these external developments, and partly as a result of the Big Push character of the HCI drive, the economy was plagued by a resurgence of high inflation rates. Since the won was pegged to the dollar, domestic inflation led to a revaluation of the won, which added to the pressures on the current trade balance. In addition, the increased demand for machinery and intermediate imports due to the HCI drive also exacerbated the balance of trade problems.

Easy availability of credit on world markets led to heavy foreign borrowing by Korea to finance its deficit and its HCI drive. Inflationary pressures were also fueled by the long gestation period inherent in HCI industries, which meant that expenditures were undertaken long before output came on line. The initial performance of the HCI industries was disappointing. The end of the period therefore also saw a scaling down of the HCI drive and a relative shift in emphasis toward the more skill-intensive electronic and machinery industries.

Nevertheless, the improvement in average social welfare was spectacular. Per capita GNP in current dollars increased almost six times, though part of the increase is illusory due to the revaluation of the won. Unemployment dropped to frictional levels. University enrollments almost tripled. There was a major improvement in the health status of the population: infant mortality decreased 60 percent; the average number of calories consumed rose to meet WHO nutritional standards, while the portion of animal proteins in the diet increased by 50 percent. The coverage of medical insurance increased dramatically; the percentage of deaths due to poor sanitation, environmental conditions and overcrowding dropped by half; and average life expectancy reached the levels characteristic of more developed NICs. And absolute poverty decreased dramatically. By 1980, the overall percentage of households below the poverty line had fallen by almost two thirds, to 9.8 percent.

Due to the rural development program, by 1981 the rural-urban gap had decreased substantially: farm incomes were only 8 percent below urban wage-earner incomes, and the gap in primary and high school enrollment ratios had almost disappeared. Nevertheless, the size distribution of income became more unequal, despite the major rural-development push.

The deterioration in the distribution of income during this period was due to many different factors. First, by 1973 the distribution of real and financial assets was no longer even. Economic growth had affected accumulation, and the size structure of firms had been concentrated. Second, there was a major increase in the capital/output and capital/labor ratios during this period. This increase was due partly to the economy having reached virtual full employment, and partly to the emphasis on the growth of capital-intensive key industries. Third, the distribution of wage income became more skewed as well, due to the relatively greater tightness in the labor market for high level manpower. The only countervailing influences were the rural development effort and rural-urban migration. The *Saemul Undong* movement and the high rice-price policy initiated in the early 1970s led to an increase of farm income above urban income. But, since the share of off-farm income in rural income also rose, the distribution of income within the rural sector deteriorated as well. Migration transferred workers from the low-productivity, low income sector to a high productivity sector; but since the high productivity sector also had a higher variance in the distribution of income, this influence too was not unidirectional. Thus, the foundations for unequalizing growth were laid during this period.

The increase in inequality after, rather than during, the takeoff runs counter to cross-country experience in developing countries. But Korea started the takeoff from an unusually even distribution of real and financial assets, and adopted a human-capital intensive development strategy during the takeoff which was coupled with an egalitarian human-capital accumulation policy. By contrast, the initial distribution of wealth with which Korea entered the seventies had become more like that of a typical developing country starting its development process. And the emphasis on the second stage of import substitution in producer goods industries, albeit selective, was typical of the development strategy followed by most Latin American developing countries. Import-substitute development strategies tend to worsen the distribution of income. Thus, at this point, it is not surprising that the relationship between Korea's economic growth and distribution became antagonistic.

TAIWAN. Despite the worldwide recession, increased protectionism and decline in the growth rate of world trade, Taiwan's average growth rate continued to be rapid, and so did structural shifts in the composition of manufacturing and exports. Recessions induced by foreign price shocks were very short. Between 1973 and 1983, GNP grew at a high average real rate of 8.8 percent annually, more than doubling in ten years. Exports expanded at an average annual rate of 14 percent, more than tripling during this period. Industrial production rose at an average annual rate of 12.3 percent, and real labor productivity expanded at an average annual rate of 5.4 percent. Structural change continued: the share of agriculture in GDP declined from 12 to 7 percent, that of industry remained essentially constant, and that of services rose from 44 to 48 percent. Structural change within manufacturing shifted production and employment into heavy industry, and into more sophisticated items such as machine tools and motor vehicles. The industrial export share in total exports went up from 83 to 93 percent.

The gains in welfare achieved with the new growth strategy were also impressive. During this period, real national income per capita rose at an average rate of 6.2 percent annually, increasing by 75 percent over the ten year period. Real consumption per capita increased at an annual rate of 5.8 percent, and real wages in manufacturing rose at an annual rate of 8.4 percent. There were large gains in education: the ratio of students in higher education to population increased by a factor of 2.65, to 16 percent; enrollment rates in junior high school became 90 percent and that in senior high school rose above 60 percent, and illiteracy declined to 9 percent. Further gains were made in health as well, with an increase in life expectancy at birth to 72, and another halving of infant mortality. But health insurance was still not universal.

Unlike in Korea, in Taiwan income distribution became even more even during this period of increase in the capital intensity of the economy.[18] The ratio of income of the richest 20 percent to that of the poorest 20 percent declined from 4.5 to 4.3 in 1983. The primary reason was the very rapid rate of increase in manufacturing wages, with production-worker wages increasing even faster than overall manufacturing wages. Differences in the size distribution of enterprises also contributed to the difference between Taiwan's income distribution performance and Korea's. While industrial concentration in Korea increased during this period, it remained essentially unchanged in Taiwan. In Korea, the share of public enterprises in value added and employment actually decreased during this period, while in Taiwan it increased.

Since the heavy industries were state-owned enterprises, industrial concentration in the private sector did not increase in Taiwan during this period. Firms with less than 200 employees still accounted for 98 percent of all firms, 36 percent of value added and 42 percent of all exports in 1992 (See Table 14.2, below).

14.2.5 Economic Liberalization and Globalization (1984–Present)

The governments of both economies embarked on a liberalization, financial liberalization, and globalization drive. But limited targeted industrial policy, centered on the development of semi-conductors and high tech industries, continued in both countries. Both countries experienced some political liberalization, and continued their high growth performance in incomes, exports, and education. Both economies became economic powerhouses, with per capita incomes exceeding $10,000.

Reforms and Policies. INDUSTRIAL POLICY. In both countries, there has been a substantial reduction in government intervention in the economy through targeted incentives and controls. Nevertheless, industrial policy has not been entirely abandoned in either country. The governments of both countries are using market and non-market mechanism to foster the development of high-tech industries such as semiconductors and computer chips, in which, with their abundant supply of well-educated engineers and scientists, they have a comparative advantage. In Korea, the Economic Planning Board, which managed industrial policy since the 1960s, was abolished in 1995.

TRADE LIBERALIZATION. In Taiwan, tariff rates were reduced, especially on raw materials and intermediate products. Receipts from customs duties as a percentage of imports were reduced and almost eliminated, but a currency appreciation of 35 percent, resulting from the continued balance of trade surplus and massive buildup of foreign currency reserves, continued to afford significant shelter to imports and spur increases in efficiency in export industries. Quantitative restrictions on imports were canceled, but presettlement requirements for imports continue. Foreign exchange controls have been abandoned.

In Korea, the average tariff rate was reduced by 30 percent between 1980 and 1988, and then cut to 8 percent by 1993. Import restrictions were first substantially diminished and then eliminated. Between 1981 and 1985, the value-weighted share of restricted plus special law items in the total number of imported commodities decreased by 40 percent, to 26 percent (Hong, 1991). Raw materials and intermediate imports were all shifted to the "automatic approval" category. But in the HCI category, while tariff protection became very minimal, quantitative import restrictions, though substantially reduced, remained. And in the electronics sector, which was favored by this period's industrial policy, the value share of restricted and special law imports dropped only from 100 percent in 1981 to 60 percent in

1985 (Hong, 1991). Between 1987 and 1988 import restrictions on 814 special law items were abolished, licensing requirements eliminated, and import-inspection and approval procedures were simplified (Hong, 1992).

MONETARY LIBERALIZATION AND MACRO POLICY. In Taiwan, there was a substantial liberalization of the banking system: interest rate ceilings were lifted. As a result of the extremely high domestic savings rate and the buildup of foreign reserves, interest rates on secured loans dropped from about 10 to 8 percent, and the spread between the lending rate and the rate offered to savers decreased from 3.5 percent to 2 percent. Substantial financial deepening has taken place: the ratio of M2 to GNP rose from 1 in 1984 to 1.8 in 1994. Money market instruments have grown rapidly. The capital market for loans and equities has expanded. New public bond issues have increased by a factor of five. Fiscal policy has continued to be conservative, with large budgetary surpluses. But the share of the budgetary surplus has dropped from an incredibly large 32 percent of government revenues in 1984 to a still very large 19 percent in 1994. There is clearly room for expansion in government expenditures or reduction in the already low tax rates.

In Korea, the previous period left the economy with substantial economic difficulties: high inflation, a large current account deficit, and a foreign debt problem. Korea therefore embarked on an orthodox stabilization program during 1979-81: monetary and fiscal stringency, a withdrawal of incentives from the HCI industries, and an incomes policy. The deflationary policy led to a downturn in the economy from 1979-1982. But, by contrast with the experience of other NICs, the Korean stabilization program was successful. It ushered in a period of price stability which has lasted to the present. Trade liberalization turned the chronic trade deficits into surpluses. As part of the domestic liberalization program, four banks were privatized, exchange controls were lifted, barriers against foreign investment were reduced and a vigorous stock market yielding high rates of return started operating. Liberalization of financial markets turned interest rates positive and led to an increase in domestic savings. Fiscal deficits and trade deficits were brought under control, with current account surpluses being achieved.

POLITICAL LIBERALIZATION. Both countries have liberalized their political systems and moved towards democracy. In Korea, the constraints on political activity by opposition parties were lifted, democratic elections for the presidency were held — leading to the first civilian president — followed by democratic elections for the mayor of Seoul. One unfortunate byproduct of this political liberalization has been an increase in overt high-level corruption, aimed at financing, *inter alia*, the activities of political parties, and indicating a shift in relative political power from the government to the *chaebols*.

In Taiwan, democratic elections for the members of the National Assembly and the Legislature were introduced in 1991 and 1992 respectively; elections for the mayors of Taipei and Kaohsiung and the governor of the Taiwan provincial government were held in 1994; and the first presidential election was held in March of 1996, resulting in the first popularly elected head of state in the 5000-year history of the Chinese culture. There has been no noticeable increase in corruption as a result of the democratization in Taiwan, since the major political party owns productive enterprises whose revenue can finance political activities.

One byproduct of the democratization of the political system common to both countries is that it imposes constraints on the ability of their governments to pursue an industrial policy. Some Korean and Taiwanese intellectuals are therefore wondering whether a reduced rate of economic growth is a price they must pay for their democratization.

Results. TAIWAN. The rate of growth of GNP has continued to be very rapid, with real GNP doubling over the last 10 years. Per capita income in US dollars more than tripled, from about 3,100 in 1984 to over 10,000 in 1992. Structural change has continued, this time in favor of services, whose share in GNP has risen from 48 to 59 percent since 1984, while that of agriculture has declined to 3.6 percent and that of industry to 37 percent. Taiwan's structure of output is now similar to that of developed economies.

Substantial gains in social welfare and political development have been attained during this period. Universal Health Insurance was implemented in 1995. A proposal for a "social security" system has been drafted and is now being evaluated by the government.

KOREA. Korea's growth rebounded to enviable levels. The HCI industries matured, became the core of the manufacturing sector, and their exports started exceeding those of light industry by 1981. Industrial concentration decreased, with the percent of value added produced by the top 1.7 percent of firms dropping from 70 percent to 56 percent in 1990, but the share of medium size enterprises did not increase markedly (Song,1994).

There has unquestionably been a very substantial improvement in Korea's average welfare. Per capita income has increased almost sixfold, and on most social development indicators Korea now stands at or near the top of the middle-income group. Tertiary school enrollment rates exceed those of 70 percent of high income industrial economies. Life expectancy at birth is now in the range of that in upper middle income economies; and under-five mortality rates have declined to levels comparable to those of New Zealand and Israel.

Government expenditures on social security tripled between 1970 and 1991 as a share of GNP. There is universal medical insurance; industrial accident insurance has been expanded to include workers in firms with 5 or more employees; the coverage of the pension program, while still not covering all those in need, has been greatly enlarged; livelihood assistance programs, while still low relative to subsistence needs, have become more generous; and minimum wage legislation has been introduced, first for manufacturing (1988) and then for all industries (1990). Nevertheless, there appears to be a national consensus that the priority accorded to social welfare has not kept pace with that accorded to Korea's economic growth (Kwon, 1993a).

INCOME DISTRIBUTION. One of the main social development issues in both Korea and Taiwan has become the distribution of income and wealth. In Taiwan, government statistics indicate that the distribution of income has become steadily less even since 1980. The cummulative increase in inequality has been substantial: between 1980 and 1993, the Gini coefficient has risen from .278 to .316 and the ratio of income of the wealthiest to the poorest fifth of the population has increased from 4.17 to 5.42 (Chu, 1995).

In Korea, government statistics show the distribution of income becoming less even in 1986 and more even thereafter. There are, however, good reasons to believe that the official Korean statistics do not reflect underlying realities.[19] The coverage of the sample on which the statistics are based is biased against the high income groups, and the sample results do not match the national income results and severely understate realized capital gains. Recalculations of the distribution of income for 1992 undertaken by the author support the view that the distribution of income in Korea has continued to become more unequal. The main feature of these calculations is a more adequate accounting for realized capital gains, which are underrepresented in the government statistics (Adelman, forthcoming; Leipziger et al., 1993). I therefore believe that the "true" distribution of income in Korea has worsened during the 1980s.

Thus, the relationship between income distribution and development in Taiwan and Korea has given rise to an *inverted* Kuznets-curve. The initial stages of industrialization were marked by egalitarian growth, whereas the later stages were characterized by unequalizing growth. This is precisely the reverse of the typical relationship postulated by Kuznets. The inversion of the distribution-growth relation in Korea and Taiwan is due to both difference in initial conditions and to the policies followed during this period. By the beginning of the 1980s, both Korea and Taiwan had developed a fairly unequal distribution of wealth, experienced asset-price inflation, and, due to changes in their relative factor endowments, had relied upon capital-intensive growth since the early 1970s. Even though the distribution of income in both countries is comparable to that in the OECD countries, the trend is disturbing.

14.3 Institutions

As has been made clear in the previous section, growth was government-led in both countries during the first forty years of their development process. The governments of both countries adopted a *dirigiste* stance with respect to the private sector. They formulated development strategies in fair detail and implemented them through a mixture of carrots and sticks that were both discretionary and non-discretionary. Both used market incentives as well as direct controls to attain their goals. Neither allowed the market to operate without significant intervention and incentive change.

The role of governments in both countries went well beyond the achievement of macroeconomic stability. Both countries designed industrial policies and both targeted their industrial policies to specific industries and, in Korea, to specific enterprises. Public investment was important in both countries not only in infrastructure projects but also in specific industrial activities. The share of government-owned enterprises continues to be large.

The governments of both countries were "strong" and "developmental." In both countries, the relationship between the government and enterprises during the first five phases of their economic development was hegemonic, with government having by far the greater power. In both countries, the liberalization phase has brought about a decline in the relative power of government in the economy and a growth in the power of enterprises. This decline is a natural consequence of economic and political liberalization: in a liberalized economic system the government has fewer carrots to dispense, and in a political system in which elections play an important role and there are no specific mechanisms to finance party activities, contributions to parties or political leaders by firms and individuals are critical. Nevertheless, the government still exercises substantial control over firms. In Korea, it still must approve large projects and it mediates territorial disputes between conglomerates. And the government still has the final word in these matters.

Both countries designed institutional mechanisms to exercise their control over the economy. In Korea, the Economic Planning Board (EPB) became all-powerful in 1964. It was most powerful in the design and implementation of the Second Five Year Plan (1967-1971), in which it formulated the plan, evaluated individual projects submitted by private entrepreneurs and directed the central bank to allocate credit and foreign exchange to those enterprises whose projects were selected for inclusion in the plan. Plan performance was monitored by the Ministry of Commerce. It allocated negotiated export targets to firms, and dispensed some of the sticks used to elicit compliance by firms, while the Ministry of Finance dispensed some of the major carrots. After the Second Five Year Plan, individual ministries selected projects in their spheres of responsibility and negotiated with the EPB about their final inclusion; subsequent five year plans included mainly the statement of targets and the selection of large key projects. But the specific performance of individual firms in the implementation of the plans continued to be monitored and punished or rewarded, as deemed appropriate. In Taiwan, the analogue of the EPB was the Council on Economic Planning and Development (CEPD).

The CEPD and EPB created various other institutions through which to exercise their control over the economy. These subsidiary institutions were more important in Taiwan than in Korea, because of the differences in the countries' industrial structures. While individual direct monitoring and negotiation is possible when, as in Korea, large firms and conglomerates control the bulk of production and exports, intermediate structures are necessary when, as in Taiwan, production and exports are controlled by small and medium-size firms. In industry, trading organizations were organized and used for this purpose, and in agriculture farmers' associations were transformed to serve this function.

Institutional mechanisms to limit the power of government, such as consultative councils, were also introduced in both countries. But the growth and influence of private interest groups, especially labor unions, has been severely circumscribed.

The real issue is not whether government exercised a leading role in the development of both economies, but rather why government intervention led to superior economic results in Taiwan and Korea, in contrast with most other developing economies. One may offer several hypotheses. First, leadership commitment to economic development started at the very top and was communicated to all branches of government and civil society. This meant that primacy was accorded to good economic policy over politics and rent-seeking. Technocrats wielded substantial influence, and were granted a great deal of autonomy in strategy and policy design. While corruption and bribes were paid, they did not distort resource allocation across sectors or the design of economic strategy and policy. Second, both countries espoused good economic policies, and pursued sound economic objectives. Their development strategies were in accord with their dynamic comparative advantage. And they adopted sound macroeconomic adjustment and stabilization policies.

Third, both countries excelled in their administrative capacities. They were fortunate in attracting able top policy makers and advisers and in having good bureaucracies. The educational system and the social prestige of civil service careers in Chinese culture resulted in a superior cadre of top policy makers and a good civil service. Confucianism inculcated a tradition of social responsibility and hierarchy, which produced a meritocratic, Weberian-type bureaucracy geared to implementing the directives emanating from the top.

Fourth, both countries developed dynamic entrepreneurial capabilities and industrial organizational structures, though the latter differed between the two countries.

Fifth, the governments of both countries took a long range view. They made decisions to generate comparative advantage through their investment strategies in capital formation. They invested heavily in education, to generate first a well educated unskilled labor force in support of a labor-intensive growth strategy, and then a skilled, technically well trained one, in support of a high-level-manpower intensive strategy. They fostered capital accumulation through heavy investment in infrastructure and the promotion of domestic savings.

Sixth, policies and strategies were pragmatic and flexible. They shifted rapidly out of mistaken government initiatives and responded quickly to changes in the internal and external environment. It was not that the targeted industrial policy did not include mistakes, even serious ones, but rather that, when mistakes were made, the government quickly shifted out of them. By the same token, the government was quick to recognize and respond to internal bottlenecks and changes in external conditions. When the labor markets turned tight, the government started shifting towards capital and skill-intensive industries. When competition in exports in labor-intensive industries became more intense, the government encouraged shifts in the commodity structure of exports. When the growth of markets in developed countries faltered, the government increased its trade with other developing countries.

Seventh, the design of policy involved continued vigilance. Performance in key indicators — such as exports, inflation, and the trade balance — was closely monitored and changes in macroeconomic policies and development strategies were undertaken in response.

How was the government's commitment to economic development created and how was it maintained? The Toynbee challenge-response thesis provides a good answer to this question. Both governments felt that national survival critically depended on achieving economic viability and outdoing their respective political rivals, North Korea and Mainland China. Pragmatism therefore was a hallmark of economic policy-making in both countries. In addition, even authoritarian governments require internal legitimacy for leadership survival. The presidents of both countries firmly believed that their legitimacy in the eyes of their citizens depended on raising standards of living, reducing poverty and sharing the fruits of economic development widely. Both leaders therefore used shared development strategies to maintain their legitimacy with their citizenries. Not only rapid development, but also equitable development, was their economic and social objective. Finally, the leaders of both countries believed that economic power led to national security. Therefore, when their sense of national security was again threatened by the rapprochement between the United States and China, the leaderships in both countries shifted their focus to increasing their countries' economic power in the world at large.

How was government accountability maintained? After all, until very recently both countries had authoritarian governments in the Chinese Imperial Tradition. Opposition was repressed, union leaders were jailed and liberals were subjected to government surveillance and harassment. One answer is that technocrats had a great deal of influence and autonomy. Second, the meritocratically recruited bureaucracy and the Confucian value of communitarianism have provided checks upon the government in the performance of its functions. Leaderships that were perceived as not acting in the public interest lost their legitimacy, as the toppling of the Syngman Rhee regime in Korea demonstrates. Third, formal and informal consultation and coordination mechanisms have played a significant role in limiting government actions. Fourth, press and student demonstrations have called attention to basic societal ills: corruption, unemployment in the 1960s, and poor and unsafe working conditions in the 1970s and 1980s. Newspaper readership in both countries is among the highest in the world, and students, newspaper publishers and editors have demonstrated a high order of civic courage.

14.4 Primary Differences between Korea and Taiwan

While initial conditions, development strategies and institutions were largely similar in both countries, there were also important contrasts between them. The contrasts, too, are rooted primarily in differences in their histories and initial conditions.

14.4.1 Development Strategy

There were two important differences in development strategy between the two countries. First, in Taiwan, the import substitution phase of her economic development was one of agricultural-development-led-industrialization. By contrast, while Korea strove to achieve self sufficiency in grains, agricultural development never played the dynamic role in its industrialization that it did in Taiwan. A primary reason for the difference was that, even though both countries were primarily agricultural at independence, Taiwan was much more suited to agricultural development than Korea. It was a subtropical island, with a climate suitable for multiple cropping,[20] and although its population density was quite high, it was only about two thirds of Korea's.[21] Historically, Taiwan's agricultural productivity was higher than Korea's and cash-crop exports, such as sugar and tea, were the major source of foreign exchange; indeed, in 1952 non-agricultural exports were only 4.5 percent of total exports in Taiwan. Taiwan also had a better agricultural physical infrastructure, in the form of roads, canals and irrigation systems, left over from the Japanese colonial period,[22] as well as a better institutional infrastructure devoted to marketing of agricultural products, agricultural exports, agricultural input delivery, and agricultural extension, partially left over from the Japanese colonial period.

The emphasis on agricultural-development-led-industrialization in Taiwan had several important consequences: it resulted in a Lewis-type process of agricultural financing of capital formation in the industrial sector; raw and processed agricultural exports were the primary source of foreign exchange for industrialization; income growth in agriculture initially provided the major source of demand for manufactured consumer goods; and, last but not least, since agricultural development started from a very egalitarian distribution of land and farm incomes rose relative to urban incomes, Taiwan's agrarian policy was one of the major reasons for its better income distribution.

Second, the dynamics of Taiwan's switches in trade and industrialization policies, especially during the heavy and chemical industry (HCI) drives, were more successful in matching her changing comparative advantage than were Korea's. The timing of the HCI drive was set by external events in both countries. By 1973, when both countries switched to capital-intensive industrialization, they had both attained the Lewis (full employment) commercialization turning point. But Taiwan had a tighter labor market than Korea since its unemployment rate was lower. In addition, the rural development drive in Taiwan, with its emphasis on rural electrification, a dense rural road network, dispersion of industrial activity and a much higher density of small towns, had fostered part-time farming. This meant that the potentially available labor force for industrialization through further employment-switching among sectors was considerably smaller in Taiwan than in Korea. Also, the domestic savings rate in Taiwan was considerably higher than in Korea, so that capital was relatively more abundant in Taiwan than in Korea. Consequently, unlike Korea, Taiwan did not have to resort to inflationary finance of its HCI drive, nor did it have to resort to heavy foreign borrowing, or starve its medium and small industries of credit. As a result, Taiwan was able to pursue capital-intensive industrial policies without resorting to unsound macroeconomic policies and without harming its egalitarian distribution of income.

14.4.2 Macroeconomic Management

Both countries used a high-investment high-growth strategy. However, the monetary and fiscal policies of Taiwan were considerably more conservative than those of Korea.

The primary reason for the conservative bias of Taiwan's macroeconomic policy was the experience of the Chinese-born Taiwanese with hyperinflation on the Mainland. They learned from this experience that high inflation rates can literally tear society apart, and they therefore dreaded inflation.

Taiwan achieved its conservative macroeconomic policy not by lowering its investment rate but rather by pursuing a high savings rate policy. The contrast between the two countries in this regard is striking: In the pre 1973 period, with comparable domestic investment rates,[23] the rate of national savings in Taiwan exceeded its investment rate by 0.6 percentage points, while in Korea the rate of investment exceeded the rate of national savings by 9.5 percentage points. After 1973, Taiwan had a lower investment rate than Korea (25.9 as compared to 31.8 in Korea), but its national savings rate exceeded its domestic investment rate by 6 percentage points, while the Korean domestic investment rate continued to exceed its savings rate by 3.6 percentage points.

The high national savings rate in Taiwan early on was achieved through both high household savings rates and conservative fiscal policies. Regression equations relating real households savings to real household disposable income (see Table 14.1) indicate that before 1980, the marginal propensity to save in Taiwan was 0.23 as compared to 0.15 in Korea, while after 1980 the relationship was reversed: the marginal propensity to save out of real household income was 0.14 in Taiwan and 0.29 in Korea. In part, Korea's low household savings rate in the early years was compensated for by a much higher corporate savings rate than in Taiwan,[24] but not entirely; the average private savings rate in the finance of gross investment during 1955-1980 was 64 percent in Taiwan, while it was only 52 percent in Korea.

Table 14.1   Household Savings Propensities

Country	Period	Constant	Marg. Propensity to save	Elasticity at mean	R–square
Taiwan	1960–79	–35909	.232	1.26	.96
	t-ratio	(–3.8)	(20.6)		
	1980–92	202226	.143	0.65	.69
	t-ratio	(2.5)	(4.9)		
Korea	1962–79	–311	.152	1.64	.89
	t-ratio	(–3.9)	(11.6)		
	1980–92	–2408	.293	1.62	.96
	t-ratio	(–5.8)	(16.1)		

Note: The dependent variable is real household savings and the independent variable is real household
    disposable income.

Why was Taiwan's household savings propensity so high in the early years? One can offer many explanations:[25] First, Taiwan's relatively higher rate of economic growth; according to the Duesenberry-Modigliani hypothesis, people's consumption expenditures in a given year are set by their peak consumption patterns in the prior years, and savings are a residual. The faster the rate of growth of income, the higher the rate of savings. Second, bonus income is a larger fraction of total employee compensation in Taiwan than in Korea; according to the Friedman hypothesis, savings rates out of transitory income, such as bonuses, are higher than out of permanent income, such as regular compensation. Third, because the government's per capita expenditure on education in Taiwan is much higher than that in Korea, Taiwanese households spend less on education than do Koreans. Fourth, Taiwan's distribution of income is more even than Korea's; a more modest consumption pattern is required to "keep up with the Joneses" in a country with a more even distribution of income. Fifth, since there are relatively more small and medium sized business enterprises in Taiwan than in Korea, many more Taiwanese save in order to open up a business. Sixth, Taiwan has pursued a tight monetary policy with positive real interest rates, while Korea's monetary policy before the late seventies was expansionist and generated low real rates of interest. On the average, between 1960 and 1980, the real rate of interest in Korea was negative 60 percent of the time and zero on average. By contrast, during the same period, Taiwan's real interest rate was been positive two thirds of the time and averaged 2.2 percent. [26] Seventh, the inflation rate has been considerably lower and less fluctuating in Taiwan than in Korea; even aside from real interest rates, high and variable inflation rates discourage savings because of uncertainty concerning the future purchasing power of savings. Eighth, Koreans, especially rural ones, mistrust official banks and, during the same period that bank real interest rates averaged zero, curb market real rates averaged 28 percent. Therefore, in Korea, much individual savings bypass the banking system and are not included in the official personal savings statistics.

Why has the savings rate accelerated in Korea and become higher than Taiwan's since the early 1980s? First, during the 1980s the real rate of economic growth in Korea has exceeded that in Taiwan; regression equations relating household savings rates to disposable household income in Korea suggest that this is the primary source of difference in savings behavior during the eighties (Collins, 1994). Second, the real rate of return on bank savings in Korea has become positive and comparable to that in Taiwan. Third, there is a great deal of target savings in Korea for the purchase of big-ticket items, such as cars, land or apartments. Fourth, after 1981, the rate of inflation in Korea dropped substantially and became stable.

Taiwan's public sector was also managed considerably more conservatively than was Korea's. Taiwan achieved budgetary surpluses early on, if aid receipts to government are included in government revenues, and continued to have surpluses throughout most of its development process. By contrast, Korea has run consistent budget deficits throughout its fifty year history.[27] Nevertheless, Taiwan's public sector has financed a considerably larger share of national investment in schooling than has that of Korea.[28] In addition, Taiwan's tax rates have been significantly lower than Korea's, especially before 1980.[29] Thus, Taiwan's public sector has been more efficient than Korea's.

Since the discrepancy between domestic investment and domestic savings is equal to the current account deficit, the savings-investment gap can also be viewed as the domestic counterpart of a country's external performance. Indeed, the trade balance has been a major guidepost of macroeconomic policy in both countries. Here, too, Taiwan has been more conservative than Korea. Except for the first oil crisis years, Taiwan's trade balance has been consistently positive since 1971 while, except for 1985-89, Korea's trade balance has been consistently negative.[30] In Korea, the trade deficit was supported first by US aid and later by foreign borrowing, as a result of which Korea has become a heavily indebted country. By contrast, in the early years, Taiwan relied primarily first on US aid and later on foreign investment by overseas Chinese. Since 1984, Taiwan has consistently been a net capital exporter and investor in the rest of the world. In the perspective of the two-gap framework, Taiwan's domestic savings rate started exceeding its domestic investment rate in the mid-sixties, and this enabled her to accumulate reserves and prosper during the seventies and beyond without accumulating foreign debt.

As a result of Taiwan's more conservative macroeconomic policies, reduction in savings propensities, and substantially higher marginal capital-output ratio,[31] Taiwan's rate of economic growth in the 1980s dropped one percentage point below Korea's. As against this, Taiwan's inflation rate, except for the two oil-shock years, has consistently been in the single digit range, while Korea averaged 20 percent annual inflation rates until 1982 and about 2.5 times Taiwan's inflation rate thereafter.[32] The lower rate of inflation in Taiwan has enabled Taiwan to pursue a stable exchange rate policy without loss of international competitiveness. It has enabled international financial liberalization without fear of capital flight. It has made possible rapid development with less social stress. And, last but not least, it has also led to a lower rate of asset-price inflation, which, in turn, has meant that Taiwan's distribution of income (including capital gains) has become more unequal at lower rate than Korea's.

14.4.3 Institutional Development

The primary difference in institutional development between the two countries is in their industrial organization. Contrary to impressions, Taiwan and Korea's size distribution of firms in manufacturing is rather similar (see Table 14.2): the proportion of firms with fewer than 10 employees is actually 20 percent higher in Korea than in Taiwan; the proportion of mid-size firms, with 50-200 employees, is 8 percent higher in Korea; and the percentage of firms with over 300 employees is 15 percent lower in Korea. The smallest firms in Korea generate almost twice the share of value added than those of Taiwan; medium-sized firms produce 22.3 percent of value added in Taiwan and 17.7 percent in Korea; and firms with more than 300 workers generate 55 percent of value added in Taiwan and 50 percent of value added in Korea.

However, in Korea, firms are aggregated into business groups (conglomerates or *chaebols*) to which there is no counterpart in Taiwan. These conglomerates are very large: they combine about 270 firms (or about 50 percent of firms with more than 500 employees) into 30 business groups that produced 33 percent of manufacturing value added and 10 percent of GNP in 1985.[33] These conglomerates are modeled on the pre-World War II *zaibatsu* in Japan, in that they are family-owned and family-managed and thus represent an enormous concentration of economic power in a few families.[34] By contrast, in Taiwan, most of the large enterprises are state-owned.

Why did conglomerates develop in Korea but not in Taiwan? One can offer several conjectures. First, there was more entrepreneurial and managerial talent available in Taiwan than in Korea at independence. Taiwanese businessmen played an important role in foreign trade, especially in tea, under Japanese colonial rule, and the immigration from the Mainland included some businessmen. By contrast, in Korea, indigenous business and managerial talent had little opportunity to develop, as the Japanese used Koreans almost exclusively in lower-level positions in the Japanese-owned corporations that operated the agricultural estates and the industrial and mining enterprises. The Japanese expropriated most of the land in Korea, oper-

Table 14.2   **Industrial Organization in Manufacturing**

# of Employees	% Firms	% Value Added
Taiwan 1986[a]		
1–9	64.7	3.4
10–19	13.8	3.1
20–49	2.1	7.5
50–99	5.1	9.4
100–199	2.8	12.9
200–299	.9	8.9
Over 300	1.3	54.8
Total	123,412	100.0
Korea 1995[b]		
1–9	80.6	6.6
10–19	28.6	6.2
20–49	20.4	11.7
50–99	6.1	9.9
100–199	2.5	10.6
200–299	.8	6.6
300–499	.5	6.8
over 500	.6	41.6
Total	271,831	100.0

Sources: a. Calculated from data from the Census Survey of Manufacturing 1986 by Prof Mei Hsu.
b. Calculated from National Statistical Office , Korea Statistical Yearbook 1995 by Prof. Song Byung Nak.

ated most of its enterprises, and exported most of its agricultural and mining output. As a result, there was a severe dearth of leadership, management, technocratic and bureaucratic talent at independence. The trading-group structure economizes on these rare skills. Second, the financial system was more repressed in Korea than in Taiwan, as a result of a higher private savings rate in Taiwan in the early years and investment finance by overseas Chinese. The Korean government therefore had a more potent instrument for encouraging the development of state-dependent conglomerates in Korea through its complete control over the allocation of finance in the nationalized and, later, government-directed banking system. Third, the Korean government did not fear the development of countervailing power in the conglomerates since they were extremely dependent on the government for their continued ability to flourish. It is only in the 1980s that the Korean government has tried to curb the growth and power of the *chaebols* — with, one might add, little success. Fourth, the development of *chaebols* involves discretionary use of the state's economic power in favor of, or against, specific individuals. Reliance upon state-sponsored privately-owned *chaebols* is therefore likely to generate less resentment in a country that is ethnically homogeneous, such as Korea, than in a country that is ethnically diverse, such as Taiwan. Finally, despite a longer history of Japanese rule in Taiwan, Korea's institutions were more closely modeled on Japan's than were Taiwan's. In the early 1960s, when the *chaebols* were first introduced, the majority of high level Korean bureaucrats had been educated in Japan, and were under the influence of the United States; the US influence favored reliance on the private sector and the Japanese example suggested the *zaibatsu* model. By contrast, the ruling elite in Taiwan had been educated in the Mainland; in Confucian tradition, bureaucrats are held in high esteem and businessmen are ranked lowest in the social hierarchy. Reliance on a bureaucratically-managed enterprise system for the achievement of public goals therefore seemed more appropriate, although there were conflicts between conservatives and liberals on this score.

What are the major consequences of the difference in industrial organization between Taiwan and Korea? It is probably incorrect to conclude from the existence of the *chaebols* in Korea and their absence in Taiwan that there is less competition in domestic manufacturing in Korea than in Taiwan. The *chaebols* are well diversified among industries and there is fierce competition within the *chaebols* among firms operating in different sectors. In addition, the competition among firms belonging to different *chaebols* that operate in the same industry is intense. Moreover, one of the major goals of government intervention into the operation of the *chaebols* in Korea has been to foster greater competition.

It is also probably incorrect to conclude that the government exercised less economic control over the manufacturing sector in Korea than it did in Taiwan. Indeed, Korea's industrial policies have been more aggressive than those of Taiwan (K. Lee, 1993), despite the fact that most of Taiwan's large enterprises are state-owned. In Korea, the government exercised almost direct control over the *chaebols* through its control of credit and use of discretionary carrots and sticks. The government could (and did) order *chaebols* to undertake or refrain from undertaking certain activities; it could (and occasionally did) force the *chaebols* to divest themselves of specific firms, even without compensation; it has interfered in the detailed operations of individual *chaebol*-enterprises with measures intended to improve their management; and it has levied "taxes" by commanding specific *chaebols* to engage in particular public works or make specific financial contributions. In short, the state has participated in *chaebol* decision making with respect to production, marketing, investment and use of earnings almost like a business partner (C. Lee, 1992). The *chaebols* were the creation of the Park regime,[35] which used its control over the banking, trading and legal systems to forge the *chaebols* into instruments of its industrial policies and development strategies. The *chaebols* were important instruments in the implementation of the export-led economic growth strategy of the mid-1960s and were the primary private vehicles used to implement the HCI drive of the seventies.

The economic and political liberalization and the economic globalization policies of the 1980s are tipping the balance of economic power between the state and the *chaebols* towards the *chaebols*[36] and it is therefore likely that the contrast between the influence of the state on the large state-owned enterprises in Taiwan and the influence of the state on the large privately-owned *chaebols* will become more pronounced in the future.

The primary result of the difference in industrial organization between the two countries can be found in the difference in the distribution of income, wealth and power within the two countries. Taiwan's use of public enterprises as compared to Korea's use of privately-owned conglomerates has led to considerably greater concentration in Korea along all these dimensions. The differences in inequality between the two countries are likely to be magnified by the introduction of democracy, which erodes the relative power of the state over private enterprises and increases the power of firms through their contributions to the finance of political activities.

14.4.4 Development Results

In terms of development results, Taiwan's per capita GNP in 1955 was roughly twice Korea's; both countries have currently exceeded per capita incomes of $10,000. The production and export structures of both countries resemble those of developed nations. But Korea's large firms have achieved leading positions globally in several capital and skill-intensive industries while Taiwan's have not. Korea is the second largest shipbuilder and producer of advanced computer chips, the fifth largest automobile producer, and the sixth largest steel producer in the world. But Taiwan's income-distribution performance has been superior to Korea's. While the size distribution of income in both countries has followed an inverted Kuznets U path, Taiwan's income distribution remains considerably more equal than Korea's.

14.5 Notes

1   I a indebted to Jeff Chung for his assistance on Taiwan and to Kim Mahn Je, Nam Duk Woo and Song Byung Nak for their insights into Korean economic development.

2   Economic assistance by the US during 1953-1961 accounted for 7-12 percent of GNP and financed 60-80 percent of imports.

3   The Korean War period was one of hyperinflation. In 1953, the urban consumer price index stood at 7000 using 1947 as a base.

4   Of total government expenditures, 8.8 percent went into research and education, 5.6 percent into health and welfare, 8.7 percent into current transfers to households and 2.8 percent into roads, waterways, fire protection, water supply and sanitation as compared with a total of only 14 percent for capital formation.

5   Foreign capital inflow financed about 55 percent of imports and 80 percent of investment during 1960-62.

6   The planning model adopted utilized employment and productivity projections to determine the potential growth of output in each sector.

7   The contribution of import substitution to economic growth during 1955-63 was estimated by K.S. Kim and Roemer (1981) to be 35.7 percent while that of export expansion was only 7 percent, the growth of domestic demand was 24.9 percent and changes in input-output coefficients accounted for 32.4 percent.

8   The absolute poverty line is defined as 121000 1981 won per month for a five person household. The data are from Suh (1985).

9   Figures in text are the unemployment rate as recalculated by Kuo (1983).

10   The discussion of market and non-market incentives in this section is based on Lee and Liang (1982).

11   In direct price comparisons of domestic with world prices, Lee and Liang (1982) report that 39 percent of commodities for which price comparisons were made had domestic prices below world prices and another 45 percent did not require the full tariff protection they received.

12   The subsidies to selective import-substitute industries included duty-free entry of machinery and equipment, tariff protection for domestic industries competing with foreign imports, income tax reductions for newly established industries, and long term low-interest loans and foreign-loan guarantees for selected sectors.

13   The tariff rate structure remained varied and ranged from 13.5 percent on mining and energy to 106 percent on beverages and tobacco.

14   The average real rate of interest on loans by deposit money banks was 10 percent during this period while the real rate on foreign loans was 2 percent. Ability to borrow abroad was rationed by the government, however.

15   The calculations cited were undertaken as part of the process of calibrating the base trajectory used to explore the relative advantages of agricultural development led industrialization and export led growth in Adelman (1984).

16   For example, during 1968-73 in Korea, domestic demand expansion was responsible for 63 percent of total growth of light manufacturing while export expansion contributed only 34 percent (calculated from Suk, 1977).

17   The key industries absorbed 73 percent or 48.1 billion won released by the fund for industrial rationalization between 1972 and 1975 (see Yoo, 1990).

18   The average marginal capital-output ratio increased by a factor of 2.5, from a very low average figure of about 2 in the labor intensive growth period to 5.3.

19   For an extensive discussion see Leipziger et al. (1993), Kwon (1993a) and Adelman (1996).

20   About 37 percent of Taiwan's agricultural land was double cropped in 1950.

21   Taiwan's total population per square kilometer of cultivable land was 630 as compared to 940 in Korea. Taiwan's agricultural population per square kilometer of agricultural land was 334 while Korea's was 535.

22   The canals were in a state of disrepair after the end of World War two, but were quickly mended.

23   The average investment share in GNP was 22.8 in Taiwan during 1952-73 ; it was 21.5 in Korea between 1962 and 1973 .

24   The average share of corporate savings in the finance of gross investment in Taiwan during 1951-80 was 6.7 percent while that in Korea for 1962-80 was 29.5 percent.

25   See Scitovsky (1986) and Song (1994) for discussions of this problem.

26 This average excludes the year 1974, when the rate of inflation shot up to 47 percent, after which it dropped to 5 percent.

27 1987-88 and 1993 are the only exceptions to this statement.

28 The share of public investment in schooling in Taiwan has been two thirds higher than in Korea.

29 The pre-1980 average tax burden ratio in Taiwan was 17 percent compared to 12 percent in Korea.

30 The assessment by Haggard (in Haggard et al., 1994) that Korea has turned the corner on its external trade balance thus seems to have been somewhat premature.

31 The marginal capital/output ratio has averaged 4.6 in Taiwan and only 3.2 in Korea during the 1980s.

32 Since 1982 Korea's inflation rate has averaged 5.7 percent while Taiwan's has averaged 2.4 percent.

33 Song, 1994: 115.

34 Unlike their Japanese counterparts, the Korean *chaebols* have not yet made the transition to professional management nor have they dispersed ownership through the stock market to any great extent.

35 There were a few *chaebols* when the military government of President Park took over in 1961. These were processing imported material financed by US aid. They were brought under government control and charged with illicit wealth accumulation.

36 Indeed, since the 1980s, there are examples of non-compliance or incomplete compliance by firms to government initiatives (see K. Lee, 1993).

14.6 References

Adelman, Irma, forthcoming. "Economic and Social Development in Korea." Seoul: Korea Development Institute.
Adelman, Irma, 1984. "Beyond Export-Led Growth," *World Development* 12: 261-78.
Adelman, Irma, 1980. *Redistribution Before Growth*. Amsterdam: Martinus Nijhof.
Adelman, Irma and C. Taft Morris, 1973. *Economic Growth and Social Equity in Developing Countries.* Stanford: Stanford University Press.
Adelman, Irma and S. Robinson, 1978. *Income Distribution Policies in Developing Countries : The Case of Korea*. Stanford: Stanford University Press.
Choo Hakchung, 1977. "Some Sources of Relative Equity in Income Distribution: A Historical Perspective," in Chuk Kyo Kim (ed.) *Industrial and Social Development in Korea*. Seoul: Korea Development Institute: 303-330.
Choo Hakchung, 1985. "Estimation of Size Distribution of Income and Its Sources of Change in Korea, 1982," Korea Development Institute Working Paper 8515. Seoul: Korea Development Institute.
Chu Yun-Peng, 1995. " Taiwan's Income Inequality in the Postwar Era," Academia Sinica Working Paper 96-1. Taipei: Academia Sinica.
Collins, Susan, 1994. "Savings, Investment and External Balance in South Korea," in Haggard et al., *op. cit.*: 231-260.
Devarajan, Shantayana, Jeffrey D. Lewis and Sherman Robinson, 1990. "Policy Lessons from Trade Focused Two Sector Models," *Journal of Policy Modelling*: 625-658.
Haggard, Stephan, Richard N. Cooper, Susan Collins, Choongsoo Kim, and Sung-Tae Ro, 1994. *Macroeconomic Policy and Adjustment in Korea 1970-1990*. Cambridge, Mass.: Harvard Institute of International Development.

Hong, Wontack, 1979. *Trade, Distortions and Employment Growth in Korea*. Seoul: Korea Development Institute.

Hong, Wontack, 1977. "Growth and Trade Patterns," in Chuk Kyo Kim, *op. cit:* 361.

Hong, Wontack, 1991. "Import Restrictions in the Process of Economic Development," in Krause and Kim, *op. cit*.: 415-453.

Hong, Wontack, 1992. "Trade Policies in Korea," in Dominick Salvatore (ed.) *National Trade Policies*. New York: Greenwood.

Kim, Chuk Kyo, 1977. *Planning Models and Macroeconomic Policy Issues*. Seoul: Korea Development Institute.

Kim, K.S. and M. Roemer, 1981. "Growth and Structural Transformation." Cambridge, Mass.: Harvard University Council on East Asian Studies.

Koo Bon Ho, 1977. " Foreign Exchange Policies: An Evaluation and Proposals," in C.K. Kim, *op. cit.:* 449- 479.

Kuo, Shirley W.Y., 1983. *The Taiwan Economy in Transition*. Boulder, Colo: Westview Press.

Kuznets, Simon, 1955. "Economic Growth and Income Inequality," *American Economic Review* 45 (1): 1-28.

Kuznets, Paul, 1977. *Economic Growth and Structure in the Republic of Korea*. New Haven: Yale University Press.

Krause, Larry and Kihwan Kim (eds.), 1991. *Liberalization in the Process of Economic Development*. Berkeley: University of California Press.

Kwon, Soonwon, 1993a. *Social Policy in Korea: Challenges and Responses*. Seoul: Korea Development Institute.

Kwon, Soonwon, 1993b. *Improvement in Antipoverty Programs*. Seoul: Korea Development Institute.

Lee, Chung H., 1992. "The Government and Financial System in the Economic Development of Korea," *World Development* 20: 387-395.

Lee, Kyun, 1993. *New East Asian Economic Development*. New York: M.E. Sharpe.

Lee T.H. and K.S. Liang, 1982, "Taiwan," in B. Belassa *et al.*, *Development Strategies in Semi-industrial Countries*. Baltimore: Johns Hopkins University Press

Leipziger, D.M., D. Dollar, A.F. Shorrocks and S.Y. Song, 1993. *The Distribution of Income in Korea*. [place]: Korea Development Institute.

Scitovsky, Tibor, 1986. "Economic Development in Taiwan and South Korea, 1965-1981," in Lawrence Lau (ed.) *Models of Development — A Comparative Study of Economic Growth in South Korea and Taiwan*, San Francisco: Institute of Comparative Studies Press.

Shen T.H., 1964. *Agricultural Development on Taiwan since World War II* . Ithaca, NY: Cornell University Press.

Song Byung Nak, 1994. *The Rise of the Korean Economy*. Oxford and New York: Oxford University Press.

Suh, Sang Mok, 1985. "Economic Growth and Change in Income Distribution: The Korean Case," Korea Development Institute Working Paper 8508. Seoul: Korea Development Institute.

Suk, Tai Suh, 1977. "Growth Contribution of Trade and Incentive System," in C.K. Kim, *op. cit.:* 401-403.

Yoo, J. H., 1990. " The Industrial Policy of the 1970s and the Evolution of the Manufacturing Sector in Korea," Korea Development Institute Working Paper 9017. Seoul: Korea Development Institute.

Westphal, Larry and Kim Kwan-Suk, 1977. "Industrial Policy and Development in Korea," World Bank Staff Working Paper 263, Washington, D.C.: The World Bank.

Westphal, Larry, 1978. "The Republic of Korea's Experience with Export-Led Development," *World Development* 6: 347-382.

Whang, In Joung, 1981. *Management of Rural Change in Korea*. Seoul: Seoul National Press.

15 LATIN AMERICA AND EAST ASIA: REVISITING THE EVIDENCE

Arnold C. Harberger

The occasion of this conference offers me an opportunity to express once again in a public forum the great esteem in which I hold the two economists whom we are here to honor — T.C. Liu and S.C. Tsiang. My friendship with them began in the summer if 1950, when we shared a suite of offices at the International Monetary Fund. Little did I know at that time that my two new friends would go on to spark the takeoff of the Taiwanese economy, and to continue for many years as the guides and custodians of this "Taiwan miracle." Nor did I realize then that they both would also soon move back into the academic world, each building there an enviable record as a teacher and a scholar. Few people in our profession have managed, as they did so amply, to contribute directly through their policy advice to the welfare of a people, to leave their mark through their teaching on a whole generation of students, and beside all this to make notable contributions to our professional literature. I am most grateful to the conference organizers for giving me this opportunity to once more pay my heartfelt homage to these two great friends, great economists, great men.

The comparison of the East Asian countries with Latin America is a natural topic for me at a meeting like this, to which I can bring something of what I have learned in over four decades of experience in and study of a number of Latin American economies, while at the same time I can add something further to my own understanding and appreciation of the miracle economies of East Asia, and, most particularly, Taiwan. The topic was even more a natural one for me, because I had addressed quite similar issues in a paper written more than a decade ago.[1] The present conference gives me the opportunity to review the findings of that earlier paper, and then to inquire whether new data, coming from years not covered in the earlier study, confirm or deny those findings. Or, put slightly differently, we can inquire whether the new data suggest any important changes in our assessment of the main characteristics of these two sets of national economies.

15.1 Basic Economic Structure

Table 15.1 presents data on thirteen Latin American countries, plus eight from the East Asian region. The figures through 1980 recapitulate the data reported on in my earlier paper; they are to be compared with those stemming from the more recent years (1990, 1992, and 1993).

Table 15.1   Shares of GDP in Manufacturing

	1960	1970	1980	1990	1992	1993
			Latin America			
Southern Cone						
Argentina	32	32			22	20
Brazil	26	29		26	25	20
Chile	21	25	21			
Paraguay	17	17	17	23	17	15
Uruguay	21		25	28	22	19
Andean Group						
Colombia	17	21	22	21	20	18
Ecuador	16	18		23	22	22
Peru	24	20	27	27		21
Venezuela		16	16	20	16	14
Central America and Caribbean						
Costa Rica	14		20	19	20	19
Dominican Republic	17	19	15	13	14	12
Honduras	13	14	17	16	17	18
Mexico	19	22	24	23	20	20
Median	18	20	20.5	23	20	19
			East Asia			
The Four Dragons						
Taiwan	22	34	42	33	32	30
Hong Kong	26	29	27	18	16	13
Korea, Republic of	14	21	28	31	26	29
Singapore	12	20	28	29	28	28
Rest						
Indonesia	8	10	9	20	21	22
Malaysia	9	12	23			
Philippines	20	25	26	25	24	24
Thailand	13	16	20	26	28	28
Median	13.5	20.5	26.5	26	26	28

Sources: World Bank, *World Development Report,* various years. For Taiwan, *Statistical Yearbook of the Republic of China,* various years.

The story told by Table 15.1 is quite straightforward. The share of GDP occupied by manufacturing has been quite constant in Latin America, at about 20 percent. In East Asia, in contrast, there was a dramatic growth of manufacturing as a fraction of total product between 1960 and 1980, after which this share leveled off at about 28 percent. This growth took place earlier in Taiwan (and Hong Kong) than in the other countries, but the broad picture still applies quite well to Taiwan. Hong Kong, on the other hand, has seen a dramatic drop in the share of manufacturing, presumably as Hong Kong firms relied increasingly on operations based on mainland China, and as the territory turned more and more to a specialization in financial services.

Table 15.2 records the growth rates of GDP and of manufacturing output during the decade of the 1970s on the one hand and in the period from 1980 onward on the other. Little need be said here of the East Asian experience, except perhaps that the Philippines is here revealed to behave more like a Latin American than like an East Asian economy — a thought that has been expressed many times before.

The Latin American story is one of quite successful growth in the 1970s followed by something close to collapse in the 1980s. But there is very little uniformity of experience underlying this pattern. Commodity booms (principally oil and coffee) benefited Colombia, Ecuador, Venezuela, Costa Rica, Honduras and Mexico in the 1970s, giving their growth rates an "artificial" boost in that decade. Argentina, Chile, and Uruguay, on the other hand, had excellent growth rates in the latter part of the 1970s which are not reflected in the decade averages because of policy-induced stagnation (or worse) in the earlier years of the decade.

For the 1980s in Latin America, one has the collapse of the commodity booms (plus the end of the Itaipu dam construction in the case of Paraguay), combined with the great international debt crisis early in the decade (which struck Argentina, Brazil, Chile, Ecuador, Mexico, Peru and Venezuela). These negative forces dominate the statistics for 1980-93, masking very significant late-period growth performances by Argentina, Chile, Peru, and, to a modest degree, Uruguay.

The contrast between Latin America and the East Asian countries (once again, except for the Philippines) is stark. For East Asia, one sees a veritable litany of repeated experiences — high GDP growth, accompanied (and probably in most cases led) by high rates of growth of manufacturing.

When reading statistics on exports, and particularly of exports as a fraction of GDP, one must be alert to the phenomena of the entrepot trade and of in-bond processing and/or manufacture. It is things like these which lead to anomalous-looking figures like exports of around 80 percent of GDP for Malaysia and of over 100 percent for Hong Kong and Singapore in recent years. (Economists should really urge the international organizations that present data in this form to simultaneously prepare other tables in which only the value added embodied in real exports is counted, and in which, to be consistent, imports are defined to exclude items that are later exported.)

Even allowing for significant differences between the two regions in the importance of *maquila* and *entrepot* operations, Table 15.3 leaves a clear impression that the role of exports is much more dominant among the East Asian than among the Latin American economies. Moreover, the idea of export-led growth is a more

Table 15.2   **Economic Growth, GDP and Manufacturing (per cent)**

	GDP growth		Manufacturing growth	
	1970-80	1980-93	1970-80	1980-93
Latin America				
Southern Cone				
Argentina	2.5	0.8	1.3	0.4
Brazil	8.1	2.1	9.0	0.2
Chile	1.8	5.1	-0.8	4.4
Paraguay	8.5	2.8	7.9	2.3
Uruguay	3.1	1.3		0.3
Andean Group				
Colombia	5.4	3.7	5.8	3.5
Ecuador	9.5	2.4	10.5	0.3
Peru	3.5	-0.5		
Venezuela	3.5	2.1	5.7	1.3
Central America and Caribbean				
Costa Rica	5.7	3.6		3.6
Dominican Republic	6.5	2.8	6.5	1.0
Honduras	5.8	2.9	6.9	3.6
Mexico	6.3	1.6	7.0	2.1
Median	5.7	2.4	6.7	1.7
East Asia				
The Four Dragons				
Taiwan	9.3	8.2	13.3	6.7
Hong Kong	9.2	6.5		
Korea, Republic of	10.1	9.1	17.7	12.3
Singapore	8.3	6.9	9.7	7.2
Rest				
Indonesia	7.2	5.8	14.0	11.8
Malaysia	7.9	6.2	11.7	10.3
Philippines	6.0	1.4	6.1	0.8
Thailand	7.1	8.2	10.5	10.8
Median	8.1	6.7	11.7	10.3

Sources: World Bank, *World Development Report,* various years. For Taiwan, *Statistical Yearbook of the Republic of China* and *Monthly Bulletin of Statistics of the Republic of China.*

ready generalization for East Asia than for Latin America. Nonetheless, it is fair to say that most of the major growth episodes that have been experienced in Latin America over the last few decades have been export-led. This is true of the so-called "Brazilian miracle" (ca. 1965-75) as well as of the two major episodes of Chilean growth (1975-81 and 1985 to date), as well as of Central American growth in the 1960s and 1970s (at least if one counts intra-regional trade as part of exports). My

Table 15.3   The Role of Exports (per cent)

	Exports of goods and non-factor services/GDP						Average annual growth of exports	
	1970	1980	1990	1992	1993		1970-80	1980-93
				Latin America				
Southern Cone								
Argentina	7		14	7	6		8.9	3.2
Brazil	7	9	7	10	8		8.6	5.2
Chile	15	21	37	31	28		9.6	6.6
Paraguay	15	10	34	22	27		6.2	8.6
Uruguay	13	9	27	21	20		5.2	2.6
Andean Group								
Colombia	14	17	20	19	17		2.6	11.0
Ecuador	14	24	31	31	26		0.1	3.4
Peru	18	24	11	10	10		5.0	-0.3
Venezuela	21	33	39	25	26		-6.8	1.7
Central America and Caribbean								
Costa Rica	28	26	34	39	40		5.3	5.6
Dominican Republic	17	17	28	29	24		6.2	-3.5
Honduras	28	37	40	28	32		3.4	1.4
Mexico	6	14	16	13	13		5.5	5.4
Median	15	19	28	22	24		5.3	3.4
				East Asia				
The Four Dragons								
Taiwan	30	54	47	43	44		17.2	11.2
Hong Kong	92	111	137	144	143		9.9	15.8
Korea, Republic of	21	37	32		24		22.7	12.3
Singapore	102		190	174	169			12.7
Rest								
Indonesia	13	31	26	29	28		6.5	6.7
Malaysia	42	60	79	78	80		3.3	12.6
Philippines	22	20	28	29	32		7.2	3.4
Thailand	15	25	42	36	37		8.9	15.5
Median	26	37	44.5	43	40.5		8.9	12.5

Sources: World Bank, *World Development Report,* various years. For Taiwan, *Statistical Yearbook of the Republic of China* and *Monthly Bulletin of Statistics of the Republic of China.*

generalization would be that most Latin American growth has been export led, but that often this growth stemmed from exogenous forces like international commodity price booms. Only on occasion in Latin America (Brazil and Chile in the episodes reported above, plus several other countries more recently) does one find programs and policies that conduce to a generalized growth of exports as a country better exploits its comparative advantage. In contrast, the East Asian countries seem to be harnessing economic policy all the time so as to ensure a full (maybe sometimes even a more-than-full) flowering of comparative advantage.

15.2 Investment and Inflation

Table 15.4 presents data on two variables that have an important influence on the rate of economic growth — the rates of investment and of inflation, respectively. The rate of investment in physical capital influences growth by augmenting the economy's resource endowment. The rate of inflation deters growth, principally by blurring people's perceptions of relative prices. The more rapid the rate of inflation, the greater the prevalence of changes in relative prices that come just from different timing of response to underlying inflationary pressures. Such changes obscure the "genuine" movements of relative prices that in a well-functioning market system serve as the main signals for resource-reallocations. In addition, the blurring of price signals inhibits the search for and the adoption of cost-reducing innovations, the main source of improvements in total factor productivity.

Table 15.4   Investment and Inflation (per cent)

	Gross domestic investment/GDP						Average annual inflation	
	1970	1980	1990	1992	1993		1970-80	1980-93
Latin America								
Southern Cone								
Argentina	25		9	17	18		134.2	374.3
Brazil	21	22	22	17	19		38.6	423.4
Chile	19	18	20	24	26		186.2	20.1
Paraguay	15	29	22	23	22		12.7	25.0
Uruguay	11	19	12	13	16		63.7	66.7
Andean Group								
Colombia	20	25	19	18	22		22.3	24.9
Ecuador	18	25	19	22	21		13.8	40.4
Peru	16	16	23	16	19		30.1	316.1
Venezuela	33	25	9	23	19		14.0	23.9
Central America and Caribbean								
Costa Rica	21	25	29	28	30		15.3	22.1
Dominican Republic	19	24	15	23	22		9.1	25.0
Honduras	21	28	13	26	27		8.1	8.2
Mexico	21	28	20	24	22		18.1	57.9
Median	20	25	19	23	22		18.1	25
East Asia								
The Four Dragons								
Taiwan	26	35	23	25	25		10.0	2.5
Hong Kong	21	29	28	29	27		9.2	7.9
Korea, Republic of	28	31	37		27		19.5	6.3
Singapore	39	43	39	41	44		5.9	2.5
Rest								
Indonesia	16	22	36	35	28		21.5	8.5
Malaysia	22	29	34	34	33		7.3	2.2
Philippines	21	30	22	23	24		13.3	13.6
Thailand	26	27	27	40	40		9.2	4.3
Median	24	29.5	31	34	27.5		9.6	5.3

Sources: World Bank, *World Development Report,* various years. For Taiwan, *Statistical Yearbook of the Republic of China* and *Monthly Bulletin of Statistics of the Republic of China.*

It is notable that in East Asia, in the three recent years 1990, 1992, and 1993, only the Philippines registers investment rates below 25 percent, while two-thirds of the other countries' observations are above 30 percent. This contrasts with Latin America, where during the same three year period only one country (Costa Rica) reaches a 30 percent investment rate just once (in 1993). And apart from Costa Rica, only three out of 36 observations are above 25 percent, with nearly half of them being 20 percent or below.

On the inflation front, the story is the same, though the inequalities obviously run in the opposite direction. Here the Asian countries have rates of inflation in single digits (except for the Philippines), and, more than that, declining as one moves from the earlier (1970-80) to the later (1980-93) period. In contrast, only Honduras, of the Latin American countries listed, posted a single digit inflation. Moreover, only Chile among the listed countries managed a reduction in its rate of inflation between the two periods.

With lower rates of investment and higher rates of inflation in Latin America than in East Asia, we have two reasons to expect the sort of difference in GDP growth rates that we actually observe. Nonetheless there remains the question of why these differences have emerged — in particular, how much of these differences can be attributed to differences in the typical policy stances of governments in the two regions?

15.3 Three Key Policy Indicators

For many years now I have gained insights from the use of three simple indicators of the policy behavior of governments. Readers should have no difficulty in seeing how these variables, which were developed in an attempt to study inflationary experiences in different countries, can also be seen as influencing private investment. In particular, private investment tends to be squeezed when the government borrows money from the banking system. Private investment tends also to be squeezed, in real terms, when people are motivated by inflation to hold lower real money balances. The consequent reduction of the liability side of the balance sheet of the consolidated banking system forces a necessary squeezing of the asset side, the most vulnerable part of which, in most if not all cases, is credit to the private sector.

In choosing the policy indicators, β, γ, and λ, I was motivated by the recognition that, as surely as the sun rises and sets, "excessive" monetary expansion lies at the root of every major inflationary episode. But this fact was known and appreciated by most of the finance ministers and Central Bank presidents who presided over these monetary expansions. It is not — certainly not — that they considered inflation to be desirable; instead, it was the pressure of forces they could not control, and the resistances encountered when other, possibly more sensible solutions were essayed, that led finally to the expansion of the money supply. I believe that the three indicators used here go at least one important step behind pure monetary expansion in seeking the deeper roots of inflation, and they do so in a way that is both: a) quantifiable, and b) broadly comparable as one moves from country to country.

First, we must define the variables. They are thought of as being policy variables that have in some sense equal (or nearly equal) validity, regardless of what exchange rate regime a country has. Obviously the public sector can refrain from pumping new credits from the banking system (β) under any exchange rate system. So, too, can it determine (over time at least) whether the accumulated volume of such credits will be large or small as a percentage (γ) of the total volume of outstanding bank credit. Finally, even though the money supply is either totally or largely an endogenous variable under many exchange rate systems (fixed exchange rate, pre-fixed crawling peg — the *tablita* of the Southern Cone countries, ordinary crawling peg, etc.), the volume of domestic credit is subject to fairly wide policy control, with expansions in credit under the indicated exchange rate regimes being largely bought at the cost of reductions in international reserves. Thus, the rate of expansion of domestic credit (λ) is subject to a degree of policy control that under many exchange rate regimes is quite a bit greater than the degree of control that the authorities can exercise over the rate of expansion of the money supply.

Explicit definitions of the three variables follow:

β = net increase, during the year, of banking system credit to the public sector, expressed as a percentage of the year's GDP. Thus, if the public sector's borrowings from the banking system stood at 200 at the beginning of the year, and went to 300 by year's end, the net increase would be 100. If GDP of the year were 800, then β would be 0.125 (= 100/800).

γ = fraction of total banking system credit going to the public sector. Thus, if at the beginning of the year total bank credit were 400, and if at the end it were 500, then (using public sector credit figures from above) γ would be 0.50 (= 200/400) at the beginning of the year and 0.60 (= 300/500) at the end. In the tables presented in this paper γ is always measured from end-of-year data. Whenever the public sector is a net lender to the banking system, γ is simply recorded as < 0.

λ = percentage increase during the year in total domestic credit of the banking system. This, with the figures just presented, would be 25 percent [= (500/400) - 1] $\times$ 100.

Tables 15.5 and 15.6 summarize the data on the listed countries for two spans of years. Table 15.5 replicates the results of my earlier paper (with the addition of Taiwan, which was not covered there). Table 15.6 uses the additional data that are available at the time of this writing (April, 1996). These tables give for each indicator for a country in a period, the median value of that indicator, over the years spanned by the period. This obviously eliminates extreme observations and at the same time has a very reasonable claim to be a "representative year's observation," half the years showing larger and half showing smaller values. In this same sense, when we try to summarize the behavior of the countries in a group, we present the median value of each indicator within that set of countries.

It is easy to see, from Table 15.5, that "high" observations on β, γ, and λ are much more frequent among the Latin American than among the East Asian countries, in a sense that is only mildly reflected in the overall group medians. The differences in group medians are sharper for the single year, 1983, as one might reasonably expect.

Table 15.5 Policy Indicators (1979–83)

	Median year, 1979-83			Latest year (1983)		
	Δ Govt credit/ GDP β	Govt credit/ Total credit γ	% Change/ bank credit λ	Δ Govt credit/ GDP β	Govt credit/ Total credit γ	% Change/ bank credit λ
Latin America						
Southern Cone						
Argentina	0.017	0.072	209.3	0.027	0.051	400.8
Brazil	0.026	0.164	83.7	0.115	0.450	178.0
Chile	0.019	0.094	47.2	0.019	0.094	10.9
Paraguay	0.005	<0	25.6	0.005	0.011	25.6
Uruguay	0.012	0.034	72.4	0.127	0.252	29.6
Andean Group						
Colombia	0.003	<0	38.3	0.017	0.148	38.3
Ecuador	0.006	<0	37.1	0.015	<0	59.1
Peru	0.028	0.410	16.4	0.104	0.440	164.6
Venezuela	0.011	<0	20.5	0.002	<0	6.2
Central America and Caribbean						
Costa Rica 1/	0.060	0.362	30.2	0.080	0.422	24.3
Dominican Republic	0.031	0.364	18.1	0.031	0.426	16.6
Honduras	0.026	0.262	15.6	0.022	0.320	17.8
Mexico	0.062	0.482	49.5	0.093	0.665	56.0
Median	0.019	0.094	37.1	0.027	0.252	29.6
East Asia						
Taiwan	0.033	0.222	18.5	0.002	0.216	15.9
Korea, Republic of	0.014	0.113	29.4	0.003	0.113	16.0
Singapore	<0	<0	42.5	0.092	<0	42.5
Indonesia	<0	<0	18.7	<0	<0	18.7
Malaysia	0.025	0.081	22.9	<0	0.098	16.1
Philippines	0.012	0.160	24.6	0.026	0.216	30.0
Thailand	0.023	0.264	18.1	0.016	0.264	26.3
Median	0.014	0.113	22.9	0.003	0.113	18.7

1/ Costa Rica's figures are for 1979–80 and 1980.
Sources: IMF, *International Financial Statistics*. For Taiwan, *Statistical Yearbook of the Republic of China*.

Table 15.6   Policy Indicators (1983–93)

	Median year, 1983-93			Latest year (1993)		
	Δ Govt credit/ GDP β	Govt credit/ Total credit γ	% Change/ bank credit λ	Δ Govt credit/ GDP β	Govt credit/ Total credit γ	% Change/ bank credit λ
Latin America						
Southern Cone						
Argentina 1/	0.038	0.391	84.0	0.009	0.299	20.5
Brazil	0.452	0.519	437.1	0.628	0.441	2665.1
Chile	0.053	0.341	20.3	0.009	0.196	24.3
Paraguay	0.009	0.219	29.7	0.011	0.264	30.3
Uruguay	0.055	0.254	59.5	0.019	0.195	43.3
Andean Group						
Colombia 2/	0.003	0.168	37.7	0.003	0.026	50.1
Ecuador 3/	0.006	0.141	38.1	0.003	0.154	46.1
Peru	0.045	0.318	146.4	0.003	0.115	77.9
Venezuela	0.010	0.057	27.0	0.045	0.317	35.9
Central America and Caribbean						
Costa Rica	0.018	0.474	19.2	<0	0.263	23.8
Dominican Republic	<0	0.273	16.2	<0	<0	15.7
Honduras	0.015	0.316	12.7	0.022	0.218	19.8
Mexico	0.057	0.615	51.3	<0	0.014	11.5
Median	0.018	0.316	37.7	0.009	0.196	30.3
East Asia						
Taiwan	0.005	0.153	17.5	0.041	0.152	19.1
Korea, Republic of	0.002	0.035	16.0	<0	0.017	12.7
Singapore	<0	<0	10.0	<0	<0	12.0
Indonesia 3/	0.002	<0	34.3	<0	<0	8.0
Malaysia	0.007	0.048	16.1	0.010	0.045	12.3
Philippines	0.005	0.182	6.2	0.180	0.387	131.2
Thailand	<0	0.141	17.8	<0	<0	22.7
Median	0.002	0.048	16.1	<0	0.017	12.7

1/ For Argentina the period is 1983–84 and 1990–93 for Domestic Credit. 2/ Colombia data does not include observations for 1986 and 1989. 3/ Period of 1983–92.
Sources: IMF, *International Financial Statistics*. For Taiwan, *Statistical Yearbook of the Republic of China.*

When we turn to Table 15.6, we find sharper differences than for the earlier period, both for the case where we work with period medians for the individual countries and for the case where we use indicators from the most recent year (here 1993). The conclusion toward which we are driving is that there has indeed been a perceptible difference in policy behavior between these two groups of countries.

Looking for a way to express the degree of "policy difference" among the regions, I gravitated toward $\chi 2$ as a simple and very attractive measure. Setting up the data in a contingency table framework, one can compare observed with expected frequencies and thus assess the likelihood that these were drawings from populations with similar overall probabilities.

Table 15.7 presents the $\chi 2$ test from my earlier paper. Note that the distributions of β were still within such bounds that they might have come from the same population, while those of γ and λ were more clearly distinct, as between Latin America and East Asia.

All in all, I find this exercise to be a convincing demonstration that economic policy was indeed quite different in the Latin American countries from that in East Asia, that the difference took the form of the East Asians being more prudent, and the Latin Americans being more prone to risky policies. Moreover, as is the case with most aberrant behavior in this world, risky policies are not an everyday event in Latin America. Policy behavior there tends to be quite "normal" most of the time; it only goes awry intermittently, but I believe this occurs at great cost to the people of the countries concerned.

When we speak of policy behavior, I believe we have to introduce a moral tone into our pronouncements. Most policy mistakes, in my view, reflect a weakness of will, a lack of spine and discipline, a drift into taking "the easy way out." Simple rules, like "the government should *never* borrow from the banking system" or that "bank credit should never expand at more than 20% per year" are surely good rules on the whole, but they are hard to implant and maintain. The trouble is, one can point to too many cases where these rules are flouted with apparent impunity. (Even noble Singapore nearly doubled total domestic bank credit in 1981.)

Though simple rules are not a bad idea, what is more urgently needed is a general sense of discipline in economic policy. The consequences should be surveyed before policy actions are taken; precedent-setting moves should be treated with particular caution. Above all, one must never lose sight of the absolute truth that the potential line of claimants on the public purse is endless. Bad policy, by caving in to some dubious claims, quite naturally invites others. It is an integral part of good policy to discourage pressures and claims, and to prevent all but the most meritorious from getting very far.

A vital part of this message is that economic policy is made by people, and that the personal force and strength of character of particular individuals can and do make a difference. Forty years of observation in Latin America has provided me with a small firmament of heroes of economic policymaking — individuals who provided leadership that enabled their countries to emerge from a profound crisis (Roberto Campos in Brazil), to turn around a situation of stagnation or retrogression (Alejandro Vegh Villegas in Uruguay), or simply to run a well-tuned policy machine for year after year in a most responsible fashion (Rodrigo Gomez and Antonio

Table 15.7   Distribution of Policy Variables (number of observations in interval)

Period 1979-83

	Interval of β					
Group	Below zero		0 to 0.04		Over 0.04	Total
a .	β = (Change in Bank credit to government)/ GDP					
Latin America	12	19%	37	59%	14	22%	63
East Asia	9	26%	22	63%	4	11%	35
Total	21		59		18		98

$\chi 2 (2)=1.96$ $[\chi 2 (2)=4.61]$
                                         0.10

	Interval of γ					
Group	Below zero		0 to 0.4		Over 0.4	Total
b.	γ = (Bank credit to government)/ Total Bank Credit					
Latin America	17	27%	35	56%	11	17%	63
East Asia	11	31%	24	69%	0	0%	35
Total	28		59		11		98

$\chi 2 (2)=6.90$ $[\chi 2 (2)=5.99]$
                                         0.05

	Interval of λ					
Group	Below 25%		25% to 50%		Over 50%	Total
c.	λ = % Increase in total bank credit					
Latin America	20	32%	21	33%	22	35%	63
East Asia	19	54%	13	37%	3	9%	35
Total	39		34		25		98

$\chi 2 (2)=9.09$ $[\chi 2 (2)=7.38]$
                                         0.025

Total $\chi 2 (6)=17.95$ $[\chi 2 (6)=16.81]$
                                         0.01

Source: IMF *Financial Statistics* and *Statistical Yearbook of the Republic of China.*

Ortiz Mena in Mexico, Jose Gil Diaz in Uruguay). There are others in that firmament in Latin America, and they certainly must have counterparts in the East Asian countries. Also, we should recognize that great performances entail not only the right man but also a reasonably receptive environment. Thus for every star that made it into my firmament, there are probably several others who might have been there had they been placed in a somewhat more receptive or favorable setting (which often means, had the crisis been more unbearable when they came on the scene, or had a different president been in office). Obviously history is the result of both individuals and "forces": I emphasize individuals mainly because that is something that we ourselves, the profession of economists, can do something about.

One of the virtues of the $\chi 2$ test is its additivity, so it is also easy to test the homogeneity of the two regions by all three criteria, taken together. In this test homogeneity is rejected at a one percent level of significance.

In approaching a similar test for the later period, I was quite prepared to find that the two regions had moved closer together. Perhaps this is because of my very close observation of the Chilean scene, where the policy indicators indeed more closely approximate those of the East Asian countries. But whatever may have been my earlier thoughts, I was shocked to find that the differences between Latin America and East Asia had become, by these measures, more clear as one moved from the earlier to the more recent period. Now (in the more recent period) all the indicators show differences that are significant as well below the .01 level, and for the joint test of full homogeneity (so far as all three indicators are concerned), the results are simply off all the charts. One in a million is a conservative estimate of the relevant probability in this case (see Table 15.8).

15.4 Real Exchange Rate Volatility

While the preceding section focused on policy weaknesses, the present one concentrates on what I consider to be somewhat adverse objective circumstances faced by a number of Latin American economies. These circumstances have their symptoms in a high degree of real exchange rate volatility, which we here attempt to document.

The concept of the real exchange rate is a tricky one, to which different authors ascribe different meanings. My thinking about the subject runs as follows. In theoretical expositions, where world prices are taken as given, the real exchange rate is the nominal exchange rate (peso price of the dollar) deflated by a general price index of the (small) country in question. This real exchange rate equilibrates the supply and demand for foreign currency, measured, of course, in foreign currency units (dollars' worth). Movements of this real exchange rate ($E/\bar{p}_d$) can occur through movements of the nominal exchange rate (E) such as would occur under a flexible exchange rate regime, or through movements of the general level of internal prices and costs ($\bar{p}_d$), such as occur under fixed exchange rates. This much is needed to establish the equivalence of real comparative-statics results under alternative exchange rate systems, and is as far as we need to go to obtain a definition of the real exchange rate for theoretical purposes.

For empirical purposes, however, a further step is necessary. World prices do not stay quietly in the pound of *ceteris paribus* as the clock and calendar move on. The dollar's worth of one year is not the same as that of another, and empirical work that traces movements of the real exchange rate through time must recognize this by defining, in a sense, the basket of goods whose prices we call a real dollar. There are reasons why this basket should in principle be a basket of tradable goods, and equal-

Table 15.8   Distribution of policy variables (number of observations in interval)

Period 1983-93

		Interval of	β			
Group		Below zero		0 to 0.04		Over 0.04	Total

a. β = (Change in Bank credit to government)/ GDP

Group	Below zero		0 to 0.04		Over 0.04		Total
Latin America	32	24%	54	41%	46	35%	132
East Asia	33	43%	35	46%	8	11%	76
Total	65		89		54		208

$\chi 2 (2)=16.97$ [$\chi 2 (2)=10.60$]
                                                          0.005

Group	Below zero		0 to 0.4		Over 0.4		Total

b. γ = (Bank credit to government)/ Total Bank Credit

Group	Below zero		0 to 0.4		Over 0.4		Total
Latin America	6	5%	91	69%	35	27%	132
East Asia	25	38%	40	62%	0	0%	65
Total	31		131		35		197

$\chi 2 (2)=46.18$ [$\chi 2 (2)=10.60$]
                                                          0.005

Group	Below 25%		25% to 50%		Over 50%		Total

c. λ = % Increase in total bank credit

Group	Below 25%		25% to 50%		Over 50%		Total
Latin America	54	41%	28	21%	50	38%	132
East Asia	53	82%	10	15%	2	3%	65
Total	107		38		52		197

$\chi 2 (2)=38.69$ [$\chi 2 (2)=10.60$]
                                                          0.005

Total $\chi 2 (6)=101.84$ [$\chi 2 (6)=18.55$]
                                                          0.005

Source: IMF *Financial Statistics* and *Statistical Yearbook of the Republic of China.*

ly good reasons why the deflating index $\bar{p}_d$ should include non-tradable goods. These considerations have led to a modest drift toward a consensus that the real exchange rate should be defined as $\bar{p}_d^* E/\bar{p}_d$, where $\bar{p}_d^*$ is a world index of wholesale prices and $\bar{p}_d$ is a domestic index of general prices (consumer price index (CPI) or GDP deflator).

I have followed this convention here. In every case the nominal exchange rate E is the local-currency (peso) price of the U.S. dollar and the deflating index $\bar{p}_d$ is the local consumer price index. There are two alternative dollar price indexes $\bar{p}_d$. The first is simply the United States wholesale price index (WPI) which in effect defines the United States WPI basket as the one whose relative price is being measured by the real exchange rate. Alternatively, a multi-national WPI is constructed, using the weights that were used to define the special drawing rights (SDR) beginning in January 1981.[2] The weights are applied to each non-dollar WPI, and converted into dollars at the prevailing exchange rate between that currency and the U.S. dollar. The result is an index of the dollar[3] price level of a basket of goods consisting of the WPI baskets of five major nations.

Table 15.9   Range of Real Exchange Rate Variation 1970–83 (high observation of period/low observation of period)

	Annual observations, 1970-83		Quarterly observations, 1980-83	
	US WPI*(E/pd)	SDR WPI*(E/pd)	US WPI*(E/pd)	SDR WPI*(E/pd)
		Latin America		
Southern Cone				
Argentina	2.90	2.68	4.62	3.98
Brazil	1.92	1.70	1.55	1.49
Chile	1.97	1.74	1.79	1.53
Paraguay	1.72	1.81	1.65	1.60
Uruguay	1.86	1.74	2.15	2.01
Andean Group				
Colombia	1.33	1.45	1.20	1.32
Ecuador	1.33	1.34	1.28	1.22
Peru	1.60	1.71	1.29	1.19
Venezuela	1.34	1.51	1.67	1.73
Central America and Caribbean				
Costa Rica	2.81	2.55	2.81	2.53
Dominican Republic	1.21	1.39	1.21	1.39
Honduras	1.21	1.47	1.21	1.47
Mexico	1.55	1.47	1.81	1.72
Median	1.60	1.71	1.65	1.53
		East Asia		
Taiwan	1.27	1.34	1.09	1.22
Korea, Republic of	1.28	1.35	1.19	1.19
Singapore	1.34	1.27	1.07	1.29
Indonesia	1.78	1.44	1.35	1.31
Malaysia	1.22	1.22	1.13	1.28
Philippines	1.24	1.20	1.46	1.36
Thailand	1.10	1.19	1.14	1.23
Median	1.27	1.27	1.14	1.28

E = nominal exchange rate in local currency units per dollar. pd = local consumer price index.
Sources: IMF, *International Financial Statistics*. For Taiwan, *Statistical Yearbook of the Republic of China* and *Monthly Bulletin of Statistics of the Republic of China*.

Table 15.9 is taken from my earlier study and presents ranges of real exchange rate variations for thirteen Latin American and six East Asian countries. The first two columns take as their basic observations the annual average nominal exchange rates adjusted by annual average price levels. The figures presented are the ratios of the highest real exchange rate to the lowest real exchange rate observed over the span of years 1970-83. The last two columns concentrate on quarterly rather than annual observations, and deal with the period 1980-83. Again, the figures recorded represent, for each country, the ratio of the highest quarterly real exchange rate to the lowest quarterly real exchange rate recorded during this period.

The differences in the range of variation between the two groups of countries is quite clear. In the annual comparisons only Indonesia among the East Asian nations shows a range of more than 1.4, while for the Latin American countries only five out of thirteen have less than this range when the United States WPI is used and only two out of thirteen have less than this range when the SDR WPI is used. In the quarterly data for 1980-83 only the United States WPI observation for the Philippines has a range of more than 1.4, while eight (col. 3) or nine (col. 4) of the Latin American countries exhibit a wider range than this.

Table 15.10 is similar to Table 15.9, but shows ranges of real exchange rate variation for more recent periods, with the annual data referring to 1984-94 and the quarterly data to the period 1990-94. For my taste, there is little to choose between Tables 15.9 and 15.10, when it comes to drawing inferences. The nuances of difference that we detect between the two tables are far outweighed by the message that is common to both of them, namely, that real-exchange-rate volatility is significantly greater in Latin America than in East Asia (once again making an exception for the Philippines).

There are various reasons why real exchange rates might be more volatile in one place than in another, but they can easily be grouped into two broad categories: reasons why the demand and supply of foreign exchange might themselves be more volatile (e.g., world prices of principal export products are more variable for some countries than for others); and reasons why a given percentage shift of the demand or supply of foreign exchange would cause a greater change in the equilibrium real exchange rate. Here I shall focus on the latter, and within it on the elasticity of supply of tradable goods.

To me, one of the biggest dividends that was produced by looking at the equilibrium real exchange rate as equilibrating the demand and supply of tradables rather than (or actually in addition to and simultaneously with) equilibrating the demand for imports and the supply of exports is the light shed by this more aggregative focus on the so-called "elasticities problem." The trouble is, the demand for imports is typically an excess demand function; so, likewise, is the supply of exports an excess supply function. Their elasticities are complex multiples of the component elasticities of total domestic demand and supply for importables in the one case and exportables in the other. When excess demand or supply is involved these elasticities will themselves be volatile, depending critically on the proportion of total demand that is met by imports or the proportion of total supply that is exported. Partly for this reason, these trade elasticities have been incredibly difficult to estimate empirically for use in practical work.

Table 15.10 Range of Real Exchange Rate Variation 1984–94 (high observation of period/low observation of period)

	Annual observations, 1984-94		Quarterly observations, 1990-94	
	US WPI*(E/pd)	SDR WPI*(E/pd)	US WPI*(E/pd)	SDR WPI*(E/pd)
		Latin America		
Southern Cone				
Argentina	3.73	3.46	3.22	3.07
Brazil	3.00	2.34	1.89	1.85
Chile	1.41	1.52	1.36	1.27
Paraguay	1.85	2.21	1.52	1.40
Uruguay	2.34	1.80	1.86	1.72
Andean Group				
Colombia	1.48	1.85	1.59	1.56
Ecuador	1.89	2.37	1.48	1.46
Peru	4.68	3.61	1.70	1.81
Venezuela	1.57	1.85	1.33	1.31
Central America and Caribbean				
Costa Rica	1.20	1.26	1.18	1.16
Dominican Republic	2.50	3.18	1.24	1.20
Honduras	1.86	2.14	1.87	2.00
Mexico	1.94	1.88	1.44	1.44
Median	1.89	2.14	1.52	1.46
		East Asia		
Taiwan	1.68	1.30	1.19	1.21
Korea, Republic of	1.56	1.33	1.13	1.14
Singapore	1.47	1.36	1.37	1.26
Indonesia	1.34	1.69	1.17	1.20
Malaysia	1.18	1.48	1.24	1.23
Philippines	1.48	1.34	1.59	1.56
Thailand	1.34	1.27	1.22	1.18
Median	1.47	1.34	1.22	1.21

E = nominal exchange rate in local currency units per dollar. pd = local consumer price index.

Sources: IMF, *International Financial Statistics.* For Taiwan, *Statistical Yearbook of the Republic of China* and *Monthly Bulletin of Statistics of the Republic of China.*

In comparison, the elasticities of demand for and supply of tradables are easy to deal with. The demand for tradables is that for a very large composite commodity, whose elasticity virtually has to be low. I think of tradables as being on the whole manufactures plus agricultural products, and of non-tradables as being predominantly public utilities, transport and services. An elasticity of substitution of 0.5 between them is not an excessively low guess. This would imply own-price elasticities of about 0.25 for tradables and for non-tradables, assuming that the two groups have about equal weight in total expenditures.[4] Just as I was always troubled by uncertainty concerning the old-fashioned trade elasticities, so now I am extremely confident that demand elasticities for the broad categories of tradables and non-tradables are quite low. (Whether they are 0.15 or 0.40 hardly makes much difference in most uses to which they are put.) Thus, if these low elasticities of demand for tradables can be put to fruitful use to solve problems whose answers were obscured by the penumbra surrounding the traditional trade elasticities, the profession will have received a great boon. I believe that this is the case.

If the demand elasticity for tradables is low everywhere, this means that the volatility of the real exchange rate in response to given percentage shifts of demand or supply will depend on the elasticity supply of tradables. My hypothesis is that this elasticity is low in countries like Chile, Argentina and Uruguay and high in countries like the Republic of Korea, Taiwan, Singapore and Hong Kong. Once again the concept of total supply versus excess supply comes to our rescue. We are not asking about how the supply of exports of Argentine wheat will change in response to a rise in its price. We are asking instead how the total supply of all agricultural goods will respond to a rise in all of their prices relative to non-tradables. Wheat supply can be expanded by constricting the planting of maize and sunflowers, but the total supply of agricultural products from the pampas is not going to be equally responsive. On the whole, we can say that the total output of the agricultural and mining sectors is likely to be quite inelastic and that the elasticity of the overall supply of tradables will depend largely on the relative importance of agriculture and mining.

Countries concentrated in manufacturing have a much greater capacity for rapid expansion of production of tradables in response to real exchange rate changes. True, it is more expensive in most cases for a factory to work multiple shifts than single shifts, but the premium required in order to make it worthwhile to add a second or third shift is typically not huge. Moreover, over a longer range, capital equipment can add almost indefinitely to manufacturing capacity, something that is not true of agriculture and mining.

In my earlier paper, I attempted to pursue the above hypothesis by constructing a very rudimentary model of a small-country economy producing "tradable goods" and "home goods." Using exactly the same model, but with a different parameter values for the two countries, I created a dynamic simulation of a "debt crisis" situation in which the net resource transfer into a country falls from 10 percent of GDP to zero. This is almost exactly the size of the fall that took place in Chile between 1981 and 1982. Most people are surprised to learn that Korea suffered a sharp drop in net resource transfer about the same time. They are surprised because the Korean economy bounced back so fast that many casual outside observers hardly noticed.

I am here reproducing just a single figure from the earlier paper. It traces the movement of the real exchange rate in Figure 15.1a and of the level of real output in the economy in Figure 15.1b. Those familiar with the relevant history in the two countries will recognize that this simulation is indeed capturing the "big picture" differences that characterized their respective responses to the drop in net resource transfer that each experienced in the early 1980s.

Now the question arises, what were the main differences in assumed parameters that caused such dramatically different trajectories to emerge? The principal differences were: a) in the long-run elasticity of supply of tradables (assumed to be equal to 4 for Korea, but only to 1 for Chile); and b) in the speed of adjustment of supply to price changes (for Korea, the full adjustment was spread evenly over four periods; for Chile, over ten periods). This latter was a reflection of what I call the "hot stove effect"; Chilean entrepreneurs had lived through so much real exchange rate volatility that they did not quickly "believe" that any given change would last.

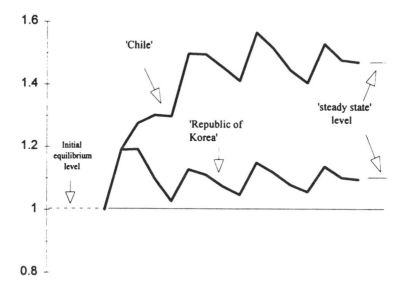

Figure 15.1a   Trajectory of Pt/Pn: Simulation of Response to Debt Crisis (plus copper shock and monetary adjustment for 'Chile')

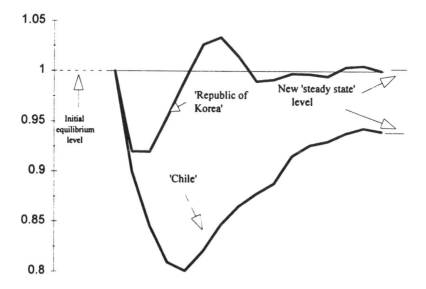

Figure 15.1b   Trajectory of Real Output: Simulation of Response to Debt Crisis (plus copper shock and monetary adjustment for 'Chile')

In addition to the above parameter changes I made an adjustment: c) that reflected the contemporaneous fall in world copper prices, amounting to an autonomous reduction in export proceeds equal to 6 percent of GDP, spread over three periods, plus a gradual reduction, d) of the Chilean demand for real money balances from 25 percent of GDP in the beginning to 15 percent of GDP in the end. This accords with what actually happened in Chile between 1981 and 1984.

The picture traced for "Chile" in Figures 15.1a and 15.1b is quite similar to the actual record. Between 1981 and 1982 real output fell by 14 percent, followed by nearly another percentage point drop from 1982 and 1983. Only in 1984 did GDP bounce back a bit, with about 6 percent real growth, but it remained far below its previous peaks until near the end of the decade. Similarly, Chile's real exchange rate in 1983 (calculated using the SDR WPI) reached a level 50 percent above its level of the third quarter of 1981; in this respect the trajectory of Figure 15.1a is quite faithful to reality.

By way of contrast, the Republic of Korea passed from a current account surplus in 1977 to a deficit of over $4 billion in 1979 and 1981, and of over $5 billion in 1980, before pulling back to a more sustainable deficit level of $1.6 billion in 1983 (Chile's deficit hit nearly $5 billion in 1981 and was back to $1 billion by 1983). But while Chile's travail was great, the Republic of Korea came off with hardly a ripple in its GDP — a fall of 3 percent in 1981 followed by growth of 6.9 percent in 1982 and 5.5 percent in 1983 — and with a real exchange rate that actually appreciated by about 10 percent *vis-à-vis* the SDR while depreciating by a similar amount *vis-à-vis* the U.S. dollar.

Some of Chile's trajectory can be traced to policy mistakes, particularly in delaying until June 1982 a policy response to a crisis that began to be perceived already in late 1981. However, certainly in terms of its overall adjustment to the debt crisis and the contemporaneous fall in copper prices, Chile gets far better marks than most of its neighbors, which highlights the principal point of the simulation exercise, that objective circumstances may cause economies like Chile's to have to pass through painful adjustments that far exceed those required by the objective circumstances of luckier economies like the Republic of Korea's.

15.5 The Sources of Growth

In this section I examine the breakdown of each country's growth rate into its familiar component parts — a contribution due to increased labor input, a contribution due to increased capital input, and a contribution (the residual) representing the percentage change in output due to changes in total factor productivity. Each country's history is broken up into periods that are, where possible, 5 years in length, and the growth rate is broken down into its component parts for each such quinquennium. This is done in Table 15.11 for Taiwan, Japan, Korea, and Thailand, and in Table 15.12 for Colombia, Costa Rica, Ecuador, Mexico, Panama, Peru and Venezuela.

Table 15.11 Rates of Return and Sources of Growth, Selected Asian Countries

a. TAIWAN

Period	Net Rate of Return	GDP Growth	Labor Contribution	Capital Contribution	Residual
1960-64	20.27%	9.08%	1.58%	3.49%	4.02%
1964-69	20.55%	9.76%	0.93%	4.85%	3.97%
1969-74	20.80%	10.27%	1.26%	6.15%	2.86%
1974-79	15.54%	10.31%	1.02%	4.75%	4.53%
1979-84	13.20%	7.21%	1.63%	3.34%	2.25%
1984-89	15.94%	9.08%	0.86%	2.77%	5.44%
1989-94	14.44%	6.51%	0.95%	3.13%	2.43%

b. JAPAN

Period	Net Rate of Return	GDP Growth	Labor Contribution	Capital Contribution	Residual
1960-64	19.61%	10.26%	0.43%	8.02%	1.80%
1964-69	14.75%	10.63%	0.38%	5.75%	4.50%
1969-74	11.53%	5.99%	2.55%	4.49%	-1.06%
1974-79	6.13%	4.60%	1.32%	2.06%	1.22%
1979-84	6.01%	3.86%	0.45%	1.78%	1.63%
1984-88	5.88%	4.30%	0.28%	1.63%	2.39%

c. KOREA

Period	Net Rate of Return	GDP Growth	Labor Contribution	Capital Contribution	Residual
1960-64	26.89%	12.27%	0.59%	3.98%	7.71%
1964-69	26.36%	11.02%	2.01%	6.51%	2.49%
1969-74	21.76%	12.10%	0.46%	6.04%	5.61%
1974-79	22.26%	15.05%	1.35%	7.07%	6.63%
1979-84	13.52%	7.08%	1.85%	4.03%	1.20%
1984-88	12.90%	10.59%	0.86%	3.91%	5.83%

d. THAILAND

Period	Net Rate of Return	GDP Growth	Labor Contribution	Capital Contribution	Residual
1970-1974	16.38%	7.26%	1.21%	3.42%	2.63%
1974-1979	14.36%	7.95%	1.71%	3.62%	2.61%
1979-1984	12.62%	3.66%	0.60%	3.11%	-0.05%
1984-1989	14.07%	10.03%	0.17%	4.11%	5.75%
1989-1991	16.80%	9.88%	-0.70%	7.45%	3.13%

Table 15.12 Rates of Return and Sources of Growth, Selected Latin American Countries

a. COLOMBIA

Period	Net Rate of Return	GDP Growth	Labor Contribution	Capital Contribution	Residual
1960-64	11.86%	4.65%	2.02%	1.79%	0.83%
1964-69	11.77%	5.77%	1.80%	1.69%	2.28%
1969-74	13.54%	7.76%	1.37%	1.76%	4.63%
1974-79	13.86%	5.10%	1.96%	1.82%	1.32%
1979-84	11.33%	3.06%	1.52%	1.80%	-0.26%
1984-88	13.20%	6.77%	0.11%	1.92%	4.74%

b. COSTA RICA

Period	Net Rate of Return	GDP Growth	Labor Contribution	Capital Contribution	Residual
1960-64	8.61%	3.81%	2.25%	1.34%	0.95%
1964-69	9.34%	7.82%	1.97%	1.61%	4.24%
1969-74	10.16%	6.75%	1.12%	2.34%	3.29%
1974-79	10.99%	12.51%	2.11%	2.74%	7.66%
1979-84	8.73%	0.88%	0.96%	2.02%	-2.10%
1984-88	7.11%	4.39%	2.18%	1.80%	0.41%
1988-92	5.99%	4.50%	-0.43%	1.67%	3.26%

c. ECUADOR

Period	Net Rate of Return	GDP Growth	Labor Contribution	Capital Contribution	Residual
1960-64	12.40%	3.72%	1.97%	1.36%	0.39%
1964-69	12.02%	4.49%	2.13%	1.46%	0.90%
1969-74	15.19%	12.51%	0.12%	2.55%	9.84%
1974-79	17.54%	7.43%	2.09%	4.16%	1.18%
1979-84	15.06%	3.37%	0.80%	2.98%	-0.41%
1984-88	13.86%	4.37%	2.10%	1.96%	0.31%

Table 15.12   (Continued)

d. MEXICO

Period	Net Rate of Return	GDP Growth	Labor Contribution	Capital Contribution	Residual
1960-64	20.53%	7.45%	1.86%	2.94%	2.66%
1964-69	20.26%	7.42%	1.93%	3.46%	2.02%
1969-74	20.00%	8.06%	2.23%	3.30%	2.53%
1974-79	17.32%	7.42%	1.87%	3.57%	1.98%
1979-84	16.87%	2.06%	-0.40%	3.55%	-1.09%
1984-88	13.51%	-1.52%	0.38%	1.63%	-3.54%
1988-92	14.81%	4.78%	0.26%	2.11%	2.41%

e. PANAMA

Period	Net Rate of Return	GDP Growth	Labor Contribution	Capital Contribution	Residual
1970-1974	10.59%	4.41%	2.91%	3.41%	-1.91%
1974-1979	7.29%	5.59%	0.98%	2.16%	2.45%
1979-1984	8.19%	4.59%	1.78%	1.92%	0.89%
1984-1989	6.63%	-0.06%	1.14%	0.25%	-1.45%
1989-1992	8.17%	7.58%	0.14%	1.22%	6.21%

f. PERU

Period	Net Rate of Return	GDP Growth	Labor Contribution	Capital Contribution	Residual
1970-1974	11.55%	5.32%	1.89%	1.48%	1.94%
1974-1979	11.59%	-0.11%	0.19%	1.19%	-1.49%
1979-1984	10.49%	2.19%	1.34%	1.81%	-0.97%
1984-1989	9.76%	0.80%	1.70%	1.62%	-2.52%

g. VENEZUELA

Period	Net Rate of Return	GDP Growth	Labor Contribution	Capital Contribution	Residual
1960-64	12.21%	8.55%	1.30%	1.17%	6.07%
1964-69	13.58%	3.93%	2.05%	2.26%	-0.37%
1969-74	14.39%	15.30%	0.51%	3.65%	11.14%
1974-79	13.19%	3.86%	3.67%	4.43%	-4.24%
1979-84	9.04%	2.64%	0.62%	1.35%	0.67%
1984-88	10.41%	0.33%	1.62%	1.21%	-2.50%

The underlying methodology is somewhat different from standard practice. Here we are using what I call the two-deflator approach. The first deflator of the two-deflator approach is a general *numeraire* price level. To my mind, there are only two plausible candidates for this role — one is the consumer price index, the other the GDP deflator. For the calculations reported here, we have used the GDP deflator. This differs from "standard" procedure in that the series on "real gross investment" used to construct the capital stock is obtained by dividing "nominal gross investment" by the GDP deflator, not by a separate deflator of capital goods.

This insight came from 30-odd years of experience in economic project evaluation. When we do an ex-post analysis of a project, we obviously have to do it in real terms. But nobody would ever think of deflating the negative flows representing investments by one deflator, and the positive flows representing the fruits of the project by another deflator. All is done in terms of a single numeraire. This is virtually essential in a proper measurement of the rate of return to capital, where the fruits of an investment should be expressed in the same units as the investment amounts.

Another important lesson from project evaluation is that one project's yield may come in the form of greater output, while another project's yield may come from changes in relative prices. Each of these sources of yield is equally valid from an economic point of view. Deflating all flows by the same numeraire (typically the CPI or the GDP deflator) is the natural and correct way to implement this lesson.

Needless to say, it is easy to implement this schema in growth analysis. The contribution of capital to NDP growth, $\rho\Delta K$, is if anything easier to identify and measure in this framework than in the traditional one. Why, then, did the traditional approach evolve, rather than this one? I can think of two main reasons: i) the traditional approach emerged out of a production function framework (in which it is natural to use different units for capital and for output) rather than a capital theory framework like ours, and ii) the traditional approach has tended to concentrate on the aggregate national level where changes in relative prices are much less important than at the sector, industry or firm level. One great advantage of the single-numeraire approach is that one can go down even to the firm level, knowing that one has a conceptually correct deflator. A production-function approach would have one forever asking, what is the right price index of capital goods for firm X, Y, or Z?

The second deflator of the two-deflator approach is a standard real wage w*. Ideally this would be the observed market wage of a category that is supposed to represent "raw labor," i.e., labor endowed with minimal human capital. For the present study we have used, as a proxy, a w* equal to 2/3 of the nation's real per capita GDP. This yields an annual income per worker which is quite similar to the annual earnings of menial labor in most countries. If now a given category of labor has a real wage wj, we simply say, under this approach, that one worker of type j is the equivalent of $w_j/w*$ standard workers. Since the total wages bill (in real terms) is $\Sigma_j\ w_{jt}L_{jt}$ at time t, this can be treated as consisting of L_t^* units of standard labor, earning a wage of w_t^*. In other words, L_t^* is defined as $\Sigma_j\ L_{jt}(w_{kt}/\ w_t^*)$. The medical doctor might count as 30 standard workers, the engineer as 18, the bilingual secretary as 8, each of these multiples simply reflecting the relative wage. The beauty of the two deflator approach is that we never have to know what is earned by doctors, engineers and secretaries. We simply take the total wages bill and divide it by w*. The resulting value of L* automatically values each worker at his/her own relative wage. In this respect we are getting infinite precision in correcting for the differential "quality" of different workers.

The contribution of labor to economic growth, in this framework, is measured simply by $w_0^* \Delta L^*$, where w_0^* is the beginning-of-period "standard" real wage. This in turn can be broken down into a part $w_0^* \Delta N$, due to the change in the "raw labor" component of the labor force (N is simply the number of workers), and $w_0^*(\Delta L^* - \Delta N)$, representing the contribution of "human capital." This breakdown of the overall labor contribution into its two main components is given in Table 15.13 for the Asian countries and in Table 15.14 for the Latin American ones.

The easiest way to present the results is by working through Figures 15.2 through 15.8. Each of these charts displays the calculated quinquennial figures for the country indicated at the left-hand axis. The Asian countries are displayed above the horizontal axis, the Latin American countries below it. The vertical dashed lines represent the first and third quartiles, the black dots the medians of the respective distributions (where there is an even number of observations, there are two black dots; the calculated median is simply the average of them). For easy reference, the numerical values of the medians and quartiles are given in the upper left (for Asia) and the lower right hand (for Latin America) corners of each table.

One of the results that flows quite naturally from the two-deflator approach is the rate of return to capital. Here, as distinct from the "standard" approach, it is a genuine rate of return, with the returns to capital being measured in the same units as the capital stock itself. It is quite clear from Figure 15.2 that the distribution of Asian rates of return lies considerably to the right of the Latin American one, though, for calculations at this level of aggregation, the Latin American one (median = 11.9 percent) is very respectable by international standards. Needless to say, a higher rate of return will contribute to a higher "capital contribution" to the growth rate, as, of course, will a higher rate of investment.

Figure 15.3 presents no surprises. The Asian countries represented here have a much better growth experience than the Latin countries, though once again the Latin American growth rate is not low by worldwide international standards.

Figure 15.4 seems reasonable enough, considering that Latin America has much higher population growth than the Asian countries considered. In this light its median labor contribution of 1.7 percent per annum seems to make sense, vis-à-vis a corresponding figure of 0.9 percent for the Asian countries.

Figure 15.5 tells us what we already know. If the Asian countries invest a greater fraction of their GDP, and get on that investment a higher rate of return, it follows that capital's contribution to the growth rate will be significantly higher — here 4.0 percent for the Asian countries versus 1.8 percent for the Latin American ones.

In Figure 15.6 we find great dispersion of the contribution of Total Factor Productivity (the "residual") in Latin America, but a notably higher average (a median of 2.7 percent) in Asia than in Latin America, where the median was 1.0 percent. This evidence seems to contradict some recent assertions that TFP growth

**Table 15.13   Contribution to Growth of Labor and Its Components, Selected
Asian Countries**

a. TAIWAN

	Contribution of Labor		
	Total Labor	Basic Labor	Human K
1960-64	1.58%	0.53%	1.05%
1964-69	0.93%	0.76%	0.17%
1969-74	1.26%	1.03%	0.24%
1974-79	1.02%	0.80%	0.22%
1979-84	1.63%	0.66%	0.96%
1984-89	0.86%	0.69%	0.18%
1989-94	0.95%	0.45%	0.50%

b. JAPAN

	Contribution of Labor		
	Total Labor	Basic Labor	Human K
1960-64	0.43%	0.39%	0.04%
1964-69	0.38%	0.51%	-0.14%
1969-74	2.55%	0.26%	2.29%
1974-79	1.32%	0.29%	1.02%
1979-84	0.45%	0.33%	0.12%
1984-88	0.28%	0.34%	-0.07%

c. KOREA

	Contribution of Labor		
	Total Labor	Basic Labor	Human K
1960-64	0.59%	0.33%	0.26%
1964-69	2.01%	0.77%	1.25%
1969-74	0.46%	0.93%	-0.47%
1974-79	1.35%	0.84%	0.51%
1979-84	1.85%	0.27%	1.58%
1984-88	0.86%	1.04%	-0.18%

d. THAILAND

	Contribution of Labor		
	Total Labor	Basic Labor[1]	Human K[1]
1970-1974	1.21%	0.28%	0.51%
1974-1979	1.71%	1.24%	0.47%
1979-1984	0.60%	1.36%	-0.77%
1984-1989	0.17%	1.80%	-1.64%
1989-1991	-0.70%	0.33%	-1.02%

[1] 1971-1974

Table 15.14   Contribution to Growth of Labor and Its Components, Selected Latin American Countries

a. COLOMBIA

	Contribution of Labor		
	Total Labor	Basic Labor	Human K
1960-64	2.02%	0.25%	1.78%
1964-69	1.80%	0.15%	1.64%
1969-74	1.37%	0.63%	0.74%
1974-79	1.96%	1.37%	0.59%
1979-84	1.52%	0.52%	1.00%
1984-88	0.11%	0.32%	-0.22%

b. COSTA RICA

	Contribution of Labor		
	Total Labor	Basic Labor	Human K
1960-64	2.25%	N/A	N/A
1964-69	1.97%	N/A	N/A
1969-74	1.12%	N/A	N/A
1974-79	2.11%	1.07%[1]	2.39%[1]
1979-84	0.96%	0.67%	0.29%
1984-88	2.18%	0.71%	1.47%
1988-92	-0.43%	0.44%	-0.88%

1/ 78-79

c. ECUADOR

	Contribution of Labor		
	Total Labor	Basic Labor	Human K
1960-64	1.97%	0.50%	1.48%
1964-69	2.13%	0.25%	1.88%
1969-74	0.12%	0.59%	-0.47%
1974-79	2.09%	0.85%	1.24%
1979-84	0.80%	-0.20%	1.01%
1984-88	2.10%	0.58%	1.52%

Table 15.14   (Continued)

d. MEXICO

	Contribution of Labor		
	Total Labor	Basic Labor	Human K
1960-64	1.86%	0.48%	1.38%
1964-69	1.93%	0.56%	1.37%
1969-74	2.23%	0.55%	1.68%
1974-79	1.87%	0.63%	1.24%
1979-84	-0.40%	0.72%	-1.12%
1984-88	0.38%	0.09%	0.29%
1988-92	0.26%	0.08%	0.18%

e. PANAMA

	Contribution of Labor		
	Total Labor	Basic Labor	Human K
1970-1974	2.91%	0.66%[1]	2.82%[1]
1974-1979	0.98%	0.29%	0.68%
1979-1984	1.78%	0.58%	1.20%
1984-1989	1.14%	0.45%	0.68%
1989-1992	0.14%	0.90%	-0.75%

[1] 1971-1974

f. PERU

	Contribution of Labor		
	Total Labor	Basic Labor	Human K
1970-1974	1.89%	0.64%[1]	1.42%[1]
1974-1979	0.19%	0.48%	-0.29%
1979-1984	1.34%	0.65%[2]	1.63%[2]
1984-1989	1.70%	0.20%[3]	0.99%[3]

[1] 71-74
[2] 80-81
[3] 87-89

g. VENEZUELA

	Contribution of Labor		
	Total Labor	Basic Labor	Human K
1960-64	1.30%	0.91%	0.40%
1964-69	2.05%	0.27%	1.78%
1969-74	0.51%	0.53%	-0.01%
1974-79	3.67%	0.82%	2.85%
1979-84	0.62%	0.70%	-0.08%
1984-88	1.62%	0.95%	0.67%

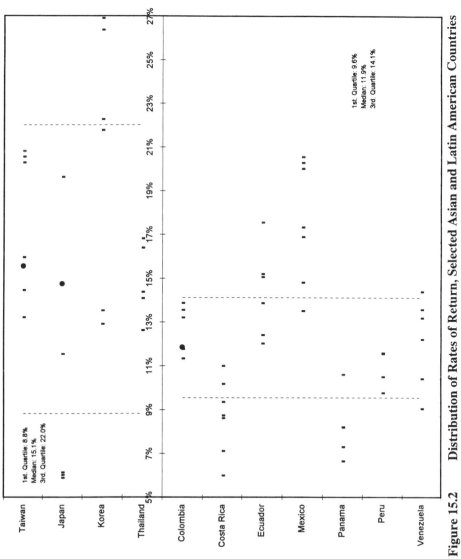

Figure 15.2   Distribution of Rates of Return, Selected Asian and Latin American Countries

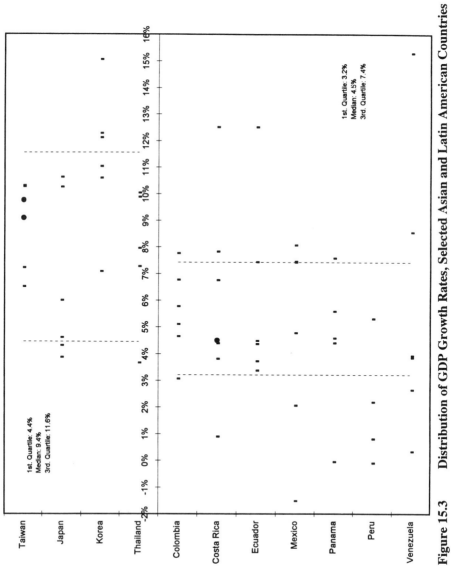

Figure 15.3   Distribution of GDP Growth Rates, Selected Asian and Latin American Countries

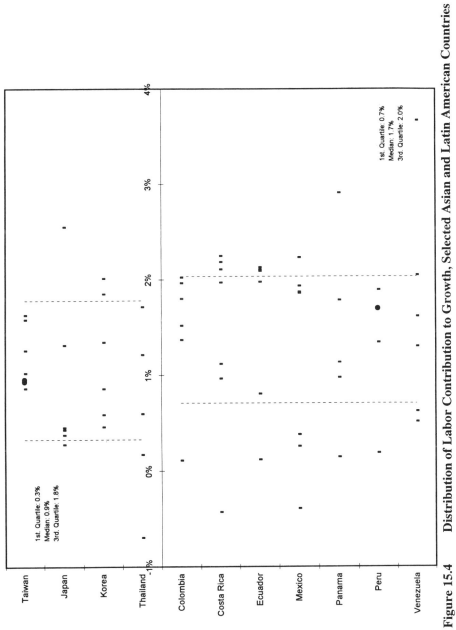

Figure 15.4   Distribution of Labor Contribution to Growth, Selected Asian and Latin American Countries

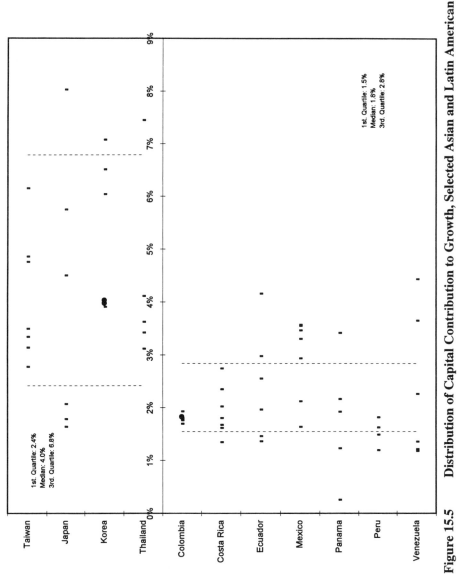

Figure 15.5   Distribution of Capital Contribution to Growth, Selected Asian and Latin American Countries

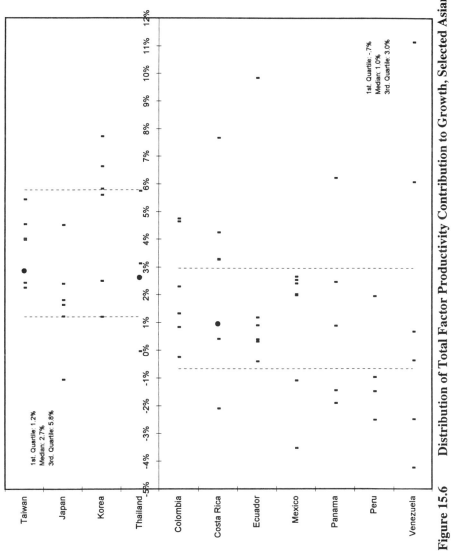

Figure 15.6   Distribution of Total Factor Productivity Contribution to Growth, Selected Asian and Latin American Countries

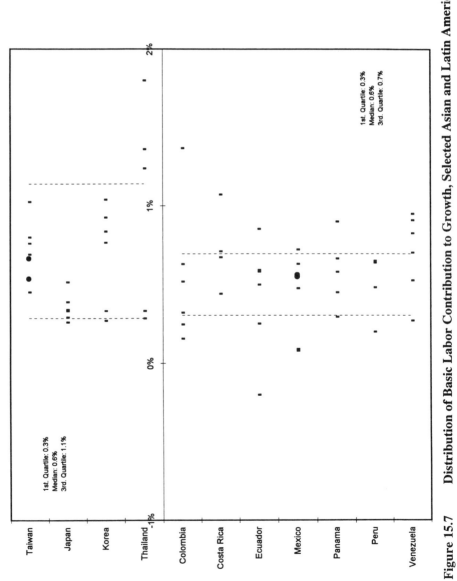

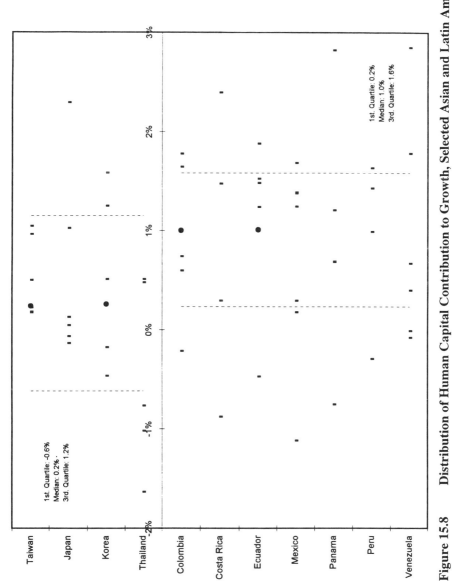

Figure 15.8   **Distribution of Human Capital Contribution to Growth, Selected Asian and Latin American Countries**

was not particularly high in the fast-growing Asian economies. These assertions certainly do not apply to our sample of results from the region.

Perhaps on this point it is worthwhile to turn to Tables 15.11 and 15.12, to see to what degree high overall growth rates are associated with high residuals. For Taiwan the five highest periodic growth rates of GDP span the five highest residuals, and the two lowest growth rates cover the two lowest residuals. In Korea the two highest growth rates accompany the two highest residuals, while the lowest growth rate (of 7.08 percent) is linked to the lowest residual (1.20 percent). In Thailand there is an almost perfect rank correlation between GDP growth rates and the residuals. Only in Japan does one find a very weak relationship between the periodic growth rate and the periodic residual.

In Latin America the relationship between GDP growth and the calculated residual is, if anything, stronger. In every country but Mexico, the highest residual is found in the same period as the highest growth rate, and in Mexico the same would be true, but for a few decimal points in the residual for 1969-74. In a similar vein, for five of the seven countries, the lowest residual appears in the same period as the lowest periodic growth rate.

This evidence supports the notion, which can be found in many other data sets, that the differences in the contribution of TFP are one of the biggest "explainers" of differences in growth rates. I continue to believe this statement to be broadly true (though it is an empirical generalization, not a theorem), and remain skeptical of assertions that it does not apply to the East Asian experiences.

Figure 15.7 brings a certain surprise, in that the medians for the contribution of raw labor for the Asian and the Latin American countries are essentially the same. I interpret this to mean that in spite of differences in population growth rates, the rates of increase of the labor force were roughly similar in the two regions.

Figure 15.8 is the most surprising of all, in that the contribution of human capital to growth turns out to be higher in Latin America than in the Asian countries surveyed. The answer, I suspect, lies in the narrowing of skill differentials that has occurred in East Asia. If educated workers averaged 10 standard units at the beginning of the period, and 9 standard units at the end, that difference would be reflected in a smaller increment ΔL^*, and with it a smaller contribution of human capital.

15.6 A Recapitulation

The messages emerging from this review of Latin American and East Asian experiences are not different in any major way from those that came out of a similar review a decade ago. Economic growth has been significantly more rapid in East Asia than in Latin America; it has been very strongly export-led, and has produced economies with a significantly higher concentration in manufactures than has emerged in Latin America. The East Asian economies have invested higher fractions of their GDP, and have been more successful than most Latin American countries in controlling inflation. When one looks behind these differences, one finds that the East Asian countries have exercised considerably more discipline in their macroeconomic policies, turning much less to the banking system to finance their governments, and at the same time maintaining significantly greater control over the expansion of total banking system credit. $\chi 2$ tests covering those dimensions of policy confirm that these differences in policy stance, as between the two regions, are genuine, with an extremely low probability of having emerged "by chance alone" from behavior patterns that were fundamentally similar.

But while some of the differences in observed results can be ascribed to differences in policy behavior, there are other respects in which objective circumstances probably play a major role. This is particularly true with respect to the rather dramatic difference, observed between the two regions, in the variability (over time) of the real exchange rates of individual countries. The East Asian countries exhibit remarkably low variability, while for the Latin American countries it is remarkably high. My hypothesis concerning this difference in variability is that it stems in considerable measure from the predominance of primary products in the structures of production and trade in the Latin American countries. This can generate greater variability of real exchange rates via the ups and downs of the world prices of key export products. But it also can generate greater variability because of the different ways in which the economies of the two regions respond to shifts of a given size in the demand or supply of foreign currency. To demonstrate how this might work, I summarize a simulation of how Korea and Chile might have responded to a major reduction in capital inflows (a "debt crisis"). I show that the very different real-world experience of Chile can have been generated by a much less elastic supply of tradable goods, together with a lower speed of response of tradables supply to relative price changes. These differences are highly plausible, given the much greater importance of agriculture and mining in the tradables production of Chile (and of the Latin American countries in general).

An analysis of the sources of economic growth reveals that the East Asian economies have a much higher rate of investment, together with a significantly higher rate of return to capital. These combine to produce a median contribution of capital to growth equal to an astounding four percent per annum (compared with less than two percent for Latin America). The other big difference is in the contribution of total factor productivity, whose median was 2.7 percent per year for the Asian countries studied here, while it was only one percent for the Latin American countries. These two factors, taken together, account for the great bulk of the observed differences in the median growth rates of the two groups of countries.

15.7 Notes

1   Arnold C. Harberger, "Growth, Industrialization, and Economic Structure: Latin America and East Asia Compared," in Helen Hughes, ed., *Achieving Industrialization in East Asia* (Cambridge: Cambridge University Press, 1988), pp. 164-94.

2   These weights are 0.42 for the U.S. dollar, 0.19 for the German mark, and 0.13 each for the French franc, the Japanese yen and the British pound.

3   It must be a dollar price index because the exchange rate is that between each given currency and the U.S. dollar. This price index would decrease, however, to reflect a depreciation of the nominal exchange rate of, say, the United Kingdom or Germany *vis a vis* the dollar.

4   For two mutually exclusive and exhaustive categories of goods, their compensated own-price elasticities of demand, summed together are equal in absolute value to the elasticity of substitution between them.

16 WHAT CAN SUB-SAHARAN AFRICA LEARN FROM THE TAIWANESE DEVELOPMENT EXPERIENCE?[1]

T. Ademola Oyejide

16.1   Introduction

Taiwan is one of the fastest growing countries in the world; its growth has been characterized by such desirable features as good income distribution and poverty alleviation, while the country's development process has been positively influenced not only by its initial conditions but also by its choice of development strategy and policies. By comparison, the Sub-Saharan Africa (SSA) region represents an example of development failure, which has been ascribed, in varying proportions, to such factors as its initial conditions, an unfavorable international environment, and questionable development strategies and policies. This juxtaposition of success and failure naturally gives rise to the question of whether SSA stands to gain by learning appropriate lessons from Taiwan on "best practice" strategies and policies for development. This is a question that has been asked in a growing list of studies, especially those relating the broad experience of Asia (or move specifically East Asia) to that of Africa (Winrock, 1991; Lindauer and Roemer, 1994; Thorbecke, 1994; Harrold et al., 1995).

What this paper seeks to accomplish has a narrower focus than what has been attempted in the literature cited above, in the specific sense of limiting the comparison of the African experience to the particular case of Taiwan. But while the base against which comparison is being made is narrow, the region for which lessons are being sought contains a large number of countries that probably have as many differences as they have similarities. Thus, a recent study (World Bank, 1995:

vii) concludes that "Sub-Saharan Africa in the mid-1990s represents a mosaic" and hence that "it is no longer possible, if it ever was, to talk of the continent as an undifferentiated whole." This is an important point to bear in mind throughout this analysis.

The rest of this paper is organized as follows. Section 16.2 concerns itself with a discussion of Taiwan's development experience, including an analysis of the role of initial conditions, development strategies and policies in the country's outstanding economic performance. In Section 16.3, the focus is on Sub-Saharan Africa and the aim is to relate initial conditions and domestic strategies and policies to the development outcome. Section 16.4 concludes the paper by suggesting areas in which lessons may be learned by Africa from the development experience of Taiwan, articulating what those lessons might be, and offering a broad development strategy for Africa that reflects these lessons.

16.2 The Taiwanese Development Experience

An analysis of Taiwan's spectacular economic performance since the 1950s that seeks not only to explain this performance, but also to draw lessons from this successful development experience, needs to relate it to both the initial conditions that set the stage for it and the development strategy and policies that facilitated and produced the performance. In the late 1940s, Taiwan was a small, labor-abundant, natural-resource poor but human-resource rich economy. It was shaped by a clear ethnic homogeneity further welded together by the realistic fear of a powerful external adversary (i.e. mainland China). Taiwan's endowment of human resources was significantly enriched by an educational system that stressed equality of access and opportunity and, in the process, achieved a relatively high level of literacy and a well educated population.

Another major legacy of colonialism was the development of infrastructure in rural Taiwan. Physical infrastructure took the form of roads, irrigation and drainage. These were complemented by a set of rural institutions (farmers' organizations, etc.) which assisted in disseminating knowledge regarding available labor-intensive agricultural technology and modern inputs, providing extension and credit services, and marketing farm inputs and outputs (Thorbecke, 1992). In this context, a series of land reform measures starting in 1905 led to a fairly equal distribution of land which, together with the development of rural infrastructures and institutions referred to above, subsequently promoted accelerated agricultural and rural development.

These initial conditions were, according to most observers, favorable for rapid economic growth in Taiwan, but more was needed. In the words of Park (1992: 82), "initial conditions are not automatically transmuted into good performance; policy is important." Hence, one must also examine Taiwan's development strategy and policies. In this connection, there is a general consensus in the literature regarding the role of a long-term perspective, shared by both government and society, in shaping Taiwan's development strategy and policies (Winrock, 1991). The broadly shared and constant vision of the importance of economic growth and development for the survival of both government and the state was implemented through a pragmatic strategy that reflected long-term considerations. This vision and its corresponding strategy were underpinned and facilitated by an enduring and stable political system; in combination, these elements generated basic stability in the focus and content of economic policy and in the general direction in which the economy and society were headed.

Taiwan's overall development strategy has emphasized the weaving together of three key strands: the maintenance of macroeconomic stability, the participation of a vibrant and active private sector, and the use of strategic and selective state intervention. These strands played complementary roles as the economy moved through a set of overlapping stages of development starting in the late 1940s, from agricultural commodity exports, through import substitution industrialization in the 1950s, to the export of increasingly sophisticated manufactures from the early 1960s.

On the macroeconomic front, the fear of inflation helped to keep fiscal deficits in check. The famous "19-points" structural reform package of the early 1960s included measures for achieving macroeconomic stabilization, as well as interest rate and exchange rate reforms which culminated in the unification of exchange rates and maintenance of a realistic exchange rate subsequently. Within the stable and favorable macroeconomic environment thus created, capital accumulation (generated primarily through the private sector) formed the most important source of economic growth in Taiwan (Kim and Lau, 1994). Gross domestic investment as a ratio of GDP almost doubled between 1965 and 1990 (Felix, 1994); Taiwan's extremely high rates of investment over this period were a reflection of high rates of *private* investment which were, in turn, derived from rapidly growing corporate profits and savings induced largely by government policies designated to promote corporate profits (Akyuz and Gore, 1994).

External sources of finance played a catalytic role in starting off Taiwan's rapid capital accumulation process. These sources were particularly important during the 1950s; they financed 45 percent of gross domestic investment between 1956 and 1960 (Akyuz and Gore, 1994). Capital inflows have remained important, although their relative contribution to Taiwan's capital accumulation has fallen substantially (Amsden, 1985). Thus, Akyus and Gore (1994: 5) conclude: "however important the initial role of foreign savings...without lifting domestic savings it would not have been possible to achieve impressive and sustained increases in investment rates from the 1960s to the 1990s." Domestic savings in fact responded vigorously. Gross domestic savings as a ratio of GDP, which averaged 9 percent during 1956-60, more than doubled during 1965-90; the ratio has averaged 30-32 percent during the late 1980s and early 1990s.

The private sector has been an important partner in Taiwan's development process and a major contributor to its growth. Government policy encouraged the participation of small and medium scale farms and firms. Taiwan's rapid growth through the late 1960s to the early 1990s is ascribed largely to the rapid expansion of these small and medium scale farms and firms (Ranis, 1992). In spite of this central role for the private sector, the "guiding hand" of the state was always in evidence in the development process, as was its continued participation in direct production. Thus, instead of wholesale privatization, Wan (1994) notes that the "private sector was allowed to overtake inefficient state industries, but not asked to take them over."

The role of the state in Taiwan's development process has been justifiably described as large, active and interventionist (Amsden, 1985; Winrock, 1991). In effect, government not only created an enabling environment for the private sector, it also skillfully orchestrated the development process by broadly influencing, guiding, supporting and coordinating the activities of private agents. In addition, the state also played and continues to play a major role in direct production. Thus, in recognition of the importance of human capital in the development process, the government invested heavily in education and other aspects of human resource development. Similarly, it provided substantial investment support for increasing agricultural productivity, while also offering protection for domestic industry and marketing support for exporters.

The interventionist posture of the state in Taiwan's development process appears to have been disciplined both by its design and the institutional mechanisms through which it was implemented. In terms of design features, Akyuz and Gore (1994: 10) finds that "an important feature of those rents created by the application of protectionist policies was that they were often linked to export performance." In addition, the same study (p. 11) finds that "rents were provided on a selective and temporary basis, and withdrawn as new industries became mature enough to face international competition." On the institutional side, Felix (1994) suggests that the military and prolonged single party dominance of the state apparatus in Taiwan insulated the economic bureaucracy from populist pressures. The autonomy that this insulation provided may have helped "in disciplining subsidy recipients by imposing on them strict and monitorable performance standards" (Hikino and Amsden, 1994: 295).

The overall development strategy and policies discussed above also have significant sector-specific dimensions, especially as they relate to key sectors such as agriculture, manufacturing industry and trade. Some of these dimensions are examined in what follows.

By all accounts, agriculture played the leading role at the beginning of Taiwan's period of rapid economic development (Ranis, 1992; Amsden, 1985). It was, in any case, the largest sector of the economy in the late 1940s, and was viewed as the source from which labor could be withdrawn, domestic savings mobilized, and foreign exchange generated. This view of agriculture changed as Taiwan progressed from an agriculture based economy in the 1950s to an industrialized one in the 1970s and 1980s. The shifts in the components of Taiwan's agricultural development strategy and policies over this period are comprehensively analyzed in Amsden (1985) and Thorbecke (1992) which also offer several key insights.

Firstly, agriculture was squeezed to provide the resources for financing the industrial sector and government in the early stages of the development process. This squeeze was achieved through the "hidden rice taxes" extracted mainly through land taxes payable in rice, compulsory purchases by government at below-market prices, and the rice-fertilizer barter system. As a result of these measures, net real capital outflow from agriculture increased from an annual average rate of 3.8 percent during the 1911-1940 period to an annual average rate of 10 percent between 1951 and 1960 (Amsden, 1985). In spite of this squeeze, however, Taiwan's agriculture produced impressive growth rates over the 1953-68 period. Secondly, therefore, agriculture received considerable government support to enable it yield substantial net withdrawals based on its rapid output growth.

The main sources of agricultural output growth up to the mid-1960s consisted of rising labor input, more intensive land cultivation and increasing application of chemicals and fertilizer. These changes were, in turn, induced by a number of institutional and policy initiatives. The three most prominent among these were the creation of the Joint Commission on Rural Reconstruction (JCRR), a set of land reforms, and foreign aid from the United States. From its establishment in 1948, the JCRR assumed the role of the premier institution for planning and implementing Taiwan's agricultural development and, in the process, energized the existing farmer's associations as a vehicle for providing the whole range of farmers services. The land reforms carried out between 1949 and 1953, and built upon the earlier (colonial) efforts in the same direction, produced an agricultural population of predominantly small scale owner cultivators. Finally, there was a significant inflow of U.S. aid, which focused on agriculture and accounted for about 60 percent of net domestic capital formation in that sector up to 1965 (Thorbecke, 1992).

As Taiwan's industrial growth and overall economic development took hold and became fairly well established, agricultural development strategy shifted. Thorbecke (1992: 34) dates the shift quite precisely:

> The major policy objective in this new phase (1973-1975) was to shift from an agricultural development strategy which had been designed to capture an agricultural surplus providing the necessary capital for the industrial take-off process towards the opposite strategy of increasingly protecting and subsidizing agriculture.

This was accomplished by a range of policy measures including abolition of various agricultural and land taxes, abolition of the rice-fertilizer barter system, and improvements in rural infrastructure, agricultural research and extension, and agricultural marketing and farm credit. Thorbecke (1992: 38) provides the following assessment:

> The greatest impact on agriculture during the present phase (since 1980) came. . .from the various measures which reduced agricultural taxation and the costs of inputs, on the one hand, and the price support programs which subsidized the prices received by farmers, on the other hand.

Taiwan's industrial development process was initiated with an inward-oriented import-substitution phase supported by high levels of domestic protection derived from import tariffs and quantitative restrictions. Some analysts claim that this phase was short and relatively mild (Winrock, 1991), while others suggest that this phase of import-substitution was not a trivial episode in Taiwan's economic history (Amsden, 1985; Park 1992). In fact, Park (1992) shows that domestic production in Taiwan enjoyed quite high nominal rates of protection and that quantitative import restrictions remained significant well into the 1970s. More specifically, Park (1992: 76) finds that:

While exporters may have faced international prices for both inputs and outputs, many producers were nevertheless protected and initiated production on the basis of protection in the domestic market.

Similarly, Amsden (1985: 89) suggests that "it was only after manufacturing had made a fair start, however, that the Taiwan government hesitantly charted a new course in the direction of export-led growth."

There are clearly two kinds of shift at work here. One was a shift toward manufactured exports and the other was a shift toward gradual reduction of domestic protection. The latter has involved the elimination of quantitative import controls and reduction of tariffs; it is a gradual process that is yet to be completed.

The shift toward an export-led growth is perhaps more intriguing. Park (1992: 84) implies that a major measure for achieving this was "the neutrality of incentives as between exports and domestic sales." This raises the issue of how "neutrality of incentives" was accomplished. Did it occur through across-the-board import liberalization or was it brought about by granting exporters access to imported inputs at international prices? A package of reforms aimed at re-oriented the Taiwanese economy toward export-led growth was implemented between 1956 and 1961 (Amsden, 1985). It supported export processing zones and allowed exporters to import their inputs duty-free. Thus, "neutrality of incentives" was achieved by granting special treatment to exporters while continuing to protect domestic production.

16.3 A Review of African Development

Unlike the experience of Taiwan, the development experience of the countries of Sub-Saharan Africa has been disappointing and unsatisfactory. This sad experience has been shaped by a set of initial conditions as well as development strategies and policies which dominated the economic scene in SSA between the 1960s and the 1980s. Various attempts have been made, particularly since the mid-1980s, to change the underlying development strategy and reform the major policies. In the process, a new set of initial conditions as well as more favorable growth-inducing environment are being established that should influence SSA's development prospect through the late 1990s and beyond. A broad review of the major trends in SSA's development experience over the last three decades should help to place in proper perspective the subsequent discussion of its future prospects.

Table 16.1 provides the evidence for making two important points regarding the economic performance of SSA between the 1960s and 1980s. Firstly, SSA's performance was more or less consistent with that of other developing countries during the 1965-73 period. Secondly, SSA's performance worsened progressively during the 1970s and 1980s in comparison both with its own record of the 1960s and with the performance of other developing countries over the period of the 1970s and 1980s.

On the first point, Table 16.1 shows that the annual growth rates of SSA's GDP, agriculture, manufacturing, and gross domestic investment were quite similar to those of all developing countries during the 1965-73 period.

Table 16.1   Selected Indicators of Economic Performance in SSA, 1965–87

	1965–73	1973–80	1980–87
Gross Domestic Product (annual average percent growth)			
Sub-Saharan Africa (SSA)	5.9	2.5	0.5
All developing countries (ADC)	6.0	4.6	6.1
Agriculture (annual average percent growth)			
SSA	2.2	–0.3	1.3
ADC	3.0	2.3	4.0
Manufacturing (annual average percent growth)			
SSA	10.1	8.2	0.6
ADC	9.1	2.1	10.3
Gross Domestic Investment (annual average percent growth)			
SSA	9.8	4.0	–8.2
ADC	9.2	7.3	10.2
Exports (annual average percent growth)			
SSA	15.1	0.2	–1.3
ADC	9.6	2.3	3.5
Gross Domestic Investment (as percent of GDP)			
SSA	14	20	16
ADC	20	25	28
Gross Domestic Savings (as percent of GDP)			
SSA	14	22	13
ADC	19	25	26
Manufacturers (as percent of exports)			
SSA	7	5	12
ADC	24	19	49

Source: World Bank, Sub-Saharan Africa: From Crisis to Sustainable Growth, 1989.

While SSA's GDP growth rate (at 5.9 percent) was virtually the same as the 6 percent recorded by all developing countries, Africa's agriculture was less robust in its performance, but manufacturing grew at 10.1 percent, somewhat better than the 9.1 percent record of all developing countries. Clearly SSA's exports performed better (15.1 percent) than the 9.6 percent growth rate turned in by the export sector of all developing countries. However, SSA's gross domestic investment and savings as proportions of GDP were lower (14 percent in each case) than the 20 percent and 19 percent respectively achieved by all developing countries. Finally, export of manufactures constituted only 7 percent of total exports from SSA; the corresponding ratio for all developing countries was as high as 24 percent.

Over the next 15 years, virtually all indicators show progressive deterioration when SSA's performance is compared with its record of the 1965-73 period. GDP growth rate declined by 50 percent in 1973-80 and ended up at 0.5 percent in 1980-

87. The growth rates of manufacturing value-added, gross domestic investment and exports exhibit a similar pattern, with the latter two becoming significantly negative during 1980-87. Both gross domestic investment and savings, as proportions of GDP, show a different pattern; they rose from 14 percent in 1965 to 20 percent and 22 percent respectively in 1980, but then fell back to 16 percent and 13 percent respectively in 1987.

A comparison of SSA's performance during 1973-87 with that of all developing countries over the same period demonstrates quite clearly that while SSA was not significantly different from other developing regions in the 1960s, it had fallen off the "growth trajectory" of all developing countries by the 1970s and 1980s. These countries experienced a general deceleration in their growth rates during 1973-80 (compared with 1965-73) but had recovered by 1980-87 and were, in fact, growing at a faster rate than they were during the period of the 1960s.

Attempts to explain SSA's progressive deterioration during the 1970s and 1980s (e.g. World Bank, 1989) have focused on the region's initial conditions, the external environment with which it has been confronted and its choice of development strategies and policies since the 1960s. Key elements of the initial conditions that have defined SSA's development prospects include the size of the countries, the structure of their economies, and the nature of their states and governments. Some of these elements (e.g. structure of the economies) have interacted with the external environment in ways that compounded SSA's development problems; while other elements (e.g. nature of the states and governments) have apparently pushed SSA into inappropriate strategic and policy choices.

The typical African economy is small, in terms of both population and gross national products. Taken together, the SSA region has a very limited human resource base, in spite of its rapidly growing population. Furthermore, these small economies suffer from inherent inflexibility and structural rigidities that constrain their ability to respond to external shocks. An important constituent of the rigid economic structures is agriculture. SSA's highly extensive and diversified farming systems have traditionally been based, essentially, on household food self-sufficiency. SSA's agricultural sector is further characterized by fragile soils, and is predominantly rain-fed agricultural and frequently exposed to unfavorable weather and other climatic conditions. Dynamism is severely limited by extremely low levels of technology and the lack of rural infrastructure such as roads and irrigation.

Most SSA countries contain heterogeneous populations in which ethnic and racial conflicts and sensitivities continue to thwart efforts at nation-building and maintenance of social and political stability. Superimposed on this structure are weak governments whose attempts to maintain legitimacy have often resulted in the use of political power to benefit the government and its close allies in the context of a system broadly lacking in transparency of government operations and deficient in terms of autonomy for economic policy-makers. These characteristics of the typical African state and government may explain why rapid economic growth and development of the nation-state has rarely emerged as the primary objective of national development strategy and policies.

Through the 1970s and 1980s, an unfavourable external environment negatively impacted upon SSA economies. In particular, terms of trade shocks and external debt overhang contributed significantly to the severe external imbalances which became an inherent feature of this period. SSA's heavy reliance on primary commodities combined with persistently declining commodity prices translated into substantial terms of trade losses suffered by the region during the 1970s and 1980s. Further losses of export earnings occurred as the share of African exports in all world trade fell from 2.4 percent in 1970 to 1.7 percent in 1985 (World Bank, 1989). In addition, SSA's total external debt ballooned from about $6 billion in 1970 to $134 billion in 1988, by which time the debt stock was 70.2 percent of the region's GNP and almost 243 percent of its export earnings. This debt overhang not only severely curtailed the region's import capacity but also generated strong disincentives against investing in these economies.

The initial conditions that characterized the SSA economies and the unfavorable external environment that they faced obviously have contributed significantly to their poor economic performance since the 1970s. The literature suggests quite strongly, however, that the region's choice of development strategy and policies probably plays a much more important role in explaining its economic stagnation and decline, partly because they aggravated the existing structural rigidities and thus reduced the capacity of the economy to accommodate external shocks. In broad terms, SSA countries pursued an inward-oriented development strategy from the early 1960s to the mid-1980s. Again in broad terms, this strategy focused primary attention on import-substitution industrialization which was financed by squeezing the agricultural sector (directly and indirectly). It was orchestrated by the state with very little room for the private sector and limited role for market discipline in the development process.

SSA's development strategy and policies during this period paid little attention to the key determinants of macroeconomic stability. Behavior with respect to the fiscal stance and exchange rate policy is of particular relevance in this regard. Reflecting the leading role assigned to the state in SSA's development strategy and the heavy financing requirements of the large number of parastatals, government expenditure rose quite rapidly. As a result, government share of the economy's total pool of resources increased significantly, and this probably impinged negatively on private sector savings and investment. The focus on expenditure did not carry over into similar concerns for raising government revenue. Hence, SSA had fiscal deficits to GDP ratios that were generally higher and exhibited greater variability than those experienced in other developing economies, such as those in Asia. The fiscal deficits reflect several tendencies; one is the penchant for incurring expenditures with little regard for their implications for macroeconomic stability, the other is the apparent inability to curb public overall expenditure effectively. The financing of fiscal imbalances through domestic and external borrowing had further negative implications in terms of inflation and external debt overhang.

During the 1960s and 1970s, SSA's development strategy lacked an explicit exchange rate policy based on some notion of an appropriate target real rate with a specific purpose, such as to promote international competitiveness, for example. Instead, most SSA countries maintained fixed exchange rates (with specific "hard" currencies or basket of currencies) over long periods of time and were unwilling to adjust these rates in spite of large and widening gaps between local inflation rates and those prevailing in trading partner countries. In addition, external imbalances were dealt with largely through ad hoc measures such as trade and payments controls, foreign exchange rationing and import licensing rather than through devaluation. As a result, most SSA economies suffered significant real exchange rate appreciation and witnessed the development of parallel foreign exchange markets.

Finally, the macro-economic framework that derived from SSA's development strategy over this period did not promote savings. On the contrary, the tendency towards high public consumption discouraged public savings, while the policy of maintaining low nominal interest rates (in the face of rising inflation rates) generated negative real interest rates which discouraged private savings.

At the sectoral level, the development strategy discriminated against agriculture and hindered its growth. On the one hand, resources were extracted from this sector "directly through low producer prices offered by state marketing boards and indirectly through a heavy implicit tax burden as a result of industrial protection, real exchange rate appreciation and changes in associated macroeconomic policies" (Oyejide, 1993: 254). On the other hand, the strategy did not provide adequate support for boosting agricultural productivity and output, which could have enabled the sector to yield the net flow of resources required from it on a sustainable basis. In particular, the strategy failed to provide for adequate investments in agricultural infrastructure, research and extension as well as input supply services.

Manufacturing was the favored sector and the target of an extensive array of government interventions. SSA adopted the classical import-substitution industrialization strategy and added a number of special African characteristics. Firstly, the public sector's leading role was reflected in the establishment of industrial parastatals which dominated the manufacturing sector. Secondly, these parastatals were nurtured behind high protectionist barriers and were provided with generous tax rebates and low interest credit. Finally, the protection and other support provided were, in many cases, neither time-bound nor performance-related. They were therefore often not subjected to either market or even bureaucratic discipline. As a result, the industries were heavily dependent on imported inputs and operated inefficiently. As export volumes and earnings declined in the late 1970's and early 1980's and foreign exchange became a binding constraint in most SSA countries, the manufacturing sector suffered sharp declines in capacity utilization and output. In the end, therefore, even the sector that was explicitly favored by SSA's overall development strategy could not lead the economy into the path of high and sustainable growth.

Thus, SSA countries were faced with a sharply worsening economic performance as well as massive external and internal imbalances. On the external front, most SSA countries faced severe balance-of-payments deficits, a rapidly increasing and clearly unsustainable external debt burden and loss of international creditworthiness. On the domestic front, these countries also faced high levels of budget deficits, which also fueled high inflation rates. The internal and external imbalances were linked by grossly overvalued exchange rates, which gave rise to parallel foreign exchange markets and rising premia between official and parallel market exchange rates. These macroeconomic imbalances were being further aggravated by endemic distortions in the factor and goods markets. This was the background against which a wide range of policy reforms was adopted and implemented, in varying degrees, in many SSA countries starting from the early 1980s. These reforms were articulated and implemented in the context of a series of structural adjustment programs (SAPs) actively supported by the World Bank and the International Monetary Fund. In essence, the reforms represented a radical change in SSA's development strategy and policies; from an inward-oriented and state dominated posture to one that is outward oriented, market-friendly and private sector-led. The new strategy focuses on restoring macroeconomic stability through fiscal adjustments and more flexible and market determined exchange rates, and promoting market efficiency by deregulating markets, reforming the financial sector and privatizing public enterprises. In addition, the new strategy seeks to enhance the private sector's role in the development process while limiting that of the state to the creation of an enabling and supportive environment for the private sector, investing in human resource development and maintaining macroeconomic stability.

A recent assessment of SSA's reform efforts in the context of the new development strategy concludes that "there has been progress on the macroeconomic front, but most SSA countries are still far from the 'policy frontier'" (World Bank, 1995: 21). In particular, while considerable changes have occurred with respect to exchange rate policy, liberalization of credit allocation, interest rate deregulation and reduction of trade restrictions, fiscal imbalances continue to pose significant problems. In addition, overall macroeconomic balance continues to be threatened by the ever increasing external debt overhang; total debt as a proportion of GNP increased from 31 percent in 1980 to 73 percent in 1993, while the debt/export ratio rose from 92 percent to 254 percent over the same period. Furthermore, much greater progress appears to have been made in terms of "getting prices right" than on the structural, institutional and infrastructural components of reform.

In spite of considerable efforts and substantial achievements in economic policy reform, SSA's economic performance between the late 1980s and early 1990s has been below expectation. Average annual real GDP growth during 1986-92 was 1.8 percent; this is lower than the average annual growth rate of 2.9 percent achieved during 1975-79, although it represents a recovery from the negative growth rates of the 1981-85 period. Compared to the 1975-79 period however, deterioration in performance were also recorded with respect to savings, investment and exports. In spite of the reform, therefore, SSA economies remain far from achieving the rapid, sustainable and equitable growth that constituted the basic rationale for the reform effort.

Various explanations have been offered for the apparent lack of (or inadequate) response to policy reforms in SSA. These include factors that revolve around the incentive regime and its structure, such as insufficient reform and the need for more time to elicit response (World Bank 1994, 1995). Other explanations stress inadequate scale of activities (or market size) as well as the continuing perception of SSA as an extremely risky region in which policies remain non-credible because they can be easily reversed by governments that are subject to weak restraints (Collier, 1994). Finally, a radically different set of explanations questions the fundamental basis of the policy reforms; the reforms are viewed as short term in orientation, focusing too rigidly on stabilization to the exclusion of longer term development needs, and emphasizing the incentive structure at the expense of the key structural, institutional and infrastructural elements without which long-term and sustainable "supply response" would not occur (Cornia *et al.*, 1992). Taken together, these explanations suggest the need to re-examine the current development strategy and policies in SSA in terms of both their design and implementation and in the light of the development experiences of more successful regions.

16.4 Lessons from Taiwan

Thorbecke (1994: 49) poses this question: "what are the key elements of successful development strategies that are transferable to the present African circumstances?" In the process of answering this question with specific reference to lessons from Taiwan, it should be noted that as Elbadawi (1996) suggests, a broad convergence is emerging which stresses market discipline, macroeconomic stability, active participation and leadership of the private sector and a redefined but critical role for the state in the development process. The devil is, of course, in the detail; and this is where the emerging broad consensus may be strained.

16.4.1 Overall Strategy

Both theories and accumulated experience of successful development elsewhere (especially Taiwan) suggest that a realistic overall development strategy for SSA should stress broad outward-orientation. The peculiar characteristics of most SSA countries as small and historically "open" economies (in the sense of high ratios of trade to GDP) are broadly consistent with this focus. SSA's failed experiment with its largely inward-oriented development strategy of the 1960s and 1970s should also quite rightly provide an additional support for a radical change in orientation. An outward-oriented development strategy assumes that aggregate economic growth will be export-led, in one way or another. This in turn, calls for the maintenance of macroeconomic balance and stability, which typically, requires sound fiscal and monetary policies that generate low and sustainable budget deficits and inflation rates combined with an exchange rate policy that maintains competitive rates.

It is generally accepted, of course, that "sound macroeconomic policy is a necessary but not sufficient condition for sustained growth with poverty reduction" (World Bank, 1995: 25). In the particular case of SSA, there are other structural, infrastructural and institutional elements of the strategy that are required to provide support and facilitate "supply response," not only in the short term but also in a sustainable way. A comparison with Taiwan suggests the crucial need for substantial and sustained investment in human capital development and rapid build-up and maintenance of infrastructure, given the current acute inadequacies in these areas.

SSA's development strategy must address the important issue of the relative roles of the state and private agents in the development process. While an outward-oriented development strategy typically regards the private sector as the main-spring of economic growth, it is not necessarily optimal to limit the role of the state to that of only providing support for and accommodating the private sector. The Taiwanese experience suggests that the state should also provide adequate public services and incentives to promote knowledge acquisition and technology diffusion, which are complementary inputs into the development process. Furthermore, the state should guide private agents and overcome "coordination failures" that occur in a private-sector-led development process (Rodrick, 1994). There exist justifiable concerns, of course, regarding the nature and capacity of the typical African State to perform these critical functions (Winrock, 1991; World Bank, 1994, 1995; Lipumba, 1994). It should be stated quite clearly that SSA cannot achieve rapid and sustainable growth unless developmental states are established that are capable of articulating a long-term vision of development and of exercising sufficient policy autonomy not only in implementing strategies constructed around such a vision but also in disciplining the private sector. Seeking refuge in a "minimalist" state could, in this context, amount to abandoning the quest for sustainable and equitable growth.

16.4.2 Sectoral Strategy

Within the broad framework of an overall development strategy for Africa, of the type briefly sketched above, three key sectors deserve specific emphasis. These are agriculture, manufacturing industry and trade (or more particularly, exports).

Agriculture. Given its relative size (in terms of contributions to GDP, exports and employment), it is clear that agriculture has to play a pivotal role in the development of SSA. This development will include a transformation during which a flow of net resources generated in the agriculture sector is transferred to the rest of the economy. SSA's failed development strategy of the past attempted to squeeze out this resource flow without simultaneously implementing the policies and providing the resources required for increasing agricultural productivity and capacity, which would enable the sector to release a net resource flow on a continuous and sustainable basis. Recent reforms of the incentive regimes in SSA countries, both at the macro and sector-specific levels, have substantially reduced anti-agriculture bias and the heavy direct and indirect taxation of agriculture. However, much remains to be done in terms of institutions, infrastructure and input supply. Particularly significant for improved agricultural productivity is the apparent lack of technological innovation immediately applicable to rain-fed agriculture in the specific context of SSA's complex farming systems, large variety of crops, fragile soils and climatic conditions.

Thus, the strategy for promoting agricultural development in SSA must go well beyond repairing the distorted incentive structure. It should include increased investment to provide the much needed support services of rural infrastructure, input and credit supply, and technological innovation as well as the agricultural extension services required for its effective diffusion. The technology development component of these services will probably have to be provided in the context of regional arrangements, given the small sizes of SSA countries, their climatic characteristics and the economies of scale and externalities typically associated with technology.

In Taiwan, there is almost a one to one correspondence between the major domestically produced agricultural crop and the most commonly consumed food crop, i.e., rice. Hence, promoting agricultural development could serve the twin objectives of enhancing food security and expanding agricultural exports. The SSA situation is more complicated. In many SSA countries , there is a lack of congruence between locally produced foods (such as coarse grains) and preferred consumption foods (such as wheat and rice). Hence, SSA's agricultural development strategy may have to place even more emphasis on agricultural exports, given the rising demand for imported cereals and other foods that has to be financed (Oyejide and Tran, 1989). Both traditional and non-traditional agricultural exports need to be promoted in SSA. In spite of the well known arguments relating to the "adding-up" problem and the long-term trend in primary commodity prices, SSA cannot afford to turn its back on its traditional agricultural exports for the foreseeable future; it should instead struggle to at least recapture its lost market shares by substantially increasing agricultural productivity.

Manufacturing Industry. SSA's development strategy should explicitly include a manufacturing industry component, given the significant role of industrialization in the process of establishing sustained economic growth, which the experience of Taiwan so vividly illustrates, and the very serious consequences of the current marginalization of the region in this respect. The industrial component of the strategy should, however, start with the recognition that the previous import-substitution-industrialization (ISI) strategy has not only failed but has also created a difficult legacy that needs to be overcome before a new push in this direction could be worthwhile.

Promoting export-oriented industrialization (which would be constituent with an overall outward-oriented development strategy) against the background of the ISI legacy, requires (i) the restructuring of the existing manufacturing sector, which evolved under the ISI strategy and whose structure may be radically ill-suited to exporting, (ii) altering the industrial incentive regime to provide exporters with access to imported inputs at tariff-and tax-free prices, and (iii) using appropriate pro-active measures to assist exporters to overcome the difficulties of gaining access to the information and technology needed to break into export markets.

The manufacturing sector is characterized by certain externalities, such as learning-by-doing, which are external to each industrial enterprise but internal to the sector as a whole. Gains from the exploitation of these externalities tend to grow as the whole sector expands, while the sector's growth feeds into and catalyzes overall growth. When this sector is marginalized, as it is SSA, overall economic growth is negatively impacted as the catalytic gains derivable from the learning-induced growth of the manufacturing sector are not realized. In addition, the presence of production externalities in this sector implies that market equilibrium may not necessarily be efficient. Hence, an industrial strategy that explicitly recognizes a significant role for pro-active measures is probably inevitable.

Trade. An outward-oriented development strategy has clear implications for the trade sector. Such a strategy obviously calls for a strong focus on exports, and therefore would include appropriate modalities for eliminating anti-export bias. One obvious way to accomplish this would be to fully liberalize imports and maintain competitive exchange rates. Since import tariffs are, in effect, taxes on exports, full trade liberalization is a first best way to remove the anti-export bias that is inherent in import barriers and trade taxes.

However, discussions of import liberalization in the context of SSA continue to confront the twin questions: how much? how soon? Recent reform efforts have achieved significant trade liberalization. A recent assessment (World Bank, 1995: 24) finds that "since the mid-1980s, most African countries have moved from complete or nearly complete government control over imports, to more open systems, and have substantially reduced the number of imports subject to quantitative barriers." It goes on to indicate that "the greatest progress has been achieved in replacing [quantitative restrictions] with lower and less dispersed tariff levels; more than half the countries now have average tariff rates of 15-20 percent, with the highest rates set at 35-40 percent, and the number of tariff categories reduced to 4-5."

Given the heavy reliance of many SSA countries on trade taxes as important sources of government revenue and strong and realistic concerns about de-industrialization, it would be difficult (and probably unwise) to push import liberalization much further beyond the current average level. Pending the full liberalization of imports and consistent with the lessons of Taiwan in this regard, other modalities for removing anti-export bias should be adopted so that labor-intensive manufactured exports can be stimulated. Taiwan offers significant lessons in the use of such modalities and instruments as zero-tariff/tax export processing zones and various forms of duty drawback arrangements.

16.4.3 Special Strategic Issues

Several cross-cutting issues of strategic importance either can be drawn from the Taiwanese experience and/or are of particular relevance for the development of the SSA region. Four such issues are identified and discussed below.

Market Orientation and Selective Intervention. By and large, a development strategy that stresses outward-orientation is also often described as "market-friendly." But, as the experience of Taiwan amply illustrates, this strategy would not necessarily preclude the use of pro-active measures or selective interventions when these seem appropriate for taking advantage of certain externalities or building dynamic comparative advantage.

Based largely on the record of past failures, the current lack of (adequate) capacity for implementing and monitoring selective interventions and a political economy that is apparently highly susceptible to rent-seeking and corruption, it is often argued that SSA countries should forego the use of such measures. Thus, it is suggested in Winrock (1991) that SSA countries should stick to policies that are simple, transparent and require the least amount of technical know-how. In a similar vein, the World Bank (1994) warns that SSA countries should use their limited state capacity sparingly by minimizing unnecessary government involvement in markets. Finally, Thorbecke (1994: 70) advises that "it may be wiser to rely on more market- and free trade-oriented policies and minimize interventionist policies."

The experience of Taiwan shows that certain pro-active and interventionist measures can play a significant role in the development process. Rather than arguing that such measures should be abandoned *ab initio*, it would be more productive to carefully identify and delineate areas in which such measures can be helpful, articulate the desirable features of the measures, and work towards enhancing the capacity for their appropriate and effective use. Taiwan shows clearly that as long as pro-active interventions are broadly supplementary to and complementary with markets, rather than market-replacing, and as long as they are temporary, transparent, and disciplined by clear and objective performance criteria, they could be usefully deployed by a competent and autonomous bureaucracy.

In SSA's development process, there are, at least, three broad areas in which the use of pro-active measures could be productive. Firstly, investment in agricultural technology is likely to have a high pay-off in terms of long run growth and improved equality; yet it is unlikely that unguided market forces will do the job quickly, adequately or unsatisfactorily. Secondly, manufactured exports are known to play a major role in sustaining high levels of economic growth; this could, in fact, be regarded as the key rationale for an outward-oriented development strategy. At the beginning, however, strong and focused pro-active measures may be required to establish foot-holds and bridge-heads in appropriate foreign markets; similar interventionist measures are often necessary to provide exporters with tax-and tariff-free access to critical inputs as well as other support services. Finally, in the area of technology adoption, adaptation and development that is so crucial both for increasing agricultural productivity and making manufactured exports internationally competitive, pro-active measures are clearly needed to build up technological capabilities (Lall, 1994, 1995).

Capacity Building. The human and institutional capacity to manage the economy and society in many SSA countries has suffered massive deterioration in the recent past; it needs to be rebuilt as an important part of articulating and implementing a realistic and viable strategy for development. Both elements of capacity should be broadly defined to include (i) capacity to design, implement and monitor public policies within institutions that are strong and autonomous, and that are subject to norms, standards and regulations which ensure integrity and accountability, and (ii) capacity of skilled workers and highly-trained management personnel required to manage the economy's production processes, including coping with new technologies. Capacity building and its effective utilization remain crucial regardless of the specific relative role assigned to the state in the development process, and whether or not pro-active measures and selective interventions are used to influence the process.

External Resources. Foreign aid played a catalytic role in the early stages of Taiwanese development. Foreign direct investment was probably much more important subsequently. Foreign aid to SSA has been large (in comparison to other developing regions), but it has lacked the sharp focus of U.S. assistance to Taiwan, it has supported public investment that has been largely inefficient, and it has not been associated with economic growth (Killick, 1991). The non-debt creating and more productive element of external resources, i.e. foreign direct investment (FDI), has not been prominent in SSA's development experience. In spite of Africa's recent policy reforms, its FDI fell by one third in 1995 to $2 billion, compared, for instance, with a 65 percent increase in South Asia and almost 50 percent increase in Eastern Europe and Central Asia (World Bank, 1996).

Given the perception of SSA as a risky region, strong pro-active measures are clearly required to stimulate joint ventures and other forms of foreign investment. To the extent that SSA's large external debt constitutes a major deterrent to private investment and a disincentive to further policy adjustment, substantial debt relief could serve as a significant boost to the region's prospects for attracting FDI.

Regional Integration. Given the small size of the typical SSA economy, a pragmatic approach to regional integration and cooperation in the context of an outward-oriented development strategy could be useful. In particular, this mechanism could be used for harmonizing and coordinating macroeconomic and key sectoral policies, and for locking in such policies with a view to enhancing policy credibility by reducing the prospects of policy reversal. To the extent that this mechanism facilitates cross-border investment, trade and payments, it could assist in attracting foreign investment for an enlarged regional market.

The region, rather than each small country, could constitute a more cost-effective basis for dealing with SSA's agricultural research and technology development needs, in view of the similarities in soil and crop characteristics across broad and well-defined agro-climatic zones. The region may also play a useful role in the promotion of manufactured exports, as a stepping stone and training ground for producers who will eventually compete in global markets.

16.5 Note

1   Useful comments on an earlier version of this paper were received from Erik Thorbecke and Henry Wan; these are gratefully acknowledged.

16.6 References

Akyuz, Y. and C. Gore, 1994. "The Investment Profits Nexus in East Asian Industrialization," UNCTAD Discussion Paper, No 91, October. Geneva: UNCTAD.

Amsden, A., 1985. "The State and Taiwan's Economic Development," in P. Evans, *et al.* (eds.), *Bringing the State Back In*. Cambridge: Cambridge University Press.

Collier, P., 1994. "The Marginalization of Africa," mimeo, Oxford.

Cornia, G. A., R. Van der Hoeven, and T. Mkandawire (eds.), 1992. *Africa's Recovery in the 1990s: From Stagnation to Human Development*. New York: St. Martins Press.

Elbadawi, I. A., 1996. "Market and Government in the Process of Structural Adjustment and Economic Development in Sub-Saharan Africa," International Conference on the World Economy in Transition, Hitotsubashi University, Tokyo, Feb.8-10.

Felix, D., 1994. "Industrial Development in East Asia: What are the lessons for Latin America?" UNCTAD Discussion Paper, No. 84, May. Geneva: UNCTAD.

Harrold, P., M. Jayawickrama, and D. Bhattasali, 1995. "Practical lessons for Africa from East Asia in Industrial and Trade Policies," World Bank Discussion Paper, Africa Technical Department Series. Washington, D.C.: The World Bank.

Hikino, Takashi and Alice H. Amsden, 1994. "Staying Behind, Stumbling Back, Sneaking Up, Soaring Ahead: Late Industrialization in Historical Perspective," in R. R. Nelson, William J. Baumol, and Edward N. Wolff (eds.), *Convergence of Productivity: Cross-National Studies and Historical Evidence*. New York and Oxford: Oxford University Press: 285-315.

Killick, A., 1991. "The Development Effectiveness of Aid to Africa," in I. Hussain and J. Underwood (eds.), *African External Finance in the 1990s*. Washington, D.C.: The World Bank.

Kim, J. I. and L. J. Lau, 1994. "The Sources of Economic Growth of the East Asian Newly Industrialized Countries," *Journal of the Japanese and International Economies*, 8: 235-271.

Lall, S., 1994. "Industrial Policy: The Role of Government in Promoting Industrial and Technological Development," *UNCTAD Review*: 65-89

Lall, S., 1995. "Structural Adjustment and African Industry," *World Development* 23 (12): 2019-2031.

Lindauer, D. and M. Roemer (eds.), 1994. *Asia and Africa: Legacies and Opportunities in Development*. San Francisco: ICS Press.

Lipumba, N. H. I., 1994. *Africa beyond Adjustment*. Washington, D.C.: Overseas Development Council.

Oyejide, T. A., 1993. "Effects of Trade and Macroeconomic Policies on African Agriculture," in R. M. Bantista and A. Vades (eds.), *The Bias Against Agriculture: Trade and Macroeconomic Policies in Developing Countries*. San Francisco: ICS Press.

Oyejide, T. A. and L. H. Tran, 1989. "Food and Agricultural Imports of Sub-Saharan Africa," in Nurul Islam (ed.), *The Balance between Industry and Agriculture in Economic Development*. Proceedings of 8th World Congress of the IEA, New Delhi.

Park, H., 1992. "Industrialization in Taiwan," in G. Ranis (ed.), *op. cit.*

Ranis, G. (ed.), 1992. *Taiwan: From Developing to Mature Economy*. Boulder: Westview Press.

Rodrik, D., 1994. "Getting Interventions Right: How South Korea and Taiwan Grew Rich," NBER Working Paper, No. 4964, December.

Thorbecke, E., 1992. "The Development of Taiwan's Agriculture," in G. Ranis (ed.), *op. cit.*

Thorbecke, E., 1994. "Performance in Sub-Saharan Africa Under Structural Adjustment and Components of a Long-Term Development Strategy," OECD Development Centre, Paris

Wan, Henry, 1994. "The Market Transition in Taiwan: Any Relevance for the PRC?" in *The Economic Transformation of South China: Reform and Development in the Post Mao Era,* Ithaca, N.Y.: Cornell East Asia Program.

Winrock, 1991. *African Development:Llessons from Asia*. Arlington, Virginia:

World Bank, 1989. *Sub-Saharan Africa: From Crisis to Sustainable Growth*. Washington, D.C.: The World Bank.

World Bank, 1993. *The East Asian Miracle: Economic Growth and Public Policy*. New York: Oxford University Press,

World Bank, 1994. *Adjustment in Africa: Reforms, Results and the Road Ahead*, New York: Oxford University Press.

World Bank, 1995. *A Continent in Transition: Sub-Saharan Africa in the mid-1990s*, Washington, D.C., The World Bank.

World Bank, 1996. *World Bank News*, xv (10), March 14.

17 THE RELEVANCE AND COMPARABILITY OF TAIWAN'S DEVELOPMENT EXPERIENCE TO INDONESIA

Mohammad Sadli and Kian Wie Thee

17.1 Introduction: Historical Overview

At first sight there is little in common between Taiwan and Indonesia. Taiwan is a relatively small, resource-poor but increasingly prosperous and relatively egalitarian newly-industrialized, densely-populated island slightly smaller than West Java, one province on the island of Java in Indonesia. Indonesia, on the other hand, is a sprawling, resource-rich but still relatively poor, rapidly-industrializing, archipelagic nation with the fourth-largest population in the world. Despite minor ethnic, cultural, and linguistic differences between the mainland Chinese and the indigenous Taiwanese, Taiwan is a relatively homogeneous society compared to the racially, ethnically, religiously, and linguistically more diverse plural society of Indonesia.

Despite these striking differences, however, both countries share some similar experiences. For one thing, both countries emerged from colonial rule after World War II as poor, agrarian economies with their physical infrastructure severely damaged because of wartime destruction and sheer neglect. In Taiwan, economic reconstruction was only started in the early 1950s, after the Kuomintang government had consolidated its political power on the island. In Indonesia, economic rehabilitation could only be started in the early 1950s after the Netherlands, following four years of armed struggle by the Indonesian nationalists, finally recognized Indonesia's independence on 27 December 1949. But then Indonesia lost 15 years of effective development because of the political turmoil during the reign of its first president, Sukarno.

While both countries have been classified as two of the high-performing Asian economies (HPAEs) by the World Bank, Taiwan's overall economic performance in terms of combining sustained rapid economic growth with equity has been superior to that of Indonesia. For this reason, this paper will attempt to assess what aspects of Taiwan's development experience is of relevance to Indonesia. First, however, we will briefly look at the initial conditions facing both countries.

17.1.1 Initial conditions

The colonial legacy. From 1895 to 1945 Taiwan was a Japanese colony. During this period, Taiwan was developed into a highly productive two-crop economy producing rice and sugar for the Japanese mainland. Most other colonies, including Indonesia, had been developed into primary export-economies based on foreign-owned and -managed large estates and mines with little favorable spillover effects on the traditional, rural sector. Primary production in Taiwan, on the other hand, was not confined to foreign enclaves with limited spillover effects on subsistence agriculture. Here many farmers with access to arable land started producing rice on a commercial basis to meet the steadily rising demand of the Japanese consumers. Unlike on Java, the sugar-producing island of the Netherlands Indies, where the large-scale, commercial production of sugar was organized by Dutch planters, sugarcane in prewar Taiwan was grown not only on a large scale by Japanese planters, but also by small Taiwanese farmers and tenants. Hence, agriculture in colonial Taiwan was quickly and generally commercialized. (Amsden 1985: 79).

The colonial government spent considerable resources on the expansion of rural infrastructure, such as roads, irrigation, and power, as well as institutional infrastructure, such as agricultural research, experiment stations, and farmers' associations. As a result of these investments, rice yields on the average rose by four percent a year during the period 1921- 1937. (Ranis 1995: 511).

The Japanese colonial government also made considerable investments in human capital. As a result, literacy rates in Taiwan were quite high compared to most other economically underdeveloped countries. For instance, by the early 1950s not less than 60 percent of the population was literate. This high literacy rate was due to the fact that the colonial government made a large effort to provide primary education for the Taiwanese population, although they were not permitted to enter higher education. The basic primary education provided to a large part of the Taiwanese population, however, enabled them to participate widely in various small and medium-scale industrial and service enterprises (SMEs). Hence, by the end of Japanese colonial rule, the initial stock of human capital was already quite considerable. (Ranis 1995: 511).

Unlike Japan, which had occupied Taiwan only in 1895, the Dutch commercial presence in the Indonesian archipelago dates back to the late 16th century. By the early 19th century the Dutch were in effective control of the fertile island of Java, the Moluccas, and some vital trading posts across the archipelago. In 1830 the Dutch colonial government introduced the forced cultivation system (*Cultuurstelsel*) on Java, under which farmers on Java were forced to grow export crops, notably sugar, coffee, and indigo, for the world market. During this period Java was in effect made into a vast government-controlled plantation which had a monopoly on the exploitation of the colony and which yielded substantial profits to the Dutch treasury.

Under increasing pressure from Dutch private interests, however, the Dutch colonial government in 1870 opened up Indonesia to private enterprise. It was during this so-called Liberal Period that Dutch and other Western private enterprise established the great agricultural (large estates) and mining export industries for which Indonesia became famous. By the time the Dutch had put the whole Indonesian archipelago under their effective control in the early 20th century, Indonesia had become an outstanding example of a *"colonial primary export economy"* in which the growth dynamics of the economy were primarily determined by the rapid expansion of primary exports (agricultural products and minerals) and diversification into other, more lucrative primary exports when the traditional primary exports began to falter (Paauw, 1983: 9). During the period of rapid expansion of primary exports (1870-1930,) the indigenous Indonesians on the whole played only a subordinate and minor role as lessors of land to the large estates and/or as unskilled workers in the large estates and mines. Notable exceptions, however, were the peasant smallholders in the Outer Islands (islands outside of Java), particularly Sumatra and Kalimantan, who since the early 20th century successfully turned to the cultivation of profitable export crops, notably rubber.

During the early period of independence, several long-run trends resulting from the colonial impact on the Indonesian economy continued to persist. These included a continued high dependence on primary exports which persisted until the late 1980s; the persistence of "technological dualism" with marked differences in productive techniques between the modern, capital intensive sector and the more traditional, labor-intensive sector of the economy (Higgins, 1968: 299-303); and the associated problem of relative weakness of indigenous Indonesian entrepreneurship in the face of continued Dutch domination of the modern sector during the early 1950s and the ethnic Chinese domination of the intermediate trade. (Thee, 1994: 146-152).

Actually, the last four decades of Dutch colonial rule (1900-1942) were not characterized by unrestrained exploitation of the economy. In fact, in the early 20th century the Dutch colonial government had introduced the "Ethical Policy," which was essentially a "developmentalist" or welfare policy aimed at uplifting the welfare of the Indonesian population, in particular the population of Java. To implement the "Ethical Policy" the colonial government designed several welfare services, including agricultural extension (involving also rice policy, notably schemes aimed at the expansion of the area for rice and other food crop cultivation), irrigation, health care, the provision of credit services, and the promotion of cooperatives (Boomgaard 1986: 58-77). In addition, the Ethical Policy also involved other schemes, such as transmigration (i.e. the resettlement of people from densely-populated Java to the sparsely-populated Outer Islands), industrialization, road-building (Cribb, 1993: 232), and education.

Although the Ethical Policy achieved some successes, notably in raising rice production, by the end of the second decade of the 20th century it ran into serious problems because of the rising budget deficits of the colonial government. The onset of the Great Depression in the early 1930s spelled the end of the Ethical Policy, although officially it was never abandoned.

Despite the demise of the Ethical Policy, however, the Dutch colonial government in the early 1930s had embarked on a modest program of import-substituting industrialization as one of the ways to overcome the adverse impact of the Great Depression on the Indonesian economy. To stimulate industrial production for the domestic market, the colonial government provided tariff as well as non-tariff protection (in the form of import quotas) which was in particular aimed at sharply curtailing imports from Japan. In addition, the colonial government also provided assistance to nascent industrialists in the form of finance and technical training. (Paauw, 1963: 162). During this period of "the industrialization of the Netherlands Indies," not only Dutch capital was invested in various light manufacturing industries, such as textile and food-processing industries, but capital from other Western industrial countries, particularly from the U.S. and Britain, also entered the economy. As a result, several American and British multinational companies (MNCs), such as General Motors (GM), British-American Tobacco (BAT), and the Good Year Rubber Company became well-known names in Indonesia (Gonggrijp, 1949: 237-238).

The relative lack of success of the Ethical Policy in achieving its overall aims is most evident in the case of education. Unlike Taiwan, where, as we have seen, the Japanese colonial government was able to provide primary education to the majority of the Taiwanese population, primary education in the Netherlands Indies was only limited to the more privileged groups in Indonesian society. As a result, according to the Population Census of 1930 only 3.7 million indigenous Indonesians were literate — less than seven percent of the population, excluding young children. Although by 1940 a relatively high 44.5 percent of Indonesian children in the six to nine age group were attending primary school, including schools providing "vernacular primary education," dropout rates were high. Only a very small minority of primary school graduates were able to continue education in secondary schools, while others were only able to pursue further education in various vocational schools, which provided training for prospective teachers for the vernacular schools, agricultural and industrial extension workers, and public health nurses (Booth, 1989: 8).

Opportunities for Indonesians to pursue university education were even fewer. According to the estimates of van der Waal, a Dutch historian, in 1939/1940 only 1,380 Indonesian students had graduated from Dutch secondary schools, compared with 1,261 European (i.e. Dutch) students and 572 "other Asian" (mostly Chinese) students. Of these, only 157 students had gained entry to tertiary education. During the period 1920-1940 fewer than 1,500 Indonesians were enrolled in the tertiary colleges in the Netherlands Indies (specifically the Schools of Law, Medicine, and Engineering), and only 230 had graduated. During this period another 344 indigenous Indonesian students had graduated from universities in the Netherlands. In contrast enrollments in tertiary colleges in British India in the early 1940s amounted to over 70,000 (Booth 1989: 8). Hence, when independence was achieved, Indonesia had a smaller number of trained people than several other former colonies in Asia, including Taiwan.

The early independence period. When the Kuomintang government retreated to Taiwan in 1949, Taiwan's economic prospects did not look bright. Although the war damage had been largely repaired and its GNP was approaching prewar levels, per capita income was still below US$ 100. Except for some modern sugar refineries and other food processing plants and some small textile plants, Taiwan lacked an industrial base, while most of Taiwan's labor force was still engaged in agriculture (Vogel 1991: 13). However, Taiwan's initial conditions in the early 1950s were relatively more favorable than those of Indonesia, which had suffered severe human loss and extensive physical damage not only during the Japanese occupation, but also during the four years of armed struggle against the Dutch. For one thing, the Kuomintang government was able to establish political stability, albeit in a heavy-handed way. Compared to Indonesia, Taiwan had a greater stock of literate and numerate human resources and a relatively well developed physical infrastructure, which had been largely repaired when the Kuomintang government retreated to Taiwan. Through a successful land reform program, the government was also able to put agriculture on a more solid base by turning tenant farmers into owner-operators. Finally, the government was also able to control inflationary pressures (Vogel 1991: 16-22).

After its defeat on the mainland, the Kuomintang government was acutely aware that the consolidation of its political power and the establishment of its legitimacy in Taiwan were linked to economic reform. This included first of all serious efforts to restore macroeconomic stability. Secondly, it included heavy investment in agricultural and rural development, and efforts to rebuild the rural organizations which had been effective during the colonial period in providing extension services, credit, and farm inputs to farmers (Haggard 1991: 83).

Although Taiwan was quite successful in increasing its agricultural exports, trade barriers hampered a return to the colonial pattern of primary exports. As a result of Japan's own reconstruction efforts and the closure of the Chinese mainland, protected or preferential markets were now closed to Taiwan's primary exports. This and serious balance of payments problems in the early 1950s thus led the Taiwan government to embark on a pattern of import-substituting industrialization (Haggard, 1991: 86). The relatively small size of the domestic market, the lack of abundant natural resources, and the impending end of American aid in the early 1960s led the Taiwanese government to shift its industrial strategy to export promotion (Ranis, 1995: 520).

Compared to the initial conditions facing Taiwan in the early 1950s, political conditions in Indonesia during this period were less favorable to economic development. When Indonesia's independence was finally recognized by the Dutch in December 1949 after four years of armed struggle, Indonesia's policy-makers were faced with the daunting task of reconciling the urgent need to rehabilitate the economy, which had suffered heavy damage during the Japanese occupation and the war of independence, with the strong popular demand to "convert the colonial economy into a national economy." Although effective political independence had been finally recognized internationally, the Indonesian government at the outset faced the politically sensitive problem that the extensive Dutch economic interests continued to be safeguarded, as stipulated under the terms of the Dutch-Indonesian agreement reached at the United Nations' sponsored Round Table Conference in The Hague, the Netherlands, in the autumn of 1949. Through their control over the modern export industries (mines and large estates) and vital services (gas, electricity, and water supply), the Dutch were still able to exert a great deal of power, particularly when it concerned the protection of what they perceived to be their vital interests. Moreover, many senior positions in the fledgling Indonesian public service were still largely occupied by Dutch officials, who numbered about 6,000 in the early 1950s (Higgins, 1990: 40).

Foreign dominance over Indonesia's economy was not only limited to Dutch dominance over the modern sector, but also involved dominance over the important intermediate trade in the rural areas and the retail trade in urban areas by ethnic Chinese middlemen. Hence, faced with this continuing "colonial" economic structure and widespread calls to convert this structure into a "national" structure, the Indonesian government took several steps to meet at least some of the urgent demands of economic nationalism. While still adhering to the Round Table Conference agreement, the Indonesian government nevertheless decided to bring vital economic institutions, such as the central bank (the Java Bank, renamed Bank of Indonesia) and several public utilities under national ownership and control. To promote indigenous Indonesian entrepreneurship and put the economically important import trade under national control, the Indonesian government in 1950 introduced the *"Benteng"*(Fortress) program, under which import licenses and import credits were allocated to some 5,000 indigenous Indonesian (*pribumi*) importers (Sadli *et al.*, 1988: 357).

Unfortunately, many of these new *pribumi* entrepreneurs did not have enough capital and business experience, and therefore sold off their licenses to the old Chinese traders whom the *Benteng* program had tried to dislodge. In view of the meager results achieved by the *Benteng* program, which had unintentionally fostered a group of "rent-seekers" instead of true entrepreneurs, this program was eventually abandoned in the late 1950s. Although only a handful of these *Benteng* importers survive today, considerations to promote *pribumi* entrepreneurs still affect current policies, reflecting the enduring strength of "economic nationalism" in Indonesia (Sadli *et al.*, 1988: 357). Aside from the widespread desire to favor *pribumi* entrepreneurs over "foreign-born" (non-*pribumi*) Indonesians, notably the ethnic Chinese (regardless of whether they were Indonesian citizens or not), in the 1950s political favoritism of the ruling political parties toward individual *pribumi* businessmen also affected the further development of the *pribumi* business class. Every time another political party came to power, different businessmen were favored. Not surprisingly, as a result of these policies, not many of these favored businessmen showed strong survival strength (Sadli et al., 1988: 357).

While the political debates about the pace at which the vestiges of Western (i.e. Dutch) capitalism would have to be eradicated in order to build up a "national economy" became increasingly vociferous, the rapidly deteriorating relations with the Netherlands about the final status of West New Guinea (West Irian, now renamed Irian Jaya) by the end of 1957 and early 1958 eventually led to the takeover and subsequent nationalization of all Dutch enterprises in Indonesia. Hence, in one stroke, the vast economic power which the Dutch had gradually accumulated in Indonesia in the course of three and a half centuries was eliminated.

As politically more radical groups gained increasing power in the ensuing years, and sound economic policies were increasingly disregarded, the economy steadily deteriorated, while deficit- financing led to inflation and subsequently to hyper-inflation in the mid-1960s. In the early 1960s Indonesia became increasingly hostile to the Western countries, particularly the U.S. and Britain, because of their opposition to Indonesia's "Crush Malaysia" campaign, which led to the subsequent nationalization of all American and British enterprises in 1963 (Sadli, 1972: 202). It would take the overthrow of the old government and the assumption of power by a new, more pragmatic government in 1966 and the restoration of political stability to turn the economy around. As a result, it was only by the late 1960s that Indonesia for the first time in its postcolonial history was finally set on a path of sustained rapid economic growth, almost two decades later than Taiwan and roughly one decade later than its neighbors in Southeast Asia, notably Malaysia and Thailand.

17.2 The Relevance of Some Aspects of Taiwan's Development Experience to Indonesia

As one of the most successful models among the high-performance Asian economies (HPAEs), Taiwan's development experience may offer some lessons for Indonesia, despite the great differences in the historical background, factor endowments, size, and level of development between the two countries. In the following pages we will look at some aspects of Taiwan's development experience which may offer some valuable lessons to Indonesia. The aspects of Taiwan's development experience of particular interest to Indonesia include those aspects of development in which Taiwan, but not Indonesia, has been quite successful. These include Taiwan's success in reducing widespread corruption within a relatively short period of time, promoting the healthy growth of economically viable and highly competitive small- and medium- scale industries (SMIs), and the related problem of acquiring and mastering foreign industrial technologies for rapid industrialization and export development. In the following pages we will elaborate further on Taiwan's experience in these three aspects of development and assess to what extent they are relevant to Indonesia.

17.2.1 The Corruption Syndrome and the Problem of Governance

The Problem. When the Kuomintang government still held power on the mainland, it was infamous for its corruption. However, after it retreated to Taiwan, this "disease" withered away. How did this happen? This issue is of particular importance to Indonesia, as Indonesia along with China and Vietnam, have, according to a poll undertaken among Western businessmen, been perceived as among the most corrupt countries in Asia. Even though corruption has apparently not hampered rapid economic growth, it may, if unchecked, seriously erode the political and moral legitimacy of the regimes in power in the eyes of its domestic constituents, which may have grave destabilizing consequences.

As the causes of corruption are rooted in the peculiar economic and political conditions of each country, these causes are as complex as the types of corruption are varied. In view of these complexities, finding practical cures to reduce, if not eradicate corruption is naturally quite difficult (Harriss-White and White, 1996: 1). Nevertheless, the problem of corruption merits serious attention. For one thing, there is a widespread perception that the level and pervasiveness of political and bureaucratic corruption in developing and developed countries alike is not only greater than many thought it was, but also that it may very well be increasing. Political and bureaucratic corruption, in Indonesia often referred to as "collusion" between senior government officials and big businessmen, is quite prevalent in many countries, including the post-communist transitional economies, particularly Russia and China, and even to a lesser extent in the East Asian newly-industrializing economies (NIEs), including Taiwan (with the notable exception of Singapore). In addition, the emergence of neoliberal ideas since the early 1980s in international aid organizations, which has become the basis of the structural adjustment measures advocated by the World Bank and the International Monetary Fund (IMF), has led to the identification of corruption as one of the adverse consequences of excessive state intervention and the resulting bureaucratic rents. The policy implications of this economic analysis are that corruption can be reduced by decreasing the role of the state through deregulation and privatization and by introducing more competition, transparency, and accountability into the political process (Lall, 1994: 65; Harriss-White and White, 1996: 2). However, the empirical evidence from several developing countries — including Indonesia — that have gone through a process of greater economic liberalization and deregulation has indicated that the overall level of corruption may not have decreased. For one thing, the opportunities for corruption facing government officials may have remained high if the regulatory responsibilities of the state in the new economic system are still considerable and the political controls over the behavior of senior government officials remain weak. Moreover, the demand for corruption may have remained high when economically powerful actors, such as big businessmen, who have been enriched and empowered by the liberalization and deregulation process, attempt to maintain and defend rents in the face of competitors (Harriss-White and White, 1996: 3).

Some possible explanation(s) for Taiwan's experience. Corruption never goes away overnight. In Taiwan it also took time to reduce corruption. The situation of a government in exile, as the Kuomintang government on Taiwan obviously was in the 1950s, was certainly quite different than when the Kuomintang government still ruled over the mainland. As a government in exile, the Kuomintang government had to establish its political legitimacy and respectability, both among the native Taiwanese who were the large majority of Taiwan's population, as well as in the world at large. Hence, the Kuomintang government became more performance oriented, in order to prove that the people who had fled to Taiwan were not "the rats who had abandoned the ship." Certainly, upon their retreat to Taiwan, the Kuomintang leaders deeply reflected on the reasons for their disastrous loss of the mainland. This critical self-analysis led to their acknowledgment that they had completely lost the support of the overwhelming majority of the Chinese people because of their utter failure to deal with pervasive corruption and to provide for a decent livelihood of the people. Hence, in order to survive and gain the political support of the Taiwanese population, the more unified Kuomintang leaders were determined to achieve a better performance in Taiwan by being more strict with corruption. To this end they resolved to create a greater distance between the government and the private sector, and to expand the role of state enterprises in a way not susceptible to private influence. For example, the government stipulated that government bureaucrats were not allowed to accept presents and dinner invitations from businessmen, and they had to avoid any social functions at which members of the business community were present. Although the government officials naturally disliked these detailed regulations, these rules proved effective in curtailing corruption. They helped to maintain a level of public support and trust before government-business relationships could be institutionalized on a non-personal basis (Vogel, 1991: 33-34).

Another factor that played an important role in pushing the Kuomintang government to establish a more viable and legitimate system of governance was the political leverage which the American government held over the Taiwan government by virtue of its vital economic and military aid. This American pressure was evident from the threat of the U.S. Congress that it would withdraw the much needed American aid if the Taiwan government faltered in its drive to control corruption (Vogel, 1991). The question arises why the American government did not do the same when the Kuomintang government still ruled over the mainland, or to the extent that it did, why this pressure at the time did not bear more palatable fruits?

Some "Theory." As noted above, corruption is the result of unchecked power: "Power corrupts and absolute power corrupts absolutely!" Unchecked political power often exists in developing countries because of the state of civil society. There are, however, a few interesting exceptions, notably Singapore. One possible explanation for the Singapore case is the role and personality of Lee Kuan Yew, who is said to have an obsessive intolerance for corruption. The government decided to give salaries to ministers and key government officials (even professors!) at least as high as those top decision-makers would receive in big companies in the West. What makes Singapore unique is that there never has been a big scandal in high government places. Even in now affluent Korea a scandal broke out when former President Roh Tae-Woo confessed in October 1995 that, during his tenure, US$ 650 million in donations from business had been amassed in a slush fund. In Thailand, money politics and vote buying are still endemic.

The experience of these two Asian countries indicates that one type of corruptive practice, namely the one related to politics, is not going away with increased prosperity in the whole country. However, to what extent is it relevant to distinguish between corruptive practices for a collective (e.g. party) purpose and one for purely individual or private gain? The dividing line is likely to be blurred, as anything can happen in the management of slush funds when accountability is not transparent. The case of former President Roh Tae-Woo illustrates this.

In the post World War II period several leading personalities of the newly-independent countries, such as Nehru, Nyerere, and even Sukarno, were relatively free of the blemish of corruption. It has been said that Chiang Kai-Shek himself was also not corrupt. But these few charismatic leaders could not prevent their courtiers, cronies, or close relatives from indulging themselves in self-enrichment at the expense of the state and society.

So there are several types of more or less illicit payments, from the blatant ones given to the top man of the country and permanently stacked in a Swiss bank, to the more subtle contributions made by business which are not one-to-one related to a favorable decision made by a senior government official. Another important distinction can be made between (illicit) payments made to a bureaucrat (not necessarily a government one) or even a "doorman" to "speed up" things, without the presence of a "yes or no" decision, and payments made to swing a decision the other way. In practice, however, there is a large gray area. Customs clearance can be delayed because of an ambiguity about whether a certain merchandise falls under one category or another. Will an "under the table" payment (only) speed up the process, or will it not also affect the judgment of the official in favor of the client concerned? "Lubrication" can improve (administrative) efficiency, but not when it creates a distortive effect.

The government bureaucracy in many developing countries has often been a part of a planned economy with socialist overtones. Hence, it has been a slow moving machine, often with a disdain for the private businessman, especially if the latter comes from another ethnic group or another caste or social class than the one controlling the government. In such an environment, one can often find the so-called lubricating type of corruptive practices. The other type is the large payments made to the top man or men. When their economies have been in steady decline, this illicitly gathered money remains stacked in Swiss banks or is at best invested in properties abroad. Such corruption hastens the process of eventual breakdown of the system, economically and politically.

While corruption has existed in several East and Southeast Asian countries, their economies have nevertheless flourished. There is apparently no one-to-one relationship between corruption and the health of the economy. But if there was economic retrogression, for instance during the later years of the Marcos regime, the question arises whether it was caused by the blatant corruption or because of the bad macro-economic policies in the first place? When Marcos was eventually removed, the economy did not jump-start right away. It would take almost another decade before the Philippine economy under President Ramos was finally set on the road to economic recovery.

It has been said that corruption in mainland China today is rampant. Nevertheless, its economy continues to grow by almost double digit figures. Similarly, several senior government officials in Indonesia have argued that the Indonesian economy has grown quite rapidly during the past few years even though corruption in Indonesia is said to be rampant. How can this be explained? Some Japanese and Dutch business friends have told us that although corruption "is rampant" in China, it consists mainly of payments on various occasions when foreign business has to meet or interact with local hosts or bureaucrats, and is therefore more comparable to the lubricating type of corruptive practices. Through the experience of "learning by doing," these "lubricating" costs can eventually be bargained down. It is therefore similar to a situation in which an uninitiated tourist has to pay more for the souvenirs he buys in Asia. One of our Sino-Indonesian business friends has denied the claim of rampant corruption in China. Can it be true that a Westerner is appalled by what he sees as rampant corruption, while an Asian (businessman) shrugs his shoulders at certain practices considered abhorrent by most Westerners? The above Sino-Indonesian friend argued that the need for these extra payments can be likened to a car driver who wants to go from place A to B at a faster pace and therefore takes the toll road and pays the required fare.

Corruption or bribes paid to high government officials are like taxes for business. Taxes that are too high can kill business, but how much is too much? It is said that in East Asian countries the local companies often avoid paying the full taxes, while the foreign companies do not have the same latitude. On the other hand, the foreign companies are more likely to be spared from the pressure of having to make various kinds of contributions. So in a way there is an equalization of the (actual) fiscal regime for domestic and foreign companies. Like in advanced countries too, high taxes can also slow down economic growth if the proceeds of such taxes are used for consumptive purposes, such as transfer payments and subsidies. On the other hand, it is conceivable that in developing countries illicit payments to high officials are (partially) turned into capital for investments in business. If senior government officials or their siblings have businesses on the side, the bureaucracy may be more "pro-business" in its judgments and decisions, or at least appreciate the need for expediency of decisions. Such an attitude can be growth facilitating if economic policies do not create too many economic distortions as a result of discriminatory policies in favor of the relatives and cronies of officials. In fact, when such blatantly discriminatory policies are being pursued, they may lead to a gross misallocation of scarce resources and widespread cynicism, undermining the political legitimacy of the government.

The Relevance of Taiwan's Experience for Indonesia. How did corruption in Taiwan wither away during the 1950s and 1960s? What happened when per capita income rose from under US$ 1000 to US$ 3000 per annum? Is there a link between levels of per capita income and blatant corruption? Or is a decline in corruptive practices more related to progressive professionalization of the bureaucracy, better salaries, development of the legal system, better functioning of the state audit agency, the growth of a more vocal press. etc.? As a country undertakes economic deregulation, the amount of illicit payments to the long chain of bureaucratic licensing required to do business is likely to decrease. Is this always true? By itself, related to the number of steps or counters to be passed, it is true and small time corruption involving petty bureaucrats declines. But big time corruption or payments made by contractors winning fat government contracts may not be affected at all, as the costs of such big projects may not always be transparent. If a power project costs significantly more than comparable projects in a neighboring country, this may or may not be the smoke indicating some fire, because no two big projects are quite identical in nature. While transparency in the tender system will help a great deal and will avoid major irregularities, it is not a watertight system.

Similarly, large defense contracts are noted for the possibility of sizable kickbacks or commissions because one deals with merchandise without a market price tag. Moreover, corrupt practices can easily be abetted by the (foreign) suppliers and thus morality must come in pairs.

While the Kuomintang government on Taiwan, through its strict regulations, was able to establish an arm's length relationship between government and private business, the same cannot be said of Indonesia. Unlike the East Asian NIEs, Indonesia cannot be considered an "insulated developmentalist state" in the sense that government has retained a sufficient degree of autonomy to pursue what it sees as its national interest without undue subservience to foreign multinational corporations or to the local business classes (Mackie, 1988: 292, 315-316). It is for this reason too that, particularly in recent years, there has been a spate of scandals involving senior government officials and shady businessmen, which have given rise to widespread public criticism of "collusion" between self-serving senior government officials and big businessmen. To reduce this big time corruption Indonesia may well learn from Taiwan's experience by establishing a more transparent and greater arm's length relationship between government and private business.

Conclusion. Corruption is too much a generic term, requiring specification for the relevant analytical purpose. Apart from a moral imperative which a priori rejects corruption, for most developing countries where corrupt practices are endemic, one important question is the nexus between corruption and (lack of) growth. In this respect not all corruptive practices inhibit economic growth. Corruptive practices are still prevalent under the surface in high growth and even advanced Asian countries such as Japan, for instance in connection with party politics.

Hence, it would be relevant to distinguish corruptive practices which distort the allocative system *too* much and adversely affect economic growth from the more benign types of the social disease which are not too costly in terms of gross misallocation of resources and thus are a phenomenon a developing country can live with.

In this regard important questions would include: first, if an economy grows (fast), to what extent and how will corruptive practices decline (and what does the Taiwanese experience tell us); second, does it require a change in political or other non-economic parameters to have corruption wither away (like the traumatic experience of the Kuomintang regime having to go into exile in Taiwan)?

17.2.2 The Growth of Small, Medium, and Large Enterprises

The Problem. Taiwan and South Korea have developed different industrial structures and scales. South Korea has the largest, heaviest, and most advanced industrial structure among the four Asian NIEs with a high level of industrial concentration (higher even than in Japan) due to the prevalence of giant, private conglomerates (*chaebols*) which were developed because of deliberate government policy. Since the 1960s, the Korean government had pursued a highly interventionist industrial policy to push industry into very large-scale, complex, technologically demanding activities with a view to develop internationally competitive industrial groups (*chaebols*) able to face head on the strongest competition in world markets. At the same time the Korean government also pursued a highly restrictive foreign investment policy to safeguard national ownership in the manufacturing sector. (Lall, 1991: 8-9).

Taiwan's industrial structure, on the other hand, is "lighter" than that of Korea, as it consists largely of small and medium scale enterprises (SMEs) which are spread over a broad base of activities, ranging from simple, labor-intensive to high skill, technology-intensive ones, many of which are export-oriented. (Lall, 1991: 7). Most of these SMEs have focused more on filling market niches rather than mass production, and, in view of their smaller size and assets, have done little in-house R & D and, with a few exceptions, have placed less emphasis on creating international brand names for their export products (Lall, 1994: 77). The great importance of SMEs in Taiwan's industrial structure is evident from the fact that in 1992 SMEs accounted for no less than 98 percent of all industrial establishments, while 60 percent of Taiwan's total manufactured exports were generated by SMEs (World Bank,1993: 162).

To a large extent, the growth of SMEs in Taiwan can be attributed to the equal distribution of land following the successful land reform and the shift towards more labor-intensive crop mixes and technologies, which caused the demand for non-agricultural goods to be increasingly directed towards the output produced by SMEs. As these SMEs were largely located in Taiwan's rural areas, mutual backward and forward linkages between changes in agricultural and non-agricultural output could be considerably strengthened. The widespread dispersion of SMEs all over the island, particularly in the rural areas, is a major factor accounting for the considerable success of Taiwan in terms of growth, employment generation, enhanced equity, and balanced regional development (Ranis, 1995: 514).

As rural labor was able to shift from agricultural to non-agricultural activities within the rural areas themselves, Taiwan's industrialization process was able to avoid the relative (and sometimes absolute) decline in rural non-agricultural activities that usually occurred in other rapidly industrializing countries. In other words, in Taiwan rural, non-agricultural activities were not eroded by more favored urban industry and services. As rural incomes in Taiwan rose, farmers' demand for domestically-produced consumer goods rose (creating forward final consumption linkages), as did demand for intermediate inputs (creating backward linkages). As a result of these developments, the ability and willingness of Taiwan's farmers to take advantage of new investment opportunities outside of agriculture also increased. Both these trends further encouraged the growth of rural SMEs in the industrial and service sectors (Ranis, 1995: 514-515). Incidentally, in Indonesia itself the expansion of off-farm job opportunities in the rural areas as a result of rapid agricultural development during the 1970s and 1980s was a major factor accounting for the rapid decline in absolute poverty in rural areas, particularly on Java.

Taiwan's model is attractive for latecomer developing countries, including Indonesia, on the road to industrialization and export development because smallness of scale is associated with a better distribution of income, wealth and economic power. This argument is based on the fact that rapid growth of small-and medium-scale industries (SMIs) absorbs large numbers of workers, particularly by attracting rural labor, and thus reduces poverty. As rapidly-growing SMEs upgrade their operations and shift to more sophisticated production and therefore raise their operational efficiency, the real incomes of SME owners and workers will increase (World Bank, 1993: 161). This equity argument is compelling in the social debate today, particularly in Indonesia, where concern is rising because of the perceived widening gap between large conglomerates on the one hand and small and medium-scale enterprises (SMEs) on the other hand. In fact, Indonesia's industrial structure shows a "dualistic" structure in which the small- and medium-scale industries (SMIs), which employ between 5 to 199 workers, in 1985 accounted for only 20.5 percent of total manufacturing value added (MVA) (Hill, 1995: 7).

Thus far the various promotion programs initiated by the Indonesian government to develop economically viable SMEs have not been very successful. For instance, in 1990 the Indonesian government terminated the nation-wide subsidized credit (KIK/KMKP) program that had been introduced in 1973 because the high default rates (27 percent) had endangered the self-sustainability of this program. To replace this program, the government in January 1990 introduced the Small Enterprise Credit (KUK) Scheme, under which all banks were required to allocate 20 percent of their loan portfolio to SMEs. While in quantitative terms the record of this KUK program has been impressive, it has not been very successful in stimulating the healthy growth of the mass of SMEs (Thee, 1993: 10-13). Similarly, the major technical assistance program for small- and medium-scale industries (SMIs), the Small-Scale Industries Development (BIPIK) program, implemented by the Directorate-General for Small-Scale Industry, Department of Industry, has not been successful in providing the necessary technical assistance for SMIs because of insufficient funding for this program and the reluctance on the part of small entrepreneurs to utilize the facilities offered under this program (Thee, 1993: 13-15). At present, the Agency for Small-Scale Industry Development (BAPIK), Department of Industry and Trade is exploring the possibility of developing promotion programs for SMIs which put a greater emphasis on the "efficiency" approach rather than the "welfare-oriented" approach. Under the former approach, promotion programs will be focused on the modern, technology-based SMEs which show greater potential to become economically viable.

The attraction of the comparison between Taiwan and Korea is that export and economic growth are seemingly not one-to-one related to scale of operation, as both countries were able to achieve scale economies and international competitiveness. But because the underlying concern is normative, i.e. that of equity and distribution, one still needs confirmation that the Taiwanese growth model produces better results in these normative aspects than does the Korean one. We should also test the hypothesis that the Taiwanese growth model has not produced large (private) conglomerates because the country may be in an earlier phase of (statist) development. Some large state-owned corporations were eventually privatized and thus became privately-owned conglomerates. Today, it is certainly not true that in Taiwan there are no private conglomerates. In heavy industry and other activities involving large economies of scale or using advanced technologies, Taiwan has some large private economic groups (for instance in consumer electronics, mini-computers, and plastics) and several large state-owned enterprises (SOEs).

However, among the East Asian NIEs Taiwan has the largest public sector (Lall, 1991: 7).

Reliable facts and figures about comparative income and wealth distribution are difficult to obtain. However, the available empirical evidence indicates that Taiwan and Korea have been doing quite well compared to the large majority of developing countries in that both countries, in particular Taiwan, have been able to combine rapid and sustained economic growth with declining income inequality and a steep reduction in absolute poverty (World Bank, 1993: 28-32). Is the explanation for this the thesis that fast economic growth per se trickles down? Or has the crucial variable been the high education rates prevailing in those East Asian countries as compared to developing countries in other areas of the world? What has been the great equalizer: economic growth per se, education per se, or some combination of the two? Have government fiscal (tax) policies also played a significant, if not a crucial role, perhaps together with spending policies directed to correcting maldistribution of income?

According to a comparative study conducted by Irma Adelman in the mid 1970s, a small number of non-communist countries (Japan, Taiwan, South Korea, Singapore, and Israel) were able to combine rapid economic growth with a steep reduction in absolute poverty and a relatively equal distribution of income by pursuing a sequential development strategy which at the outset implemented a radical distribution of assets (i.e. land reform), followed by a massive investment in human capital, and a subsequent labor-intensive, export-oriented pattern of industrial development (Adelman, 1975: 302-309). Taiwan's development experience certainly appears to confirm Adelman's thesis that the sequential development strategy of redistribute first, invest in human capital, and then grow by pursuing a labor-intensive, export-oriented pattern of development has indeed led to the favorable mix of rapid growth with equity.

The Relevance for Indonesia. Indonesia is still in the early stages of its industrialization and export drive. While per capita income has recently reached the US$ 1000 per annum level, the export orientation of the manufacturing sector only started in earnest since the mid 1980s. As a result, Indonesia's total manufactured exports in 1992 accounted for only 0.6 percent of world exports, while those of Taiwan had a 2.8 percent overall market share (Lall and Rao, 1995: 9). However, although Indonesia still lags behind Taiwan in exporting manufactured products, it has made rapid progress in raising its manufactured exports from only US$ 809 million in 1982 to US$ 16.1 billion in 1992. This performance has not only been achieved by large-scale industries (LIs), but also by small-scale industries (SIs), as indicated by the fact that these SIs accounted for 10.0 percent of Indonesia's total manufactured exports in 1983 and for 13.2 percent in 1992 (Hill, 1995: 16).

Indonesia's manufacturing sector (including both its oil and gas subsector and the larger non-oil and gas subsector) now accounts for 24 percent of total GDP. So far the bulk of manufactured exports consists of textiles and garments, footwear and plywood, and to a lesser extent electronics, while other exports, such as electrical goods and petrochemicals, are increasing, but are individually far from reaching the level of US$ 1 billion of annual exports. But non-oil and non-gas exports have been growing at double digit levels, namely in the range of 11 to 14 percent during the period 1993/94 - 1994/95. Although the growth of non-oil and gas exports, particularly manufactured exports, slowed down in 1993 and 1994, their performance showed an improvement in 1995. In fact, non-oil and gas exports during the first nine months of 1995 grew by 14.2 percent over the same period in 1994, up from 11.4 percent growth the previous year. For manufactured exports the comparable figures for 1994 and 1995 respectively were 9.0 percent and 13.6 percent. However, the three "problem" export industries, plywood, textiles, and garments, continued to perform poorly, although the latter two showed some slight improvement (Bird, 1996: 15-16).

Another phenomenon during the past 10 years in Indonesia has been the growth of large, diversified conglomerates. These are private groups of family-owned corporations, usually still controlled by their founders — mostly people of Chinese origin who migrated to Indonesia during the Dutch colonial period. The second and later generation Chinese families, who have culturally been more integrated with the indigenous Indonesians since the Dutch colonial era (the so-called *"peranakans"*) only form a minority among the ethnic Chinese families owning and controlling these large conglomerates. A fewer number of conglomerates owned and controlled by indigenous (*pribumi*) Indonesians have emerged during the past 25 years, although only two or three are among the top ten in terms of estimated size of assets. The dominance of ethnic Chinese-owned and controlled large conglomerates is, for instance, indicated in the respected Indonesian magazine EKSEKUTIF, which in its February 1994 issue published a list of the 100 largest diversified conglomerates ranked by estimated size of assets. This list showed that no less than 75 of these top 100 business groups could be identified as being owned and controlled by ethnic Chinese businessmen, while ethnic Chinese almost certainly also had a stake in several of the *pribumi* owned conglomerates. However, Indonesia's non-oil export surge since the mid 1980s has by and large not been due to these large conglomerates, most of which are still largely oriented towards the still protected large domestic market, because they generally do not control the export-oriented textile and particularly the garment industries. However, a small number of these private business groups do own and control large-scale, integrated textile plants, including spinning, weaving, dyeing, finishing, and printing operations. Nike shoes for exports and other brand name footwear are currently made in large quantities in Indonesia by joint ventures with Asian NIE firms, particularly Korean firms, which have relocated to Indonesia since the late 1980s because of their loss of comparative advantage in labor-intensive industries in their home countries. The garment industry consists largely of domestic, (including *pribumi*-owned) SMEs, although several export-oriented, large-scale operations have since the late 1980s been set up by Asian NIE firms, particularly Korean and to a lesser extent Taiwanese firms. However, the rapid mandatory rise in minimum wages in recent years, which has not been matched by a commensurate rise in labor productivity, has led to a relocation of several of these NIE firms to lower-wage countries in the region, such as Vietnam.

Indonesia's labor-intensive exports have to a large extent been triggered by foreign (mostly Asian NIE firm)-controlled joint ventures which have been relocating to Indonesia and elsewhere in Southeast Asia from Northeast Asia since the mid 1980s, when they started looking for cheaper production locations or countries with still unused quotas at the time. The important contribution of foreign direct investment (FDI) projects to Indonesia's effort to increase its non-oil and gas exports is clearly indicated by Bank of Indonesia estimates, which indicated that the contribution of FDI projects (joint ventures) to total non-oil and gas exports steadily rose from 14 percent in 1987 to 20 percent in 1988, 30 percent in 1989, 38 percent in 1991, and 40 percent in 1993 (Wibowo, 1995: 4).

There is now a public image in Indonesia that the rise of domestic conglomerates has little to do with superior productivity and international competitiveness. This image appears to be borne out by the findings of a recent World Bank study, which has indicated that the export performance of highly-concentrated industries in Indonesia in which there is a large presence of firms owned by large private conglomerates or state-owned enterprises (or SOEs), such as the non-metallic (particularly cement), metal goods, chemicals, food, and basic metals industries, has been poor, while industries with low four-firm concentration ratios, such as the textile, garments, and footwear industries, have shown a much better export performance (Iqbal, 1995: table 18). Hence, the conglomerates are seen as the result of deliberate government policy which did not link preferential treatment (directed subsidized credit, high protection, government procurement, and other government facilities) with certain performance criteria, such as proven export performance, as has been the case in South Korea where the late President Park Chung-Hee himself personally monitored the export performance of the *chaebols*.

In retrospect one can see the remarkable growth of conglomerates in Indonesia as not only related to preferential government policies, but also to a particular group of domestic entrepreneurs — i.e. the ethnic Chinese minority and the handful of migrants — who have had an unusual head start from the Dutch colonial period and considerable leeway since then.

In the 1970s and first half of the 1980s economic growth and industrialization were state directed. SOEs occupied the commanding heights of the economy, especially in the large-scale basic (resource-processing) industries and also in banking, where SOEs accounted for roughly 85 percent of total bank assets. During that period the government offered lower than market interest long term credits (so-called liquidity credits) for investments to a number of prioritized industries, such as plywood and shipbuilding. On the other hand, the incoming foreign companies were until recently barred from obtaining credits from the state banks, even for working capital. The idea was that foreign MNCs should import their own capital and not compete for scarce capital in the local capital market.

The availability of cheap credits from the dominant state banks (at the time private banks had only around seven percent of market share, while by foreign banks operating in the country had an eight percent market share) was certainly not designed to feed the Chinese enterprises. In fact, since 1974 ethnic Chinese businessmen were discriminated against in favor of indigenous (*pribumi*) enterprises. However, nature seemed to be stronger than man-made rules. The fact can be verified that behind the fast growth of the ethnic Chinese-owned enterprises there have been willing government banks which trusted them with their money.

The dominance of Chinese enterprises has led to social tensions that increase the risks that the country will experience a nasty political sting, or even that riots will erupt that could endanger political stability as well as the country's investment climate. The present government's approach to this problem is, on the one hand, to recognize and deal with the social prejudices by introducing various equity- and poverty-oriented programs. On the other hand, the government also regards the (domestic) Chinese enterprises and entrepreneurs as "national assets" which should not be left by the wayside in the national drive for economic growth, industrialization, and modernization. Even if the available evidence indicates that the conglomerates are not more efficient and productive, in contrast to SMEs and large firms not affiliated with the conglomerates (and there are quite large number of these), at least the conglomerates have been in the forefront of asset growth and diversification, especially in new modern ventures (such as financial services), often aligning themselves with international sources of know-how and capital.

The Indonesian conglomerates have grown very fast since deregulation policies were introduced after 1985 with a view to promote a more efficient private (including both domestic and foreign) sector which could generate the non-oil and gas exports needed to offset the decline in oil export earnings following the end of the oil boom in the early 1980s. But can one really say that conglomeration was the product of deregulation and a liberalized business environment? The social critics doubt this, because the Indonesian business environment has never been free of controls, and those critics do claim that the recent extra growth has also been a result of "collusion" between high government circles and the captains of business. But this mutual trust and close government and business relations have been mentioned as one of the causal factors for the "Asian miracle." It has been said that such government-business relations have been lacking in Africa and South Asia, which has been the reason of the lack of or slower growth in these countries.

A country such as Indonesia, where various manufacturing industries display high four-firm concentration ratios, is also interested to learn about the experience of Taiwan and Korea regarding philosophy, legal system and practice with respect to "competition policy" and the prevention of monopolistic practices.

What makes the Taiwanese experience so intriguing, and attractive, is that without the dominance of large private conglomerates, its export growth performance has been as impressive as that of South Korea with its *chaebols.* This is clearly indicated by the fact that in 1992 Taiwan's manufactured exports had a 2.8 percent overall world market share, with low- skill exports accounting for 4.7 percent and high skill exports accounting for a 2.2 percent world market share. The corresponding figures for South Korea's manufactured exports were an overall market share of 2.6 percent (second-best performance among the NIEs after Taiwan), with low skill exports accounting for 4.2 percent and high skill exports accounting for a 2.1 percent world market share (Lall and Rao, 1995: 9). In other words, in South Korea the impressive performance of manufactured exports was mainly achieved by the *chaebols,* while in Taiwan it was the SMEs which generated the bulk of the country's manufactured exports. On the other hand, in Indonesia SMEs have, as indicated earlier, accounted for 13.2 percent of total non-oil and gas exports in 1992. In the export-oriented textile, garments, and footwear industries, however, SMEs accounted for no less than 57.3 percent of the combined exports of these three industries (Hill, 1995: 16).

17.2.3 Industrial Policy and the Acquisition and Mastery of Foreign Industrial Technologies for Industrialization and Export Development

The Problem and Its Options. The countries of East and Southeast Asia have pursued different strategies or routes to acquire and absorb technologies from outside to boost their industrialization process. The choice in a particular country has been the result of domestic conditions and policies and the prevailing international situation and the trends of the time.

When Japan started to look for and acquire western know-how and technologies at the start of its modernization efforts in the second half of the 19th century, the world was not yet an open place, buttressed by modern means of transport and communications. At the time the now ubiquitous (western) multinational enterprises were still an unknown phenomenon. Despite the different conditions, however, some of the things Japan did can still be repeated at present — for instance sending many people abroad to look around, compare and absorb new technologies. In our time this process has even been facilitated by international aid — providing, among other things, scholarships to students of the developing countries and technical assistance from donor country experts — and has hence became less costly for the developing countries. On the other hand, as has been the case in Indonesia, because of the existence of foreign aid there was less technological effort, insistence and sacrifice on the part of the receiving government to actively pursue a policy like that of Japan (e.g., selection and choice) in the Meiji period. In several developing countries (though not Indonesia since the introduction of an open capital account in 1972) a shortage of foreign exchange reserves and a foreign exchange control regime has also made it much more expensive for families to send their children overseas for further study.

In today's world, technology acquisition can also follow the FDI (foreign direct investment) route, as occurred in countries in Southeast Asia and Hong Kong in East Asia. In fact, FDI has generally been the dominant form of resource and technology transfer from developed to developing countries. It is and has been the most "packaged" form of technology transfer, combining the provision of capital with technical know-how, capital equipment, management, marketing, and other skills (Lall,1993: 95). This route, however, has its own limitations. FDI in Indonesia, for instance, has been more inclined to tap the potentially large domestic market for which technological improvements were needed only when threatened by greater import or domestic competition. Depending on the strength of the domestic enterprises, technology acquisition through technical licensing agreements has also been an effective option which many Indonesian enterprises have taken.

On the other hand, Taiwan and particularly Korea after the Second World War have not depended too much on FDI for the acquisition of advanced industrial technologies. Nonetheless, through FDI in Taiwan foreign firms did play an important role in introducing new products and process technologies in the automotive and the automotive parts and components industries as well as in the electrical appliance, electronics, and plastic and plastic products industries.

However, in the textile and machinery industries foreign firms played only a minor role (Chi, 1990: 37).

Taiwan's early industrial strategy was focused on providing strong support to its small- and medium-scale industries (SMIs) which provided greater flexibility while, unlike Korea, it held back large, risky investments in industrial technologies by large enterprises. In other words, in contrast to South Korea, the Taiwan government pursued a more cautious, less interventionist, more incremental industrial strategy which, however, later hampered efforts to develop high technology industries. Like South Korea and other developing countries, Taiwan too protected its emerging industries, guiding the expansion of certain industries along certain lines, and pursuing an active technology development policy (Lall, 1991: 176). When economic growth was mainly spurred by labor-intensive industries and manufactured exports in the late 1950s and early 1960s, very little scientific research and development (R & D) was carried out, except in the field of agriculture. However, since the early 1970s Taiwan's National Science Council (NSC) began to actively promote R & D cooperation between Taiwan's public research institutes and various state-owned and private enterprises, and increased its grant support for basic and applied research. After the mid 1970s the NSC expanded its support for R & D activities with a view to build up a modern defense industry as well as "upgrade" Taiwan's industrial structure. To that end, the NSC in 1980 established the Science- based Industrial Park in Hsinchu, a new type of industrial zone geared in particular to upgrade Taiwan's electronics industry. In addition to promoting its own R & D efforts, Taiwan was also able, as mentioned above, to make good use of the multinational corporations (MNCs) from the advanced countries as sources of industrial technologies, and therefore was able to successfully integrate foreign technology transfer into its own strategy to advance its own indigenous science and technology (S& T) capabilities (Arnold, 1990: 84-85). A few years earlier the Ministry of Economic Affairs had also established the Industrial Technology Research Institute (ITRI), which was entrusted with conducting applied industrial research and with providing technical services to industry as well as coordinate defense-related research. Over time, ITRI was able to establish itself as Taiwan's leading institution for R & D activities to enhance the international competitiveness of its manufacturing industries, including its SMIs (Arnold, 1990: 86-87). Actually, because of its earlier "hands off" policy regarding the promotion of large-scale firms, however, the Taiwan government in later years had to promote more actively Taiwan's industry and technological development. This was, for instance, reflected by the establishment of an SOE to produce semiconductor (DRAM) chips. Moreover, the Taiwan government also intervened by coordinating related technology imports, design, manufacture, and marketing by several private firms, including SMEs (Lall, 1991: 176).

In other words, since the Taiwan government, unlike Korea's government, did not attempt to create and develop giant private conglomerates which were expected to act as the spearhead for the push into capital-intensive and high technology industries, its later attempts to develop heavy industries had to be led by large, state-owned enterprises. As a result, among the four East Asian NIEs, Taiwan has the largest public sector (Lall,1994: 77). Moreover, to offset the competitive disadvantages for technical and industrial upgrading associated with the proliferation of SMEs, the Taiwan government provided a wide range of technology support services, including R & D. These effective technology support services as well as the inherent flexibility associated with SMEs, most of which were led by highly entrepreneurial owners, has accounted for the fact that Taiwan has managed to keep up high rates of manufactured export growth comparable to those of Korea (Lall, 1994: 77).

In contrast to Taiwan, the South Korean government has pursued a much more ambitious and hence more interventionist industrial strategy, which has involved the promotion and strong protection of a number of selected "strategic" industries, (sometimes set up as state-owned enterprises, such as the highly efficient Pohang steel plant), the direction of investment at the sectoral and often even at the firm level, the strong promotion of manufactured exports by direct measures (including linking the various incentives provided to the various enterprises to their actual export performance), intervention in technology transfer agreements and technology development (as in the petrochemical industry), the restructuring of industry, and the enforced training of labor. Despite considerable liberalization, a strong element of government guidance has persisted until today (Lall, 1991: 176).

The Relevance for Indonesia. For a country like Indonesia the experience of Taiwan, and a comparison of the industrial strategies of Korea, Taiwan and Singapore to acquire up-to-date technologies to strengthen their industrial development and export performance, are very important matters. In this regard it is also very important to understand the special and specific circumstances in which Taiwan could operate. For instance, is it is true that Taiwan made maximum use of the presence of a great number of Chinese scientists and professionals working in Silicon Valley in the United States? Certainly Taiwan's policy of unrestricted emigration led to a "brain drain" as large numbers of Taiwanese scholars and scientists trained overseas, particularly in the U.S., chose not to return to Taiwan. However, in recent years an increasing number of Taiwanese scientists and engineers who were trained overseas have returned to Taiwan in response to the expanding employment and career opportunities in their own country. According to a recent estimate, out of the 128,000 Taiwanese students holding foreign university degrees from the early 1960s up to the present, 44,905 were recorded as having returned to Taiwan (Tsiang, 1996: 5, 14). This was an avenue that countries such as Thailand, Malaysia and Indonesia are not able to travel, as there are not many Indonesian, Malaysian, or Thai scientists and engineers who upon their graduation from foreign universities decided to stay in the countries where they had studied in order to work in high-tech industries. On the other hand, India could most likely emulate Taiwan's experience in the near future in view of the presence of a large number of Indian scientists and engineers who studied in the U.S. and other advanced countries and upon their graduation decided to stay in these countries. If India sets out to embark on an ambitious export-oriented pattern of industrialization, the ensuing rapid economic growth might open up good employment and career opportunities which could tempt the overseas Indian scientists and engineers to return to their country.

It also appears that Taiwan made good use of export processing zones (EPZs), such as Kaohsiung, to attract FDI from the U.S. and other advanced countries to make use of Taiwan's cheap but skillful labor. Malaysia also followed this route in the Penang area, but the question arises why a copy-cat entrepreneurial group did not develop in Malaysia to clone the electronic and electrical products assembled in Malaysia? One reason given is that the Malaysian entrepreneurs, most of whom are ethnic Chinese, did not have the same mental horizon as their Taiwanese counterparts. The Sino-Malaysian entrepreneurs, like most Sino-Indonesian entrepreneurs, historically were steeped in the tradition of trading and dealing in primary commodities. As a result, they were much less oriented towards industrial ventures than their Taiwanese counterparts.

A popular explanation given to explain the success of Taiwan and Korea in industrialization is that they had been Japanese colonies before World War II, and that the Japanese overlords had given these colonies mass primary education and effective rural development that distinguished them from the European colonizers. Is that a valid, though partial, argument?

The first author of this paper was most impressed and gratified that the first affordable desk computer he could buy ten years ago was an Apple II clone made in Taiwan which was a trouble free machine for a long time. How did Taiwan manage cloning this popular product and marketing it successfully in Southeast Asia? Why did Korea come later in producing personal computers and selling them abroad? Nowadays, the technology is mature and therefore widespread enough that countries like Indonesia could emulate the process, but as a latecomer the juicy markets overseas appear to be gone.

As an anecdote, the Liem Sioe Liong conglomerate, Indonesia's largest private conglomerate and one of the largest in Southeast Asia, has been able to produce Walkman clones in the backyard of its industrial area, adjacent to its giant cement plant in Cibinong, West Java, and to export these to the United States. The technology was acquired from Taiwan.

Hence, with a limited technological basis in Indonesia, but noting the fact that, in time, some entrepreneurs could emulate the producers in industrially more advanced countries such as Taiwan, in making popular consumer electronics products and selling them in overseas markets, the question arises whether this feat would reflect real domestic technological capabilities or rather entrepreneurial ones?

Mr. Gerrit Zalm, the Dutch finance minister, in late 1995 observed at a seminar on Indonesia organized by the Erasmus University in Rotterdam, the Netherlands, that developing countries need not develop new technologies. For them it is enough to move up to the frontier of it, and this "catching up" process is less difficult than developing new technologies. By nature this is true but a developing country must certainly master a number of basic technologies and know-how, such as reverse engineering and production technologies. It has been argued that a developing country needs a number of supporting industries, most of which would consist of SMEs which would supply parts and components to the downstream assembly industries, particularly the engineering goods industries. Is there something in the present international, and East Asian, setting that could facilitate this development? For instance, can Japan, Korea or Taiwan help Indonesia in setting up and/or upgrading these industries, and in the process train the required managers, technicians, and shopfloor workers? What would be the incentives, or compulsions, in the international or Asia-Pacific regional setting at the moment to do so?

Certainly in the case of Indonesia the absence of a strong base of supporting industries at present is a major factor which may adversely affect the international competitiveness of export- oriented assembly industries, such as the consumer electronics and electrical appliance industries. Because of the absence or lack of an adequate number of efficient supplier industries, these assembly industries have to import more expensive parts and components from Japan, Korea, Taiwan, and other Southeast Asian countries, such as Malaysia and Thailand, which adversely affects the international competitiveness of these local assembly industries. In view of the need for short lead times and lower transaction costs (just-in-time delivery of the required parts and components) and the need for flexible operations in order to respond quickly to changes in market trends, the need to develop efficient supporting industries is crucial to developing internationally competitive consumer electronics and electric appliance industries (FIAS, 1995). Hence, there is an urgent need to establish and strengthen these supporting industries, lest the existing ones be wiped away by import competition after AFTA (ASEAN Free Trade Area) is established in 2003. Interviews with some small- and medium-scale supplier firms in Indonesia have indicated that in the face of these developments, there is a desire to tie up and establish joint ventures with Japanese and Korean small-and medium-scale supplier firms in order to survive, even if they would be minority partners in these joint ventures. In time, of course, it is hoped that such Indonesian supplier firms can enhance their performance through technology transfer and absorption from their Japanese and Korean partners.

Indonesia's public S & T infrastructure should, like that of Taiwan, be able to provide needed technology support services to upgrade the capabilities of these supporting industries, most of which consist of SMEs. While there has been a lot of rhetoric about the need for the domestic S & T infrastructure to assist national industry in raising its technological capabilities in order to raise its competitiveness, as has been the case in Taiwan, thus far Indonesia's public S & T institutions, including the technology support institutions, have not yet been very effective in providing these essential services. In attempting to improve the performance of Indonesia's S & T infrastructure in this regard, steps need to be taken to make this infrastructure more "demand-driven" rather than continuing to be merely "supply-driven" as has been the case thus far. In order to achieve this goal, the public S & T institutions, including the technology support institutions, need to be freed from the bureaucratic constraints which have thus far hampered their efforts to forge more effective and mutually profitable linkages with private companies. Once freed from these bureaucratic constraints, these S & T institutions could become more "demand (market)-driven" and be more responsive to the actual technological needs of private industry.

17.3 Concluding Remarks

In the preceding pages, three aspects of Taiwan's development experience were discussed in which Taiwan has achieved some notable successes, namely in the rapid reduction of corruption within a relatively short period of time, the successful promotion of economically viable and highly competitive small- and medium-scale industries (SMIs), and the acquisition and subsequent mastery of foreign industrial technologies. These three aspects of Taiwan's development experience are of interest to Indonesia, as it is precisely in these fields that Indonesia has not been quite successful.

In regard to Taiwan's relative success in reducing widespread corruption, a relevant lesson for Indonesia could be to create a greater distance between government and the private sector, so as to make senior government officials less susceptible to private influence. In addition, corruption can also be gradually reduced by decreasing the role of the state through deregulation and privatization and by introducing more competition, transparency and accountability into the political process.

In regard to the role of small- and medium-scale industries (SMIs), Taiwan's development experience has indicated that a good performance in manufactured exports is not necessarily dependent on large-scale enterprises, as in Taiwan it has been the SMEs which have generated the bulk of the country's manufactured exports. Hence, the relevant lesson for Indonesia would be that a policy bias in favor of large conglomerates is not necessary to sustain Indonesia's manufactured exports. In fact, to promote a more efficient manufacturing sector, existing policy biases in favor of the large conglomerates as well as existing policy biases against SMIs need to be eliminated.

In regard to the acquisition and mastery of foreign industrial technologies for rapid industrialization and export development, Taiwan has been able to make good use of the multinational corporations (MNCs) from the advanced countries as sources of industrial technologies, and to integrate these technologies into its own strategy to advance its own technological capabilities.

Taiwan has also been able to establish a highly effective science and technology (S & T) infrastructure which has been conducting valuable R & D activities and providing valuable technology support services for private industry, including the SMIs. In this regard one relevant lesson for Indonesia would be that the Indonesian government could play an important role in enhancing the supply-side capabilities of manufacturing firms by improving existing S & T infrastructure and by removing the bureaucratic constraints facing S & T institutes, which have thus far prevented these institutes from establishing effective and mutually profitable linkages with private industry.

17.4 References

Adelman, Irma, 1975. "Development Economics — A Reassessment of Goals," *American Economic Review — Papers and Proceedings* (May): 302-309.

Arnold, Walter, 1990. *Science and Technology Development in Taiwan and Korea, The Republic of China on Taiwan Today — Views from Abroad*, 2nd Edition. Taipei: Kwang Hwa Publishing Company.

Amsden, Alice H., 1985. "The State and Taiwan's Economic Development," in P. Evans et. al., (eds.), *op. cit.*: 78-106.

Bird, Kelly, 1996. "Survey of Recent Developments," *Bulletin of Indonesian Economic Studies*, 32 (1): 3-32 (April).

Boomgaard, Peter, 1986. "The Welfare Services in Indonesia, 1900-1942," *ITINERARIO - Special Issue: India and Indonesia from the 1920s to the 1950s - the Origins of Planning*, no. 1: 57-82.

Booth, Anne, 1988. *Agricultural Development in Indonesia*. Sydney: Allen and Unwin.

Booth, Anne , 1989. *The State and Economic Development in Indonesia: The Ethical and New Order Eras Compared*. Canberra: mimeo.

Chi, Schive, 1990. *The Foreign Factor: The Multinational Corporation's Contribution to the Economic Modernization of the Republic of China*. Stanford: Hoover Institution Press, Stanford University.

Cribb, Robert, 1993. "Development Policy in the Early 20th Century," in Dirkse, et al., (eds.), *op. cit.*: 225-246.

Dirkse, Jan-Paul, Frans Husken, and Mario Rutten (eds.), 1993. *Indonesia's Experience under the New Order*. Leiden: KITLV Press.

Drysdale, Peter (ed.), 1972. *Direct Foreign Investment in Asia and the Pacific*. Canberra: Australian National University Press.

Evans, P. et. al., 1985. *Bringing the State Back In*. Cambridge: Cambridge University Press.

FIAS, 1995. *Promoting Backward Linkages in Indonesia's Manufacturing Sector*. Washington, D.C.: Foreign Investment Advisory Service, May.

Gonggrijp, G, 1949. *Schets ener Economische Geschiedenis van Nederlandsch Indie* [Sketch of an Economic History of the Netherlands Indies]. Haarlem: De Erven F. Bohn.

Haggard, Stephan, 1991. *Pathways from the Periphery: The Politics of Growth in the Newly Industrializing Countries*. Ithaca, NY: Cornell University Press.

Harriss-White, Barbara and Gordon White, 1996. "Corruption, Liberalization, and Democracy: Editorial Introduction," *IDS Bulletin - Liberalization and the New Corruption*, 27 (2): 1-5 (April).

Higgins, Benjamin, 1968. *Economic Development: Problems, Principles, and Policies, Revised Edition*. New York: W.W. Norton.

Higgins, Benjamin, 1990. "Thought and Action: Indonesian Economic Studies in the 1950s," *Bulletin of Indonesian Economic Studies*, 26 (1): 37-47 (April).

Hill, Hal, 1995. "Small-Medium Enterprise and Rapid Industrialization: The ASEAN Experience," *Journal of Asian Business* 11 (2): 1-30.

Hughes, Helen, 1988. *Achieving Industrialization in East Asia*. Cambridge: Cambridge University Press.

Iqbal, Farrukh, 1995. "Deregulation and Development in Indonesia," Paper presented at the Conference on "Building on Success: Maximizing the Gains from Deregulation," Jakarta, 26-28 April.

Ichimura, Shinichi (ed.), 1988. *Indonesian Economic Development - Issues and Analysis*. Tokyo: Japan International Cooperation Agency (March).

Lall, Sanjaya, 1991. "Emerging Sources of FDI in Asia and the Pacific," Paper presented at the Round Table on Foreign Direct Investment in Asia and the Pacific in the 1990s, Honolulu: East-West Center, March 26-28.

Lall, Sanjaya, 1992. "Technological Capabilities and Industrialization," *World Development* 20 (2): 165-186.

Lall, Sanjaya, 1993. "Promoting Technology Development: The Role of Technology Transfer and Indigenous Effort," *Third World Quarterly*, 14 (1): 95-108.

Lall Sanjaya, 1994. "Industrial Policies: The Role of Government in Promoting Industrial and Technological Development," *UNCTAD Review* 1994: pp. 65-89.

Lall Sanjaya and Kishore Rao, 1995. *Indonesia: Sustaining Manufactured Export Growth, Vol. 1: Main Report* (Revised Draft). Report submitted to the Asian Development Bank, Manila. (August).

Mackie, J.A.C., 1988. "Economic Growth in the ASEAN Region: The Political Underpinnings," in Hughes (ed.), *op. cit.*: 283 - 326.

McVey, Ruth (ed.), 1963. *Indonesia*. New Haven: HRAF Press.

Paauw, Douglass S., 1963. "From Colonial to Guided Economy," in McVey (ed.), 155-247.

Paauw, Douglass S., 1983, "The Economic Legacy of Dutch Colonialism to Independent Indonesia," Paper presented at the "Conference on Indonesian Economic History in the Dutch Colonial Period," Canberra, December.

Ranis, Gustav, 1995. "Another look at the East Asian Miracle," *The World Bank Economic Review* 9 (3): 509-534 (September).

Sadli, Mohamad, 1972. "Indonesia," in Drysdale (ed.), *op. cit.*: 201-226.

Sadli, Mohamad, Dorodjatun Kuntjoro-Jakti, and Toshihiko Kinoshita, 1988. "Private Sector and Public Sector," in Ichimura (ed.), *op. cit.*: 353-372.

Thee, Kian Wie, 1993. "Industrial Structure and Small and Medium Enterprise Development in Indonesia," EDI Working Papers. Washington, D.C.: Economic Development Institute, The World Bank.

Thee, Kian Wie, 1994. "The Impact of the Colonial Past on the Indonesian Economy," in Kian Wie Thee, *Explorations in Indonesian Economic History*. Jakarta: Lembaga Penerbit Fakultas Ekonomi Universitas Indonesia: 133-154.

Tsiang, Grace Ren-juei, 1996. "Human Capital Creation and Utilization in Taiwan," Paper presented at the "Conference on Government and Market: The Relevance of the Taiwanese Performance (1945-1995) to Development Theory and Policy," Cornell University, 3-4 May.

Vogel, Ezra F, 1991. *The Four Little Dragons: The Spread of Industrialization in East Asia*. Cambridge: Harvard University Press.

Wibowo, Y. Santoso, 1995. "The Importance of Foreign Direct Investment Data on the Balance of Payments," Paper presented at the workshop on the Foreign Direct Investment Data Base, Jakarta, 8 November.

World Bank, 1993, *The East Asian Miracle: Economic Growth and Public Policy*. New York: Oxford' University Press.

PART VI
CONCLUSIONS AND EPILOGUE

18 SOME FURTHER THOUGHTS ON TAIWAN'S DEVELOPMENT PRIOR TO THE ASIAN FINANCIAL CRISIS AND CONCLUDING REMARKS

Henry Wan and Erik Thorbecke

In this chapter we draw some further thoughts on what lessons can be drawn from the Taiwanese experience compared to that of the other High Performance Asian Economies more particularly as it relates to the degree of government intervention in its industrial policy and relative performance of key industries prior to the onset of the Asian Financial Crisis.

In the next and final chapter we address specifically Taiwan's response to the Asian Financial Crisis and argue that existing policies and institutions left Taiwan largely unscathed from the economic and social devastation that affected most of its neighbors.

18.1 Why Study Taiwan?

Why is it important to study Taiwan's experience? To provide some perspective, we begin by plotting the recent levels and growth rates of per capita GNP for the 8 High Performance Asian Economies (viz., Japan, South Korea, Taiwan, Hong Kong, Singapore, Malaysia, Thailand and Indonesia), prior to the onset of the Asian Financial Crisis (Figure 18.1). Among this group, the Taiwanese economy qualifies as a role model in two senses:

(a) It is inferior to none: no other economy with the same per capita income level enjoyed a faster growth rate, and no other economy with the same growth rate had a higher per capita income; and

Taiwan among the "High Performance Asian Economies"

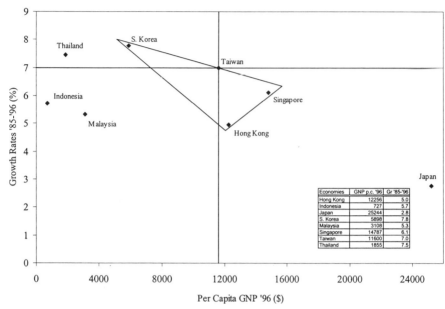

Source: for all other countries except Taiwan from World Bank, *World Development Indicators.*

Figure 18.1   Per Capita GNP (1994) and Growth Rates (1985–94)

(b) It is non-idiosyncratic: it occupies a middle ground within the four NIEs (viz.,
South Korea, Hong Kong, Singapore and Taiwan itself) that form a 'central
subgroup' among the entire group of eight.

Next, we focus upon the four NIEs and zero in on two specific dimensions: 1)
their 'size'; and 2) the degree of 'activism' of the government in the realm of industrial policy.

Regarding size, the rankings of the four NIEs by area and mid-1996 population
included in the World Development Tables among all 217 economies are tabulated
below together with their total nominal GNP in 1994:

Economy	Area Rank	Population Rank	GNP (billion $)
South Korea	108	26	366
Taiwan	138	44	244
Hong Kong	179	94	126
Singapore	187	130	66

Area and population are correlated; therefore, it seems reasonable to use the
1996 population as 'size.' Regarding the degree of 'activism' of the government in
industrial policy, the following description is not far off the mark:

i)   The Hong Kong government never attempted industrial targeting;

ii) Through alternative means, the governments of Korea and Singapore have the
most influence over the industrial structure by 'governing the private enterprises';

iii) In Taiwan, government plans to start new industries are often allowed to fail.

Thus, schematically, one may represent the situation as follows (Figure 18.2):

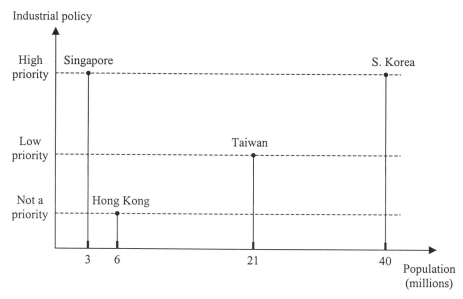

Figure 18.2   Extent of Government Intervention in Industrial Policy and Population Size

The adoption of an (active) industrial policy is determined by both the government's *intention* and its *capability* to intervene. We shall turn to the question of capability first. For any developing economy, *size* matters for industrial policy in two respects:

(a) Size influences *implementation*. A *small* economy does not have the option of supporting its own industries by fencing off its domestic market with protective barriers. Thus, tariffs and quotas were not adopted by either the *laissez faire* Hong Kong or the interventionist Singapore. For industry targeting, Singapore selectively attracted direct foreign investment, on a case-by-case basis (thanks to its Lilliputian size) through various inducements. It paid for such inducements (which included, among other things, a stunningly clean environment) out of the forced savings in payroll deductions (the Central Providence Fund). Taiwan also realized that, for many products, its domestic market was too small to support domestic production at an efficient scale. Taiwan thus adopted a two track policy. Resources were allocated to attract selected investors to the Hong Kong-like or Singapore-like environments replicated in the Export Processing Zones and the Science-based Industrial Parks. To generate spill-over effects from these enclaves and to reinforce their attractiveness, foreign investment in general was encouraged, and trade was greatly liberalized on an economy-wide basis, in order to make Taiwan a favorable export platform.

(b) Size influences *command and control*. A *large* economy faces the challenge of steering the private sector so that it conforms to the industrial policy. On this score, South Korea adopted a two-pronged strategy: first, much of the economy was concentrated in the hands of a few business groups (*chaebols*) and then, *directed credit* was used to bring the latter to heel. Allegedly, the Hyundai Group's reluctance to build supertankers evaporated in response to a veiled hint suggesting that President Park was becoming impatient (See Stern et al., 1995: 19).

In Taiwan, on the other hand, the government repeatedly had difficulties making private firms invest in targeted industries: integrated steel, petrochemicals and semi-conductor foundry (in the beginning) and civil aircraft (later on), to name only a few. However, it should be noted that when the 'national interest' was really viewed as being at stake, the same government did successfully persuade the Formosa Plastic Corporation to shelve its multi-billion investment project in Mainland China. Thus, the apparent 'inability' of the government to impose its will reflects a lack of intention, not capability. In Taiwan, *the South Korean game is presumably not worth the candle*. This is discussed further below. As Chen (Chapter 11) illustrates, the performance of the Taiwanese economy often deviates greatly from government targets and as Kuo (Chapter 3) notes, announced policy measures in Taiwan often are either not carried out or are modified in practice, though not in name.

18.2 What Does the Record Show about Taiwan?

Rather than joining the raging debates about whether any or all of the Asian NIEs have ever followed the Neoclassical *laissez faire* script, or whether they owe their performance to such a stance or, alternatively, to government intervention [See for example, chapter 1 in Wade (1990), Amsden and Singh (1994), and Bhagwati, Chapter 2], we focus on three narrowly defined issues:

Question (A). Are policies in force in Taiwan identical or similar to those used in South Korea or Singapore?

Question (B). Is the performance of the Taiwanese economy inferior to that of South Korea or Singapore?

Question (C). Are the specific strengths of the Taiwanese economy a testimony to the need for an active industrial policy?

A negative answer to either (A) or (B) would mean that the Taiwanese economy need not be studied. A negative answer to (C) would suggest that an optimal policy stance should be less interventionist than that of Taiwan (closer to that of Hong Kong) rather than the other way round (closer to that of South Korea and Singapore).

We examine these questions further below, specifically comparing Taiwan's experience with that of Singapore and of South Korea, respectively.

18.2.1 The Singapore-Taiwan comparison
Taiwan first set up its Export Processing Zones to replicate a Hong Kong-like environment, where bureaucracy and distortion are reduced to a minimum. The success of these zones has made an impact on the attitudes of both foreign businessmen and

the public in Taiwan: the former have been persuaded that Taiwan could be a competitive source for a broad variety of industrial products, and the latter has become convinced that continued trade liberalization is beneficial in creating jobs and generating foreign exchange revenue. Through backward linkages, the development of Export Processing Zones has also nurtured supporting institutions and satellite industries outside of the zones and parks. By the time the Science-based Industrial Parks were set up to house skill-intensive industries such as personal computers, application-specific microchips, etc., indigenous firms were ready to join the multinational enterprises, sometimes as their suppliers, but also sometimes as their rivals, both in Taiwan and on the worldwide stage. Such interactions are present also in Hong Kong, but rather rare in both Korea and Singapore, though for quite different reasons.

In contrast to such a gradualist approach, Singapore sought out and attracted multinational high tech firms with individualized package deals. It has become a favorite export platform for high value-added goods such as computer hard drives. These foreign firms are served by government-linked companies which supply land, public utilities, communication, transportation, etc. Their competent and effective operations are no less efficient than any public enterprises anywhere, but they are neither innovative, nor do they engage in direct export. Together, this modern sector forms an 'enclave' that is quite delinked from indigenous private enterprises, which consists essentially of traditional or service trades of a strictly low tech nature. Efforts to bridge this gap have not yet succeeded.

Part of the reason that backward linkages have failed to develop in Singapore may be cultural. What often escapes casual observers of Singapore is that, crosscutting the multi-ethnic society of Chinese, Malay and Indian heritage, there is also a fault line between the English-school educated elite and the non-English speaking majority. A policy environment that emphasizes the cosmopolitan patina may succeed admirably in attracting expatriate elite and ameliorating intercommunal conflict. At the same time, it may also relegate the traditional sectors of the Chinese majority to the backseat. It is a dilemma perhaps only time can resolve in the best of circumstances.

The weakness of the indigenous Singaporean entrepreneurship has already been noted by Krause et al. (1987). The backwardness of the small and middle sized Singaporean firms is further commented upon in a World Bank monograph edited by Meyanathan (1994), whereas the vitality, flexibility and continued growth of their Taiwanese counterparts is emphatically recognized in that same volume.

Actually, the small and middle sized firms in Taiwan (as in Hong Kong) have not only helped that economy in niche marketing, but have also formed a spawning ground for large firms as well. Taking the information industry as a specific example: Acer, based in Taiwan, has become a respectable computer supplier on the world stage; Wyse, initially founded by a group of Hong Kong engineers, is also a world class producer of computer monitors. There is no comparable indigenous firm from Singapore.

The development of indigenous entrepreneurship is especially important for economies like Taiwan and Singapore. They have progressed by now to a point that any further growth is likely to depend upon how innovative their economies are, and whether the innovative profit will accrue to the local economy. Their role models might be the small economies in North-West Europe, like Denmark, Belgium or the Netherlands, where indigenous entrepreneurship is increasingly decisive in determining further growth.

18.2.2 The South Korea–Taiwan comparison

The South Korean economy developed under state guidance. This can be understood by the nature of its three distinct components: (a) the leadership, (b) the institutions, and (c) the major policy goal. Schematically, this is depicted below:

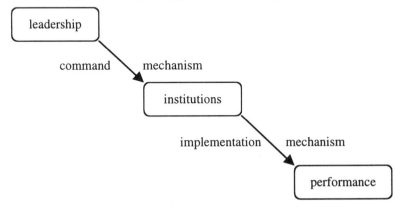

The Leadership — Personal Micro-Management. South Korea industrialized under President Park, a military man committed to *micro-managing the economy in person.* He religiously attended the monthly economic activity briefings and the export promotion meetings (Sakong, 1993) and spent 30-40 percent of his time on the Heavy and Chemical Industry Drive (Stern et al., 1995:17). Early on, export targets were set indicating what commodities should be produced for export to which countries and by which firms. The government was also able to redirect the management of a particular enterprise from one business group to another with a superior management record. Bold decisions were made, and actions could also easily be followed by quick policy reversals.

Institutions — Control by Directed Credit. As discussed in Jones and Sakong (1980), after taking power, the Park government (i) did not restore to business groups the ownership of financial institutions, which had been seized, (ii) deprived the private stockholders of Korean banks of their voting rights, and (iii) forbade private firms from borrowing foreign funds without government approval. Using the banking system it controlled, the government then (iv) granted the business groups short term 'policy loans' at interest rates below the inflation rate. This led to the desired results:

1. The business groups grew faster than the rest of the private sector
2. Their debt/equity ratios remained precarious,
3. The government—through its control of banks—could bankrupt any business group, anytime if desired, with no explanation necessary to anyone.

Thus, from its immediate point of view, the government had a perfect control mechanism over the economy, much more nimble than the police power. Yet, this situation did give rise to some undesirable 'side effects' (not shared by Taiwan) such as:

4. A worsening income distribution,
5. A barrier to new entry into industries, thus eroding efficiency,
6. Persistent double digit inflation,
7. Low saving/ income rate throughout the period of inflationary finance,
8. Repeated need for exchange rate depreciations,
9. Persistent deficits in the balance of payments, and growing foreign borrowing,
10. A weak financial structure for banks, due to non-performing 'policy loans', and
11. The alienation of the workers (leading to strikes and the assassination of Park)

Policy Goal — Economy of Scale. Like its Japanese role model, the goal of the Korean development strategy was to realize scale economies. Thus, in a perceived world market where *the large overpowers the small*, a less developed economy must concentrate its strength through cross-subsidization. We may consider the Hyundai Group for example (see Kirk, 1994):

1. Domestic sales subsidize foreign sales

    Thus, behind protective barriers, a Korean may pay three times more than an American to buy the same Hyundai car.
2. Products sold in markets with less stiff competition subsidize those sold in markets with strong rivals. Thus, with the presence of conglomerate business groups, a Korean buyer of a Hyundai machine may subsidize an American buyer of a Hyundai car.
3. Service exports subsidize goods export

    Thus, in the form of service exports, the Korean construction workers on Hyundai's Mideast construction projects who may be underpaid are subsidizing American buyers of the Hyundai car.

To break into the export market, Hyundai initially planned to lose $1,000 per car exported to America (Stern et al., 1995: 18). It built upon its past experience in assembling cars for Ford, relied on an Italian design, advice from a British consultancy team and bank loans ordered by President Park, while all America-bound units carried Mitsubishi engines. This exercise may be either viewed as a subsidy from the present operations to the expected future economic gain, or perhaps to the present glory of Park's Korea.

Turning now to Question (A), we note that, quite clearly, *Taiwan is not a second South Korea*. The key differences between the two economies are tabulated in Table 18.1.

The government in Taiwan regards itself as a regime in exile. The policy of the state is dictated by the survival imperative, and the structure of the economy also follows from this consideration. K. T. Li, a chief architect of Taiwan's economic policy has remarked that the government in Taiwan would always prefer a stable economy to a 2 percent increase in annual growth. In fact, having lost the Mainland in the civil war, the ruling party was most sensitive to speculations about possible inflation as well as to charges of a 'conspiracy to benefit *others*' (meaning favoritism

Table 18.1   Key Institutional and Policy Differences

Aspects	South Korea	Taiwan
Guiding principle of the state policy	'Growth first'	'Progress through stability'
State dominated banks	Using *policy loans* for control	Lending 'like a pawnshop'*
Industrial *institutions*	*Chaebols* in control	Proliferating small enterprises
Prominent operating mode	Cross subsidy between products	Firms competing for niche markets
Goal of operations	Economy of scale	Flexible response to market

* i.e., based upon available assets as securities rather than earning prospects

towards officials' relatives and friends to benefit oneself or one's own family) (As Wade [1990: 391] mentions, the temporary loss of power of the economic policy maker K. Y. Yin in 1955 was due to this charge). Given the preoccupation of the government with its confrontation with Beijing, to adopt any policy akin to that pursued by South Korea (such as inflationary finance, growth before equitable distribution, accumulation of foreign debt, etc.) would have been courting oblivion. In any case, *form decides function*, and an economy configured like Taiwan's is in no position to micro-manage the economy in Park's fashion.

A selective summary about some of Taiwanese own efforts on industry-targeting further illustrates some of the differences between Taiwan and Korea:

(a) Projects which the government had to 'go it alone': Integrated steel mill
(b) Projects which were abandoned: General trading companies, Mass-producing automobile factory, and Civil aircraft
(c) Projects for which the government could initially find only foreign partners: Petrochemical, and Semi-conductors

In comparison, the Korean record is certainly much more impressive in terms of getting things started. Yet, the final outcome is more mixed. According to Hong (1994), this includes the 'well-known notorious failure cases' such as 'the investments in non-ferrous metal manufacturing, large petrochemical complexes, large fertilizer plants, capital intensive armament factories, a gigantic heavy-machine factory, shipping and overseas construction sectors.'

We now address Question (B): how has Taiwan fared relative to South Korea. There have already been quite a few studies that have taken up this comparison. The early work of Scitovsky (1986) favored Taiwan over Korea on various general economic indices. The well-known study undertaken at the Korean Development Institute by Yoo (1990) viewed the Heavy-Chemical Industry drive of Park as being highly costly without creating an industrial structure superior to that which has naturally evolved in Taiwan. In contrast, in an assessment of the micro-electronic industry, Mody (1990) has predicted that the Korean industry will be far more successful than that of Taiwan in the long term. (Yet as we shall see below, for the same electronic industry, the in-depth industry analysis of Ernst and O'Connor [1992] argues that not all the advantages belong to the Korean side.) So far, there is no consensus about which economy has followed a better strategy, from the long term perspective.

Leaving aside the question of long run advantages, we can still say that the Korean economy is out-performed by Taiwan, in two senses. First, if the purpose of economic development is to improve the welfare of the people (rather than the power and glory of the state — which the heavy-chemical industries signify), then a battery of social-economic indicators show that in Taiwan people live better than in South Korea. This may be seen in the 'radar chart' in Figure 18.3. Thus, not only in GNP per capita, but according to such socioeconomic indicators as infant mortality, both female and male life expectancies, electricity consumption per capita, car and television ownership, residential room/person ratio and teacher/student ratio in primary schools, Taiwan is ahead. Most recently, Korea has overtaken Taiwan in calories intake per capita, but this is more than offset by Taiwan's strong lead in the percentage of calories consumed in high-protein food.

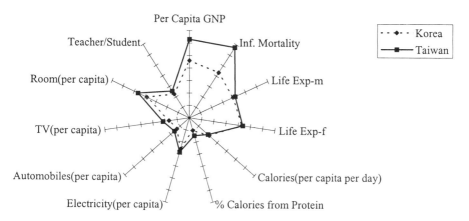

Figure 18.3   Radar Diagram of Socioeconomic Indicators: Taiwan vs South Korea (early 1990s)

One may question whether the above snapshot only reflects the situation at a particular instant in time. Figure 18.4 below tracks the purchasing power parity measure of 'relative per capita incomes' of the Asian NIEs and Japan, in relation to the United States. Two facts stand out, (a) throughout the period of study, South Korea might have narrowed the gap vis-à-vis Taiwan, but never closed it, (b) Japan, the usual role model for South Korea, by 1996 had been surpassed by Hong Kong, the paragon of laissez faire, and by Singapore. Naturally, such information may be interpreted in many ways. Taiwan's historical head start over Korea may be a matter which provides a partial explanation for. But interestingly, the argument that an urbanized population tends to be 'richer' at least on paper would work the other way, since Korea is more urbanized than Taiwan.

To put it mildly, Taiwan is not a bad role model at all, relative to South Korea. But the matter does not stop there, for four reasons. First, Korea is hard to emulate. It has a 'goldilocks' size, neither 'too small', nor 'too large': smaller economies (like Singapore) would not have the aggregate domestic purchasing power to cross-

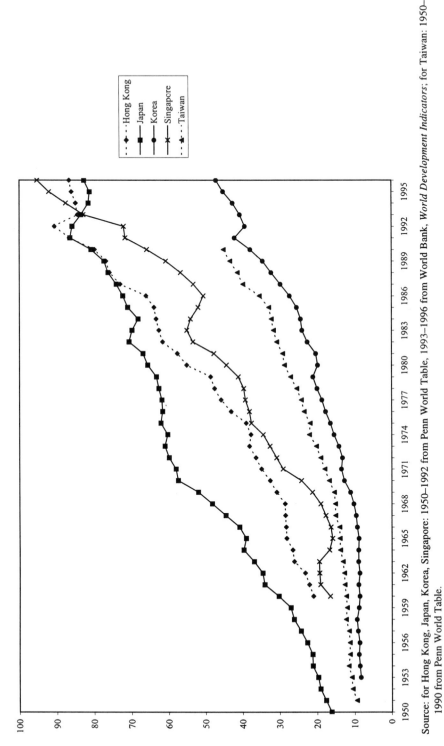

Source: for Hong Kong, Japan, Korea, Singapore: 1950–1992 from Penn World Table; 1993–1996 from World Bank, *World Development Indicators*; for Taiwan: 1950–1990 from Penn World Table.

Figure 18.4   Per Capita GNP (Corrected for Purchasing Power Parity), Selected Asian Countries Relative to U.S., 1950–1996

subsidize the targeted industries, and larger economies like India would defy micro-management in the style of President Park, with or without the Korean-style industrial concentration and 'directed credit.'

Second, the Korean emphasis on Heavy Chemical Industries is a game only one country can play at any one time. If more than one developing economy tries to get a large market share in shipbuilding, Korean-style, then each would suffer financially much more than Korea has. In short, the Korean policy may suffer the 'fallacy of composition.'

Third, in terms of such economic indicators as inflation, trade and current account deficit as well as foreign debt/GDP ratio, the Korean performance differs from that of Brazil only as a matter of degree. A developing economy which emulates the fiscal brinkmanship of South Korea may well end up with the sort of troubles that plagued Brazil. Korea suffered from double digit inflation for more than 20 years out of the period 1960-1989, while inflation in Taiwan was in the double digits only for about six years during the same period. Korea had an export surplus for only about 25 percent of the period 1972-1989, while Taiwan had an export surplus for more than 90 percent of the same period. As we shall discuss later, this picture reflects some resource misallocations in Taiwan, while the Korean situation also suggests an imbalance induced by inflation, with the constant shadow of a debt crisis.

Last but not least, although by using 'directed credit' the Korean state has in principle acquired an irresistible influence over any heavily leveraged *chaebol*, in practice the state's control is not always absolute. Once a *chaebol* has reached a certain importance in the economy, the argument that it is 'too big to fail' usually prevails in times of difficulty. Surely, no policy maker would like to test the column in the Temple of Gaza (See Sakong, 1993: 185).

To sum up, in comparison with both Singapore and Korea, Taiwan appears to be a case worthy for study by development economists. Of course, this is not to deny that Taiwan also has had its share of policy failures, most notably including the under-valued exchange rate.

Finally, we now consider Question (C): to what extent 'interventionist' policy measures are responsible for Taiwan's favorable performance. We shall approach this issue now at an industry-specific level. The growth of an economy must be reflected in the growth of its component industries, and it is at the latter level that we can see more clearly the policy factors that are at work. Four sectors will be briefly reviewed here: the textile industry, the machine tool industry, the bicycle industry and the computer industry.

18.2.3 The textile industry

Birth and Transition from Import Substitution Phase to Export Promotion Up to Early 1970's. In East Asia, the modern textile industry originated in Meiji Japan. It eventually also took roots in China. In Colonial Taiwan, it developed relatively late: in 1940 the island was 10-30 percent self-sufficient in textiles, with Japan supplying the rest. In Hong Kong, the first textile factory was constructed only about 1949. With the end of the Chinese Civil War, part of the same textile industry in East China was relocated to both Taiwan and Hong Kong, respectively, under protectionism and *laissez faire*. Both industries grew rapidly, yet with widely different performances.

Government control of the Taiwanese textile industry took many forms: tariff, exchange control, raw material rationing, state trading, price control, control of entry, etc. At one time, the government allotted U. S. aid-provided cotton to private and public mills, to produce cotton cloth for a generous fee, and then traded the output to farmers for food grain. For a while, even cotton cultivation was encouraged with import tariffs.

The eventual growth of the textile industry is often cited in defense of import substitution in Taiwan (see Lin, 1995). The truth is far more complex. Although production soared and self sufficiency was reached in 1954, the policy was far from rational, and the industry was not competitive for a long time. Three types of evidences from various sources point to this conclusion:

• Opinions from Contemporary Observers:
  (a) In a report on his Hong Kong trip, Y. C. Shu, then the CEO of the government-owned Yung-hsing Textiles, noted that, in the 1950s, Hong Kong was exporting shirts to England and America by relying on low wages. He was bitter that bureaucratic rules prevented Taiwan from competing. [Memorial volume for Mr Shu by Wang (1974)].
  (b) The Shanghai-born capitalists in Hong Kong interviewed by Siu-lun Wong (1988) did not have a high opinion of the industrial environment in Taiwan at that time.
• General Considerations:
  (c) For a while, cotton — a crop patently unsuitable to Taiwan — was grown under tariff protection, in the spirit of self-sufficiency (Lin, 1995.). This is hardly rational.
  (d) The producers of synthetic fiber and woolen yarn developed a 50 percent excess capacity, forcing the government to forbid new entries in 1958 and 1959 (Liang and Liang, 1981). Clearly this implies inefficiency.
  (e) Early protection was concentrated on cotton textiles; the eventual growth of the industry after the policy reform of 1958, was in products of artificial fiber in the 1960s. The benefit of protection, if any, is not clearcut.
• Statistical evidence
  (f) Evidence in Table 18.2 (see Wan, 1978) suggests that during the transition from the import substitution phase to that of export promotion, Taiwan's *protected* textile industry was generally outperformed by the *unprotected* textile industry of Hong Kong.

Growth from the early 1970's up to the mid-1980s. From the 1985 Yearbook of the Textile Industry Export Promotion Commission of Taiwan, the relationship between the textile industries of Japan and Taiwan may be gauged as follows (See Lau and Wan, 1993):
  (1) In the sub-industry of dyeing and finishing, Taiwan lagged behind Japan, not so much in equipment, but in skilled personnel;
  (2) In the sub-industry of artificial fiber, Japan's superiority in material science and market research caused many types of products to be developed

Table 18.2   U.S. Market Shares of Selected East Asian Countries in Textiles and Clothing, 1962–71, and Loom Activities, 1965

	1962	*1965*	*1968*	*1971*
1. U. S. market shares				
i) SITC 8411 (textile)				
Japan	35.3%	35.3%	31.9%	21.8%
Hong Kong	27.7	27.4	29.1	28.2
Taiwan	3.7	3.8	5.3	10.0
Korea	0.3	3.8	5.8	12.9
ii) SITC 8414 (clothing, etc.)				
Japan	17.0	14.9	11.4	13.2
Hong Kong	11.5	23.0	25.2	20.8
Taiwan	10.9	1.3	7.9	26.4
Korea	0.0	1.1	10.9	13.5

and

	# (thousands)	*% automatic*	*Hrs. worked/yr.*
2. Loom activities (1965)			
Japan	371	14	6,786
Hong Kong	20	100	8,161
Taiwan	16	63	4,864
Korea	9	52	6,401

there first, and introduced to Taiwan only later when the technology had matured, but the profit rate had also declined;

(3)   Over time, Taiwan did manage to catch up with Japan to a certain degree, judging from the relative wage rate in textiles:

	1975	*1980*	*1981*	*1983*
Taiwanese wage/Japanese wage	24.8%	34.3%	40.6%	46.5%

According to Lin (1995), the growth of the Taiwanese apparel industry is due to the recession in the Japanese artificial fiber industry, making the Japanese more willing to transfer the downstream technology. The outward oriented reform of the Taiwanese trade regime (including the Export Processing Zones) further facilitated such development.

According to Morawetz (1981), speedy delivery in textile exports is a key advantage enjoyed by the East Asian economies over their Latin American rivals. Hence, it is no surprise that Hong Kong, the least regulated of the East Asian economies, has become the most successful in exporting design clothing. At the same time, given its limited local market, clearly Taiwan can hardly expect that its R & D in textile can be encouraged by protectionism. (See Lin and Wan, 1996, for a theoretical analysis.)

Decline after the mid 1980s. According to Lin (1995), the falling birth rate and the rising college enrollment in Taiwan imply a growing shortage of the young female labor force that is the backbone of the textile industry. Under the 'reform and openness' policy in Mainland China, a large number of Taiwanese factories are being induced to migrate across the Taiwan Strait, in spite of the government efforts to stem the tide. If the force of the product cycle has proved to be the strongest determinant of the decline of the Taiwanese textile industry presently, it is likely to be the best explanation of the rise of the same industry in the past. Lin noted that the textile industry evolved at a rhythm of its own, irrespective of the change of the Taiwanese saving/income ratio, from 20% to 30% to 40% and then down again.

For a considerable period, the textile industry was the predominant sector in Taiwan, with important linkages to both the machinery and the petrochemical sectors. In sum:

• The Taiwanese textile industry is a large industry which started under import substitution and had its share of success on the world market in its hey day. Yet by various indicators and in comparison with its Hong Kong counterpart, one can hardly claim that it has benefited from government assistance.

18.2.4 The Machine Tool Industry

As discussed in Lin and Wan (1993), as part of the engineering industries, the machine tool industry is regarded as a heavy industry. It has considerable strategic importance, both because of its use in weapon production and because of its 'forward linkages' ('as the machine to produce machines'). For that reason, this is a sector much protected in most developing economies such as Argentina, Brazil, India, Korea and Mexico, with Taiwan being a conspicuous exception: the sector receives hardly any support from the government (see for instance, Amsden, 1977). The growth of the Taiwanese machine tool industry came during the 1970s, much after the reform of the trade regime. It is far more competitive than its counterparts from any other developing economy (South Korea included) on the world market, gaining and holding remarkable market shares and exhibiting resilience against the impact of foreign quota.

Evidence of the competitive success of the Taiwanese machine tool industry is provided by the fact that in the mid 1980s, Taiwan was one of only four economies which were asked by the U.S. to impose "voluntary" export restrictions (the other three being Japan, Germany and Switzerland).

The firms in the Taiwanese machine tool industry are mostly small, and their labor force is noted for experience, not academic credentials. The key to the success of the Taiwanese machine tool industry is its ability to adjust to highly variable market needs with reliable quality and punctual delivery, at competitive prices. Its considerable design capability and extensive subcontract network grew over time because of the lack of bureaucratic constraints on trade in Taiwan. The major firms are neither state-owned nor part of any business group: their independence lends them flexibility, which is their major strength. They rely on Japan for key components, such as the controller of the computer numerically controlled machines. Nor does the industry attempt to produce top-of-the-line products. In sum:

• The Taiwanese machine tool industry has become a small but very successful industry on the world market without ever receiving much government assistance. It has outperformed its counterparts in all other developing economies (South

Korea included), all of which have received far more assistance from their governments. Firms of this industry are small and none produces top-of-the-line products.

18.2.5 The Bicycle Industry

Bicycle production is a light industry, with about a hundred parts, and little asset-specificity. Assemblers produce the frame but few parts. As in Korea, the Taiwanese bicycle industry started under import substitution. When Americans placed large orders to meet surging domestic demand in the early 1970s, many more small Taiwanese firms than Korean ones were ready to enter the market. After entry, the Taiwanese firms got advice from their American clients and used their industry scale to improve productivity with finer division of labor. The Taiwan government provided product inspection for the industry to ensure that the products were safe. By 1980, Taiwan replaced Japan as the leading exporter of bicycles in the world. The exchange rate appreciation in the mid-1980s and the reform of the PRC made the Taiwanese firms shift the production of low value units to the Mainland and upgrade their product by using more Japanese high quality parts. Today, Giant Bicycle from Taiwan is the largest bicycle supplier in the world. In sum:

• While the Taiwanese bicycle industry showed many of the same characteristics as the machine tool industry, it received protection at the outset, while the machine tool industry did not. One can speculate whether performance would have been even superior without this import-substitution phase. The quicker response of the Taiwanese than the Koreans to market changes in the early 1970s is due to the Korean weakness in small and medium-sized enterprises, which were neglected under an industrial policy favoring large business groups. Part of the Korean rationale is that small firms from the developing economies may find it hard to survive in the world market. The history of Giant Bicycle shows this is not so.

18.2.6 The Computer Industry

Any discussion of the roles of government and market in the Taiwanese growth will be incomplete without mentioning the computer industry: it is a high tech sector, important to both the world and the Taiwanese economy (as well as to that of Singapore and Korea), for now and the near future; it is a sector over which observers like Mody (1990) had rated Taiwan's prospect as inferior to that of Korea, where the state has played a far more active role; it is also a sector in Taiwan where the government has played a much more active role than it has in the machine tool sector. Three points will be made briefly:

Industry Performance. The Taiwanese computer industry is doing well, both absolutely and relative to South Korea. Three news items suggest the vitality of this sector, in its own right:

(i)   In a joint venture with the Taiwanese firm Mosel-Vitelic, Siemens AG of Germany plans to set up a $1.7 billion foundry in Taiwan;

(ii)   The licensed clone makers for the Apple Mac OS include Umax Data Systems Inc. from Taiwan;

(iii) As Samsung from Korea, the world's largest memory chips supplier, plans to enter the more challenging market of logic chips, Business Week (June 2,

1997) predicts that it will face tough competition from such rivals like the Windbond Electronic Corporation from Taiwan.

Also, the following Korea-Taiwan interactions are well-known:

(i)   Hyundai produced 64 DRAM, 16SRAM and 256 DRAMS in 1986; all were designed by Vitelic of Taiwan (see the OECD study by Bloom, 1992, p. 82);

(ii)   Ernst and O'Connor (1992:153) reveal that Koryo Systems in Korea declined to launch its own brand, stating that Acer of Taiwan sells under its own brand because it has its own PC sets and is hence able to offer new products at the same time as its major American and Japanese rivals (apparently, Koryo Systems lacked that capability). They then state that the Taiwanese had demonstrated more innovativeness than the Koreans (ibid.: 154.). (In their view, all other developing economies are far behind Taiwan and Korea in the computer industry.)

The Source of Comparative Strength. In their study for OECD, Ernst and O'Connor (1992: 238-9) found that the current strength of the Taiwanese computer industry in relation to its Korean counterpart arises from differences in industrial policy, and consequently differences in industrial structure. The smaller Taiwanese firms focus on their own strength. Suppliers form an extensive network, with each firm free to work for any client. The Korean industry is highly vertically integrated. Further, suppliers are limited to their respective specific clients, viz., the few giant *chaebols* which arose from government subsidized credit and now dominate the industry. Suppliers are not supposed to serve any other firm.

Initially, the Korean system of high volume, low cost production also economized on entrepreneurship and product design, which were (allegedly) scarce in South Korea (and Singapore) but not in Taiwan (or Hong Kong) (see also Bloom, 1992: 86). This conglomerate structure was well suited to the earlier period of rapid growth of the firms, with each producing relatively standard goods. This structure became an obstacle when rapid product differentiation gained importance for both the electronics industry as a whole and the NIEs faced with rising domestic wages and new competitors. Ernst and O'Connor state (1992: 248), "Large firms, such as the Korean *chaebol* or state-owned companies in Brazil and India, tend to be more susceptible to hierarchical and bureaucratic inefficiencies than smaller ones."

Korean R & D is centralized within the in-house laboratories of the giant *chaebols*. The drawbacks of this arrangement are:

(i)   it tends to slow down product development in response to market conditions;

(ii)   it reduces flexibility in a world of uncertainty;

(iii)   it weakens technologically the suppliers outside the *chaebols*, making it hard to reduce the dependence on the Japanese supply of key components.

In comparison, the Taiwanese institutions are better adapted to today's world.

In corroboration of the opinion of Ernst and O'Connor, one may cite Professor Linsu Kim, a worldwide authority on Korean industrialization and the current head of the Korean Science and Technology Policy Institute: "Korea has militaristic corporations that must change." (Business Week, June 2, 1997.)

State Policy and Institutions. Based on Ernst and O'Connor, we may compare government policies related to the computer industry in all four NIEs according to the four following criteria:

Policies	On trade	On foreign investment	On financing	On research
Singapore	Free	Selective inducement	Support	
Hong Kong	Free	Free	Free	
Taiwan	Inputs not protected	Some mild selective inducement	Subsidy up to 2.5%	Government-linked labs
Korea	Chaebols use some own inputs	Inducement early on; restriction later in the 1980s	Subsidy makes real interest negative	Government labs

Unlike Singapore, where the market is smothered by multinational firms, or South Korea, where the industry is dominated by giant conglomerates, Taiwan has many electronic firms which started small, but shared access to the R & D fruits from the government-affiliated laboratories in the Industrial Technological Research Institute (ITRI): an advantage not available to their counterparts. Repeatedly, staff members of the ITRI left to set up businesses on their own. In sum:

• The Taiwanese computer industry has a record clearly not inferior to its counterpart in any NIE, owing to its appropriate policy environment. A careful consideration indicates this record is not a testimony and argument for industrial policy. The electronics industry thrives well in the United States – the current unquestioned leader of that industry in the world – where firms like Microsoft, Intel, The Sun Systems and the like arose as small start-up firms and proved their worth under the baptism of competitive fire. Institutions such as independent research labs (including Battelle Memorial Institute) and markets for venture capital are active, but industrial policy is conspicuous by its absence. ITRI as well as Taiwan's subsidized credit for a vibrant sector like the computer industry are just temporary substitutes for the absence or weakness of certain non-government institutions.

Overall Assessment of Taiwan's Industrial Policy. We can now provide a more conclusive answer to Question (C): a more interventionist policy environment would not likely have improved Taiwan's economic performance, and the record of Taiwan does not prove the merit of industrial policy. It does not mean, however, that Hong Kong provides a superior environment to Taiwan just because of its thoroughly non-interventionist policy. The lack of research institutions in Hong Kong slowed down innovations. In fact, the efforts made by the government of Hong Kong in the last a few years (such as the setting up of Hong Kong University of Science and Technology) is an attempt to remedy such defects.

The industries we considered have some common features. They all rely on mature foreign technology, imported foreign parts, components or material and ship a major portion of their labor-intensive outputs to American and European markets initially supplied by Japan. Small firms, often organized in subcontractor networks, provide such industries the advantages of punctual delivery and flexible response in a world of short product cycles and variable market demand. Similar industries are also active in Hong Kong, Malaysia and Thailand as well as Mauritius.

However impressive, the Korean policy is neither universally applicable in the developing world, nor quite the best available. According to Bloom (1992: 84), South Korea in 1992 still did not have the design ability that Japan already possessed in 1955, when two technical breakthroughs were made by the latter to commercialize the transistor radio. This seems to be related to the fact that, once returned from abroad, talented Koreans usually go to work for one of the hierarchical *chaebols*.

One may cite the OECD study by Bloom (1992), as an indication of the working environment in South Korea, at least prior to the reorganizations in the late 1980s. In one case, considerable product overlap developed between subsidiaries in the same conglomerate, in another, almost all senior executive came from the founders' families (p. 91), and in a third, almost all foreign-acquired researchers in semiconductor production left in 1988, due to "differences in approach" (p. 83). These represented three of the top four Korean firms which together produced 56.3% of Korea's electronic output in 1988. Such a high industrial concentration and the concomitant hierarchical corporation organization which survive and thrive in it cannot be separated from Korea's industrial policy.

In contrast the dynamic industrialization process of Taiwan illustrates how many latecomer firms were able to overcome the disadvantages of small scale. As Hobday (1995) aptly concludes after an exhaustive analysis of technological innovations and industrial development in South Korea, Taiwan, Singapore, Hong Kong and Japan "The scale-intensive approach of South Korean chaebols contrasted sharply with the actions of small and medium enterprises in Taiwan. Taiwan's success in electronics relied on the speed, skill and agility of hundreds of local entrepreneurs, rather than the scale and financial power of the chaebol." (Hobday, 1995: 132).

The extent of the Taiwanese success in this evolution from small to very large enterprises, at least compared to South Korea, can be judged by the number of firms in the list of top one hundred firms ranked according to total sales in the so-called emergent markets. Whereas in 1993, twenty Taiwanese firms and twenty-three Korean firms appeared in the list of top one hundred firms, by 1998, sixteen Taiwanese firms made the list but only three Korean firms (Business Week, various issues).

Evidences at this disaggregated level are consistent with the main views of Bhagwati (Chapter 2) on the main issues of this conference. Specifically,

1. In broad lines, the Taiwanese experience is widely replicable, since the major industries which fueled the sustained growth of Taiwan are already blossoming from Mauritius to Thailand to the People's Republic of China.
2. Since foreign technology, foreign inputs and foreign markets play such essential roles, trade — hence, an outward orientation — is indispensable for such development, which takes advantage of the product cycle. It is a matter of semantics whether trade is counted as a source of growth.
3. The sustained expansion of output per worker is accompanied by constant compositional changes in outputs, trade and jobs. It calls for an increase in human capital, secured by education, on the job experience or, most likely, both. This usually is accompanied by changing demography and thus a bell-shaped

evolution of the saving/income ratio. The growth-accumulation nexus is as intimate as the growth-trade nexus and any causal attribution may well be a matter of taste.

4. Growth is impossible without a stable macro-economic environment and an adequate supply of infrastructure. This calls for a government of a certain capability under which nurturing institutions such as subcontract networks and financial intermediaries would take form. Thus, the government is always crucial just as the market is, in Hong Kong no less than in Singapore and Korea. On this, there has never been any disagreement.

5. Over all, there can always be both government failures and market failures. The ultimate check is the competitive pressure: the Darwinian mechanism has the chance of cauterizing some of the inefficiencies. That is why both the Singaporean and the Korean policies carry some danger of entrenching the oligopolistic incumbents, multinationals in the former and domestic conglomerates in the latter. In either case, to some extent the local talent may be prevented from realizing their full potential.

18.3 How Can the Contributions of Liu and Tsiang be Placed in Context?

The Chinese ideograms for economics carry the ideal of 'providing norms for the world and benefits for the people.' Both Professors Liu and Tsiang were brought up in the classical Chinese tradition, and trained professionally respectively in the United Kingdom and United States. They were dedicated to using their expertise in public service. According to Tsiang's Reminiscences (1992), his concern in his study of economic issues was always how can this make a poor country like China rich. As recalled by one of us, to Liu the point of economic development in Taiwan was to make sure that people there did not have to eschew Western style democracy just because of destitution. This explains why these two distinguished academic economists eventually got involved with Taiwan's economic development.

When China was at war in World War II, both Liu and Tsiang served in the diplomatic corps, and their devotion and service were well noted. After the war, both joined academia , Liu in Tsinghua University and Tsiang in Peking University, and contributed critical journal articles on economic policy. Through the recommendation of Dr. Hu Shih, founder of the vernacular Chinese movement and then the President of Peking University, both were personally invited by President Chiang Kaishek to Nanking, the seat of Republican China, to advise on economic policy. Judging that no useful purpose could be served, both declined at the last moment. At the same time, the death of Jan Masaryk also convinced both Liu and Tsiang that, as Western-trained liberals, neither could they serve any purpose in Mainland China after 1949, so they left, first for the IMF and eventually for American academia.

In the decade after World War II, it was the consensus of development economists that (i) basic industries should be the top priorities for developing nations, (ii) the export prospects of these economies were bleak, (iii) government intervention was crucial in launching industrialization, and (iv) the Keynesian doctrine of easy money fit well the needs of all economies at all times. Based upon the time dimension of production, Tsiang already wrote in *Economica* in the late 1940s, against the fashionable view that poor countries should focus on the heavy industries, given their very low output/capital ratios. On his sabbatic visit, he introduced J. E. Meade's book, *Planning and the Price Mechanism* , to K. Y. Yin. This led to the invitation for Tsiang and Liu to advise on Taiwan's exchange rate reform in 1954. Their proposal was adopted four years later which 'set the fundamentals right for Taiwan' (See Shea, Chapter 8). As related by Tsiang, he and Liu could not find contemporary literature appropriate to Taiwan's needs. In any case, their proposals refuted the views of export pessimism, of development via inflationary financing, and of the need for massive government interventions.

Not all of their views were accepted immediately by the government in Taiwan. Many of their calls for reform, and their advice about taxation (to which T. C. Liu devoted much effort) and financial and exchange rate liberalization (a principal concern of S. C. Tsiang) were implemented only after years of delay, due to recalcitrant officers as well as powerful lobbying from the private sector. Liu's econometric expertise and Tsiang's macro-economic insights as well as their selfless dedication were deeply respected in Taiwan by all, from the topmost government circles to academia to businessmen, even by those who opposed their views. They helped to strengthen economic research and education in Taiwan, training future leaders in the Taiwanese economic profession. They provided leadership by their personal example. After the untimely passing away of T. C. Liu, S. C. Tsiang founded two major research institutions in Taiwan and used his prestige to influence economic policies both in private consultations and in policy debates through various media. Their caution saved the Taiwanese economy from both over-ambitious ventures in industrial policy and the vested interests which attempted to sway government trade and monetary policies in their own favor.

Both Liu and Tsiang were pragmatist and not the least 'ideological.' It is wrong to view them as advocates of *laissez faire* for its own sake. After all, Tsiang's first action on the Taiwanese economic scene was to introduce Minister Yin, the policy maker, to Meade's precept of how the government should intervene. Certainly they were well aware of the arguments regarding public goods, externalities, increasing returns, etc. But they were both painfully aware of the reality of 'government failures,' 'rent seeking' and all the considerations of what is now called 'political economy'. Their policy proposals for Taiwan were anchored not only on theoretical understanding but also on practical judgments concerning which was the greater evil: corruptive influence and bureaucracy or the tolerance of a degree of market failure, in the context of Taiwan of that day.

With the possible exception of what prevailed in Hong Kong, what was implemented in Taiwan was the closest, though quite imperfect, policy environment they would endorse, and the bias was what was implemented was still not liberal enough, in their view. The delays in exchange appreciation and financial market reform were, to Tsiang, lost opportunities for upgrading the industry and wasted resources idling in foreign reserves. Much of this came about because the business lobby favored easy export environments. As it stands, the performance of the

Taiwanese economy, as chapters in this volume can testify, has been highly successful and worthy to be studied by scholars and policy makers alike.

18.4 References

Amsden, A.H., 1977. "The Division of Labor Is Limited by the 'Type' of Market: the Taiwanese Machine Tool Industry," *World Development* 5: 217-34.

Amsden, Alice H. and Ajit Singh, 1994. "The Optimal Degree of Competition and Dynamic Comparative Advantage," *European Economic Review* 38: 941-51.

Bloom, Martin, 1992. *Technological Change in the Korean Electronic Industry*, Paris: Development Center of OECD.

Business Week (various issues)

Ernst, Dieter and David O'Connor, 1992. *Competing in the Electronics Industry, The Experience of the Newly Industrialized Economies*, Paris: Development Center for OECD.

Hobday, Michael, 1995. *Innovations in East Asia: The Challenge to Japan*. Aldershot: Edward Elgar Publisher.

Hong, Wontack, 1995. *Trade and Growth, a Korean Perspective*. Seoul: Kudara International.

Jones, Leroy P. and Il Sakong, 1980. *Government, Business and Entrepreneurship in Economic Development: The Korean Case*, Cambridge, MA: Harvard University Press.

Kirk, Donald, 1994. *Korean Dynasty: Hyundai and Chung Ju Yung*. Armonk, NY: M.E. Sharpe.

Krause, Lawrence B. et al., 1987. *The Singaporean Economy Reconsidered*, Singapore: Institute of Southeast Asia Studies.

Liang, K. S. and C. H. Liang, 1980. *Trade Strategy and the Exchange Rate Policies of Taiwan*, Taipei: National Taiwan University.

Lin, Chung-cheng, 1995. "Study of the Policies on the Development of Taiwan's Textile Industry." *Report to the National Science Council*, Republic of China, Taipei, Taiwan.

Lin, Yongchih and Henry Wan, Jr. , 1996. "Laissez Faire as Source of Comparative Advantage: What Price Protectionism?" Mimeo, Cornell University.

Meyanathan, Saha Dehevan (ed.), 1994. *Industrial Structures and the Development of Small and Medium Enterprise Linkages: Examples from East Asia*. Washington, DC: World Bank.

Mody, Ashok, 1990. "Institutions and Dynamic Comparative Advantage: The Electronic Industry in South Korea and Taiwan," *Cambridge Journal of Economics* 14(3):291-314.

Morawetz, D. 1981. *Why the Emperor=s New Clothes Are Not Made in Colombia: a Case Study of Latin American and East Asian Manufactured Exports*, New York, NY: Oxford University Press.

Sakong, I., 1993. *Korea in the World Economy*, Washington, D. C.: Institute for International Economics.

Scitovsky, Tibor, 1986. "Economic Development in Taiwan and South Korea, 1965-1981," in Lawrence Lau (ed.) *Models of Development—A Comparative Study of Economic Growth in South Korea and Taiwan*, San Francisco: Institute of Comparative Studies Press.

Stern, J.J., Kim, J.-H., Perkins, D.H. and Yoo, J.-H., 1995. *Industrialization and the State: The Korean Heavy and Chemical Industry Drive*. Cambridge, MA: Harvard University Press.

Tsiang, Sho-chieh, 1992. *Chiang Shuo-chieh hsien sheng fan wen chi lu / fan wen Ch'en Tz'u-y, Mo Chi-p'ing; chi lu Ch'en Nan-chlh, Ts'al Shu-hsan, P'anShu-fen*. T'al-pei shih Nan-kang: Chung yang yen chiu yan chin tai shih yen chiu so, Min kuo 81.

Wade, R., 1990. *Governing the Market: Economic Theory and the Role of the Government in East Asian Industrialization*, Princeton, NJ: Princeton University Press.

Wan, H., 1978. *Manpower, Export-led Growth and Industrialization: The Taiwan Experience*, Occasional Papers/Reprint Series in Contemporary Asian Studies, School of Law, University of Maryland, College Park, MD.

Wang, Chu-I (ed.) 1974. *Annals for Mr. Yun-Chang Shu*, prepared by P'ei-lien Chu, Historial Sources Reprint Series, 15, Nankang, Taipei: Institute of Recent History , Academia Sinica.

Wong, Siu-lun, 1993. *Emigrant Entrepreneurs: Shanghai Industrialists in Hong Kong*, New York, NY: Oxford University Press.

Yoo, J.H., 1990. "The Industrial Policy of the 1970's and the Evolution of the Manufacturing Sector in Korea". Korea Development Institute Working Paper 9017. Seoul: Korea Development Institute.

19 EPILOGUE: HOW DID TAIWAN WITHSTAND THE ASIAN FINANCIAL CRISIS?

Erik Thorbecke and Henry Wan

Eighteen months after the breakout of the Asian Financial Crisis the Taiwanese economy remains largely unscathed in dire contrast with the economic and social havoc that the crisis brought on most of its neighbors in East and Southeast Asia. Why was Taiwan able to withstand successfully the onslaught of the tidal wave that engulfed most of its neighbors? In order to answer this question, we need to rehearse the major underlying causes of the Asian financial crisis and identify the specific structural, institutional and policy elements which protected the Taiwanese economy from this onslaught. Hence, in what follows, we review the generally agreed upon causes of the crisis before analyzing, first, in a general way and subsequently, in much greater detail, the particular and specific characteristics of the Taiwanese socioeconomic and policy environment that allowed Taiwan to escape being more than only slightly and temporarily affected by the crisis. Hence, this chapter is subdivided into the following sections: 1) The Fundamental Causes of the Asian Financial Crisis and Taiwan's Response to It; 2) Financial Factors; 3) The Industrial Structure; 4) Political Economy Factors; and, 5) Reflections on the Nature of the Crisis and Growth Prospects in the Long Run.

19.1 Fundamental Causes of the Asian Financial Crisis: How Did Taiwan Overcome Them?

The consensus among experts is that a set of fundamental causes was responsible for the onset of the Asian Financial Crisis. One of the most authoritative analysis of the Asian Financial Crisis by Corsetti, Pesenti and Roubini (1998) identifies the following fundamental causes: 1) significant real appreciation of currencies because most of the currencies of the East and Southeast Asian countries were pegged to the U.S. dollar, while enjoying large capital inflows and somewhat higher inflation rates than those prevailing in the U.S.; 2) large and growing trade current account deficits explained by a combination of real appreciation and loss of competitiveness, and investment boom, and a slowdown in Japanese growth in the 90's that translated into a slowdown of these countries' exports to Japan, and the large Chinese devaluation of 1994; 3) a vicious circle of "competitive devaluations" starting in the summer of 1997 that eroded the equilibrium value of the other currencies that had not yet depreciated and led to contagion; 4) excessive investment in risky and low profitability projects facilitated by an exchange rate policy that kept borrowing costs low, and low interest rates in Japan that led to large capital movements from Japan to the higher yielding Asian countries; 5) over-borrowing and over-lending in the financial sector because of the moral hazard effects of implicit or 'explicit government bail-out guarantees and fragile financial institutions (e.g. inappropriate supervision and monitoring by the Central Bank and other public authorities); 6) current account deficits were financed with the accumulation of foreign debt in the form of short-term foreign-currency denominated and unhedged liabilities leading to a mismatch between short-term foreign liabilities and longer term domestic assets; and, finally, 7) excessive lending by international investors in the 90's and sharp reversal of capital flows starting in mid-1997.

How did Taiwan perform compared to its regional neighbors in East and Southeast Asia in the extent to which it was affected by the above causes—taking them one at a time. First, as the value of the U.S. dollar became stronger in the 90's, the New Taiwan dollar was gradually depreciated in contrast with the currencies of countries such as Malaysia, Thailand and Indonesia that continued to be pegged to the U.S. dollar, causing their trade deficits to accumulate. The inflation rate (i.e. the consumer price index) in the five years preceding the Asian Financial Crisis (i.e. 1993-1997) was also relatively very low in Taiwan, i.e. 2.9% annually. In comparison, the corresponding annual inflation rate over the same five-year period was significantly higher in South Korea and Thailand (about 5% per annum), Hong Kong and the Philippines (about 7.5% per annum), Indonesia (8.4%), and China Mainland (13.2%). Only Singapore had a somewhat lower inflation rate of 2.1% during this period. (Hu, Lin, Shea and. Wu, 1998).

Secondly, Taiwan maintained large and growing current account surpluses in the period preceding the crisis, while all the other High Performing Economies in Asia except for China, Singapore and Malaysia faced relatively large and growing current account deficits (see Table 1 in Hu, et al, 1998). Taiwan was also much less affected by the Chinese devaluation of 1994 and the stagnation of the Japanese economy in the 90's than other countries in the region for at least two reasons: 1) approximately 80% of Taiwan's exports consisted of intermediate and high-tech products in 1996 that were largely sheltered from the typical exports from China and other Asian countries; and 2) Taiwan is much more dependent on the U.S. market than the Japanese market for its exports.

Thirdly, Taiwan was largely successful in resisting the contagion caused by the vicious circle of competitive devaluations for the reasons previously noted, i.e.

because it maintained an essentially equilibrium exchange rate and enjoyed large and growing current account surpluses, in addition to being endowed with an enormous level of foreign exchange reserves amounting to about 90 billion dollars at the onset of the financial crisis—a level bound to discourage most currency speculators.

Fourth, Taiwan in recent times has been a net exporter (not importer) of capital to other Asian economies and the rest of the world. Its foreign debt is insignificant and by mid 1997 foreign capital accounted for only 3% of the value of the stocks traded in the TAIEX stock market (compared to 30% in most other Asian stock markets). Hence, Taiwan was much less vulnerable to a withdrawal and outflow of short term capital by foreigners following the onset of the crisis. Furthermore, strict banking regulations and relatively strong financial institutions—discussed in some detail subsequently—protected Taiwan from excessive investment in risky and low profitability projects. Taiwan also learned from a mini-bubble crash in the early 90's.

Fifth, the relatively robust financial institutions, Central Bank supervision and monitoring, prevailing norms (e.g. the pawnshop mentality discussed below) and the strong reluctance to borrow abroad—which could have weakened the economic and political independence of the regime—kept the flow of external and internal borrowing within a safe limit.

Finally, the last two fundamental causes of the Asian Financial Crisis listed above (6 and 7) do not apply to Taiwan since it enjoyed current account surpluses and a very low level of foreign debt.

19.2 Financial Factors

The immediate causes of the resilience of the Taiwanese economy is financial. They can be grouped under three categories. First, there are the 'fundamentals': a) the sustained rapid growth which reflects the vitality of the economy, b) an insignificant inflation rate which buttresses the real exchange rate, c) the government budget, balanced year after year until 1989, that lends additional confidence to the financial discipline, and d) the habitually low rate of unemployment which provides further proof that the economy is performing well. A fly in the ointment is that these reassuring signals set Taiwan apart only from Brazil and Mexico (when they were hit by the "Latin" crisis of the early 80's and 90's), but not Korea (nor Thailand nor Indonesia), which are currently in distress. Table 19.1 gives the GDP growth rates and the debt service ratios (in parentheses) before financial crises affected selective economies in Latin America in the early 80's and 90's and Asia in 1997.

A perusal of Table 19.1 suggests that items (a) through (d) are necessary but insufficient for financial health. Second, there are facts distinguishing Taiwan from Korea: a) the insignificant level of foreign debt, b) between 80 and 90 billion U.S. dollars' worth of foreign reserves (approximately double the level of reserves of Korea for a population only half that of Korea), and c) a record of export surplus rarely broken over three decades (Korea has had frequent import surpluses). For example, the current accounts of these economies in the recent years are shown in Table 19.2.

Table 19.1   GDP Growth Rates and Debt Service Ratios Prior to Financial Crises: Selective Countries

Latin Crisis, '80s	1981	1982	1983
Argentina	–6.3 (n.a.)	–4.0 (n.a.)	3.0 (n.a.)
Brazil	–1.6 (72%)	0.9 (97%)	–3.2 (91%)
Mexico	7.5 (28%)	–0.6 (33%)	–5.3 (36%)
Mexican Crisis, '90s	**1993**	**1994**	**1995**
Mexico	0.7 (36%)	7.0 (28%)	–6.2 (40%)
Asian Crisis, '90s	**1994**	**1995**	**1996**
Thailand	8.7 (38%)	8.7 (31%)	6.0 (38%)
Malaysia	9.2 (19%)	9.5 (15%)	6.2 (15%)
Indonesia	7.5 (69%)	8.2 (63%)	7.8 (67%)
The Philippines	4.4 (43%)	4.8 (39%)	5.5 (29%)
South Korea	8.6 (6%)	8.9 (5%)	7.1 (6%)
Taiwan	**6.5 insign**	**6.0 insign**	**5.7 insign**

Table 19.2 Current Accounts: Selected Asian Countries, 1994–1996

			(billion U.S. $)
	1994	1995	1996
Thailand	–8.1	–13.6	–14.7
Malaysia	–4.5	–7.4	–3.6
Indonesia	–2.8	–7.0	–7.0
The Philippines	–2.9	–2.0	–4.8
South Korea	–3.9	–8.3	–21.8
Taiwan	**6.2**	**4.8**	**10.5**

There is little doubt that the above facts played some role in discouraging speculators from selling the new Taiwan dollar short. But this is not the entire story either. After all, at the end of World War II, many countries in the British Commonwealth possessed huge blocked Sterling balances accumulated during the war. Such balances melted away like springtime snow. The rapid rise of the Korea foreign debt during the mid-1990s is another piece of evidence: what counts most are not assets but the persons and institutions behind those accumulated assets.

There are institutional and social factors underlying the behavior of financial agents that may be less tangible than assets but much more resilient. Throughout East Asia, individual habits and behavior differ widely from the Western world, even where income levels have converged to the latter. Households in Taiwan rarely make payments with checks; they often keep savings in post offices which are under the direct control of the Central Bank. Hence these savings are protected from the type of risk they could be subjected to if they had been deposited in commercial banks and lent out to finance real estate and other speculative ventures.

Until 1991, 21 of a total of 24 banks in Taiwan were government owned, and the interest rate was set by a committee. When bad debts arose, lending officers were not reprimanded by superiors for mismanagement, but investigated by the Control Yuan (this permanent organization for 'independent prosecutors' is co-equal to the cabinet and to the legislature, according to the Nationalist constitution) which considered it as *prima facie* evidence of collusion with the borrowers. The present situation remains essentially the same.

In granting loans, collateral is more important than business prospects. To Western observers, such 'pawn-shop mentality' is not congenial to financial intermediation. In addition, the lending operations of banks are regulated by the Finance Ministry and come under its regular supervision. For example, banks are precluded from lending such large amounts to private firms that they would, in fact, control—if not own—those firms. In practice, through their political connections, a few 'trust companies' had received special licenses to take on banking operations. Their real estate speculations led to bankruptcy. The political scandals ended the careers of some high government officials and led to renewed government efforts to control banks.

The composition of the source of funds is little known, for business groups resist disclosure of their operational secrets. Estimates differ widely, but it is generally believed that the debt/equity ratios are between American corporations, on the low side, and the Korean and Japanese firms, on the high side. Fields (1995) used two studies in 1967 and 1980; both come up with a debt/equity ratio near 1.5.

Until quite recently, the curb market conducted a significant portion of intermediation. But the foreign exchange operations remain the preserve of government banks. The ruling Nationalists regard themselves as constituting a government in exile, over an island economy constantly susceptible to destabilization from the Mainland. In that perspective, the borrowing of foreign loans by local firms (including state enterprises) is naturally suspect, and requires special licenses from the government.

The other important financial institution is the stock exchange. Although many households own stocks nowadays, only a relatively small portion of business enterprises have shares traded publicly. Furthermore restrictions have always been imposed upon the ownership of Taiwanese stocks by foreigners. In October 1997, only 3.32% of Taiwan's stocks were owned by foreigners (compared to 60% for Indonesia), a fact that contributes to the stability of the economy against outside volatility via capital flight.

Overall, the financial institutions in Taiwan are not perfect in their function as financial intermediaries, but they contain features which are more prudent than those of other Asian economies, in trouble today. At least, in the Taiwanese financial sector, there seems to be less rent-seeking and government failure. The reason may be attributed to the industrial structure relying on Small and Medium Enterprises (SMEs) enterprises which are export-oriented and can adjust quickly to changing world market conditions. Powerful business groups have more resources to lobby successfully. They are also less flexible than SMEs to make adjustment when things turn bad.

In a special column of a news journal, S. C. Tsiang had remarked a dozen years ago that what Taiwan needed is the gradual development of better institutional safeguards, side by side, with the gradual liberalization of the institutions for financial intermediation. It appears that Taiwan heeded his wise advice!

19.3 The Industrial Structure

As a benchmark in comparison with Taiwan, we choose Korea, rather than Thailand or Indonesia for three reasons because i)its record is better documented; ii) prior to the Asian Financial Crisis it was held up as a model by both Southeast Asian policy makers and development economists; and iii) some writers claim that the approach of Taiwan is either sufficiently similar to Korea, or else somewhat inferior to it.

Unlike Taiwan, banks in Korea were used very aggressively to implement the industrial policy, under President Park. That episode had effectively transformed the Korean industrial structure in favor of *chaebols* (business groups). Our discussion here proceeds under the following headings. a) How was the Korean industrial policy implemented?; b) How different was the Taiwanese industrial policy compared to Korea?; c) What industrial structure has emerged in the Taiwanese policy environment?; and d) What are the implications of this structure for Taiwan in confronting the Asian Crisis?

19.3.1 How was South Korean industrial policy implemented?

In successfully implementing his industrial policy, especially the Heavy Chemical Industrial (HCI) drive, President Park granted short-term policy loans at negative real interest rates, to co-opt, promote, control and steer business groups toward his policy goals, a topic extensively studied in Stern et al. (1995) and discussed in Chapter 18 of this volume. This allowed the business groups to grow at a rate faster than the rest of the economy. It also produced a highly concentrated industrial structure, so that Park could interact personally with business leaders in his monthly Export Promotion Meetings, etc. (See for example, Jones and Sakong, 1980).

Professional Korean economists to their credit, for years and decades, have looked at such development with concern and dread (see Stern et al., 1995) even though a large corps of non-Korean economists seemed to be mesmerized by the spectacle, and rose to Park's defense.

After displacing the elected government through a coup, the promotion and harnessing of such giant firms served as a justification for Park to amass state power and concentrate it in his own hands. He wrote:

> In human life, economics precedes politics or culture. . .the gem without lustre called democracy is meaningless to people suffering from starvation and despair. . . . Mammoth enterprise. . .plays. . .a decisive role in the economic development and elevation of living standards. . . . The key problems facing a free [sic] economic policy are coordination and supervisory guidance, by the state, of mammoth economic strength. (See for example, Fields, 1995: 50).

In this process, the chaebols gained the haft to lobby successfully for their own agendas, seeking expansion to reach scale economies (Sakong, 1993, contains an interesting account of the growth of chaebols during the HCI drive). In reality, the expanded scale of production often exceeded their ability to manage effectively. According to Bloom, (1992:90-93) their returns were too low to cover their financial charges without the subsidy. Samsung, for example, earned 1% of profit in 1996 on its total sales. The autocratic chaebols alienated Korean workers, making Korean strikes far more disruptive than the Japanese ritualized one-day strikes. This same process also facilitated rent-seeking by Park's military successors, as revealed in the trials of Presidents Chun and Roh. As some astute observer noted, "the presidential Blue House used the credit. . .to control the chaebol, and make sure generous campaign contribution kept rolling in."

Initially, the high debt/equity ratios of the chaebols and the short-term maturities of their bank loans gave the state a Damocles sword over its creatures. Yet the bankruptcy of the Kukje Group (which accounted for 3.6% of Korean exports in 1984, with a debt/equity ratio above 900%, and constituted one-fourth of the loans of the Korean First Bank) became *a cause clbre*, because its chairman backed the opposition, and refused to contribute to a foundation bearing President Chun's name, and also because other chaebols were in similar positions. However, once fully grown, the bankruptcy of any one major chaebol would destabilize the economy, making the threat of government action less credible. In fact, the crisis of 1997 followed the collapse of the Hanbo and Kia groups. To make matters worse, by mid-1997, eight of the largest thirty conglomerates in South Korea were de facto or de jure bankrupt (Corsetti, et al., 1998).

One can argue that there is a direct link between the HCI drive of Park and the financial debacle of 1997: the economy had become irreversibly tied to the large but unprofitable chaebols which were weighed down by top-heavy debt/equity ratios. To support such an industrial structure, the financial sector was constantly burdened with non-performing loans. Hoping to break out of the cul-de-sac, and to earn returns higher than what was locally available, the Korean financial sector borrowed low interest foreign loans under government guarantees and invested in risky projects in Southeast Asia and Russia. By late 1997, the crisis erupted.

19.3.2 Taiwan's industrial policy compared to that of South Korea
The development of the Taiwanese industry differs significantly from the Korean scenario in each of the following aspects:
a) The *industrial policy* proclaimed by the government was never forced on the private sector. In Taiwan there was never the type of carrot and stick, nor political will, to follow through with a Korea-style policy. In steel and shipbuilding, the government went it alone; in petro-chemicals and integrated circuits, the government signed on a foreign partner, instead of domestic firms; in auto-making and aerospace, the government simply called off the projects, after much fanfare to the amusement of its critics. Chu (1994) reported a successful case, when Taiwan launched its first petrochemical plant, no private firm participated, and the government had to enlist a foreign firm as partner. Once the profitability was demonstrated, local private firms rushed to join all later projects.

b) The *policy loans* (i.e.loans at favorable terms satisfying some policy objectives) in Taiwan represent a much smaller portion of the total bank lendings and provide much less advantages than their Korean counterparts. As Little (1979) observed, even the most favored customer pays a positive real interest rate. Never baited by loans with negative interest rates, local firms have not gone deeply into debt, Korean-fashion.

c) Although *public firms* in the petrochemical and steel industries are not particularly competitive in either Taiwan or Korea, relative to the private firms in those industries, the Taiwanese public firms are much less debt-financed and debt-burdened than their Korean counterparts.

d) Taiwan also has *business groups* (guanhsichiyie). Relative to their Korean counterparts, they are neither heavily leveraged, nor dominant in the economy. The data of the top 5 business groups in each economy in 1983 is somewhat dated but remains quite interesting. In each economy, each business group consisted of about 24 to 25 firms, on average. Each firm employed, on average, 3,600 workers in Korea and 1,100 in Taiwan. Their total sales were 44 billion U.S. dollars in Korea, amounting to 52.4% of the GNP, and a little over 5 billion U.S. dollars in Taiwan, amounting to 10.3% of GNP. Given the relative size of Taiwanese groups, the economy could not be destabilized if any one of such groups became insolvent. Given their smaller average size, the Taiwanese enterprises are unable to cajole accommodating loans and all firms have to remain profitable to survive in contrast with South Korea. Korean economists have observed that although Taiwan does not play an active role in the world market for automobiles and shipbuilding (in contrast with South Korea), Taiwan was still able to develop almost as large a set of heavy and chemical industries as Korea *without*having launched a costly HCI drive.

19.3.3 The Taiwanese Industrial Structure

What characterizes the industrial structure of Taiwan is not so much the presence of the few relatively small and healthy business groups as the preponderance of SMEs. Without denying the proper role of such firms as Acer, in computer, or Evergreen in transportation, one can still argue that at this stage, that the vitality of the Taiwanese economy derives from the dense cluster of interconnected SMEs relying on mutually reinforcing subcontracting. The nature and contributions of SMEs to the Taiwanese economy is still not adequately understood. In the present context, it is relevant to analyze how an industrial structure based on SMEs helped Taiwan overcome the Asian Financial Crisis:

a) SMEs in Taiwan today are no longer a collection of isolated firms. They form a self-emerging network, with fine specialization and capable of taking on large international subcontracts. They offer punctual delivery, strict specifications, at competitive prices.

b) Such a development is not an anomaly but akin to the structure that evolved in Hong Kong, in small European countries (like Switzerland and Belgium), and in the Silicon Valley of America.. Such clusters of interconnected firms emerge in economies with an outward orientation, in the absence of an excessive bureaucracy or the dominance of business groups of the Korean type.

c) These firms, in their present status and by themselves, may be too small to conduct sustained, organized research. However, some of them grew to become giants. Acer emerged out of the ranks of such firms in Taiwan, as recently as 1976 with an initial capital of U.S. $25,000. So did Giant, the Taiwanese bicycle producer which ships more product, in value terms, than any other firms in the world today. In America, Apple and Microsoft also arose in similar fashion. As a matter of fact, Japan, a country which is usually associated with gargantuan enterprises has spawned Sony and Shimano in like manner. Thus, even an economy which started exclusively with SMEs can expect some 'native daughters and sons' becoming world class giants. From this viewpoint the emphasis of President Park (of Korea) on promoting large business from scratch was simplistic, if not self-serving.

d) The government in Taiwan did not provide much specific help to SMEs. The only institutional innovation was to set up the Industrial Technological Research Institute (ITRI) which offers cooperative research facilities to some of these firms. It also spins off certain small enterprises in the high tech sector. Specifically, one must note that the spin-off firms are placed in a sink-or-float position, with no guarantee of ultimate success. As a matter of fact, back in the early days, the views of K. Y. Yin (1954), to some, 'the father of Taiwan's industrialization' deserve to be cited in full:

> It is only too common to find in Taiwan today industrial units whose equipment is antiquated, whose scope (scale) is exceedingly small, whose technique is inferior, whose management is inefficient, whose proprietors completely devoid of the modern enterprising spirit, often seek short-term advantages but ignore the long-range development of their own enterprises.

Such firms both in the past and today would be subjected to Darwinian elimination, and Yin need not have worried.

e) Finally, the prevailing type of industrial structure is an important determinant of how well an economy can weather a financial crisis. The special strengths of an economy with vibrant SMEs are *adaptability* and *resilience*. *Adaptability* comes from a new approach to fabrication. Firms specialize in sets of modular basic operations and new skills can be developed for additional chores. Customers' orders, novel though they might appear at first glance, can be decomposed into sequences of such operations and matched with various enterprises. *Resilience* comes from the fact that skills and knowledge in such a network are retained and internalized by workers and not firms. The entry and exit of any particular firm cannot degrade much of the capability or performance of a system. An added factor concerns labor relations. Due to the small size of the labor force in each firm and the close relationship between workers and owners in such firms, strikes rarely occur. This would give the economy additional room to maneuver, in confronting a financial crisis.

In contrast, flexibility is often lacking in an economy dominated by large firms, whose outputs are concentrated on a few standard items. Again taking Korea as an example, at the eve of the current financial crisis, the business groups cut prices to expand their export of steel, petrochemicals and DRAMs, in the face of market saturation—rather than diversifying their products as Taiwan did.

19.4 Political Economy Factors

One of the cardinal objectives underlying the economic evolution of Taiwan is the Principle of Progress within Stability adopted and embraced faithfully by the ruling party in Taipei, throughout a span of half a century. The tightly controlled government budget, the carefully maintained price stability, the patiently accumulated balance of foreign exchange reserves, the manpower policy which maintained full employment throughout five decades and a reasonably equitable income distribution sustained for decades can be all viewed as corollaries of this successfully upheld policy goal. The steady, rapid growth of income was and still is strictly a welcome byproduct of a development strategy guided by this principle. Likewise, the acquisition of modern technology is a humble handmaiden, and not the mistress, in , assisting the achievement of progress within stability.

Institutions were designed and put in place not so much to aim for fast growth, but to fend off unwelcome contingencies in the best possible way—whatever their nature might be. It is this political economy background which gives the Taiwanese economy its special resilience vis-à-vis the Asian financial crisis, up to this stage. A major worldwide depression, say, triggered by a 'total meltdown' (whatever that means) of the Japanese economy could still impose havoc and misery upon the Taiwanese economy. But as likely as not, the people would hang together somehow to ride out the storm as they did when they confronted the two oil shocks.

From the political point of view, the *fruits* of such a policy emphasizing progress within stability appear to have won the respect from all quarters, even opponents of the regime are reduced to argue that the main credit is not due to the stewardship of the regime, and that even better results could have been obtained through a different set of policies. Ten years after the end of the Martial Law, the voting public, though fully aware of the imperfections of the present system, remains hesitant to change the political guard in elections that are considered reasonably fair and representative by most observers.

As development economists, the performance of the Taiwanese economy contains much useful information to be learned. And that is what we have tried to do in this volume and the present epilogue. The current Asian Financial Crisis serves as a litmus test for alternative development policies, and we social scientists should learn lessons whenever Nature provides us with the equivalent of a laboratory. In East Asia, less developed economies of all sizes and ideological persuasion can continue to enjoy successful growth based on an outward oriented reform, be it South Korea or Vietnam. The main benefit of such a strategy results from technological spillovers. To wit, when the transfer of technological information becomes freer, between Korea and America, say, there is no way America can gain 'to the same degree' as Korea in the bargain. Thus, when Korean growth has reduced the technology gap, the benefit of trade, hence growth, slackens.

Some readers may prefer a discussion of the realities behind the Principle of Growth amid Stability, and we are glad to oblige, even if only in the most sketchy terms. The political status of Taiwan today can only be understood in the context and the aftermath of both the Chinese Civil War and the Cold War. The former was a seven-decade contest between two parties, both organized on Leninist principles.

The latter protected the integrity of Taiwan as a state. In what ways did these historical facts shape the economic policies of the government in a much more risk-averse and decidedly less pro-business direction than its Korean counterpart? Since its withdrawal to Taiwan in 1950, the major goal of the Chinese Nationalists was to preserve Taiwan as its means to have its say in the future of the Chinese Mainland. When it lifted the Martial Law, the regime began rapidly losing its Leninist features and changing into the stance of a parliamentary party, familiar to the rest of the world. Since the government is recognized by only few nations and excluded from most international organizations (that refuse to grant it full membership rights) and since the ruling party has steadily lost its legislative majority, it is keenly aware that any economic debacle may end its five and one-half decades' control over Taiwan. Hence, stability and risk aversion are crucial principles and requirements to the survival of the regime and the relative independence of Taiwan as a separate territorial unit.

To understand the Taiwanese reluctance to endorse an extreme pro-business stance one has to recall that the party ideology originated with Sun Yatsen, a socialist who admired the writings of Henry George, and advocated the control of 'capital'. Along with the Land-to-the-tiller program in the country side, the fidelity to Sun's socialist ideology in Taiwan was also politically useful against Maoist pronouncements on the Mainland, that Taiwan catered only to the interest of capitalists, of imperialist or domestic stripe. The Nationalists were fully aware that their debacle in the Chinese Civil War was attributable more to the disaffection of the impoverished mass than to the business elite.

On the whole, the residents of Taiwan, are mostly non-ideological and non-political. They are interested to prolong whatever is good in the status quo, averting risks to the best of their ability. Thus, the 'Progress amid Stability' Principle answers quite well both to the survival requirements of a small island state and to the psychological needs of the people.

19.5 The Nature of the Crisis and Growth Prospects in the Long Run

The Asian Financial Crisis of 1997 is neither the death knell of the East Asian Miracle, nor a definitive repudiation of the outward-oriented development policy. It does not establish at all that East Asia grew only on the strength of capital accumulation, which has already reached its limit. At the same time, it illuminates some facts only dimly perceived before. We turn to these in quick succession.

First, in 1997, the Asian crisis came under a conjunction of circumstances: a) the domestic recession of Japan lingered on into its seventh year, while banks were burdened by non-performing loans and over-exposed in lendings to Korea and Southeast Asia; b) Southeast Asian economies had negotiated huge loans (by the end of 1996, the foreign debt/GDP ratio was 43% for Thailand, 39% for Malaysia, 48% for Indonesia and 48% for the Philippines *before devaluation*) and over-expanded production in several industries which developed market glut; c) the Korean banks shared the problem of Southeast Asian exposure with their Japanese counterparts; Korean industries faced an export glut (in DRAM, petrochemicals and steel) and were forced into an involuntary retrenchment along with other Southeast Asian countries; and foreign debt rose 84% over 1994-96; d) some Chinese firms relying on investments from Japan and Taiwan gained market share at the expense of Southeast Asia (in particular, Malaysia and Thailand during 1996) but with the massive layoffs of workers in the restructured state firms, the general market demand weakened.

Hence, what happened was coordination failure on an international scale, triggering immiserized growth in several particular industries simultaneously. It is a cautionary story against the 'feeding frenzy' of industrialists who compete to build up capacities in the same industries in vogue—some of whom even going as far as borrowing short term loans in foreign currency to finance such folly.

Overall, the world market has not disappeared for developing economies. The product cycle remains in force. There is no general glut of capital funds. The opportunity to gain information and technology in foreign transactions is still there. Both trade and direct foreign investment are channels for technology spill over. The resilience of the Taiwanese economy is a testimony that appropriate institutions and policies can shelter a small country relatively well against exogenous shocks and allow it to continue to grow.

Secondly, there has never been that much truth that East Asia grew only as a result of capital formation and scale economies. As export market opened, the acquired information boosted labor skills, especially in handling more sophisticated equipment. This raised the profitability of more capital intensive processes and products and caused sectoral shift as well as structural change. The brightened investment prospects provided the incentive for saving. The causality goes from trade to technology, hence to investment prospect and the incentive to save. For this view, one may refer to Van and Wan (1997). The measured increasing returns are partly agglomerative rather than internal to the firm. In other words, the marginal *social* productivity of investment and technological acquisition by any given firm is likely to exceed greatly the marginal *private* productivity of that investment. This is just as true for Taiwan, with its SMEs, as it is for Korea with its large plants. The belief that such externalities can only be achieved through large scale economies is clearly erroneous.

East Asia, in general, still has much to learn from abroad so that its growth potential is far from having reached its limit. The Japanese growth rate did not decline towards the American level until its per capita real income had approached the American figure. There is every reason to expect that the rest of Asia can follow the same growth pattern and reach its ultimate potential.

Perhaps a final lesson that could be learned from the history preceding and during the Asian Financial Crisis is that too much volatility in the exchange rate is not desirable, but nor is too much rigidity. The ultimate test is to keep the domestic economy at an even keel. It is the interest of the people which must be served and not their vanity.

19.6 References

Bloom, M., 1992. *Technological Change in the Korean Electronic Industry.* Paris: Development Centre of the OECD.

Chu, W.-W., 1994. "Import Substitution and Export-Led Growth: A Study of Taiwan's Petro-chemical Industry."*World Development* 22(5): 781-94.

Corsetti, G., P. Pesenti, and N. Roubini, 1998. "What Caused the Asian Currency and Financial Crisis?" Unpublished paper, Yale, Princeton, and New York Universities, March.

Fields, K.J., 1995. *Enterprise and the State in Korea and Taiwan.* Ithaca, NY: Cornell University Press.

Hu, S.-C., J.-L. Lin, J.-D. Shea and C.-S. Wu, 1998. "The Asian Financial Crisis: A Comparative Analysis of Taiwan Experience," mimeo, Taipei Institute of Economics, Academia Sinica and Central Bank of China.

Jones, L.P. and I. Sakong, 1980. *Government, Business and Entrepreneurship in Economic Development: The Korean Case.* Cambridge, MA: Harvard University Press.

Little, I.M.D., 1979. "An Economic Reconnaissance." In: W. Galenson (ed.), *Economic Growth and Structural Change in Taiwan: The Post-War Experience of the Republic of China.* Ithaca, NY: Cornell University Press.

Sakong, I., 1993. *Korea in the World Economy.* Washington, DC: Institute for International Economics.

Stern, J.J., J.-H. Kim, D.H. Perkins and J.-H. Yoo, 1995. *Industrialization and the State: The Korean Heavy and Chemical Industry Drive.* Cambridge, MA: Harvard University Press.

Van, P.H. and H. Y. Wan, 1997. "Emulative Development Through Trade Expansions: East Asian Evidence," in: J. Piggott and A. Woodland (eds), *International Trade Policy and the Pacific Rim,* London: Macmillan Press, forthcoming.

Yin, K.Y., 1954. "Adverse Trend in Taiwan's Industrial Development." *Industry of Free China* 2(2):1-6.

INDEX